ASPEN PUBLISHERS

Teacher's Manual

to

TORTS

Cases and Questions

Second Edition

Ward Farnsworth
Professor of Law
Boston University

Mark F. Grady
Dean and University Professor
George Mason University School of Law

Wolters Kluwer
Law & Business

AUSTIN   BOSTON   CHICAGO   NEW YORK   THE NETHERLANDS

ISBN 978-0-7355-8295-8

This manual is made available as a courtesy to law teachers with the understanding that it will not be reproduced, quoted or cited, except as where indicated. In the event that anyone would like to cite the manual for thoughts drawn from it, a reference to the relevant page number of the materials text (with the formula "suggested by") may be appropriate.

Copies of this manual are available on computer diskette. Teachers who have adopted the casebook may obtain a copy of the diskette, free of charge, by calling the Aspen Publishers sales assistant at 1 – 800 – 950 – 5259.

Aspen Publishers
Attn: Permissions Department
76 Ninth Avenue, 7th Floor
New York, NY 10011-5201

Table of Contents

INTRODUCTION TO SECOND EDITION

As the new preface in the casebook explains, the changes made in the new edition of the casebook are modest. Mistakes and typos here and there have been corrected; more facts have been added to some cases; more excerpts from the Third Restatement are included. Here are the *cases* and other substantive notes that have been added, subtracted, or substantially changed:

White v. University of Idaho (in the battery section) was changed from a case to a problem.

Mohr v. Williams added as lead case in the section on consent in battery cases.

Rains v. Superior Court and *Freedman v. Superior Court* have been omitted from the section on consent in battery cases.

Lubner v. City of Los Angeles and *Carrol v. Allstate Ins. Co.* have been omitted from the section on negligent infliction of emotional distress (in the Duty chapter).

Note on Vioxx litigation added to end of chapter on Cause in Fact. Note from Glen Robinson's article dropped from the same space.

Some commentary on *Palsgraf* has been added after that case.

Blankenship v. General Motors Corp., *Bruce v. Martin-Marietta Corp.*, and *Lewis v. Coffing Hoist Div., Duff-Norton Co.*, were omitted from the section on design defects in the Products Liability chapter. *Green v. Smith & Nephew* has been added to that same section, along with a note on *Wyeth v. Levine*.

Eyoma v. Falco was dropped from the section on hedonic damages in the chapter on Damages. Notes on the Sept. 11 Victim Compensation Fund, and on workers' compensation recovery schedules, were added to that section.

Marshall v. Ranne was made a lead case in the section on Secondary Assumption of Risk in the chapter on Defenses.

All these changes were in reply to suggestions or requests from instructors who have been using the book. Our apologies to those who liked it better the old way! Some teaching notes on the new materials just shown have been added to this manual. This manual also includes, a few pages below, a sample syllabus for a one-semester course based on the new edition of the casebook.

INTRODUCTION TO FIRST EDITION

Welcome to the electronic version of the teacher's manual for *Torts: Cases and Questions*. If you obtained it from the publisher, you may also wish to contact Farnsworth so that he can email you a more up-to-date version if there is one. We expect that this electronic version will be the most useful format in which to use the manual, since this way it becomes searchable and enables you to cut and paste anything you like. It also contains ongoing updates, additions, and improvements over the bound version. The only thing it doesn't have is the page-numbered table of contents; any such page numbering we offered here likely would have become wrong as soon as you opened this document and it was formatted on your machine. But the good news is that now you can reformat it however you like. You may wish to enlarge the font or make other adjustments to enhance its readability.

We hope you will find the materials in the casebook as exciting and interesting to teach as we do. The premise of the book is explained in its preface, so we won't belabor it here. In brief, the book offers lots of cases that reach different results on related facts and challenges the student to draw distinctions between them. As a result of this approach the students quickly come to understand how to prepare for class, and the process of sorting out the cases leads to absorbing and instructive discussions that can explore the logic of the rules from a variety of different normative perspectives.

This purpose of this manual is to provide plenty of raw materials to help you get those good classroom discussions off the ground. Its main features are these:

1. *A sample syllabus* for use of the book in a one-semester, four-credit course.

1. *Questions and answers*. We teach our courses in more or less Socratic fashion, calling on students without notice to ask them questions. This manual is written to support that sort of approach. Most of the materials here are presented in a Q and A format that can be adapted directly to classroom use. We do not expect such direct adoption to occur very often; teachers all have their own ideas about what questions to ask and how to work with the answers. But our hope is that any ideas you like here are presented in a fashion that will make them easy to integrate into your own lesson plans.

2. *Hypotheticals*. The questions and answers here focus first on the distinctions between the cases in the text. The second focus of the manual, however, is on hypotheticals. No torts teacher wants to enter a classroom unarmed; hypotheticals enliven classroom discussion, teach students to think on their feet, and provide useful illustrations in reply to points and questions that arise during class. They also allow you to control the clock, adding material to the discussion and subtracting it so that your coverage matches the time you have allotted for it. We like hypotheticals based on real cases, so the manual frequently presents facts followed by key excerpts from the opinions addressing them. The manual also contains excerpts from the opinions that serve as the basis for the "problem" cases that appear frequently in the book.

3. *Secondary sources*. While the casebook is little lighter than some others on secondary materials, this manual is heavier on them than most. The reason for the arrangement is our view

that instructors vary a great deal in the theoretical ideas they want to discuss with their students. So in several areas of this manual—the ones that are theoretically the richest—we provide excerpts from interesting academic writings on the issues under consideration. Our hope is that among them you will find ideas you can weave into your class discussions to enliven and enrich them. The disadvantage of this approach is that the students will not have read the materials themselves; the advantage is that you can decide which ideas to emphasize and regulate their flow into the conversation. For examples of this feature of the manual, have a look at its treatment of the *Palsgraf* case (toward the end of the chapter on proximate cause) or design defects (in the middle of the chapter on products liability). Here as elsewhere our goal has been to create materials flexible enough to support a variety of approaches to teaching the course.

4. *Coverage.* The structure of the book lends itself to a fast-paced, action-packed approach to the subject; there are lots of cases on the table during a typical class meeting. If your own pace inclines you to move a little more slowly, there are various solutions: assign everything but only discuss some of it; assign little and convey the rest as hypotheticals as time permits; or assign fewer than all the cases but try to cover all that you assign. The manual offers suggestions about what to cut if you want to go the latter route. They are contained at the start of the sections within each chapter. Mind you, we don't *recommend* cutting anything; everything in the book is there because we think it teaches well and adds value to the course. But we know that those who do plan to make cuts might appreciate some guidance about where to make them, so we have done our best to identify the cases that can be sacrificed with the least pedagogical loss.

Planning the course.

Most users of this casebook will be teaching a one-semester course; longer torts courses have become increasingly rare. The book can be used to fill a six-credit course if the whole thing is taught in an unhurried fashion. If you do have just one semester, however, you will not be able to cover the whole thing. The syllabus that appears below suggests how the time might best be spent.

There also are some standard choices to make about the order of the course. The first choice is whether and when to cover intentional torts. Many instructors start with that material, finding it a nice warm-up for the materials on negligence that consume the greatest share of time in the course. But of course intentional torts also can go at the end or be skipped entirely. Second, there is the question of whether to cover duties before or after the negligence standard. Again, instructors vary in their views on this, and the chapters of the casebook are written to work in either order (we have done both in our own classes). Third, one must decide when to cover defenses to negligence claims and in what depth. That chapter appears relatively late in the book, but you might prefer to cover it a bit earlier.

Whatever else you do, we recommend assigning the introduction to the casebook at the start of the course. It contains some useful context for the students, particularly on the subject of procedure; it explains the L and NL designations that we use all the time in the casebook, which can cause some confusion at first. More generally, many students come to a better understanding of certain aspects of procedure—especially summary judgment— during their torts course than they do in their formal course on civil procedure. But to achieve that goal requires constant mindfulness of the procedural postures in which the cases arise, so we like to emphasize those issues from day one, with particular focus on them during the materials on negligence per se and res ipsa loquitur.

We wish you well with your course, and welcome your suggestions for future editions of the casebook and this manual.

Ward Farnsworth
Mark F. Grady

The sample syllabus shown below shows how the high points of the subject matter and the casebook (2d ed.) can be covered in a four-credit, one-semester course. It makes many painful omissions, of course; those are inevitable in a shorter course on large topic. Its general goal is to provide students with some exposure to the most important ideas in tort law, and to allow use of the most interesting cases in the book—all without hurrying too much (usually covering five to ten pages per class).

Let me just note a few somewhat idiosyncratic choices that this syllabus reflects and that many instructors might prefer to change. First, in the strict liability chapter it covers liability for harm done by animals, but not *Rylands v. Fletcher*; some instructors might prefer to reverse that (or cover neither or both). This syllabus contains no formal coverage of joint and several liability; there is a brief treatment of that subject at p. 345 of the casebook if one wants it. It provides no coverage of the history of products liability law (*MacPherson*, etc.); that material appears at pp. 449-462 for those who want to cover it. There is no coverage of "secondary" assumption of risk (pp. 605-611). More generally, longer lead cases are sometimes left out; instructors who like those will want to add more back in. Room for all these additions might be made by trimming out some material the syllabus includes (and that I enjoy teaching) but that many teachers omit: the unit on discipline as a source of privilege to commit battery, and/or the units on the intentional torts that follow battery (trespass, conversion, outrage (intentional infliction of emotional distress), and invasion of privacy). Some instructors prefer not to teach a unit on damages, but that seems to me one of the most interesting parts of the course. I might skip *Palsgraf*, but I realize that many instructors would consider that heretical.

—Ward Farnsworth

The Negligence Standard

The Reasonable Person.

> 122-127
> 133-137 (through note 1)

Risks and Precautions.

> 140-top of 145
> 151-152
> 154-157

Custom.

> Bottom 158-top 160
> Bottom 162-top half 169

Negligence Per Se.

> Bottom 170-178 (through note 8)
> #13 on page 184
> Bottom 188-191 (through note 5)

Res Ipsa Loquitur.

> 192-top 201
> Bottom 204-top 207
> 208-214

Duties and Limitations

Affirmative Acts; Undertakings.

> 217-first half of 223
> Bottom half 224-top 226
> Bottom half 231-top 233
> #8 on 235

Special Relationships.

> 236-237
> 239
> Bottom 241-middle 247
> Bottom 251-255

Owners and Occupiers of Land.

> Bottom 255-top 257
> Bottom 258-269

The Privity Limitation.

> Bottom 272-279

Pure Economic Losses.

> 280-top 286

Negligent Infliction of Emotional Distress.

> Bottom 290-298

300 (start with #8)-top half 303

Cause in Fact

But-for Causation.

> 307-309
> 317-top 324
> Bottom 328 (start with #5)-top 332

Alternative Liability.

> Bottom half 332-344

Proximate Causation

Remoteness and Foreseeability.

> 351-365 (through #14)

Intervening Causes.

> Bottom half 368-376

Palsgraf, etc.

> Bottom half 378-393

Strict liability

Liability for Animals.

> 395-406

Abnormally Dangerous Activities.

> Bottom half 416-top 425
> Bottom half 426-top 432

Respondeat Superior.

> Bottom half 433-448

Products liability

Manufacturing Defects.

> Bottom half 462 (starting with #2)-top half 470
> 477-top 479 (stop before #10)

Design Defects.

> Bottom 479-486
> Bottom half 489-492 (through #7)

Warning Defects.

> Bottom half 499-top half 502
> Bottom half 509-515

Damages

Lost Earnings.

> Bottom half 526-532

Pain and Suffering.

> 538-top half 541
> Bottom 549 (start with #14)-top 552

Punitive Damages.

> 552-565 (through #9)

Defenses

Contributory and Comparative Negligence.

> Bottom half 577-581
> 584 (start with #5)-top 587

Primary Assumption of Risk.

> Bottom 596-top 605

Battery

Intent and Voluntariness.

> 1-11 (through #12)

Consent.

> 19-top half 24
> Bottom half 227

Trespass

> 29-top half 37

Conversion

> Bottom 40-top half 49

Outrage

> 70-71
> Bottom 73 (start with #1)-83

Privileges to Commit Intentional Torts

Defense of Person and Property.

> 85-94 (stop before #10)

Private Necessity.

> Bottom half 97-top 99 (stop at end of *Ploof*)
> 100-top half 106

Public Necessity.

> Bottom half 107 (start with #2)-top 110

Discipline.

111-top half 116

Invasion of Privacy

Disclosure of Embarrassing Private Facts.

696
Bottom 700-top half 706

Intrusion upon Seclusion.

Bottom half 710-717
721-722

Appropriation of Name or Likeness.

723-top 724
733-top 737 (through #8)

CHAPTER 1

INTENTIONAL TORTS:
THE PRIMA FACIE CASE

SECTION A. BATTERY

1. Intent and Volition

This subsection teaches well in one class day, typically with some spillover to the following session. There are three basic themes to cover. The first involves the meaning of the intent requirement. The second involves the requirement that the defendant commit a voluntary act. The third involves transferred intent. For some instructors this will be the first unit of the course (and perhaps of the student's first year), in which event a slower pace naturally may be appropriate. Some instructors (not us) like to start the course with a whole day or more on *Vosburg* alone.

This isn't a great section in which to make cuts; everything in it serves an independent purpose. You probably could drop *White* and/or *Laidlaw v. Sage*, but both—and especially *Laidlaw*—are great teaching cases. You also could cover transferred intent by using just *Keel* or *Manning* and dropping the other; *Keel* probably is better, especially when combined with a few hypotheticals.

Vosburg v. Putney (the L case of the kick in the schoolhouse)

We stylize (and the casebook presents) *Vosburg* as a case of liability even though the decision printed in the casebook actually resulted in reversal and a new trial because of erroneous evidentiary rulings. There is some interesting background on *Vosburg* given in Zigurds L. Zile, *Vosburg v. Putney: A Centennial Story*, 1992 Wis. L. Rev. 877 (1992). The case generated an expensive series of criminal and civil trials and appeals at the behest of Andrew Vosburg (the injured boy) and his father, Seth, against George Putney (the kicker). Andrew never did win anything; his victories at trial were overturned on technicalities and his case finally was dismissed for failure to pay the costs of one of his appeals. His father won $1,200 in medical expenses that he probably was not able to collect. Explains Zile:

> [T]he total of the direct costs in the three cases was $953.54, of which $22.19 was absorbed by Waukesha County, $715.03 fell on Andrew and Seth Vosburg, Andrew's guardian-ad-litem, and $216.32 on George and Henry Putney, George's guardian-ad-litem. The evidence is persuasive that neither child owned property. As a consequence, collection of the taxed costs was a matter between the warring fathers who had stood in for their sons during the four-year contest. A payment of $451.66 ($370.82 plus $189.00 less $108.16) by Seth Vosburg to Henry Putney would have put the matter to rest. Yet this amount was roughly equal to Seth's annual income and, thus, probably beyond his means. Furthermore, we have no evidence whatsoever of any money having changed hands to compensate the other party for costs.

> Attorney's fees were a separate matter. As arrangements entirely between the client and his counsel, professional fees, whether merely agreed upon or actually collected, leave tracks only in private files where passage of time typically erases them faster than notations in the public record. Because of this, we can only speculate about this potentially large cost item in the series of judicial proceedings that George Putney had kicked off. But there are some guides to what the lawyers generally expected in those days and, thus, what the parties and their counsel might have

arranged. [...] [Assuming that the plaintiff's lawyers] took the Vosburgs' civil actions on a contingent fee, we can construct a summary showing the approximate financial results of the four-year contest and compare them with the terms of the settlement proposed in the late summer of 1889. Two sets of calculations may suffice to illustrate the contest's ultimate futility in purely monetary terms. One variant posits actual transfer of money in satisfaction of awards of damages and costs and in fulfillment of agreements for reasonable attorney fees; the other, uncollected awards, no fees for [the plaintiff's lawyers] and reasonable fees for [the defendant's lawyers].

According to the first variant, it would have cost the Vosburgs $955 to collect $1,200 in damages. The cost figure includes a modest 20% of the recovery, or $240, for the contingent fee. Had the agreement, in the event of a recovery, called for a fee based on the kind and quantity of service performed (i.e., $560) the Vosburgs' total litigation expenses would have exceeded the amount of damages awarded by $75. The Putneys, on their part, would have spent $776 for the privilege of transferring $1,200 to the Vosburgs, that is, for an ultimate loss of nearly $2,000.

The other variant, which probably approximates what actually transpired, changes the figures but not the message. The Vosburgs would have incurred costs in the amount of $263 in order to get nothing. Although the Putneys paid nothing to the Vosburgs, they would have given $560 to their attorneys and absorbed their own costs which added up to $667, for a combined expenditure of $1,227.

These figures tell that litigation, under the first set of assumptions, neither appreciably improved nor worsened the Vosburgs' financial situation compared with what it would have been had they accepted the Putneys' $250 settlement offer. The Putneys would, of course, have been far better off by responding positively to the Vosburgs' demand for $700 in settlement of their claims. The preferability of the attempted settlement stands out even more starkly against the backdrop of the second variant. The Vosburgs would have been spared an expenditure of $263 on costs and received, as a minimum, $250, for a total gain of $513. Payment of the $700 which the Vosburgs had demanded would have yielded the Putneys a net gain of $527. Any settlement figure between $250 and $700 would have further improved the position of both parties.

As for the plaintiff's subsequent life:

Despite the gloomy medical prognosis which took Andrew's handicap to be permanent and allowed for the possibility that his right leg might have to be surgically removed, Andrew resumed his education. After leaving school, he was briefly employed as an office worker, either as a bookkeeper or stenographer. In 1900, he took a job of a utility trainman with The Milwaukee Electric Railway and Light Company in Milwaukee, just ahead of his younger brother John. He was made assistant yard foreman in 1903 and promoted to foreman in 1906. During the early phase of his Milwaukee job, Andrew continued to live with his parents and siblings in Waukesha. Around 1908, however, he moved to Milwaukee and, on August 10, 1909, married Kathryn Louise Kimbel. She blessed him with a daughter, Florence Kathryn, and two sons, Andrew Clarence and Warren Harding, the latter born on November 2, 1920—the fifty-fifth birthday and the day of the landslide victory of his namesake. Andrew and his wife frequently changed their residence, as it was their wont to buy and resell houses they had refurbished in the interim. Much of this work fell on Kathryn because Andrew's leg, on which he wore a laced leather brace, was too weak for climbing ladders. This went on until about 1930, when the Vosburgs bought a more permanent home on the city's northwest side. Here, their daughter Florence, a physician's assistant, died at the age of twenty-one. Here, Andrew lived out the remainder of his life vexed by worsening hypertension and asthma. He died on October 4, 1938, at sixty-four, a respected member of his company's supervisory staff. He left to his wife real property valued at $9,000 and a $1,000 insurance policy on his life. Andrew Vosburg was buried in the Prairie Home Cemetery of Waukesha.

Some interesting thoughts on teaching *Vosburg* were offered in James A. Henderson, *Why Vosburg Comes First*, 1992 Wisconsin L. Rev. 853:[*]

> We then [on the second day of class, after much time spent on procedural issues] turn attention to the third substantive issue on appeal—whether the defendant is liable for all of the plaintiff's harm, even if much of it would not have been expected to follow from a gentle tap on the shin. [...] "The holding on appeal that an actor is liable even for unforeseeable harm seems to undercut the first issue regarding what the actor intended, does it not? If you're liable for causing freakishly unexpected injuries when you intentionally touch someone, then intent to cause harm cannot matter for much, can it?"
>
> The answer, of course, is that the so-called "thin skull" (or "thin shin") aspect of *Vosburg* presumes tortious conduct. Only wrongdoers fall prey to the rule, and intent remains relevant to whether Putney was or was not a wrongdoer. After eliminating this red herring, the students consider the substantive merits of the thin skull rule. What happened to the notion that the punishment should fit the crime? Given the jury verdict of no intent to harm the plaintiff, the defendant cannot have acted all that badly. Putney might have deserved to stay an hour after school for breaking the rules. But why should he be liable for thousands of dollars for harm that no reasonable person could have foreseen?
>
> Finally, we turn to the issue for which *Vosburg* is most widely known, the issue relating to the wrongfulness of the defendant's behavior in the absence of any intent to harm. I ask the students to consider how the plaintiff might have tried to prove at trial that the defendant did, after all, intend to cause substantial injury. Of course, the jury believed the defendant and found no intent to harm. But it is interesting to observe that before that finding was made the plaintiff was free to argue that there was intent.
>
> So what was the first issue on appeal? "Did the trial judge err in entering judgment for plaintiff notwithstanding the special verdict of no intent to harm?" And what is the substantive issue on appeal? This is a critical juncture. If the student frames the substantive issue: "Must a defendant intend to cause harm in order to commit a battery?" and answers that question "No," she may conclude that intent to harm is never required for a battery—that all intended contacts that cause injury, even unforeseeable injury, constitute batteries. And yet all would agree, intuitively, that gentle, inoffensive touchings are not tortious, even if they freakishly happen to cause injury. So another substantive issue is presented: "Given no intent to harm, what, if anything, supports the conclusion that defendant Putney committed a battery?"
>
> Clearly, the Supreme Court of Wisconsin required more than merely an intended contact causing harm. Exactly what more the court required is debatable. The analysis in the opinion is terse and murky, with several examples of what could pass for circular reasoning. That is what makes *Vosburg* so marvelous from the pedagogical perspective. The students confront a court, fairly early in the development of the American law of battery, struggling with a case which, on its facts, is painfully close to the boundary between acceptable and unacceptable behavior. [...] Whatever substantive test the court adopted, that test eventually developed into what today would be referred to as one defining "offensive contact." The primary interest that is being protected is

one of personal dignity. Depending on time and place, every individual has the right not to be contacted intentionally in ways that offend a reasonable sense of self. In effect, the defendant has trespassed on the plaintiff's person, and is strictly liable for harms that follow directly from that transgression.

The third and final dimension that justifies *Vosburg's* coming first in the torts course is the extent to which it presents the most fundamental question in the jurisprudence of torts: What set of values justifies assigning the underlying legal entitlement to one party or the other? I realize that virtually every tort decision presents the same opportunities, at least to some extent; but *Vosburg* does so more vividly and in a more interesting fashion than most others. This is because *Vosburg* combines two essentially contradictory features. On the one hand, because it is a battery case, students tend to share an intuitive feeling that it is self-evident that when someone kicks another person, as between the kicker and the kickee the former is the "aggressor" and the latter is the "victim," and that the victim should always enjoy the entitlement. (What they do not realize, of course, is that by casually characterizing the defendant's act as a "kick," the underlying value judgment is well on its way to being made.) On the other hand, because *Vosburg* involves childish horseplay by an actor who was so young as to be incapable of negligence, it is possible to characterize this plaintiff's conduct as innocent and the liability imposed, strict.

Q. How would you restate the holding of *Vosburg* regarding the intent required to commit a battery?
A. Perhaps that it is an intent to commit the touching in a setting where there is no implied license to touch. The court's notion of an "unlawful intention" is confusing; it seems just to mean an intent to commit an act that the defendant has no permission to commit, and that thus is "unlawful" in a broad sense.

Attempts to define the intent required to support a battery claim tend always to be vexed by this ambiguity: is it merely an intent to complete the touching, or must the intent be tainted by some sort of inappropriate wish to harm or offend—or by some other feature of the facts that makes the touching inappropriate? Courts don't always treat the issue in the same way, and it's probably a mistake to allow students to become too sure about it. The Second Restatement takes an approach that seems a little different from that in *Vosburg*:

§18. Battery: Offensive Contact

(1) An actor is subject to liability to another for battery if

(a) he acts intending to cause a harmful or offensive contact with the person of the other or a third person, or an imminent apprehension of such a contact, and

(b) an offensive contact with the person of the other directly or indirectly results.

(2) An act which is not done with the intention stated in Subsection (1, a) does not make the actor liable to the other for a mere offensive contact with the other's person although the act involves an unreasonable risk of inflicting it and, therefore, would be negligent or reckless if the risk threatened bodily harm.

Here's one way to think about the problems raised by this aspect of the battery tort. In battery cases everyone agrees that the defendant has to have intended the touching itself. And the touching has to lead to harm or offense. Those are the two uncontroversial elements of battery; but there also is a sort of semi-element that also must be present: something wrong with the defendant's act besides the fact that it happened to lead to harm. The "something wrong" could be an intent to actually cause the harm. It could be that there was no intent to harm or offend, but that a reasonable person would have realized that offense was likely even if the defendant didn't (the boor who gropes or bestows an unwelcome kiss on a woman, unreasonably thinking she really will like it). It could be that the act violated a rule or norm (*Vosburg* itself?). Or it could be that there was no consent—in a situation where consent is important. The Restatement's standard can be read as consistent with liability for the boor (and with *Vosburg*, for that matter); it's a little ambiguous as to whether the defendant must intend harm or offense, or whether the actor merely must intend a touching (that turns out to be harmful or offensive).

The reason that either reading creates a mess is that some of the considerations just listed really have nothing to do with the defendant's intent as such. The boor has an intent to complete the touching, and that is all (except for his additional wish to bestow what he believes is a favor on his victim—but surely this can't add to the case against him). What makes the case "go" are facts about what he reasonably should have understood. But that is an awkward consideration to try to shoehorn into the intent element of the tort. If it doesn't go there, the intent needed is just the intent to commit the touching itself, and the "harmful or offensive" requirement has to be expanded to ensure that the defendant has done some additional something wrong to support liability.

Q. What was the significance of the fact that the kick occurred in the classroom ("after it had been called to order," as the court says), rather than at recess?

A. See above. It could be said to go less to intent than to whether the "harmful or offensive touching" element of the battery tort was satisfied. On this view, the idea would be that at recess there was implied consent to some contact, as there would be in a football game. In a classroom called to order no such implied license exists; whether the defendant committed a literal infraction of school rules is neither here nor there (there may have been a literal infraction on the playground as well). Since there was no implied license, the intended act was unlawful in the sense relevant to battery. But this leads to problems of the sort suggested a moment ago: it might be thought to imply that the battery was complete when there was a touching against the rules, regardless of whether the plaintiff was hurt or offended by it; for it was against the rules.

Q. Suppose that A intentionally exceeds the speed limit while driving, and as a result unintentionally runs over B. Has A committed a battery?

A. Surely not, though it might be useful to have a student try to work out the analogy and its limitations. One author has suggested that an affirmative answer is implied by *Vosburg*: "By the reasoning in *Vosburg*, A's unlawful act implies an underlying unlawful intent. In [the hypothetical case of the speeder], as in *Vosburg*, the unlawfully intended act results in a harm. The law of negligence per se is replete with cases in which an actor's conduct in violation of a statute has harmed the plaintiff. Under the right conditions, that plaintiff is permitted to plead the violation as establishing the actor's negligence. If *Vosburg's* unlawful-intent principle were correct, the law of battery would swallow much of the law of negligence per se." Craig M. Lawson, *The Puzzle of Intended Harm in the Tort of Battery*, 74 Temp. L. Rev. 355 (2001). The author adds, however: "*Vosburg's* discussion of unlawful intent is short and leaves open at least one possible narrower reading. The court explicitly declined to predicate liability on intent to harm, but perhaps an actual intent to make contact is required. The opinion mentions no such requirement, but the defendant did tap or kick the plaintiff, purposely making contact with the plaintiff's leg."

You can, of course, use *Vosburg* to explore the eggshell-skull principle a bit, though it is a distraction from the main theme of the section (it's revisited more directly in the chapter on proximate cause).

Knight v. Jewett (D inadvertently steps on P's finger during touch football game; NL).
White v. University of Idaho (problem—piano teacher drums fingers on student's back; L)

Q. What is the distinction between *Knight v. Jewett* and *Vosburg v. Putney*?

A.   In *Vosburg* the defendant intended the touching that harmed the plaintiff; in *Knight* the defendant did not intend the touching that harmed the plaintiff (a finding based on the plaintiff's admission in a deposition, rather than on a special verdict).

Q.   But didn't the defendant in *Knight* intend some contact with her? What does the case say about this?
A.   It seems likely that he intended to have some contact with her, but he did not intend the contact with her finger. Notice that Jewett's account of his behavior might seem to rule out any intent to have contact with Knight, since he said that he stepped backward onto her hand. But Knight's account was that Jewett ran over her on the way to catch Knight's teammate, which would suggest that he did intend contact with Knight. Since this case was decided on Jewett's motion for summary judgment, Knight's account is the one that matters.

There are more notes on *Knight v. Jewett*, and its relationship to transferred intent doctrines, at the end of this section.

Q.   What result in *White v. University of Idaho*?
A.   The court of appeals affirmed the grant of summary judgment:

> The tort of battery requires intentional bodily contact which is either harmful or offensive. The intent element of the tort of battery does not require a desire or purpose to bring about a specific result or injury; it is satisfied if the actor's affirmative act causes an intended contact which is unpermitted and which is harmful or offensive. Indeed, the contact and its result may be physically harmless. Thus, a person may commit a battery when intending only a joke, or a compliment—where an unappreciated kiss is bestowed without consent, or a misguided effort is made to render assistance.
>
> It is undisputed that Professor Neher intended to touch Mrs. White, though he did not intend to cause harm or injury. His lack of any specific intent to harm or injure Mrs. White is immaterial. Professor Neher's affirmative act caused an intended contact which was unpermitted, offensive and, apparently, harmful. Such voluntary contact constitutes the tort of battery.

This result seems questionable, which is why the case is presented as a problem rather than on its own.

Q.   Does *White* follow *Vosburg v. Putney* or extend it?
A.   It is an extension in that there were no overtones of rulebreaking here, or of any intent to cause a negative result at all: apparently Neher's gesture was meant to be playful or affectionate. The case stands for the idea that there must be an intent to commit the touching, and the touching must not be permitted—but expands "impermissible" to include unwelcome touchings regardless of whether they were "unlawful" in *Vosburg's* sense.

Q.   What is the distinction between *White v. University of Idaho* and *Knight v. Jewett*?
A.   In *White*, Neher intended the touching that occurred; the defendant in *Knight* did not.

Q.   What if Neher had been in love with White, and drummed his fingers on her back because he thought it would be romantic or titillating or at least feel good; assume that he thought that White would consent to this, and his intention was to provide a benefit (a kind of backrub) rather than any harm. Liability (for Neher)?
A.   Yes: the relevant intent is an intent to commit an act that turns out to have been unauthorized, not an intent to commit an unauthorized act (much less an intent to harm her). The defendant's *motive* is not relevant. The court makes this clear when it says that a defendant can commit a battery in an attempt to bestow a compliment.

Q. What if Neher had done this many times before, and White had always said, "I love when you do that"? (But not this time…)

A. No liability: there probably would then be an implied authorization to keep doing it. Neher would have an intent to commit a touching that turned out to be harmful, but no intent to commit a touching that was (from an objective standpoint) *unpermitted.*

Q. Is the test for whether the touching was unauthorized subjective or objective? What's the difference?

A. An objective test would focus on whether a reasonable person would have understood themselves to be allowed to commit the touching. A subjective inquiry would ask whether the plaintiff in fact welcomed the touching or consented to it. There is language in the *White* case suggesting that the test is subjective: it reports the plaintiff's testimony that she would not have consented to Neher's contact and found it offensive. But that can't quite be the whole issue; a touching that a reasonable person would expect to be permitted, but to which the plaintiff secretly did not consent, could not become a battery just for that reason. You can try a hypothetical in which the plaintiff has aphenphosmphobia—fear of being touched—but nevertheless ventures onto a crowded subway. So what is the relevance of the plaintiff's inner wishes? They must be relevant only (a) if they destroy the plaintiff's claim because it comes out that she secretly welcomed the touching before she knew what its consequences would be (there's more on this in the upcoming materials on consent); or if (b) the inner wishes manifest in signals that a reasonable person would understand as a lack of permission. Since no such signals were given in *White*, the lack of authorization must have arisen simply from the context: nobody should expect that they can do to others what White did to the plaintiff.

It seems to follow that Neher committed a battery every time he drummed his fingers on anyone, unless they had sent unusual signals that such a touching *was* authorized or unless they secretly welcomed it. This might seem odd because one might imagine that once the touching occurred and caused no harm, its recipients might have regarded it as unobjectionable. Perhaps the plaintiff here would have been content with the touching if it merely had tickled. The implication of this ex post method of evaluating the issue is that we don't learn whether a touching is a battery until we see how much harm it causes. This can't be right as a matter of theory, but it seems like an accurate description of how some of the cases play out.

Q. What if Neher had killed White? He drums his fingers on her back, and she keels over right away; she had a weak heart, and the shock of the experience kills her. Assume this was totally unforeseeable. What result?

A. Under *Vosburg's* eggshell-skull principle, Neher would be liable for all resulting damages regardless of how unforeseeable they were. The extent of the harm was unforeseeable in *Vosburg*, too.

Q. Why hold Neher liable? Is it fair to hold a person liable for doing something they thought would cause no harm? If it doesn't seem fair, is it a good idea for some other reason?

A. Well, what is the point of having an intent requirement in the first place—and especially a requirement that can be satisfied by a mere intent to touch without any intent to harm? From the standpoint of corrective justice you might expect someone who performs an act deliberately to be more blameworthy than someone who acts inadvertently. But that reasoning would seem to suggest an intent requirement that can be satisfied only if the defendant intended to cause some harm; it doesn't explain liability for Neher, who did not want or expect to cause any harm, or for a child or insane defendant who likewise expects to cause no harm. Maybe none of these defendants formed a culpable intent; yet all are held to be intentional tortfeasors.

Could the point be administrative? Is figuring out whether a defendant intended to touch someone else simpler than figuring out whether the defendant intended harm? Or it might be possible to defend the logic of the rule with a different policy justification: people who act deliberately, even without intending harm, may be easier to deter than people who act entirely inadvertently, since the former are in a position to reflect in a more focused way on the likely consequences of their acts. Since by assumption the defendant is making a choice to commit a touching, we throw onto him (by holding the intent requirement then satisfied) the burden of determining whether the touching is authorized. This sounds right if you imagine that the people subject to the rule have knowledge of it, but in battery cases that's unlikely to be true, at least outside of institutional settings like hospitals.

Maybe the surface appeal of the deterrence argument suggests that it is aligned with some intuition about fairness—that someone who acts at all deliberately is blameworthy even when unintended harm results because they committed an invasion of the plaintiff's physical integrity. In a related vein, one can look at the problem this way: harm has been done, so the only question now is who should pay for it. White and Vosburg, the plaintiffs, are 100% blameless. Neher and Putney at least have deliberately done things that, even if not meant to be harmful, should have been understood to be unwelcome (and that turned out to cause much harm). So better that they should pay than the plaintiffs.

Or perhaps *White* is just wrong. Notice that the case involved a statute exempting the university for liability for an employee's battery. Is the intent requirement adopted in the case likely consistent with the point of that statute? Did Neher commit the sort of act for which it might make particular sense to let his employer off the hook? What sorts of acts best fit that category?

Q. Hypothetical: in *Garratt v. Dailey*, 279 P.2d 1091 (Wash. 1955), the defendant, Brian Dailey, was a five year old boy. One day he was visiting with two adult friends, Naomi and Ruth Garratt. Ruth Garratt claimed that as she started to sit down in a wood and canvas lawn chair in her back yard, the defendant deliberately pulled it out from under her. This caused her to fall to the ground and suffer a broken hip. The judge, who tried the case without a jury, did not accept the plaintiff's version of the facts, but instead found that the defendant moved the chair away from its spot without any desire to cause her to strike the ground. The judge entered a verdict and judgment for the defendant. The plaintiff appealed. What result?

A. *Held*, for the plaintiff, that the case should be remanded to the trial court for consideration of whether the defendant knew with substantial certainty that the plaintiff would strike the ground as a consequence of the his act. Said the court:

> A battery would be established if, in addition to plaintiff's fall, it was proved that, when Brian moved the chair, he knew with substantial certainty that the plaintiff would attempt to sit down where the chair had been. [...] The mere absence of any intent to injure the plaintiff or to play a prank on her or to embarrass her, or to commit an assault and battery on her would not absolve him from liability if in fact he had such knowledge.

On remand, the trial court found additional facts and held Brian Dailey liable for battery. The Washington Supreme Court affirmed. 304 P.2d 681 (1956). The main point the case makes is rarely important in battery cases, but it ends up being useful as a reference point if you go on to teach the other intentional torts later in the chapter; with respect to some of them the general idea in *Garratt* recurs: substantial certainly that a consequence will follow from an act, whether or not it is desired, may be enough to satisfy the intent requirement.

Some questions on the case:

Q. What does *Garratt* add to the cases already considered?
A. Two points. First, and not directly related to the intent element, you can commit a battery without touching the plaintiff by merely causing contact between the plaintiff and something else (e.g., the ground). Second, there need not even be an intent to cause contact. There need only be substantial certainty that the contact will result. The first point most often becomes important in cases where people throw or fire things at each other. The second point is not often important; the difference between a person intending that a touching result from his actions and a person merely being certain a touching will result is most likely to matter in cases involving children (like Dailey) or insane people who may be able to realize that a consequence will follow from their actions without quite forming an *intent* that it occur.

Q. There's an old Charles Addams cartoon where a miscreant—perhaps a member of the Addams family—driving on a mountain road waves another driver past him; we can see (and so can the miscreant) that in doing this he's going to create a collision between the other driver and an oncoming truck in the other lane. Liability for battery under *Garratt*? There's another Charles Addams cartoon where a miscreant parks his trailer next to the edge of a cliff and then invites his wife to step outside (and off the edge of the cliff). Liability?

A. Liability in both cases. Either case would be like telling the plaintiff to have a seat while knowing there's no chair there. That intermediate hypo serves as a bridge between the problems; it probably is indistinguishable in a principled way from *Garratt* and from the Addams cases.

Polmatier v. Russ (the L case of the insane defendant who shot his father in law)
Laidlaw v. Sage (the NL case of the philanthropist who used his clerk as a human shield)

Q. Suppose the defendant in *Polmatier* had been firing the gun as a demonstration of his omnipotence, claiming that he could cause the shot from the rifle to veer around his father in law?

A. No liability—for battery. The question in these cases is simply whether the defendant intended to cause the touching. The fact of insanity by itself adds nothing; it doesn't figure into the analysis. If it causes a defendant to have no intent where an ordinary person would, then there's no liability, though of course there may be liability for negligence, where again the courts make no allowance for lunacy.

Q. Do these rules seem likely in the long run to make insane people better off or worse off?

A. They probably make them worse off in the sense that they result in more liability than would exist if insanity somehow were factored in to the intent calculus. True, a lunatic escapes liability if he doesn't expect his behavior to result in any contact at all. But it seems likely that the more common fact pattern is the one represented by *Polmatier*. On the other hand, making the insane easier to sue might also make them better off by encouraging others to work with them. That is why the right to "sue or be sued" is important and desirable. Nobody wants to get sued; but if others know you can't be sued, it naturally may affect their willingness to put themselves at risk of your misbehavior. Might some of those who work with the insane be expected to charge a premium if they know the patient effectively will be impossible to sue if trouble arises?

Q. Is it fair to hold someone liable who was incapable of appreciating that what they were doing might be harmful, or who was unable to control her behavior?

A. How fair is it to let the injuries the insane person inflicts go unredressed? One can consider again the point suggested earlier about *White*: as between the injured plaintiff and the insane defendant, the one who caused the harm ought to pay for it. But this sort of thinking seems to suggest liability regardless of whether there even was an intent to make contact. Surely the actual reasons for liability, as the court in *Polmatier* suggests, have to do with policy: liability gives the kin and other watchers of lunatics an incentive to be more careful with them, since they may have an interest in their property in the long run. And disallowing an insanity defense obviates the need to separate sound from spurious insanity claims (though there remains the need to figure out what the insane person actually did intend).

Q. What is the distinction between *Polmatier v. Russ* and *Laidlaw v. Sage*?

A. The first thing to clarify is that strictly speaking we are worrying in this section about two elements of the battery tort. The first is *intent*, which is satisfied in both cases. The second is that the defendant have committed a voluntary act, which was found to be satisfied in *Polmatier* but not *Laidlaw*. But why? Russell Sage appeared to make a choice for himself, whereas Norman Russ was in the grip of delusions—voices (auditory hallucinations) telling him what to do or at least describing circumstances to him that might have been as frightening as those confronted by Russell Sage. Both defendants *thought* their lives were in danger. One possible distinction is that Russ didn't believe he was in imminent danger in the way that Sage did; the imaginary threat posed by his father in law was not an emergency. If he were sane and his father in law really *had* been an agent of the Chinese planning to kill him, he would have had no right to make a preemptive strike of this kind and his decision to do so certainly would be considered voluntary. The question this raises is whether Russ would have been held not liable if he had been seized upon by a delusion that his life was in imminent danger. It's hard to say (but we expect that he would have been). The court thinks it relevant that Russ at least was able to make a "crazy choice," and it's not clear whether that would also cover the case where he had a crazy belief that he was in immediate danger.

Another way to come at the cases is to ask whether it matters if the force that overrides the defendant's capacity for voluntary action is real or imagined, or if it matters whether the force was one that a rational person would find irresistible. When it comes to intent courts seem not to draw this distinction: we simply ask whether the defendant intended the contact and ignore whether the basis for the intention (or lack thereof) was an insane belief. (This was the point of the hypothetical above in which Russ intended the bullet to veer around the decedent.)

Still another way to put the question: is the test for "voluntary action" objective or subjective? It's tricky: one might say that it's objective in that the circumstances must be such that a reasonable person would have thought he had no choice in responding to them. *Laidlaw v. Sage* seems to imply as much. But that doesn't quite address the question of whether the facts underlying the danger must have been ones that a reasonable person would have perceived. In other words, a reasonable person might grab a human shield if he thought he was otherwise about to be killed (of course this can be contested, but assume it for now since the court evidently does); but should we also ask whether a reasonable person would have thought he was, in fact, about to be killed given the evidence at hand? If we ask the latter question it sometimes would bear very hard on insane defendants in cases where they do not draw reasonable inferences from their circumstances. It's tempting to say that since Russ lost in *Polmatier* the court must have been taking this ungenerous view of voluntarism, but we can't quite go that far because, as noted a moment ago, Russ didn't seem to believe—even on a crazy basis—that the threat he faced from his father in law was "pressing."

Q. If Sage did commit a battery (i.e., if his actions had been considered voluntary), when was it complete?

A. There were two potential batteries: one when Sage touched the clerk to guide him into the path of the blast, and another when the clerk was hit by the shrapnel. Whether these both were batteries has to do with the "contact" element of the battery tort, which is treated a little later in this section. The first touching might seem problematic as a battery because in itself it was not harmful or offensive; the second touching might seem problematic as a battery because it was not a contact between *Sage* and the clerk. But one can commit a battery by causing a contact between the plaintiff and some other surface or object (as illustrated by *Garratt* and by *Keel*, the next case). And a touching on the shoulder, not offensive in itself, might become a battery once its true nature or purpose was revealed (as the *Desnick* case discusses in the section of the chapter on trespass, and as other cases partially illustrate in the upcoming materials on consent).

Q. Suppose Sage learned that he was going to die unless he obtained a kidney transplant, and no kidneys were available. He drugs his clerk and harvests one of his kidneys while he is unconscious. Liability for battery? How would that case be distinguishable from *Laidlaw*?

A. The harvested kidney hypo is an obvious case of battery, of course, though in either case Sage would have sacrificed his clerk for the sake of "self-preservation." In the hypo, the invasion of the clerk's rights by Sage is greater, though then again the clerk may have suffered greater injury in the actual *Laidlaw* case than in the case of the stolen kidney. But the hypo also differs from *Laidlaw* because there was no comparable time pressure. This may have significance in at least two ways. First, the heat of the moment would provide no justification for Sage's decision to harvest the organ (but was Sage acting in the "heat of passion" in the actual case?). Second, there was plenty of time for Sage to try different ways of getting a kidney. Most importantly, he could have tried to obtain his clerk's consent as a donor; and perhaps where there is time do that, it must be done. In any event, in the kidney case there is time for the deterrent pressure of the law to take effect and make a difference. (We don't *want* Sage to take advantage of the clerk in either case, but trying to stop him from doing so on the facts of the actual *Laidlaw* case may be futile.)

In economic terms, the kidney hypo is a case of low transaction costs. We will return to this theory when we consider the necessity privilege and Posner's analysis of it. But note if the reason for no liability in Sage is that transaction costs were high (there was no time for discussion), the implication is that the ultimate arrangement (the use of the clerk as a human shield) is the one the parties would have reached if they could have. That seems unlikely, to say the least; if the clerk were to consent to such treatment, he presumably would demand very considerable compensation. Again, this foreshadows necessity cases like *Vincent*, which suggest that if the reason for no liability here is a kind of privilege created by the threat to Sage, then the clerk at least ought to be entitled to compensation for being used in this way. The point of *Laidlaw* itself seems to be different: there is no liability not because Sage faced great danger per se, but because he was not acting voluntarily.

Q. Was *Laidlaw v. Sage* correctly decided? Do the distinctions we have been considering make sense? What arguments would you make for or against its result?
A. You might invite students to look at the case from the standpoint either of corrective justice or of deterrence. As a matter of corrective justice Sage might seem less sympathetic than the defendant in *Polmatier*. He appears to have made a pretty cool decision to manipulate his clerk into harm's way. Having so chosen to sacrifice the welfare of another to save his own, perhaps the least he can be expected to do from an ethical standpoint is provide compensation. On the other hand, the court's "law of nature" remark might be understood as meaning that no person reasonably could be expected to do anything other than what Sage did under the circumstances, which (if true) might be thought to make Sage less blameworthy. But this point also leads to a policy argument: maybe the point is that it's unrealistic to imagine that we can deter people in Sage's circumstances from doing what he did; when confronted with immediate threats to their lives, people are going to grasp for survival any way they can, so from an economic standpoint liability will serve no purpose. On this view "involuntary" again is just one way of saying that someone is beyond the deterrent reach of the law. This helps distinguish the case of the stolen kidney. For whatever reason (what is the reason?), ordinary people who need kidneys do not try to harvest them from others without their consent; apart from the immorality of doing so, the law (criminal as well as civil) may be able to serve as a more effective deterrent in such circumstances that it can in cases like Sage's. There is plenty of time for the potential tortfeasor to contemplate the consequences of his actions.

Keel v. Hainline (D participates in eraser fight; eraser thrown at him hits P; L);
Manning v. Grimsley (pitcher throws baseball toward hecklers to scare them, but hits them instead; L)

Q. If one of the boys in *Keel* had been injured, would he have a good battery claim against the other boys? If so, what is the relationship between *Keel* and *Vosburg*?
A. The opinion implies as much. At first this part of *Keel* seems to be in tension with *Vosburg*, because the boys in *Keel* were engaged in the kind of horseplay that would seem to create the implied license missing in *Vosburg*; their horseplay was in a classroom that had not been called to order, which the court in *Vosburg* considered significant. But the defendant in *Keel* tried that argument and it failed: the court said the conduct was wrongful anyway. Therefore the intent was wrongful, and could transfer to the girl.

The idea that the boys could sue one another is the implication of the court's holding, not a dictum, since it is necessary to support the result here: there needs to be a battery in the background so that the intent from it can transfer to the plaintiff. But against this perhaps it could be argued that the boy in *Keel* merely would have a complete *prima facie* case against whoever hit him with the eraser; he nevertheless would lose because a defense would be available against him that would not be available against the girl: that he assumed the risk or should be barred from suit by his complicity in conduct that was against public policy.

An interesting intermediate hypothetical to consider is a simple game of catch with a ball or Frisbee. The Frisbee sails over the head of the person who was supposed to catch it and instead hits a bystander in the back of the head. Set aside possible claims of negligence; does the bystander have a good claim for battery? Probably not: the thrower did intend the Frisbee to come into contact with his partner, but this is not the kind of intent that can "transfer" to a third-party victim. Is *Keel* distinguishable?

Q. Suppose that the plaintiff in *Manning* had sued the hecklers that goaded Grimsley into throwing the ball in the plaintiff's direction. Could the hecklers be held liable for battery under *Keel*? (Or suppose we're playing poker and I accuse you of cheating. You pull out a gun. I declare that you're a coward and wouldn't dare use it. You shoot at me, but hit the person next to me. Am I liable?)

A. Probably no liability in either case, but it's an interesting issue. The jury instruction in *Keel* includes a long list of things that the defendant could have done to support liability: "aiding, abetting, encouraging, procuring or instigating." But "provoking" is not on the list. Arguably it could be squeezed into the word "instigating," but this seems doubtful. The court probably was trying to capture a notion of mutuality between the parties that was absent in Grimsley's case. A core case of mutuality would be one where two people are playing catch with a hand grenade that explodes between them, hurting a third person. Either of the two people could be held liable: it takes two to make this kind of trouble, and whether any given defendant was on the throwing or catching end when the grenade went off is fortuitous and shouldn't make a difference. Both are putting the plaintiff in danger, are blameworthy, and should be deterred. True, *Keel* was different from the core case of the grenade because the boys were throwing things *at* each other, not playing catch; in this sense the hecklers in *Manning* may not seem too different from the appellant in *Keel*. But the fight in *Keel* did have a back-and-forth mutuality, even if this is not captured well in the language of the jury instruction, which allows a finding of liability on the basis of encouragement alone.

You might ask how *Grimsley* could be made more like *Keel*. What if the hecklers had been throwing things at Grimsley? What if they had dared him to throw the ball their way? These hypos, especially the first, would bring *Grimsley* closer to *Keel*, but it still is hard to imagine liability for the hecklers. Provocation is no defense to battery of any sort (though it can be used to mitigate damages), and it might thus seem incongruous to say that the provocateur is responsible. Then again, encouragement is not a defense to battery, either, but the encourager in *Keel* is still held liable; and the taunting in the hypo is something that did put others at risk and that probably should be deterred.

Q. Suppose the boy who threw the eraser had grabbed a chair and made a throwing motion with it in the direction of his friend (the *Keel* appellant), but without letting go, in hopes of giving him a start. He doesn't actually intend to throw the chair at his friend or at anyone else. But the momentum of the fake throw causes the chair to slip out of his hands and to fall onto someone sitting right in front of him. Liability?

A. Yes, under *Manning v. Grimsley*. There was an intent to commit an assault, which is intent enough to support liability for the battery that actually resulted.

Q. Think back to *Knight v. Jewett*. If Jewett intended one sort of contact with Knight and committed another—as seemed to be the case there—then shouldn't the doctrine of transferred intent (as later described in *Keel* and *Manning*) have resulted in liability?

A. Only if the contact actually intended was itself a battery or was otherwise intentionally tortious. Perhaps the point here is that the contact Jewett did intend (the intent to at least jostle Knight) was lawful. It was within the "implied license" of the game, as Putney's kick might have been if it had occurred at recess. Yet the extent of Jewett's license is not so clear: there were no explicit rules laid down for the game, but Knight had told Jewett to stop playing so rough. If a jury could find that Jewett's intended contact with Knight was outside the license she had granted to him, couldn't it then find that there was sufficient intent to support a battery claim against him for stepping (inadvertently) on her finger?

2. *Minimum Requirements*

These materials and the set that follow (on consent) will take a couple of days to cover if you want to talk about all of the cases. This initial batch of four involves the minimum sorts of touchings that will be considered invasive or offensive enough to amount to a battery. These cases don't take long to cover. The next batch, though—*Grabowski* through *Werth*, and on to *Neal*—are very rich and make for lively, interesting, and sometimes long class discussions as the students try to figure out what principles might explain them. If you want to streamline your coverage of these pages and just spend a single day on them, you can skip the first set of cases—*Leichtman* through *Wallace*—and then assign just a selection from the rest: perhaps *Grabowski* and *Werth*, and then *McNeil* and the Restatement note that follows it. You can then use *Brzoska* and *Neal* as hypotheticals as time permits.

Leichtman v. WLW Jacor Communications, Inc. (D's radio host blows cigarette smoke in P's face; L)
Madden v. D.C. Transit System (D's bus sprays fumes at P; NL)

Q. What is the distinction between *Leichtman* and *Madden*?
A. The contact was similar in the two cases, but in *Madden* it was unintentional.

Q. Suppose the bus in *Madden* had been like the Batmobile (or perhaps some James Bond movie), so that the driver could pull a lever and send oily fumes out the back. Seeing the plaintiff, the driver pulls the lever as the bus is passing him. Liability?
A. Yes; that probably would be indistinguishable from *Leichtman*.

Q. What is the superficial similarity between *Madden* and *Garratt v. Dailey* (if you covered the latter case as a hypothetical)? What is the distinction between them?
A. In *Madden*, as in *Garratt*, the driver may have been substantially certain that fumes from the bus would contact the plaintiff. The distinction has to be on policy grounds. We want buses, and don't want every bus company held liable for battery when it drives past somebody and blows fumes their way. We don't want people to pull chairs out from under others, and need not worry about discouraging a valuable activity if we find liability in the *Garratt* case.

Q. Suppose you're at a restaurant where the person at the next table is (lawfully) smoking. The smoke drifts into your face, annoying you immensely. You ask the smoker to put out the cigarette. The smoker replies with a rude gesture. The smoke continues, as does your annoyance. Do you have a claim for battery under *Leichtman*? What if he deliberately moves his ashtray closer to your table?
A. The court went out of its way to disclaim liability in the first circumstance: "We do not, however, adopt or lend credence to the theory of a "smoker's battery," which imposes liability if there is substantial certainty that exhaled smoke will predictably contact a nonsmoker." If the smoker deliberately blows smoke in your direction the case becomes closer, for then we have the overtones of humiliation that worried the court in *Leichtman*. Perhaps the courts want to provide remedies for such provocations because without them there is a greater danger of attempts at private justice. The plaintiff's actual likelihood for recovery probably would depend on the court's patience with seemingly trivial lawsuits. Again from the *Leichtman* opinion:

> Arguably, trivial cases are responsible for an avalanche of lawsuits in the courts. They delay cases that are important to individuals and corporations and that involve important social issues. The result is justice denied to litigants and their counsel who must wait for their day in court.

However, absent circumstances that warrant sanctions for frivolous appeals under App.R. 23, we refuse to limit one's right to sue. [...] This case emphasizes the need for some form of alternative dispute resolution operating totally outside the court system as a means to provide an attentive ear to the parties and a resolution of disputes in a nominal case. Some need a forum in which they can express corrosive contempt for another without dragging their antagonist through the expense inherent in a lawsuit. Until such an alternative forum is created, Leichtman's battery claim, previously knocked out by the trial judge in the first round, now survives round two to advance again through the courts into round three.

Q. Suppose you're on the bus and someone sneezes on you. Later it turns out that the sneeze infected you with smallpox or some other dread disease—or for that matter the flu. Liability for battery?
A. Probably—at least in the smallpox case. The contact would be sufficient under *Leichtman*; the question would be whether sneezing on someone is within the society's "generally acceptable standards of conduct" (and whether the sneeze can be understood as sufficiently voluntary and intentional).

Q. Suppose there's a solar eclipse and I sell you a pair of sunglasses to use to look at it that I assure you are adequate for the purpose. Actually the sunglasses are made of cheap plastic; I know this, but I lied because I wanted the sale. You go and gaze at the eclipse, and it causes damage to your eyes. Liability for battery?
A. Possibly. The rays of light might be analogized to the particulate matter in *Leichtman*. If so (i.e., if there was sufficient contact in the case to support a battery claim), the rest of the case becomes analogous to *Garratt v. Dailey* and the Charles Addams hypotheticals that followed it: my statements caused contact between you and something else; I knew it was likely to happen, regardless of whether I *wanted* it to happen.

Morgan v. Loyacomo (the plaintiff's box is seized by a suspicious store manager; L)
Wallace v. Rosen (the plaintiff falls downstairs when given a push by the defendant; NL)

Q. I deliberately knock the baseball cap off of your head. Liability for battery?
A. Yes.

Q. What if I toss a firecracker in front of the horse you're riding, causing it to charge off into a gully. Have I committed a battery against you?
A. Probably so, at least if you suffer any harm as a result. You might build there by asking whether placing a lit firecracker in someone's shoe is a battery (yes; see *Waters v. Blackshear*, 591 N.E.2d 184 (Mass. 1992), and whether it would be a battery to punch the horse in the jaw (yes—a battery against the rider; see *Van Eaton v. Thon*, 764 S.W.2d 674 (Mo.App. 1988)). This hypothetical is distinguishable because the firecracker did not touch the horse, but perhaps transferred intent applies (though you can't assault a horse...). The point to stress is that there is some interaction between the elements of the tort. If the defendant meant to offend, then a smaller contact will considered enough to support a battery claim. The Restatement excerpts make this clear.

Q. What is the distinction between *Morgan v. Loyacomo* and *Wallace v. Rosen*?
A. First note the similarities, and the respects in which *Wallace*—which is NL—seems the worse case. The touching in *Wallace* was not insulting, but it turned out to be physically a lot more harmful than the touching in *Morgan*. Indeed, in *Morgan* the plaintiff's body was not touched at all; in *Wallace* it was. In both cases one can argue that there was some sort of emergency or exigent circumstance. In neither case was there consent in fact on the plaintiff's part. The difference seems to involve notions of consent implied in law. People have to be able to push other people a little when a fire alarm goes off, but apparently there is no comparable felt need to let managers seize boxes from customers. Query, though,

whether the result in *Morgan* would have been different if the box had turned out to contain stolen merchandise.

Q. What is the distinction between *Wallace v. Rosen* and *Vosburg v. Putney*?
A. The point of the question is to get students to think about the different elements of the tort and see the relationship between them. There evidently was intent in both *Vosburg* and *Wallace*, though one way to look at *Wallace* is to say that the full required intent was lacking: there was intent to commit the touching, but not in an environment where it was in any sense unlawful. Whether any consent to the touching could be implied in fact may be questioned (compare *White*), but then perhaps implied license can be found from the emergency circumstances: even if the plaintiff didn't consent, we insist that her consent be found in law because the good of everyone else (the students trying to get down the stairs) requires it. In any event the court framed in a related by slightly distinct way: as whether the touching itself was harmful or offensive. Notice how this question can merge with the aspect of the intent question that focuses on whether the intent was "unlawful" (In *Vosburg's* unfortunate phrasing).

3. Consent and its Limits

See notes to previous section for suggestions on what you might cut here.

Mohr v. Williams (doctor operates on wrong ear; L)
Grabowski v. Quigley (ghost surgery: L)
Brzoska v. Olson (dentist with AIDS: NL)
Cohen v. Smith (Woman touched by male nurse against her wishes; L)
Werth v. Taylor (Jehovah's witness receives transfusion; NL)
Neal v. Neal (problem: battery suit against husband who had an affair; L)

Q. Mohr consented to an ear operation, and that is what she got. Why isn't that statement a good defense for Williams?
A. Because the issue isn't semantic. It's whether she understood herself, in agreeing to the procedure, to be consenting to an operation on one ear in particular or on any ear as needed. One can imagine the latter circumstance, but evidently there was no evidence of such a state of mind in this case.

Q. All right, but suppose Williams had asked Mohr before the operation: "If I find that the right ear is okay and that the left is not, should I take care of the left one?" Isn't it obvious that she would have said "yes"? What rational basis could there be for consenting to the work on the right ear but not the left ear?
A. Perhaps none; that affirmative answer probably would have been her reply. But consent to battery cannot generally be founded on beliefs about what the plaintiff would (definitely) have consented to if she had been asked. *Actual* consent must be obtained. There are exceptions—cases where good guesses about consent are permitted—when transaction costs are prohibitive, as when (in the situation the court mentions) there is an emergency. But here there was no obstacle to either securing Mohr's consent either in advance or waiting to operate until it was obtained afterwards.

Q. Can you think of an argument that Mohr was made *better* off by Williams's decision that she would been if he had waited until her permission had been obtained?
A. She was under a general anaesthetic, which always has risks (especially a hundred years ago). Operating on the spot spared her a second round of exposure to those risks. But she would have been best off of all if Williams had asked her *in advance* for permission to work on both ears; and this decision gives future doctors in the position of Williams an incentive to take that first-best route.

Q. Turning to *Grobowski v. QuigleyI:* What were Grabowski's damages? (What were the damages in *Mohr v. Williams*?)

A. From the *Grabowski* opinion:

> Where it is proven that an unauthorized invasion of a person's personal integrity has occurred, even if harmless, the person is entitled to nominal damages. Prosser and Keeton, *Law of Torts* § 9 at p. 40 (5th ed.1984). In *Perna v. Pirozzi,* 92 N.J. 446, 457 A.2d 431, (1983), the New Jersey Supreme Court further explained:

> "The plaintiff may further recover for all injuries proximately caused by the mere performance of the operation, whether the result of negligence or not. If an operation is properly performed, albeit by a surgeon operating without the consent of the patient and the patient suffers no injuries except those which foreseeably follow from the operation, then a jury could find that the substitution of surgeons did not cause any compensable injury. Even there, however, a jury could award damages for mental anguish resulting from the belated knowledge that the operation was performed by a doctor to whom the patient had not given consent. Furthermore, because battery connotes an intentional invasion of another's rights, punitive damages may be assessed in an appropriate case."

Q. What is the distinction between *Grabowski* and *Brzoska v. Olson*?

A. In both cases the plaintiffs received treatment that they would have rejected if they had known the truth about the person performing them. In *Grabowski* the issue was the truth of the doctor's identity; in *Brzoska* the issue was the truth about the doctor's medical condition. It may be hard to see in the abstract why a line should be drawn between them. A patient may be more or less indifferent to a doctor's identity, so long as he is competent, but keenly interested in whether the doctor has medical problems that put the patient at risk. Of course part of the court's reasoning in the dental case was that Owens' condition *didn't* put his patients at risk. But the patients' belief that they were threatened by AIDS, even if unreasonable, may be matched by Grabowski's belief, perhaps also unreasonable, that it mattered whether his doctor was Quigley or Bailes. (Maybe Bailes was *better* than Quigley.) It's a useful exercise to tell a student to imagine arguing the *Brzoska* case for the plaintiffs, and to ask how the *Grabowski* case should then be described; in other words, they should complete the sentence "*Grabowski* stands for the proposition that...." in a way that suggests there should be liability in *Brzoska*.

The distinction between the cases probably has to do with administrative convenience and some other policy concerns. If we recognize a battery claim in *Brzoska*, then the general principle (the proposition that the case will be understood to stand for) has to be that such claims arise whenever health care providers fail to reveal some facts about themselves that would have caused their patients (or perhaps a reasonable person) to seek treatment elsewhere. This would create several kinds of problems. First, it opens a can of worms concerning what such providers have to disclose about their personal situations: diseases of all kinds? Drinking problems? Pending malpractice suits brought by other patients? Second, after the fact, when a plaintiff announces that such a disclosure would have prevented his consent, a jury would have to decide whether such claims such claims are true. Some plaintiffs may be telling the truth; some may be lying; some may think they are telling the truth but be misjudging what their own reaction would have been. Juries inevitably will screw up in trying to sort these possibilities out. Finally, normative problems would arise in deciding which objections to honor. Suppose the plaintiff is a bigot who discovers late that his dentist is Jewish and announces that he never would have consented to treatment if he had known this. It is hard to imagine a court upholding a claim for battery on these facts, though they do indulge other idiosyncratic claims when based on different sort of religious preference—as *Cohen v. Smith* shows.

A bright-line rule regarding the identity of the physician is a different matter. It reflects a generalization about a feature of the physician—his identity—that most people might agree they regard as material to their consent, at least as a default principle (as the Restatement excerpt says, it's often different as a matter of contract). More to the point, it's an easy rule to state and enforce without most of the line-drawing principles that would arise with liability in *Brzoska*.

Q. What is the distinction between *Cohen v. Smith* and *Brzoska v. Olson* (the NL case of the dentist who had AIDS)?

A. Liability in *Cohen* might seem inconsistent with the analysis just offered, because the plaintiff's sensitivity here was idiosyncratic. Again, challenge someone to state what *Brzoska* stands for in a way that suggests there shouldn't be liability in *Cohen v. Smith*. The cases seem similar because in both of them the plaintiff had objections that might not have been shared by a "reasonable person"—though there are some nice definitional problems here. An average member of the community probably wouldn't have minded the defendant's conduct in *Cohen*; an average member of the community might have objected to having dentistry performed on them by someone with AIDS, but in the judgment of the court those people, while possibly average, wouldn't be *reasonable*. So query whether reasonable means average, and whether a reasonable person means a person with typical religious views. The court in *Cohen* seems inclined to take as a benchmark the reasonable person *with* the plaintiff's religious views. (The *Friedman* case in the "reasonable person" section of the negligence chapter raises similar questions.) Perhaps the point is that the court is more comfortable second-guessing strong reactions against people with AIDS than it is second-guessing unusual religious views.

But the key point is that in *Cohen v. Smith* the idiosyncratic preference was registered in advance. This obviates many of the administrative problems considered above: the post-hoc guessing games about the veracity of the plaintiff's claim, and the provider's uncertainty about what has to be revealed. The implication is that *Brzoska* would have come out differently if the plaintiff had said to the doctor in advance that his consent was conditioned on the doctor not having AIDS. This is plausible, though it is made difficult by the fact that some of the dentist's patients claimed that they asked him whether he had the disease and he denied it. Still, perhaps this is not quite the same as making a clear statement in advance that consent is conditioned on the state of his health. (Suppose the plaintiff in *Cohen* merely had asked whether there were male nurses at the hospital, and incorrectly had been told there were not. Without more, this probably wouldn't have been enough to support her battery claim.) It is possible that a court would reject a battery claim even if a clear statement *were* made in advance on the ground that an objection to a dentist with AIDS is irrational and can't be honored as a matter of public policy; this probably is the result we would expect if the patient told the dentist that his consent was conditioned on assurance that the doctor was not Jewish, which assurances later turned out to be false.

The general lesson is that consent with conditions made clear in advance receives greater judicial solicitude than claims after the fact that consent wouldn't have been given if the truth had been known. This may not always seem fair to plaintiffs, who in a case like *Brzoska* had no reason to make their conditions clear in advance since they didn't think Owens had AIDS (though apparently a few of them did ask him about this). But there are other truth-seeking advantages that make explicit conditions in advance preferable to objections raised in hindsight, as explained above.

Q. What is the distinction between *Werth v. Taylor* and *Cohen v. Smith*?

A. The distinction has a bit of a Hand-formula quality to it. As the costs of honoring the patient's preference get higher, we require a clearer statement of it. In Werth's case, the costs seem extremely high: likely death. Under this circumstance the presumption that the patient would want the procedure becomes very powerful, both as a generalization about what most people would want if they could be asked and because as a social matter we place a high value on saving a life. The same points can be viewed from the doctor's point of view: if he decides to honor his rough sense of the patient's preference and lets her die as a result, his potential exposure if he made a misjudgment is enormous. The costs of making an error the other way seem much smaller, though of course they are hard to quantify: we are talking now about the cost of violating the plaintiff's religious wishes.

Anyway, the lesson is that the doctor has to have more than a rough sense; he has to have a perfectly clear demand from the patient before withholding a life-saving procedure. Indeed, the standard the court imposes is so high that it's not clear there is anything Werth could have done to avoid having the transfusion: the court says that the refusal has to be contemporaneous and informed, and obviously that will be impossible if the crisis arises while she is unconscious. But maybe it also mattered that Werth and her husband showed the slightest signs of irresolution when questioned by the doctor in advance. An iron-clad declaration in advance that she would rather die than receive a transfusion might have been enough to support a battery claim afterwards, but nothing less would do.

Q.   Suppose that a man falls unconscious behind the wheel of his car and drives into a tree. An ambulance takes him to the hospital, and a doctor concludes that the man had a heart attack and will die unless he receives requires heart surgery. He performs the surgery successfully. The man wakes up and is appalled; he is a Christian Scientist, and would not have consented to the operation. The operation requires a long and painful convalescence. He sues the doctor for battery. Liability?

A.   No liability. We can assume it's 100% clear that there would have been no consent if the plaintiff had been awake. Where consent is implied in law, we aren't interested in finding out later whether there really would have been consent. The point is that ex ante, the benefits of operating reasonably appeared to dwarf the costs. We want doctors to operate in these circumstances, not hesitate because this might be the one case in a million where the patient would rather die. A comparison of the costs of making a mistake either way make the result clear.

Q.   What result in *Neal v. Neal*?

A.   Liability(!). The trial court gave summary judgment to the defendant:

> [W]e conclude that Thomas' failure to disclose his relationship with Jill LaGasse did not invalidate Mary's consent to engage in sexual intercourse with him. Although Thomas deceived Mary as to the exclusivity of their relationship—a factor arguably bearing upon her consent to sexual intercourse with him—it did not directly or substantially relate to the essential nature of the physical contact she consented to.

Then the Idaho Supreme Court reversed:

> Mary Neal's affidavit states that: "[I]f the undersigned had realized that her husband was having sexual intercourse with counterdefendant LaGasse, the undersigned would not have consented to sexual intercourse with counterdefendant Neal and to do so would have been offensive." The district court opined that because the act was not actually offensive at the time it occurred, her later statements that it would have been offensive were ineffective. This reasoning ignores the possibility that Mary Neal may have engaged in a sexual act based upon a substantial mistake concerning the nature of the contact or the harm to be expected from it, and that she did not become aware of the offensiveness until well after the act had occurred. Mary Neal's affidavit at least raises a genuine issue of material fact as to whether there was indeed consent to the alleged act of battery.

> The district court also noted that Mary Neal's later sexual relations with her husband after becoming aware of his infidelity, extinguished any offensiveness or lack of consent. The fact that she may have consented to sexual relations on a later occasion cannot be said to negate, as a matter of law, an ineffective consent to prior sexual encounters. Again, her affidavit raises a question of fact regarding whether these prior sexual encounters were nonconsensual. This factual issue precluded the dismissal of the battery claim by the district court.

Q.   Can the result in *Neal* be squared with *Brzoska v. Olson* (the NL case of the dentist who did not tell his patients that he had AIDS)?

A. *Neal v. Neal* may seem a surprising result. To say that the "fraud" went to the essence of the consent implies a quite particular view of the sexual act—that Mrs. Neal was not consenting to sex with her husband so much as to sex with her *faithful* husband. Then again, it seems plausible on its face that a spouse who learns of the adultery of her husband might well not consent to sex with him—though in this case the plaintiff apparently *did* so consent later on. One can suggest that in *Neal* the wife's objection included not only the changed feelings she would have had for her husband but also the risk that she might get some sort of disease indirectly from LaGasse; but this doesn't distinguish the case from *Brzoska*, where the dentist's patients likewise may have had general worries of that sort.

Then there are additional puzzles on the policy side. The decision discourages adultery, since it makes all adulterers potentially liable for battery for having sex with their spouses. But it also encourages vigorous efforts to avoid confessing adultery, since the case arms the betrayed and infuriated spouse with a mighty legal weapon: a claim for battery for any sexual acts in which they have engaged since the affair started. This would seem a particularly serious threat as an adjunct to the divorce proceedings that sometimes are a sequel to revelations of infidelity. We find it doubtful that *Neal* represents the view most courts would take.

Q. What is the distinction between the two illustrations given from § 57 of the Second Restatement of Torts? (In the first, A uses a counterfeit bill to buy sexual favors from B and is not held liable; in the second, A uses a counterfeit bill to induce B to submit to a blood transfusion and *is* held liable.)
A. From § 57 of the First Restatement:

> b. *Liability for bodily harm when assent fraudulently obtained.* The fact that an assent is procured by fraudulent misrepresentations of a collateral matter does not prevent it from being effective to protect the actor from such liability as is predicated solely upon the fact of the intentional invasion. The purely dignitary interests of personality, such as the interest in freedom from a merely transitory confinement, are protected only against intentional and unpermitted invasion. Therefore, the assent, though procured by fraud, protects the actor from liability. On the other hand, interest in freedom from bodily harm is protected from any form of conduct which is intended or likely to cause it. Therefore, while the fraudulently procured assent protects the actor from liability predicated upon the mere fact that the contact has been inflicted, he is still subject to liability for any bodily harm which results from the contact to which he has fraudulently induced the actor to submit, not because of any lack of consent to the contact, but because of the fraudulent, and therefore tortious, means by which the assent has been procured, with knowledge that the contact will or may prove harmful.

So the difference is that the blood transfusion causes more than dignitary harm.

Hart v. Geysel (battery during illegal prize fight; NL)
McNeil v. Mullin (battery during impromptu brawl between buggy drivers; L)

Notice that the Restatement recommends the minority position; this might be a good time to explain that the Restatement view and the majority view are not always the same thing.

Q. Should people who agree to fight be able to collect damages from each other?
A. Some ways of looking at the problem are suggested by the opinions in *Hart* and *McNeil*: on the one hand, there is a reluctance to financially "reward" the person who consented to fight and got the worst of it (how were his rights invaded?); on the other hand, there is a sense that the public is made worse off by these fights, and that they ought to be discouraged.

Another way to look at this question, as suggested by the note following these cases, is to ask which rule will better discourage fights. Presumably people who fight usually expect to win, which means inflicting more costs on their opponent than they incur themselves. Such people would not want liability; liability makes losers better off. So if the rule is going to have any effect on fights, the majority rule holding mutual combatants liable to each other is more likely than the minority rule to discourage them.

For those students having trouble conceptualizing this, the choice between the two rules can be compared to a choice between two messages being sent to brawlers: "you guys are on your own" vs. "you both are going to pay for whatever damage you do to each other." The latter seems more likely to discourage a fight, does it not? For both sides probably think they will win, which means they both will have to worry about paying out more in damages than they are able to collect.

Q. Is it realistic to think that decisions to fight will be affected by the tort rule?
A. Perhaps it's not realistic if you imagine that every fight looks like the one in *McNeil*. People who get into impromptu fights are usually acting in the heat of passion, and the inducement for the fight and the blows struck usually follow in rapid succession without great reflection—even assuming they have any idea what the rule is, which they probably don't. But what about fights like the one in *Hart*? That case involved an illegal prize fight. In other words, it was planned, and indeed it presumably was staged largely for the money; people who so plan ahead—or *some* of them, which is all that's necessary for the law to have some effect—might well worry about the legal rules. There's a loose comparison possible to earlier points made in the voluntary act cases (the kidney harvesting hypo, etc.): people with time to reflect are easier to deter.

Hollerud v. Malamis (battery claim against bartender for indian wrestling match; plaintiff claims his consent was ineffective because given while drunk; L)

Q. Suppose the bartender had been drunk. Would this be a good defense to the plaintiff's battery claim? To what element would it be potentially relevant? What case that we have considered is most on point?
A. It could undercut the defendant's voluntariness, or more plausibly his intent. But intoxication is not otherwise a defense to a battery claim. We read no cases precisely on point, but if insanity is no defense, then a fortiori intoxication should not be.

Q. So why does the court say that Hollerud's consent is ineffective if he was incapable for "expressing a rational will"? Why might we treat intoxication as undercutting consent but not intent?
A. Think of it in policy terms. We are suspicious of prima facie batteries and want to err on the side of deterring them; if we overdeter them, that is not likely to be much of a loss. We so err on the side of deterrence by being tough on people who commit apparent batteries (letting the intent requirement be easily satisfied), and easy on their victims (and thus additionally tough on the batterers) by being slow to find consent. If we are too slow to find consent, the worst that can happen is that some people will forego indian wrestling matches, boxing matches, and perhaps sexual encounters that they might have enjoyed. If we are too quick to find consent, we may give the go-ahead to some situations that end in broken hands and much worse. These latter costs seem more serious than the costs of foregoing the prima facie batteries.

Miller v. Couvillion (problem: karate demonstration; NL)

Q. What result in *Miller*?
A. The court found no liability, reasoning as follows:

> [B]y striking the concrete pad with his foot, the defendant, Savage, was not directing his act to the person of the plaintiff. Nor was his act offensive or insulting so as to result in personal indignity to the plaintiff. His act was directed toward striking the concrete pad for whatever consequences

it might have on the concrete pad. The fact that his act was in poor judgment, reckless, or negligent because of plaintiff's position in relation to the concrete pad, does not equate to his act being an intentional contact with the person of the plaintiff. It is simply negligence. A similar incident could be envisioned where the defendant strikes a wooden stake being held by plaintiff with a sledge hammer, causing the wooden stake to shatter and injure plaintiff's hand, or even causing the sledge hammer to glance off the stake and strike plaintiff in the head. These acts would not constitute a battery against the person or dignity of the plaintiff. There is no contact intended with the person or dignity of the plaintiff. The intent of the defendant obviously is not to cause contact with the plaintiff's person. While it is foreseeable the plaintiff could be injured, this foreseeability involves negligence, and not an intentional act.

The court's reasoning is a good example of how hypothetical variations can be used to create effective legal arguments. You might ask whether the problem facts can be distinguished from a case involving a sledge hammer and stake of the sort that the court describes.

Q. What are the issues in the problem?
A. Did the defendant have the necessary intent to support a battery? Did he commit a harmful or offensive touching of the plaintiff?

Q. What are the most useful intent cases to bring to bear on the problem?
A. *White v. University of Idaho* holds that a defendant can be held liable for battery even if a touching was not intended to be harmful at all—so long as it was unpermitted (see below). But it does also require an intent to complete the touching.

Q. What are the most useful "touching" cases to bring to bear on the problem?
A. *Morgan v. Loyacomo* holds that the touching requirement can be satisfied by contacting something the plaintiff is holding, but is distinguishable because the touching here was not done in a rude or insolent manner (which the court in *Morgan* thought was important). Was there consent to the contact here? Perhaps only at first, and not when Miller climbed down: maybe Savage then went too far. You might also then try analogies to the mutual combat cases: was this a type of consent that we do not want to honor, perhaps because we don't want to encourage informal exhibitions of karate? Or do you lean the other way and say that Miller got himself into this and has nothing to complain about now? The demonstration was not illegal, after all, much less a breach of the peace. Was it against Chuck's rules? Does it matter?

Section B. Trespass

If you want to make cuts, the best candidates are the two cases at the end of the chapter, *Edwards* and *Smith*, which discuss liability for trespass by aircraft or entrants into caves under the plaintiff's land. The issues are interesting, but they take some time to discuss, and the general ideas in them usually get covered in the first-year property course.

Desnick v. American Broadcasting Co. (D's investigative reporters enter P's clinics pretending to be patients; NL for trespass)

Q. In *Desnick*, investigative reporters posed as patients and underwent eye examinations at the plaintiff's clinics. The court accepted that the plaintiff would not have consented to the entry of the phony patients if he had known of their motives. Why was it nevertheless held that the reporters were not liable for trespassing?

A. Because (the court said) there was no invasion of the plaintiff's interest in the inviolability of his property. The meaning of this is not entirely clear—perhaps even to the court, which works toward its result largely by feeling its way through strings of other L and NL cases. Explaining when the use of fraud to obtain consent gives rise to a trespass or battery claim is quite difficult. The courts talk about a line where the fraud somehow starts going to the essence of what the plaintiff thinks he is getting, but the line is hazy and sometimes seems unsatisfactory. In *Desnick* it also seemed to matter that the defendants had thrown open their doors to the public. That is how the court distinguished *Dietemann v. Time, Inc.*

A possible objection to the result in *Desnick*, and a way to distinguish it from the NL cases the court describes, is that in those other cases there is generally some sort of potential benefit that the plaintiff gains if the defendant's entry is allowed. The restaurant might get a good review; the car dealership might sell a car; etc. But it's not clear that there was any possible upside for the plaintiff in *Desnick* here: if the defendants had found no evidence of wrongdoing, they would have had no story. Well, but maybe you could suggest that eye clinics generally (though not the Desnick clinic in particular) are made better off if they can be inspected by undercover reporters like this, because then they get policed and the public can have confidence in the good ones. And of course there is a public benefit to having the wrongdoing exposed—a benefit which, however, might arguably be better captured under a First Amendment analysis than through an inquiry into whether the defendant committed a private trespass. (For a different result from *Desnick* on similar facts, see *Food Lion, Inc., v. Capital Cities/ABC, Inc.*, 194 F.3d 505 (4th Cir. 1999)).

Q. The court says that the distinctions between fraud that does and does not vitiate consent "are the traces of the old forms of action, which have resulted in a multitude of artificial distinctions in modern law. But that is nothing new." What does this mean?
A. It's a little puzzling. If you assigned the portion of the introduction to the casebook that discusses the old forms of action, you can tie it in here. Apparently the idea is that in the old days when cases of battery or trespass qcf were all brought as suits claiming *trespass vi et armis*, the harm had to be incurred "directly" for liability to result. Perhaps the court is perceiving a link between that old requirement and the modern idea it suggests that a battery or trespass only occurs when there is an invasion of the plaintiff's right to the inviolable integrity of his person or property.

Q. Does the false motive idea familiar from *Rains* and *Freedman* (in the battery section) explain *Desnick?*
A. No; there was a false motive in *Desnick*, but no liability. Surely part of the reason for the *Desnick* decision was that there is a possible social benefit from the type of investigative reporting at issue. Here as in *Madden* (the NL case of the bus fumes), courts are reluctant to open the floodgates to a new types of intentional tort suits, and reluctant as well to deter activities that may have substantial upside.

Q. Can *Desnick* be distinguished from *Neal v. Neal* (the L case in the battery section where the wife sued her husband for having sexual relations with her once she learned he had been having an affair)?
A. They seem similar because in both cases the defendant was hiding something that would have caused the plaintiff to withhold consent. *Neal* does not seem consistent with the discussion in *Desnick* that tries to link liability to whether the plaintiff's right to physical integrity was violated; but maybe one could make something of the risk in *Neal* that the wife risked contracting a venereal disease from her unfaithful husband, and thus analogize it to *Crowell v. Crowell* (the L case mentioned in the *Desnick* opinion where the plaintiff got a venereal disease from the defendant and sued for battery).

Pegg v. Gray (D's dogs run onto P's land and frighten his cattle; L)
Malouf v. Dallas Athletic Club (D's golfers hit balls onto P's land; NL)

Q. How should the cases be stylized (i.e., what factual assumptions should we make) if we are to consider *Pegg* a case of liability and *Malouf* a case of no liability?

A. The question is asked because *Malouf* is a "no liability" case in a weaker sense than most of the NL cases in the book: the court affirms a jury verdict for the defendant rather than saying the club was entitled to judgment as a matter of law. So it's worth taking a minute to clarify how the procedural posture affects accurate thinking about the facts. In *Pegg* the defendant won the equivalent of judgment as a matter of law in the trial court, and this was reversed; so we just look at the plaintiff's evidence, which was the basis for the appellate decision. That means we assume that the defendant knew his dogs were headed onto the plaintiff's property (intent to send them there would suffice for liability as well, but if we want to find the outer boundary of the rule it makes more sense to focus on the lesser requirement of *knowledge* that the court says is enough). Indeed, the court refers even just to "constructive" knowledge, which might mean that the defendant should have known the dogs were headed onto the plaintiff's property, or perhaps that he knew enough other facts to make him chargeable with knowledge of this fact as well—regardless of whether he was conscious of it (a subjective inquiry that a court might sensibly like to avoid where it can).

In *Malouf* the defendant won judgment after a trial, so this time we interpret the facts as favorably to the defendant as is reasonable; thus we assume that the golfers intended to hit the balls to the sixth hole, not toward the plaintiffs' properties. In this way—i.e., with those assumptions in place—the cases can pretty robustly be styled L and NL even though the court didn't say that these parties *had* to be held liable and not liable respectively. We compare the plaintiff's side of the story in *Pegg* with the defendant's account in *Malouf*.

Q. What is the distinction between *Pegg* and *Malouf*?

A. First clarify the superficial similarity. In both cases the defendants were engaged in a sporting activity that created a risk of damage to a neighbor's property; in both cases the neighbor's property was in fact damaged. In *Pegg* the defendant loosed dogs, knowing they might well run onto the plaintiff's land; in *Malouf* the defendant loosed golfers, perhaps knowing that they might well hit balls that sliced onto adjacent properties.

It's tempting to say the difference is that in *Pegg* the dogs' owner intended to send them onto the plaintiff's land, whereas in *Malouf* the golfers didn't intend to send their golf balls onto the plaintiff's cars. But that may be too strong. Remember that in *Pegg* it is said to be enough if the dogs' owner has "knowledge, actual or constructive" that the dogs are likely to end up on his neighbors' land. If we focus on that minimum requirement and assume it is all the plaintiff in *Pegg* was able to show (see previous question), we have two ways of thinking about the difference between the cases. One is that maybe in *Malouf* the legal standard is just different. The court speaks only of intent, not of knowledge, so maybe it thought knowledge wasn't enough. A true intent standard makes life much easier for a defendant: obviously the golfers here didn't *intend* to hit their balls onto the plaintiffs' automobiles. But this seems a little hard to swallow; suppose the defendant golfers mistakenly hooked shots every day onto the plaintiffs' cars. Eventually wouldn't we expect their knowledge of this likely outcome to turn them trespassers, even if it never was the result they *wanted*? This suggestion is not quite consistent with the court's phrasing, so perhaps it isn't correct; maybe instead the facts just described would give rise to claims for negligence. But if one does accept that a defendant's knowledge of a likely invasion can be enough to satisfy the intent requirement for a trespass, the distinction between these two cases would have to be that the defendant in *Pegg* had a higher degree of certainty that his dogs would go onto the plaintiff's land than the golfers in *Malouf* had that their balls would leave the course.

The interesting question then becomes how often such an invasion has to accidentally occur before we start calling it "intentional" despite the fact that it isn't actually desired by the defendant.

Q. What if I get lost in the woods between our properties and wander onto your property accidentally—"accidentally" in the sense that I have every intention of staying on my side of the boundary, but fail to do so. I neither intend to be on your property nor know that I am on your property. Am I a trespasser?

A. Yes. The point is that you intended to be where you were; you intended to take the steps you took. The relevant intent is not the intent to trespass; it's the intent to enter the land (which turns out not to be your own). This is the point of part (a) of section 164 of the Second Restatement.

Q. What if the golfers in *Malouf* saw some laundry hanging on a line behind the plaintiff's house, mistook it for the flag on the sixth green, and therefore shot in that direction?

A. Liability. This is the implication of the answer to the previous question about mistaken entries. But the Restatement provision on mistaken intrusions suggests that there would be no trespass here if the plaintiff had erected a flag in hopes of luring golf balls onto his land.

Q. What is the relationship between the standards of intent in battery cases and trespass cases?

A. They are similar in that the intent for battery requires an intent to complete the touching, just as the intent required for trespass is an intent to enter (or to cause a thing to enter) the defendant's property. You need not intend to invade anyone's rights. The "actual or constructive knowledge" of *Pegg* is a little like the intent standard seen in *Garratt v. Dailey*, a hypothetical offered to accompany the battery section. The difference between intent and knowledge is less likely to be an issue in battery cases than in trespass cases, because usually if you touch a person you intend to do so, whereas causing things to fly onto someone else's land can more easily be done with knowledge but without intent. But the difference is one of practical likelihood, not formal doctrine. Thus if the golf balls in *Malouf* had hit the plaintiff on the head, there would be no liability for battery just as there was no liability for trespass in the actual case. If either event happened often enough, there might eventually be liability for an intentional tort, at least in a jurisdiction that recognized that knowledge without desire can satisfy an intent requirement.

Q. Hypothetical: in *In re Air Crash Disaster at Cove Neck, Long Island*, 885 F.Supp. 434 (E.D.N.Y. 1995), the defendant's Boeing 707 aircraft crashed into the back yard of the plaintiffs, a Long Island family named Tissenbaum, who suffered considerable damages as a result:

> When the firefighters first arrived they sprayed the deck with a chemical foam to protect it from any possible fire damage if there were a post-crash explosion. After securing the house against possible fire damage, rescue workers were in and out of the Tissenbaum household all night asking for water, using the bathrooms, and borrowing their linens and tools. The Tissenbaum garage became in effect "command central." Curious observers also entered the Tissenbaum property all through the night.

> The evacuation of the passengers finally ended at about 6:00 a.m. The dead bodies were placed on the Tissenbaums' driveway and in their garage. For days plaintiffs had no electricity, telephone service or running water, and they could not leave their home as rescue vehicles blocked their passage. For weeks the wreckage of the plane and heavy equipment remained on their property.

What result on the resulting claim for trespass against the defendant airline?

A. No liability—though it might have been different if the plane had been intentionally grounded there. Said the court:

> The tort of trespass is the intentional and unlawful invasion of another's land. To meet the intent requirement the tortfeasor "need not intend or expect the damaging consequences of his intrusion," rather he need only "intend the act which amounts to or produces the unlawful invasion, and the intrusion must be ... the immediate or inevitable consequence of what ... he does so negligently as to amount to wilfulness." *Phillips v. Sun Oil Co.,* 307 N.Y. 328, 121 N.E.2d

249, 250 (1954).

Plaintiffs maintain that their complaint sets forth a prima facie case for the intentional tort of trespass: to wit, that the Avianca flight #052 crashed onto plaintiffs' property and that the crash was the result of defendant's knowing, reckless and willful misconduct in exhausting its fuel supply so as to inevitably result in a crash. Defendant's response is that no evidence was adduced that suggests Avianca acted with deliberate disregard for life and that the crew of Flight 052 intentionally grounded the plane into the plaintiff's property.

This Court holds that there is no genuine issue of fact to support a claim for the tort of intentional trespass as there is no evidence to prove the necessary intent to invade unlawfully. There was never a legal finding in this case that Avianca acted in a manner which rose to the level of wilful misconduct in the invasion of property or that the crew in this case, all of whom perished but one, voluntarily crashed the flight into the plaintiffs' yard. Rather, when the plane ran out of gas, after holding over the airport for hours, it became impossible for any human being to act voluntarily and control the aircraft and it unfortunately and accidentally crashed into the Tissenbaum's yard.

Other theories of liability may have been available, of course, and the onlookers who came onto the plaintiffs' property presumably were trespassers (but they caused little damage and so were not attractive defendants). The trespasses committed by the rescuers would have been privileged by the doctrine of necessity, on which see the next chapter.

Van Alstyne v. Rochester Telephone Corp. (D's workmen leave lead droppings on ground that poison dogs of landowner, P; L)
Hollenbeck v. Johnson (D's cow wanders onto P's property and causes the floor of P's barn to collapse; NL when P later falls through the resulting hole)

Notice that there are two distinct issues in *Van Alstyne*: first, whether the defendant's workmen became trespassers when they dripped their lead; and then secondly, and assuming there was a trespass, whether the defendant was liable for the death of the plaintiff's dogs as a result even if this was an unforeseeable consequence. (The court's answer to both questions: yes.) The first proposition seems questionable. The second one is solid.

Q. What is the distinction between *Van Alstyne v. Rochester Telephone Corp.* (the L case of the lead droppings left behind by the defendant's workers) and *Desnick v. American Broadcasting Co.*?
A. In both cases parties on the defendant's property exceeded the scope of their permission to be there. The tension between the cases arises because in *Van Alstyne* so much seemed to turn on the idea that the defendant's workers had a right to be on the property only for a limited purpose; straying from that purpose one iota resulted in liability. In *Desnick* the defendant's workers strayed very far from the purpose for which they were admitted to the clinic, yet there was no liability. Maybe part of the formal reason for the difference is, again, that in *Van Alstyne* the workers were on the plaintiff's property pursuant to a narrow easement—an exception to a usual presumption that no strangers were allowed there; whereas in *Desnick* the clinic's doors were open to the public and everyone was presumptively allowed. Still, suppose someone decided that the Desnick clinic's waiting room was warm and comfortable and had good magazines to read. Could they settle in there day after day, perhaps saying that they were still thinking about whether to make an appointment? Surely not. So in the end perhaps the cases are better explained by references to policy goals: we want to discourage workers from leaving junk behind and we want to discourage people from squatting in waiting rooms where they have no real business; but we don't want to discourage investigative reporting that produces valuable social benefits.

Q. What is the distinction between *Van Alstyne v. Rochester Telephone Corp.* and *Malouf v. Dallas Athletic Club*?

A. The superficial similarity is that in both cases the defendants sent something (golf balls or lead droppings) onto the plaintiff's property without authorization and without intent (we can assume an absence of intent in the *Van Alstyne* case because the court says that "[s]uch an invasion of the premises of another renders the invader liable whether it be intentional or not"). To make the similarity between the cases sharper you can ask what legal result would have followed in *Malouf* if the plaintiff's dog had tried to eat one of the golf balls that sailed onto the property and choked to death. Presumably that remains a case of no liability (it's difficult to see why it would make the plaintiff's case stronger than it already was). Yet in *Van Alstyne* there was liability. Why? Presumably it matters that in *Malouf* the defendants didn't enter the plaintiff's property and leave things behind; rather, only the things themselves (the golf balls) entered the property. But why should so much depend on this point?

Van Alstyne* is a hard case. The idea here must be that the defendants had a limited right to be on the plaintiff's property: consent (or more precisely an easement) only to certain acts there, and not to others—whether the others were intentional or not. There was consent to the intrusion to fix the line, but no consent to an intrusion that included spilling lead on the ground, and the courts police that consensual line very carefully. Here it helps to refer to the Restatement provisions that follow the *Desnick* case: a person can consent to an entry onto his land for a limited purpose, and liability can be quite strict for departures from that purpose. The Restatement examples don't perfectly explain *Van Alstyne* because they all seem to involve acts more intentional than spilling lead droppings without realizing it, but at least they provide some toehold for the notion that accidentally leaving something behind when one shouldn't can amount to a trespass.

So suppose you let a plumber into your house to fix your pipes. He drops some gaskets on the floor and leaves them behind. Is he a trespasser—an "intruder" in the court's terminology? That seems a hard result. Maybe the point is that the repairmen in *Van Alstyne* had even lesser rights than the plumber because they merely were exercising an easement. Another possibility—especially tempting after all these headahes—is that *Van Alstyne* was just badly decided.

Q. What case of battery would be analogous to *Van Alstyne*?

A. Perhaps a case where a surgeon leaves a sponge inside a patient—which generally would be a case of no liability for battery (though likely a good case of negligence). There would be liability for battery if a physician intentionally worked on a part of the plaintiff's body for which there was no authorization, as in *Mohr v. Williams*—a well-known case not in the book where the plaintiff goes in for an operation on the right ear but the surgeon decides to operate on the left ear instead. But that isn't analogous to *Van Alstyne* because the surgeon there does intend the contact that occurs. So again one wonders whether *Van Alstyne* was quite right on the intent issue.

Of course there is a second point to *Van Alstyne*, which is that once the defendant is found to have trespassed (in other words, once the intent question is behind us), the defendant is then on the hook for all damage resulting from the trespass whether it was foreseeable or not. Here the *Van Alstyne* ruling is more clearly consistent with the rest of the case law. Someone who trespasses and causes a fire is liable for the fire damage regardless of whether he started the fire intentionally, negligently, unwittingly, etc. The rationale for this is given in the opinion excerpts from *Van Alstyne*: once someone is so in the wrong as to be called a trespasser, it is thought fairer that he should pay for every consequence than that the plaintiff should have to bear any of the consequences without compensation. Of course this hard statement of the rule doesn't explain the *Hollenbeck* case, which brings us to the next question.

Q. What is the distinction between *Van Alstyne v. Rochester Telephone Corp.* and *Hollenbeck v. Johnson*?

A. This is tricky. The first question is whether *Hollenbeck* is really a trespass case at all. The court does speak of the cow as trespassing, but of course cows cannot literally trespass; it's an intentional tort.

And the cow's owner may not have had the needed state of mind, either. It might seem easy to run *Hollenbeck* together with the other cases on animals, like *Pegg v. Gray*, because liability is said to be strict for trespassing cattle—but that's only for damage done by grazing. We take up these issues under the heading of trespass because that's how many courts discuss them, but really the theory of liability ought to be considered distinct. Liability is *strict* for damage caused to crops by wandering cows (i.e., the true theory is strict liability rather than trespass), at least at common law, but the point of *Hollenbeck* is that liability for personal injuries nevertheless is limited to those caused directly by the animals, or (on other formulations) to those harms which lie within the foreseeable scope of the risk created by the "trespass." The rules of causation when animals trespass thus resemble the principles of causation governing other sorts of strict liability claims—but differ from the less forgiving rules that govern liability for human trespasses, as *Van Alstyne* illustrates. Thus suppose that in *Hollenbeck* the defendant himself had been snooping in the plaintiff's barn and fell through weak floorboards; then the plaintiff came into the barn and fell into the hole left behind by the defendant. This would almost certainly be a case of liability on the theory of *Van Alstyne*.

The reason for treating the cow differently seems to involve the expected costs and benefits of restraining farm animals. Dogs are allowed a certain liberty to roam without creating liability for trespass, as *Pegg v. Gray* explains; but dogs don't eat crops. Since farm animals do present that hazard, the rules governing trespass are less forgiving toward them. But the unforgiving attitude is limited. It does not create liability for every kind of harm an animal can cause if it walks onto a neighbor's land, probably because in an agrarian community it can be hard to prevent the occasional animal from wandering off the property. Those wanderings do create some risk of freak accidents like the one in *Hollenbeck*, but the chances of such things occurring are remote and perhaps also reciprocal: it would be easy to be on either end of such an event. So the rule is that there is strict liability for damage done by trespassing animals for the harm they *characteristically* inflict. A trespass by a person is different because it's much easier to prevent. We expect humans to understand the rules, so if they break them we expect them to pay for the resulting damage, even if freakish.

These rules get a little intricate, but they are a nice opportunity to help students see how different circumstances in the world, and the different policy considerations they generate, can put pressure on tort doctrines and cause them to defy oversimple restatement. As a matter of abstract principle it is hard to square these cases, but there are ways to view them as presenting different practical problems that understandably generate different solutions.

Once you have brought out the logic of *Hollenbeck*, you have the option of using a couple of additional questions to illustrate how the doctrine it represents works in other cases. For example:

Q. Hypothetical: in *Harvey v. Buchanan*, 49 S.E. 281 (Ga. 1904), the defendant's mule, Maud, wandered onto the plaintiff's property and killed the plaintiff's goat with its "mouth and fore feet." Liability under the principle of the *Hollenbeck* case?
A. No. Said the court:

> A careful examination of the record fails to disclose any evidence that the owner of the mule knew that the animal was vicious and dangerous. Hence there was no liability upon him for damages, whether he was at fault in allowing the mule to go at large, or whether he had a right to release it from his premises. The killing of stock is not the natural or usual consequence of allowing the ordinary mule to go at large. The destruction of or injury to crops or herbage would be. Hence, in the one case, proof of the scienter as to the mule's habits and tendencies is necessary as a part of the plaintiff's case, and in the other it is not.

Q. Hypothetical: in *Adams Bros. v. Clark*, 224 S.W. 1046 (Ky. 1920), the defendant's chickens—several hundred of them—crossed onto the plaintiff's property and ate large quantities of the plaintiff's grain and vegetables. Liability on the principle of *Hollenbeck*?
A. Yes. Said the court:

It is argued in brief of counsel for [the defendant] that the right to freely range their chickens is of the utmost importance to that "great number of people in all the towns and cities and in the rural districts all over the state who, by raising and keeping flocks of these valuable fowls, are endeavoring to meet the high cost of living and make their small salaries and small business enterprises carry them and their families through the year"; but the equally important and sacred right of the same class of citizens, equally great in number, to plant and raise a garden or truck patch on their own premises, without annoyance or trouble to neighbors, to help feed themselves and families, and thus tide over the high cost of living period, is wholly overlooked and forgotten. The right of free range to the chicken ends where the equal right of the gardener begins.

Incidentally, the defendant also argued that the plaintiff's barn full of grain was an attractive nuisance. The court disagreed:

The attractive nuisance doctrine has no application to the facts of this case. It is lawful to have and keep upon your place a barn with grain in it, and it has never been held that such is an attractive nuisance, even to fowls. This doctrine has only been applied to cases where one erects upon his premises and leaves unguarded a contrivance or device which in its nature is calculated to entice children or other thoughtless persons onto the premises to their personal injury, but has never, so far as we are able to ascertain, been applied to a situation where animals have crossed a lawful fence and committed depredations, to the injury of the person on whose premises they entered.

Edwards v. Lee (L for entering cave that leads under plaintiff's property)
Smith v. New England Aircraft Co. (L for flying airplanes low over plaintiff's property)

One could spend a great deal of time on these cases, working out whole theories of the purpose and extent of property rights from them; but that probably is best left as a task for the courses on property law. The placement of those cases here is meant just to flag some of the interesting basic issues they raise. The cave case, *Edwards*, raises a tension between formal notions of property (I own everything above and below my parcel of land) and economic conceptions of property intended to create incentives for people to maximize the value of resources. From the latter standpoint it makes obvious sense to give the property right to the owner of the mouth of a cave; otherwise he may have no incentive to develop it. Well, of course he can negotiate with the owner of the land that lies over the cave's passageways, but in some cases the transaction costs will be high (there may be many owners, holdout problems, bilateral monopolies, and so forth); and anyway it seems entirely clear that the rights will be more valuable to the owner of the mouth than to everyone else, since those who merely live over the cave have no ability to take advantage of it. So perhaps the rights should be assigned there straightaway—an application of Coase's analysis.

The airplane case raises some similar tensions, but this time the logic is a little different. It's not the case that the landowner can get no benefit from his right to the airspace far overhead, for he *can*; he might prefer skies free of airplane noise. Yet at some point in the sky this right gives out by force of statute as well as common law, not because the owner loses interest altogether but because (a) the interest weakens as the planes get higher, (b) we want air travel, and (c) there is in-kind compensation to the owner: in the end almost everyone puts up with planes traveling over their property, and has the reciprocal right to ride on them. Low overflights are a different matter because now the inconvenience may be very great and not so evenly distributed: we don't all bear it alike. So the court allows liability there, using as a rough measure the height in the sky that anyone's enterprises—tall buildings and the like—ever reach, which might seem a bit arbitrary but perhaps no more so than any other measure one might care to name.

SECTION C. CONVERSION

If you want to make cuts, consider dropping *Palmer* and *Spooner* early in the chapter and *Kremen v. Cohen* and the *CompuServe* case at the end.

Q. In *Russell-Vaughn Ford, Inc., v. Rouse*, the plaintiff appears to get quite a deal: $5,000 in damages for being deprived of his car for an hour. What is the sense of this? Another way to put the point: When a court sustains a claim for conversion it effectively orders a judicial sale of the item at issue; but in this case Rouse got to keep his Falcon *and* the $5,000. What gives?
A. Think of it this way: a thief steals your car and drives off with it, then at the end of the day decides to give it back. What are your damages in that case? Possibly none as a practical matter. The thief nevertheless is liable for conversion and will be required to pay over the value of the car. The reason can be viewed as involving deterrence. If the thief only is liable for your actual damages, he may pay nothing and thus be encouraged to do it again. One way to discourage him would be with a stint of jail time, but not all civil conversions rise to the level of criminal theft, and even if they do they are not all likely to be prosecuted. In low-level cases the civil tort of conversion thus seems to do a little of the work that might be associated normally with criminal law, thus letting the private plaintiff, rather than the government, foot the bill for bringing the defendant into line. The discrepancy between actual and awarded damages here makes the case resemble one in which punitive damages are awarded; and indeed in *Kemezy v. Peters*, a lead case on punitive damages (printed in the chapter on damages), we see some of the same sorts of points made as just suggested: the use of civil suits to take some pressure off the criminal law, and the use of extra damages to discourage defendants from misbehaving in ways that would not be effectively deterred by mere compensatory damages.

That whole line of thinking assumes that we're dealing with a thief or someone else who needs a good hard lesson. The defendants in the *Russell-Vaughn* case weren't thieves but their behavior seemed pretty atrocious, especially in view of the evidence that they made a practice of "losing keys" of customers on a regular basis. Again, this fact would have supported an award of punitive damages, and perhaps it would indeed have been more precise here to award a small amount of compensatory damages but a large amount in punitives. But the net effect of the award is similar. The car dealer's salesmen, or their replacements, probably will behave a little better next time.

Palmer v. Mayo (D lends out rented horse for unauthorized use; L for conversion)
Spooner v. Manchester (D takes horse to unauthorized town because he gets lost; NL)
Wiseman v. Schaffer (problem: tow truck driver takes car at the behest of an imposter; L)

Palmer v. Mayo is a little complicated; the facts and the court's rulings may take a few minutes to sort out. Mayo hired a horse and carriage from Palmer and then decided to lend it to Cook and one Scott (try to ignore him), who rode off and demolished it. The defendants were Mayo and Cook. Evidently they blamed each other for the loss of the horse and carriage; both were held liable. The case against Mayo was reasonably straightforward: he hired the apparatus for one purpose, then used it for something else—in the course of which it was destroyed. True, Mayo didn't crash it himself, but that's not necessary for liability. You can ask what trespass case would serve as an analogy here; the answer probably is *Van Alstyne v. Rochester Telephone Corp.*, where the defendants dripped lead on the plaintiff's property and were held responsible for all resulting consequences, foreseeable or not. The idea is that once you step into the wrong, all consequences are your to bear. Mayo did this by lending out the carriage for unauthorized use.

Then there is the case against Cook. The court said that if Cook was in control of the carriage and knew that he was using it without authorization, then he was on the hook for any damage caused to it—even if there was no negligence on his part. Apparently the jury found the facts to be precisely those.

Again, this is like the holdings in the trespass cases that one who trespasses is liable for damage of any sort that results. What makes the case complicated are the limitations the court puts on this rule. Evidently Cook would *not* be liable if he wasn't in control of the carriage, and he might not have been liable either (the court doesn't reach the question) if he thought the carriage belonged to Mayo and that his borrowing of it therefore was legitimate. The trial court thought this might matter, but on appeal there was no occasion to settle the point because the jury found that Cook knew he had no business in the carriage.

To put the open question precisely, it is this: if X borrows a carriage from a friend without realizing that this is an unauthorized act (because the carriage really is owned by Y), and then the carriage is damaged through no fault of X, is X liable for conversion? The trespass cases would seem to suggest that it's a case of liability (see Restatement (Second) §164, regarding mistaken intrusions, in that section of the chapter). But perhaps one can argue that Cook ought to be able to rely on Mayo, and therefore that Cook should get off if Cook (a) wasn't negligent and (b) didn't know that Mayo was acting beyond his powers when he lent out the carriage. *Wiseman v. Schaffer* also seems to suggest that there is liability in these circumstances, as we shall see.

Q.   What is the distinction between *Spooner v. Manchester* and *Palmer v. Mayo*?
A.   The superficial similarity is that in both cases the defendant hired a horse and took it where he was not supposed to go, and in both cases the horse then came to grief (we may assume) through no fault of the defendant's. We can also assume that in both cases the defendant knew at the time of the accident that the carriage was someplace it wasn't supposed to be. The difference is that in *Spooner* the defendant was trying at all times to get the horse back to its owner. Putting weight on this point may sound inconsistent with the trespass cases that hold people liable even for mistaken intrusions, but the lesson of the inconsistency is just that trespass and conversion don't work quite the same way. Conversion requires an exercise of dominion by the defendant that is inconsistent with the owner's rights. This is well illustrated by the Restatement examples at the start of the conversion section: walking out with the wrong umbrella at a restaurant is not necessarily a conversion; it depends why you do it and whether you promptly return it. Trespass law is not contingent and forgiving in this way. The interesting question then becomes *why*. Presumably the reason has to do with the costs of avoiding two kinds of invasions: entering, perhaps mistakenly, onto someone else's land (which should be relatively easy to avoid), and misappropriating someone else's movable property (which can happen more easily and thus is harder to avoid).

Q.   What result in *Wiseman v. Schaffer*?
A.   Liability. This may seem a hard result, since it is easy to sympathize with the tow truck driver and to want him to be able to rely on a plausible-sounding request to tow a car. The result can be viewed formally or functionally. From a formal perspective the point to emphasize is that the tow truck driver had no right whatsoever to take the car, and that this can't be changed by the utterances of some third party to the contrary. If I tell a moving company to come take all my goods and then direct them to your house when you are out of town, the point is the same: entering your house and walking out with your television set is a conversion (and a theft), period. It's even worse than *Palmer v. Mayo* because at least there Mayo legitimately had possession of the horse and carriage, even if he shouldn't have been lending it out. (There is an analogy to the difference between the rights of purchasers from thieves and from frauds, as we will see soon.) From a functional standpoint the idea is that the tow truck driver is the party in the best position to prevent nasty scams like the one seen in *Wiseman*. We need to put the pressure of tort law on the driver to deter him from taking orders casually and perpetuating this sort of theft.

In the actual case the jury brought in a verdict for Schaffer (the tow truck driver) and the trial court entered judgment upon it. The court of appeals reversed and remanded for a new trial:

Construing the evidence most favorably to Schaffer, including the testimony of the two tow truck operators, there is substantial evidence to support a verdict on the issue of negligence. However, a verdict for Schaffer on the issue of conversion is not supported by the evidence. [...]

The evidence shows that Schaffer exercised dominion or control over the Wisemans' pickup inconsistent in fact with the Wisemans' right of ownership. [...] [T]he law of conversion does not relieve an actor of liability due to his belief, because of a mistake of law or fact not induced by the other, that he has the consent of the other. Restatement §244. Furthermore, to create liability for conversion it is not necessary that the actor intends to commit a trespass or a conversion; and the actor may be liable where he has in fact exercised dominion or control, although he may be quite unaware of the existence of the rights with which he interferes.

The evidence shows the second element of conversion was also satisfied. Schaffer's interference with the Wisemans' right of control ultimately resulted in the loss of the Wisemans' pickup. The jury could have found otherwise only if they postulated that the deprivation of possession did not follow "consequently" from Schaffer's actions because the pickup apparently was stolen by an unknown third party. Such reasoning by the jury might have been consistent with the judge's instructions—and defense counsel's arguments—on the negligence theory of liability, but it was not appropriate under the conversion theory. The judge's instruction on conversion did not excuse liability if property were lost due to theft by a third party after the defendant wrongfully exercised dominion.

O'Keeffe v. Snyder (P sues D to retrieve stolen painting that D innocently purchased; L)
Phelps v. McQuade (P sues D to recover jewels that P lost to a fraud; NL)
Kelley Kar Company v. Maryland Casualty Co. (P sues D to recover stolen cash; NL)
Anderson v. Gouldberg (P recovers logs from defendants who took them, even though P may have unlawfully taken them himself)

Q. What is the distinction between *Phelps v. McQuade* and *O'Keeffe v. Snyder*?
A. In *O'Keefe* the plaintiff was the victim of a theft. In *Phelps* the plaintiffs were the victims of a fraud. Formally the point of the distinction is that the plaintiffs in *Phelps* voluntarily handed over the jewels to the bad guy, whereas in *O'Keefe* the paintings were simply stolen with no involvement by the plaintiff. This way of looking at the cases might suggest that the plaintiffs in *Phelps* share a bit of culpability for the outcome, and as a matter of fairness perhaps that is true. But this also can be turned into a functional point: people who deal with potential frauds have opportunities to take protective measures that aren't available to victims of thieves. They can do more careful background checks and the like, and we *want* them to do this.

Q. What is the distinction between *Kelley Kar Company v. Maryland Casualty Co.* and *O'Keeffe v. Snyder*?
A. The similarity is that in both cases a thief outright stole property from the plaintiff and then transferred it to the defendant; but in *Kelley* the property could not be retrieved. The reason is that the property was cash. The rationale for the distinction between cash and other types of property is that a purchaser or seller—the innocent party who receives the stolen property in return for comparable value—is in a far worse position to inspect or research the pedigree of the property when it is cash than when it is a chattel (such as the paintings in the *O'Keeffe* case).

Actually there was a second type of property at issue in *Kelley* as well: an automobile the thief had traded in. But this wasn't stolen; it was bought with stolen money. This implies a good practice for thieves: steal cash, not chattels. It might seem that the thief should be indifferent, for if he is caught with either type of property it can be taken away from him. But the point is that stolen cash is more valuable than a stolen chattel of the same market value, because a merchant can accept cash without a worrying about whether it is stolen but cannot accept a car with the same sense of indifference.

Regarding *Anderson v. Gouldberg*, there is an interesting comment on the issue in R.H. Helmholz, *Wrongful Possession of Chattels: Hornbook Law and Case Law*, 80 Nw. U. L. Rev. 1221 (1986). The article examine the courts' use of the rule in *Anderson v. Gouldberg* nearly a century later and finds the case still to be good law on its facts, but suggests that broad statements of its holding are potentially misleading:

> [A] gap exists between the decided cases and the hornbook rule that possession of chattels, however acquired, prevails against anyone but the rightful owner. First, ordinary statements of the rule exaggerate the frequency of disputes between two wrongdoers. Most cases involving purely possessory claims are not like *Anderson v. Gouldberg*. Second, when possessory claims arise in litigation, courts regularly reject them if they stem from wrongful possession. Courts examine the quality of possession as well as the fact of possession. Third, the most common use of the hornbook rule in judicial opinions has been to permit courts to disregard technical flaws in one person's title when those flaws might permit a wrongful possessor to prevail. Without recognizing the apparent incongruity, American courts have used an apparently amoral rule to buttress moral claims.

Q. How does *Anderson* extend *Armory v. Delamirie?*
A. In *Anderson* we may assume the plaintiff was not merely a finder but a thief.

Q. What rationale can there be for using the courts to restore stolen property to a thief? Why does he have any better right to it than anyone else?
A. The formal answer is that possession alone is treated by the law as giving rights to the possessor—rights not as strong as those of the legitimate owner, but rights still stronger than those of anyone else not in possession of the thing. The policy rationale, as suggested by the court in *Anderson*, is that under any other rule stolen property would fall outside the law and be subject to attempts at theft with impunity, which in turn would cause thieves to take the law into their own hands (these are the "reprisals" of which the court speaks).

Moore v. Regents of the University of California (NL—at least for conversion—for taking P's cells to create patented cell line)
Kremen v. Cohen (D registry gives away P's domain name; L)
CompuServe, Inc. v. Cyber Promotions, Inc. (D spammer held liable for trespass to chattels)

Q. How does *Moore v. Regents* fit into the line of cases considered in this chapter?
A. The cases thus far have shown that there are a couple of different aspects of the conversion tort that can raise complications. One involves the sorts of actions that give rise to conversion in the first place; the other involves the consequence for others who later come into possession of the converted property. On the first score *Moore* might seem to bear some resemblance to a case like *Phelps v. McQuade*, where a fraud took P's jewelry. The point of *Phelps* was that later good-faith purchasers of the jewels couldn't be held liable for conversion, but of course there was no question about the fraud's liability if he could be found. *Moore* might seem similar because the plaintiff voluntarily relinquished his cells to the defendant, who then turned around and made unauthorized use of them. It's a little different, of course, not least because the plaintiff in *Moore* did not understand himself to be selling his cells to the defendant in the first place; the cells were not the subject of a transaction in the way that the jewels were. Nor is it clear that the cells were of any value to the plaintiff, at least before the defendants got hold of them (maybe he should be regarded as having property with value that he did not appreciate). The defendants did

appreciate it, though, which creates an interesting question about the impact of asymmetrical knowledge in a conversion case. From the dissent of Broussard, J.:

> [I]t is easy to lose sight of the fact that the specific allegations on which the complaint in this case rests are quite unusual, setting this matter apart from the great majority of instances in which donated organs or cells provide the raw materials for the advancement of medical science and the development of new and beneficial medical products. Ordinarily, when a patient consents to the use of a body part for scientific purposes, the potential value of the excised organ or cell is discovered only through subsequent experimentation or research, often months or years after the removal of the organ. In this case, however, the complaint alleges that plaintiff's doctor recognized the peculiar research and commercial value of plaintiff's cells before their removal from plaintiff's body. Despite this knowledge, the doctor allegedly failed to disclose these facts or his interest in the cells to plaintiff, either before plaintiff's initial surgery or throughout the ensuing seven-year period during which the doctor continued to obtain additional cells from plaintiff's body in the course of periodic medical examinations. [...]
>
> If defendants had informed plaintiff, prior to removal, of the possible uses to which his body part could be put and plaintiff had authorized one particular use, it is clear under the foregoing authorities that defendants would be liable for conversion if they disregarded plaintiff's decision and used the body part in an unauthorized manner for their own economic benefit. Although in this case defendants did not disregard a specific directive from plaintiff with regard to the future use of his body part, the complaint alleges that, before the body part was removed, defendants intentionally withheld material information that they were under an obligation to disclose to plaintiff and that was necessary for his exercise of control over the body part; the complaint also alleges that defendants withheld such information in order to appropriate the control over the future use of such body part for their own economic benefit. If these allegations are true, defendants clearly improperly interfered with plaintiff's right in his body part at a time when he had the authority to determine the future use of such part, thereby misappropriating plaintiff's right of control for their own advantage. Under these circumstances, the complaint fully satisfies the established requirements of a conversion cause of action.

These front-end considerations may have some importance in the case, since on the majority's view they make the "theft" from Moore seem less egregious than the ordinary conversion case. But evidently what most drives the result is the court's concern about the other end of the conversion tort: it might imply liability for all who later do research on the cell line. Again one can return to *Phelps* and wonder if those later researchers might somehow be conceptualized as bona fide purchasers for whom there is no liability, at least if the taking of the cells is regarded as more like a fraud than a theft. True, this logic would fail once Moore announces that the cells were his, since then subsequent researchers would be on notice that they are dealing in filched property; but the court's concern seems to be with those researchers who aren't on notice. The problem is that the *Phelps* pattern is difficult to map onto situation in *Moore*, where "cell lines are routinely copied and distributed to other researchers for experimental purposes, usually free of charge." Apparently the Industrial Biotechnology Association filed an amicus brief in *Moore* arguing that bona fide transferees of the cells could still be held liable. See Appelbaum, *Moore v. Regents of the University of California: Now That the California Supreme Court Has Spoken, What Has it Really Said?* 9 N.Y.L. Sch. J. Hum. Rts. 495 (1992). The majority evidently agreed:

> If the use of cells in research is a conversion, then with every cell sample a researcher purchases a ticket in a litigation lottery. Because liability for conversion is predicated on a continuing ownership interest, "companies are unlikely to invest heavily in developing, manufacturing, or marketing a product when uncertainty about clear title exists." In our view, borrowing [from

Brown v. Superior Court, 44 Cal.3d at 1065], "[i]t is not unreasonable to conclude in these circumstances that the imposition of a harsher test for liability would not further the public interest in the development and availability of these important products." [...]

Nor would it significantly ameliorate the threat to research to limit conversion liability to cases in which the patient's consent was invalid. One cannot know with certainty whether a consent is valid until a lawsuit has been filed and resolved. Moreover, since liability for conversion is based on a finding that the plaintiff has a continuing ownership interest, the threat of a lawsuit against anyone in the chain of title would place the ownership of research materials in doubt. [...]

In order to make conversion liability seem less of a threat to research, the dissent argues that researchers could avoid liability by using only cell lines accompanied by documentation of the source's consent. But consent forms do not come with guarantees of validity. As medical malpractice litigation shows, challenges to the validity and sufficiency of consent are not uncommon. Moreover, it is sheer fantasy to hope that waivers might be obtained for the thousands of cell lines and tissue samples presently in cell repositories and, for that reason, already in wide use among researchers.

But a possible implication of this reasoning, as argued by Broussard, J., is that the defendants would not be liable for conversion even if they had stolen the cells outright (e.g., against the plaintiff's clearly expressed wish to keep them for himself)—for then the policy issues regarding future researchers would remain the same. In any event, Broussard also suggested that the liability of subsequent researchers would not be so great as the majority says:

> If, as the majority suggests, the great bulk of the value of a cell line patent and derivative products is attributable to the efforts of medical researchers and drug companies, rather than to the "raw materials" taken from a patient, the patient's damages will be correspondingly limited, and innocent medical researchers and drug manufacturers will retain the considerable economic benefits resulting from their own work. Under established conversion law, a "subsequent innocent converter" does not forfeit the proceeds of his own creative efforts, but rather "is entitled to the benefit of any work or labor that he has expended on the [property]...." (1 Harper et al., The Law of Torts (2d ed. 1986) §2.34, p. 234.)

As the text notes, the majority did uphold the plaintiff's claim for breach of fiduciary duty. But Mosk, J., thought this remedy inadequate:

> There are two barriers to recovery. First, "the patient must show that if he or she had been informed of all pertinent information, he or she would have declined to consent to the procedure in question." The second barrier to recovery is still higher, and is erected on the first: it is not even enough for the plaintiff to prove that he personally would have refused consent to the proposed treatment if he had been fully informed; he must also prove that in the same circumstances no reasonably prudent person would have given such consent.

But couldn't the plaintiff simply argue that while he would have gone forward with the procedure, he would not have relinquished—at least for free—the rights to his cells? In any event, Moore's case was settled a few years later for a "token" amount. Daar, *Informed Consent: Defining Limits Through Therapeutic Parameters*, 16 Whittier L. Rev. 187 (1995).

Q. What's the best that can be said for the defendant in *Kremen v. Cohen*? To what prior case in the chapter is *Kremen* most analogous?

A. The district court put the case for the defendant in this way:

The foundation of the action rests neither in the knowledge nor intent of the defendant.... Therefore, questions of the defendant's good faith, lack of knowledge, and motive are ordinarily immaterial." *Burlesci v. Petersen*, 80 Cal.Rptr.2d 704 (1998). The following example is illustrative of the tort's severity: "where a warehouseman delivers stored household goods to a corporation which appears to have a bona fide claim of ownership, the warehouseman will be liable for conversion if the corporation is eventually unable to establish its title." *Gonzales v. Personal Storage, Inc.*, 65 Cal.Rptr.2d 473 (1997). As the warehouseman in the latter scenario, domain registrars such as NSI would be exposed to liability every time a third party fraudulently obtained the transfer of a domain name. The Court finds it inherently unjust to place NSI in this untenable position by virtue of innocently performing a purely ministerial function. Furthermore, the threat of litigation threatens to stifle the registration system by requiring further regulations by NSI and potential increases in fees.

The best analogy probably is to *Wiseman v. Schaffer*, where another innocent defendant—the tow truck company—converted the plaintiff's property at the behest of a crooked third party. Just as the decision for the plaintiff in *Kremen* may have resulted in some increased fees, the result in *Wiseman* may well have caused towing fees to be raised slightly (or it may just have made the process of getting a car towed a little more cumbersome).

Q. Suppose you receive an annoying email—or eight dozen annoying emails—offering products to enlarge parts of your body that, let us suppose, you do not care to enlarge. Can you sue the sender for trespass to chattels under *CompuServe, Inc., v. Cyber Promotions, Inc.*?

A. Probably not. The key to the court's decision was the observation that "[t]o the extent that defendants' multitudinous electronic mailings demand the disk space and drain the processing power of plaintiff's computer equipment, those resources are not available to serve CompuServe subscribers." So a single user bringing a complaint about spam would presumably have to show some respect in which the arrival of the unwanted email imposed costs on him. One cost is the lost time in reading and deleting the emails; any problems with treating that loss as an adequate basis for a claim? Well, it would open the doors to liability—however trivial in amount—every time someone uses your resources to make unwanted contact you. Thus we would have to consider similar tort claims on the basis of ordinary junk mail and telephone solicitations. Courts get nervous about extending liability in that direction for First Amendment reasons, among others. Similar objections arise if you point not to the loss of time involved in receiving spam but in the trivial losses caused when the spam temporarily takes up space on your computer or delays your receipt of other more pressing email.

So sure, a court *could* come up with a theory of liability on those bases, just as it did in the *CompuServe* case. The question is whether we want this problem handled through the extension of common law tort actions or through a legislative approach. A problem with judicial solutions is that judges are not likely to be in a great position to grasp the costs and benefits of finding tort liability in a case like this. An advantage, of course, is that judges are not subject to the kind of lobbying that may occur in the legislative setting.

D. FALSE IMPRISONMENT

This section isn't all that long. If you want to make cuts, we recommend not teaching it at all, though conceivably you could just assign the first two cases to give students a nodding familiarity with the tort.

Peterson v. Sorlien (P is kidnapped for deprogramming; NL for false imprisonment)
Eilers v. Coy (P is kidnapped for deprogramming; L for false imprisonment)

Q. What is the distinction between *Eilers v. Coy* and *Peterson v. Sorlien*?

A. The court in *Eilers* thought it critical that the plaintiff there, unlike the plaintiff in *Peterson*, had not passed up any chances to escape. The plaintiff's apparent (but feigned) consent was treated as irrelevant:

> Relying on the Minnesota Supreme Court's decision in *Peterson v. Sorlien*, 299 N.W.2d 123, 129 (Minn.1980), the defendants contend that there was no actual confinement because there is evidence that the plaintiff consented to the defendants' actions, at least by the fourth day of his confinement. The plaintiff, in contrast, has testified that he merely pretended to consent in order to gain an opportunity to escape. The plaintiff's apparent consent is not a defense to false imprisonment. Many people would feign consent under similar circumstances, whether out of fear of their captors or as a means of making an escape. But in this case, unlike the *Peterson* case relied on by the defendants, it is undisputed that the plaintiff was at no time free to leave the Tau Center during the week in question, nor were any reasonable means of escape available to him. Under these circumstances, the Court finds, in agreement with many other authorities, that the plaintiff's apparent consent is not a defense to false imprisonment. The Court therefore holds, as a matter of law, that the plaintiff has proven the necessary elements of false imprisonment.

Also, *Eilers* involved a suit for false imprisonment just against the deprogrammers; the plaintiff's parents were not made defendants. It's not clear if this made any difference. Both types of defendants were held not liable for false imprisonment in *Peterson*. It's possible that the court in *Eilers* would have taken a different view of the plaintiff's family members if they had been sued.

Many students will have strong views about the correct result in these cases.

Bright v. Ailshie (D wrongly taken into custody by bounty hunter; L)

Baggett v. National Bank & Trust Co. (P taken into custody because he unknowingly handed paper to bank teller that made him appear to be a robber; NL)

Melton v. LaCalamito (P taken into custody when he refused to give his blankets to U-Haul dealer; L)

Q. What is the distinction between *Bright v. Ailshie* and *Baggett v. National Bank & Trust Co.*?

A. In both cases private defendants had good reason to believe that the plaintiff was a felon. In both cases the defendants therefore caused the plaintiff to be arrested. But there was liability only in *Bright*. The first reason is that in *Bright* the plaintiff was taken into custody by a private person; in *Baggett* a police officer made the arrest. The rules governing the former situation naturally are more demanding than they are in the latter. In effect the Michigan statute imposes strict liability on a private citizen who detains the wrong person: he is liable no matter how good his reasons were for making the arrest. The common law was more forgiving, as the Restatement excerpts after *Bright* show (so the result in *Bright* might well have been different in a common law jurisdiction, or in a state like California that allows citizens' arrests supported by "reasonable cause").

Q. Suppose a private person makes a citizen's arrest that is supported by probable cause but that turns out to be mistaken—as perhaps occurred in *Bright*. Now suppose the same citizen instead tells the police to arrest the plaintiff, and they do; again, the citizen had probable cause but was mistaken—as perhaps occurred in *Baggett*. Evidently there is liability in the first case, at least in Michigan, but there probably is not liability anywhere in the second case. Why? (Or put it this way: suppose the bank teller in *Baggett* had arrested the plaintiff herself. In Michigan that would be a case of liability, wouldn't it? But as a matter of policy why would any state want to treat that case differently from the real *Baggett* case where there was no liability?)

A. The participation of the police officer makes abuses less likely and thus reduces the need for a strict rule. It's true that in either case a mistaken belief by the defendant could result in an arrest, and sometimes the officer's involvement won't do anything to prevent this, as when the officer simply acts on the defendant's urgings. But in some cases the officer can evaluate the defendant's claims and consider them more objectively;—whereas if the police officer isn't present, the defendant is left to his own judgment, which may be defective and go unchecked. In addition, a private citizen's arrest presents some collateral dangers. The arrestee may resist, especially if the arrest is based on a mistake, and this could lead to a serious altercation and breach of the peace. A police officer, even when mistaken, is in a better position to control that risk.

Q. What is the distinction between *Baggett v. National Bank & Trust Co.* and *Melton v. LaCalamito*?
A. This time both arrests were made by police officers, so the distinctions have to lie either in the quality of the defendant's reasons for insisting upon the plaintiff's arrest or on the relationship between the defendant's urgings and the police officer's decision. Perhaps both considerations played roles. The court in *Baggett* said the defendants did not request that Baggett be taken into custody, but merely told the police what happened. The court in *Melton* said that the defendant there also did not request that the plaintiff be taken in custody; but the defendant did insist that the blankets belonged to him, and the court thought that this was important. Perhaps the difference was that the apparent robbery attempt in *Baggett* was over and finished, and the bank was not "out" anything; a decision to release Baggett thus would have had little effect on the bank. But in *Melton* there was a live disagreement over who owned the blankets. If the plaintiff had been allowed to keep them, he might have been getting away with a theft. So the defendant's insistence that the blankets belonged to him put the officer in *Melton* into a harder position than the officer in *Baggett*, and the defendant in *Melton* was therefore held more accountable.

The court in *Melton* also said that the defendant lacked probable cause to support his "instigation" of the arrest. Presumably the distinction on this score would be that in *Melton* the plaintiff was actively protesting his innocence and had a plausible explanation for the facts; and perhaps the defendant in *Melton* was in a pretty good position to determine the accuracy of the plaintiff's claims, but failed to do so (as by calling the company to check its records?). In *Baggett* the bank was not itself confronted with an innocent explanation by the plaintiff, and was not in a good position to figure out whether his apparent robbery attempt was a real one.

Q. Would the plaintiff in *Bright* have had a good claim for false imprisonment against his brother? Would the plaintiff in *Baggett* have had a good claim for false imprisonment against the author of the language on the back of the deposit ticket?
A. Possibly. There may not have been *instigation* in either case, since neither Vincent Bright nor the author of the fake stick-up note asked the police to do anything. But there can be liability if a defendant gives a police officer false information leading to the defendant's arrest; this is Prosser's point in the excerpt from *Melton*. The conventional case under this rule would be one where the defendant accused the plaintiff of a crime in bad faith. That isn't precisely what Vincent Bright did, and indeed he might have hoped that his brother would *not* be arrested. He just wanted to escape himself. But think of a case where X commits a theft, and then when the police arrives he points at Y and says that *he* should be arrested for the crime. X says this so that he can make his escape, and the ruse succeeds. Clearly that would be a case of liability for X; and how is it really any different from Vincent Bright's behavior?

In *Baggett* the facts are a little different. Whereas Vincent Bright furnished misinformation to the police, the miscreant in *Baggett* didn't give any information to the police. He simply committed an act that was calculated (let us assume) to give the bank teller, and then the police, the wrong impression about some other random customer. Still, the natural effect of the act was to lead to the arrest of somebody who was innocent, and it seems no less reprehensible than the lies told in the *Bright*, so perhaps there is no real difference.

Q. Suppose it turned out that the miscreant who wrote the robbery note(s) in *Baggett* was not trying to create trouble for another customer; rather, the deposit ticket that the plaintiff presented had been used by the miscreant as a rough draft of a real robbery note that he had intended to present himself (perhaps he went off to look up how to spell "stick up" and planned to return afterwards). How would this affect the miscreant's liability?

A. In that case his act *vis a vis* Baggett would look more like negligence: he did something that inadvertently caused another person to fall under suspicion of being a bank robber. But false imprisonment is an intentional tort, making such claim difficult to analyze on these facts. See, e.g., Restatement (Second) of Torts sec. 35, comment h: "It is not enough that the actor realizes or should realize that his actions involve a risk of causing a confinement, so long as the likelihood that it will do so falls short of a substantial certainty."

The leading view on negligence in this area generally seems to be that a defendant can be held liable if he urges the police to make an arrest when he has not used due care to check the basis for his request; but there is no liability if the defendant simply makes a negligent statement to the police that causes them to go off and arrest the plaintiff. See *LaFontaine v. Family Drug Stores, Inc.*, 360 A.2d 899 (1976) ("There may be a duty on the part of a citizen to use reasonable care to ascertain the true facts when he insists upon, demands or pressures the police to make an arrest."); Restatement (Second) of Torts sec. 653, comment g ("Where a private person gives to a prosecuting officer information which he believes to be true, and the officer in the exercise of his uncontrolled discretion initiates criminal proceedings based upon that information, the informer is not liable under the rule stated in this Section even though the information proves to be false and his belief therein was one which a reasonable man would not entertain."). The stronger the role the defendant plays in securing the arrest, the more careful he has to be. And notice that where liability arises in either situation, the defendant has committed an intentional act: intentionally lying or intentionally (though mistakenly) urging the police to make an arrest.

The miscreant who tries to draft a stick-up note, but then walks away and leaves it behind, thus is in a funny position and probably cannot be held liable for false imprisonment. The closest case we could find—and another good hypothetical for class—was *Green v. Donroe*, 440 A.2d 973 (Conn. 1982). The defendant, who was emotionally disturbed, worked at a package store. He was distraught over a marital dispute and shot himself in the shoulder. When the police arrived, the defendant was too embarrassed to admit that he had shot himself, so he said that he had been shot by a black man wearing a green jacket. The police went out and detained the plaintiff, a black man wearing a green jacket. He was released when the defendant did not identify him as the culprit. When the true facts of the case became known, the plaintiff sued the defendant for false imprisonment and negligence. The court dismissed the false imprisonment claim, citing the comment to sec. 35 of the Restatement quoted a moment ago. The court did say that the plaintiff could have recovered for negligence, but the complaint did not allege this.

E. ASSAULT

This is a short section that serves in part as a run-up to the materials on intentional infliction of emotional distress. The *Grimsley* case in the section on battery gives you a chance to do a quick overview of the assault tort, and you may not want to bother with more. If you do, these materials should take about half a class section to cover. Again, it's too short for cuts to make sense.

Brower v. Ackerley (P is threatened by D on the phone; NL for assault)

Bennight v. Western Auto Supply Co. (P is sent to work in part of warehouse infested with bats; L for assault)

Langford v. Shu (P opens box said to contain "mongoose," and is scared by prank inside; L)

Tuberville v. Savage (P sues for battery, and D defends on ground that P assaulted him; held no assault because P's words negated his threatening gesture; in effect an NL case)

Newell v. Whitcher (problem: D comes on to blind woman in her bed; L)

Q. Suppose that in *Brower v. Ackerley*, one of the Ackerleys had taken Brower aside after a city council meeting about the billboards, and had said essentially the same words he used on the phone: "Ooooo, Jordan, oooo, you're finished; cut you in your sleep, you sack of shit." Liability?

A. Probably not for assault. It's a closer case than the real *Brower v. Ackerley* because here the defendant would have had a present ability to carry out his intentions. But it sounds like he still isn't threatening any imminent harm. It becomes more clearly a case of no liability if the defendant adds language like, "when you least expect it, expect it." Facts like those might seem to cry out for liability, but that's what the outrage tort is for. Indeed, one purpose of these cases is to help motivate the upcoming inquiry into intentional infliction of emotional distress. Still, one might ask *why* the courts insist on apprehension of "imminent" contact, just letting the maker of a more vague threat off the hook. The result of the doctrine is that a serious and frightening threat that refers to the future may result in no liability, while a more minor threat of imminent harm—but that creates little real fear—can result in liability. Presumably the reason involves the fact that most threats don't pan out, thus leading to administrative difficulties in separating the serious from the unserious threat made in advance. The imminence requirement, while seemingly focused on how close the threat is to occurring in time and space, really is being used to isolate the cases where the threat is most likely to be carried out.

Q. What is the distinction between *Bennight v. Western Auto Supply Co.* and *Brower v. Ackerley*?

A. The assault in *Bennight* consisted in ordering Mrs. Bennight into the bat-infested part of the warehouse. This placed her in imminent fear of attack, not fear of attack at some later time.

Q. Suppose none of the bats had bitten Mrs. Bennight, gotten tangled in her hair, or otherwise contacted her. The bats nevertheless gave her the heebie-jeebies and she was no longer able to work as a result. Would the defendant still be liable?

A. Yes—or at least the defendant still would have committed an assault. Whether he would have been *liable* would depend on the details of the statute. Probably he would be. The assault is complete once there is apprehension.

Q. What is the intent required to support an assault claim? Is it analogous to the intent required to support a claim for battery?

A. It's just the intent to commit the act that puts the plaintiff into apprehension of the contact. It need not be an intent to cause the apprehension or any other harm. The rule is analogous to the holdings of battery cases like *White v. University of Idaho*, where the music teacher intentionally drummed his fingers on the plaintiff's back. He intended no harm, but was held liable anyway because his act was intentional. *Bennight* adds the point that an assault can occur if the defendant makes the plaintiff apprehend an imminent touching from some other source—e.g., the bats. There is an analogy to cases like *Laidlaw v. Sage*, where the defendant might have committed a battery by bringing his clerk into the path of the blast threatened by the bomber. Or *Garratt v. Dailey*, mentioned as a hypothetical in the notes to the battery chapter, where the defendant did not touch the plaintiff but caused her to strike a surface (the ground).

Q. Think back (if it was read) to the false imprisonment case *Baggett v. National Bank & Trust Co.* The plaintiff, Richard Baggett, entered the defendant's bank to deposit a check. He filled out a deposit slip from a supply provided for customer use and handed it to the teller along with his check. Unbeknownst to Baggett, on the back of the deposit slip someone had written "This is a stek up." When the teller saw this message she walked away from her window and phoned the bank manager, telling him to call the police. Baggett was taken into custody, leading him to bring an unsuccessful claim for false imprisonment against the bank. The question for now, however, is this: did Baggett commit an assault?

A. You can take apart the issue by asking first whether it would have been an assault if the note's *author* passed it to the teller. Probably so: the note does not make an explicit threat of violence, but the implication of it is that the teller had better hand over the money or else suffer violence. This kind of conditional threat—"your money or your life," etc.—is an assault; it's distinguishable from *Tuberville v.*

Savage because the condition on the threat depends in the stick-up is a demand the thief has no right to make. The next question is whether the case is changed by the fact that Baggett passed the note unwittingly. It nevertheless (let us assume) caused an apprehension of an imminent touching. But did Baggett have the needed intent? He intended to hand the paper to the teller, but he did not intend to convey the language that had been written on it. Since the words themselves made the assault, and since Baggett did not intend to say them, an assault claim against him probably fails.

Q. Suppose defendant threatens to shoot plaintiff with a gun. Defendant believes the gun is loaded; plaintiff knows it is not. Liability for assault?
A. No. An intent to cause apprehension not only is not necessary to support a claim for assault; it also isn't sufficient to support such a claim (though it is sufficient to satisfy the *intent* element of the tort). In this hypothetical the defendant has such an intention but the desired apprehension is not, in fact, created.

Q. What is the superficial similarity between *Tuberville v. Savage* and *Langford v. Shu*? What is the distinction between them?
A. In both cases the plaintiff evidently was not facing any imminent danger of a battery. The difference is that in *Tuberville* the defendant made this clear to the plaintiff, while in *Langford* the defendant deliberately helped to create the opposite impression.

Q. Suppose A, a notorious gangster known to have killed other men, telephones B and tells him that he will shoot him on sight. Coming around a corner, B encounters A standing on the sidewalk. Without moving, A says to B, "Your time has come." Liability?
A. Yes; this is Illustration 4 to section 31 of the Second Restatement. Words can constitute an assault even when there is no physical gesture to accompany them, just as they can *negate* an assault that otherwise would be the result of a threatening gesture (as in *Tuberville v. Savage*).

Q. What result in *Newell v. Whitcher*?
A. Liability. From the court's opinion:

> The approach to her person in the manner her testimony tends to prove—sitting on the bed and bed-clothes that covered her person, and leaning over her with the proffer of criminal sexual intercourse; so near as to excite the fear and apprehension of force in the execution of his felonious purpose, was an assault. The whole act and motive was unlawful, sinister and wicked. The act of stealing stealthily into the bed-room of a virtuous woman at midnight to seek gratification of criminal lust, is sufficiently dishonorable and base in purpose and in act; but especially so, when the intended victim is a poor, blind girl under the protecting care of the very man who would violate every injunction of hospitality, that he might dishonor and ruin at his own hearthstone this unfortunate child, who had the right to appeal to him to defend her from such outrage.

Incidentally, the court actually went farther and said that the defendant was a trespasser—in his own house:

> [W]e think that [the plaintiff's] right to her private sleeping-room during the night under the circumstances of this case, was as ample and exclusive against the inmates of the house, as if the entry had been made into her private dwelling house through the outer door. Her right of quiet occupancy and privacy was absolute and exclusive; and the entry by stealth in the night into such apartments without license or justifiable cause, was a trespass; and, if with felonious intent, was a crime.

Q. Suppose the defendant hears thieves rustling in his watermelon patch. They start to run when he approaches. In order to frighten them away on a more permanent basis, the defendant fires his gun into the air away from where he thinks they are running. Has he committed an assault?

A. Yes; the only question is whether it is justified by the privilege to defend his property. The court in the case on which this question is based, *Brown v. Martinez*, 361 P.2d 152 (N.M. 1961), held that firing his gun exceeded the privilege. It mattered because the bullet ended up striking one of the fleeing thieves. The watermelon farmer was held liable to him; it was a case of transferred intent like *Manning v. Grimsley*. This case also is discussed in the section of the manual covering privileges.

F. OUTRAGE (INTENTIONAL INFLICTION OF EMOTIONAL DISTRESS)

If you want to trim this section, we suggest dropping the *Van Duyn* and *Walko* cases toward the end, as they discuss the definition of "public figure"—an issue that you may want to touch on only briefly in a first-year, common law course, and that is introduced adequately in the *Hustler* case.

Q. Why might a threatened claim of outrage be thought to provide a particularly potent bargaining tool to a party with few resources?

A. You can pursue this question by asking others: how does the likely expense of pressing such a claim compare with the expense of pressing a claim for negligence? Which type of claim is likely to be more worrisome to a defendant? The answer is that outrage claims are relatively inexpensive to assert, as they don't generally require any expert testimony (except, perhaps, for establishing damages). This is a consequence of the tort's reliance on community standards of outrageousness. Such a claim also is likely to be especially worrisome because a defendant is unlikely to have insurance that covers it. To put the point in a more concrete factual context, a claim for IIED can be a particularly unwelcome form of counterclaim if a debtor is sued. Givelber enlarges on these issues in portions of his article that aren't included in the casebook but that are given at the end of this section of the manual.

Roberts v. Saylor (patient's former doctor is mean to her before she goes in for surgery; NL)
Greer v. Meddars (patient's current doctor is mean to him and his wife; L)

Q. What is the distinction between *Roberts v. Saylor* and *Greer v. Meddars*?

A. One distinction is that in *Roberts* the plaintiff did not have any sort of contractual or otherwise special relationship with Saylor when the incident occurred; these cases are useful partly because they illustrate how outrage claims often arise from within particular types of relationships where the courts set higher standards than they do between strangers. Saylor *had* performed surgery on the plaintiff, but it seems clear that their doctor-patient relationship had been terminated—with prejudice, one might even say, since it was unlikely they would resume professional relations after the hard words Saylor earlier had spoken to the plaintiff and the lawsuit she had filed against him. So when Saylor told the plaintiff that he didn't like her, she didn't have the kind of vulnerability to him that the Greer had in *Greer v. Meddars*. This isn't entirely clear-cut because the plaintiff in *Roberts* might have worried (and to some extent said that she did worry) that Dr. Saylor had the power to enter the operating room and hurt her, or maybe to persuade his colleagues at the hospital to do so. But perhaps the courts think they have to draw a line someplace between those situations where verbal abuse is out of bounds and those situations where it has to be tolerated, and the formal existence of a doctor-patient relationship seems like the line that is most manageable as an administrative matter. This still leaves open the question of Dr. Meddars' liability to *Mrs.* Greer, who was not his patient; but she had a certain vulnerability to him as well, since he was caring for her husband.

Muratore v. M/S Scotia Prince (P is hounded by obnoxious photographers on cruise ship; L)

Pemberton v. Bethlehem Steel Corp. (D circulates embarrassing photographs and information to P's wife and colleagues; NL)

Q.   What is the distinction between *Muratore v. M/S Scotia Prince* and *Pemberton v. Bethlehem Steel Corp.*?
A.   The results might seem curious, since the harm allegedly suffered by Pemberton—the loss of his marriage—is worse than the more transitory embarrassment and annoyance experienced by Muratore. But the cases show how strongly context affects claims for outrage. The court in *Pemberton* holds the plaintiff's claims to a more demanding standard because of his "personality"—that of a "rough and tumble labor official." Apart from the details of the plaintiff's personal style, presumably the idea is that the rules are different in a labor dispute than they are on a cruise ship. In the latter case the plaintiff is a captive on the defendant's property and reasonably expects to be treated with courtesy. In the labor setting, where the stakes are high and proceedings can be openly adversarial, perhaps everyone has to expect a measure of brutality. If they don't like it, they can find a tamer line of work.

It also appears that the court discounted Pemberton's claims because the embarrassing pictures and information were true and had possible value to others. Perhaps they left his wife and colleagues more knowledgeable about him than they had been before. This ties in to the controversies over the scope of tort liability for disclosing embarrassing private facts about a person, an issue taken up in the chapter of the casebook on invasion of privacy. By revealing the truth about Pemberton his employer might be understood to be doing some social good, inadvertently or otherwise; maybe Pemberton was a fraud. But no similar good is achieved by bothering Muratore and directing lewd remarks toward her. The point can be stated in forward-looking terms: if liability were found in *Pemberton*, then parties in the defendant's position might be deterred from informing the members of a union that its leader—or a leader they are considering—has a criminal record that they hadn't heard about. And the principle might be hard to contain; it might spread to any situations where true, embarrassing, but important revelations are made about someone. Are we sure we want to deter this? But in *Muratore* there is no such policy interest in the picture; there is no apparent risk that a finding of liability will deter socially useful conduct.

Figueiredo-Torres v. Nickel (D marriage counselor has affair with his client's wife; L)
Homer v. Long (hypothetical; D psychiatrist seduces P's wife; NL)

You can teach *Figueiredo-Torres v. Nickel* just as a quick look at the overlap between the outrage tort and sexual misconduct; or, if time permits, you can use the *Homer* case (below) as an in-class hypothetical to go farther with the theme.

Q.   What is the analogy between *Figueiredo-Torres v. Nickel* and *Greer v. Meddars*?
A.   In both cases the defendant's conduct would not have supported a claim for outrage ordinarily, but did here because the defendant had a special relationship with the plaintiff and abused it.

Q.   What is the distinction between *Figueiredo-Torres v. Nickel* and *Pemberton v. Bethlehem Steel Corp.*?
A.   In *Figueiredo-Torres* the defendant had an affair with the plaintiff's wife, resulting in liability; in *Pemberton* the defendant told the plaintiff's wife about an affair the plaintiff had with someone else, resulting in no liability. Again, one key reason for the difference is that in *Figueiredo-Torres* the plaintiff was in a vulnerable relationship with the defendant. Another is that *Pemberton* involved conduct by the defendant that may have had some value to others, as discussed above. *Figueiredo-Torres* did not.

Q.   Hypothetical: in *Homer v. Long*, 599 A.2d 1193 (Md.App. 1992—the same jurisdiction that decided *Figueiredo-Torres*), a woman named Vicki Homer became depressed and attempted to commit suicide. She was admitted to the Howard County hospital and soon came under the care of one Eugene Long, a psychiatrist. Long persuaded Vicki Homer's husband, James, to keep her at that hospital; from James he also obtained a detailed statement of sensitive information about Vicki Homer that he said he needed to treat her effectively. Long often prevented James or the Homers' children from visiting Vicki, saying that her therapy required her to remain out of contact with them. And then once she was discharged from the hospital, Long told James Homer that his wife's therapy required that she live away from home—as a result of which she went to live with a cousin. It turned out that all the while, Long had been seducing Vicki Homer and was conducting an affair with her. The affair finally resulted in the collapse of the Homers' marriage. These at least were the allegations in James Homer's complaint, which sought damages from Long for intentional infliction of emotional distress. What result? Can the case be distinguished from *Figueiredo-Torres*?

A. On these facts the court of appeals affirmed the dismissal of the complaint. It found *Figueiredo-Torres* distinguishable:

> There is no doubt that Dr. Long's conduct, as alleged, would be extreme and outrageous as to Ms. Homer, who, so far at least, has not chosen to complain of it. And, as *Figueiredo-Torres* makes clear, had Mr. Homer also been a patient of Dr. Long, it could be regarded as outrageous to him as well: "[A] jury may find extreme and outrageous conduct where a psychologist who is retained to improve a marital relationship implements a course of extreme conduct which is injurious to the patient and designed to facilitate a romantic, sexual relationship between the therapist and the patient's spouse." 584 A.2d 69. But that is not the case here.

> There are situations in which conduct directed principally at one person has been regarded as extreme and outrageous as to another, but normally the other person must be present to witness the conduct in order to recover. [...] We see no reason not to apply the general rule, for the pragmatic reason noted in the Restatement and by Prosser and Keeton. The emotional and economic trauma likely to arise from the seduction of one's spouse is not limited to the case where the seducer is the spouse's therapist. The conduct may be just as outrageous and the harm may be just as great where the seducer is a neighbor, a good friend, a relative, an employee or business associate of the plaintiff, or indeed anyone in whom the plaintiff has imposed trust or for whom he or she has special regard. To relax or abrogate the presence requirement in such cases would greatly expand the scope of the tort as framed and adopted by the Court of Appeals, which we are unwilling to do.

    Figueiredo-Torres isn't the only case in the chapter that one has to worry about distinguishing. James Homer also might seem a bit analogous to Mrs. Greer in *Greer v. Meddars*, the L case where the bad-tempered doctor had harsh words for his patient and his patient's wife and was held liable to both of them. It might seem especially strange for liability to exist to Mrs. Greer in that case but not here, since what Dr. Long did in *Homer v. Long* seems considerably more serious than the abuse Dr. Meddars offered in the *Greer* case. As a matter of doctrine the distinction is that Mrs. Greer was present for the abuse and was the direct object of some of it. As a matter of policy the idea evidently is that the class of potential plaintiffs in these cases remains tolerably limited so long as they have to be present or involved themselves in the abuse in order to sue. The courts especially worry about this in cases like *Figueiredo-Torres* and *Homer v. Long* because they don't want litigation to become too quick a recourse for betrayed spouses. (But is the worry exaggerated in *Homer v. Long*? The husband there did put a large and unusual measure of trust in the defendant even if he was not his patient.)

    The result here is a corrective to a misimpression the students otherwise might get—viz., that the courts are quick to find liability for outrage whenever a special relationship exists. It's not quite as simple as that. The details matter.

Hustler Magazine v. Falwell (D magazine publishes offensive cartoon about P; NL)
Van Duyn v. Smith (D follows around P, director of an abortion clinic, and publishes posters about her; L)

Walko v. Kean College (D publishes offensive satire about P, a college professor; NL)

Q. What is the distinction between *Hustler Magazine v. Falwell* and *Van Duyn v. Smith*?
A. The more precise question to ask is why Jerry Falwell, a minister, is considered a public figure, but Van Duyn, the director of an abortion clinic, is not. The reason is that Falwell has achieved a position of fame and influence in public life. This not only makes it important that he be subject to criticism (for many people might think it important that Van Duyn be subject to criticism as well), but also gives him plenty of ways to respond publicly to the defendant's speech. True, this rationale is limited to outrage claims based on *speech*; but then so is the doctrine: it's not at all clear that Falwell would have to meet a heightened standard if he sued to recover for IIED that took some form other than speech.

Q. What is the distinction between *Van Duyn v. Smith* and *Walko v. Kean College*?
A. This pair is harder than the previous one, though the conduct in the two cases is easy enough to distinguish. In *Van Duyn* the defendant followed the plaintiff around, which the court thought was important; it did consider the posters a legitimate part of the plaintiff's case, but said that it probably would affirm the dismissal of the complaint if only the posters had been at issue. In *Walko* there just were the satirical advertisements. There was nothing comparable to the stalking from *Van Duyn*. The trickier part is the question of the plaintiff's status. Walko was held to be a limited purpose public figure; Van Duyn was not. It's a little hard to understand the difference between them. Both were involved in controversial activities—Van Duyn perhaps more so. Maybe Walko, as an administrator, had somewhat better access to channels of rebuttal within the relevant community—the campus—than Van Duyn did in her neighborhood. And perhaps Walko, again by taking a position as an administrator, assumed a role of authority in her community that made it important for those under her authority to be able to question and ridicule her.

Murray v. Schlosser ("Berating the Brides" contest; L)

Q. What result in *Murray v. Schlosser*?
A. The court allowed the claim to go forward. For a similar result with a better discussion, see also *Esposito-Hilder v. SFX Broadcasting Corp.*, 665 N.Y.S.2d 697 (App.Div. 1997). In *Esposito-Hilder*, the plaintiff's bridal photograph, along pictures of other newlyweds, was published in the *Schenectady Daily Gazette*. The hosts of a program on a local radio station entered her picture into an "Ugliest Bride" contest each week in which they made insulting remarks about women whose pictures appeared in the newspaper's wedding announcements. In the plaintiff's case they also took certain other atypical steps: they disclosed her full name, her place of employment (a competing radio station), her position there, and the identity of her superiors. The plaintiff sued for intentional infliction of emotional distress. The defendant moved to dismiss the complaint; the trial court denied the motion, stating that "The First Amendment was not enacted to enable wolves to parade around in sheep's clothing, feasting upon the character, reputation and sensibilities of innocent private persons." The court of appeals affirmed:

> [W]e attach particular significance to several factors. First, plaintiff is a private individual and not a "public figure". Second, the nature of the communications made by defendants involved a matter of virtually no "public interest"; there is an inference that defendants' conduct represented a deliberate intent to inflict injury upon plaintiff based upon the claimed unprecedented expansion of its standard "routine" of the "Ugliest Bride" contest to include particulars concerning plaintiff's name, employer, supervisors and the like, and the fact that the parties are business competitors in the radio broadcast industry.
>
> We are not unmindful of the constitutional issues implicated in this case and in our resolution thereof. In the quest for the proper accommodation between the right of redress for infliction of injury and the freedoms of speech and expression protected by the 1st Amendment, we have

determined that the State's relatively strong interest in compensating individuals for harm outweighs the relatively weak 1st Amendment protection to be accorded defendants. It is elementary that not all speech or expression is to be accorded equal 1st Amendment protection; the most jealously protected speech is that which advances the free, uninhibited flow of ideas and opinions on matters of public interest and concern; that which is addressed to matters of private concern, or focuses upon persons who are not "public figures", is less stringently protected. Moreover, among the forms of communication, broadcasting enjoys the most limited 1st Amendment protection.

As to defendants' alternative contention that their conduct is protected comedic expression, we note that comedic expression does not receive absolute 1st Amendment protection. Instead, it can be actionable where "humor is used in an attempt to disguise an attempt to injure," *Frank v. National Broadcasting Co.,* 119 A.D.2d 252. The allegations of the amended complaint allege an intent to injure, which satisfies the limited inquiry before us.

Another issue. If you are looking for more issues to discuss regarding the outrage tort, there are interesting questions concerning the type of intent needed to support such claims. An example that makes a nice in-class hypothetical is *Potter v. Firestone Tire and Rubber Co.,* 863 P.2d 795 (Cal. 1993), a case included in the Duty chapter of the casebook (in the section on Negligent Infliction of Emotional Distress). The plaintiffs lived next to the Crazy Horse landfill in Salinas. The defendant, Firestone, dumped toxic industrial waste in the landfill despite being told not to do so by the company managing it. The chemicals, many of which were carcinogens, seeped into the plaintiffs' wells and contaminated their water. The plaintiffs could not prove that they had suffered any physical injury as a result, but they sued Firestone to recover for their fear that their ingestion of the water eventually would cause them to develop cancer. If you're interested you can go to that part of the book and read the holding on the defendant's liability for NIED (basically there was liability only if the defendant made the plaintiffs more likely than not to get cancer). But the plaintiffs also brought IIED claims. There was evidence that the defendants had a policy against dumping toxins in the landfill and knew it was risky, but went ahead and did it anyway. The question was whether this sort of behavior could support a claim for outrage. Here is the analysis the court offered:

> The elements of the tort of intentional infliction of emotional distress are: "'(1) extreme and outrageous conduct by the defendant with the intention of causing, or reckless disregard of the probability of causing, emotional distress; (2) the plaintiff's suffering severe or extreme emotional distress; and (3) actual and proximate causation of the emotional distress by the defendant's outrageous conduct...." Conduct to be outrageous must be so extreme as to exceed all bounds of that usually tolerated in a civilized community.' [Citation.] The defendant must have engaged in 'conduct intended to inflict injury or engaged in with the realization that injury will result.'" *Christensen v. Superior Court,* 820 P.2d 181 (Cal. 1991).

> In *Christensen,* we held that "'[t]he law limits claims of intentional infliction of emotional distress to egregious conduct toward plaintiff proximately caused by defendant.' The only exception to this rule is that recognized when the defendant is aware, but acts with reckless disregard, of the plaintiff and the probability that his or her conduct will cause severe emotional distress to that plaintiff. Where reckless disregard of the plaintiff's interests is the theory of recovery, the presence of the plaintiff at the time the outrageous conduct occurs is recognized as the element establishing a higher degree of culpability which, in turn, justifies recovery of greater damages by a broader group of plaintiffs than allowed on a negligent infliction of emotional distress theory."

Thus, "[i]t is not enough that the conduct be intentional and outrageous. It must be conduct directed at the plaintiff, or occur in the presence of a plaintiff of whom the defendant is aware." "The requirement that the defendant's conduct be directed primarily at the plaintiff is a factor which distinguishes intentional infliction of emotional distress from the negligent infliction of such injury."

In this case, it is ambiguous whether the lower courts determined that Firestone's conduct was directed at these particular plaintiffs in the sense intended by *Christensen*. Although the Court of Appeal correctly rejected Firestone's contention that Firestone was not liable because it did not know the particular names of any individual whose groundwater was contaminated by the hazardous waste, it is unclear whether it believed that Firestone was actually aware of the presence of these particular plaintiffs and their consumption and use of the water.

Furthermore, it is questionable whether the trial court made a finding that Firestone possessed the requisite knowledge, and if so, whether such a finding would be supported by substantial evidence. Although the trial court concluded that Firestone "had to realize" that the eventual discovery of the toxic contamination "by those drinking the contaminated water would almost certainly result in their suffering severe emotional distress," this may be interpreted in one of two ways. First, this may have been a finding that Firestone actually knew of these particular plaintiffs and their consumption of the water, and nevertheless sent prohibited wastes to Crazy Horse despite a realization that plaintiffs would almost certainly suffer severe emotional distress upon their discovery of the facts. Alternatively, this may have been a finding that Firestone had to have realized that its misconduct was almost certain to cause severe emotional distress to any person who might foreseeably consume the water and subsequently discover the facts. Although the knowledge requirement is met under the first interpretation of the court's ruling, it is not satisfied under the second because knowledge of these particular plaintiffs is lacking.

This conclusion is consistent with the result reached in *Christensen* itself. There we held that, even though it was alleged that defendants' conduct in mishandling the remains of deceased persons was intentional and outrageous and was substantially certain to cause extreme emotional distress to relatives and close friends of the deceased, the plaintiffs' cause of action for intentional infliction of emotional distress was not sufficiently supported where there was no allegation that the defendants' misconduct was directed primarily at plaintiffs, or that it was calculated to cause them severe emotional distress, or that it was done with knowledge of their presence and with a substantial certainty that they would suffer severe emotional injury.

The court added in a footnote:

Firestone asserts in its brief on the merits that there is no evidence in the record showing that it knew of anyone living near Crazy Horse or that it had any interaction with plaintiffs. Plaintiffs do not specifically contest these assertions. Rather, they point out that Firestone was informed that Crazy Horse was not equipped to prevent toxins from leaching into the groundwater, that Firestone agreed not to send any toxic materials to the landfill, and that despite its knowledge that the reason for the no toxic requirement was to protect "plaintiffs' water source," Firestone chose to return the toxins to Crazy Horse where they found their way into the water source.

More reading. Givelber's article, quoted in the text, makes a number of other interesting points about the outrage tort. Here are some more of them:

The absence of insurance obviously enhances the pain of money damages and exacerbates the unfairness of indeterminate standards. One is far more likely to be insured against liability for negligence than for outrageousness. The widespread existence of insurance also affects the "practicability" of the respective standards for resolving disputes informally. Courts are not actively involved in the resolution of the vast majority of disputes concerning who should bear the cost of accidental physical injuries. These disputes are settled informally by liability insurance companies. These companies possess the expertise, information, and resources to process cases efficiently. They are not immobilized by the indeterminacy of the negligence standard; indeed, their agents reduce the vagueness of "reasonableness" to a series of rather clear rules to facilitate the processing of claims and the resolution of disputes. Comparable institutional arrangements for the resolution of "outrageousness" disputes do not exist since most people are not insured against such liability. Moreover, even those insurers who do provide coverage probably do not process a sufficient number of claims to achieve the same kind of efficiency or to establish the same kind of informal working "rules." The indeterminateness of the outrageousness standard, then, may confound the informal resolution of disputes about emotional injuries to a considerably greater extent than the indeterminacy of negligence retards the resolution of disputes about physical injuries. [...]

Outrageousness, then, is a hybrid tort: it resembles intentional torts in that the distinction between behavior and injury is blurred, and it resembles negligence in that the defendant's conduct is evaluated in terms of a vague standard. The resemblance to either form of tort ends, however, when we look for the definitional elements that limit the dangers inherent in these features: there is neither the precise definition of the prohibited behavior that is characteristic of intentional torts nor the requirement of a palpable, physical injury characteristic of the unintentional ones. [...]

The results in these two categories of cases reflect when and why people sue, and for what, as well as a court's need to ground its decision as to the socially intolerable in something other than its own vision of the good (or, more accurately, the bad). Since we do not have a fully developed social response to the problem of severe emotional injuries (or, indeed, even a consensus that relatively brief interactions between people can produce them), courts cannot look for guidance to a rich body of law, or social or industrial customs, or a set of governmental regulations or administrative practices. Rather, courts have found the necessary context in the social and legal responses to a series of specific problems arising out of economic legal relationships-employer-employee, creditor-debtor, landlord-tenant, insurer- insured. The law of outrageousness has developed interstitially—by filling gaps in the law governing these relationships. [...]

It is not surprising that most of the cases dealing with outrageousness arise in the context of disputes concerning legal rights. These disputes make it likely that a potential plaintiff would come in contact with a lawyer in any event. The tort provides those who would normally be defendants in a contract action with a mechanism for taking the offensive while giving those who are owed money under the contract a means for pushing the potential recovery beyond mere contract damages. In disputes between creditors and debtors, insurers and the insured, employers and employees, and landlords and tenants, it provides a potent bargaining tool for the party who is traditionally without much leverage. The decided cases may be the tip of a potentially much larger iceberg.

Modern procedure makes it a simple matter to add a claim of outrageousness to a suit that would be brought in any event, or to interpose it as a counterclaim if one has been sued. As we have noted, it is also a relatively easy suit to bring in its own right. While the high cost of personal injury litigation is a significant limitation on the proliferation of these suits, it is still a great deal cheaper to litigate such a case than it is to try a malpractice or personal injury or products liability case. Since it is the moral quality of defendant's conduct, and the inferences to be derived from it, that dominate the proof, the plaintiff can typically present evidence sufficient to support a finding of all elements of the tort without the heavy reliance on expert witnesses and exhaustive discovery that are so characteristic of many personal injury cases. If the defendant's conduct is outrageous (a matter as to which the opinions of experts are irrelevant) this may support an inference that the defendant caused plaintiff's suffering, and that the plaintiff's suffering was severe. [...]

In sum, we have a doctrine that defies consistent definition, and presents all the problems inherent in that lack of definition compounded by a prominent punitive component. This same doctrine, however, permits courts to achieve justice in specific cases without the costs in terms of dissembling and distorted rules often associated with that conduct. The doctrine has typically been invoked, and is likely to continue to be invoked, on behalf of the noninstitutional, nonprofessional party to a variety of significant economic and commercial relations. While there is no way of accurately measuring costs, there is at least no reason to believe that the doctrine redounds to the disadvantage of those in whose behalf it is typically invoked. Although there is little evidence that this tort will ever provide the basis for principled adjudication, it has provided and probably will continue to provide the basis for achieving situational justice. That, rather than the general protection of emotional tranquility, is the major mission and justification for this tort.

CHAPTER 2

INTENTIONAL TORTS:
PRIVILEGES

SECTION A. DEFENSE OF PERSON AND PROPERTY

This section presents a number of good opportunities to identify superficial similarities between cases that come to different results and then draw distinctions between them. Sometimes the rhetoric of one case suggests a conflict with another, but the conflict can be resolved or relieved once the factual distinctions between the cases are fully taken into account—a good lesson for students to remember when they are confronted with a case that contains language unhelpful to their problem but has distinguishable facts. There also are recurring substantive themes that run through these cases and that can form the basis of analogies between decisions on seemingly different facts: proportionality, and the leeway that court give defendants who have no alternative but to commit apparent violations of the proportionality principle.

If you are looking to make cuts (it would be a shame in this section), consider skipping *Crabtree*, *Hull v. Scruggs* (a case we ourselves would not skip under any circumstances, however), and the Restatement excerpts at the end ("Rules of Engagement").

Katko v. Briney (P shot by spring gun when trying to burglarize D's unattended house; L)
Crabtree v. Dawson (Innocent P hit in face with musket; NL)
Wright v. Haffke (D store owner shoots P thief in the back; NL)
Woodbridge v. Marks (P bitten by D's watchdog; NL)

Q. Would the court in *Katko* have been satisfied if the Brineys had posted huge signs saying "Spring gun inside; trespassers will be shot"?
A. No. The court's emphasis is on proportionality, not notice.

Q. Suppose Katko had been a member of the Manson family who showed up at Briney's farmhouse with a gun, hoping to find him and kill him—but finding an empty house with a spring gun inside instead, and getting maimed by it. Different result?
A. Not clear. The trial court's instruction suggests that a spring gun might be legitimate to repel a felony of violence or a felony punishable by death. If the landowner were present he would be able to use deadly force in such circumstances. But if he were present the level of danger to him obviously would be much greater than if he were absent, and it seems a little odd to suppose that his liability for setting up the spring gun depends not just on whether it shoots a criminal but on the intentions in the criminal's mind. Meanwhile the public policy objections to unattended spring guns are intact no matter who is shot by them: they indiscriminately threaten firemen or children who may wander into the house innocently, so perhaps we want to discourage their use as a matter of policy even if a defendant in a particular case might have been able to use comparable force if there in person.

Q. Suppose Edward Briney had been sitting in the house smoking a pipe when Katko arrived to steal the Mason jars. What would Briney have had the right to do? Would his use of the spring gun have been permissible then?
A. He could have ushered him off the property, as explained in the notes following *Katko*; that much would indeed be justifiable even if Katko weren't a thief. Since he was trying to commit a crime, Briney

could have used a measure of actual force to deal with him. Could Briney have beaten him into submission with the butt end of his rifle? Well, a judicious beating would probably be all right; it would not involve deadly force. Could Briney have tied him to a chair? Yes; that would be mere detention. It all depends heavily on what Katko was trying to do. Some case law (see *Wright v. Haffke*, about to come), and the Restatement excerpts later in the chapter, suggest that Briney could use lethal force to repel an attempted invasion into his home (the cases are the basis of hypotheticals given below). Notice again an odd quality to statements equating what Briney can do if he is there and what he can do if he isn't there. If he is there his rights are greater than they are if he were absent: since if he were present he would face personal danger, Briney might then have had the more expansive entitlement commonly given to people who shoot burglars that threaten them while they are in their own houses.

Q. Why can't a property owner shoot a trespasser, even after giving a clear warning ("I'll count to ten, then I'm going to shoot you if you don't leave")?
A. This is a question that merits some discussion and has no single answer. There is a problem of proportionality to which we will return in almost every case in this section. If you are fortunate some student will take the position that the property owner ought to be able to do whatever he wants to a trespasser. That vision of absolute vision of property rights (and the right of an owner to protect them) obviously is not the basis of the law in this area; instead we find something closer to a utilitarian calculus. You might ask what the rights of a student should be if he catches someone—a stranger—trying to steal one of his pens. Can he stab the stranger? What would be the problems with a regime that allowed such measures? Consider the dangers of escalation, and the absence of marginal deterrence: if a petty thief knows you can kill him if you catch him, what are *his* incentives? Not to get caught, of course, but what if he finds that he is about to get caught?
      What is the relationship between the rights of the property owner against the thief and the sort of sanction the *criminal* law imposes once the thief is caught? Note that shootings sometimes are "allowed"—i.e., privileged—even where the crime would not warrant the death penalty—as in *Wright v. Haffke*.

Q. Since Briney couldn't be there himself, what was he supposed to do about the recurring thefts? Does Katko have immunity as a practical matter?
A. Katko can of course be sued as well as jailed if he is caught. That is Briney's right: to collect from Katko through the courts, not to maim him. Since catching Briney may be difficult, Briney has some other options, too: invest in non-threatening security measures (and perhaps buy a dog; see *Woodbridge*, infra); and call the police.

Q. What is the distinction between *Katko v. Briney* and *Crabtree v. Dawson*? Is the outcome in *Crabtree* fair?
A. Dawson behaved reasonably; the Brineys didn't—if we measure the reasonableness of the behavior (as we must) ex ante, by reference to what they reasonably knew and understood. From a corrective justice standpoint these decisions may rankle when taken together; Crabtree, who did not necessarily do anything wrong, nevertheless collects nothing because Dawson was acting the way we want him to act. But perhaps this is no different from other areas where there is no liability without some sort of fault—the driver who has a heart attack, etc.

Q. What is the superficial similarity between *Wright v. Haffke* and *Katko v. Briney*? What is the distinction between them?
A. The similarity between the cases is that in both a defendant was shot while in the act of trying to steal property, and in neither case did the defendant appear to threaten any (further) physical harm to the plaintiff.
      Distinctions: It may be helpful for students to imagine that they represent the shooter (Haffke), and have to think of ways to avoid losing their case on account of *Katko*. Some possible distinctions are

that in *Wright* the defendant had assaulted the plaintiff; that in *Wright* the amount of property at stake appears to have been greater, and the crime more serious; that in *Wright* the defendant was present to assess the situation before firing; and that in *Wright* the defendant appeared to have had no other means available to stop the thieves. To test the significance of those possible distinctions, it helps to consider whether they likely would have changed the result in *Katko*. So:

The value of the threatened property. Would *Katko* have come out differently if Briney had some valuable oil paintings stored in his house? What if a museum sets up nozzles to spray lethal mustard gas if sensors detect thieves trying to remove paintings from the wall after hours? There's probably still liability in both cases, though no doubt those facts would have made the court more nervous. Certainly the language of the *Katko* opinion provides no toehold for this distinction.

The assault. What if Briney had been present and Katko had pushed him out of the way to steal the Mason jars? This would have helped the Brineys a lot. This question invites the students to try to rewrite the facts of *Katko* to make them like *Wright*. If Katko had pushed Briney and then been shot while leaving the house, the cases would look more similar, and the court might have been more sympathetic to the Brineys.

The presence of the defendant. But this still brings us to the third point: in *Wright*, the defendant was *present*. There might be good reasons in policy for allowing people to use force in person that they could not use if absent. A spring gun is indiscriminate, and will shoot anyone who trespasses. A clerk with a gun is able to be more sensitive to the details of the circumstances. So even though a thief got shot in both cases, one can imagine courts being more eager to condemn the use of spring guns generally by imposing liability.

No feasible alternatives. Finally, what if there was nothing else the Brineys could have done to protect their property? There is a strain in the cases in this section (see *Hull v. Scruggs*, below) that allows seemingly disproportionate responses if it's clear that the defendant has no other recourse. Are there senses in which the *Wright* defendant might have had recourse after all in the sense (also present in *Katko*) that he could have taken better precautions against theft ex ante?

Q. What is the superficial similarity between *Woodbridge* and *Katko v. Briney*? What is the distinction between them?

A. In both cases a defendant suffered (we may assume) great bodily harm because he invaded the defendant's property; in neither case did the defendant threaten harm to anyone (indeed, *Woodbridge* seems the stronger case for liability since the plaintiff was not committing a crime at all, unless it was a trespass). Here was how the court in *Woodbridge* distinguished that case from one involving a spring gun:

> A spring gun is more than likely to take human life. It is placed, not for the purpose of warning others off, but with the design to do them great injury, even if life is not taken should they come in contact with it. A dog is rarely so vicious or powerful that it would endanger a man's life. And the watch dog is used, not so much for the purpose of injuring an intruder, but rather as a means for warning and frightening him away. A dog gives notice of his presence and attack. A spring gun kills without any notice whatever. There is a marked distinction between the cases, and the rule which should condemn the use of a spring gun as a lawless and cruel method of protection does not apply to a case like this.

The chief distinction between the cases is that a dog, unlike a spring gun, is both visible and audible. This distinction is not completely satisfying, because spring guns result in liability even if accompanied by warning signs; but as a *class*, it nonetheless is easy enough to see on these grounds why dogs would not receive the same broad condemnation given to spring guns. The court in *Woodbridge* also emphasized that watchdogs are common precautions, and seemed reluctant to condemn their owners to liability whenever intruders get bitten. Dogs confer many different sorts of benefits on their owners. Spring guns do not. Notice that this is an exception to the usual rule of strict liability for vicious dogs.

Q. What if the Brineys had bought a vicious dog and kept it in their house; the dog then attacks Katko and chews off his leg when he tries to enter. Liability?

A. Probably not; obviously *Woodbridge* suggests not. A student once asked if the outcome here would be different if the Brineys had removed the dog's vocal cords, as some criminals have been known to do with their watchdogs; naturally that would make the case a lot more analogous to *Katko*. (The court in *Woodbridge* left liability for watchdogs to be determined on a case-by-case basis, and on these hypothesized facts that qualification might have bite.) It's also worth noting that in *Woodbridge* the court seemed to care that the dog was posted where it could guard against thefts from the chicken house, and not where it would menace pedestrians on the nearby walkways; this suggests a greater possibility of liability if such a dog were used just to guard against mere trespassers.

Hull v. Scruggs (D shoots incorrigible egg-sucking dog; NL)

Q. What is the superficial similarity between *Hull v. Scruggs* and *Katko v. Briney*? What is the distinction between them?

A. They seem similar because in both cases the property owner had put up with a series of intrusions and seemed to be at wits' end. But the two cases can be distinguished on the basis of the two general threads that seem to wind through these cases. With respect to proportionality, taking life to save property generally is not permitted; taking property—even expensive property—to save other property is easier to forgive. And while it's true that both defendants had been suffering repeated invasions of their rights, the *Katko* defendant still had other things he could have done short of using a spring gun to protect his rights—things that seemed reasonable (cost-effective) to require, given the high costs of using a spring gun. The only precautions still available in *Hull v. Scruggs* were fences that the court apparently did not consider reasonable to require given the stakes involved.

Now here are some hypotheticals to consider.

Q. Hypothetical: in *Brown v. Martinez*, 361 P.2d 152 (N.M. 1961), the trial court found that Brown, a teenage boy, went to Martinez's farm one evening with several friends to steal watermelons. Brown waited at the southeast corner of the property while his confederates entered the garden to seize the melons. Martinez emerged from his house with a rifle and called to the boys to get out of the garden. They ran toward the southwest corner of his property. Martinez fired his rifle into the air in a southeasterly direction to scare them; the bullet unexpectedly struck Brown in the leg, and Brown sued Martinez for battery. What result?

A. The trial court dismissed Brown's claim. The New Mexico supreme court reversed, holding that judgment must be entered for the plaintiff as a matter of law:

> There is no question that appellant, together with his companions, was engaged in an illegal undertaking, viz., trespassing on land occupied by appellee and stealing his crop; also that they had done some very minor injury to his fence. The question thus presented is whether or not injury resulting from the use of such force as a rifle to prevent a trespass or loss of property is actionable. [...]

The court concluded that Brown and his friends were committing a misdemeanor; they had violated a New Mexico statute that provided as follows:

> Every person who shall wilfully commit any trespass, by entering upon the garden, orchard, vineyard, or any other improved land belonging to another, without the permission of the owner thereof, with intent to cut, take, carry away, destroy or injure the trees, grain, grass, hay, fruit, or

vegetables there growing, shall be punished by fine not exceeding twenty-five dollars ($25.00), nor less than three dollars ($3.00).

In finding for the plaintiff, the court quoted approvingly this passage from *Carpenter v. State*, 62 Ark. 286, 36 S.W. 900, 907:

> [T]he right to defend property against one who manifestly intends or endeavors, by violence or surprise, to commit a known felony, to the extent of slaying the aggressor, does not include the right to defend it, to the same extent, where there is no intention to commit a felony. A man may use force to defend his real or personal property in his actual possession against one who endeavors to dispossess him without right, taking care that the force used does not exceed what reasonably appears to be necessary for the purpose of defense and prevention. But, in the absence of an attempt to commit a felony, he cannot defend his property, except his habitation, to the extent of killing the aggressor, for the purpose of preventing a trespass; and, if he should do so, he would be guilty of a felonious homicide. Life is too valuable to be sacrificed solely for the protection of property. Rather than slay the aggressor to prevent a mere trespass, when no felony is attempted, he should yield, and appeal to the courts for redress. Ordinarily the killing allowed in the defense of property is solely for the prevention of a felony.

The trial court in *Brown* found that Martinez had not intended to shoot anybody; he fired his gun away (he thought) from the fleeing thieves in order to scare them. Why was he was held liable anyway? Because it was a case of transferred intent like *Manning v. Grimsley*: the defendant had the intent necessary to support a claim for assault against him, and this intent carried over to support liability for battery when one of his bullets struck the fleeing thief.

Q. Hypothetical: in *Bennett v. Dunn*, 507 So.2d 451 (Ala. 1987), Dunn's wife awoke in the middle of the night to the sound of the family's dogs barking in their back yard. She woke her husband (the defendant), who looked out the window and saw the brake lights flashing on his truck. The truck was parked 20 to 30 feet from his infant son's bedroom. Dunn ran to the front door, stuck his head out, and yelled at the "dark blob" in the truck. Realizing that he did not know whether the intruder had weapons or whether there were accomplices elsewhere in the yard, Dunn shut and locked the door and told his wife to call the police. He put on some clothes, loaded his .22-caliber rifle, and went back to the front door. With rifle in hand, Dunn walked almost to the end of the walk leading to his driveway and kept yelling for the "dark blob" to leave. The windshield wipers in the truck were being turned on and off. The truck's radio was on and the volume was being turned up and down. The intruder in the truck was not deterred by the barking of the dogs, Dunn's yells, or the sight of Dunn's rifle. Dunn fired three or four shots into the air in an attempt to scare the intruder into leaving or to evoke a response. The shots apparently accomplished neither purpose, and Dunn retreated to his living room. The intruder cranked the truck and Dunn stepped out of the living room and unsuccessfully attempted to shoot out its tires. The truck rammed into the back of Dunn's car. The intruder, Bennett, opened the door to the truck. Dunn, unsure what the "crazy" intruder would do next, took five shots at the windshield of the truck, aiming at the dark blob. The truck then backed out of the yard, crossed the street, went into a drainage ditch, and then made it onto the road and pulled away.

One of Dunn's bullets hit Bennett. Bennett later was arrested and pled guilty to stealing the truck. He also sued Dunn for battery. What result?

A. No liability. The trial court gave summary judgment to Dunn, and the Alabama supreme court affirmed:

> [W]e find that Dunn acted out of a reasonable and well founded apprehension that he, his wife, and his 11-month-old baby were in danger. The law does not require that a man retreat when defending his home and allows him to use whatever force is necessary to remove the danger.

Q. Hypothetical: in *Bruister v. Haney*, 233 Miss. 527 (1958), the plaintiffs, Mr. and Mrs. Floy Haney, sued the defendant, H. W. Bruister, for poisoning their cows. The Haneys' evidence was that they grazed 8 to 10 cows on their unenclosed oat field about a quarter of a mile from Bruister's unfenced field. On several occasions in the months preceding the death of their cattle, the Haneys' cows strayed from their field and grazed in Bruister's field. After telling the Haneys to keep their cows out of his field, Bruister mixed some "Paris green," a poison containing arsenic, with whole oats. He placed two dozen piles of the mixture in his field near its border. The piles were about three inches high and placed six feet apart, with oats at the base, then the poison, then oats on top. Bruister did not tell the Haneys that he had done this. The Haneys' cattle strayed from their pasture onto the edge of Bruister's field and ate some of the piles of oats and poison. Three of their cows died as a result, and two cows and a bull became sick and lost weight. They sued Bruister to recover for the loss of the animals. What result?

A. Liability: The jury held Bruister liable for the damage to the cattle, and the Mississippi Supreme Court affirmed:

> The established rule in this respect is stated in 3 C.J.S. Animals sec. 213, page 1330: "In accordance with the general rule that a landowner has no right unnecessarily to kill or injure trespassing animals, * * * where a person places poisoned food on his premises with the intention to injure or kill animals of others trespassing on his land, he is liable for the injury to or the loss of such animals as may be poisoned by eating the food, although he notifies the owner of the animals of his intention to put out the poisoned food...."

Q. What is the superficial similarity between *Bruister* and *Woodbridge v. Marks*? What is the distinction between them?

A. The cases seem similar because both involved unattended traps. Some possible distinctions:

Audibility; visibility. The dog was audible and visible, whereas the oats were set out as a trap. But to test this distinction we have to ask whether it would have mattered in *Bruister* if there had been a sign posted saying that the oats were poisoned. Presumably not, since cows can't read. Might it have been different if Bruister had warned the Haneys? The court thought not, though this was dicta. So the audibility/visibility point alone doesn't seem to be critical to the outcomes.

Poisons vs. dogs. What if Bruister kept a dog that attacked the Haneys' trespassing cows? Liability? This would be a harder case—and hard to distinguish from *Woodbridge*. Perhaps the next two animal cases shed light on it. As a policy matter (analogies to some of the earlier battery cases are possible here), if a court comes down hard on poisoned oats it runs no risk of deterring a good or reasonable activity; but liability for damage done by dogs to trespassing animals on a farm is another matter. Farmers may need dogs to keep away predatory animals, and it may not be reasonable to demand that they discriminate between such predators and mere cows. Bruister's oats, however, were targeted to have the effect that they did have.

Alternatives. There are better ways of safeguarding a house than using a spring gun, and better ways of dealing with trespassing cows than by poisoning them. But there may not be many better means of keeping away trespassers than buying a watchdog.

Proportionality. The issue of proportionality comes back to the fore here. Bruister may as well have simply shot the cows for eating his grass. What would be wrong with this? The later blurb from *Kershaw* suggests one answer: allowing farmers to shoot each others' cows for eating their grass is not a promising prescription for civil order in an agrarian society. It's easy to imagine escalation and nasty feuds resulting. Everyone is better off using milder sanctions, and here Bruister did have obvious alternatives: impound the cows and collect damages from the Haneys. We see the courts trying to promote the cheapest way of resolving the problems presented by these conflicts. (The relevance of cheapness is seen most clearly by focusing on the fact that the cows are property. It is misleading to analogize *Bruister* to *Katko* on the ground that both involved threats to life, or "fatal" injuries inflicted to prevent the loss property. Animal lovers might like that suggestion, but it doesn't do much to explain the cases; so far as the common law is concerned, *Bruister* is a property-vs.-property case, not a life vs. property case.)

The single owner. An economic way to interpret this case, suggested by the quote from Baron Bramwell at the end of the section, is to ask how you might expect a single owner to have handled this sort of problem (e.g., if a single owner found that his cows were eating grass that was earmarked for other purposes; or perhaps imagine a corporation that owns two farming subsidiaries that get into a conflict like this). He would not kill the cows. He would build a fence or take other—measures the cheapest measures he could come up with to solve the problem. The law can't force that precise sort of solution, though there's an interesting literature running from Coase to Ellickson on whether such a solution might be expected anyway. But the law can discourage measures that obviously are way outside what any single owner would want; and perhaps damages will cause the owners of these properties (or the owners of other properties confronting similar situations) to think about ways of settling these problems that are preferable to constantly paying to get their cows back.

Q. What is the superficial similarity between *Hull v. Scruggs* and *Bruister v. Haney*? What is the distinction between them?
A. The similarity is that in either case, the defendant killed the plaintiff's animal (a prima facie tort of conversion) to save his crops (here, eggs that presumably were destined to be eaten; note that the hens and turkeys in *Scruggs* apparently were not being threatened).

Some distinctions: The disparity between the value of the properties involved was greater in *Bruister*. More strikingly, the defendant in *Hull* had no unexhausted alternatives except to allow his property to be taken. He could not impound the dog; the dog was wilier than the Haneys' cows. The court dismisses the various ex ante precautions the defendant might have taken (e.g., installing fences); why? Presumably because they are too costly, and (unlike in *Bruister*) the costs can't necessarily be recouped from the dog's owner. The owner may have been impossible to identify, and in any event allowing people to recoup the costs of fences in cases like this would create difficulties in determining whether the fence was really necessary, or was just something the owner of the birds wanted for other reasons. There are few doubts of that sort when a cow has been impounded or a dog killed.

The court points to the simple fact that the property belongs to the defendant, not to the dog. That also was true in *Bruister*; but in *Bruister*, the costs of impounding the cow could have been charged to its owner. In a sense, *Hull* is to *Bruister* as *Wright* is to *Katko*. In the former cases, force is authorized to protect property where there seem not to be plainly cheaper ways of preventing it from being taken.

Notice the relationship between rhetoric and result in these cases. In *Katko* we are told that the value of human life and limb outweighs the value of mere property; but then in *Woodbridge* we find no liability for the owner of a dog that may have maimed the plaintiff. Likewise, it might be tempting if one had only read *Bruister* to imagine it standing for a broad rule that you can't kill an animal to save crops. After reading *Hull* one sees that the common law's approach to these problems is more nuanced than that.

Kershaw v. McKown (D shoots dog that menaces his dog; L to dog's owner depends on dog's value)

Q. Notice that everyone agrees the defendant must be held liable for killing the dog if it was worth "greatly more than the goat." (The plaintiff wanted an instruction that he should win if the animals' worth was about the same.) Is it true that if the dog was a valuable one—perhaps a known purebred—the defendant is obliged to watch his goat get killed, but if it's a mutt the defendant is authorized to kill it? Why?
A. Yes, that's pretty much the rule of *Kershaw*. Again, the single-owner idea is of some help. A person seeing his purebred dog threaten his more common goat might decide to let the goat die rather than kill the dog, if those were his choices. So that is the outcome the law encourages—followed, of course, by the payment of damages from the dog's owner to the owner of the goat. (What if the dog's owner were unknown? Then this case would come to resemble *Hull v. Scruggs* a bit more.)

Q. What is the superficial similarity between *Hull v. Scruggs* and *Kershaw v. McKown*? What is the distinction between them?

A. In both cases the plaintiff owned a dog that was killed by the defendant. In both cases the dog was threatening the defendant's property. In both cases, we may assume (by stylizing the cases accordingly), the dog was worth more than the property. This seems plausible in *Hull v. Scruggs* (dog vs. eggs), and it was one of the conclusions the jury would have been permitted to reach in *Kershaw v. McKown*. Yet only in *Kershaw* would this result in liability. It might seem especially strange because in *Kershaw* the owner seemed to be out of options for stopping the attack; his goat was about to be killed. But he did have one option that apparently wasn't available in *Hull v. Scruggs*: he could let the goat die and collect from the owner of the dog. In *Hull v. Scruggs* the owner's identity evidently wasn't known, so sending him a bill for the eggs wasn't feasible. In that case the law gives the owner of the threatened property more leeway to reply.

Q. What if the dog were a purebred but the defendant was sentimentally attached to the goat?

A. When it can, the common law usually measures value by reference to the market (you can discuss reasons why this is so, especially if you won't be teaching the damages chapter where the issue is covered in more detail). The result is that on facts like those the law would give the goat's owner a choice: he can kill the dog and pay the dog's owner; or he can let the goat die and collect from the dog's owner. He has to decide whether he would rather have the plaintiff buy him a new goat, or keep the old goat but buy the plaintiff a new dog. The first choice normally will seem preferable (again, we're still assuming that the dog is a purebred and plainly worth more than the goat; it might be easier to imagine a hog and a chicken, as suggested by the next note in the text). It doesn't cost the defendant anything (or at least not much). The second choice leaves the defendant out of pocket whatever the replacement purebred will cost (say, $500). But it might be worth it to him if he values the goat $500 more than the market does.

SECTION B. PRIVATE NECESSITY

If you are looking to trim something you can cut the *Rossi* case (right after *Ploof*), but it teaches pretty well. Otherwise there is nothing to cut here unless you just want to assign *Ploof*, *Vincent*, and an item or two from the public necessity materials afterwards; this would enable you to cover all aspects of necessity in one day or less, while using all the cut cases as hypotheticals as time permits.

Ploof v. Putnam (L for pushing plaintiff's boat away from dock during an emergency)
Rossi v. DelDuca (L for defendant whose dog bites girl while she is trying to escape being bitten by another dog)

Q. How is it that the privilege of necessity was turned into the basis of a *plaintiff's* claim in this case?

A. The point of the question is just to enable the students to see that while necessity most naturally is invoked as a defense to an intentional tort claim, it also can become the basis of a claim for damages if the party holding the privilege is denied access to the property of another when he is entitled to be there.

Q. What if the defendant's servant, rather than pushing the plaintiff away, had simply refused to take a rope that the plaintiff threw his way?

A. That case would have been distinguishable from *Ploof* because it would have required affirmative efforts by the defendant to make the dock available to the Ploofs—whereas in the actual case the defendant's servant expended resources to drive the Ploofs away. The necessity privilege seems to require that the plaintiff allow the defendant to trespass and take no steps to impede him. It may even require the plaintiff to absorb some costs (temporarily, as in *Vincent*). But it does not create a duty to rescue or otherwise require the defendant to actively expend resources to help the plaintiff. The reasons presumably are the same ones that are invoked against a general duty to rescue.

The harder intermediate case is the text question where Putnam stations a vicious dog so as to prevent people from trespassing in a time of need. The next case, *Rossi*, addresses that possibility.

Q. What is the superficial similarity between *Rossi v. DelDuca* and *Woodbridge v. Marks* (the watchdog case from the section of the chapter on defense of property)? What is the distinction between them?
A. In both cases the plaintiff was doing nothing very wrong and was bitten by the defendant's dog, which was not capable of exercising much discretion. But in *Rossi* the plaintiff had a right to be on the defendant's property. The dog in *Rossi* thus is analogous to the servant in *Ploof* who pushed the plaintiff's boat away. The plaintiff in *Woodbridge* was not threatening any harm, but evidently he had no privilege to be on the defendant's property, so he had to take his lumps as a trespasser.

Q. How was the dog in *Rossi* supposed to know whether the plaintiff was a casual trespasser or someone trying to avoid peril?
A. Obviously the dog wasn't charged with any knowledge; the dog wasn't being sued. The dog's inability to exercise discretion apparently is regarded as the problem of its owner rather than the problem of the trespasser. It's as if the defendant in *Ploof* built a robot to push away all unauthorized boats. The servant wasn't allowed to do this, and the defendant can't use automated means (robots or dogs) to accomplish what he couldn't accomplish in person. If you do use a robot or dog, you are taking a chance that someone will be pushed away who has a right to be there, resulting in liability for you. In this respect it's a little like using an unattended spring gun, despite the outcome in *Woodbridge* suggesting that for other purposes dogs and spring guns are distinguishable.

Q. Suppose the *Rossi* defendant had kept his Great Danes on chains, and the sight of them had kept the plaintiffs from entering his property. What result?
A. The plaintiff in *Rossi* is suing to collect for a dog bite; it's not quite a *Ploof*-style suit for damage caused by the plaintiff's refusal to permit a privileged trespass. But *Rossi* does imply that the plaintiff had such a privilege. The first question is whether she would have had a good *Ploof* claim if this case were more like *Ploof* itself—i.e., if the defendant pushed her off of his property and into the jaws of the Weimaraner. That seems like a clear case of liability indistinguishable from *Ploof*. Same result if she had been deterred from entering the defendant's property because of a snarling Great Dane waiting at the border, and as a result had been bitten by the Weimaraner? Probably, but it's harder because it is not clear what other measures the defendant was supposed to take to protect his property. It's one thing to tell the defendant not to interfere with the plaintiff's attempt to enter the property; it's another to hold him blameworthy for having a guard dog that can do a lot of good (cf. *Woodbridge*). That is why the defendant in *Ploof* generally arouses more indignation than the defendant in *Rossi*. But it might seem formalistic for the defendant in *Rossi* to lose on the actual facts of that case but not in this hypothetical, since his actions and the basic result (the plaintiff gets bit by a dog) are about the same.

Q. What if the *Rossi* defendant had a barbed wire fence along his property rather than a dog? If the plaintiff couldn't make it over the fence, and was injured by the barbed wire or bitten by the Weimaraner as a result, would it be a case of liability?
A. This case is tricky to distinguish from the prior hypothetical as a formal matter, but it seems like a sure loser for functional reasons: it would be hard to effectively tell the defendant he can't fence his property (or more precisely that he will be held liable if he does and someone needs to get through in an emergency). There are lots of efficient and otherwise desirable reasons for erecting fences. (What if he built the fence to keep the Great Danes from biting people?) Liability for a fence thus would impose considerable costs on the defendant, and perhaps considerable social costs—assuming the defendant responds by not having a fence and suffering thefts, etc. If the defendant responds by doing nothing—by keeping the fence in place and just paying the bills—then liability seems to serve little purpose as a matter

of policy. The necessity doctrine does not seem intended to impose such costs. Here again we see part of the logic of the cases on the self-defense privilege: if the least costly means of securing property is used, the law is reluctant to fault the owner.

Perhaps we have liability in *Rossi* because in *Rossi* we are not in the pure common law world on which the preceding discussion was based. Instead there has been a legislative decision to impose liability for dog bites. The court construes the exception for trespassers as itself including the common law exception for privileged trespasses.

Vincent v. Lake Erie Transportation Co. (L for damages for defendant who damages the plaintiff's dock by lashing a boat to it during a storm)

Q. What tort was the owner of the *Reynolds* committing that required his assertion of a necessity defense?
A. This becomes surprisingly puzzling. It seems like a trespass, but the plaintiff did not forbid the defendant to keep his boat where it was. The plaintiff could argue that the defendant still was a trespasser, but that he (the plaintiff) simply declined to eject him because of the harm that would result. Another possibility is conversion: the defendant appropriated the plaintiff's dock and wrecked it.

Q. What's left of *Ploof* after *Vincent*?
A. A privilege to be on the defendant's property. The boat owner has a *right* to be there. The point of *Vincent*, of course, is just that the privileged trespasser has to pay for any damage done. It's a forced transaction.

Q. What should be the measure of damages under *Vincent*?
A. There's a little exercise that can be conducted here in thinking through the incentives created by different damages rules. What should be the measure of damages: the benefit to the boat owner (i.e., restitution, which may be enormous if the boat was expensive), or the cost to the dock owner (which may be small)? The answer has to be the cost to the dock owner. If the answer is the restitution measure, you are making the boat owner pay over the entire value of the boat, and thus making him indifferent between asserting the privilege and saving the boat in the first place or just letting it be lost. But the point of the privilege is to get the boat saved and keep everyone happy. That's done by compensating the dock owner for his losses. The point can be seen by imagining the figures reversed, so that the boat is cheap and the damage to the dock is great. In that case we don't want the boat owner to exercise the privilege; we want the boat to be destroyed. That incentive is preserved best by making the boat owner pay for the damages to the dock. We want the boat owner to act as he would if he owned both the boat and the dock, and he'll do that if he has to pay the dock owner's costs regardless of what happens.

Q. What if the owner of the dock had cut loose the *Reynolds* to save *his* property?
A. This is fun to think about; conundrums arise as we try to imagine the dock's owner cutting the ropes while the boat's owner keeps trying to retie them. Whose privilege trumps whose? It helps cut through the conundrums to keep the goal in view, whether it's viewed a defense of property case like *Kershaw* (from the previous section) or a necessity case like *Vincent*: we want the solution that keeps the overall cost of the disaster to a minimum, or (equivalently) that a single owner of all the resources would reach. Turning to doctrine, the dock owner's claimed privilege probably is best viewed as defense of property, something like *Kershaw v. McKown* in the previous section of the casebook: in either case the plaintiff's property is threatening the property of the defendant (his goat there, his dock here), and the defendant destroys the plaintiff's property to prevent this. The rule of *Kershaw* is that the defendant doesn't owe the plaintiff anything unless the boat turns out to have been worth "greatly more" than the dock. This gives the dock's owner the same general incentives that *Vincent* gives to the owner of the boat. The dock's owner will jettison the boat if it's worth less than the dock, but leave the boat there (and collect from the

boat's owner—unless *he* decides to cut it loose) if the boat worth is more than the dock—with the understanding that the dock's owner gets the benefit of the doubt on close calls (the *"greatly* more" proviso).

So let's summarize by running through a couple of different states of affairs.

a. *The damage to the dock will be more expensive than the damage to the boat if the boat is cut loose.* In this case the dock's owner will want to cut loose the boat (and will pay nothing for doing so) and the boat's owner will want to do the same (because otherwise he pays for the damage to the dock, which is more than he would pay for the wreck of his boat).

b. *The damage to the dock will be less expensive than the damage to the boat if the boat is cut loose.* In this case the dock's owner will want to leave the boat where it is, since this way he will be compensated for the harm to his property (and otherwise he has to pay the boat's owner for the damage to *his* property). The boat's owner will want to keep the boat there, too, and pay compensation; this will be cheaper for him than seeing his boat wrecked.

In other words, if the boat stays, its owner pays for any damage it does (*Vincent*). If the boat goes at the plaintiff's own behest, each side bears its own losses. If the defendant forces the boat away, he pays if the decision is an economic mistake (*Kershaw*).

Geraldon v. Texas & Pac. Ry. Co. (family forced out of train station and into the rain; L for the railroad)
Borough of Southwark v. Williams (homeless people squat in public housing; L for the squatters for trespassing)

Q. What would be the application of *Vincent* to the *Geraldon* case?
A. It would require the plaintiffs to pay for any damage they did to the train station, of course; but presumably it also would require the plaintiffs to compensate the railroad for whatever costs it incurred in allowing the plaintiffs to stay overnight: costs of keeping the building open, keeping a watchman around, and so forth. In effect the railroad can charge rent.

Q. What is the superficial similarity between *Borough of Southwark* and *Geraldon* (L for ejecting plaintiffs from railroad station)? What is the distinction between them?
A. In both cases someone in dire straits wanted to occupy a private dwelling as a shelter. The main distinction between the cases seems to involve policy fears: the consequences of finding liability in the two situations are likely to be quite different. If the necessity privilege is limited to cases of acute and unexpected distress it seems unlikely to open a nasty can of worms. If the privilege is read to encompass cases of chronic and predictable distress, the parade of horribles feared by the *Southwark* judges seems more possible. "Acute" and "chronic" point to questions of timing, and suggest an analogy to *Laidlaw v. Sage* and the hypo in which Sage harvests one of Laidlaw's kidneys. Acute distress implies high transaction costs: not much time to negotiate. (But are we to imagine that with more time and no bilateral monopoly, the plaintiff and defendant in *Geraldon* would have reached a deal?)

Students sometimes wonder whether *Geraldon* really means that a person can force a business (or residence?) to allow them to stay inside through the night if they are sick and the weather is bad. It is helpful to work through the factual details of *Geraldon* that courts probably would focus on to prevent that case from leading to too great an erosion of property rights. Indeed, the "next case" scenario that one might fear after *Geraldon* is more or less presented by *Southwark*, where the court draws a line. One may be excused for doubting that *Geraldon* comes out the same way today—but just why do those doubts arise?

Q. Hypothetical: in *Greyvensteyn v. Hattingh*, [1911] A.C. 355 (P.C.), a swarm of locusts invaded the plaintiff's farm in the Cape of Good Hope. The locusts were "voetgangers": young insects that had not yet acquired the use of their wings and that trekked across the country on foot, eating grass and crops on their way. The locusts entered the plaintiff's farm from the north. The defendants, who also were farmers, had their lands to the south of the plaintiff's, separated from his only by a narrow strip of veldt. As the locusts finished working their way south across the plaintiff's farm, the defendants took up positions on the veldt and shooed the locusts in various directions away from where their own farms lay. The result of the defendants' acts was to increase the damage to the plaintiff's lands and crops, and the plaintiff sued to recover for these damages. What result?

A. The trial judge found that the effect of the defendants' acts might have been to drive some of the locusts back onto the plaintiff's land, but he entered judgment for the defendants on the ground that "there was no willful or malicious driving and the defendants were entitled to do what they did." On appeal to the Privy Council, plaintiff's counsel argued that the defendants "drove the locusts away in such manner and direction as certainly to damage the appellant's land. They did so in order to avoid risk of injury to themselves which could only be regarded as contingent and perhaps probable, while the resulting damage to the [plaintiff] was certain and very serious." The Privy Council held that that the plaintiff's appeal should be dismissed and the judgment below affirmed:

> [The appellant's] case is that locusts are like flood water, and that their natural course must not be diverted, even in self-defense, if injury is thereby caused to a neighboring proprietor. [...] In *Menzies v. Breadalbane*, the defendant was erecting an embankment which would have the effect of throwing the ordinary flood stream of the river Tay off his lands and entirely on the lands of his neighbour. The House of Lords held, on the facts of that case, that the embankment was an obstruction and diversion of the natural and ancient course of the stream in times of flood and that the natural course of a river could not legally be altered by one proprietor so as to create a new waterway to the prejudice of other proprietors. [...] [B]ut the principles of law laid down for preserving or regulating the settled course of a river, on which may depend so many of the rights and benefits of adjacent owners, are not necessarily appropriate to the course of an insect pest, which it is the interest of every one concerned to repel or destroy. The supposed analogy between the two things is wholly fallacious. The pest has no settled course, and whatever its course may be, no one is bound to respect it. Indeed, the progress of a fire would be a much nearer analogy to the moving horde of locusts than the course of a river.

> In *Whalley's Case*, Lindley L.J. points out that, if an extraordinary flood is seen to be coming, the owner may protect his land from it, and so turn it away without being responsible for the consequences. Visitations of locusts, though no doubt unpleasantly frequent, are in the nature of extraordinary and incalculable events, rather than a normal incident like the rise of a river in the rainy season. [...] Even if the invasion be regarded as a normal incident of agricultural industry in South Africa, the respondents would be entitled, as an agricultural operation, to drive the locusts away just as they are entitled to scare crows, without regard to the direction they may take in leaving.

SECTION C. PUBLIC NECESSITY

Mouse's Case (D passenger throws P's property overboard to prevent barge from sinking; NL)
Surocco v. Geary (D mayor orders P's house torn down to stop fire in San Francisco; NL)
Struve v. Droge (landlord damages tenant's property because he mistakenly thinks his apartment is on fire; L)

Q. What is the distinction between *Mouse's Case* and *Vincent v. Lake Erie Transportation Co.*?

A. In both cases one person's property was sacrificed for the benefit of others, but only in *Vincent* was the beneficiary required to make compensation for the sacrifice. The distinction is not that life was at stake in *Mouse's Case* but only property was on the line in *Vincent*; for while this seems to be true, the principle in *Vincent* appears to extend to cases like *Ploof v. Putnam* where life is indeed at stake (we are told as much in *Vincent*, though it's a dictum). The real distinction is that in *Vincent* only the defendant benefited from the sacrifice of the plaintiff's property. In *Mouse's Case* everyone on the ship benefited. But why does this matter? Why shouldn't the owner of the casket receive compensation from all those who benefited?

From a policy standpoint the answer might be understood in terms of the incentives it creates in a situation like the sinking barge. We want a passenger to feel free to fling whatever property overboard he thinks will save the lives of everyone; the costs of throwing too little overboard (i.e., the loss of the barge and all hands) will tend to be a lot higher than the costs of throwing too much. But the passenger might hesitate if he has to worry about compensating the property's owner. Of course he won't hesitate too long if he thinks he's going to die otherwise, but there may be situations where it's not so clear cut and the passenger dithers when he should be hurling things overboard. Those worries about compensation may seem needless if the cost of compensation will be spread among all the passengers. But notice that since Mouse was suing the individual passenger who threw his property overboard, it would fall to that passenger to turn around and try to collect from all of the other passengers. What if he can't find them? What if they are insolvent? What if they protest that he made a bad choice in picking Mouse's property to jettison? All these worries might cause a passenger to hesitate before acting next time.

There may be a certain unrealism in this analysis of the passenger's incentives, since it might seem implausible to imagine a passenger on a barge knowing all this, much less thinking it over at the moment of action. But the principle established here also has possible application in situations where the actors involved are more likely to understand the rules and have a little time for reflection. Some of those cases may involve sea captains; others may be like *Surocco v. Geary* and the fire in London in 1666, discussion of which follows next. These cases may illustrate a margin where the policy analysis takes its bite. And even if the analysis of incentives never does have bite, it can be turned into a moral point: someone who throws property overboard to save others, and not just himself, should not have to bear all the resulting costs; and he shouldn't even be put at *risk* of having to bear them by being saddled with a judgment that he may or may not be able to pass on to the other passengers as a practical matter.

Q. Maybe the plaintiffs in these cases lose for a different reason: there is no causation. If Mouse's property hadn't been jettisoned, the whole barge would have gone down and the property would have been lost anyway—as well, perhaps, as Mouse's life. Might this be the best way to understand the doctrine?

A. No. First of all, this interpretation wouldn't explain *Surocco v. Geary*. In that case the plaintiffs claimed that even if their house had been doomed, they would have been able to evacuate more of their personal effects if the house hadn't been torn down at the mayor's insistence before the fire arrived. So there was causation in that case in a straightforward sense, but still no liability. Even in *Mouse's Case*, though, making the rule turn on this sort of finding about causation might create some of the same sorts of policy problems described a moment ago. What if the plaintiff can show that there was other less valuable property that could have been thrown overboard instead of his casket, and with equal good effect? What if it turns out that the casket might have survived a sinking, since Mouse was busy trying to attach a buoy to it—but that the defendant grabbed the casket and threw it overboard before the work was done to be on the safe side? We don't want passengers like the defendant in *Mouse's Case* to have to worry about these considerations, and (equivalently) we don't want them to suffer later if it turns out that they were wrong about them.

Q. Is the result in *Mouse's Case* consistent with what Mouse reasonably should have expected when he got onto the barge?

A. You can pursue this by asking students what legal rule they would want to see in place if they were passengers on a similar barge. What would they expect (or want) the rule to be if they were the ones about to jettison someone else's luggage to save the boat? What would they expect or want if it was their own luggage about to be jettisoned by someone else for the same reason?

Q. Why is there a separate privilege of public (rather than private) necessity? What is the difference between them, and what is the rationale?

A. Again, the difference is that a defendant who successfully invokes the public necessity privilege does not have to pay anything to the plaintiff, unlike in the private necessity cases epitomized by *Vincent*. As we saw in *Mouse's Case*, the rationale is clearest in cases where the defendant invoking the privilege is a private citizen who destroys someone else's property to prevent great and general harm to the community. Since the benefits of the destruction are reaped by others (they are "external"), the defendant must be allowed to externalize the costs of it as well; otherwise he may not have an adequate incentive to destroy the property even if the overall benefits of doing so outweigh the costs. Contrast *Vincent*, where the destroyer internalizes all the benefits of appropriating the defendant's property. In that case it works to make the owner of the boat pay the owner of the dock, as this induces him to think about whether the destruction he is about to cause is worth it (i.e., whether the benefits it will bring his way will be enough to offset his obligation to reimburse the dock's owner).

You can comment here on the ancient (and still living) admiralty doctrine known as the "general average." It provides that if a portion of a ship's cargo is jettisoned to avert a common danger (common, that is, to everyone and everything on board), the owner of the lost cargo is entitled to compensation; the loss is divided among the owners of the ship and cargo in proportion to the size of their stake in the venture. (The doctrine also can apply more broadly to other expenses incurred to save the ship and its cargo.) Interestingly, however, no compensation is due from those whose lives were saved. (What incentives do these rules create in a moment of peril?) If *Mouse's Case* arose now, the doctrine of general average thus probably would allow Mouse to recover, though not from the defendant he sued in that case. Whether the doctrine was available to the plaintiff on these facts in 1609, and whether any attempt was made to use it, we do not know.

Q. But then how do we explain *Struve v. Droge*? Doesn't this case create exactly the kind of uncertainty and risk for the defendant that we just said the public necessity doctrine is meant to avoid?

A. To clarify, the rule of *Struve v. Droge* is that defendants invoking the public necessity privilege have to be correct; they are strictly liable for any mistakes, meaning that they have to compensate the owner of the destroyed property if it turns out that they were wrong in believing there was sufficient public reason to sacrifice it. This might seem at odds with the discussion just offered, the premise of which was that in times of crisis a defendant needs to be able to act for the common good without hesitating to worry about whether he himself can pay for the damage. But the cases can be reconciled by distinguishing between two kinds of decisions and the worries that accompany them. The first determination involves whether there *is* a crisis that calls for the destruction of property. At this point we do want defendants to think, hesitate, and worry, precisely because the cost of such a determination is so high: innocent plaintiffs will see their property destroyed without compensation. Once we get over that threshold and a public emergency is found to exist, however, we want the defendant to put less energy into worrying and more into acting. We don't want him pausing to reflect on whether he will be able to collect reimbursement from those he is helping, or on whether the property he is destroying is sure to be lost in the disaster anyway if he *doesn't* destroy it.

It might seem that this division could be preserved by letting the defendant off so long as there was reasonable grounds for believing that there was an emergency and that the destruction of the property was needed to prevent catastrophe; why impose strict liability for such mistakes? Again, perhaps the reason is that the stakes are so high. Allowing one citizen to destroy the property of another without paying for it is strong medicine. We don't want it to happen unless we're very sure there is a crisis that requires it. One way to achieve that certainty would be to raise the standard of proof, so that the privilege only applies if the apparent need for the destruction is established on some stronger showing than mere reasonableness shown by a preponderance of the evidence. But another way to help achieve the certainty is to simply throw the entire risk of error onto the defendant. Knowing that reasonableness is not enough, the defendant will make double sure that the occasion really does call for the destruction of the plaintiff's property.

Once more the point can be restated in the language of fairness if the policy analysis seems strained. Maybe a plaintiff should be required to absorb his own involuntary losses if they were necessary to avoid a public calamity. But this is such a brutal doctrine that we can't apply it in good conscience where the sacrifice wasn't really necessary. As between the plaintiff (the utterly innocent property owner) and the defendant (the almost-but-not-quite innocent destroyer of the plaintiff's property, who at least was mistaken, however reasonably), it's fairer that the defendant suffer the loss.

Q. But then how is *Struve v. Droge* distinguishable from *Crabtree v. Dawson*, the NL case from the section on self-defense where the defendant hit the plaintiff in the face with a musket because he thought the plaintiff was someone else?

A. Since the defendant's belief in *Struve* was reasonable, he was not held liable. The moral point offered a moment ago seems to create a problem here: again the plaintiff is entirely innocent but the defendant is not; the defendant made a mistake, however reasonably. Yet we don't tax the defendant in *Crabtree* with the costs of his error. Maybe the difference again goes back to the fact that once the public necessity privilege is triggered, the consequences can be very severe. This may not be evident on the facts of *Struve* because there we were just dealing with a possible fire in one apartment. But rulings made about public necessity have broader potential application. Saying that a reasonable mistake can trigger the doctrine could cause lots of houses to be brought down. Perhaps reasonable mistakes about self-defense have less potential to expand.

Another consideration: in cases of self-defense or private necessity the party invoking the privilege usually (though not necessarily) will be doing so to protect himself or his family. In public necessity cases the person invoking the privilege is trying to save others from harm to which he himself may not be exposed. Which of these two types of invokers is more in need of a rule to discipline their judgment? The answer is not obvious; nor is it clear which invoker should have a better claim on our sympathies.

The way this last point was stated may cause a natural question to occur to some students: *Crabtree* was a case of self-defense, and *Struve* was a case of public necessity; so which rule about mistakes applies in cases of *private* necessity? Section 197 of the Second Restatement, "Private Necessity," says that "One is privileged to enter or remain on land in the possession of another if it is or *reasonably appears* to be necessary to prevent serious harm…" (Emphasis added.) On the other hand, the Restatement's provision on public necessity—sec. 262—likewise refers to reasonable beliefs, which is inconsistent with *Struve v. Droge*. Perhaps published opinions on the doctrines do not arise often enough to allow the issue to be considered settled. The logic of the previous paragraph would suggest that a reasonableness defense generally should apply in cases where private interests are at issue, because then the damage likely to be done as a result is more likely to be self-limiting. But again the point is far from obvious, since since cases of public necessity will tend to be cases where the cost of the apparent disaster will be largest: if we're going to forgive reasonable mistakes anyplace, shouldn't it be in *those* cases?

Finally, you may wish to ask why *Struve v. Droge* is considered a case of public necessity at all, since in that case, as in *Vincent v. Lake Erie Transp. Co.*, the defendant was trying to save his own property. The answer presumably is that where fire is concerned, there always is a danger that it could spread as well to the property of others. There didn't seem to be any comparable danger of spreading on the facts of *Vincent*.

Q. What result in Restatement sec. 262, Illustration 2, if the infection of B's bull was caused by A's earlier act of negligence?

A.   Liability for A. There is an English case discussing facts a bit like this. In *Esso Petroleum Co. v. Southport Corp.*, 3 All E.R. 864, A.C. 218 (H.L. 1956), one of Esso's oil tankers was attempting to traverse a narrow channel near Liverpool when it ran against an wall used to support the channel's embankment. The tanker became stuck in a perilous position; the captain concluded that it was in danger of breaking up and that the lives of his crew were at risk. He ordered that the cargo of oil be jettisoned into the water to lighten the tanker and enable it to float freely. The crew discharged 400 tons of oil and the ship was saved. The oil washed ashore on Southport's property, causing extensive damage. The case produced interesting opinions finding no liability for Esso. On the trespass count, Devlin, J. found (and the House of Lords agreed) that the defendants had a good necessity defense. Said Devlin, in the course of ordering no compensation: "The safety of human lives belongs to a different scale of values from the safety of property. The two are beyond comparison and the necessity for saving life has at all times been considered a proper ground for inflicting such damage as may be necessary upon another's property." But it also was made clear that if Esso's agents had been negligent in navigating the tanker into the situation where the discharge became necessary, Esso would have had to compensate after all. In the *Esso* case no negligence was found.

Q.   Hypothetical: suppose the defendant ingests some fruit punch at a party. Unbeknownst to him, the punch is laced with a hallucinogenic drug or some other mind-altering agent. Once the drug takes effect, the defendant comes to believe that he is a CIA agent and that he needs to steal a car to go stop a threat against the President's life. None of this turns out to be true. Is his theft of the car privileged?
A.   The only excuse for offering such a preposterous hypothetical is that these facts actually arose in a California case, *People v. Scott*, 194 Cal.Rptr. 633 (Cal. App. 1983). Since that was a criminal case it does not settle the question on the civil side, but the court did cite the Restatement provision on public necessity in the course of finding no criminal liability:

> It is clear that in attempting to commandeer the vehicles defendant acted under a mistake of fact: he thought he was a secret government agent acting to protect his own life or possibly that of the President. When a person commits an act based on a mistake of fact, his guilt or innocence is determined as if the facts were as he perceived them. If in fact defendant were a government agent and either his life or the life of the President were in danger and defendant attempted to commandeer the vehicles for the purpose of saving his own life or that of the President, his actions would have been legally justified under the doctrine of necessity. Cf. *People v. Patrick* (1981) 126 Cal.App.3d 952, 960, 179 Cal.Rptr. 276; Rest.2d Torts, §§ 262....

The court assumed that the mistake of fact had to be reasonable—but found that it was, since the defendant was involuntarily intoxicated. The result on the civil side presumably would be different if *Struve v. Droge* were held to control the case. Should it?

SECTION D. DISCIPLINE

This whole section is more optional than most, but it raises interesting issues. You certainly shouldn't pass on *Forbes v. Parsons* without first reading it, and the materials on spousal abuse at the end are of great interest to many students.

Forbes v. Parsons (sea captain beats incompetent cook; NL)

Q.   What is the best that can be said for the result in *Forbes v. Parsons*?
A.   The point of the question is to force the students to think about the context of the decision and reasons why it might have seemed reasonable at the time even if it now seems brutal. At the time the

decision was made, travels over the ocean by ship were more perilous than they now are; there was no way to communicate to the shore. (The invention of the telegraph, and of Morse code, was only just occurring; the development of wireless communication would have to await the early twentieth century.) If order disintegrated, everyone on board could be placed in jeopardy. And meanwhile sea captains sometimes did not have many internal options for dealing with misbehavior. If the crew was not large and not skilled, locking up the cook or some other important member of the crew might not be a satisfactory response to his delicts; one needed him to *perform*. (Imagine a situation where there are five people on the space shuttle and the one who knows how to cook won't do it. What do you do with him? What do you do *to* him?) Finally, there may have been some sense of assumption of risk at work here: crewmen who signed on for these voyages understood that for these reasons, or perhaps for others, captains were given a freer hand to discipline the crew than would be found on land.

Lander v. Seaver (teacher whips student for showing him disrespect outside the classroom; "L" in that the student won the appeal, but NL on remand unless the punishment was clearly excessive; the trial court had incorrectly made the teacher's good faith an absolute defense)
Rinehart v. Board of Education (teacher paddles student who called him a "dickhead"; NL)
Hogenson v. Williams (teacher strikes student to "fire him up"; L)

It is hard to teach these cases in conventional fashion because corporal punishment in public schools is now widely regulated by statutes and regulations that vary considerably from one state and school district to the next—and that have been changing fairly rapidly. From 1974-1994, the number of states banning it outright went from two to twenty-seven (typically with explicit or implicit exceptions for cases where physical force is needed to prevent one student from hurting others—if those cases are considered matters of punishment at all). See Edwards, *Corporal Punishment and the Legal System*, 36 Santa Clara L. Rev. 983, n. 230 (1996); Bloom, *Spare the Rod, Spoil the Child? A Legal Framework for Recent Corporal Punishment Proposals*, 25 Golden Gate U. L. Rev. 369 (1995). In other states, such as Georgia, there are statutes leaving the question entirely to the local school districts (or to the governing bodies of private schools); in still others, such as North Carolina, there are statutes authorizing corporal punishment to maintain "order" unless the local school district says otherwise, or (as in Illinois) leaving the matter to the local districts but requiring them to make their rules within certain guidelines—e.g., that no paddling or slapping is allowed. The statutes are not interpreted to apply to college students, as they are considered adults for whom the educational institution does not act *in loco parentis*.

So on the question of discipline at school, as well as on the common law's historical treatment of spousal abuse, we have little enough to say about the best way to lead a conversation in the classroom; since there really aren't cases that lend themselves to doctrinal analysis, the discussion has to become one of policy, and instructors will vary in how they want to approach it. As just noted, the trend now is strongly against corporal punishment in the schools. One can ask why this should be. (Incidentally, the common law traditionally did not allow civil suits by children against their parents for damages caused by physical discipline. Such suits were prevented by combinations of parental tort immunities and the parent's privilege to inflict reasonable chastisement. There have been some cracks emerging in this wall as well. For discussion, see the Edwards article cited a moment ago—36 Santa Clara L. Rev. 983, 1007-10 (1996).)

Similarly, on the material regarding the rights of married women, one question to ask is *why* many ideas about their rights that seemed so plausible to many people (not to all of them, of course) a hundred or so years ago now seem so counterintuitive and offensive. What engines drove this change? There have been many economic changes during that time; household labor has become much less time-consuming, and birth-control technologies have put married women into stronger positions than before as well; for these and other reasons, married women entered the labor force in far greater numbers at the end of the twentieth century than they did at the beginning. What relationship might we expect between developments like these and the evolution of their legal rights to protection against domestic violence? (A larger question: what is the relationship between the development of various sorts of wealth on the one hand and the advancement of rights on the other?) Did the advent of women's suffrage play a role? Was the extension of the vote to women a cause of these changes, an effect of the same (other) forces that caused the changes in the common law—or both?

CHAPTER 3

THE NEGLIGENCE STANDARD

SECTION A. THE REASONABLE PERSON

These materials are pretty thick; it can take a couple of days to cover everything in the section on mental states, and then another day to cover physical impairments and age, especially if you are starting the course with this chapter. If you're in a hurry and want to abbreviate the coverage, we suggest using *Williams v. Hays* and *Vaughan v. Menlove*; then skip the next few cases and jump to *Fredericks v. Castora*; then assign the rest of the cases in the section, which gets lighter as it goes on.

1. Mental ability and mental states

Williams v. Hays (captain goes insane and grounds ship; L; but NL if the insanity was caused by his efforts to save ship from storm)
Vaughan v. Menlove (D, whose lawyer says he lacked the highest order of intelligence, creates fire hazard that results in loss of P's cottages; L)
Lynch v. Rosenthal (mentally retarded P hurt by D's corn picker; L)

Q. What is the (combined) holding of the opinions in *Williams v. Hays*? What rules emerge?
A. The holding of the first opinion is that lunacy is no defense to a claim of negligence. The more general lesson, which is repeated in the next case (*Vaughan v. Menlove*), is that the negligence standard is objective. It doesn't matter how good the defendant's intentions were, or how hard he tried to be careful; he is required to behave as a reasonable person would—and not like a reasonable person with the defendant's mental condition.

The holding of the second opinion is harder to state. Narrowly it is that Hays cannot be held negligent if his behavior was the result of insanity brought on by his efforts to save the ship. A partial statement of the broader principle might be that a defendant's insanity will excuse his negligence if a reasonable person would have gone insane under the same circumstances. But perhaps that can't quite be right; it might seem to imply that there would be no liability for an overworked doctor who finally lost his mind and committed malpractice. No doubt there would be liability in most such cases, though perhaps not all of them (see below). Maybe the point can be restated: there is no liability for acts by the insane if a the insanity resulted from reasonable behavior—which the overworked captain might have engaged in, but not the overworked doctor. The court seems to have been sure of the fair result on the facts of this case, but it did not feel ready to set out its position as a rule, preferring to wait for other cases involving such claims of justifiable insanity—if any—and to compare them to *Williams v. Hays* on their facts. As it turns out, we are aware of no other cases where this second aspect of *Williams v. Hays* has been put to use.

If you are starting the course with this case, you may wish to back up and consider the problem it presents from the ground up. A captain tries to fight off a storm, eventually loses his mind (let us assume—it's a question of fact), refuses offers of help, and wrecks the ship. How should the obligation to pay for this mess be allocated? Why liability for anyone? If there is to be potential liability, what are some possible rules that might be used to govern it? What goals should guide the creation of those rules? Etc.

Q. Why does the court say that it may be "unjust" (or "cruel" in the words of the trial court) to hold insane people liable for negligence? Why does it say they should be held liable anyway?

A. The rule might seem cruel because it requires some defendants to meet a standard that they cannot possibly reach. (Note the tension with the "impossibility" maxims at the end of the *Williams* court's second opinion.) The court says the rule is based on notions of policy: the desirability of giving the kin of lunatics incentives to supervise them carefully; the fear of false claims of insanity (a worry especially in case involving a claim of *temporary* insanity; does that feature of this case make it an inapt one for crafting general rules?); and the sense that as between two "innocent" people—the insane defendant and the plaintiff—it is more fair that the costs of an accident be paid by the person who caused it (but on that reasoning why not skip the inquiry into the defendant's fault altogether?). As a policy matter, too, holding defendants liable for failing to meet a standard they cannot reach might be understood as operating like strict liability to give such defendants a reason to avoid certain activities altogether—a point that has application to the insane person deciding whether to drive a car, though probably not to Hays.

Q. Suppose an overworked, underslept doctor (or lawyer) loses his grip on reality and commits malpractice. Liability under *Williams v. Hays*? How is *Williams* distinguishable? What facts would you need to add to the hypothetical to make it a case of no liability?

A. Assuming that the medical case arose at an ordinary hospital, it would be distinguishable from *Williams v. Hays* because doctors more easily can step aside and be replaced by others if they feel their faculties slipping away from them. But not necessarily; some hospitals are understaffed, and most ships—perhaps including the ship in *Williams*—have mates to whom exhausted captains might yield. There no doubt are additional policy considerations to explain liability in the medical hypo: allowing doctors or the hospitals that employ them to use insanity as an excuse creates bad incentives; hospitals can foresee the likelihood of exhaustion and malpractice, and we don't want them thinking that they face less liability exposure if understaffed.

The specific fact pattern of *Williams v. Hays*, by contrast, depends on a confluence of factors that are hard to predict and unlikely to be deliberately manipulated by anyone: terrible weather that typically will threaten the life of the potential defendant as well as the ship's cargo. If you have covered intentional torts already, there is a possible analogy from this reasoning to cases like *Geraldon* in the section of the casebook on the necessity privilege: an exception to a general rule is unlikely to unravel a rule or create temptations for abuse if it is confined to circumstances involving unpredictable circumstances that threaten the party asserting the privilege—the family in *Geraldon*, and the captain in *Williams*.

Still, it's a little curious that the court in *Williams* does not suggest an inquiry into whether the captain was indeed reasonable in the first place in driving himself over the edge. Asks the court: "What careful and prudent man could do more than to care for his vessel until overcome by physical and mental exhaustion? To do more was impossible." But might it have been more prudent to do *less*? Do we want future captains in Hays's shoes to handle these situations the same way Hays did? If the answer is "no," then perhaps this court was torn between trying to make good policy and trying to give some effect to feelings of sympathy for a defendant who pushed himself in ways that, reasonable or not, seemed heroic. Or maybe the court was reluctant to put pressure on captains to relieve themselves of command. The costs of a captain stepping aside too quickly may be higher than the costs of a doctor doing so—at least in a maritime environment where firm discipline from the captain on down is considered highly valuable in preventing the whole enterprise from ending in a wreck.

Q. What is the point of holding someone who is stupid to the standard of a person with a reasonable degree of intelligence? To what extent do the rationales offered for liability in *Williams v. Hays* continue to apply here?

A. Foolish people do not have keepers for whom the law can provide incentives, but some of the other reasoning behind *Williams* still makes sense in this context. From a corrective justice standpoint it may be hard to see why the cost of the accident should be borne by the entirely innocent plaintiff rather than by the non-innocent-but-stupid defendant. Again, though, this point can be used to introduce questions about why we insist on a showing of fault at all. The basic argument—as between the blameless plaintiff and the blameless defendant who caused the harm, why shouldn't the latter pay?—is available against anyone who causes harm. A defendant who who has an unforeseeable heart attack while behind the wheel and runs over the plaintiff is not held liable (see, e.g., *Cohen v. Petty*, 65 F.2d 820 (D.C.Cir. 1933)); how is he different from the defendant in *Vaughan*? Why punish someone who (by hypothesis) did his best?

Then one can come at the issue from a policy standpoint. Stupidity is even more subject than temporary insanity to the danger of false claims by defendants; it's harder—both more expensive and more unreliable—to establish the extent of a defendant's intelligence than it is to determine his sanity. And while our sympathies are with the insane (the court in *Williams v. Hays* makes reference, via Cooley, to "the inexpressible calamity of mental obscurity"), we are less patient with people who just aren't very thoughtful. Perhaps there is a sense that the latter have the power to cure themselves if they are willing to work at it. *Vaughan* gives them incentives to work at it. (Yet are stupid people unlikely—almost by definition—to be aware of such rules and the incentives created by them?)

Q. What is the superficial similarity between *Lynch v. Rosenthal* and *Vaughan v. Menlove*? Between *Lynch v. Rosenthal* and *Williams v. Hays*? What is the distinction between them?

A. The first thing you have to clarify is that the plaintiff in *Lynch* did seem to get a break on account of his mental condition. Lynch's own expert said that Lynch lacked the ability to comprehend the danger presented by moving machinery, and Lynch's theory was that the defendant should have provided him with a warning tailored to his lack of comprehension. An ordinary ("reasonable") person almost certainly would have appreciated the danger and so would have needed no direct warning; in any event, Lynch built his case around his own particular mental limitations, not around his reasonableness by ordinary standards. The court was fine with this, and Lynch won the case, having been found free from contributory negligence. Thus *Lynch,* like the other cases, involved a party who may well have failed to act in the way a reasonable person would have acted, because he was unable to do so; but in *Lynch* the court made allowances for this, or at least seemed to allow the jury to make an allowance for it.

As for the distinctions, *Vaughan* involved a mere claim of stupidity. *Williams* involved a claim of temporary insanity. Neither claim was recognized by the courts; the parties asserting the claims were held to ordinary standards of reasonableness (subject, of course, to the qualification at the end of *Williams*). *Lynch,* however, involved a claimed mental impairment: retardation, rather than insanity or stupidity. Most often the courts treat such impairments just as they treat insanity, and for all the same reasons given in *Williams*. But here the mental impairment is asserted by a *plaintiff* to excuse what otherwise might be contributory negligence on his part. (If this is the students' first brush with contributory or comparative negligence, then it's a good time to introduce those doctrines.) Courts occasionally, as here, will cut a party some slack as a plaintiff that would not be given to the same party as a defendant. Why? Perhaps the reason relates to the policy logic described a moment ago. The insane person can avoid liability for many sorts of harms by avoiding (or by being restrained by their kin from engaging in) activities that put others at risk. But it is another matter to keep people with mental disabilities away from situations where others might injure them. It is the difference between a rule that essentially tells lunatics not to drive (because they may hit people, and will then be held to an ordinary standard of care as defendants) and a rule telling them not to be pedestrians (because they might be hit by cars, and will then be held to an ordinary standard of care as plaintiffs). The latter seems harsher, which is why many courts make allowances for the mental states of plaintiffs that they would not make for defendants. Notice the difference here from a corrective justice standpoint as well: the question is not which of two innocent parties should bear the loss; it might be framed as which of two parties, each of whom might be considered culpable, should bear the loss.

To say that the defendant in *Lynch* should be considered culpable might be considered a bit circular; the very question is whether he was obliged to take account of the plaintiff's mental deficiencies.

Here it's worth teasing out the difference between two questions to which a victim's mental state could be relevant: was the defendant obliged to take precautions predicated on the assumption that the plaintiff might have these problems? And was the plaintiff contributorily negligent, or did he do enough so long as he used all of his (limited) faculties to try to protect himself? Both questions seem to be in play in *Lynch*. The case against the defendant (as opposed to the plaintiff's case in mitigation of his own acts) is supported by the fact that the defendant knew of the plaintiff's disability, had a close relationship with him, and was giving him instructions. The case of the mentally retarded pedestrian who is hit by a car and becomes a plaintiff—and the previous cases in the chapter—are not *quite* like this. Asking a defendant to take account of a plaintiff's limitations often seems unrealistic (how should the defendant know of them?), but *Lynch* is perhaps the easiest case one can imagine for making such a demand.

Q. If discussion goes down the path sketched in the previous paragraph, you can introduce as a hypothetical the battery case *McGuire v. Almy*, 8 N.E.2d 760 (Mass. 1937). It's a bit of a detour since it involves an intentional tort, but it shows that this rule about making no allowances for insanity carries over to the intentional side of tort law—and it creates a chance to explore the rationales behind *Lynch* a little further. (If you prefer to keep things simple you can restyle the facts on *McGuire* as a negligence suit against the plaintiff rather than a suit for battery.) The facts were these: The plaintiff, a registered nurse, was employed to take care of the defendant, who was insane. On the day in question, the plaintiff heard a crashing of furniture from the defendant's locked room and from past experience knew that the defendant was "ugly, violent and dangerous." The defendant told the plaintiff and a maid who was present that if they came into her room she would kill both of them. The plaintiff and a maid looked into the defendant's room and saw that she had broken some of the furniture. They decided it would be best to take it away before she did any harm to herself with it. They sent for the defendant's brother-in-law, who was living elsewhere in the house. When he arrived, the defendant was in the middle of her room holding a lowboy leg as if she were going to strike. The plaintiff stepped into the room and walked toward the defendant, while the other two remained behind. As the plaintiff tried to grab the lowboy leg, the defendant struck her in the head with it, causing injuries for which she sued. What result?
A. The Massachusetts court held the evidence of battery sufficient to support the verdict; it made no allowance for the defendant's mental condition, using reasoning similar to what we see in *Williams v. Hays*. (The result in *McGuire* surely would have been the same if the claim had been based on negligence; imagine that the plaintiff was flailing around with the lowboy leg, causing an unreasonable risk of harm to her keepers but with no intent to hit them.) This result might seem at odds with some of the ideas discussed in connection with *Lynch*, because in *McGuire* the plaintiff knew the defendant was insane and could have taken precautions accordingly. But of course there's a difference: the mentally impaired person was the aggressor, not (as in *Lynch*) the victim of the harm. So the "relational" point in *Lynch* may be part of the story there, but it's not the whole thing.

Q. Does Holmes's notion of a "distinct defect" shed light on the cases so far?
A. "Distinct" in Holmes's usage can be viewed as referring both to how discrete the problem is (i.e., how readily it can be measured, and how easily real claims can be separated from spurious claims ex post), or to how visible the defect is to others ex ante (before the accident occurs). Stupidity generally (as in *Vaughan*) is not a distinct defect, both because it is hard to measure and because it cannot be seen by others who might be in a position to compensate accordingly with extra precautions. Lunacy is somewhat similar, though as Holmes says it presents a harder problem. In any event, courts generally take neither defect into account. The court does take into account the mental problems of the *Lynch* plaintiff, and those problems *generally* were no more visible to others than the mental impairments in the other cases; but Lynch's problems both were easy enough to measure (the easiest of any of those seen in these first three cases—remember the expert testimony) and they were known to the *Lynch* defendant, and so in a sense were "distinct" after all as a practical matter.

Weirs v. Jones County (P drives over condemned bridge because he can't read "bridge unsafe" sign; NL; city need only anticipate "reasonable" people, not people who can't read English)

Friedman v. State (girl jumps from chair lift to avoid spending night with man in violation of her religion; no contributory negligence).

Q. What is the superficial similarity between *Weirs v. Jones County* and *Lynch v. Rosenthal?* What is the distinction between them?

A. The superficial similarity is that in each case a plaintiff who had difficulty appreciating warning signs of danger was injured. In *Lynch* the plaintiff won in the sense that the court said the defendant may have been obliged to take the plaintiff's difficulty into account to some extent. In *Weirs* the plaintiff lost; the court held that the defendant was not obliged to take the plaintiff's difficulty into account.

The difficulty in *Weirs* (English illiteracy) might be distinguishable from the difficulty in *Lynch* (retardation) because illiteracy can be corrected. But are we therefore to imagine that if the *Lynch* plaintiff had ridden his wagon over the bridge with the same result, he would have won (i.e., fared better than the *Weirs* plaintiff)? Probably not; but why? For one thing, in the actual *Lynch* case the plaintiff's defect was distinct in the sense noted earlier: the defendant enlisted the plaintiff's help while knowing of his problems. But in the hypothetical just offered the defendant county would be in no better position to know of the plaintiff's difficulties than it was in *Weirs*. *Weirs* would have been more closely analogous to *Lynch* if the county had hired the plaintiff to perform deliveries in this area while knowing of his illiteracy (telling him it wouldn't matter, etc.). Then in both cases the defendant would have been aware of the plaintiff's limitations, perhaps resulting in a different outcome in *Weirs*.

A related distinction involves policy considerations. Liability in *Lynch* is not likely to create great costs; it might make it a little harder for people like Lynch to get jobs, or require people like the *Lynch* defendants to spend more resources on warnings; but these costs do not seem likely to be all that large. The court's discussion in *Weirs* suggests that it might have been worried about creating a rule that generally means signs in English aren't enough to protect the government from liability. Such a rule might more require expensive compliance measures (signs in many languages, as the court notes, or costly measures other than signs). Common law courts often are reluctant to require other branches of government to make expensive changes in their way of doing things. Should they be? (We'll revisit this point in the part of the book covering the public duty doctrine.)

You can make a related hypothetical out of Restatement (Second) of Torts, §289, Illustration 5: "A, driving an automobile, approaches a strange town in which the signals in use are different from those to which he is accustomed. It is negligent to go on without ascertaining the meaning of these strange signals."

Q. What is the superficial similarity between *Weirs v. Jones County* and *Friedman v. State?* What is the distinction between them?

A. The superficial similarity is that in both cases the plaintiff differed from an average person in a particular way: in *Weirs* because he spoke (let us imagine) French, and in *Friedman* because she held certain unusual religious beliefs. In *Weirs* no allowance was made for the plaintiff's inability to read English. In *Friedman* an allowance was made for the plaintiff's nonstandard moral opinions. *Weirs* actually might seem the more sympathetic case, at least as we look at the defendant's conduct. Which was more foreseeable: that someone might use the bridge in *Weirs* who could not read the sign, or that someone might get stuck on the chair lift in *Friedman* who felt obliged for religious reasons to jump off of it? Surely the latter was less foreseeable, and so should produce a lesser sense of culpability for the defendant. But here it is worth spending some time straightening out the students' likely puzzlement about whether the plaintiffs' unusual qualities are being made relevant to whether the defendant was negligent or to whether the plaintiff was contributorily negligent. In *Weirs* the plaintiff's illiteracy is relevant to both issues: whether the county did enough to protect Weirs depends on whether its literacy assumptions were reasonable; and whether Weirs did enough to protect himself depends on whether his failure to learn to read English (or his decision to proceed in the face of a sign he could not understand) was reasonable. In *Friedman*, however, it seems clear that the state was negligent irrespective of the plaintiff's religious beliefs. Her beliefs only become relevant in assessing whether she (then) negligently contributed to her own injuries. So in this sense it is a red herring to focus on whether the plaintiff's idiosyncracies were more foreseeable in the one case than in the other—though if the *Friedman* situation were a common enough one, presumably the case against the defendant would become simpler and stronger.

In any event, why treat language and religion differently? Maybe because asking people to learn to read English in this country—or at least in Iowa in 1892—seems pretty clearly to have more benefits than costs. Requiring people to conform their moral beliefs to some norm, directly or indirectly (by denying them compensation when they are hurt by their adherence to them), involves a more complex calculus; for historical, constitutional, and other reasons we aren't comfortable associating legal penalties with systems of religious belief. Does this imply too casual a view of the value of language as a repository of culture and identity? Not necessarily; for one can learn an additional language without giving up a prior one. Religious beliefs are more like a zero-sum game: you can't just add more of them; the plaintiff in *Friedman* would have to abandon her views in favor of others.

If students suggest that the key point in *Friedman* is that the defendants put the plaintiff into her hard situation, or that she might foreseeably have been made hysterical by it, you can try this variation: imagine the illiterate plaintiff in *Weirs* was on the chair lift when it stopped; and suppose there was a sign on the chair lift advising users that rangers came by every hour. Since he was unable to read the sign, the plaintiff jumped off. He, too, would have been put into the bad situation by the defendant, and he may have been made hysterical by it; would he be able to recover? It seems doubtful.

Can one imagine a case where the *Friedman* plaintiff's beliefs were invoked by her as a defendant rather than as a plaintiff fending off a claim of contributory negligence? We like to wonder whether the plaintiff would have had a good defense—perhaps on necessity grounds—if she had been moved by her beliefs to push her companion off the chair lift.

Q. Is the point of *Weirs* that the plaintiff was unreasonable? Can the plaintiff be *faulted?*

A. Perhaps so. The opinion does not make clear which was the case here, though its references to "the English language" might imply that the plaintiff could read some other language; you may be able to catch a student making a hasty assumption on the point. Either way you can have a lively discussion about whether a reasonable person in this country today can be expected to read English. Is it a descriptive point, so that whether it's reasonable to expect people to read English depends simply on whether most people in the community can? Or is there a normative dimension, so that we expect people to learn English and tell them that they fail to do so at their peril? You can ask about the costs and benefits of requiring precautions to be taken in languages other than English in areas where many people may speak other languages, such as ethnic neighborhoods in big cities or parts of the American southwest.

Moving closer to the facts of *Weirs*, one can argue that apart from whether the defendant was reasonable in confining its sign to English words (rather than multi-lingual signs or pictures or other precautions, like chains), it is unreasonable for a plaintiff to venture over a bridge with a sign posted next to it (written in English in a country where English is the primary language) if you aren't able to read the sign.

Q. How far does the principle of *Friedman* go? Suppose the plaintiff is injured in a car accident and then declines medical treatment because she is a Jehovah's Witness and thus is forbidden by her religion to receive blood transfusions. Is the plaintiff on the hook for all of the resulting damages she suffers?

A. This is the more common scenario in which *Friedman*-type issues arise: with respect to mitigation of damages, not contributory negligence in causing the harm in the first place. You may or may not want to get into these waters at this point; they become interesting and involved in a hurry, and can end up being a substantial digression. (The beliefs of Jehovah's Witnesses raise many interesting tort problems; we consider them in the casebook in the sections on battery and assumption of risk.) Most courts say that the plaintiff's efforts to mitigate damages are to be judged against the benchmark of a reasonable person, not a reasonable Jehovah's Witness (or Christian Scientist or member of whatever other religion is involved). But courts sometimes are skittish about this because they do not want to be understood as imposing a burden on the plaintiff's religious choices in violation of the First Amendment. Thus in *Williams v. Bright*, 658 N.Y.S.2d 910 (App. Div. 1997), which involved facts like those just described, the court had this to say:

> No one suggests that the State, or, for that matter, anyone else, has the right to interfere with that religious belief. But the real issue here is whether the consequences of that belief must be fully paid for here on earth by someone other than the injured believer. According to the trial court, the State has little interest in enforcing its general rule of damage mitigation simply to rescue a wrongdoer from the full consequences of his tortious conduct. This simplistic formulation has little application to the realities of this case. Here, the "wrongdoer," who fell asleep at the wheel, paid for his "fault" with his life. The respondents in damages (defendant car leasing company and its insurance carrier) must answer for the harm under the derivative liability imposed by Vehicle and Traffic Law § 388, which expresses the State's interest in cost allocation among that segment of the public that pays automobile insurance premiums.

> Of course, the State does not have any interest in the question of who wins this lawsuit, or the extent to which one party prevails over the other. But the State does have a compelling interest in assuring that the proceedings before its civil tribunals are fair, and that any litigant is not improperly advantaged or disadvantaged by adherence to a particular set of religious principles. The State also has a compelling interest, by constitutional command under the Fourteenth Amendment, to extend equal protection of the law to every person haled before its courts. A derivative tortfeasor is certainly entitled to no less equal protection, in this regard, than an individual under criminal indictment. [...]

> An order emanating from a State court constitutes "state action" which, under the Fourteenth Amendment, would trigger First Amendment protections. The trial court's instruction to the jurors on mitigation directed them to pass upon the reasonableness of plaintiff Robbins' objection, on religious grounds, to a blood transfusion. The fallacy in this instruction was that the jury never received any evidence pertaining to the rationale of her religious convictions, nor how universally accepted they may have been by members of her faith. True, there were entries in her medical records that she refused blood transfusions because she was a Jehovah's Witness, and there was brief testimony (in the context of presenting her diminished physical capabilities) that she attended Jehovah's Witness prayer services. But there was no evidence of the basis for the religious prohibition of blood transfusions. The charge thus created a sham inquiry; instead of framing an issue on how plaintiff Robbins' religious beliefs impacted on mitigation, the court foreclosed the issue in her favor without any supporting evidence. Let us recall, the jurors were told that they must ask themselves whether this plaintiff's refusal to accept a blood transfusion was reasonable, "given her beliefs, without questioning the validity" of those beliefs. Having thus removed from the jury's consideration any question as to the validity (that is to say, the reasonableness) of plaintiff Robbins' religious convictions, the court effectively directed a verdict on the issue.

> Of course, the alternative—the receipt of "expert" testimony on this subject—presents an even worse prospect. Such evidence, if any conflict developed, would present a triable issue as to whether the conviction against transfusions was heretical—or orthodox—within the Jehovah's Witness faith. [...]

> In espousing the objective standard and remanding this matter for a new trial, we take note of an obvious problem with strict adherence to the pattern jury instruction that is provided as a general

guide. We conclude that the unmodified application of that formulation would work an injustice in this case, as well as in others of a similar nature. It seems apparent to us that a person in plaintiff Robbins' position must be permitted to present to the jury the basis for her refusal of medical treatment; otherwise, the jury would simply be left with the fact of her refusal, without any explanation at all. Once such evidence is (as it should be) received, the court is called upon to instruct the jurors as to how such evidence should affect their deliberations. Addressing this issue, we hold that the pattern jury instruction must be supplemented here with the following direction:

> In considering whether the plaintiff acted as a reasonably prudent person, you may consider the plaintiff's testimony that she is a believer in the Jehovah's Witness faith, and that as an adherent of that faith, she cannot accept any medical treatment which requires a blood transfusion. I charge you that such belief is a factor for you to consider, together with all the other evidence you have heard, in determining whether the plaintiff acted reasonably in caring for her injuries, keeping in mind, however, that the overriding test is whether the plaintiff acted as a reasonably prudent person, under all the circumstances confronting her.

[...] Our modification of the PJI charge is intended to strike a fair balance between the competing interests of these parties. And in pursuit of that goal, we reiterate that the court is not to permit the introduction of any "theological" proof, by way of either expert or lay testimony, as to the validity of religious doctrine, nor should the court issue any instructions whatsoever on that score.

Q. Hypothetical: in *Padula v. New York*, 398 N.E.2d 548 (N.Y. 1979), two heroin addicts were committed to a rehabilitation center run by the State of New York. They got into a print shop located on the premises, and found there a chemical called Ditto (apparently for making "dittoed" copies of documents) that contained ethyl alcohol. They mixed it with the orange breakfast drink known as Tang and drank the resulting beverage. One of them died; the other went blind. Suits were brought to collect from the state for these results. The theory of the suits was that one of the guards at the facility negligently had allowed the two addicts into the print shop where the chemicals were located and had failed to intervene when he saw the men drinking. The plaintiff claimed that the men were powerless to resist the temptation to drink the alcohol because their addiction created an uncontrollable urge to get "high" by any means at hand. What result?

A. New York's Court of Claims found for the plaintiffs, concluding that the state's agents had been negligent and that the plaintiffs had been free from contributory negligence. The Court of Appeals affirmed:

> [W]e think that in relation to persons in the custody of the State for treatment of a drug problem, contributory (or comparative) negligence should turn not on whether the drug problem or its effects be categorized as a mental disease nor on whether the injured person understood what he was doing, but on whether based upon the entire testimony presented (including objective behavioral evidence, claimant's subjective testimony and the opinions of experts) the trier of fact concludes that the injured person was able to control his actions. As Mr. Justice Simons put it in *Mochen v. State of New York*, 352 N.Y.S.2d 290, 293, in holding it a question for the jury whether an inmate of a mental institution was guilty of contributory negligence in jumping out a window: "The disability may fall short of psychosis or severe retardation and the act may be a voluntary judgment by the patient but still be the product of impulse or irrational behavior beyond his control. Under such circumstances, a plaintiff should not be held to any greater degree of care for his own safety than that which he is capable of exercising."

Tested by that standard, the weight of the evidence in the instant case favors the finding of the Trial Judge that Padula and Modafferi were not guilty of contributory negligence. The evidence shows that the accepted practice in institutions such as that in which they resided was to keep close watch on chemicals such as methyl alcohol because addicts were constantly looking for something to get high on, that at the Iroquois Center alcohol and drugs were not permitted, urine tests were taken at random to see whether residents had ingested any chemical, spot inspections of lockers for chemicals were carried out, and chemicals used in the shops were closely controlled. Thus, the fact that Padula and Modafferi had been screened and accepted for the program cannot be read as meaning that the institution believed them wholly free of the effects of the addiction which brought them to the institution in the first place.

The expert testimony on behalf of claimants came from Doctors Herbert Wender and Daniel Casriel. Dr. Wender testified that it was common medical knowledge at the time of the incident that drug abusers motivated by the desire for the gratification induced by a high would deny the reality of the damage that methyl alcohol could do and drink it, even if told it was poisonous and could cause death or blindness. Dr. Casriel's opinion was that it was common knowledge at the time that a drug addict is an emotional infant who will insert any available chemical into any bodily orifice by any means available in order to obtain an affective change, for which reason any chemical that could possibly be taken to change mood, whether poison or not, had to be kept locked away, that the institution had to protect the addict against his own proclivity for danger, and that a certified addict, unless his personality is totally restructured, has a lifelong psychological dependence on drugs, as a result of which if he cannot get heroin he will take other substitutes. Both also testified in response to hypothetical questions that Padula and Modafferi could be expected to ingest the Ditto-Tang drink.

Testifying on behalf of the State, Dr. Jerome H. Jaffe stated that there was no consensus among medical experts, that the majority view was that heroin addicts are not emotional infants and will make choices between good and bad substances. He conceded, however, that as to persons in a facility such as Iroquois "much of the expert opinion, and, incidentally, backed by practical and actual experience of and with heroin addicts is that such addicts do not have the ability to resist temptation to ingest a substance that might make them euphoric or 'high', even if such substance is harmful or dangerous to the human body if ingested", though he gave it as his personal opinion that such an addict had discretion to say "no".

The testimony of those present at the print shop drinking session was that Joseph Perrone read from the Ditto can, on which there was a skull and crossbones, a warning that it was poisonous and could cause blindness or death, and Modafferi testified that Perrone said "We've got to be crazy to drink this", but that both he and Perrone drank it nevertheless, that he was aware when he drank it that it could cause blindness or death but could not resist doing so because he felt he needed it and wanted to believe it was all right to do so.

Weighing on the side of the finding by the Court of Claims are the procedures imposed by the institution in question and such institutions generally, the clearly stated opinions of Doctors Wender and Casriel, and the fact that not only Padula and Modafferi but six other residents drank the Ditto-Tang concoction notwithstanding that the warning on the can had been read to them. Weighing against the Court of Claims finding is the self-interest of Modafferi and the opinion expressed by Dr. Jaffe. Bearing in mind the opportunity of the Trial Judge to see and hear Modafferi and thus use his demeanor in evaluating his evidence and Dr. Jaffe's concession that there was a substantial body of expert opinion contrary to the opinion he expressed, we conclude that the weight of the evidence is with the findings of the Court of Claims rather than those of the Appellate Division.

Fredericks v. Castora (D truckers held to ordinary standard of care, not heightened standard; NL)
Restatement (Second) of Torts §298

Q. Can the decision in *Fredericks v. Castora* be squared with the Restatement provisions that follow the case?
A. Well, maybe not. Illustration 12, involving the doctor, seems distinguishable because it isn't all that hard as an administrative matter to identify doctors and what we expect them to know. It's more difficult to figure out which drivers we expect to be better than average and to state what we expect them to be able to do differently than other drivers. Driving is not a regulated profession in the same way that medicine is. But Illustration 1 seems to look the other way, calling for a specialized inquiry into the defendant's strength. Still, maybe it's easier for the jury to estimate a defendant's strength than it is to estimate driving ability based on experience.

Q. The standard of care demanded of professionals is treated in more detail in the section of the chapter on custom. But it you want to look at it here, you can create a good hypothetical out of *Heath v. Swift Wings, Inc.*, 252 S.E.2d 526 (N.C. App. 1979). In that case several people were killed when a Piper 180 Arrow airplane crashed immediately after takeoff from the Boone-Blowing Rock Airport in North Carolina. The accident resulted in several lawsuits. In one of them, the administrator of the estates of two of the passengers brought suit against the estate of the pilot, Fred Heath, claiming that Heath had been negligent. The trial court instructed the jury as follows:

> Negligence, ladies and gentlemen of the jury, is the failure of someone to act as a reasonably and careful and prudent person would under the same or similar circumstances. Obviously, this could be the doing of something or the failure to do something, depending on the circumstances. With respect to aviation negligence could be more specifically defined as the failure to exercise that degree of ordinary care and caution, which an ordinary prudent pilot having the same training and experience as Fred Heath, would have used in the same or similar circumstances.

So instructed, the jury found that Heath had not been negligent. The trial court entered judgment for the defendants, and the plaintiff appealed, complaining that the instruction was erroneous. What result?
A. The court of appeals reversed:

> It is a familiar rule of law that the standard of care required of an individual, unless altered by statute, is the conduct of the reasonably prudent man under the same or similar circumstances. While the standard of care of the reasonably prudent man remains constant, the quantity or degree of care required varies significantly with the attendant circumstances.

> The trial court improperly introduced a subjective standard of care into the definition of negligence by referring to the "ordinary care and caution, which an ordinary prudent pilot having the same training and experience as Fred Heath, would have used in the same or similar circumstances." We are aware of the authorities which support the application of a greater standard of care than that of the ordinary prudent man for persons shown to possess special skill in a particular endeavor. Indeed, our courts have long recognized that one who engages in a business, occupation, or profession must exercise the requisite degree of learning, skill, and ability of that calling with reasonable and ordinary care. Furthermore, the specialist within a profession may be held to a standard of care greater than that required of the general practitioner. Nevertheless, the professional standard remains an objective standard. For example, the recognized standard for a physician is established as "the standard of professional competence and care customary in similar communities among physicians engaged in his field of practice."

Such objective standards avoid the evil of imposing a different standard of care upon each individual. The instructions in this case concerning the pilot's standard of care are misleading at best, and a misapplication of the law. They permit the jury to consider Fred Heath's own particular experience and training, whether outstanding or inferior, in determining the requisite standard of conduct, rather than applying a minimum standard generally applicable to all pilots. The plaintiff is entitled to an instruction holding Fred Heath to the objective minimum standard of care applicable to all pilots.

Q. How is *Heath v. Swift Wings* (if you used it as just described) distinguishable from *Fredericks v. Castora*?

A. In both cases the defendant was a professional operator of a vehicle that most people don't use, and had (or may have had) a level of ability beyond that of the ordinary person. In *Fredericks* the defendants nevertheless were judged against the plain benchmark of the reasonable person, or reasonable driver; in *Heath* the defendant was held to the standard of the reasonable pilot. The reason has to do with the benefits of drawing such distinctions vs. the administrative cost involved. An unvarnished "reasonable person" in the sense of an *ordinary* person has no ability to fly a plane, so obviously that can't be the standard. But an ordinary level of care in driving is an understandable idea, familiar to most jurors, and while the gains from holding professional truckers to a higher standard might be worth something if it could be done costlessly (for as the Restatement excerpt says, we do want people to use all the ability that they have), it would likely be very difficult to do in a way comprehensible to jurors and to parties negotiating in the shadow of their verdicts.

Q. What is the analogy between *Heath v. Swift Wings* and *Vaughan v. Menlove*?

A. In both cases the defendant was required to measure up to a standard of care that may have been impossible for him to meet. *Heath* says that defendant was pressing for a subjective standard, but that's potentially a bit misleading; a true subjective standard is one like the defendant wanted in *Vaughan*: the defendant wins if he was trying to the best of his ability. The defendant in *Heath* was not quite asking for that. He wanted a standard that was "subjective" in the sense of being highly particularized. But this sometimes can come to resemble a real subjective standard; that is what often happens in cases involving children, where the standard is so tailored to the child's level of maturity and education that it can operate much like a simple inquiry into whether the child did the best he could.

2. Physical impairments

From the Restatement (Second) of Torts (1965):

> Sec. 283B. Mental Deficiency
>
> Unless the actor is a child, his insanity or other mental deficiency does not relieve the actor from liability for conduct which does not conform to the standard of a reasonable man under like circumstances.
>
> Sec. 283C. Physical Disability
>
> If the actor is ill or otherwise physically disabled, the standard of conduct to which he must conform to avoid liability is that of a reasonable man under like circumstances.

Perhaps the wording of these provisions is not as clear as it could be. The upshot is that illness and physical disability are considered part of the circumstances under which the defendant was operating; in other words, an allowance is made for them, unlike mental deficiencies. The Restatement attributes the different treatment to "the greater public familiarity" with physical difficulties and "the comparative ease and certainty" with which they can be proved. You can tie this into the excerpts from Holmes regarding "distinct defects" and the accompanying discussion in the previous section.

Kerr v. Connecticut Co. (deaf P hit by D's train because he didn't hear it coming; NL, as P was contributorily negligent)

Davis v. Feinstein (blind P falls through D's cellar door despite using his cane; L, as P was not contributorily negligent)

Q.   What is the superficial similarity between *Kerr* and *Davis*? What is the distinction between them?

A.   In both cases the plaintiffs had disabilities and were hurt in circumstances where ordinary people without those disabilities probably would not have been injured; in that sense neither of the plaintiffs acted as an ordinary person of reasonable prudence would have acted. The distinction is that in *Davis* the plaintiff was taking all precautions that we would expect a reasonable blind person to take; in *Kerr* the defendant did not act like a reasonable deaf man.

The cases so far in the chapter all involve decisions about whether to include some feature of a party's condition—the party's mental state or mental ability, the party's beliefs, or the party's physical condition—in the reasonable person standard (making it "the reasonable deaf man," or the "the reasonable person with retardation"), in which case the costs of their inability to act like an average person are shifted to the defendants; or whether to exclude those features from the standard, so that the party fails to measure up to the reasonable person standard at his peril and bears the costs of his inability to do so. In the case of blindness, the costs created by a blind person's inability to act as an average person would actually are divided between himself and the other side. He does not have the right to collect for accidents caused by his disability regardless of the steps he took to correct for it (that's *Kerr*); but if he does take reasonable steps to correct for it, he can collect for accidents even if a person with the disability could have avoided them (that's *Davis*).

Q.   What is the superficial similarity between *Davis v. Feinstein* and *Weirs v. Jones County*? What is the distinction between them?

A.   In both cases the plaintiff sustained a fall because he was unable to protect himself from it in the way an average person might have done; for either defendant to have protected the plaintiffs from the harm they suffered would have required special efforts beyond what would be necessary to protect average people. *Davis* in effect required the defendant to take those precautions for the benefit of the plaintiff. This is the practical result of the holding; the implication of the case is that an average person with sight might well be held contributorily negligent on similar facts, leaving the defendant with no liability. Perhaps one reason for treating blindness and English illiteracy differently is that illiteracy can be surmounted. Other mental limitations, such as insanity, might not be surmountable and thus not distinguishable from blindness on that ground; but then there are administrative issues that separate those cases: there are more worries about false claims of insanity than there are about false claims of blindness.

Notice, too, that this is another case where the injured plaintiff is the one who is accused of being unreasonable. Same result if a blind person knocks over a bystander and thus becomes a defendant?

Q.   Hypothetical: in *Stephens v. Dulaney*, 428 P.2d 27 (N.M. 1967), the plaintiff and defendant were traveling together in a the defendant's pickup truck. At one point after they had stopped to fill the gas tank, the plaintiff stood smoking a cigarette near the truck. The cigarette ignited gasoline fumes that had leaked out of a defective valve on the truck's gasoline tank, which the defendant recently had filled. An explosion resulted that caused the plaintiff various injuries for which she sued to recover. The plaintiff's evidence was that the defendant earlier had fiddled with the valve in an attempt to repair it, and that his negligence caused it to become loose and leak the fumes that gave rise to the explosion. The defendant's evidence was that the plaintiff was negligent to light a cigarette in the presence of the fumes; to this the plaintiff replied that she had a disability: she lacked any sense of smell. How should the jury have been instructed?

A. The court approved the substance of the following instruction, though it criticized its form as prolix:

> You are instructed that a person under a physical disability, such as not having a sense of smell, which may reasonably be calculated to increase the possibility of her being injured must nevertheless exercise ordinary care to avoid injury commensurate with her known disability, and if she fails to exercise that degree of care which a reasonable person so disabled would exercise and such failure contributes proximately to cause the injury, she is guilty of contributory negligence. Such a person is not required to exercise a higher degree of care to the end of protecting her safety than is required of a person under no disability, but ordinary care of a person under like circumstances is what is required.

> In determining whether the plaintiff exercised ordinary care for her own safety, this disability of loss of smell, if any, is a circumstance which may be considered. In other words, ordinary care, in such a case as this, is such care as an ordinary prudent person under the same disability would exercise under the same or similar circumstances.

Q. Hypothetical: in *Mahan v. State ex rel. Carr*, 191 A. 575 (Md. 1937), the plaintiff's decedent, a young boy, was struck and killed by the defendant's taxicab. The driver, Mahan, was eighty years old and was four feet, ten inches tall. He defended on the ground that his short stature made it impossible for him to see the boy until it was too late. What result?

A. Liability. Said the court:

> The jury were also authorized by the evidence to find that his failure to see the child was due to the facts, first, that he was not looking at the road immediately before him, but at a car in the next block, and, second, that because of his stature the hood of his own automobile prevented him from seeing objects in front of and close to him. It is true that persons of small stature may and do lawfully operate automobiles, but if that condition makes it more difficult for them to discover the presence of children, or objects in the highway, it imposes upon them the duty of exercising greater watchfulness to avoid injuring others also in the lawful use of the highway than would be necessary for one of normal stature.

Or perhaps he should have sat on a phone book.

3. Age

Purtle v. Shelton (D shoots P while hunting; D wins when his negligence is assessed by reference to the degree of care expected of a minor of his same age and intelligence; NL)
Roberts v. Ring (old D runs over young P; P gets allowance for his age, but D does not)
Dellwo v. Pearson (D runs across P's fishing line in motorboat; held to adult standard of care; L)

Q. What is an "adult activity"? Why is it an element of the test for deciding whether a child will be held to an adult's standard of care?

A. It usually just means an activity normally engaged in only by adults. But consider whether the standard has normative as well as descriptive force. If it's purely descriptive, perhaps the sense of the rule is that all who engage in "adult" activities generally assume that all others will be using an adult level of care, and so can coordinate their own precautions accordingly. Or maybe it's just a concession to reality: if an activity commonly is engaged in by children, it might seem futile to apply an adult standard of care. From a normative standpoint the "adult activity" point could be a way of saying that only adults *should* engage in certain activities—or more precisely that people should engage in them only if they're ready to meet the adult standard of care, perhaps because the activity is so dangerous if done carelessly (or because others who may be hurt by the activity have no ability to perceive that it is being carried out by a child and thus no reason to take extra precautions). The normative angle can in turn be viewed from a standpoint of fairness or incentives. On the latter point the question is whether the legal decision about standard of care is entirely exogenous to the activity, or whether it might be expected to have some effect on who participates in it. It probably depends on the activity; the question is whether one can come up with plausible examples of activities children might like to engage in that are surrounded by an institutional structure (whether it's parental or organizational) that is likely to know about the rules either directly or through the indirect promptings of insurance premiums.

Q. Why make allowances for youth but not for old age?
A. While both youth and old age may impair an actor's ability, youth is more likely to be associated with an inability to perceive and appreciate those impairments. The elderly have been through normal adulthood and understand what is expected of them, so they are in a better position to make judgments about what they can and cannot do. In addition, an allowance for youth helps facilitate the learning process: the young have to acquire the ability to do things; they have to start somewhere. The impairments of the elderly do not similarly tend to occur on the way up the learning curve; they represent deterioration. So there is not a comparable social good in giving them a break. We would be subsidizing below-average performance without the payoff of later mastery.

Q. What is the distinction between *Purtle v. Shelton* and *Dellwo v. Pearson?*
A. In both cases the defendant was engaged in an activity creating dangers to others. But the court thinks it relevant in *Dellwo* that the plaintiff had no way of knowing that the defendant was so young, unlike a plaintiff run down by someone on a bicycle. In the latter case, as in *Purtle*, youth becomes a kind of "distinct defect" for which the plaintiff can compensate. But would *Purtle* have come out any differently if the defendant had shot a stranger who did not see Bubba Shelton and did not realize there was an armed minor in the woods? The plaintiff realized he was with a minor; the question is whether other hunters assumed—or should have assumed—that there probably were minors hunting in the woods who would be acting their age and not necessarily using the care expected of adults.

Q. Hypothetical: in *Stevens v. Ventura*, 573 N.W.2d 341 (Mich. App. 1998), the defendant, Aaron Veenstra, was a fourteen-year-old student enrolled in a driver's education course at his high school. (State law permitted minors who had reached 14 years and 9 months to obtain a "learner's license." Veenstra had skipped four grades during elementary school and thus was preparing to graduate and head to college; he wanted to learn how to drive first.) Veenstra never had driven before. On his first day in the "road" portion of the course, Veenstra made a right turn too sharply and drove into the plaintiff, who was exiting his parked car. The instructor in the passenger's seat of Veenstra's car tried to stop him but was too late; Veenstra testified that when he turned toward the plaintiff he may mistakenly have hit the accelerator instead of the brake. How should the jury be instructed?
A. Veenstra was held to an adult standard of care. Said the court:

> Veenstra defines the activity he was involved in as not simply driving an automobile, but driving an automobile as part of a driver's education course to satisfy the legislative requirements placed upon those under eighteen years of age seeking to obtain an operator's license, and claims that because he was engaged in an activity, which by definition is limited to minors, he was not engaged in an adult activity and should not be held to an adult standard of conduct. We disagree.

One rationale behind holding a minor driving an automobile to an adult standard of conduct is that, because of the frequency and sometimes catastrophic results of automobile accidents, it would be unfair to the public to permit a minor operating an automobile to observe any standard of care other than that expected of all others operating automobiles. See *Dellwo v. Pearson*, 107 N.W.2d 859 (Minn. 1961). It would seem illogical to think that the dangers associated with driving are lessened when the activity is undertaken by a minor with little or no experience. While we concede that Veenstra was attempting to satisfy requirements placed only upon minors, we do not think that changes the nature of, or danger associated with, driving an automobile. In our opinion, defendant defines the activity he was engaged in too narrowly. Veenstra was engaged in the adult activity of driving an automobile, and we do not consider the reasons behind his undertaking the activity to justify departure from the general rule that all drivers, even minors, are held to an adult standard of care. The licensing statutes cited by Veenstra are important in determining the qualifications required to drive an automobile and assuring a minimum level of driver competence. We find no authority in these statutes to apply a lesser standard of care to those seeking to satisfy the statutory qualifications and are not persuaded that the policy behind the rule applying an adult standard of care to minors driving automobiles should be set aside under these circumstances. If a lesser standard of care is to be applied to minors in Veenstra's circumstance, it should be imposed by the Legislature. As a result, the trial court erred in instructing the jury to consider the degree of care that a reasonably careful minor of the same age, mental capacity, and experience as Veenstra would use under the circumstances.

The standard instruction the court approved for the case therefore was as follows:

When I use the words "ordinary care," I mean the care a reasonably careful person would use under the circumstances which you find existed in this case. The law does not say what a reasonably careful person would do or would not do under such circumstances. That is for you to decide.

SECTION B. RISKS AND PRECAUTIONS

The materials in this section primarily are meant to start students toward a sense of comfort with analysis based on the Hand formula, while also starting them toward an appreciation of possible critiques of the formula from both descriptive and normative standpoints. We find the Hand formula a useful tool for analysis and refer back to it at many points in the book; this makes the section an important one for students to grasp, but we think it also makes it important to introduce them to skepticisms about the Hand formula before they become uncritical fans of its analytical power.

If you want to make cuts (we don't recommend them), you can pass on *The Margharita* (great case, though), the *Davis* problem, and the note on compliance errors.

United States v. Carroll Towing (no bargee on D's barge; L; Hand formula introduced)

The facts and parties in this case can cause some confusion; you have to decide how much class time to spend sorting them all out vs. summarizing them and cutting straight to Hand's analysis.

Q. What did the Grace Line employees (the harbormaster and his helper) do wrong in the first place?
A. They failed to retie the *Anna C*'s lines properly; as a result the lines loosened, which allowed the *Anna C* to drift into the harbor where she collided with another vessel. Applying the Hand formula to this part of the case, the burden of tying the lines properly was low, and this untaken precaution would have reduced a significant probability (P) that the *Anna C* would break away—as well as the probable

magnitude of the resulting injury (L) would have been large if the *Anna C* did break away. So under the Hand formula the Grace Line employees committed a clear breach of duty. Hand did not explicitly apply his formula to the Grace Line's negligence, which he took as a given that did not need elaborate analysis, probably because their conduct amounted to an obvious "compliance error"—a failure to take a precaution that everyone would understand to be important.

Q. What untaken precaution was alleged against the Conners Company (the owner of the *Anna C*) as its breach of duty?
A. Its failure to have a bargee on board. (A bargee is the person who watches the barge; for those few students not entirely clear on the subject, a barge is a flat boat often used to haul bulk goods such as grain or coal.)

Q. How do we determine, using the Hand formula, whether the absence of the bargee was a breach of duty?
A. The burden of having a bargee was small relative to the probability that the *Anna C* would break away if no bargee were present, multiplied by the gravity of the injuries that could be expected to then result. The important question, of course, is the size of those variables as they reasonably appeared ex ante. When he offered the "formula," Hand seems to have been thinking of cases where the untaken precaution would have reduced the probability of an accident to zero. In that case, the simple comparison of the burden of the untaken precaution (B) with the total risk (P times L) is the appropriate one. The next question explores the more common case where a precaution will reduce but not eliminate the risk of trouble.

Q. Assume that the probability (P) that an automobile driver will sustain head injuries is one percent over the life of a car and that head injuries impose an average cost (L) of $1 million when they occur. Thus the expected value of these injuries (P times L) is $10,000. Suppose it would cost the manufacturer $100 to bundle a safety helmet with the car, and that wearing the helmet would reduce the injuries to zero. Would it be a breach of duty for the automobile manufacturer to fail to include a safety helmet with each car sold?
A. No. Although the risk of head injuries is large, a bundled safety helmet would not much reduce this risk because most drivers of cars are not going to wear helmets. Correct use of the Hand formula compares the cost of the precaution with the *risk reduction* that the precaution would yield. Under this modified analysis, appropriate when the untaken precaution does not reduce the risk to zero, no breach of duty would exist unless the cost of providing a helmet was less than the reduction in the risk of head injuries. In this sense the Hand formula can be rewritten as asking whether the burden of the untaken precaution was less than the *change* in risk that it provided.

Another illustration of the same point is a hypothetical obligation of an employer to issue parachutes to window washers. Although the PL involved in window washing may be substantial (or we can so hypothesize), and the B of giving parachutes to window washers is small, the parachutes will not much reduce the risks of window washing. So while the cost of parachutes may be less than the total risk from window washing, the cost would be greater than the risk reduction yielded by taking the precaution; B might be less than PL but greater than the *reduction* in PL. Although he did not explicitly say so, Hand clearly meant to measure a precaution's burden against its effectiveness, not against risks that it would leave unaffected.

Adams v. Bullock (NL when boy swings wire so it contacts trolley line running under the bridge)
Bolton v. Stone (plaintiff struck on head by cricket ball; NL)

Q. What happened in *Adams v. Bullock*? Describe it.

A.   The point of the question is to get students to think carefully about the facts of the case. Many of them will imagine a child throwing a wire over a four-foot wall on the side of a bridge, an image that seems weird—but isn't quite right. The opinion never tells how high the "parapet" was. We only know it was four and a half feet from the top of the parapet down to the defendant's trolley cable. It couldn't have been too high, since the parapet rested on the bridge, and some of the 4.5 feet had to be consumed by the bridge itself. The record of the case (which we obtained) reveals that in fact the parapet was about twenty inches high—which was pretty short. It's not clear whether the plaintiff was walking alongside the parapet or on top of it.

The case that the boy was contributorily negligent seems pretty strong. He testified that he knew that electric trolley wires were strung under the bridge, knew that a wire hung over the side could touch them (other boys were trying to do this deliberately with their own wires), and knew that if his wire did touch them, he would get shocked and hurt. But he said he didn't intend that his wire contact the trolley wires; he said he was just swinging the wire near them because he "was in the habit of swinging things like that." The presence of other children swinging wires over the edge of the bridge, which from the testimony does not sound like an uncommon occurrence, makes the accident seem more foreseeable and less freakish than Cardozo's opinion may suggest. One may wonder whether Cardozo, in writing his opinion, was thinking about contributory negligence but found it hard to say so because it's difficult to reverse a jury determination applying a child's standard of care (the charge to the jury was in the classic form—the plaintiff was "only required to exercise such care and prudence for his own safety, as children of that age, intelligence, and judgment usually exercise under the circumstances.").

Q.   How would you analyze *Adams v. Bullock* using the Hand formula?
A.   You can march through the excerpts from Cardozo's opinion, asking students to restate his analysis in the language of the Hand formula. Clearly L was very high and difficult to quantify. As often is true in cases involving serious accidental harm, the analysis focuses more on the relative sizes of B and P. The court says that "[r]easonable care in the use of a destructive agency imports a high degree of vigilance. But no vigilance, however alert, unless fortified by the gift of prophecy, could have predicted the point upon the route where such an accident would occur." This can be restated as the idea that if L is high, it may justify a high B; but if P is so small that PL seems negligible ex ante, the obligation to take precautions may vanish after all. Another way to put this is in terms of information costs: asking a defendant to think of the possibility that a child would do this is just too much to expect. This ties the negligence issue into questions of foreseeability and thus causes it to resemble some of the proximate cause issues we will be covering later. Another way to interpret the B described here is to say that since an accident like this could have occurred anyplace, the true B of preventing it actually was extremely high, since it would require precautions wherever the wires run. On the other hand, "Chance of harm, though remote, may betoken negligence, if needless. Facility of protection may impose a duty to protect." Thus if the P of an accident is very small, precautions against it still may be required if B is very low as well. But "[w]ith trolley wires, the case is different." B is very large, because the defendant would have to put the wires underground.

But *Adams* also is a useful case for thinking critically about B, P, and L, and not accepting the court's descriptions of them passively. Was B *really* all that large? Wouldn't shields protruding from the bottom of the bridge and over the trolley cables have been pretty easy to install? Indeed, wouldn't they be pretty common now? In thinking about the usefulness of such guards, should we take into account the good that shields (or higher railings) would do besides just preventing accidents like this? (They might prevent falls or prevent people from dropping things onto the trolleys.) Then again, it wasn't the defendant's bridge; it was the railroad's bridge. Is the defendant responsible for the railroad's failure to take these precautions?

In G. Edward White, *Tort Law in America: An Intellectual History* 298-300 (2003), the author discusses students' suggestions that the railroad could have done more to prevent the accident in *Adams v. Bullock*. He describes a response that he probably would not offer too early in the year:

> [T]he suggestions follow from an individualized conception of justice in negligence cases—something that resembles a corrective justice approach in modern torts scholarship—but that negligence cases invoke more than corrective justice considerations, they also invoke public policy concerns. The central premise of Cardozo's opinion in *Adams v. Bullock*—one he never explicitly articulates—is that trolley cars are a socially useful means of transportation even though the means by which they are propelled, overhead uninsulated electric wires, pose some risks. For the risks to be completely eliminated, the means of transportation would have to be completely overhauled, perhaps even eliminated. […]

White goes on to suggest that the *Adams* case contains competing considerations: those of "private law" that center on justice to the individual plaintiff, and those of "public law" that focus on the social consequences of the decision. He suggests that the result in the case might have been different if the boy had fallen off the bridge onto the live wire, since then the "situational" features of the case—the private law considerations—might have looked different. They likewise would have seemed different if an adult had been swinging the wire, in which case White thinks "it is unlikely that the case would ever have reached the New York Court of Appeals."

> From Sugarman, *Assumption of Risk*, 31 Val.U.L.Rev. 833 (1997):
>
> The only problem I have with Cardozo's opinion in [*Adams*] is that, when discussing the possible precautions, he talks about the railroad having no "duty" to underground the wires. This, unfortunately, is a common formulation in judicial opinions. But, to be precise, what Cardozo means is that the defendants did not "breach" their duties to take reasonable care by failing to take the precaution in question. This imprecision would not be a serious problem but for the fact that there is a separate defendant's legal doctrine called "no duty," and this case is not an example of it.

Q. What were the B, P, and L in *Bolton v. Stone*?
A. The B was building a higher fence or playing cricket elsewhere. L was the sort of injury that apparently occurred here, which we can assume was serious. P is impossible to estimate with any precision, but the thrust of the court's reasoning is that it was so small that neither precaution described above was in order.

Q. Suppose the ball had flown through an opening in the existing fence; imagine that the opening was a gate that the team usually kept closed but forgot to close on the day in question. Different result?
A. Probably. The marginal B would then be very small, and a party's failure to take a precaution that it had set for itself as routine sometimes will make liability more likely.

Q. Is *Bolton v. Stone* a good example of the Hand formula in action?
A. Maybe; maybe not. The opinions do seem to reject liability on the ground that the P of the accident here was too small to require precautions by the defendant. But Lord Reid's opinion seems to embrace the idea that there is liability for the creation of significant foreseeable risks, which is not the same as the balancing called for the Hand formula. He says "In considering that matter I think that it would be right to take into account not only how remote is the chance that a person might be struck, but also how serious the consequences are likely to be if a person is struck, but I do not think that it would be right to take into account the difficulty of remedial measures." Thus P and L are relevant—but not B, which is irrelevant once substantial risks are present, for reasonable men do not impose substantial risks on others. Lord Radcliffe's opinion is more ambiguous, and seems to us to imply that B might be relevant as well as P and L.

In *The Emergence of Cost-Benefit Balancing in English Negligence Law*, 77 Chi.-Kent L. Rev. 489 (2002), Stephen Gilles offers this critique of Reid's reasoning:

[T]here is a real tension between Lord Reid's approach and the conventional understanding of the reasonably prudent person standard, which requires the plaintiff to identify some precaution that a reasonable person allegedly would have taken (but that the defendant failed to take) and that would have avoided the accident. Recall that the substantial risk approach holds that reasonable persons must do everything possible—including curtailing their activities—to avoid creating substantial risks of harm to others. One would therefore expect plaintiffs, under that approach, routinely to argue that the defendant should simply have refrained from engaging in whatever activity occasioned the accident. But while such arguments are sometimes made, plaintiffs normally try to identify some precaution the defendant could have taken while engaging in the same underlying activity. Why go to all that trouble, if the substantial risk approach is good law? It would be much simpler just to point out that the defendant could have avoided the underlying activity. Thus, the way in which the untaken-precaution framework is normally employed implies that the standard for breach does not focus solely on foreseeable substantial risk (or danger).

Gilles's article undertakes a close reading of *Bolton v. Stone* and English cases before and afterwards; it's a nice compliment to his piece on the use of the Hand formula by American courts, which is referenced and quoted in the text. In this second piece he offers the following interesting summary of his conclusions regarding the standard of care in English negligence law:

Assuming the defendant owed the plaintiff a duty of reasonable care, the first question is whether the risk was reasonably foreseeable. Here the broader version of reasonable foreseeability championed by Lord Reid is frequently used. Yet one occasionally encounters cases in which judges choose to apply the older judgments suggesting that only likely risks are reasonably foreseeable. Overall, however, the not-reasonably-foreseeable defense, while hardly moribund, enables only a small percentage of defendants to evade scrutiny of whether they took reasonable care.

If the risk is reasonably foreseeable, then the question of avoidability—that is, whether the risk was avoidable by reasonable care—becomes decisive. Here, as in American negligence law, the reasonable person standard is the first-cut source of content for the duty of reasonable care. Consequently, notwithstanding its practical and doctrinal importance, the balancing of costs and benefits is in an important sense a derivative norm in English negligence law. Specifically, it derives from the reasonable person standard: reasonable persons, the argument goes, consider the burdens and disadvantages of precautions when deciding how far to go in eliminating foreseeable risks to others.

Precisely because it is derivative, the balancing approach can be bypassed by a judicial finding that is couched directly in terms of what a reasonable person would or would not have done. The upshot is that cost-benefit balancing coexists—on the whole, remarkably peacefully—in English negligence law with what one might call the "imaginative" use of the reasonable person as a device for determining how the defendant ought to have behaved in the circumstances. English judges who favor balancing are free to balance, and English judges who distrust balancing are free simply to ask whether a reasonably careful person would have avoided the risk.

Thus, Landes and Posner are wrong insofar as they suggest that cost-benefit balancing has simply supplanted the reasonable person—or, alternatively, that when judges (or juries) apply the reasonable person standard, they should be presumed to engage in implicit cost-benefit analysis. Conversely, however, Weinrib and Wright are wrong to treat cost-benefit balancing as an exceptional and marginal feature of English negligence law. Cost-benefit balancing is far more widespread and important than the substantial risk approach Weinrib and (to a lesser extent) Wright endorse.

Indeed, in the context of workplace accidents, cost-benefit balancing has become the normal method of applying the reasonable person standard. In other types of accident cases, judges seem comparatively more likely to evaluate untaken precautions by simply imagining what a reasonable person would have done. Yet as [other] cases […] attest, English judges have employed cost-benefit balancing in a wide range of contexts. And I have found no context in which cost-benefit balancing is forbidden.

In making regular, and in some contexts routine, use of cost-benefit balancing, however, the English judges have not adopted a Posnerian interpretation of the Hand Formula as calling for razor's-edge balancing of costs and benefits. Under the English balancing approach, actors must take all "reasonably practicable" precautions to guard against reasonably foreseeable risks. What is reasonably practicable depends on balancing the severity of the risk (PL) against the burden of avoiding it (B). But in conducting that balancing, there is no rule that the judge is to decide for the defendant if the costs of avoidance are found to be even a tiny bit larger than its benefits. Indeed, I have yet to come across a judicial statement to that effect. The "mood" in which English judges balance seems more akin to the disproportionate-cost test that continues to be used to implement the statutory "reasonably practicable" defense.

Yet it would be an exaggeration to claim that English judges routinely make explicit use of the disproportionate-cost test in negligence cases at common law. One occasionally encounters disproportionate-cost language in a common- law negligence case, but for the most part the judges simply speak of balancing in general and qualitative terms. The point is further muddied by the fact that the defendant bears the burden of proof on the statutory "reasonably practicable" defense, whereas the plaintiff bears the burden of proving negligence at common law. Perhaps most puzzling of all, there is no debate on the subject, indeed no recognition that there is even an unsettled question here.

How can this be, and what does it mean? I am inclined to infer that there just isn't that much at stake. Because it requires that the risk be "insignificant" as compared to the "sacrifice," defendants are somewhat less likely to prevail under the disproportionate-cost test than under a razor's-edge balancing test. But given that the balancing is being done intuitively and qualitatively, the difference may not be all that significant.

English cost-benefit balancing also departs from the Posnerian model in another way. Whereas for Posner the Hand Formula factors are to be quantified in terms of willingness-to-pay, there is no indication that English judges are thinking along those lines. Again, however, it is not as if there is an explicit consensus in favor of some other approach to the evaluation of costs and benefits. Judges occasionally refer to social costs, and they occasionally refer to social norms, such as that pecuniary costs are of relatively little weight when compared to the risk of serious injury or death. But I have found no self-conscious discussion of how judges should go about balancing costs and benefits.

Moreover, English lawyers do not offer—and English judges do not invite—evidence about how valuable the competing interests in negligence cases are. Although the question certainly deserves further study, English judges seem just as reluctant as their American counterparts to make the evaluative dimension of balancing explicit. Their value judgments—and the process whereby they arrive at them—typically remain implicit in informal, qualitative assessments of the costs and benefits of untaken precautions. Because the English negligence standard is applied by judges who give reasons for their decisions, one at least gets a comparatively good look at how they find, structure, and analyze the facts. But when it comes to the values that determine whether the facts amount to negligence, the judges' motto might almost be "the less said, the better." Thus, although the English have taken the jury out of the courtroom in negligence cases, they have not taken (and perhaps they do not want to take) the juror out of the judge. Cost-benefit balancing has emerged as a major feature of English negligence law, and there is no indication that this development is an impermanent one. But cost-benefit balancing has also remained an informal—one is tempted to say rudimentary—technique; and that too may be a permanent condition.

Q. Do you agree with the result in *Bolton v. Stone*?

A. This question is meant to provoke some general discussion of the justice of liability only for negligence; such discussion can also be postponed until the concept of strict liability is introduced if that it as not been done already. Students naturally differ in their view of whether someone who causes harm necessarily should pay for it, or whether the obligation to compensate attaches only to harm caused in manner that somehow is blameworthy. In insanity cases like *Williams v. Hays*, the courts sometimes will suggest that as between the blameless plaintiff and the blameless defendant, neither of whom has done anything wrong, it's most fair for the party who caused the harm to pay for it. Is that reasoning persuasive here? *Bolton* might be distinguished from *Williams v. Hays* on policy grounds: Liability in *Williams* might have the positive consequences mentioned there (incentives for lunatics to be supervised by their kin, etc.). Liability in *Bolton* arguably will not lead to any improvement in anyone's behavior, if you assume that B exceeded PL; it merely will cause the defendant to internalize the cost of its activities. But that internalization might be considered a good thing, since it would cause the defendant to make its own comparison of the costs and benefits of it actions, rather than leaving that judgment to a court. What considerations lie on the other side? Perhaps Holmes's arguments about encouraging action; perhaps an ethical sense that if the defendant did nothing wrong he should not pay anything (against which can of course be set the ethical sense that if the *plaintiff* did nothing wrong and was hurt, she ought to be compensated by the defendant); and the consideration that the negligence rule may result in more lawsuits, though with strict liability those suits that do result are simpler.

Marginal analysis problem.

The important thing to see is that while the 10 foot fence looks like a cost-justified improvement over a state of affairs in which there is no fence at all, due care (economically interpreted) does not require it. The costs of moving to ten feet instead of seven outweigh the benefits. The goal of the Hand formula—again, on an orthodox economic view—is to create incentives for actors to take cost-justified precautions: spending the right amount, neither too much nor too little. In this example the "right amount" to spend, at least as between the possibilities offered, is $2,000. But this is not to say that American courts would give the defendant judgment as a matter of law on these facts even if they were stipulated.

The casebook describes this as an exercise in "marginal" analysis. Another way of looking at it, favored by Grady, is that it calls for "incremental" analysis. The difference is that if courts could conduct a true marginal analysis they could see where the marginal cost line intersects the marginal benefit line and identify the precautions that minimize social cost. Then they could simply compare the defendant's actual precaution level to the set of precautions that they would have identified as efficient and see from the comparison whether there has been negligence, something like the way the problem suggests.

In the real world, however, courts do not get (or even ask for) nearly the amount of information that would make marginal analyis possible. Instead they require plaintiffs to provide information about untaken precautions and then compare the cost of each untaken precaution to the benefits (in the form of risk reduction). Although some people might loosely call this a "marginal analysis," an economist would not. The reason is that the untaken precaution often is a significant precaution—certainly bigger than the infinitesimal change that marginal analysis requires. Moreover, the courts' actual untaken precaution approach (conducted over significant intervals) produces results different than a true marginal analysis would achieve. Under a true marginal analysis of the casebook example, if the defendant had no fence, the plaintiff could not prove that a ten-foot fence was a breach of duty. The court would know that a ten-foot fence was above the seven-foot optimum (because the court could see where marginal cost equals marginal benefit—right at seven feet). Under the untaken precaution approach Grady regards as the courts' actual practice, by contrast, the defendant's failure to build a ten-foot fence *will* be a breach of duty when the defendant has built no fence (but not when the defendant has built a seven-foot fence). Grady has argued that the courts' actual adoption of the untaken precaution approach, besides reducing information requirements, also produces more balanced incentives for potential tortfeasors. See Mark F. Grady, *A New Positive Economic Theory of Negligence*, 92 Yale L. J. 799 (1983).

Eckert v. Long Island R. Co. (plaintiff's decedent is killed when he rushes onto railroad tracks to save child; no contributory negligence)
The Margharita (ship does not stop to get aid for seaman whose leg had been bitten off; NL)

Q. How does the Hand formula apply to *Eckert*?
A. The application of the formula here usually takes students a moment to understand. The important thing to grasp is the untaken precaution: the railroad says it wanted Eckert to restrain himself from charging onto the tracks. In applying the B, P, and L analysis to Eckert's conduct, it's easiest to begin with "PL"—the expected harm that could have been averted if Eckert had taken the precaution of refraining from his rescue attempt. P is the likelihood that Eckert would be killed attempting the rescue; L is the value of his life. The cost of the precaution the railroad was urging—B, in other words—would have been the loss of the child's life, or in any event the loss to the child of the chance of being saved created by Eckert's rescue attempt. An apparent difficulty in this analysis, of course, is quantifying the value of a lost life. We can and do put dollar values on lives for the purpose of assessing damages in wrongful death cases, but those may not be appropriate figures to use in conducting an *ex ante* Hand formula analysis. (This essentially is the Pinto problem, and also is raised by the *Margharita* case that follows.) But nailing down such a figure may not really be necessary here: there is life at stake on either side of the equation (the child's life, or Eckert's); so long as we assume their lives have the same value (whatever that value may be), we can proceed to focus on the P involved instead. So far as the Hand formula is concerned, Eckert's task was to decide which course of action was more likely (P) to avoid the loss of life: trying to rescue the child, or not trying, perhaps bearing in mind that both of them could have been killed by a bad rescue attempt.

Q. Is there a difference between Posner's contractual analysis and Terry's Hand-like analysis?
A. Not much. The assumption behind Posner's contractual counterfactual is that parties in a world without transaction costs (including the timestream) would bargain to results that maximize their joint wealth—which effectively would mean using the Hand formula to find those precautions that are cost effective. But when parties negotiate contracts they also have the ability to walk away from the table in disgust, an option not in view when we engage in cost-benefit analysis in the abstract. (Is disgust a transaction cost?) This split can be discussed further in connection with the next case, *The Margharita*.

Q. What was the "B" in *The Margharita*?
A. This case, like *Eckert*, illustrates that "B" can itself sometimes involve a "PL" calculus, so that the actual Hand formula inquiry is not so much whether B < PL as whether PL < PL. Here the B confronting the defendant if it detoured to Port Stanley consisted of a series of risks that seemed to vary in both magnitude and likelihood of occurrence. The court apparently was worried about the dangers involved in detouring to a harbor unfamiliar to the captain, the delays that would be caused by the detour, and the extra costs that the owner of the boat would incur in having to pay and feed the crew. It's not clear

whether these risks involved threats to anyone's life or health. Perhaps the route to the foreign harbor was thought to create risks that the boat would sink; perhaps the provisions that would be depleted by the journey would not be so easy to replace (cf. *Forbes v. Parsons* in the Privileges chapter, and earlier discussions in that chapter about how the value of life and the value of property ought to be weighed).

Q. What were "P" and "L" in *The Margharita*?

A. It's probably best to start with L. One way to quantify it is to imagine that this turned out to be a case of liability after all. What would be Martinez' damages? The trial court set them at $1,500. (That's anywhere from about $28,000 to $40,000 in year 2000 dollars, depending on the conversion method used.) If that award of damages were a fair measure of L, then we would multiply it by P: the likelihood of the suffering occurring if the captain did not make any stops until reaching Georgia. That likelihood might be reckoned at 1.00 or close to it; it must have been exceedingly clear that Martinez would endure great suffering on the way home if no stops were made. So the case turns into a straightforward comparison of the costs entailed and risked by (a) detouring to Port Stanley and (b) Martinez' suffering ($1,500)—though perhaps from an *ex ante* perspective it was possible that the decision to press on to Savannah *could* have caused Martinez to end up much worse off than that, which risks might be figured into the calculation.

What makes this way of looking at the problem troubling, in any event, is that the award of damages Martinez would have received may be a highly imperfect way of valuing his suffering. If Martinez had that sum of money on his person during the voyage, would he have been ready to pay it to persuade the captain to stop at Port Stanley? Might he have been ready to pay much more? Here, as in the fabled Ford Pinto case, we find a tension between the different purposes an award of damages might be understood to serve: ex post it might be considered an amount that is in many ways unsatisfactory but nevertheless is the best we are ready to do to compensate the plaintiff. But *ex ante* the damage award might also serve as the price we want potential defendants to consider when deciding how many precautions to take to prevent such injuries from occurring. The figures we want used for the ex ante and ex post purposes may be different. Hence the discomfort some might feel at using the damage award to Martinez as the sum of "PL" in the Hand formula, and the occasional imposition of punitive damages on parties who use it too self-consciously.

Q. Suppose the captain had bargained with Martinez and other members of the crew to obtain their services on the *Margharita*. If one of them had raised the possibility that this sort of fact pattern might arise, how do you think it would have been handled in their negotiations? [Or the question can be put this way:] This case appears to be laying down rules for ship captains about their legal obligation (or lack thereof) to stop for help when a member of the crew is injured. The rough rule seems to be that detours into port are likely to be required if failing to do so will cause death or additional permanent disability to a crewman, but not if the only result of pressing on will be transitory suffering. Can you imagine an argument that this case will have no bearing on that question—in other words, that captains will stop for help about as often no matter what the court says here?

A. These two questions are meant to point in the same direction: toward exploration of an analysis based on the Coase theorem. Captains (or boat owners) and their crew members bargain over the terms of employment. One of those terms, whether it is discussed or not, is the extent of the ship's obligation to detour into a port if one of the crew is injured. The Coasean argument would be that the decision in *The Margharita* merely sets a default rule that serves as a backdrop for those negotiations; the parties are likely to bargain their way to the same outcome regarding the extent of the obligation no matter what the court says. If the court's decision represented the usual understanding of parties to these deals, then the decision will have no effect. If the background custom had been harder on the boat owners than the court's decision was (perhaps the previous custom required captains to take detours to spare their men suffering), then the court's decision suddenly makes life harder for the crew members than it used to be, and the crew members will therefore either demand additional compensation or require that the boat owner opt out of the *Margharita* rule in writing. But this assumes that transaction costs are low. Are they? What are possible impediments to this fantasized bargain? Shortages of information? Of bargaining power? Should these be considered transaction costs that help justify the court in trying to fashion a rule for the situation that might reflect what the parties would have agreed to if those impediments to complete bargaining were absent? You can have a quite interesting discussion about what negotiations between owners of ships and their crew might have sounded like before and after the decision.

And then what are the implications of the Coasean interpretation if it is correct? The economic argument probably would be that the court should simply have asked what the custom was and deferred to it; any other rule simply forces the parties to consume transaction costs by bargaining around the court's result. (More on this in the subsequent section of the chapter.)

Q. How would the *Margharita* be analyzed by Professor Wright?
A. We went ahead and asked Richard Wright for his views. He was kind enough to respond at length; we will present excerpts from his views (representative ones, we think) here:

> [I]n this case, there is a very special relationship—of not merely employer to employee but master to sailor—that arguably creates a duty to aid with a standard of care that is the same as the standard applied in misfeasance cases involving participatory plaintiffs (actually, any misfeasance case not involving on-premises risks to noninvitees): the "prohibitive cost" test [quoted in the extract from his article]: if the risk is significant, it is unreasonable unless it is justified by its presumed acceptability to those put at risk due to its benefits to them, including both direct benefits to them as participants in the risky activity and indirect benefits due to the socially valuable nature of the activity ("socially valuable" being interpreted in an equal-freedom-enhancing way rather than an aggregate-risk-utility tradeoff way). In general, this will be true only if the risks are necessary to obtain the desired benefits to those put at risk, reduced to the maximum extent possible without significantly impairing those desired benefits, greatly outweighed by the desired benefits, and not too serious.
>
> A key point in these seafaring injury/illness cases is noted by the Court in *The Iroquois*: "A seafaring life is a dangerous one, accidents of this kind are peculiarly liable to occur, and the general principle of law that a person entering a dangerous employment is regarded as assuming the ordinary risks of such employment is peculiarly applicable to the case of seamen." In other words, the risks of not being able to get immediate or the promptest possible medical treatment, if doing so would seriously impair the successful operation of the enterprise in which the sailor is employed, is understood and accepted by the sailors involved. But if no such serious impairment of the business in which both master and sailor are involved and from which both seek to benefit would occur, or (the *Margharita* court implies) if the risk of delayed treatment were too serious (permanent injury or disability), the duty to put into the nearest known port with surgical facilities would apply, without regard to whether the costs of doing so might or might not (marginally) outweigh the benefits to the injured sailor.

Wright suggests that the *Margharita* really is not distinguishable from *The Iroquois*. In the latter case a ship's master was held liable for failing to get aid for a crewman likewise injured (this time on the ship's deck) while the boat was rounding Cape Horn. The Supreme Court affirmed the finding that the master should have taken a detour to get aid for the crewman at Valparaiso (in northern Chile). In the *Margharita* it's not quite clear how long the detour would have taken, but it seems to have been similar to that in the *Iroquois*. (The evidence in the *Margharita* was conflicting. The district court opinion had the master saying about 17 days and the crewman saying less than a week. The judge seemed to believe the crewman, but also appeared to indicate that he was inclined to find liability on either view of the facts. The court of appeals, meanwhile, didn't discuss the timing issue in detail. The reference to "three weeks" in the casebook text may be a little misleading, as the court of appeals' opinion does mention 23 days but is ambiguous regarding how much of that time would have been at the expense of the ship's normal journey.)

In any event, the *Margharita* court distinguished the *Iroquois* because in the latter case the seaman ended up having his leg amputated, a result that could have been avoided with more prompt medical attention. In the *Margharita* the court found that treatment at Port Stanley wouldn't have made a difference (except to the pain and suffering the libellant endured). More from Professor Wright:

> [A] failure to put in somewhere along the way seems outrageous, even if countenanced by the Hand formula. Arguably, the circuit court's opinion is wrong even under the Hand formula, unless minimal weight is given (as by the circuit court) to the sailor's intense pain and suffering over so long a period and one implausibly assumes, as the circuit court seems to, that after the first few days no medical treatment would have benefited the sailor, apart from avoiding prolongation of his (intense) pain and suffering. But then, no one knows how to put numbers to the Hand formula, right?

Davis v. Consolidated Rail Corp. (problem)

Excerpts are given below from Judge Posner's opinion and from Richard Wright's critique of it. To summarize Posner's application of the Hand formula to these facts, Lundy's failure to radio the train crew may have involved a small burden, but also might have reduced the risk by just a trivial amount. In most cases in which the radio call would be made, it would turn out to be a wild goose chase. And perhaps B is high after all if you assume that Lundy would have to make calls every time someone was seen near the tracks. The second untaken precaution also flunks Hand's test, since it would be very burdensome to look under the train every time it was moved; this precaution also might fail to reduce P substantially, because the train was so long that by the time someone had looked under every car, someone else might have slipped under the first car that had been checked. The third untaken precaution was the winner for the plaintiff, because it would have been cheap for the train crew to have blown the horn before the train was moved, and this precaution would have reduced multiple risks. People in front of the train and those leaning on it would have opportunities to get out of the way, along with people like the plaintiff who were working underneath it. Davis's failure to heed the blue flag rule does not necessarily excuse the railroad's negligence (if negligence it was); the railroad is entitled to assume that others will use due care, but not that others will exercise such care perfectly.

Wright, by contrast, views the case as more plausibly explained by a principle of liability for defendants whose behavior subjects the plaintiff to substantial foreseeable risks.

One can ask what sort of advice a lawyer can give to a railroad client based on the actual result in *Davis*: does the case mean a railroad is liable every time a plaintiff is injured by a train if the crew didn't blow the horn before it was moved? No; and this is a good time to straighten out the significance of the procedural posture in cases where a court affirms a jury verdict. The court says that a judgment that it was negligent not to blow the horn was not crazy, but also makes clear that no such finding was *required*. The precise thing to tell a client is that in a case like this where the plaintiff's evidence is that the horn was not blown, it will not be possible to keep the case away from a jury (e.g., via summary judgment).

a. From *Davis v. Consolidated Rail*, 788 F.2d 1260 (7th Cir. 1986):

> On the question of Conrail's negligence, Davis presented three theories to the jury. The first was that Conrail's employee Lundy, whose auto was equipped with a two-way radio, should have notified the crew of the train that an unknown person was sitting in a van parked near the tracks. We consider this a rather absurd suggestion. Lundy had no reason to think that the man in the

van would climb out and crawl under a railroad car. If he had called the crew and told them there was a man in a van by the tracks, they undoubtedly would have replied, so what? [...]

In the famous negligence formula of Judge Learned Hand, which is recognized to encapsulate the more conventional verbal formulations of the negligence standard, a defendant is negligent only if $B < PL$, meaning, only if the burden of precautions is less than the magnitude of the loss if an accident that the precautions would have prevented occurs discounted (multiplied) by the probability of the accident. If P is very low, elaborate precautions are unlikely to be required even if L is large, and here the necessary precautions would have been elaborate.

Davis's second theory of Conrail's negligence is even more fantastic. It is that before the train was moved a member of the crew should have walked its length, looking under the cars. The probability that someone was under a car was too slight, as it reasonably would have appeared to the crew, to warrant the considerable delay in moving the train that would have been caused by having a crew member walk its entire length and then walk back, a total distance of a mile and a half. It might have taken an hour, since the crew member would have had to look under each one of the train's 50 cars, and since the cars were only 12 inches off the ground, so that he would have had to get down on all fours to see under them.

Davis's third theory is more plausible. He argues that it was negligent for the crew to move the train without first blowing its horn (also referred to as the whistle) or ringing its bell. Since no member of the crew was in a position where he could see the train's western end, which was now its rear end, a reasonable jury could find—we do not say we would have found if we had been the triers of fact—that it was imprudent to move the train without a signal in advance. Although the crew had no reason to think that Davis was under a car, someone—whether an employee of Conrail or some other business invitee to the yard (such as Davis)—might have been standing in or on a car or between cars, for purposes of making repairs or conducting an inspection; and any such person could be severely, even fatally, injured if the train pulled away without any warning or even just moved a few feet. Regarding the application of the Hand formula to such a theory of negligence, not only was B vanishingly small—for what would it cost to blow the train's horn?—but P was significant, though not large, once all the possible accidents that blowing the horn would have averted are added together. For in determining the benefits of a precaution—and PL, the expected accident costs that the precaution would avert, is a measure of the benefits of the precaution—the trier of fact must consider not only the expected cost of this accident but also the expected cost of any other, similar accidents that the precaution would have prevented. Blowing the horn would have saved not only an inspector who had crawled under the car (low P), but also an inspector leaning on a car, a railroad employee doing repairs on the top of a car, a brakeman straddling two cars, and anyone else who might have business in or on (as well as under) a car. The train was three-quarters of a mile long. It was not so unlikely that somewhere in that stretch a person was in a position of potential peril to excuse the crew from taking the inexpensive precaution of blowing the train's horn. Or so at least the jury could conclude without taking leave of its senses.

The defendants' strongest argument is that Conrail had no duty to warn persons who might be in or on or under the train—given the blue flag rule. There is in general no duty to anticipate and take precautions against the negligence of another person. Such a requirement would tend to induce potential injurers to take excessive safety precautions relative to those taken by potential victims; the cost of safety would rise. Thus, "If the motorist on the through highway had to travel at such a speed that he could stop his car in time to avoid collisions with vehicles which ignore stop signs on intersecting roads, the purpose of having a through highway in the first place would be entirely thwarted." *Hession v. Liberty Asphalt Products, Inc.*, 380 N.E.2d 17, 22 (Ill. 1968). It is true that if precautions necessary to prevent an undue risk of injury to persons who are exercising due care are omitted and a careless person is injured as a result, then in a jurisdiction such as Illinois where the complete defense of contributory negligence has given way to the partial defense of comparative negligence the careless victim can recover some damages. But he can do so, in general, only if there was a breach of duty to the careful.

The defendants argue that the rule regarding blue flagging excuses the crew from any duty of care to persons who might be injured by a sudden starting of the train, because all such persons can protect themselves by blue flagging and are careless if they fail to do so. There is some evidence, however, that the rule was honored in the breach. Davis inspected cars at the yard three or four times a week, never posted or requested the posting of a blue flag, and was seen by many employees of Conrail without remonstrance from them. Maybe all these people were careless but maybe the rule of blue flagging is not so universal as the defendants claim. Common sense tells us that there must be times when there are no blue flags handy; and if the railroad thought it could prove that the rule of blue flagging was so steadily observed (though not in this instance) that the probability that someone, not careless, would be working on or in or under a train that had not been blue flagged was so small as to excuse the crew from a duty to sound any warning signal before moving the train, it should have put in evidence to this effect—evidence, for example, of where the flags are stacked. [...]

[W]e were careful to qualify our statement of the rule that a potential injurer is entitled to assume that potential victims will exercise due care, by saying that this was true "in general." A certain amount of negligence is unavoidable, because the standard of care is set with reference to the average person and some people have below-average ability to take care and so can't comply with the standard, and because in any event efforts at being careful produce only a probability, not a certainty, of avoiding careless conduct through momentary inattention. Potential injurers may therefore be required to take some care for the protection of the negligent, especially when the probability of negligence is high or the costs of care very low. You cannot close your eyes while driving through an intersection, merely because you have a green light. If, as the jury could have found, Conrail could have avoided this accident by the essentially costless step of blowing the train's horn, it may have been duty-bound to do so even if only a careless person would have been endangered by a sudden movement of the train. [...]

b. From the same article of Wright's that is excerpted in the text:

Davis alleged three distinct instances of negligent conduct by the railroad. The first instance was the failure of one of the railroad's employees—who had seen Davis sitting in his van near the train as or shortly after the train pulled into the yard and, not recognizing him, had thought it was queer that he was there—to use the two-way radio in his auto to notify the second locomotive's train crew that an unknown person had been seen sitting in a van parked near the train. Posner dismissed this alleged negligence as "a rather absurd suggestion. [The railroad employee] had no reason to think that the man in the van would climb out and crawl under a railroad car." This might be a plausible finding that, as a matter of law, the railroad's employee had no reason to foresee any risk to Davis. Posner, however, sought to explain this holding as an application of the Hand formula: "If P is very low, elaborate precautions are unlikely to be required even if L is large; and here the necessary precautions would have been elaborate." This reference to the Hand formula is superfluous and implausible. The precaution of using the two-way radio to notify the second locomotive's crew (or the yard dispatcher) of an unknown person sitting in a van by the train would hardly have been "elaborate" or burdensome. If there had been any foreseeable possibility, no matter how slight, that Davis might crawl under or between the train cars, the great magnitude of the potential injury (L) surely would have required taking this minimal precaution to protect him, since he was a business invitee on the railroad's property.

The second instance of alleged negligence, which Posner described as "even more fantastic," was the failure of one of the second locomotive's crew-members to walk the train's entire length and look under each car prior to moving the train. Posner stated:

> The probability that someone was under a car was too slight, as it reasonably would have appeared to the crew, to warrant the considerable delay in moving the train that would have been caused by having a crew member walk its entire length [checking under each car] and then walk back, a total distance of a mile and a half.

This holding seems correct, for reasons independent of the Hand formula. Even if it were foreseeable that someone might be under one of the train's cars, the probability was remote, and even under the justice-based theory of liability, a person is not required to take burdensome precautions against insignificant foreseeable risks. Moreover, the proposed precaution would do little to reduce the remote risk: during the extended time required to check under every car of the long train, a person could have climbed under or between previously checked cars. On the other hand, if there were a significant foreseeable risk that an invitee might be under or between the cars, and no less burdensome and equally effective precaution were available, the railroad might well be required to undertake the car-by-car inspection, even if the burden of doing so might be thought, quantitatively or otherwise, to be greater than the foreseeable risk.

The third instance of negligence alleged by Davis was the failure of the second locomotive's train crew to blow the train's horn or ring its bell prior to moving the train. Posner held that the jury could reasonably find that the failure to take this minimal precaution had been negligent, given the foreseeable, albeit perhaps not significant, risk that some railroad employee or business invitee such as Davis might be working on, under, or near the three-quarter-mile-long train, the end of which was not visible to any of the crew: "It was not so unlikely that somewhere in that stretch a person was in a position of potential peril to excuse the crew from taking the inexpensive precaution of blowing the train's horn. Or so at least the jury could conclude without taking leave of its senses." However, Posner stated that "we do not say we would have found [the railroad negligent] if we had been the triers of fact." Given the admittedly foreseeable (albeit remote) risk, the great magnitude of the potential harm, and the extremely minimal burden of precaution, Posner's inability to draw a definite conclusion while supposedly applying the Hand formula demonstrates, once again, that the Hand formula is, at best, merely window-dressing for conclusions reached on independent grounds.

The Malibu litigation (*Anderson v. General Motors Corp.*) and the Ford Pinto case (*Grimshaw v. Ford Motor Co.*), etc.

The discussion of this issue generally propels itself. If you are going to discuss the famous case of the Ford Pinto, though, here are some interesting factual notes on it from Gary Schwartz, *The Myth of the Ford Pinto Case*, 43 Rutgers L. Rev. 1013 (1991):

> I have suggested that the Ford Pinto case is mythical in the sense that several misconceptions burden the public's understanding of the case. What, then, are those misconceptions? One of them—indeed, a set of misconceptions—concerns the significance of what has become a much-publicized Ford report. In pre-trial discovery in *Grimshaw*, the plaintiffs secured from Ford what Stuart Speiser calls "possibly the most remarkable document ever produced in an American

lawsuit." In this report, Ford compared the "costs and benefits" of reducing the chances of certain fuel-tank fires. The safety device considered by the document would have cost $11 per vehicle; multiplied by 12.5 million vehicles, the total cost would thus have been $137 million. According to the document, the added safety provided by the device would have resulted in the avoidance of 180 deaths and another 180 serious burn injuries. Setting $200,000 as the value of life and $67,000 as the value of injury avoidance, the document calculated the total safety benefit at $49.5 million, much less than its $137 million cost.

As described by Speiser, this document specifically dealt with the problem of fuel tank integrity in the event of rear-end impact, and hence was quite relevant to the accident in *Grimshaw*. The description is, however, inaccurate. When the document was prepared, NHTSA was considering a combination of regulations that related to the problem of fuel-system fires. One of these proposed regulations concerned the rear-end-impact problem; another such regulation related to lateral collisions; yet another proposal concerned the problem of fuel leakage in the event of a vehicle rollover. It was the rollover situation, and not the rear-end-impact situation, that was the subject of the Ford document. To be sure, the document added the thought that "analyses of other portions of the proposed regulation would also be expected to yield poor benefit-to-cost ratios." Given, however, the document's focus on rollover, the *Grimshaw* plaintiffs did not even claim that the document was relevant to the issue of liability; rather, they attempted to introduce it on the issue of punitive damages, as indicative of Ford's corporate mentality. After considering the matter over a period of several weeks, the trial judge ruled against admissibility.

A second common understanding of the Ford document is that it put on display Ford's consideration of its tort liability; the document is said to show Ford officials internally reaching the conclusion that it would be less expensive to absorb the cost of tort judgments than to incorporate safety modifications into the Pinto. Yet, as suggested above, this document was not prepared with tort liability in mind, but rather for purposes of submission to NHTSA. Specifically, this Ford report was part of a petition that Ford filed in September 1973, urging NHTSA to reconsider the rollover portion of its recently promulgated standard. Contrary to the common understanding, the report was not really "about" the Pinto. Its calculations—12.5 million vehicles, 180 deaths—referred not to Pintos, but rather to all cars (as well as light trucks) sold by manufacturers in America in a typical year; the $137 million figure concerned the annual cost to be borne not by Ford alone, but by the entire auto industry.

An additional point frequently heard about the Ford report is that its $200,000 life-valuation figure was so deplorably low as to justify our condemnation of Ford. The NHTSA context of the report, however, helps show why this point is somewhat unfair: $200,000 is the value-of-life that NHTSA itself had developed in a 1972 study calculating the social cost of motor-vehicle accidents. Indeed, a 1972 article by William Greider reported that $200,000 was the life-value figure upon which NHTSA was then relying in setting vehicle standards. That article identified a proposed standard, relating to rear under-ride bumpers on trucks, that NHTSA "killed" because the monitorized safety benefits of the proposed regulation were significantly lower than its associated costs.

What I had learned from the Greider article was in harmony with what I knew of the 1966 Motor Vehicle Safety Act. Accordingly, in last summer's discussions I expressed the view that Ford's invocation of the $200,000 figure in its presentation to NHTSA was clearly proper, since it employed the same datum that NHTSA would be utilizing in deciding whether to promulgate the standard. Having now done further homework, however, I find that the Greider article does not quite have its story right. While NHTSA has long accepted the idea that it must give serious consideration to costs, the agency has always resisted the notion that it must employ anything resembling a formal cost-benefit analysis; and it has definitely rejected the claim that, in issuing standards, it should place an explicit value on life and serious injury. In interpreting its obligations under the Act, NHTSA has taken the position that while it should gather and consider all information relevant to the safety benefits and the likely costs of a proposed standard, the decision whether to adopt a standard is then a judgment call on the part of the NHTSA Administrator. In the early 1970's, NHTSA did indefinitely table the rear under-ride guard truck proposal on grounds that compliance costs would plainly be disproportionate to safety benefits. Nevertheless, this was an exercise of judgment rather than an arithmetic calculation; and the NHTSA Administrator reached this decision only after agonizing with an associate as to what a proper result would be.

Contrary, then, to my earlier understanding, in its standard-setting NHTSA was not, in the early 1970's, relying on a $200,000 life-value figure. In setting standards, however, NHTSA was indeed taking both monetary costs and safety benefits into account; in doing so, the agency was essentially finessing the question of the monetary value of life, while at the same time releasing documents that set forth a $200,000 life-value datum. Given these circumstances, it is proper to conclude that Ford's utilization of this figure in its submission to NHTSA was not deplorable, but was within the range of expected and acceptable advocacy.

SECTION C. CUSTOM AND THE PROBLEM OF MEDICAL MALPRACTICE

The first chunk of these materials discusses the use of custom to set standards of care generally. The second part focuses on the use of customs in cases of medical and other professional malpractice. If you want to abbreviate the coverage, we suggest skipping *Ellis v. Louisville & Nashville Ry.*, *MacDougall v. Pennsylvania Power and Light Co.*, and *Gambill v. Stroud*.

The T.J. Hooper (L for not having radios on tugs)
Ellis v. Louisville & Nashville Ry. (NL for not giving worker a mask)
MacDougall v. Pennsylvania Power & Light Co. (L for customary but negligent placement of dangerous fuse box)

Q. How would the Hand formula apply to *The T.J. Hooper*?
A. It's a case where the Hand formula seems to be in tension with custom. The cost of radios (B) had become low (this is a good occasion on which to review the point that B can change with time, so that precautions that the law did not require at one point becomes mandatory as technology becomes cheaper), and the *reduction* they could cause in PL made them seem plainly cost-justified.

Q. What risks would have been reduced by the untaken precaution of having a working radio on board the tug?
A. The tug, the crew, the barge, and its cargo all would have been safer. Again, here is a chance to review another point about the use of the Hand formula: courts may (as in *Davis v. Consolidated Rail Corp.*) look at all of the risks that would have been reduced by the untaken precaution, and not just the reduced risk of the bad thing that happened here.

Q. The *T.J. Hooper* is the leading case for the proposition that adherence to a custom is not a complete defense to a negligence claim. But why not? What does a custom consist of?
A. It depends on the custom, of course. Sometimes the custom may be out of whack with the Hand formula or other norms in the community; sometimes it may impose costs on parties who can't very well respond. In other cases, particularly where parties are coordinating their activities and precautions,

customs may be welfare-maximizing. This section seeks in part to consider which cases fit each of these descriptions. The main doctrinal point to understand about the role of custom in tort law is that it is evidence, not proof and not a definition of the standard of care—except in medical cases, where it does set the standard. But you can also have a nice discussion of where customs come from, who they might be expected to benefit, and why anyone would prefer them to a simple cost-benefit analysis. If we were sure such that a cost-benefit analysis analysis could be done perfectly in every case, there might indeed be no argument—at least from an economic perspective—for bothering with custom. The problem is that a good cost-benefit analysis is often very hard for the trier of fact to conduct, and it's also hard for jurors to figure out what "reasonableness" means in an unfamiliar environment. In some situations customs may represent efficient efforts by the parties to them to come up with practices that maximize their joint welfare; it may be hard for a jury to improve on them.

A first reason for nevertheless objecting to attempts to give conclusive weight to custom is the one given in the *T.J. Hooper*: "a whole calling may have unduly lagged in the adoption of new and available devices"; an industry may decide it is better off with a custom that is cheap for its members to observe but creates high costs for others. A second and related objection is that turning custom into a complete defense might give industries and other potential defendants an incentive to stick with customary precautions even after they have been shown to be deficient; any effort to experiment with an idea that looks better becomes risky, since the actor then loses the shield furnished by sticking within the custom. A final objection is that customs tend to be rules of thumb that are too tenuous to support a judgment in litigation. Thus Restatement (Second) of Torts sec. 295A, illustration 1:

> It is the usual custom of railroads to couple cars by bumping them together. On a day when the tops of the cars are covered with ice, and brakemen are required to stand on top of them, the A Railroad follows this custom. When the cars are bumped B, a brakeman, loses his footing on top of one of the cars, falls off, and is injured. A Railroad may be found to be negligent toward B.

As we shall see, some of these objections may lose some force when the parties are in contractual or other sorts of consensual relations with each other.

Notice that custom can have two sorts of significance: it can serve as a sword used by a plaintiff who argues that the defendant should be held liable because it did not adhere to customary standards of care; and it can serve as a shield used by a defendant who argues that it should not be held liable because it did adhere to a customary standard of care. The *T.J. Hooper* was the second sort of case, and as a practical matter appeals to custom tend to be given less force in this setting than they do in the first scenario. But the force given or not given to custom usually is a matter for the trier of fact to decide.

Richard A. Epstein, *The Path to the T.J. Hooper: The Theory and History of Custom in the Law of Tort*, 21 J. Leg. Stud. 1 (1992), contains a number of provocative views on where customs come from and why they should be valued in consensual settings. He also has some interesting views on the *T.J. Hooper* itself:

> Even the most casual armchair empiricism, whether of the 1920s or today, would lead anyone to conclude that radios are an unmixed blessing for ocean transport. [...] If the world were as Hand described it—one in which no custom had emerged on the use of radios—there is powerful, if not conclusive, evidence of a gap between common practice and due care that it was imperative for the law to bridge.

> Te difficulty with Hand's decision is the factual premise on which it rests. The imperative need for radio communication was apparent to outsiders to the business. [...] That radio sets were in widespread use on vessels of all kinds is clearly indicated by the testimony in this case. [...] The testimony further indicated that at least 90 percent of the tugs in the defendant's company and others along the coast relied on the receiving sets. [...] Given the state of the record and the findings of the district court, why did Hand strike out so boldly with his attack on custom? The

best guess for his behavior rests on a combination of three factors. First, his decision did not reverse but rather affirmed the decision down below. Under those circumstances, it matters less that Hand took a somewhat different view of the facts than did the trial judge. [...] Second, it seems clear that Hand harbored some doubts about the nature of the custom in the case. In his bench memo, he expressed much uneasiness about the question of *who* was charged with the duty to carry the radio on board. Was it the tug-owner, or could it have been delegated to the master of the tug? Third, Hand did believe that the overall cost-benefit calculations yielded a simple and clear result that avoided all the complications of delegated responsibilities otherwise raised in the case.

Epstein then quotes from Hand's bench memo:

> I should be disposed to say that regardless of custom we might hold [radios] a reasonable necessity. To do so would certainly not be an innovation. Concededly, the Southern Transp. Co. had installed them. Apparently the other lines rely upon their masters', who have them partly for amusement, partly for safety. We can hardly say that these other lines have charged themselves with radios as part of their equipment; but it is fair on the other hand to suppose that they do rely upon them, as on their masters' binoculars. Should we say that if they do, they are responsible for their fitness? The custom hardly goes that far; apparently they are hal[f] a toy, half an equipment. On the whole I doubt we should say that the custom extends to more than that. If so, it would be a little extreme to say that there is any custom that tugs should carry proper radios.

Epstein goes on to make a provocative condemnation of the influence the *T.J. Hooper* had on products liability law, where litigation over design defects

> became big business once custom was no longer the standard by which the safety or defectiveness of products was judged. It became possible to challenge an entire industry whose custom "lagged" behind what reasonable prudence dictated, as the famous quotation from the *T.J. Hooper* is trotted out at critical junctures to justify the movement away from any market-based standard of liability. Assumption of risk is no longer an absolute defense against charges of liability unless it is unreasonable, and it thus becomes a species of contributory negligence. Liability is not restricted to latent defects, where there is a colorable claim tha the condition of the product was misrepresented by the manufacturer to the consumer. Common practice is never an absolute defense but is admissible as evidence on the state of the art.

> The overall pattern is clear. The successive layers of protection against government intervension are thus pierced one at a atime, so that in the end it is possible to attach liability to known defects sanctioned both by common practice and individualized assumption of the risk. With all the limitations on liability put to one side, there was but one technique by which such a development could take place: the cost benefit of the Hand formula in *Carroll Towing*, championed by both Landes and Posner and by Shavell, ironically becomes the "risk/utility" test of Wade that has received such prominence in the decided cases. The rhetoric of Hand has fit in perfectly with the antimarket rationales that dominate this area of thought, so that *The T.J. Hooper* has its greatest influence and vitality in an area that lies far removed from the admiralty controversy that gave it birth. [...] It is always open season on an established practice, as the cost-benefit approach can be used, without rudder or compass, to override the established custom: "[A] who calling may have unduly lagged in the adoption of new and available devices." There are many competitors for this questionable honor, but Hand's famous bon mot is perhaps the most influential, and mischievous, sentence in the history of the law of torts.

Q. Is the *Ellis* case inconsistent with *The T.J. Hooper*, or are the cases distinguishable?

A. The positions the courts take may be less different than they appear. Both courts seem to agree that custom ordinarily may be probative of what care reasonableness requires. The cases might be distinguished on the ground that in the *Hooper* case at least *some* tug lines had started using the precaution that the libelant said should have been used by the defendant. The famous language from *Hooper* does not suggest that this point is decisive, but Hand seems to give it some weight. It may also be that the Hand formula just did not suggest an outcome as clearly in *Ellis* as it did in *The T.J. Hooper*. The language the court recites in *Ellis* refers to cases where "a common practice has existed for years without resulting in an injury, and that has nothing about it which shows a want of due care." That description may well have fit the facts of *Ellis* better than the facts of *The T.J. Hooper*: the B in *Ellis* of providing a mask seems pretty low (cf. *Paris,* the goggles case), but the foreseeable prevention of harm they would achieve might have seemed slight as well.

Q. Is there a satisfactory distinction between *Ellis* and *MacDougall*?
A. *MacDougall*, like the *T.J. Hooper*, might be considered a case where the Hand formula cut pretty decisively against the custom. The court says that "vigilance must always be commensurate with danger," and says that custom only is important where the conduct involved is not "inherently dangerous." This might be understood as a way of saying that where P and L are very high, the required B may well be set high regardless of custom. The danger of setting out a fuse box that conducted high voltage where unsuspecting people could bump into it was evident. The court says that common sense therefore requires either safer placement of the box or warnings for the unwary. In *Ellis*, as noted a moment ago, apparently the PL that was seen to result from not providing masks, or perhaps the reduction in PL thought to be achieved by masks, did not clearly justify the precaution.

An additional point is that in *Ellis* the parties had a contract (employer and employee), which might be thought to represent acquiescence to whatever precautions were considered customary unless the contract stated otherwise. In *MacDougall* there was no contract, so if the defendant was taking too few precautions there was no way for the plaintiff, and others similarly situated, to retaliate with market sanctions or increased contract demands. Posner's opinion in *Rodi Yachts* (and similar academic writing elsewhere) argues that this sort of analysis is a key to understanding the weight that customs ought to be given, though of course the courts in *Ellis* and *MacDougall* do not discuss the point.

Q. Is there a satisfactory distinction between *The T.J. Hooper* and *Rodi Yachts*?
A. Perhaps not. Posner has suggested elsewhere that *The T.J. Hooper* may indeed have been wrongly decided on its facts. The parties had a contract. If radios were a cost-effective way of preventing damage to barges, presumably it would be in the interest of the tug company to use them or the barge company to demand them. To turn the point around, the barge owners were compensated *ex ante* for the lack of radios on the tugs; they paid less for the tug services than they would have had to pay if the tugs had been equipped with radios. Are there respects in which these facts might suggest market failure? Perhaps the tort sanction still might be useful in cases where contracting parties have trouble enforcing the precautions the Hand formula seems to require because one of the parties might shirk without the other being aware of it.

The hypotheticals after the *Rodi Yachts* case are intended to make the contractual logic clearer. If a railroad steams through an intersection without blowing its horn and therefore causes damage, the people injured cannot retaliate in the market by ending their contract with the railroad; by hypothesis they have no such contract. And if the railroad is considering adopting safety precautions (installing gates and flashing lights might be a better example here than blowing a horn, which is cheap—see *Davis*), it knows it cannot pass on the costs to the people in the town the precaution will benefit. So the railroad will not have good market incentives to bother with the precaution, even though it would create more benefits than costs. The resulting custom may therefore be inefficient or otherwise undesirable. Against this is a possible argument that the railroad's customers would want to reward the railroad for blowing its horn, because blowing the horn cuts down on delays caused by accidents. One can also imagine a town responding to the railroad's custom by installing flashing lights and gates of its own—which might be a more expensive solution to the problem than just blowing the train's horn. Perhaps the towns affected could offer to pay the railroad to adopt a practice of blowing its trains horns; but this suggestion then raises other sources of high transaction costs, including the costs of coordinating the various parties benefited by such a deal and the costs of monitoring the resulting agreements.

Where the storage of baggage on trains is concerned, the market would seem able to operate better. If customers want safer ways to store their bags, some railroad will be able to gain an edge—temporarily—by being the first to offer them. Railroads that do offer them can charge more to the people benefited by the precaution. The resulting custom does not impose external costs on anyone, so perhaps it should be given more weight. Naturally the defendants in both hypos may have general reputational worries, too, apart from the fear of losing contracts; the economic account stylizes this point away for comparison's sake. The point is just that in the contractual setting there is at least some additional pressure to make the custom efficient, because all the parties affected by it (by assumption) are "at the table" in a sense, and being represented when the custom is made.

There is a comeback to the economic argument: when the risk of injury seems small, it may not pay consumers to incur additional the search costs needed to find the seller offering the most safety. But then there are comebacks to the comeback—more reasons to wonder whether it makes sense to use the courts to enforce technological progress by requiring more of industries than custom already does. First, judicial standards of care may be more inflexible and general than people want. In the context of *The T.J. Hooper*, for instance, it is conceivable that some shippers wanted state-of-the-art tugs and were willing to pay for them, while others would have preferred less fancy tugboats and lower rates. Hand's rule may have made it more difficult (or at least more *cumbersome* as a matter of contract) for the industry to serve customers with different preferences. Second, imposing liability for failure to adopt a new technology increases the insurance component of the liability for negligence. If radios are required, occasionally they will be out of order because of "efficient compliance errors"—cases where radios fail not because anyone was negligent but because due care does not guarantee perfectly working radios all the time. There nevertheless will be liability in these cases, and the defendant then becomes an insurer. Sellers will charge consumers for this insurance, and the insurance is income-regressive: when accidents occur, rich people collect more for lost wages than poor people do. The poor will end up subsidizing the rich unless sellers are able to charge the poor less. This concern may be more important in the medical malpractice area than in the maritime industry where sellers can easily charge a higher premium to those with valuable freight.

Brune v. Belinkoff (rejects locality rule for medical malpractice cases)
Gambill v. Stroud (NL for D doctor who met standards set in localities "similar" to his own)
Johnson v. Wills Memorial Hospital & Nursing Home (NL for facilities that satisfy locality rule)
Cook v. Irion (NL; applies locality rule to legal malpractice)

Q. Among other things, *Brune* reiterates the general background point that the standard of care in medical malpractice cases is defined by reference to custom. Why? What is the distinction between this case and, say, *MacDougall v. Pennsylvania Power & Light Co.*, which rejects the use of custom to set the standard of care?
A. There are a couple of ways to understand the use of custom in cases involving medical or other professional malpractice. One is the rationale already considered: the parties have a contract; they presumably are contracting for the customary level of care unless they say otherwise. But the more usual explanation involves the problem of expertise. Courts generally will have difficulty acquiring the competence to judge medical decisions under the Hand formula or against freestanding norms of reasonableness; evidence of custom, provided by expert witnesses, is used as a substitute for an independent inquiry that would be prohibitively expensive.

Q. The other point of *Brune v. Belinkoff* is that it rejects the locality rule; the relevant custom is a national one. Why?

A. In its heyday the locality rule required a plaintiff to get a local medical expert to opine that the untaken precaution was dictated by medical custom in the particular geographic area where the alleged malpractice took place; it was thought that only a local expert would know the relevant customs and practices. The rule thus placed a particular burden on small-town plaintiffs who would have few possible experts from which to choose; many of the possible experts may be reluctant to testify against other doctors in the area either out of fear of reciprocation or out of fear of violating norms of camaraderie in their small professional circle.

In support of the locality rule, it might be argued that doctors compete to be able to practice in markets where the level of wealth is high enough to support a high standard of care; one way that large, wealthy markets drive up the standard of care is by making specialization feasible. It therefore may seem unrealistic to impose the same standard of care on country doctors even if their nonhuman capital resources are equal to those of city doctors. But courts abandoning the locality rule have been impressed by the rise of national standards in medical education and board certification.

Gambill v. Stroud offers an interesting intermediate solution to the problem: a type of locality rule that sets the standard of care by reference not to the defendant's particular locality but to localities that are similar. This makes it easy enough for plaintiffs to find experts who are qualified to testify without being members of the defendant's own community; and if national standards really are so pervasive, then the experts who testify in the case can say so and the jury can hold the rural practitioner to the same standards as the urban doctor after all. But of course this approach creates a new variable for the parties to argue about: what counts as a similar locale? As for the benefits and burdens of the approach, they are hard to identify with confidence. Holding rural doctors to lower standards than urban doctors keeps down the rural doctors' costs, and so may make their services more accessible to more patients; on the other hand, it also may remove a valuable incentive for the rural doctors to keep up with their urban colleagues and therefore cause some of those patients to get hurt. How these consequences can be expected to shake out will depend on part on the magnitude one expects each of those effects to have, which is an empirical question with no clear answer.

Q. What is the basis for the distinction the court in *Johnson* draws between medical care and medical facilities?

A. The most appealing answer is that the quality of a hospital's facilities, more than the knowledge of its doctors, seems likely to be a function of the community's wealth. Doctors come from medical schools and take tests that are geared toward national standards, and the cost to them of keeping up with those standards increasingly is thought to be small as the technology for transmitting new knowledge gets cheaper and more effective. Perhaps there are no comparable innovations to support a view that the equipment at a rural hospital will be just as good as the equipment in an urban hospital.

That account seems plausible, but then one must ask about its fit to the *Johnson* case. Challenge the students to figure out what the plaintiff's precise claims must have looked like and to consider how they intersect with the logic sketched above. The plaintiff's claim wasn't that the hospital lacked a fancy gizmo (or even heavy-duty unbreakable windows) that would have helped save the decedent, nor was the problem of expensive technology quite the basis for the court's decision. Rather, the court's claim was that "The protection of patients is not a medical function of a hospital; rather, it is a service provided by a hospital to its patients, and the ability of a small rural hospital to provide such a service is limited by its location and resources." So in this case it apparently might have turned out that the defendant's negligence was found in the incompetence of its orderlies—human error, not a failure of technology—and that this failure still was judged under a locality rule. What sense does this make? Suppose the plaintiff had been burned by coffee negligently spilled on him by a waitress in the hospital's cafeteria (or by a nurse trying to be helpful in the recovery room). Serving coffee is not part of a hospital's "medical function," but we wouldn't judge the negligence of the coffee spill according to a locality rule. So why is the conduct of the orderlies in *Johnson* arguably different?

Maybe the idea is that protecting patients is a function of expense after all. True, bad judgment by the orderly may have contributed to the outcome in *Johnson* (he should have checked on the patient more often), but in the end it's the hospital that is being threatened with liability here. And an adequate institutional response by the hospital if it is found liable in this sort of situation may not just be to tell the orderly to check on the patient more often; it may be to hire more orderlies or guards or to spend more on the training of them. But this is an expense-driven issue much like the decision to buy fancy gizmos; urban hospitals may be able to afford more patient-protecting personnel than rural facilities. Well, at leat that's the best face we can put on it; some of the plaintiff's grounds for complaint do seem to us to have little to do with expensive staffing or training decisions, and therefore to provide little basis for use of a locality rule. The only consolation is the self-correcting point offered by the court in *Gambill*: if the meaning of "reasonableness" in measuring an orderly's behavior has nothing much to do with where the hospital was located, then there won't be much difference between using the locality rule and a national rule, and it didn't really matter which approach the court used.

Q.   But this still leaves the second question posed in the text: why are we worried about custom at all when assessing the plaintiff's claims in *Johnson*?

A.   This is a hard question; we think it's not at all clear that custom should be given such weight as the court assigns it. The reasons for using custom as the standard in medical cases involve, as noted before, the inability of the usual jury or trial judge to understand medical controversies well enough to say how they should be resolved. But if a hospital isn't acting in its medical capacity (as the court says—see previous question), why give custom any more weight here than we would in judging the alleged negligence of a school's assistant principal in protecting his charges against self-destructive behavior? In other words, why not just stick to the usual standard of reasonable care and let the defendant introduce evidence of custom without instructing the jury to make it decisive? The best answer probably is the thought that training and staffing decisions within a hospital, even if not involving medical matters, are too complex for a jury to be likely to understand; the flip side of the point is that allowing juries to pass judgment on those issues is likely to force hospitals into screwy allocations of their limited resources (or else turn them into insurers). But this argument seems about equally available in other complex institutional settings—schools, prisons, and police departments, for example. We don't use locality rules to judge behavior in those settings (though we sometimes have other doctrines—such as immunities or limited duty rules—that seem to give effect to similar reservations about whether juries in tort cases can be expected to improve those institutions' performance).

Q.   Is the rationale for relying on custom as strong in cases of legal malpractice as it is in cases involving medical malpractice?

A.   Perhaps not—but it may well be plenty strong nevertheless. Medical treatment decisions often involve assessments of risks and benefits that a jury would be entirely unable to conduct for itself without guidance from a professional stating how most doctors would balance them. Disputes over a lawyer's alleged slip-ups are more likely to be explainable to a jury in a period of hours or days. The law of civil procedure is complicated, for cxamplc, but not quitc as complicated as open heart surgery. But even if arguments about strategic decisions such as those made in *Cook* do not require huge amounts of technical knowledge, they may nevertheless depend on subtle judgments of many factors that are hard to accurately convey—both individually and in the relationships of the factors to each other—to a jury. In a close case it may be that only someone with a feel for the enterprise of litigation is really in a position to make an intelligent criticism of the balance the defendant struck. This logic might seem to apply to many professions, but then so does the rule that custom sets the standard: it may be used in may sorts of cases of professional malpractice—in architecture or accounting or engineering. The question the courts often will ask in these cases is whether the conduct at issue is within the jury's competence (or its "experience and knowledge"). If not, expert testimony is required to make the plaintiff's case and the standard of care becomes more likely to be set by reference to custom within the profession. (But then why is it considered within the court's competence to decide what technology should be used to protect barges from bad weather?)

An additional argument for relying on custom is that law, like medicine, is a learned profession in which customs are more reliable than they are in other sorts of businesses. They are set by people who are committed to particular ethical standards, which in turn are policed by professional boards (and those boards sometimes create the customs at issue).

Q. Any particular reason why the relevant locality in legal malpractice actions should be the state?
A. It's (a) because in our legal system, each state gets to make its own laws, which in turn vary a good deal across state lines; and relatedly (b) because lawyers are certified to practice on a state-by-state basis via bar exams. Of course the wisdom of some decisions lawyers make may have nothing to do with state law or with state-sensitive considerations, but those reasons just given are the ones used to justify the general approach most commonly used.

Other uses of custom. The cases in this chapter involve attempts to use custom to define negligence, but of course there are other ways of using customs in tort cases that are worth noting. Morris, *Custom and Negligence*, 42 Colum.L.Rev. 1147 (1942), notes three uses of custom: If an industry adheres to one way of doing something, a court might put a heavier burden on a plaintiff who claims that there's a better way; even if the plaintiff can show a feasible alternative, its rarity suggests that it may have been reasonable for the D to be unaware of it; and the existence of a custom may suggest large transition costs if the defendant is found negligent. Likewise, a plaintiff may use custom to show that some precaution was feasible even if not pervasive. Custom may also be relevant to what the plaintiff reasonably expected the defendant to do, an important point if a case involves questions of contributory negligence.

SECTION D. NEGLIGENCE PER SE

Apart from its doctrinal importance, this section of the chapter (along with the following section on res ipsa loquitur) provides a good occasion for discussing the role of juries in tort litigation. Negligence per se is a doctrine that allows issues that ordinarily would be decided by juries to be taken away from them; res ipsa loquitur is a doctrine that allows issues that normally might be taken away from juries to be sent to them. This is a helpful time to pin down the operation of summary judgment and the distribution of questions to judges and juries in the American civil system, as well as to inquire about the merits of using juries in tort cases generally; most countries, of course, do not (England discontinued them in the 1930s).

If you are looking for material to cut from the section on statutes, we suggest dropping *Tingle v. Chicago B & Q Ry.*, *White v. Levarn*, and *Sparkman v. Maxwell*.

1. Violations of criminal statutes

Cases where a statute provides for civil liability as well as a criminal penalty for its violation usually are simple enough: the courts follow the statutory instructions and find that the violation amounts to negligence as a matter of law. The problems arise in the many cases where the legislation does not spell out its own implications for civil suits. In those situations courts develop default rules and then doctrines that make exceptions to them. The Second Restatement offers this formulation:

§286. When Standard Of Conduct Defined By Legislation Or Regulation Will Be Adopted

The court may adopt as the standard of conduct of a reasonable man the requirements of a legislative enactment or an administrative regulation whose purpose is found to be exclusively or in part

> (a) to protect a class of persons which includes the one whose interest is invaded, and
> (b) to protect the particular interest which is invaded, and
> (c) to protect that interest against the kind of harm which has resulted, and
> (d) to protect that interest against the particular hazard from which the harm results.

Martin v. Herzog (P's decedent had no lights on his buggy; contributory negligence as a matter of law)
Tedla v. Ellman (Ps hit by car when walking in same direction as traffic; statute required them to walk against thr traffic; verdict for Ps affirmed)

Q. What is the superficial similarity between *Martin* and *Tedla*? What is the distinction between them?
A. In both cases the plaintiffs violated statutory requirements regulating behavior on the highways, but only in *Martin* did the violation prevent the plaintiffs from recovering. The cases can be distinguished, first, because the *Tedla* plaintiffs had an excuse for their violation: their actual conduct was safer—and comported better with the Hand formula (by reducing P)—than compliance with the law would have. Second and relatedly, the law in *Tedla* was one that selected one option—walking against the traffic—rather than another option that may in some cases have distinct advantages. The law in *Martin* required behavior—using lights on a buggy—that always will be advantageous; it doesn't involve a generalized trade-off that could come out differently under special circumstances. Third and also relatedly, the law in *Tedla* codified a common law presumption that had been qualified by common law exceptions; the court assumed that the legislature intended to preserve the exceptions. There was no such tradition of exceptions in *Martin*.

Q. What is left of the rule in *Martin* once the court in *Tedla* finishes with it? Has the court replaced the law with a holding that a party should just do whatever is safest?
A. First, it may be worth pointing out that the law in either case still is enforceable through criminal penalties. The question is just whether to *add* civil liability, via a finding of negligence per se, to whatever sanctions the law explicitly provides. Second, the statute in *Tedla* still provides a default rule in negligence cases—a presumption that can be rebutted only if reasonableness (or the Hand formula—however one wants to look at the negligence standard) cuts decisively the other way, and then only if statute that can be understood to resolve a safety trade-off that may change. *Martin* was not such a case, as we have seen.

Tingle v. Chicago B & Q Ry. (D's train runs over P's cow on a Sunday, when statute forbids trains to run; NL)
White v. Levarn (D shoots his hunting companion on a Sunday, when statute forbids hunting; L)
Selger v. Steven Bros. (P slips on dog excrement outside D's store; NL)
Sparkman v. Maxwell (problem: D turns left because she misunderstands the significance of the red arrow light; NL)
Vesely v. Sager (negligence per se for D that served drinks to intoxicated customer; overruled by statute)

Q. Is there an argument that both of these cases were decided incorrectly?
A. The argument would be that in *Tingle,* one can imagine animals being let loose by their owners on Sundays because no trains are expected; in other words, there is possible reliance, so the defendant's violation of the statute made it more likely that an accident of this sort would occur. But possibly the result in *Tingle* can be defended on the ground that the statute's purposes had nothing to do with protecting the plaintiff or preventing the type of harm he suffered. *White* seems less defensible because there appears to have been no possible reliance: the parties headed into the woods together. (The result

of the *White* case would seem more attractive if the defendant had shot a stranger taking a Sunday walk in the woods—perhaps in his squirrel suit—because he thought he would be safe there.) Similarly, it can be argued that the statutory violation made the accident in *Tingle* more likely to occur. The accident in *White* seems equally likely to have occurred whether the parties went hunting on a Sunday or a Monday. (This foreshadows some of the reasoning that is introduced in the chapter on proximate causation: the idea that causation requires a showing that the defendant's negligence increased the likelihood of the harm that occurred.)

In stylizing these cases for purposes of discussion it helps to isolate the statutory theory of negligence as the only basis of the plaintiff's claim: we can assume *White* would have been a case of no liability if it had occurred on a Monday. And we can assume that apart from operating its train on a Sunday, the railroad in *Tingle* was using due care.

Q. What is the difference between the use of the statute in §288B of the Second Restatement and in cases like *Martin v. Herzog*? What is the role of the jury in the two situations?
A. This is basically answered in the note before the *Selger* case: the Restatement allows the statute to be used as evidence when the harm that occurs is outside the scope of the risks the statute was intended to address; in that case liability (including satisfaction of the negligence element of the plaintiff's case) still is a jury question.

Q. What is the distinction between *Selger v. Steven Bros.* and *Martin v. Herzog*?
A. It's important to note that discerning or constructing legislative intent is the key in these cases. The purpose of the ordinance in *Selger*, unlike the law in *Martin*, probably was not to prevent the type of harm that befell the plaintiff; probably the main purpose of the ordinance was to keep sidewalks attractive. But this isn't a complete answer because, as the note in the text says, this case represents the general approach courts take in all cases of this type, including cases involving slips on ice where the purpose of the ordinance unquestionably *does* include prevention the kind of accident that occurred. The point is that these cases can raise more than one sort of issue about legislative intent. First there can be questions about whether the harm that occurred was the sort the law was intended to prevent or whether the plaintiff was among the class of people the law intended to protect. Second, there can be additional questions about legislative intent: whether the legislature would have wanted civil liability given the relationship between the extent of the misconduct involved and the size of the penalty that civil liability would create. In this case (or in a case involving a slip on ice) a $402,050 penalty assessed against the defendant for failing to clear its sidewalks might seem out of proportion to its culpability, to create exaggerated incentives to fuss over the cleanliness of the sidewalk, and to result in unfair outcomes in cases when the defendant had no opportunity to clear the sidewalk before the plaintiff came along. In *Martin v. Herzog* these proportionality concerns aren't pressing in the same ways: asking a buggy driver to maintain working lights on the vehicle is not as onerous as asking a city resident to keep the sidewalk clean at all times, and the result of failing to keep the buggy's lights working more predictably might be a catastrophe—not just a slip and fall, but a collision of heavy, fast-moving (well, *relatively* fast-moving) vehicles.

Q. What possible distinctions are there between the case against the store for violating the sidewalk-cleaning ordinance and a hypothetical case against the dog's owner for violating the pooper-scooper ordinance?
A. Pointing to the evils the laws are meant to address may not help much: as noted above, it may be that the primary purpose of the ordinances in both cases is aesthetic, rather than to prevent slipping accidents, though undoubtedly one purpose of pooper scooper laws is to prevent the risk that unsuspecting pedestrians will feel the repulsive squish underfoot and be left with a frustrating cleaning task. But there is another point as well: whereas most courts find it hard to believe the legislature meant to create civil liability every time someone slips on an "unwholesome" sidewalk, it is a little less startling to suppose that the legislature might have meant to create civil liability for accidents resulting when dog

owners who do not clean up after their dogs. The reason in Hand formula terms is that the B of perfect compliance is very great for the *Selger* defendants: they have to constantly monitor their sidewalk to see whether it has been messed up, and it may get messed up anyway when they leave town or close up shop overnight. A dog owner, on the other hand, can and should be present whenever the dog defecates, making the burden of compliance with the pooper scooper ordinance less severe. So it's easier to imagine the legislature meaning to create civil liability in the one case than in the other. On the other hand, the pooper scooper ordinance set a $20 fine for offenses, which may be the legislature's way of saying that it does not consider an infraction to be high culpable—and in that case we again would have to wonder whether a $400,000 penalty would be a reasonable result.

Q. What result in *Sparkman v. Maxwell*?

A. No liability. Said the court:

> In *Impson v. Structural Metals, Inc.*, we discussed excuses for violating a legislative enactment and approved the general rules found in Restatement, Second, Torts §288A. One of the recognized excuses is that the actor "neither knows nor should know of the occasion for compliance." As pointed out in *Impson*, this category would include cases where a night driver has a tail light go out unexpectedly and without his knowledge. The truck driver in *Impson* attempted to pass to the left of another vehicle within 100 feet of an intersection. He admitted that he was aware of the intersection but sought to excuse the violation by proof that he momentarily forgot about the intersection, which was obscured to some extent by trees or houses, and that the sign warning of its presence was small. It was held that the evidence did not raise an issue of a legally acceptable excuse for the violation but showed simply inattention and errors of judgment.
>
> The present case is quite different. Mrs. Sparkman was confronted with a traffic signal that she had never seen before, one that evidently had never been used in this state. The evidence shows that other motorists were confused by the signal. If Mrs. Sparkman had taken time for deliberation, she might have decided to stop rather than proceed to the intersection. It was not wholly unreasonable under the circumstances, however, for her to move in response to the direction in which the arrow was pointing rather than stop in response to its color. In our opinion there is no material difference between a situation in which a driver is reasonably unaware of an event that gives rise to a duty to act as in *Taber* and the present case where the driver may have been reasonably confused by the traffic signal that triggered her duty to stop. This is not to say that confusion on the part of a driver constitutes a legal excuse, but the evidence here will support the conclusion that Mrs. Sparkman's confusion was caused by an unreasonably confusing traffic signal. It was for the jury to determine whether her conduct was reasonable under the circumstances. Where as here the evidence raises an issue of fact as to a legally acceptable excuse, the burden was on the opposite party, Mrs. Maxwell, to obtain a finding by the jury that Mrs. Sparkman was guilty of negligence by the common law standard. Since the jury refused to find that Mrs. Sparkman was guilty of common law negligence, she is not liable to Mrs. Maxwell.

> Steakley, J., dissented: "Unwittingly or not, as I see it, the majority has in practical effect rendered impotent the doctrine of negligence per se. Perhaps this is well and good; if so, why not abolish the doctrine?"

Q. *Taber v. Smith*, 25 S.W.2d 722 (Tex. App. 1930), cited in the above excerpt from *Sparkman*, makes a nice follow-up hypothetical. The defendant's deliveryman caused an accident with his truck after sundown. State law required the truck to have working lights; the defendant's truck did not. The defendants made the following claims in defense:

that their deliveryman was out delivering clothes before sundown; that he had completed his deliveries in the east end of town before time to turn on his lights; that when said truck left the defendants' place of business, it had been in constant use and was in good running order, and defendants did not know or anticipate that the lighting system was not in good working condition; that the driver of said truck, just prior to the time of the accident, had turned on the ignition switch and found that something had, temporarily, gotten out of order, and that his lights would not burn; that the defendants knew nothing of this condition; that said ignition system had been in good condition prior to that time and they did not know, and could not have known, prior to that time, that the lights were not in good working order.

It is further alleged that the weather conditions were very bad; that it was extremely cold and snowing and sleeting and the streets and roads were covered with snow, sleet, and ice, and that their driver, when he learned of the condition of the lights, stopped at a private residence and telephoned defendants that said car was not working well, that his lights would not burn, and requested that someone come for the car.

They further allege that they had no other car or means of conveyance to send for the truck, and made every effort to get the garages in said town to go for the truck, but, owing to extreme weather conditions and other circumstances, they were unable to procure assistance; that the driver called the second time and told defendants he was about 400 feet from Barbour's Garage and Filling Station on the main highway above mentioned; whereupon, defendants instructed their driver to drive very slowly, upon the extreme right-hand side of the road, and take the car to Barbour's Garage, that being the nearest place where the car could be repaired; that the driver then proceeded only a short distance when the truck was struck by plaintiff's car without any warning of any kind.

They assert that the driving of said car without lights was due to unavoidable condition and accident; that said car being temporarily without lights and the ignition system being out of repair, could not have been foreseen or prevented, and that they used every reasonable means and method to get the car to a place where it could be repaired, which was only about 400 feet from where the defect was discovered, and denied that the driving of said car without lights, under said circumstances, was negligence.

What result?

A. The trial court instructed the jury to assume that the defendant was negligent because of its violation of the statute. The court of appeals held that this assumption was erroneous in view of the facts just recited.

Q. Another hypothetical: In *Clinkscales v. Carver*, 136 P.2d 777 (Cal. 1943), the defendant drove through a stop sign and collided with the plaintiffs in the middle of an intersection; he had looked both ways and thought he saw no one coming. The plaintiffs attempted to proceed against him on a theory of negligence per se. The defendant replied that the stop sign had been posted illegally by a road foreman to give gravel trucks the right of way at the intersection; the defendant showed that the statute authorizing the stop sign never became effective because of technical defects in how it was published. What result?

A. Negligence per se anyway. Said the court:

> Even if the conduct cannot be punished criminally because of irregularities in the adoption of the prohibitory provisions, the legislative standard may nevertheless apply if it is an appropriate measure for the defendant's conduct. When the court accepts the standard it rules in effect that defendant's conduct falls below that of a reasonable man as the court conceives it. It does no

more than it does in any ruling that certain acts or omissions amount as a matter of law to negligence. Restatement: Torts, sec. 285. An appellate court is concerned with determining whether the trial court arrived at a proper standard in a particular case. In this case the trial court rightly instructed the jury that measured by the standard set up by the resolution of the board of supervisors and the Vehicle Code it was negligence as a matter of law to disregard the stop-sign. Failure to observe a stop-sign is unreasonably dangerous conduct whether or not the driver is immune from criminal prosecution because of some irregularity in the erection of the stop-sign. If a through artery has been posted with stop-signs by the public authorities in the customary way and to all appearances by regular procedure, any reasonable man should know that the public naturally relies upon their observance. If a driver from a side street enters the ostensibly protected boulevard without stopping, in disregard of the posted safeguards, contrary to what drivers thereon could reasonably have expected him to do, he is guilty of negligence regardless of any irregularity attending the authorization of the signs. Such irregularity does not relieve a person from the duty to exercise the care of a reasonable man under such circumstances. Otherwise a stop-sign would become a trap to innocent persons who rely upon it.

Q. Which institution acquitted itself better in *Vesely v. Sager*: the court or the legislature?

A. The case illustrates the possibility of dialogue between the branches: a statute is passed; the court finds civil liability under it; the legislature reverses the decision; the court sustains the reversal against constitutional challenge despite having taken an evidently different view of the policy issue the first time around. The case provides a chance to talk about the comparative strengths of legislatures and courts as lawmakers. It helps drive the comparison to start by considering why the prospect of civil liability for bars in these circumstances might be problematic. The incentives created by liability might well reduce the number of drunk driving accidents as taverns take more care not to overserve their patrons. But civil liability is a crude tool for that purpose, as it also may create liability—and at a minimum creates great difficulties of application—in cases where it is questionable whether the marginal drink served by the defendant was the one that made the difference, or where the driver jumped from one bar to another, or where (for that reason or others) it's hard to say whether the bartender should have realized how much the patron already had imbibed. And then behind all this is the larger sense that the driver, not the bar, is the really culpable party, and that it therefore is unjust to put the bar on the hook in a plaintiff's wrongful death suit for doing nothing more than serving drinks to a paying customer. Then again, the drunk driver often may have inadequate assets to satisfy a judgment, and in that case the loss will have to fall on either the innocent plaintiff or the obly-somewhat-innocent tavern. So negligence per se may save some lives, but at a possibly high (though contestable) price in fairness.

What are the pros and cons of having the balance struck by courts vs. legislatures? To the extent the issue depends on empirical details, the legislature is in a far better position to gather the relevant information; the court does not have access to information about the world unless it is supplied by the parties, amici, or in academic writing, whereas a legislature can hold hearings and create fat reports. But then legislatures are confronted with pressures that courts don't have to worry about: aggressive lobbying by the restaurant industry to eliminate their liability. This may have been the court's meaning when it said "We do not speculate on the influences that might have prompted the Legislature to answer this acute and growing problem by narrowly *restricting* rather than *enlarging* civil liability."

Brown v. Shyne (chiropractor practicing without license injures P; no negligence per se)

Q. What is the distinction between *Brown v. Shyne* and *Martin v. Herzog*?

A. In both cases the defendant disobeyed a statute that was intended to protect the plaintiff. Yet there is no liability in *Brown*: the court says that if the defendant performed his treatments negligently, he will be held liable regardless of the licensing question; and if he was free from negligence it wouldn't seem right—or intended by the legislature—to hold him liable for the plaintiff's injuries just because he wasn't licensed. The difference seems to involve causation. In *Brown v. Shyne* the harm was not so clearly a direct result of the defendant's failure to have a license. It's not even clear that the lack of a license made the harm more likely to occur; it could be that licensed chiropractors were widely available and that they were no more or less likely to injure the plaintiff than was the defendant here. One might like to know more about whether the alleged negligence by the defendant in *Brown* involved a mistake that studying for a license would have prevented him from making. In *Martin v. Herzog*, meanwhile, the absence of a light contributed directly to the accident; it wouldn't make sense to suggest that the driver used all due care despite the absence of the light (setting aside *Taber v. Smith*), given that the defendant's claim is precisely that the absence of a light itself made the accident more likely to occur.

Q. How would the logic of *Brown v. Shyne* apply to cases involving other types of licensing, such as a driver's license?

A. Play it out this way: Suppose your driver's license expires, and you then get into an accident despite using due care; perhaps your car skids in terrible weather. Are you automatically liable for any resulting damage because you are unlicensed? No—though perhaps the want of a license could be admitted as some evidence suggesting negligence. To impose liability here, as in *Brown*, would amount to imposing strict liability on the unlicensed defendants for any harm that results from their activities no matter how carefully undertaken. The expiration of the license did not make it more likely that your car would skid. But might it be different if you were driving without ever having earned a license in the first place, and then caused an accident by failing to obey a rule of the road? Now the case is closer. It's still true that the absence of a license did not contribute directly to the accident in the same way that the absence of a light did in *Martin v. Herzog*. But obtaining a license requires the applicant to go through a process that involves learning some rules, so it might be argued that failing to obtain a license did make the accident more likely. Yet if the driver broke a rule of the road, you don't need to point to the absence of a license: the violation is negligence per se in any event. And what if the driver *didn't* violate any rule of the road? Imagine he was a 13-year-old who took his parents' car without their knowledge, managed to drive with all the care any adult would have used, but ended up in an accident for reasons beyond his control. Why negligence per se? For a case finding no (contributory) negligence per se when the plaintiff was driving with a suspended license, see *Fuller v. Sirois*, 82 A.2d 82 (N.H. 1951).

By the way, *Brown* is a good example of a case where the statutory violation was used by the trial court as mere evidence of negligence, much as a violation of custom would be. It is important to note that even if a statutory violation results in harm of the sort the statute was meant to prevent, not all courts will conclude that a finding of negligence per se is in order; some courts instead will consider the violation to have evidentiary significance.

Q. Hypothetical: in *Romero v. National Rifle Association*, 749 F.2d 77 (D.C. Cir. 1984), the defendant, Robert Lowe, was an NRA employee. He owned a .22 caliber target pistol and ammunition which he regularly used for recreational shooting at the firing range at the NRA building in Washington. When he left work Lowe kept the pistol in his office, locking it and the ammunition in a closet and hiding the key in his desk. Four burglars broke into the building one night, found the key to Lowe's closet, and stole the gun and ammunition. Four days later, after committing several robberies with the gun, one of the burglars and an accomplice used it to shoot and kill Orlando Gonzalez-Angel during a robbery. His administrator brought a suit for wrongful death against Lowe. The trial judge refused the plaintiff's request to instruct the jury that a violation by Lowe of the District of Columbia Firearms Act would constitute evidence of Lowe's negligence or negligence per se, based on his finding that no violation had occurred. The Act provided as follows:

> Except as otherwise provided in this chapter, no person or organization shall within the District receive, possess, have under his control, transfer, offer for sale, sell, give, or deliver any destructive device, and no person or organization shall, within the District possess or have under

his or its control any firearm, unless such person or organization is the holder of a valid registration certificate for such firearm.

The jury brought in a verdict for Lowe. The plaintiff appealed, arguing that that the jury had been improperly instructed. What result?

A. No liability. The D.C. Circuit (per Scalia, J.) held that the district court properly refused to instruct the jury that his violation of the Firearms Act was negligence per se (or even that it was evidence of negligence) because the purpose of the statute was not to prevent harm from stolen guns:

> It is not at all apparent that a purpose of this registration requirement is to prevent criminal acts with stolen firearms. The statutory requirements for registration contain many disqualifications bearing upon the registrant's own responsible use of the weapon (e.g., conviction of certain crimes, adjudication as chronic alcoholic, commitment to mental institution, adjudication of negligence in a firearm mishap causing injury, lack of knowledge of the laws of the District pertaining to safe and responsible use of firearms, and even faulty vision) but none that appears designed to render the weapons secure against theft. By contrast, the provisions of the Act pertaining to licensed firearms dealers do contain requirements that relate to the safeguarding of weapons from theft. The only provision relating to the storage of weapons by owners is §6-2372, which requires firearms kept at home to be unloaded and disassembled or bound by a trigger lock—which renders them less likely to cause home accidents or acts of violence by family members, but hardly less vulnerable to theft. The legislative history of the Act contains no mention of theft of personal firearms. It sets forth the general purpose of "reduc[ing] the potentiality for gun-related crimes and . . . deaths," but that seems less likely to refer to the prevention of theft than to the "new and stringent [registration] criteria [which] relegate guns . . . to demonstrably responsible types of persons." It points out that very few guns used in crimes and recovered by the police are registered—but again, that seems less designed to suggest that registered guns are rarely stolen than to suggest that registered owners are rarely criminals.

Q. Is the *Romero* hypothetical analogous to *Selger v. Steven Bros*? How are they similar? How are they different?

A. In both cases the defendant violated a statute but was not held negligent per se. In both cases the reason for this involved the court's view of the legislature's intent. But in *Selger* the point is that the legislature probably did not intend to create civil liability. In *Romero* the point is slightly different: it is that the evil that occurred here was not what the legislature was trying to prevent. The case might seem a bit like the Sunday cases, where the purposes of the laws seemed unconnected to the harms that befell the defendants.

Q. Does it matter whether the defendant would have been able to register the gun if he had tried?

A. If the gun could have been registered easily, it seems doubtful that the failure to register had any causal connection to the theft; it would have been stolen anyway. If he would not have been able to register the gun, it would strengthen somewhat the case against him; there is an analogy to the analysis of *Brown v. Shyne*. But still missing would be any sense that the registration requirement (and any restrictions on registration) were related to the prevention of theft.

Gorris v. Scott (problem)
Ross v. Hartman (problem)

Q. What result in *Gorris v. Scott*?

A. No liability—or more precisely, no negligence per se. This is a classic case where the class of injuries against which the statute was meant to guard did not include the harm that befell the plaintiff. The result is foreshadowed by the excerpt from Restatement (Second) §288B earlier in the section. Said

Pollock, B.: "Admit there has been a breach of duty; admit there has been a consequent injury; still the Legislature was not legislating to protect against such an injury, but for an altogether different purpose; its object was not to regulate the duty of the carrier for all purposes, but only for one particular purpose." The issue is not causation; the failure to obey the statute was a but-for cause of the loss of the sheep, and also made their loss more likely. Since the legislature evidently did want the animals to be put into pens, why not assume civil liability in this case? Perhaps because it would upset the scheme of penalties the legislature already devised. Well, but allowing civil liability at all (i.e., in cases where animals transmit diseases to each other) already does that, does it not?

And how can this result be squared with the principle, discussed in the section of this chapter on the Hand formula, that in deciding whether a defendant was negligent a court looks at all the harms that would have been prevented by an untaken precaution, not just the harm the plaintiff suffered? Landes and Posner say that "there is a severe practical problem with using this insight as a basis for liability in *Gorris*-type cases. It requires the court to consider a type of accident not before it in the litigation—in *Gorris*, to weigh the costs of the pens against their benefits in disease prevention, though the accident being litigated involved the washing overboard of plaintiff's animals in a storm." Landes & Posner, *Causation in Tort Law: An Economic Approach*, 12 J. Leg. Stud. 109 (1983). Yet we know that courts do sum multiple risks in other types of negligence cases—including Posner's own *Davis v. Consolidated Rail Corp.*, the problem case at the end of the section on the Hand formula. Maybe the idea is that the multiple harms one can foresee from failing to (say) blow a train's horn are not so dissimilar in kind from what happened to the plaintiff; in *Gorris* the harms were quite different. But the simpler point is that we are only talking here about negligence per se. It still would (or should) have been possible to argue in *Gorris* that the defendant was negligent in the common law sense (setting aside negligence per se) for failing to pen the sheep—and that in support of *this* claim it would have been possible to point to several different types of risks the pens would have reduced. In negligence per se cases, courts are more stingy; perhaps because the doctrine is such strong medicine, they insist that the statute be meant to prevent the very harm that occurred.

Q. What result in *Ross v. Hartman*?
A. Liability. Said the court:

> Everyone knows now that children and thieves frequently cause harm by tampering with unlocked cars. The danger that they will do so on a particular occasion may be slight or great. In the absence of an ordinance, therefore, leaving a car unlocked might not be negligent in some circumstances, although in other circumstances it might be both negligent and a legal or 'proximate' cause of a resulting accident.

> But the existence of an ordinance changes the situation. If a driver causes an accident by exceeding the speed limit, for example, we do not inquire whether his prohibited conduct was unreasonably dangerous. It is enough that it was prohibited. Violation of an ordinance intended to promote safety is negligence. If by creating the hazard which the ordinance was intended to avoid it brings about the harm which the ordinance was intended to prevent, it is a legal cause of the harm. This comes only to saying that in such circumstances the law has no reason to ignore and does not ignore the casual relation which obviously exists in fact. The law has excellent reason to recognize it, since it is the very relation which the makers of the ordinance anticipated. This court has applied these principles to speed limits and other regulations of the manner of driving.

> The same principles govern this case. The particular ordinance involved here is one of a series which require, among other things, that motor vehicles be equipped with horns and lamps. Ordinary bicycles are required to have bells and lamps, but they are not required to be locked. The evident purpose of requiring motor vehicles to be locked is not to prevent theft for the sake of

owners or the policy, but to promote the safety of the public in the streets. An unlocked motor vehicle creates little more risk of theft than an unlocked bicycle, or for that matter an unlocked house, but it creates much more risk that meddling by children, thieves, or others will result in injuries to the public. The ordinance is intended to prevent such consequences. Since it is a safety measure, its violation was negligence. This negligence created the hazard and thereby brought about the harm which the ordinance was intended to prevent. It was therefore a legal or 'proximate' cause of the harm. Both negligence and causation are too clear in this case, we think, for submission to a jury.

The fact that the intermeddler's conduct was itself a proximate cause of the harm, and was probably criminal, is immaterial. *Janof v. Newsom* involved a statute which forbade employment agencies to recommend servants without investigating their references. An agency recommended a servant to the plaintiff without investigation, the plaintiff employed the servant, and the servant robbed the plaintiff. This court held the agency responsible for the plaintiff's loss. In that case as in this, the conduct of the defendant or his agent was negligent precisely because it created a risk that a third person would act improperly. In such circumstances the fact that a third person does act improperly is not an intelligible reason for excusing the defendant.

There are practical as well as theoretical reasons for not excusing him. The rule we are adopting tends to make the streets safer by discouraging the hazardous conduct which the ordinance forbids. It puts the burden of the risk, as far as may be, upon those who create it. Appellee's agent created a risk which was both obvious and prohibited. Since appellee was responsible for the risk, it is fairer to hold him responsible for the harm than to deny a remedy to the innocent victim.

Some students may think this case analogous to *Romero*, if you used that hypothetical. In both cases a miscreant seizes upon an opportunity for mischief created by the defendant's statutory violation. But the question is whether the mischief is one of the risks the statute was meant to reduce, and whether allowing the car to be taken away by a joy-rider increased the risk of accidents. On the first point the statute in *Ross* is open to interpretation: some may suggest that it was meant to prevent cars from rolling away. But if we assume, as the court here found, that the point of the statute was at least in part to prevent joy-riding by miscreants, the case for liability becomes stronger. And no doubt a joy-rider is a lot more likely to get into accidents that would be the car's owner, so the negligence does increase the risk of the type of harm that occurred.

It still is possible to interpose a *Selger*-style argument that civil liability, perhaps for enormous damages, is disproportionate to the offense of leaving keys in an unattended car, and thus should not be thought to have been intended by the legislature—but B is much smaller here than it was in *Selger*. Meanwhile is *Ross v. Hartman* more like *Martin v. Herzog* or *Tedla v. Ellman?* At first there might seem to have been no excuse for leaving the keys in the car, but perhaps doing so was the most efficient way for the garage to run its parking services (suggesting that B was higher than first appears). But this is not a case like *Tedla* where the plaintiff's disregard of the law actually better serves the law's purposes than would compliance; and there seems little risk that overcompliance with the law will lead to hazards of its own. In any event, the court found liability here, which is a common but not unanimous result on facts like these.

Other uses of statutes. You may wish to note the possibility of a defendant claiming as a defense that he *complied* with a statute and therefore was free from negligence as a matter of law. This type of argument rarely succeeds; compliance with a statute typically is treated evidence of freedom from negligence, not as decisive proof of the point. You also can flag the possibility of preemption of state law claims by federal statute or regulation, but we make no effort to get into that in a first-year course.

2. Judge-made rules

The section isn't long, and it can be made even shorter if you skip *Theisen* and *Blaak*. Those two cases illustrate some modern courts' struggles with judge-made negligence rules.

Baltimore & Ohio R.R. v. Goodman ("Stop, look, and listen" rule adopted)
Pokora v. Wabash Ry. (Same rule rejected)

Goodman and *Pokora* comprise a well-known story about the temptations and difficulties involved in fashioning judge-made rules about negligence. *Pokora* should not be understood to mean that judges never can take the negligence question away from the jury in a railroad-crossing case; *Pokora* approved the particular result in *Goodman*, and other courts have relied on *Goodman* to find contributory negligence as a matter of law on similar facts. What *Pokora* did establish is that there is no precise rule that a driver must stop, look, and listen or else be held negligent. The business in *Goodman* about getting out of the car was not absolute anyway; notice that it was hedged with "ifs." Cardozo's opinion sometimes is taken to show a skepticism about the use of rules, but it may be more a question of (as he says) "caution in framing standards of behavior that amount to rules of law. The need is the more urgent when there is no background of experience out of which the standards have emerged. They are then, not the natural flowerings of behavior in its customary forms, but rules artificially developed, and imposed from without." This may especially have been a difficulty for Holmes, who never had driven a car.

Jason Johnston, *Uncertainty, Chaos, and the Torts Process: An Economic Analysis of Legal Form*, 76 Cornell L Rev 341 (1991), suggests an interesting theory concerning the cycling of rules and standards in tort law. The handiest brief summary of Johnston's idea for our purposes probably can be found not within his piece but in Vermeule, *The Cycles of Statutory Interpretation*, 68 U. Chi. L. Rev. 149 (2001):

> Suppose that courts developing tort doctrine initially choose a rule—say, that drivers at train crossings must stop, get out of the car, and check the track in both directions. But litigants, knowing of the rule, will tend to pursue precisely those cases in which the rule fits exceptionally poorly with its underlying justifications, and thus displays even more than the usual over-and underinclusiveness of rules (perhaps a case in which leaving the car would increase the danger to the driver). If judges evaluate the utility of the rule by reference to the sample of litigated cases brought before them, they will eventually come to consider the rule remarkably mistailored, and the temptation to substitute an equivalent standard will be great.

> Litigants' responses to the new standard, however, will eventually cause an equal and opposite reaction. Under a standard or a balancing test, extreme cases will go unlitigated or will quickly be selected out of the litigation system through settlement. If the standard instructs drivers to "behave carefully at train crossings," the estate of the driver who crossed the tracks at breakneck speed will not contest a suit based on the resulting death, while the driver who engages in extensive precautions at crossings will not suffer an injury in the first place. Rather, under a standard, the most frequently litigated cases are the intermediate cases, those in which the defendant drove with some care and yet happened to be killed or injured. Observing a stream of rather similar, intermediate cases, judges will be tempted to generalize a rule, such as the stop-and-check rule. After all, the similarity of the litigated cases ensures that the rule will not prove terribly over- or underinclusive, so that the usual benefits of rules—their relative certainty and adjudicative efficiency—can be obtained at a reasonable price. The cycle begins again when litigants probe the new rule by bringing to court not the typical cases from which the rule was generalized, but the atypical cases that arise in the zone of the rule's over-and underinclusion.

It is a nice exercise to invite students to propose their own rules of negligence per se: some not uncommon behavior that always can be said to be negligent without worrying about claims that it was reasonable in any given case. (How about running out of gas while in the left lane of an interstate highway?) The cases that follow present chances to think about such possibilities.

Thiesen v. Milwaukee Automobile Mut. Ins. Co. (D falls asleep at wheel; L)
Blaak v. Davidson (D rear-ends P during dust storm; NL)

If you want to ask students to distinguish these cases, some bases for doing so are brought out by the following questions.

Q. To what case in the materials on statutory compliance (in the previous section of the chapter) is *Blaak v. Davidson* most analogous?
A. Probably *Tedla v. Ellman*. In both cases the details of a party's situation made it seem unreasonable to hold them to a bright-line rule governing their obligations; in both cases the party's decisions about what to do involved trade-offs between different safety advantages. In *Tedla*, the decision to walk in the same direction as traffic had the disadvantage of making it easier for the plaintiffs to be hit by any oncoming cars, but reduced their overall likelihood of being hit because there were fewer cars on their side of the road. In *Blaak*, slowing down but not stopping had the disadvantage of creating the risk that the defendant would rear-end someone, but the advantage of reducing the risk that the defendant would himself by rear-ended. Where trade-offs of this sort are involved, rules creating "negligence per se" don't work well; the question of reasonableness is too sensitive to little changes in the facts.

Q. To what case in the materials on statutory compliance (in the previous section of the chapter) is *Thiesen v. Milwaukee Automobile Mut. Ins. Co.* most analogous?
A. Perhaps *Martin v. Herzog*. In both cases the court was comfortable holding the defendant to a *rule* that defined reasonable care. In both cases the rule was one that involved no trade-offs. It's never safer to drive without lights on your buggy, and falling asleep at the wheel is never safer than staying awake. The court in *Thiesen* thus saw sleep as a case where no potential excuses or factual permutations would make the application of a rule unjust (yet even here there may be different outcomes in the related cases of fainting or epilepsy that the court describes).

Q. Should the failure to wear a seat belt be considered negligence per se (setting aside the possibility of a statutory requirement to wear one)? How about a motorcyclist's failure to wear a helmet?
A. In a regime of comparative negligence these questions are less important than they used to be; whereas an affirmative answer might once have resulted in a certain finding of no liability for the defendant, nowadays it is common for a plaintiff's failure to take such precautions to be sent to the jury as part of the inquiry into comparative negligence. But it still can matter whether a plaintiff's conduct is considered negligence per se. If it was, the jury may be precluded as a matter of law from finding all the responsibility for the accident lies with the defendant; the jury may be given a basis for finding negligence on the plaintiff's part when it otherwise (i.e., without the negligence per se instruction) would find none; and then there are those rare cases where the *defendant's* failure to wear a seat belt may be part of the plaintiff's case, as in *Kington v. Camden*, 507 P.2d 700 (Ariz. App. 1973): the plaintiffs claimed that when the defendant's car was cut off on the highway by a truck, the defendant lost control of her vehicle and caused a collision; as she swerved to avoid the car that cut her off, she slid out from behind the wheel of her car—because she wasn't wearing a seat belt.
From *Swajian v. General Motors Corp.*, 559 A.2d 1041 (R.I. 1989), holding as a matter of law that there is no duty to wear a seat belt in Rhode Island:

> The law on the admissibility of safety-belt evidence has encountered mixed judicial and legislative reception. Compare *Waterson v. General Motors Corp.*, 111 N.J. 238, 544 A.2d 357

(1988) (admissible) with *Welsh v. Anderson*, 228 Neb. 79, 421 N.W.2d 426 (1988) (inadmissible). During its infancy, the safety-belt defense was overwhelmingly rejected by court decision and legislative enactment mainly as a variant of contributory negligence. With the advent of comparative-negligence principles, however, a ripple of judicial and legislative approval of this defense has spread throughout a number of jurisdictions, particularly in products liability "crashworthiness" cases. Nevertheless, a majority of states which have addressed the issue continue to reject the safety-belt defense. See Westenberg, *Buckle Up or Pay: The Emerging Safety Belt Defense*, 20 Suffolk U.L. Rev. 867 (1986).

A plethora of cases and scholarly articles have explored in depth the various reasons given by courts for either admitting or barring safety-belt evidence in civil actions for damages. See *Spier v. Barker*, 323 N.E.2d 164 (N.Y. 1974); *Miller v. Miller*, 160 S.E.2d 65 (N.C. 1968); Ackerman, *The Seat Belt Defense Reconsidered: A Return to Accountability in Tort Law?*, 16 N.M.L. Rev. 221 (1986). [...] Consequently, for purposes of answering the question certified to this court, we need only highlight these conflicting rationales.

There is a sharp split of authority amongst courts that have considered the admissibility of safety-belt evidence. Courts barring the use of such evidence under any theory of civil litigation have generally relied on one or more of the following reasons: there is no duty to mitigate damages prior to sustaining an injury; the defense fails to conform with traditional elements of assumption of risk; a defendant must take plaintiffs as he or she finds them; the matter involves considerations properly left to the Legislature; the efficacy of safety belts in preventing injuries is questionable; few motorists actually utilize safety belts; the evidence leads to excessive speculation by experts and protracted litigation; and absent a statutory standard of care, most courts refuse to find a common-law duty to wear a safety belt. The plaintiff in the instant case advances many of these arguments in support of precluding all evidence relating to Mrs. Swajian's safety-belt usage or nonusage.

Other courts have admitted safety-belt evidence for purposes of determining whether the plaintiff breached his or her duty to mitigate damages under the so-called doctrine of avoidable consequences. Courts have also allowed this evidence on the issues of contributory or comparative fault. In addition, the safety-belt defense has been employed to show that the plaintiff misused the product or voluntarily and knowingly assumed the risk of injury resulting from the failure to wear a safety belt. Arguing for admission of safety-belt evidence, GMC strenuously asserts these contentions in its brief.

Appellate court approval of the safety-belt defense appears to be aimed at reducing the human carnage on public highways through promoting increased safety-belt use. In every jurisdiction allowing this defense, however, the defendant must demonstrate by competent evidence that a causal relationship exists between the injuries sustained in the accident and the plaintiff's failure to wear an available safety belt. [...]

We recognize the safety-belt defense for what it is worth—a manifestation of public policy. This court believes that any attempt at reducing highway fatalities through promoting the increased use of safety belts is best accomplished by legislative action. Recent studies indicate that the vast majority of Rhode Islanders refuse to buckle up. If we were to impose a duty to wear safety belts, in essence this court would be condemning most motor-vehicle occupants as negligent. Such a determination, if desirable, is properly left to the Legislature. Arguably, in light of the child-passenger-restraint law—which precludes all safety-belt evidence in civil trials—the General Assembly has already indicated its unwillingness to allow juries to consider this evidence. Moreover, should recent safety-belt-use studies prove reliable, it could be argued that manufacturers should design vehicles in a manner safe for those who foreseeably will not wear safety belts. The above discussion smacks of public-policy considerations more appropriately addressed by the Legislature. In any event, we are doubtful that a contrary holding would encourage increased use of safety belts.

SECTION E. RES IPSA LOQUITUR

This section of the chapter is divided informally into three parts. The first focuses mostly on how courts decide whether an accident probably was caused by negligence—or probably *enough* was caused by negligence, since most courts aren't very rigorous in stating how probable the negligence must have been to clear the res ipsa threshold. We thus focus on the somewhat crude but helpful distinction between cases where the optimal number of accidents of the type that occurred is zero or close to it, and cases where the optimal number is positive and perhaps substantial. The excerpt from Guthrie et al. at the end of the first section puts some more starch into the analysis, as does the Grady excerpt a few pages below in this manual. The second part of the section, starting with *Judson v. Giant Powder Co.*, consists of a little batch of cases on the use of res ipsa loquitur to deal with cases where neither side has any evidence to show how the accident occurred. The last part, starting with *Ybarra v. Spangard*, discusses the use of res ipsa in cases where the plaintiff is unsure which of several defendants caused the harm.

If you want to abbreviate the coverage, we think the most important things to assign are *Byrne v. Boadle* and *Combustion Engineering Co. v. Hunsberger*; the "likelihood of negligence" and "procedural consequences" notes before *Judson*; the *Archibeque* problem; and then *Ybarra v. Spangard* and *Wolf v. American Tract Society*. Then you can weave in some of the other cases and problems as hypotheticals as time allows.

Byrne v. Boadle (barrel falls on P's head; L)
Combustion Engineering Co. v. Hunsberger (wedge falls on P's head; NL)

Q. What is the superficial similarity between *Byrne v. Boadle* and *Combustion Engineering Co. v. Hunsberger*? What is the distinction between them?
A. In both cases a plaintiff was hit by a falling object that had been under the defendant's control. But in the *Hunsberger* case, the B of preventing tools, wedges, and other geegaws from ever falling was too large (in view of the harm they were likely to cause if they fell) to permit a conclusion that if such an object did fall, it must have been the result of negligence.

Q. What small changes could you make in the facts of *Hunsberger* to cause it to become analogous to *Byrne*—and a case of liability?
A. Suppose Durdella had bumped a cinder block off of his platform and it had fallen onto Hunsberger's head. That probably would be a good res ipsa case. The Hand formula can be used to demonstrate the difference between this hypo and the actual case. In a world where everyone is just as careful as they should be, we still expect wedges to fall from time to time; the B of never allowing that to happen would be great, and the PL of allowing it to happen occasionally is not so great. Cinder blocks are different. In a world of due care they probably would never fall from great distances into populated areas; the PL if something that heavy were to plummet from 30 feet would be very great, and the B of fastening down heavy objects is not as great as the B of fastening down wedges and sundry other small objects. So while the "optimal" number of wedges to fall is some positive number, the optimal number of falling cinder blocks is zero. If one falls, we probably can assume that someone wasn't being as careful as they should have been.

Q. What if the plaintiff in *Byrne* had been hit by a falling wedge or screw from a construction site? Would the res ipsa presumption apply there?

A. That would be an intermediate case between *Byrne* and *Hunsberger*. The point of *Hunsberger* is that we don't expect perfection in keeping small objects from falling on construction sites. That might seem to support a more general argument that we don't expect perfection in keeping small objects from falling, period (B remains high); but when they fall on members of the public (not workers within construction sites) the PL may be higher, too, since the public is not on guard against such things. It's probably a good res ipsa case.

Q. Hypothetical: In *Worland v. Rothstein*, 49 N.E.2d 165 (Ohio 1943), the defendants were window washers. One day they were washing the windows of a Woolworth's store in Cleveland. One of them dropped a sponge and some water onto the plaintiff, who was walking along several floors below. She was drenched. Her evidence was that she had to wait twenty minutes for a streetcar to take her home. The temperature was below freezing. She developed chills and an earache. Eventually she became partially deaf in that ear. Her expert testified that the drenching of the ear, followed by the exposure to the cold, could have caused an infection that resulted in her hearing loss. What result?

A. Liability: the court found it a good case for res ipsa loquitur. The court's opinion was uninformative, but the facts bear some interesting discussion as a follow-up to the previous two cases. The B for a window washer of keeping his gear (bucket, squeegee, rope, etc.) secure is not as great as the B for a construction worker using lots of tools. There also is a possible distinction based on the amount of care the plaintiff can be expected to be using. As Posner says in the *Davis* case (considered as a problem in the section of this chapter on risks and precautions), due care is the amount of care the defendant should use given the assumption that others also will be using due care. In Hunsberger's case it may be that construction workers are expected to take a few precautions against being hit by falling debris: wearing hard hats, keeping an eye out, and so forth. A pedestrian is not likely to be taking any such precautions, so the precautions we want the window washer to take will be greater. The optimal number of falling buckets of water from a window washer's scaffold probably is zero. Similar reasoning also can be applied to other accidents where construction workers drop things on pedestrians. The B in that case may not be the cost of fastening down all the tools and wedges and the like; it might just be the lower cost of building a platform over the sidewalk, as the court notes is common. This may not be feasible on a construction site where people are working at many different vertical levels, and where such protective platforms might affirmatively obstruct the work that needs to be done.

Larson v. St. Francis Hotel (P hit on head by armchair thrown from hotel window; NL for hotel)
Connolly v. Nicollet Hotel (P hit in face by mystery substance thrown from hotel window; L for hotel)

Q. What is the distinction between *Larson v. St. Francis Hotel* and *Connolly v. Nicollet Hotel*?

A. In *Connolly*, the B of intervening to prevent the accident was lower because the hotel had several days' worth of notice that the guests were acting abominably. V-J Day caused spontaneous pandemonium that could have been prevented only if the hotel either had been on guard against its arrival every day for some long period of time (high B), or if it had acted instantly to put down the disturbance (also a high B).

Q. What change in the facts of *Larson* would make it analogous to *Connolly,* and a case of liability?

A. Suppose that these chaotic celebrations happened every year on the anniversary of V-J Day, or every New Year's Eve. Eventually a presumption might arise that the hotel was failing to use due care; the B of taking precautions would be decreasing over time as the damage that occurred became easier to predict.

Q. What precautions might the hotel in *Connolly* have taken? (What B that would have helped could possibly have been small enough to be the basis of a finding of negligence?)

A.   If throwing out the conventioneers was not feasible, perhaps warnings could have been given to pedestrians—especially since bottles and other items had already been thrown out of the hotel's windows. It presumably was open to the hotel to argue at trial that it had in fact taken such precautions, and that these were all that reasonable prudence required.

Q.   Why wasn't the hotel's lack of control over its guests fatal to the res ipsa claim in both cases?
A.   The "exclusive control" issue is a little tricky in cases where the immediate cause of the harm was someone other than the defendant but over whom the defendant had some limited powers. Again, it helps to consider the costs, or level of difficulty, in restraining the guests, rather than looking at the case as involving an absolute right or lack of right to do so. With the foresight created by the signs of trouble that had accumulated in *Connolly*, it becomes easier to take measures to keep guests under control.

There are some more thoughts on these cases in the Grady excerpt below.

Brauner v. Peterson (D's cow strays through fence onto road; NL)
Guthrie v. Powell (D's cow falls through ceiling onto plaintiff; L)

Q.   What is the distinction between *Brauner v. Peterson* and *Guthrie v. Powell*?
A.   First, the B seems to have been higher in *Brauner*. When the court says that a cow "can readily escape perfectly adequate confines," this might sound to some like a contradiction in terms: if a cow can readily escape its confines, how can the confines be considered perfectly adequate? The answer here, as in the *Hunsberger* case, is that complete prevention of escapes by cows, like perfect prevention of falling debris at a construction site, is too expensive to be worth the bother. Ranchers could build brick walls around their land or post guards to prevent their cows from escaping, but we don't require this; lesser fences will restrain most cows, and the damage done by the occasional cow who slips out is not great enough to warrant further preventive measures. That is why it is possible to say that a cow can end up in the highway without any negligence by its owner—though some courts *do* allow the res ipsa presumption on these facts.

Meanwhile the B in *Guthrie*, at least at first glance, seems low or even negative: while it might be expensive to build a ceiling strong enough to support livestock without fail, the simpler precaution would simply be to keep the cows on the ground floor rather than driving them upstairs. (But perhaps that approach would have hidden costs after all, making the first floor a less attractive destination for guests at the fair.) The B of keeping the cows downstairs might seem negative here because this would spare the owners of the pavilion the bother of moving the cows upstairs. But what if the thing that fell through the ceiling was not a cow but a heavy object such as a sofa or printing press? There might be good reasons for wanting to keep such things on the second floor of the building rather than the first, so in that sort of case B becomes higher after all.

But PL also differs because of the force of gravity. If a cow escapes through a fence, it may stand around and do no harm. If a cow (or a sofa, or a printing press, etc.) escapes "vertically" through a ceiling, it is certain to fall with great force onto the floor below, damaging property and seriously injuring anyone who happens to be there. So while we expect some optimal number of cows to escape through their fences each year, the optimal number of cows that should fall through ceilings—like the optimal number of falling barrels of flour, or falling cinder blocks—probably is zero or close to it.

Procedural points.   It is important for students to understand the procedural consequences of res ipsa loquitur: that it is a way for plaintiffs to avoid summary judgment. If you emphasize that point, however, occasionally some students may become confused and lose sight of the fact that res ipsa then also becomes the basis of a jury instruction that allows the plaintiff to win at trial despite having no untaken precaution to use as the basis of the negligence claim. Here are a couple of sample jury res ipsa jury instructions in case you run into this difficulty:

Florida Standard Jury Instruction 4.6:

If you find that the circumstances of the occurrence were such that, in the ordinary course of events, it would not have happened in the absence of negligence, and that the instrumentality causing an injury was in the exclusive control of the defendant at the time it cause the injury, you may infer that the defendant was negligent unless, taking into consideration all of the evidence in the case, you conclude that the occurrence was not due to any negligence on the part of the defendant.

Wisconsin Jury Instruction—Civil 1145:

If you find (defendant) had (exclusive control of) (exclusive right to the control of) the (name the instrument or agency involved) involved in the accident and if you further find that the accident claimed is of a type or kind that ordinarily would not have occurred had (defendant) exercised ordinary care, then you may infer from the accident itself and the surrounding circumstances that there was negligence on the part of (defendant) unless (defendant) has offered you an explanation of the accident which is satisfactory to you.

Food for thought. The text soon (after the next batch of cases) includes an excerpt from From Mark F. Grady, *Res Ipsa Loquitur and Compliance Error*, 142 U. Pa. L. Rev. 887 (1994). Here's some more from the article for those who may be interested in additional ideas about how we identify cases where accidents probably were caused by negligence:

The modern economic theory of accident law is principally a mathematical description of the conditions that will yield zero negligent behavior. A large literature has now concluded that if the rule is negligence, if courts and private parties make no errors about the legal standard, if precaution is not random, and if private parties have uniform precaution costs (that is, no one is specially challenged), there will be no negligent behavior. Modern economic tort theory is thus analogous to the traditional economic theory of industrial organization, which posited that prices will be competitive if information is perfect, if buyers and sellers are numerous, if inputs and outputs are divisible, and so forth. For many modern tort theorists, finding an actual instance of negligent behavior is analogous to finding a monopoly price. It suggests an "imperfection."

Res ipsa is a legal rule that lets plaintiffs avoid proving specific negligence when they can show that the type of accident speaks of the defendant's negligence. The courts' surprising premise is that some accidents are usually caused by negligence. When the plaintiff brings his case within the doctrine, the judge tells the jury that it may infer negligence from the accident's very occurrence. This is why the doctrine embodies a theory of accidents. Although res ipsa forms an important part of negligence law, up to this point economic theorists of tort law have scarcely mentioned it in their writings. The reason for the omission is implicit in their theory. If one's overriding concern is to define the sufficient conditions for zero negligent behavior, one is unlikely to have much interest in a legal doctrine that says that negligent behavior is sometimes probable.

When we take the economic assumptions that yield nonnegligent equilibria and try to use them to explain res ipsa cases, we get confusion. When a commercial airliner crashes, the courts apply res ipsa loquitur. Even when no one knows anything about how the plane crash occurred- maybe the aircraft disappeared without a trace-courts infer that someone's negligence probably caused the accident. There is nothing in the current economic theory of tort to justify this inference while there is much to oppose it. Interestingly, courts have not applied the res ipsa doctrine as readily to small plane crashes, and the res ipsa puzzle is only compounded if we try to use the standard economic explanations for negligent behavior as a positive tool to distinguish the private plane cases from the commercial ones.

The current economic theory of tort could suggest either that courts are mistaken about res ipsa cases or that the whole doctrine is just a fictional form of strict liability. Based on my informal surveys, most economic theorists of tort opt for the "strict liability in disguise" theory, and usually stress that many res ipsa cases, including airplane crashes, are "unilateral care" accidents: only the airline can use precaution; the victims cannot. Since the 1960s economists have argued that strict liability is appropriate for unilateral care accidents. Coase and Calabresi, both of whom assumed that the unilateral case was normal, said that strict liability should be imposed on the cheaper cost avoider.

The "strict liability in disguise" theory does not really explain the res ipsa doctrine. For instance, how would it explain why small plane crash cases come out differently than commercial aircraft ones? Both seem equally unilateral. Moreover, if res ipsa is really strict liability, why does the airline get off if it can show that it was not negligent? The doctrine merely shifts the burden of persuasion. Moreover, some applications of res ipsa do indeed occur in "bilateral" situations where both injurers and victims could have used precaution and where strict liability is economically inappropriate.

[...]

Economists have a maxim: Tasks are more costly the shorter the period of time given for their accomplishment. Courts applying the res ipsa doctrine seem to follow this same rule. The economists' explanation is that a longer time period allows use of all available short-term techniques as well as techniques that are only available over a longer period of time. Thus, because there is a greater set of techniques available in the longer time period, costs are apt to be lower, as with any task where choice and flexibility are unconstrained. Applying this maxim to accidents yields a useful generalization: High precaution rates imply low compliance rates.

A lapse is more likely for a precaution that has a required rate of sixty times a minute (looking for pedestrians) than for one that has a rate of once every 100 years (replacing a fire escape). The high-rate precaution requires compliance within one second intervals. In contrast, the interval for the low- rate precaution is measured in years (one or two). Accordingly, there are techniques available for remembering the low-rate obligation that are simply unavailable during the one second or one minute intervals of a high-rate obligation. Suppose that negligence law requires a building superintendent to have the boiler inspected once every year. It is unlikely that he will forget, since he has a year to remember and ample opportunities to remind himself. Perhaps he will make a list; maybe his computer will remind him. On the other hand, a driver may have to look for other cars every second or two. Putting such an obligation on a list would be preposterous, and for a computer to beep at her every time she forgets-if that were possible-would simply make things worse. Even relatively low precaution rates can be demanding. For instance, a driver that is obliged to look for pedestrians six times per minute cannot perform all six looks during the last ten seconds of the minute. Nonetheless, even this standard has more flexibility than one that requires sixty looks a minute. The latter standard is so demanding that no rational person would comply with it every single minute.

If courts follow the economists' time maxim, res ipsa cases are especially strong when the precaution rate is high. With a stipulated rate of unavoidable accidents, a higher precaution rate implies a higher rate of compliance error and therefore a higher proportion of negligent accidents to unavoidable accidents. In fact, there are two other reasons why high precaution rates imply

strong res ipsa cases. First, a high precaution rate reduces the rate of unavoidable accidents. The more often precautions have to be taken, the smaller the window of opportunity for unavoidable accidents to
occur.

The second reason—really the converse of the first—why high precaution rates yield high rates of negligent harm is that a high precaution rate makes it difficult for an accident to slip through required precautions. Suppose that a pedestrian is walking through a museum. The required rate of looking out for people and objects might be five times per minute. If someone or something stumbles into the pedestrian's path and is damaged, there is a substantial possibility that the damage was not negligently caused. Each minute there would be five relatively long windows in which a nonnegligent collision could occur. Now, imagine that the pedestrian is given an extremely valuable Ming vase to carry from one part of the museum to another. Because of the higher danger rate, the required precaution rate increases, let us say to fifty times a minute. Under these new circumstances it is difficult for a nonnegligent accident to slip through the net of required precautions, because the net is now fine. Hence, as the rate of required precaution increases, the rate of expected compliance error increases, even assuming a relatively obsessive porter and the rate of unavoidable accidents decreases. Each of these effects makes res ipsa cases strong. Given a sufficiently high precaution rate, the mere fact of an accident carries an almost irrebuttable presumption that it had a negligent cause. Such would be the case when a nuclear reactor melts down.

Because the *Byrne* workers were moving barrels of flour, and not feathers, above a public sidewalk, the danger rate was high, implying a high precaution rate. That high precaution rate implied a low rate of unavoidable accident and a high rate of (expected) compliance error. Therefore, *Byrne v. Boadle* was a strong res ipsa case.

[...]

Anything that increases the required rate of precaution makes res ipsa cases stronger. As already noted, there are two separate reasons for this phenomenon. First, a high rate of precaution snags most accidents and makes them avoidable by due care. Indeed, with a high enough required rate of precaution, it is impossible to have a nonnegligent accident. Second, high rates of precaution are especially costly to achieve. Hence, the rate of compliance error increases with the rate of precaution. Therefore, high precaution rates simultaneously reduce the rate of nonnegligent accidents and increase the rate of negligent ones. The combination of these two effects produces strong res ipsa cases. Although the precaution rate is key, it is useful to analyze cases using some other factors as well.

High danger rates

High danger rates usually imply high precaution rates. The correlation between danger and precaution rates explains why dangerous activities, such as moving barrels above sidewalks, make such strong res ipsa cases when they go awry. For instance, the Marine Corps' accidental bombing of the plaintiff's oyster boat during practice exercises over Pamlico Sound presented a strong res ipsa case. Dropping practice bombs is even more dangerous than moving barrels, and requires such a high rate of precaution that little room is left for unavoidable accidents. Moreover, with such a high rate of precaution, a fair amount of compliance error is inevitable.

Effective durable precaution

Highly effective durable precaution usually increases the productivity of complementary nondurable precaution, and thus its required rate. As a result, the crash of a modern commercial airliner makes a much better res ipsa case than the crash of an airplane that takes place at the birth of aviation. It was more likely that Amelia Earhart's airplane would crash without negligence than it is that a modern airplane will crash without negligence.

Low-cost nondurable precaution

Some nondurable precautions are very cheap, and that factor can create strong res ipsa cases. For instance, in *Swiney v. Malone Freight Lines*, the defendant owned an eighteen-wheel truck equipped with dual tandem wheels. As the defendant's driver was travelling down the road, first one wheel, then the second, became detached. The plaintiff, who was driving in his car, avoided the first wheel but was struck by the second and was injured. In its opinion the court stressed that the tractor-trailer wheels required frequent inspections. Moreover, checking whether wheel lugs have loosened was both easy and highly effective. In holding that the evidence was sufficient to send the case to the jury on a res ipsa theory, the court distinguished two other cases in which nondurable precaution was less productive.

When compliance error is impossible, res ipsa is usually an unsuccessful theory. Consider *Bolton v. Stone*, in which the plaintiff, standing outside her garden gate on the street that ran between her house and the defendant's cricket grounds, was struck by a particularly well hit cricket ball. Balls were hit out of the park extremely infrequently. The plaintiff alleged two untaken precautions: failing to erect a fence of sufficient height to prevent balls being struck into the road, and placing the cricket pitch too close to the road. Her third claim was that failing to ensure that cricket balls would not be hit into the road amounted to general negligence. In response to this allegation of general negligence the court took up the question of res ipsa loquitur, as well as the specific negligence put at issue by the two untaken precaution allegations. he specific negligence counts failed, as did the res ipsa count, despite the superficial similarity that the case bore to Byrne v. Boadle (the case of the falling barrel). In Byrne the harm very probably resulted from compliance error, whereas in Bolton, compliance error was impossible: the batter was trying to hit the ball out of the stadium. If any precaution was reasonable, it was some durable one, like the two specific untaken precautions mentioned in the plaintiff's declaration. [...]

Chronic vs. Acute Danger

Rapidly accelerating danger rates-acute dangers-imply high rates of unavoidable accident and weak res ipsa cases. The reason for this implication is that precaution is cheaper when it can be planned over a longer period of time. The cases bear out the prediction that acute danger situations will not succeed on a res ipsa theory. In *Larson v. St. Francis Hotel*, the plaintiff was walking on the street when she was struck by an armchair that someone had thrown out of a hotel window. She was nonsuited. In *Connolly v. Nicollet Hotel*, the plaintiff was struck by a mud-like substance while she was passing the defendant's hotel. Here, however, the plaintiff was allowed to recover under the doctrine. In both cases, the objects were thrown by celebrating guests; thus, the hotels' negligence would consist in the failure to exercise more restraint. In the St. Francis case, the cost of this precaution would have been great, due to the fact that the guests were celebrating the end of World War II and their celebration developed rapidly over a few hours. In the Nicollet case, however, the rate of unavoidable accident was less because the celebration, a Junior Chamber of Commerce convention, accelerated less rapidly over several days.

[...]

The preceding positive economic analysis indicates that there is a counterintuitive idea at the very center of res ipsa doctrine. The more advanced the safety technology present in the relevant activity, the more loudly an accident speaks of negligence. The orthodox economic theory of tort, with its emphasis on the Learned Hand formula and durable precaution, might suggest exactly the opposite conclusion. Under the conventional analysis, it might seem that the safer the technology is, the less likely is a judicial finding of negligence. Nonetheless, the counterintuitive idea of the actual doctrine makes more sense once we account for the importance of the pocket of strict liability within the negligence rule. Elaborate durable precaution increases the likelihood that a given accident will fall within the pocket, a point that legal economists have, up to this point, neglected to notice.

Judson v. Giant Powder Co. (defendant's gunpowder factory explodes; L: res ipsa applies)
Haasman v. Pacific Alaska Air Express (D's airplane vanishes without explanation; L)
Walston v. Lambertson (D's boat sinks without explanation; NL)
Archibeque v. Homrich (problem: car crashes without explanation; L)

Q. If the plaintiff is given the benefit of the res ipsa presumption in *Judson*, how can the defendant respond?
A. The defendant probably can't respond effectively. All the witnesses to how the explosion occurred are dead, and all the evidence has been destroyed. In this way the use of res ipsa on facts like these resembles strict liability.

Q. How certain are we that if an accident occurred, it must have been because the defendant was negligent? (Or: What is the distinction between *Judson* and *Brauner v. Peterson* (NL where defendant's cow escapes onto highway and is struck by P's car))?
A. It's likely that the accident was caused by negligence. The court says this without quite explaining why it is a reasonable conclusion. The logic can be brought out by comparing the case to *Brauner*, the matter of the cow in the road. In *Judson*, as in the case of the falling cow or falling cinder block (but unlike in *Brauner* or *Hunsberger*), the L that would result from an explosion at the defendant's factory was so large that very great precautions would be justified, much as in the case of a nuclear power plant. The optimal number of accidents of this sort is none. So if an accident occurs, it is likely that someone wasn't being as careful as they should have been. This case thus is analogous to *Guthrie* (the cow that fell through the ceiling). A general point helpful to reinforce here (because some students find it hard to accept) is that sometimes, as in *Hunsberger* and *Brauner*, accidents and injuries can occur even if everyone involved is being just as careful as we think they should be. We don't expect people in those situations to be so careful that no harm ever results from their activities. Applying res ipsa is partly a matter of separating those cases from the ones like *Judson* where if an accident occurs, it almost certainly means someone was not being as careful as we want them to be—cases, in other words, where we do expect sufficient precautions to be taken to prevent the harm from ever occurring.

It's true enough, however, that if there were an explanation for the explosion in which at least the defendant was innocent (like what?—maybe that it was the fault of one of the defendant's suppliers?), the defendant will be stuck with the bill anyway.

Q. What would be the consequences of *not* applying res ipsa loquitur here?
A. No liability. Again, the absence of any surviving witnesses or evidence means that neither side is going to be able to make much of a case. The final result essentially boils down to which side wins the benefit of the presumption. The presumption against the defendant may rankle students who take an "innocent until proven guilty" view of liability. But a presumption in favor of the defendant has consequences of its own: not only no liability here regardless of how negligent the defendant may have

been, but probably no liability generally for defendants in cases involving explosions like this. This is another way to understand the underlying logic of the court's decision: we can't tolerate a regime that creates pockets of immunity for defendants that will enable them to continually get off scot free—though "scot free" might not be the most apt description of the outcome of this case for the defendant, given the losses it suffered. Then again, consider the racist *New York Times* article excerpt included in the text, which perhaps suggests a perception that lives of certain ethnic groups had diminished value.

Q. What is the meaning of the *Haasman* court's distinction between equality of knowledge and equality of ignorance?

A. The court apparently was in a jurisdiction that did not allow res ipsa loquitur to be used if both sides had equally good access to the evidence concerning whether the defendant was negligent. One way of looking at the logic behind such a limitation is to consider res ipsa a way of dealing with defendants who try to win by concealing evidence: we threaten them with liability to loosen their tongues. But that makes sense only where the defendant has better access to the evidence than the plaintiff does, since only then will sitting on the evidence be an effective strategy for the defendant; so res ipsa is limited to such occasions. If that is the rationale for the court's approach, it suggests that res ipsa should not apply in *Haasman,* because the defendant isn't hiding any knowledge; he doesn't have any knowledge to hide.

A different way of understanding the logic of the limitation the court describes, however, is that it is meant to prevent plaintiffs from making defendants do work that the plaintiffs should be doing themselves. Again, this explains why res ipsa doesn't apply if the parties have equal access to the evidence ("equality of knowledge"). But it also suggests, consistent with *Haasman,* that res ipsa has a place even if the defendant knows nothing, so long as the plaintiff also knows nothing ("equality of ignorance")—for then there is no fear that the plaintiff is using the rule to make the defendant do his work for him.

Q. What is the analogy between *Haasman* and *Judson v. Giant Powder Co.?*

A. First, in both cases an accident resulted in the elimination of all evidence and witnesses, so the winner of the case was very likely to be whichever side was given the benefit of the presumption that the accident was or wasn't caused by negligence. Second and relatedly, both are cases where holding res ipsa inapplicable might create a pocket of immunity for the type of defendant at issue: airlines, like powder factories, might have a good chance of getting off without liability every time a catastrophic accident occurred that destroyed all the evidence. Finally, both cases involved activities where the cost of an accident (a plane crash or an exploding dynamite factory) is very high, and justifies great precautions; if an airplane crashes, it therefore is very likely that someone wasn't being as careful as they should have been. (But how sure can we be that it was the airline or its employees, rather than the maker of the plane?)

Q. What is the superficial similarity between *Haasman* and *Walston v. Lambertson?* What is the distinction between them?

A. Again, in both cases (as in *Judson*) an accident resulted in the elimination of all evidence and witnesses, so the winner of the case was very likely to be whichever side was given the benefit of the presumption that the accident was or wasn't caused by negligence. And perhaps *Walston* creates some danger of immunity for boat owners whose vessels vanish. But here, like in *Brauner* but unlike in *Haasman,* the court is not ready to say that if a boat sinks it probably is because someone was negligent. A boat might sink even if everyone is being as careful as we want them to be. "The sea itself contains many hazards," as the court says—reefs, marine monsters, and so forth. Eliminating the risks posed by those hazards would involve an intolerably high B: everyone would have to use expensive ships (just as preventing cows from ever escaping might require brick walls around farms rather than barbed wire fences). True, when it comes to air travel we are ready to make everyone use relatively expensive planes. But if a boat sinks, the PL is not as high as in the case of a plane crash; the crew often will survive. That is one of the reasons why airplane cockpits are loaded with precautionary features, while crab fishing boats tend to have fewer. And it is why a sinking boat does not necessarily suggest that anyone was being less careful than they should have been, whereas a vanished airplane does suggest that. There is some more on these cases in the Grady excerpt in the casebook.

Q. What result in *Archibeque v. Homrich*?
A. The court found the case adequate to send to a jury on a res ipsa theory. Compare Restatement 328D ("Res ipsa loquitur"), Illustration 12:

> A's son, with A's consent, takes B for a ride in A's automobile. Under a statute of the particular state, A is liable for any negligence of his son in driving the car. The car is found in the ditch with both B and the son dead, the son seated behind the steering wheel. There is no evidence as to how or why the car left the road, and it clearly appears that A does not have and cannot possibly obtain such evidence. It may be inferred by the jury that B's death was due to negligence of the son, for which A is subject to liability.

The court's opinion does not add much to the points already described in the casebook text. But as an interesting additional twist to the problem, the plaintiff argued that the defendant hitchhiker was negligent per se: he was driving the car, and it was evident that he had failed to stay on the right side of the road as statute required (the inference seems sound inasmuch as the car was found in a ditch on the left side of the road). The court didn't buy this:

> Whom the legislature sought to protect is not explicitly stated; however, it is reasonable to assume that it is the motoring public in general, including passengers such as the plaintiff. The harm sought to be prevented by the statutes apparently is head-on collisions or sideswiping the opposite moving traffic. It is doubtful that the statute could have been intended by the legislature to apply to a situation such as this. Thus, the district court properly refused to submit this instruction to the jury.

Ybarra v. Spangard (P wakes up from surgery with mysterious new ailment; L for all present)
Wolf v. American Tract Society (P hit on head by brick on construction site; NL)
Bond v. Otis Elevator Co. (P sued building and elevator company after being injured by elevator's free fall; res ipsa applies to both)
Actiesselskabet Ingrid v. Central R. Co. of New Jersey (dynamite goes off and destroys plaintiff's boat; NL for maker of dynamite, the railroad that transported it, and the owner of the ship that was moving the dynamite when it exploded)

Q. In what ways does *Ybarra* follow *Judson v. Giant Powder Co.*? In what ways does it go farther?
A. In both cases the plaintiffs were in no position to figure out how their injury was sustained. But in *Ybarra,* as the court views the case, there is none of the symmetrical ignorance we saw in *Judson.* The plaintiff cannot know what happened; the defendant might. This is the classic asymmetry often used as a rationale for res ipsa (see Bramwell's remarks in *Byrne v. Boadle*). So *Ybarra* is less extreme than *Judson* because it puts the defendants in a less difficult position: they may well be able to respond with evidence to rebut the presumption. In another sense *Ybarra* resembles *Judson*: in either case the injuries that occurred are of a type that we expect not to occur if everyone is being as careful as they should be; the care we expect of doctors is care sufficient to prevent injuries to parts of their patients on which they are not operating. So in both cases there is a strong inference that someone was negligent.

But *Ybarra* of course goes beyond *Judson* in that it applies the res ipsa presumption to a group of defendants, any given one of whom probably did not commit any acts of negligence—or at least no negligent acts that caused the plaintiff's injury. In *Judson*, the defendant apparently had responsibility for the behavior of all of the employees who could have caused the blast; in *Ybarra*, the defendants did not all have a like ability to control one another. Indeed, given the result on remand in *Ybarra*, the case goes very far indeed and is open to strong criticism: if the defendants all testified honestly and knew nothing, then the use of res ipsa in the case is doing no work to loosen their tongues and in effect just results in holding liable a bunch of defendants who must have been innocent in every sense of the word.

The harshness toward the defendants in these two cases thus differs: *Judson* is harsh because it creates a presumption that probably is impossible for the defendant to overcome; even without the result on remand, *Ybarra* is harsh because it applies a presumption to defendants each one of whom probably is innocent of any wrongdoing. Yet both kinds of harshness might be explained in part by a similar rationale: they are ways of preventing a pocket of tort immunity from being created for the defendants. The court in *Ybarra* makes the point explicit ("if we accept the contention of defendants herein, there will rarely be any compensation for patients injured while unconscious"). The same might be said in *Judson* or *Haasman* to justify the way res ipsa is used in those cases.

Ybarra is an interesting example of a court using res ipsa loquitur as a rather blunt instrument of policy. It is used not because the presumption it creates is likely to be accurate and thus fair, but rather because the court wants to make the parties do something (i.e., talk), and res ipsa is an expedient way to get this to happen.

Saul Levmore, *Gomorrah to Ybarra and More: Overextraction and the Puzzle of Immoderate Group Liability*, 81 Va. L. Rev. 1561 (1995), is an interesting piece on group liability. Here are some excerpts from it; if you like them, you may want to read the whole thing:

> Imagine that you are jostled in an office building elevator and you sense that your wallet, with $100 in it, has been taken. There are five fellow passengers in the elevator, and as the door opens a police officer stands before you. The officer is sympathetic to your problem, but is unable to narrow the group of suspects in order to carry out a search. None of the five suspects volunteers to be searched. There is the possibility that the victim could be made whole by a recovery of twenty dollars from each of the five suspects. We might think of such liability as a form of communal responsibility, familiar since the Biblical story of Sodom and Gomorrah[.] [...] A modern, perhaps more functional, justification for this kind of joint liability is that it might encourage otherwise silent witnesses to help identify the chief culprit who would then bear the entire liability (and perhaps criminal punishment as well).

> This kind of "information forcing" rule, or explanation for a rule, [is] surprisingly similar to the famous case of *Ybarra v. Spangard*, where a patient was able to recover from a number of health professionals for an injury sustained during an operation. The facts suggested that one (unidentified) defendant negligently caused the injury, and the decision can be read as hinting that a plaintiff should not go uncompensated simply because doctors and nurses may be unlikely to testify against one another and identify the wrongdoer. *Ybarra* is not a startling case, although it represents a minority view, and yet there is something startling about applying its principles to force passengers in an elevator to compensate a pickpocket victim. We sense that these passengers will not, and should not, be held liable. [...]

> If *Ybarra* is an example of shrewd, judge-made law because of its information-forcing potential, then a more clever rule would not only encourage witnesses but also persuade the wrongdoer to confess or to right the wrong. If the *Ybarra*-style rule calls for each of the five suspects to pay twenty dollars, then we might contemplate a radical rule requiring all six passengers to pay more than $100 each, perhaps $150, into the hands of a police officer or other third party. This stakeholder would return all funds if the stolen wallet and money are immediately returned, but otherwise would give it all to a charity or to the government, where it might be earmarked for crime-fighting or prison construction. The scheme would only be used when there appeared to be no other means of identifying the wrongdoer and imposing criminal or tort penalties. The idea is to make the thief an offer that will not be refused. If the thief keeps the wallet, the thief

loses the $150 "overextracted" by this immoderate group liability rule; if the thief returns the wallet, then the thief enjoys the $150 returned from the stakeholder. The rational thief will presumably return what has been stolen, spending $100 to make $150. When the thief responds "rationally," all passengers receive their money back. Thus, the success, and perhaps even the popularity, of this "overextraction rule" depends rather plainly on the empirical question of how often pickpockets will return wallets and how much crime will be deterred in the first place once potential wrongdoers know that the rule will preclude gainful theft. [...]

If *Ybarra* is confined to hospital settings, it is of limited precedential importance because in such situations it will often be the case that the plaintiff can sue the hospital and through vicarious liability overcome the defense that the identity of the actual wrongdoer is unknown. If the hospital is vicariously liable for all its employees, then the plaintiff will win when it is clear that an injury was caused by some employee in the operating room and that all present in the operating room, aside from the patient, were hospital employees. Indeed, in *Ybarra* itself, where some of the "suspects" were not employees of the hospital, the court implied that it would be prepared to hold that these non-employees were nevertheless agents of the surgeon, so that vicarious liability would solve the plaintiff's doctrinal difficulty. [...]

There is, however, much more group liability than first meets the eye when the identity of the wrongdoer is uncertain. I have already alluded to the first reason for this conclusion by implying that *Ybarra* may be of limited precedential importance because in so many like cases the plaintiff will succeed with a claim based on vicarious liability, even though it is impossible to identify the wrongdoing agent. Put simply, the doctrine of vicarious liability often places liability on an innocent member of a "group."

Products liability law is perhaps the most important reason for my description of the real scope of *Ybarra*. If an automobile explodes, a victim may collect from the manufacturer of this apparently defective product without pointing to the precise component (and therefore subcontractor) of that product that was negligently made and that caused the explosion. Products liability law looks to the least-cost avoider—where that expression refers not only to direct precautions but also to the ability to contract with other precaution takers. Indeed, once we recollect that the historical, doctrinal obstacle in the way of products liability was lack of privity between consumer and manufacturer, it is easy to see that in the absence of that obstacle vicarious liability and products liability are close relatives. [...]

There is also a more dramatic and less doctrinally driven reason to think that group responsibility, as in *Ybarra*, is commonly the de facto rule when the identity of the (causal agent and) wrongdoer is uncertain. When victims are repeat players, they will generally be able to share losses with other innocent players and perhaps with a group that includes both innocents and unidentifiable wrongdoers. Thus, shoplifting raises prices in a way that forces all shoppers (including most shoplifters, who are likely to acquire some of their goods through normal purchases) to bear the cost of this crime; tax fraud probably imposes costs on all citizens and surely on all taxpayers; and unsolved burglaries and many other crimes impose costs on all property owners. The costs of some crimes and torts are borne more broadly than others but the point is that in the long run the cost of undeterred wrongdoing is shared by many innocent people through higher prices and taxes, the costs of taking precautions, and the hidden costs of avoiding certain activities or locations.

In the case of the pickpocket on the elevator, there is less potential for loss sharing because there is little repeat playing. Once the wrongdoer has struck, passengers are unlikely to agree to share the loss (much less agree to a less moderate group liability rule) even though some of these passengers might have agreed on such a scheme ex ante, before they knew who among them would become the victim. To the extent that many passengers would agree ex ante to an *Ybarra* rule or more, there is of course the familiar argument for imposing (legislatively or judicially) that which citizens would bargain for in the absence of transaction costs. Some measure of group responsibility may satisfy this criterion.

If most passengers would in fact decline an ex ante opportunity to opt in to an *Ybarra*-style rule, they might do so because of a kind of confidence or fear of the moral hazard that some of their fellow passengers are more likely, or will now be more likely, to fall prey to the pickpocket than they. It is no accident that more people purchase insurance covering the theft of their automobiles, for example, than purchase traveler's checks or other forms of pickpocket insurance. Even in a world without insurance many people might decline to share losses more than they must, but the point is that a great deal of sharing will occur naturally. In its simplest form, this sharing comes from repeat playing, so that the elevator case may be unusual because it is a scenario that is not often repeated with the same passengers. If it were repeated, it would make little difference whether the apparent rule was no liability or *Ybarra*, or whether passengers agreed ex post or ex ante or even through insurance contracts to share in the losses. In the long run, given the pervasiveness and costs of crime, group liability is the de facto rule for people who work or live near one another. [...]

[A]t a less refined level there is almost no end to the list of measures that can at least in part be described as spreading costs in the manner of *Ybarra*. Many taxes, affirmative action plans, curfews and reporting requirements can be viewed in this way. In all these cases we might well choose to impose liability on known wrongdoers if we could do so costlessly; it is in the face of uncertainty that we share burdens more widely for reasons of deterrence or compensation or both. If *Ybarra* is about providing some deterrence (even if only at the activity level), some insurance, and some incentive to report wrongdoing by others, then an enormous amount of government regulation can be described as of a piece with *Ybarra*. If there was something remarkable about the decision in *Ybarra*, perhaps it was simply the fact of its judicial rather than legislative origins. [...]

One obvious problem with the political or judicial adoption of an overextraction rule is that the immediate costs of unsuccessful overextraction are painful to contemplate. In contrast, if overextraction is successful, some of its benefits are hidden because they involve the decline of activities such as pickpocketing. Similarly, the popularity of broad but modest group liability can be ascribed to the dispersed and often hidden costs of such burdens. Much as the enactment of a government spending program is often explained as the product of encouragement by coordinated beneficiaries (who face little opposition from relatively dispersed taxpayers who pay for the program), we can explain many loss-sharing arrangements as satisfying relatively organized interests at the expense of less identifiable, dispersed losers. The puzzling absence of overextraction in a world where there are other group liability schemes can in this way be solved with the observation that the relative advantages of overextraction go unnoticed, while the costs tend to attract attention.

A slightly different and more cynical version of the hidden costs explanation is that most people (including legislators and judges) abhor forcing contributions from innocents only when they can identify with these innocent losers. When the defendants are businesses, for example, the reaction to group liability is less negative than where individual defendants are concerned (perhaps because the effect of such liability on prices is hidden or not fully understood). It is no accident, I think, that outside of the medical context the cases which most resemble (or even expand upon) *Ybarra* involve defendants that are common carriers, warehouse owners, manufacturers, and other business enterprises. And to the extent that the most important examples of group liability are accomplished through vicarious liability or products liability law, as suggested earlier, judgments normally fall on business enterprises rather than (uninsured) individuals. *Ybarra* itself involved a hospital, doctors, and other health professionals who are normally insured. In contrast, the decisions most striking in their refusal to follow or to expand upon *Ybarra* involve preparers of turkey salad, smokers in a hotel room that later catches fire, and jeering onlookers who might know the identity of the person who assaulted a misbehaving police officer—cases where the defendants are nonbusiness individuals.

Q. What is the distinction between *Wolf v. American Tract Society* and *Byrne v. Boadle*?
A. In both cases it seems clear enough that *someone* was negligent. But in *Wolf* the object may not have been dropped by the defendants or by anyone under their control (and apparently it was not possible to sue the owner of the building project under respondeat superior because the workmen were independent contractors). In *Byrne* the barrel of flour was under the defendants' exclusive control.

Q. What is the superficial similarity between *Wolf* and *Ybarra v. Spangard*? What is the distinction between them?
A. In both cases the defendant was injured, in both cases it seemed likely that the injury was the result of negligence, and in both cases the plaintiff was unable to identify the person whose negligence was responsible. In both cases the defendant could only narrow down the field to some possible suspects who did not (all) have control over one another. In both cases there is a policy danger (identified by the dissenter in *Wolf*) that a pocket of immunity will be created if the res ipsa presumption is not applied.

The *Ybarra* approach was not in vogue in 1900. But the cases are distinguishable anyway, and *Wolf* probably comes out the same way now that it did then, even in California and even if all of the workmen are sued rather than just two of them. The key difference is that in *Wolf* there appears not to be any reason to suspect a conspiracy of silence. True, the worker who dropped the brick can keep his mouth shut, but the point of *Ybarra* seems different: in that case it was possible that many or all of the defendants might well have known what happened, but might be protecting each other. That seems less likely in *Wolf*. Holding a random (and probably innocent) mason liable is not going to accomplish anything if he has no knowledge that can be pried out of him—unless one thinks it generally more just to hold the random mason (who *might* be guilty, but probably isn't) liable than to let the injury go unredressed. Indeed: as between the plaintiff, who is entirely innocent of any negligence, and the mason, who has, say, a 1/19 chance of being guilty of the negligence, why not foist the loss onto the mason?

Some students will focus on the fact that the plaintiff in *Wolf* only sued a couple of the workmen, not all of them; but the court's opinion makes clear that the result would have been no different if all the workmen had been sued, so imagining that they were makes *Wolf* a better discussion piece.

Q. What is the superficial similarity between *Bond v. Otis Elevator Co.* and *Wolf v. American Tract Society*? What is the distinction between them?
A. In both cases a plaintiff was injured and was not in a good position to figure out who caused the injury; in both cases the defendant therefore sued multiple potential culprits on a res ipsa theory. But in *Bond* the defendants had shared control over the instrument that harmed the plaintiff, whereas in *Wolf* the brick was under the control of one or another workman at the construction site, but not under the joint control of all of them. Yet what exactly is "joint" control? It could mean (a) that either side could and should have prevented the accident; or (b) that each side was involved enough in the control of the instrument to know how the accident was caused. What does the court seem to mean here? Apparently (b).

Q. What is the analogy between *Bond v. Otis Elevator Co.* and *Ybarra v. Spangard*? Which is the more radical decision?

A. In each case the plaintiff was injured by negligent behavior on the part of someone; in each case the plaintiff did not know whose negligence it was, and so sued more than one possible culprit; in each case the court was struck by the defendants' superior access to information about how the accident occurred, and so held all (both) of the defendants presumptively negligent. Perhaps *Bond* seems easier to defend because it should be straightforward enough for the two defendants to get together and determine exactly how the accident occurred; perhaps it also is a more sympathetic case because only two defendants are being presumed negligent, rather than six or seven.

Q. What is the distinction between *Bond* and the *Ingrid* case?

A. One possible distinction is that in *Bond* the defendants were working more closely together than they were in *Ingrid*. Another possible argument is that in the *Bond* case it seemed highly likely that one of the two defendants should know or be able to determine how the accident occurred, so res ipsa served the useful purpose of forcing them to do so. In the *Ingrid* case the evidence was destroyed by the accident, so it didn't seem particularly likely that any of the defendants would have the key information to dispel the mystery surrounding the case. Applying res ipsa to them would thus amount to strict liability—but in a case where two out of the three defendants, at least, probably were blameless. And in the *Ingrid* case the court noted the possibility that the accident might have been caused by outsiders unconnected to any of the defendants.

Q. What is the distinction between *Judson* and *Ingrid*?

A. Both involved explosions that apparently destroyed all evidence of their cause, but in the *Ingrid* there was not the sort of exclusive control found in *Judson*, and thus not the same confidence that res ipsa would pin liability on a party fairly likely to have been responsible for the damage.

Q. What result in *Samson v. Riesing*?

A. No liability. Like *Ybarra*, it's a case where one (or perhaps more than one) of a group of defendants negligently injured the plaintiff. And as in *Bond v. Otis Elevator Co.*, the defendants arguably had some sort of "joint duty" to the plaintiff. They were working together in making the turkey salad. But the no-liability result becomes pretty clear if we look at the cases in this section of the chapter as being driven largely by two policy considerations: overcoming a possible conspiracy of silence between defendants who all are in a better position to finger the culprit than the plaintiff is; and avoiding the creation of a pocket of immunity created in situations where the plaintiff will be unable to pin down which of several associated defendants caused an injury. On the first score *Samson* is more like *Wolf* than *Ybarra* (or *Bond*) in that there was no apparent danger of a conspiracy of silence: it seems unlikely that the ladies who cooked the turkeys know or are in a position to learn which of them was negligent (the negligent party herself may not know), so imposing liability would not serve much purpose as a policy matter. And it seems unlikely that we need to worry about a pocket of immunity for future people who contribute undercooked turkeys to a similar turkey salad project. (Why?)

CHAPTER 4

DUTIES AND LIMITATIONS

SECTION A. DUTIES ARISING FROM AFFIRMATIVE ACTS

If you want to shorten this section, you can skip *Weirum* and focus just on the thread in *Yania* concerning the duty to rescue (and not on the thread concerning the absence of liability for goading another). If you want to abbreviate things even further, you can assign only the *Yania* case from this section (perhaps also adding *Soldano*) and then combine it into one assignment with a few items from the section that follows on undertakings, such as *Lawter* and *Frank* and then the problems at the end of that part (*Bloomberg* and *Marsalis*).

Yania v. Bigan (D goads P into jumping into water, then doesn't rescue him; NL)
Weirum v. RKO Radio General (D goads teenagers into driving fast to reach promotion site; P's decedent is killed in resulting accident; L)

From Jack Balkin, *The Rhetoric of Responsibility*, 76 Va. L. Rev. 197 (1990):

> Varying the relevant time period in which facts are to be considered is a frequently used device for characterizing the responsibility of the parties. Professor Kelman first demonstrated this point in the context of criminal law[.] [...] Kelman showed how alternatively viewing events from a broad or narrow time frame, or from a unified or disjointed perspective, enables courts to justify particular conclusions about criminal responsibility. [...]

> Moral and legal responsibility often depends on whether a person has acted or merely omitted to act. For example, this distinction is important in tort law because in many circumstances there is no affirmative duty to rescue a stranger, although one can be held liable for placing strangers in unreasonably dangerous situations and then failing to rescue them. In *Yania v. Bigan*, [...] The court's argument becomes increasingly plausible the more we focus on Bigan's behavior at the moment Yania leapt in. In doing so we exclude the previous history that gave rise to this situation: the invitation and the subsequent tauntings and inducements which, after all, are verbal acts justly attributable to Bigan. In Kelman's terminology, the defendant's counsel and the court have chosen a narrow time frame in which to view Bigan's behavior. The plaintiff, however, probably would adopt a broad time frame to characterize the situation. The plaintiff would argue that Bigan's previous behavior constituted an integral part of an ongoing course of action—taunting plus failure to rescue—that ultimately resulted in Yania's death.

> The defendant's and plaintiff's arguments employ another pair of opposed rhetorical devices in addition to broad and narrow time framing. Because in this case choosing a narrow time frame also separates the acts of taunting from the failure to rescue, defendant's strategy is to emphasize a disjointed perspective of events. Conversely, the plaintiff's use of a broad time frame implicitly relies on a unified perspective of events—a continuous course of conduct or a coherent and interrelated system of action on the part of Bigan, rather than discrete and isolated instances of Bigan's behavior.

Q. Is the Restatement illustration a fair interpretation of *Yania v. Bigan*?

A. Perhaps. We don't know that Bigan was a strong swimmer or that he harbored unreasonable hatred toward Yania, but the *Yania* holding seems to encompass those cases. The complaint was dismissed, and in that procedural posture the plaintiff is entitled to the benefit of any assumed facts of that sort that might be unearthed during discovery. There is no general duty to rescue.

One of the puzzles of *Yania,* and a way to distinguish it from the Restatement example, is that the incident occurred on premises owned by Bigan, onto which he had invited Yania. That would seem to make Yania an invitee to whom Bigan owed a duty of care. But perhaps that duty was not implicated on these facts; perhaps the court saw this as akin to a case where a customer is invited by the proprietor of a store to set himself on fire, and does so. (Would the proprietor have a duty to rescue in that circumstance?)

Q. Suppose Bigan had advised Yania to go ahead and jump into the water while knowing that it was more shallow than it appeared, or while knowing it contained crocodiles. Liability for Bigan? Does it matter whether Bigan's omission of a warning was deliberate or negligent?

A. If Bigan suggested that Yania dive into the water, and Bigan knew it was shallower than it appeared (and Yania did not know), it would seem like a case of battery by rough analogy to cases like *Garratt v. Dailey* (a hypo in the battery chapter) where the defendant causes a harmful contact between the plaintiff and some surface or object. Telling the plaintiff to have a seat when there is no chair present seems indistinguishable from pulling the chair out from under the plaintiff as she sits down; the latter is *Garratt* and the former is like our current hypothetical.

If Bigan merely is negligent in failing to inform Yania of the hidden hazard, it becomes a tricky case. Bigan is not responsible for what Yania does, and perhaps Yania should not jump into the water without checking for hazards regardless of what Bigan says. There is a tort of negligent misrepresentation, and it can be the basis of a claim for personal injuries; but generally the courts require that the speaker have a duty of care to the listener, and that the listener's reliance be justifiable. Thus in a case a little like this current hypothetical, *Heard v. City of New York*, 623 N.E.2d 541 (N.Y. 1993), a lifeguard at Rockaway Beach told the plaintiff, Heard, to get off of a jetty where he was standing. Heard said he wanted to take one more dive into the water. The lifeguard told him to go ahead. The plaintiff did so—but the water turned out to be shallow, and he suffered the common and terrible fate of divers in such situations: paralysis. He sued the city, saying the lifeguard's negligent misrepresentation was to blame for his injuries. The Court gave judgment as a matter of law to the defendant. Its opinion is worth a look if you want to explore these variations on *Yania*:

> If the evidence shows that Heard dove into the water in justifiable reliance on the lifeguard's negligent words or acts, a prima facie case was made and properly presented to the jury. It is not enough for plaintiffs to say that defendant could have prevented Heard's conduct by withholding permission (see, Restatement [Second] of Torts §314). The issue is causality—in short, not what defendant could have prevented but what defendant proximately caused by inducing reliance. It was plaintiffs' failure to establish reliance that was a central contention in the City's motion to dismiss at the conclusion of plaintiffs' evidence, and on that basis the motion should have been granted. [...]

> In the context of this case, two theories of reliance are available to plaintiffs. First, an "assumed duty", or a "duty to go forward", may arise once a person undertakes a certain course of conduct upon which another relies. In determining whether a cause of action lies in such instances, "[t]he query always is whether the putative wrongdoer has advanced to such a point as to have launched a force or instrument of harm, or has stopped where inaction is at most a refusal to become an instrument of good" (*Moch Co. v. Rensselaer Water Co.*, 247 N.Y. 160). Put differently, the question is whether defendant's conduct placed plaintiff in a more vulnerable position than plaintiff would have been in had defendant done nothing (*Nallan v. Helmsley-Spear, Inc.*, 407 N.E.2d451 (1980)). In *Nallan*, plaintiff alleged that defendant was negligent in performing its

assumed duty by not providing a lobby attendant in a building on the night plaintiff was shot there. We suggested there that the assumed duty theory would have been viable if defendant's prior conduct (i.e., the provision of an attendant on other nights) had foreseeably led plaintiff to change his own conduct—for instance, by giving him a false sense of security. In such an instance, defendant's actions could properly be deemed to be a legal cause of plaintiff's harm.

No such causal connection is to be found in the present case. The mere fact that the lifeguard undertook to remove the boys from the jetty neither enhanced the risk Heard faced, created a new risk nor induced him to forego some opportunity to avoid risk. Simply stated, the lifeguard's actions created no justifiable reliance. Heard was in no worse position once the lifeguard acquiesced in his dive than if the lifeguard had stood by and done nothing. Thus, in looking at plaintiffs' evidence under an assumed duty theory, we conclude as a matter of law that the lifeguard's failure to insist that Heard leave the jetty was not a breach of duty proximately causing Heard's injuries.

The second theory of reliance available to plaintiffs would hold that the lifeguard's assent to the dive was a negligent misrepresentation as to the safety of the dive and that Heard foreseeably relied upon it to his own detriment.

At common law, mere statements, even those upon which persons were likely to act, were not grounds for an action in tort, unless fraud or deceit was alleged. Only negligent conduct, and not "negligence in word", was actionable. New York abandoned that distinction long ago. [...] Though initially the cause of action arose solely in commercial litigation, misrepresentation now may be asserted as grounds for recovery in personal injury litigation as well.

Not every misstatement, however, gives rise to a valid cause of action. For there to be an actionable claim, the defendant must be under a duty to the plaintiff to exercise reasonable care in giving the information, and plaintiff's reliance upon the information must be foreseeable. In elaborating on this test, we stated: "There must be knowledge or its equivalent that the information is desired for a serious purpose; that he to whom it is given intends to rely and act upon it; that if false or erroneous he will because of it be injured in person or property. Finally the relationship of the parties, arising out of contract or otherwise, must be such that in morals and good conscience the one has the right to rely upon the other for information, and the other giving the information owes a duty to give it with care."

There can be no doubt that a prima facie case is made out when one familiar with a hazard offers direct assurances of safety to one who is unfamiliar with the hazard and who foreseeably relies upon those assurances. In *Kriz v. Schum*, 549 N.E.2d 1155, we concluded that a facially sufficient complaint had been made where a diver using defendant's poorly lighted pool for the first time acted, in part, on defendant's assurances that diving was safe. Similarly, when one party seeks specific information from a second party, and the second party exclusively controls the information and purports to investigate the matter before responding, liability may be found (*International Prods. Co. v. Erie R.R. Co.*, 244 N.Y. 331).

No liability arises, however, when the statements are made in circumstances where reliance is unforeseeable or unjustified. Thus, in *Webb v. Cerasoli*, 87 N.Y.S.2d 884, we affirmed a decision holding that plaintiff, a painter, had no cause for action based on negligent misrepresentation when he overheard defendant property owner tell plaintiff's supervisor that it was safe to stand on a building's marquee while working and the marquee subsequently collapsed causing him injury. Similarly, the particular nature of the communication may serve to defeat plaintiffs' claim of reliance. A casual response given informally does not stand on the same legal footing as a deliberate representation for purposes of determining whether an action in negligence has been established.

In sum, our cases make clear that the determination of whether defendant, by negligent misrepresentation, breached a duty to plaintiff and proximately caused the injury turns on the reasonableness of both parties' conduct. Defendant must have imparted the information under circumstances and in such a way that it would be reasonable to believe plaintiff will rely upon it; plaintiff must rely upon it in the reasonable belief that such reliance is warranted (Restatement [Second] of Torts § 311, comments b, c).

Here, plaintiffs' evidence, when viewed in the light most favorable to them, is insufficient to establish the necessary reliance under a misrepresentation theory. Heard and his companions had been jumping and diving from the jetty for several minutes. They had done so earlier in the day as well. Thus, while the lifeguard may have been informed of the general hazards of their conduct as part of his training, Heard had at least some familiarity with the area based on his immediate experience and that of his companions. In fact, Heard exhibited his appreciation for the hazards involved by employing a shallow-water racing dive. In making his request of the lifeguard, he was not a person wholly without knowledge seeking assurances from one with exclusive knowledge. Moreover, the lifeguard made no explicit representation that diving was safe. Nothing about the exchange suggested that the lifeguard was imparting exclusive information about safety upon which Heard should rely. To the contrary, he clearly communicated to the boys that they were to leave the jetty. While his decision to permit Heard one last dive was inconsistent with that message, such inconsistency did not revoke the prior admonition or, according to the testimony, even create an ambiguity in the minds of the divers as to whether they were to leave the jetty. The evidence establishes that the lifeguard initially refused Heard's request and gave in only after Heard continued to press for permission.

At best, then, the lifeguard's statement was a reluctant assent that may have implicitly minimized the risk. In looking at the nature and context of the lifeguard's statement as presented in plaintiffs' evidence, however, we conclude that no reasonable person in Heard's position would have relied on such a statement in deciding to dive and that no jury could reasonably have found to the contrary[.] In the context of his continuing order that the jetty be cleared and his obvious reluctance to accede to Heard's wishes, the lifeguard was as much warning of danger as vouching for safety. In the face of such ambiguity, a reasonable person would not have relied upon the lifeguard's reluctant assent to decide to undertake an obvious hazard. That being so, as a matter of law, the lifeguard's statement was not a breach of duty that proximately caused Heard's injuries.

The court added in a footnote: "This case, like others involving reliance, may be analyzed as raising either an issue of proximate cause or scope of duty. Under either view, the question is whether the defendant had a duty to protect the plaintiff against the harm that occurred. Prosser and Keeton, *Torts* §42 at 274 (5th ed.).

Q. Can *Yania* be squared with §322 of the Restatement?
A. The idea would have to be that the defendant in *Yania* did not perform an "act" at all by goading Bigan.

Q. What justification can there be for the result in *Yania v. Bigan* and the nonduty to rescue?
A. Some thoughts on this are given in the literature excerpts later in the section. Posner has offered this summary of the pragmatic objections to a duty to rescue: the person who declines to throw a lifeline to a drowning man "is acting (or failing to act) in what most of us would consider a profoundly immoral way.

It is true that he is not punished, but this merely illustrates the imperfect overlap between law and morality. He is not punished for a variety of practical reasons: Such cases are rare. Amateur rescuers often make things worse. Punishing for not rescuing would make people steer clear of situations in which they might be in a position to perform a rescue. It is difficult to identify cases in which the rescuer would not have been imperiling himself. And imposing a legal duty of rescue would discourage altruistic rescues by making it more difficult for a rescuer to be recognized as an altruist[.]" *The Problematics of Moral and Legal Theory* 125-126 (1999).

Cf. Ian Ayres, *A Theoretical Fox Meets Empirical Hedgehogs: Competing Approaches to Law and Economics*, 82 Nw. U. L. Rev. 837 (1988), a review of Landes and Posner's *The Economic Structure of Tort Law* (1987):

> While Landes and Posner's stated goal is explicitly non-normative, there is the risk that in testing their efficiency theory they have become emotionally invested in its conclusions. Indeed, at times it seems that they [...] are laboring under some kind of burden to find efficiency explanations of common law rules.
>
> This is nowhere clearer than in Landes and Posner's analysis of the common law's refusal 'to impose liability for failure to assist a stranger in distress no matter how low the costs of assistance would be or how great its benefits.' Landes and Posner trot out an elaborate model to suggest that this common law rule of no liability may be efficient even when encouraging rescue is efficient. They argue that imposing liability on potential rescuers will cause them to avoid activities in which they might encounter a duty to rescue—so that there might actually be less rescuing if liability is imposed. A closer look at their model, however, leads to exactly the opposite conclusion. The assumption that potential rescuers will be motivated by the potential of liability to change their behavior indicates that they would fail to rescue if they came upon a victim and there was no threat of liability. Thus, within their model there would be no rescues in a no-liability world, because potential rescuers encountering a victim would not choose to incur the costs of rescue. Landes and Posner must compare a zero-rescue equilibrium under the no-liability rule with possibility of rescue (albeit with ex ante substitution) under the liability rule. Since something is always bigger than nothing, the logic of their model indicates that the common law rule is inefficient.

Q. What is the superficial similarity between *Weirum v. RKO General* and *Yania v. Bigan*?
A. In each case the defendant inveigled someone into doing something dangerous.

Q. What is the distinction between the two cases? Why was a duty found in *Weirum*, but not in *Yania v. Bigan*? (Or: why was the goading in *Weirum* treated as an affirmative act that could create liability, while the goading in *Yania* did not seem to count as an affirmative act at all?)
A. (1) In *Yania v. Bigan*, the inveigled person was a responsible adult, whereas in *Weirum* the inveigled people were irresponsible teens. (2) In *Weirum* the person hurt was an innocent third party, whereas in *Yania v. Bigan* the injured person was the same one who performed the irresponsible act in response to the inveigling.

Q. Suppose that in *Weirum* one of the teenagers had been hurt. Would the radio station have a duty in that case? What would be the analogy to *Yania v. Bigan*?
A. That would probably be a case of no liability, but it is hard to be sure. This hypothetical case would be analogous to *Yania* because the inveigled person would be the plaintiff. To create liability in this more extreme situation would be to impose a liability on the defendant for harm that was most directly caused by the plaintiff's own highly negligent (reckless) behavior toward herself. The *Weirum* teens were financially irresponsible, so their recklessness arguably should not bar suit against the radio station by an innocent third party; but they were old enough to know better and did not need the tort system to

subsidize their own irresponsibility toward themselves. Another possible way of looking at the point is that courts sometimes seem to allow people to collect only from those more irresponsible than themselves. The plaintiff in *Weirum* was able to collect from both the radio station and the teens, since both were more culpable than he; but if the teens were hurt they would not be able to collect from the radio station, since they were more blameworthy than the station was. We sometimes see this sort of logic in cases where social hosts are sued for damage done when their drunken guests drive home. In many jurisdictions third parties who are hurt by such guests can sue the hosts, but the guests themselves cannot sue.

Q. Suppose the party who drove recklessly in *Weirum* had been an immature adult—say, Donald Trump. Liability for the radio station?
A. Probably not, given the court's emphasis on the irresponsibility of the teenagers in *Weirum*. But query whether the point is that minors get special treatment or that we simply can foresse teenagers are likely to overreact to goading. If the latter is the correct point, so that it's a question of foreseeability rather than paternalism, it might follow that there would be liability for misbehavior by adult contestants, too, so long as it had happened often enough to put the radio station on notice of the danger.

Globe Malleable Iron & Steel Co. v. New York Cent. & H.R.R.Co. (D's train blocks fire cart; L)
Soldano v. O'Daniels (D refuses to allow telephone in bar to be used to call for help in stopping deadly assault; L)
Stangle v. Fireman's Fund Ins. Co. (D refuses to allow phone to be used to call for help in catching thief; NL)

Q. What is the distinction between *Globe Malleable Iron & Steel Co. v. New York Cent. & H.R.R.Co.* and *Yania v. Bigan*?
A. In both cases the defendant refused to go out of his (or its) way to help a party in trouble; the defendants in both cases basically stood still and watched. The distinctions here are, first, that in *Yania* the defendant refused to aid the plaintiff's decedent, whereas in *Globe* the defendant obstructed rescue efforts by others. (Nobody in the railroad cases was claiming that the railroads' employees would have been obliged to help put out the fires if help from the fire department had been unavailable.) Second, in *Yania* the defendant was exercising his right to do nothing in an entirely private setting, whereas in *Globe* the court views the defendant's behavior in blocking the street as occurring in a semi-public setting; there is a sense that the railroad has been granted special permission to run its tracks across a street, and that in return it is only fair to require the railroad to get out of the way when others need to move past. Third, there are distinctions between the cases on policy grounds. The policy basis of *Yania's* non-duty to rescue might be understood as involving a fear that if we require people to rescue others, they will make things worse, or that they will avoid situations where they might end up obliged to help, or that it might be hard to figure out which bystanders are within the range of the duty and which are far enough away to remain outside it. None of these considerations are very troublesome in the railroad cases. The railroad doesn't have to rescue anyone. It just has to make way for fire trucks and the like within a reasonable period of time.

 Yania might seem an even more promising case of liability than *Globe* if Bigan's goading were regarded as an "act" akin to pushing Yania into the water (or starting a fire, etc.). But as we have seen, mere goading of an adult is not considered an affirmative act that creates a duty.

Q. What is the analogy between *Soldano v. O'Daniels* and *Globe Malleable Iron & Steel Co. v. New York Cent. & H.R.R.Co.*?
A. In both cases the defendants are required to get out of the way so that others can try to assist a party in peril.

Q. What is the distinction between *Soldano* and *Stangle*?

A.   First, *Soldano* involved a threat to life; *Stangle* involved a threat to property. Second, Happy Jack's Saloon was under common ownership with the Circle Inn, so arguably a special relationship, maybe almost of innkeeper/guest, existed between the deceased and the defendant—though the court finds to the contrary.   In *Stangle* we see the predictable attempts to cabin the *Soldano* principle with various limitations before it gets out of hand. But does it make sense to draw the line based on considerations that may only be clear ex post? Some thefts are worse than some assaults, and in *Soldano* it may not have been clear to the defendant that a life was hanging in the balance when he denied permission to use his phone.

Here's what the court in *Stangle* said about *Soldano*:

> Whether a duty to plaintiff exists is primarily a question of law. *Weirum v. RKO General, Inc.* (1975). […] A narrow exception to this often harsh rule has been forged by the court when physical violence is threatened. *Soldano v. O'Daniels* [cite]. In *Soldano*, it was held that a restaurant owner owed a murder victim a duty to permit a third person the use of a telephone to call police when a death threat was made. In reversing summary judgment, the court rejected the restauranteur's argument that common law never imposed a duty to rescue one in peril. The court held there was a duty to permit use of the telephone to summon emergency aid, but underlined the narrow scope of the new rule: "[T]he duty would arise if and only if it were clearly conveyed that there exists an imminent danger of physical harm." The plaintiff herein argues by analogy that the rule announced in *Soldano* should be extended to "emergencies arising from all criminal conduct." Such a ruling would be a vast departure from the rule of nonliability for inaction, and we believe it would be ill-advised and unwarranted.

Q.   What is the superficial similarity between *Stangle* (or *Duncan*) and *Globe*? What is the distinction between them?

A.   In both cases the defendant obstructed efforts by others to save the plaintiff's property. Again, the policy considerations are different. A duty of a railroad to move its trains is not likely to get out of hand. A duty in *Stangle* might seem to have more potential to expand.

Q.   Why is there no duty on the part of a homeowner to allow strangers in distress to use the phone? Does the answer depend on considerations of morality and autonomy, or on policy considerations, or both?

A.   A home, unlike the restaurant in *Soldano*, is not open to the public, so an obligations to allow strangers to use the phone would create obvious dangers for homeowners, and indeed obvious incentives for thieves and marauders to feign emergencies (as the court in *Soldano* notes in its allusion to *A Clockwork Orange*).

Q.   How might you distinguish between *Soldano* and *Yania v. Bigan* without advocating a new rule?

A.   In Yania the defendant was called upon to perform a rescue; in *Soldano* the defendant was only entitled to make his property available for use in a rescue.

Q.   What is the analogy between *Stangle* and *Yania v. Bigan*?

A.   Each defendant was guilty of nonfeasance. The *Stangle* defendant's employee refused to allow the plaintiff's agent to use the defendant's telephone, and the *Yania* defendant failed to rescue the plaintiff. Indeed, misfeasance more plausibly occurred in *Yania*, because the *Yania* defendant encouraged the plaintiff to place himself in a position of danger and to use his premises as a place of business, whereas the *Stangle* defendant apparently did not encourage the plaintiff to use its business premises as a place to conduct the transaction.

Q. If the *Stangle* defendant were liable, how might it affect the incentives of the plaintiff or others in the future who are similarly situated? How easy would the defendant find it to avoid this type of negligence in the future? Did the defendant have a significant opportunity to control the risk created by Richards' jewel selling operations?

A. Extending liability to Fireman's Fund might reduce the plaintiff's incentive to avoid the harm. Indeed, liability in this case might, in a small way, encourage people with dubious transactions to conduct them in the lobbies of the richest corporations: if anything were to go awry, the defendant would be obliged to allow its resources to be used to stop a theft. The defendant would not find it easy to reduce this liability to zero. Although the receptionist was wrong to deny the plaintiff's agent the chance to use the phone, her type of lapse would be difficult for employers wholly to eliminate. Perhaps more plausibly, it might be argued that if the *Stangle* defendant were liable it would acquire a socially counterproductive incentive to ask building visitors to state their business with the company before being admitted onto the premises.

Q. What is the distinction between *Stangle* and *Ploof v. Putnam* (if you have covered the chapter on the necessity defense to intentional tort claims)?

A. The cases are difficult to distinguish. In both cases the plaintiff's property was at risk, and the plaintiff wanted to appropriate the defendant's property as part of a rescue effort; the defendant's failure to allow this was a source of liability in *Ploof* but not in *Stangle*. The plaintiff in *Stangle* apparently didn't press a private necessity theory, so it's hard to know what the court would have said about it.

Q. Suppose it was a public pay phone and the defendant's receptionist placed her body between the phone and Britt, refusing (unaccountably) to move. Would that be a case of liability?

A. It probably would be a case of liability on the ground that the defendant's employee would have committed an affirmative act. The analogy would be to fire cases like *Globe*, but the general question of liability for active interference with a voluntary rescue attempt is not well-settled.

Q. What if a stranger knocks on the door of a homeowner and asks that an ambulance be called because there is some sort of emergency occurring outside?

A. That could be a hard question in some jurisdictions, though we're not aware of any case quite like it. *Soldano* would be distinguishable because a public establishment was not involved; but the *Clockwork Orange* worry is not present, either, since the homeowner is not being asked to take any risks. The problem raises a few different threads that run through these cases: the distinction between non-obligations of people in private settings (*Yania*) and the partial obligations that may be imposed on them in more public contexts (*Globe, Soldano*); and the tension between the libertarian thread (*Yania*) and the more utilitarian thread (*Soldano*) we also see here and elsewhere in the course. The utilitarian or Hand formula calculus in duty cases tends, of course, to be conducted at the "macro" level: the question is whether the imposition of a duty will result in more benefits than costs in the long run, with both terms broadly understood (and with costs read to include the expense resulting from multiplication of suits).

SECTION B. DUTIES ARISING FROM UNDERTAKINGS

Lawter and *Frank* probably are the best teaching cases in this batch; the ones we would cut if pressed are *Ocotillo* and *Cuppy v. Bunch*.

Hurley v. Eddingfield (D doctor fails to come when summoned by P's decedent; NL)
O'Neill v. Montifiore Hospital (doctor tells P's decedent to come back later; L)

Q. What is the distinction between *Hurley* and *O'Neill*?

A. The superficial similarity is that in each case the plaintiff's decedent sought medical help and the defendant declined to furnish it. In both cases there apparently was some reliance. But in *Hurley* the reliance apparently was general (the defendant was the decedent's family doctor), and was not made on the basis of any particular promise or undertaking. The doctor in *Hurley* did not undertake to treat the plaintiff at all. The doctor in *O'Neill*, on the other hand, did offer the plaintiff a bit of advice. Advising O'Neill to come back later might have been interpreted as a diagnosis of his condition as unserious, and thus as an undertaking. To make the cases more analogous, one could imagine a case like *Hurley* in which the doctor listened to an account of the decedent's symptoms, then referred the plaintiff to some other doctor. Or a case like *O'Neill* where Dr. Graig flatly refused to advise the patient, and thus assumed no duty.

Q. What is the superficial similarity between *O'Neill* and *Yania v. Bigan*? What is the distinction between them? What is the analogy between *Hurley* and *Yania v. Bigan*?

A. In both *Yania* and *O'Neill* the defendant advised the plaintiff's decedent to do something that turned out to be fatal. But in *Hurley* the giving of the advice was said to amount to an undertaking to aid the plaintiff's decedent. The key distinction is not just that *O'Neill* involved a doctor (which might go to the existence of a special relationship—another possible ground for imposing a duty), but the existence of reasonable reliance in *O'Neill*. A rational adult doesn't jump in the lake just because someone tells him to, but he might go home from the hospital if a doctor so instructs.

Q. Hypothetical: in the classic case of <u>*Erie R. Co. v. Stewart*, 40 F.2d 855 (6th Cir. 1930)</u>, the defendant railroad maintained a watchman at a crossing in Cleveland. The plaintiff approached the crossing in a truck. The watchman did not make it out of his guardhouse in time to warn the plaintiff that a train was coming; as a result the plaintiff was hit by the train and sustained various injuries. The railroad argued that it had no duty to warn the plaintiff of the train; it provided the watchman on a voluntary basis and without legal obligation. What result?

A. Liability; the court of appeals affirmed a jury verdict for the plaintiff:

> Where the voluntary employment of a watchman was unknown to the traveler upon the highway, the mere absence of such watchman could probably not be considered as negligence toward him as a matter of law, for in such case there is neither an established duty positively owing to such traveler as a member of the general public, nor had he been led into reliance upon the custom. The question would remain simply whether the circumstances demanded such employment. But where the practice is known to the traveler upon the highway, and such traveler has been educated into reliance upon it, some positive duty must rest upon the railway with reference thereto. The elements of invitation and assurance of safety exist in this connection no less than in connection with contributory negligence. The company has established for itself a standard of due care while operating its trains across the highway, and, having led the traveler into reliance upon such standard, it should not be permitted thereafter to say that no duty required, arose from or attached to these precautions.

> This duty has been recognized as not only actual and positive, but as absolute, in the sense that the practice may not be discontinued without exercising reasonable care to give warning of such discontinuance, although the company may thereafter do all that would otherwise be reasonably necessary. Conceding for the purposes of this opinion that, in cases where a watchman is voluntarily employed by the railway in an abundance of precaution, the duty is not absolute, in the same sense as where it is imposed by statute, still, if there be some duty, it cannot be less than that the company must use reasonable care to see that reliance by members of the educated public upon its representation of safety is not converted into a trap. Responsibility for injury will arise if the service be negligently performed or abandoned without other notice of that fact. If this issue of negligent performance be disputed, the question would still be for the jury under the present

concession. But if the evidence in the case justifies only the conclusion of lack of due care, or if the absence of the watchman or the failure to give other notice of his withdrawal be wholly unexplained, so that but one inference may be drawn therefrom, the court is warranted in instructing the jury that, in that particular case, negligence appears as a matter of law.

So, in the present case, the evidence conclusively establishes the voluntary employment of a watchman, knowledge of this fact and reliance upon it by the plaintiff, a duty, therefore, that the company, through the watchman, will exercise reasonable care in warning such travelers as plaintiff, the presence of the watchman thereabouts, and no explanation of the failure to warn. Therefore, even though the duty be considered as qualified, rather than absolute, a prima facie case was established by plaintiff, requiring the defendant to go forward with evidence to rebut the presumption of negligence thus raised, or else suffer a verdict against it on this point. No such evidence was introduced by defendant. No other inference than that of negligence could therefore be drawn from the evidence.

Tuttle, D.J., concurred, arguing that the plaintiff should collect regardless of whether he could show actual reliance:

I am satisfied that where, as here, a railroad company has established a custom, known to the general public, of maintaining a watchman at a public crossing with instructions to warn the traveling public of the approach of trains, such railroad company, in the exercise of that reasonable care which it owes to the public, should expect, and is bound to expect, that any member of the traveling public approaching such crossing along the public highway is likely to have knowledge of, and to rely upon the giving of such warning. Such knowledge, with the consequent reliance, may be acquired by a traveler at any time, perhaps only a moment before going upon the crossing, and this also the railroad company is bound to anticipate. Having, in effect, given notice to the public traveling this highway that it would warn them of trains at this crossing, I think that it was bound to assume (at least in the absence of knowledge to the contrary) that every member of such public would receive, and rely on, such notice. Under such circumstances such a railroad company, in my opinion, owes to every traveler so approaching this crossing a duty to give such a warning, if reasonably possible, and a reasonably prudent railroad company would not fail, without sufficient cause, to perform that duty.

Q. Hypothetical (at the intersection of duty and proximate cause—you may want to hold off on it if you haven't covered the latter subject yet): in *Hieber v. Central Kentucky Traction Co.*, 140 S.W. 54 (1911), the plaintiff was a blacksmith and horseshoer. The defendant operated a rock quarry nearby. As the court recounted it, the plaintiff alleged that he "was daily, constantly, and habitually engaged in shoeing various horses of every disposition and temper for the public generally that would reasonably be frightened by the reports of the blasts made by the defendant in the quarry; that the plaintiff would thereby be placed in a position of great danger whenever such blasts should occur; that on November 5th, well knowing these facts, while the plaintiff was in the usual position of his trade underneath a mare engaged in shoeing her, the defendant negligently without notice to him set off various blasts of heavy explosives in the quarry in quick succession, creating loud noises calculated to frighten the mare, and which did frighten her so that she plunged and reared and jerked and wrenched the plaintiff, seriously injuring him to his damage in the sum of $12,000." To fend off the defendant's claim that he had no duty to warn the plaintiff, the plaintiff averred that prior to the accident "he had notified [the defendant] of the dangers to which he was subjected by the blasts and requested it to notify him when the blasts were to be exploded, so that he could avoid the danger; that thereafter the defendant did habitually notify him when it intended to fire a blast, but on the occasion in question it neglected to give him notice, and fired the blast at an unusual and unaccustomed time of the day when the plaintiff could not and did not know or expect it to be fired, by reason of which he was injured." The defendant demurred. What result?

A. No liability:

> The fact that the defendant voluntarily did for a season what it was not required to do is not sufficient to impose a liability on it. The rule that, where a private crossing has been treated by a railroad company as a public crossing, it will be held liable if the proper signals are not given of the approach of a train, has no application; for there the train itself does the injury. Here there was no injury done by the blasting; the injury was inflicted by the horse, and the case would not be different if the horse had been frightened by one of the defendant's cars running past the shop without notice of its approach, when it was usual for the cars to give notice of their approach to a crossing near by. In such an action it would add nothing to the petition to aver that the car ran unusually and excessively fast and made great and unnecessary noises. The result that happened here would have followed a sudden clap of thunder, or any like noise on adjacent property while the plaintiff was under the mare. The plaintiff does not show that the blasting was a nuisance or objectionable in any way, except that it was fired when he was under the mare without notice to him. There is no greater liability for the noise made in blasting than for any other like noise lawfully made by one on his own premises.

United States v. Lawter (D tries to rescue P's decedent but drops her from helicopter; L)
Frank v. United States (D tries to rescue P's decedent but can't reach him when he falls overboard on way to shore)

Q. What is the distinction between *United States v. Lawter* and *Frank v. United States*?
A. There was no evidence (and no suggestion either in the evidence or—importantly—in the allegations of the plaintiff) that Frank fell into the sea because of any negligence by his rescuers. The Good Samaritan doctrine requires a rescuer to use due care in carrying out a rescue, even if gratuitously undertaken, perhaps on the theory that the rescue attempt discouraged others from trying (though usually no showing of the latter condition is required for the doctrine to apply); but it does not make the rescuer responsible to the plaintiff if the situation worsens in some way for which the rescuer is not responsible. In other words, the Coast Guard would have been liable in *Frank* if they had operated their rescue boat negligently, and this caused Frank to fall into the water and drown. Then the case would be like *Lawter*. Instead we have a case where the Coast Guard undertook and non-negligently attempted to rescue Frank; but the situation then worsened when Frank fell overboard, and the Coast Guard was not ready to handle this situation. It's as if Frank's boat had sprung a leak while being towed back to shore: the fact that the Coast Guard crew had started to tow the boat did not oblige them to be ready to handle the more difficult situation that could arise if the boat sank.

The oddity of resolving the case on duty grounds, though, is that it implies there would be no liability if the Coast Guard, after seeing Frank fall into the water, simply pressed on to shore with his boat without making any effort to rescue him. These facts smell like liability, though the court's approach suggests otherwise. Perhaps the court should have held this to be a case of duty but no breach. You can build various hypotheticals to explore these ideas—they circle back for him; they don't circle back for him; they circle back but then change their minds and head for shore; etc.

Here is what the court in *Frank* said to distinguish that case from *Lawter*:

> On appellant's own theory the effect of the alleged faults of the Coast Guard was to prevent its own rescue party from reaching the drowning man soon enough to save him. There has been no showing that any fault of the Coast Guard contributed in any way to Frank's falling into the sea. Nor did the Coast Guard in any way worsen his plight thereafter. In saying this we have not overlooked a suggestion on this appeal that the Coast Guard may have worsened Frank's position by taking the cruiser in tow. No such finding was made below and on the evidence such a finding could not reasonably have been made. The present claim must stand or fall on the theory that the

Coast Guard was at fault solely in failing to get help to the decedent as soon as would have been the case had the rescue vessel been in proper condition and properly equipped and manned.

In the absence of any duty creating relationship the responsibility of a volunteer is strictly limited. He may be liable if the injured person has been harmed because of reliance upon some representation concerning the voluntary service. More generally, if an attempted rescue or other voluntary service is so conducted that it affirmatively injures the one in distress or worsens his positions, there may be liability. *United States v. Lawter*, 5 Cir., 1955, 219 F.2d 559; [...] Restatement, Torts, secs. 323, 324. But again, we have in this case none of these special liability creating factors. We have only a diligent rescue effort which proved ineffectual for lack of adequate equipment, preparation or personnel. For such ineffectual effort a private salvor is not liable.

Cf. *Daley v. United States*, 499 F.Supp. 1005 (D. Mass. 1980) (some citations omitted):

To return to plaintiff's contention that undertaking a search obliges the Coast Guard to conduct it carefully, this is true if the Coast Guard thereby worsens the subject's position, as by causing affirmative injury. E. g., *United States v. Lawter*, 5 Cir., 1955, 219 F.2d 559 (negligence in hoisting seaman without safety harness). Or there may be indirect harm, as by causing other searchers, or possible searchers, to "rest on their oars," in reliance on the Coast Guard's undertaking and its presumed, unless affirmatively disclaimed, competency. If, on the other hand, there were no such reliance, as here where no one else was available, a negligent failure to confer a benefit which more careful conduct would have achieved will not impose liability. *Frank v. United States* [...].

Q. What if the government in *Lawter* could show that if it had not tried to rescue the Lawters, they would have drowned?
A. Such a showing would suggest that the bungled rescue didn't make Mrs. Lawter any worse off than she would have been if the rescue had not been attempted at all. Yet it still would be a case of liability on the "good Samaritan" reasoning described a moment ago. Maybe the idea is that we don't want to create a pocket of immunity in which people like Antle are immune from liability for their carelessness once they start rescuing someone who would be a goner without their help. (See the notes on *Marsalis* for a bit more about this general issue.) An interesting related question is whether this might nevertheless be made relevant to damages.

Q. Return to *Yania v. Bigan*. Suppose Bigan goes and gets a rope to rescue Yania. As Bigan is lowering the rope it slides through his fingers and both ends end up in the water, ruining the rescue attempt. Yania drowns. Liability?
A. Probably not, since so far as the hypo reveals Yania didn't rely on Bigan in any way. It would be about the same as a case where Bigan volunteers to go get a rope, then gets lost or gets in an accident or forgets about it and never returns. Yania can only win in that case by showing that the undertaking and its failure made him worse off than he would have been if there had been no undertaking at all—perhaps by showing that he somehow relied on Bigan (didn't yell for other help?) and so lost other possible opportunities to obtain aid.

Q. Now suppose the rope does reach Bigan and Yania begins hoisting him up out of the water; but at the last minute Bigan negligently lets the rope slip away, causing Yania to fall onto some rocks and die. Liability?
A. Yes; that would be analogous to *Lawter*.

Q. What if Bigan is pulling Yania to shore (horizontally, not up a cliff), but then loses interest, drops the rope, and walks away?

A. A close and unsettled case, as the Restatement acknowledges. Bigan has left Yania no worse off (and perhaps a little better off) than he would have been if there had been no rescue attempt at all, and he has not affirmatively harmed him.

Ocotillo West Joint Venture v. Superior Court (D takes car keys from country club and gives them to drunk friend—P's decedent; L)
Cuppy v. Bunch (D invites drunken friend to follow him in his car; drunken friend hits other driver, who sues D; NL)

Q. What is the distinction between these cases?

A. Perhaps White never had control over Bunch (in *Cuppy*) quite like the control that Easley had over Zylka (in *Ocotillo*). Easley undertook a responsibility as custodian of Zylka's car keys. That assumption of responsibility caused other rescuers (at Ocotillo) to "rest on their oars" and give up on their own attempts to help Zylka. White, on the other hand, never undertook to do more, or assumed more responsibility, than to drive in such a way that Bunch could follow him. It's not clear that White was ever in a position to stop Bunch from driving, except perhaps by declining to wake him up at all—but waking a sleeping passenger surely does not amount to the assumption of a duty to him or to others. If we assume that Bunch was then going to drive one way or another, White's undertaking and his performance of it made it less rather than more likely that Bunch would cause an accident. It would be different if White "led the way" negligently and increased the likelihood that Bunch would hit someone.

Marsalis v. LaSalle (problem: D promises to keep cat inside, but then doesn't, so P has to get rabies shot to which she reacts badly; L)
Bloomberg v. Interinsurance Exchange of the Automobile Club of So. Cal. (problem: P's decedent calls D to request tow truck that never comes, and is hit by drunk driver while waiting for it; L)

Q. What result in *Bloomberg*?

A. The trial court dismissed the complaint; the court of appeals reversed:

> Based on [the facts alleged in the complaint], we cannot say that respondent owed no duty of care to appellants' son. The undertaking to send the tow truck clearly did affect his interest. Had they not expected respondent to send assistance, the boys may have made other arrangements. They could have called their parents, a friend or even CHP to be driven home or at least to a safer location. Appellants allege that the Auto Club failed to locate the stalled vehicle due to its negligence. If appellants can prove respondent's negligence, respondent will be held liable for its breach of duty.

Q. Suppose that in *Yania v. Bigan*, Bigan promises to go get some helpers to rescue Yania. He takes an unreasonably long time to do this, or perhaps never returns at all. Yania drowns. Liability under *Bloomberg*?

A. Not unless Yania had some alternative means of obtaining help that he could have used if he had known Bigan would not return. (But perhaps he did: the *Yania* opinion mentions the presence of another person at the scene of the drowning, a companion of Yania's named Ross.)

Q. What result in *Marsalis v. La Salle*?

A. Liability—not for the scratch, but for the consequences of the treatment afterwards:

Perhaps the defendant, LaSalle, initially owed no duty whatever to Mrs. Marsalis, but when he once agreed to restrain and keep the cat under observation, he was bound to use reasonable care and prudence in doing so and to assume and exercise reasonable care and common humanity. It may be that Mrs. Marsalis had open to her some other course by which she could have had the cat incarcerated and examined in order to determine if it was rabid, but she unquestionably and in good faith relied upon defendant to carry out the agreement which he voluntarily made, thus forgoing such other possible available protection. It was of extreme importance to know if the cat had rabies so she could regulate her course of conduct with reference to the injury. We do not doubt for one moment that both defendant and his wife were fully cognizant that such injures could be quite serious and exceedingly dangerous in the event the offending animal was infected with rabies.

Q. What would have happened if the owners of the store in *Marsalis* had not agreed to keep an eye on the cat?

A. Hard to say, but liability is conceivable. The reason there was no liability here for the cat scratch itself was that the one bite rule (roughly speaking) applied, and the cat had been well-behaved in the past. But a duty to the plaintiff might have arisen anyway under the logic of section 321 of the Second Restatement, quoted in the text after *Yania v. Bigan*: if a defendant injures a plaintiff, even without negligence, a duty of care is triggered to take reasonable steps to help reduce the resulting damage. The plaintiff was one of the defendant's customers, so a duty of care might well be founded on that ground as well.

Q. Why wasn't *Marsalis* a contract (or promissory estoppel) case rather than a tort case?

A. Probably because it can be hard to collect personal injury damages under a contract theory. Note that the defendants are being held liable for the plaintiff's injuries not because their cat bit the plaintiff, but because they promised to keep the cat under observation and then didn't.

Q. For Mrs. Marsalis to win, should it be necessary for her to show that she would have been able to get the cat quarantined in some other way if the defendants had refused to help?

A. Perhaps so. We're assuming now that the undertaking theory was the plaintiff's only argument that the defendants had a duty. The idea then would be that the defendants might argue that there was no reliance on their undertaking, and thus that the rationale for turning it into the source of a duty was not present: the defendants' promise and subsequent carelessness didn't make her any worse off than she would have been if they had not agreed to do anything. But one of the vexing issues in undertaking cases is the extent to which the plaintiff must show damaging reliance on the defendant's efforts. We suggested in the *Yania* hypo a minute ago that such reliance would have to be shown, and in *Bloomberg* it seemed important, but then in the *Lawter* case it didn't seem necessary after all. What gives? Maybe the best explanation is this: if you try to rescue someone and negligently hurt them, you are held liable regardless of whether it can be shown that your attempt actually caused others to "rest on their oars" because we want you to have an incentive to be careful once you have singled yourself out as a rescuer and have put yourself in a position to make the rescuee worse off than you found him. But if you merely announce an intention to try to rescue the person yet don't actually go through with it, the same policy worries aren't quite in place; you aren't doing anything *to* him that creates a risk of injury and that therefore should be disciplined by the threat of liability. There still *can* be liability, but first we want to see evidence that they victim was worse off in some other sense—some variety of reliance by the victim or by other potential rescuers.

Q. What is the analogy between *Bloomberg* and *Marsalis*?

A. In both cases the defendant made a representation on which the plaintiff (or plaintiff's decedent) reasonably relied, forgoing other avenues of assistance; in both cases a duty resulted that was breached when the defendant didn't follow through.

SECTION C. SPECIAL RELATIONSHIPS

1. Duties to rescue or assist others

We find the *Trans-Pacific* case a good one for drawing out the general logic of special relationships. *Brosnahan* and *Boyette* are expendable if you want to shorten the section.

Petition of Trans-Pacific Fishing & Packing Co. (L when D's captain failed to go look for crewmen washed overboard)

Q. What is the distinction between *Petition of Trans-Pacific Fishing & Packing Co.* and *Yania v. Bigan*?
A. In both cases the defendant did nothing to rescue someone who was at risk of drowning. But in the *Trans-Pacific* case the defendant was a captain of a ship on which the plaintiffs (or the plaintiff's decedent, in one case) were crewmen. It seems intuitive that this would make a legal difference—but *why*, exactly? True, the crewmen are highly dependent on the ship for rescue—though not 100% dependent, as the rescue of two of the men in this case by other boats illustrates. Yet Yania, too, may well have been utterly dependent on Bigan if he was to have any hope of being rescued. One also might try to distinguish the cases on the ground that the crewmen were swept overboard by a wave, whereas Yania foolishly jumped into the water on his own. But *Gardner* (in the chapter on cause in fact) makes clear that the duty to rescue applies even if the crewman purposely jumps into the water because he is bent on self-destruction. So maybe the result in *Trans-Pacific* involves the implicit contract terms the court imagines the parties would have devised if the parties had foreseen the situation in advance, but then why can't that also be true in *Yania*?

In the end, the best way to understand the cases may be from a policy standpoint. To impose a duty on Bigan could have implications that are tricky to contain. To impose a duty on captains of ships is less tricky: "men overboard" present a particular scenario where the dangers involved in creating duties to rescue seem less pronounced than they would be in the world at large. Rescuers on ships will not generally be at risk of putting themselves in great danger; they will tend to be reasonably well-equipped and less likely to be amateurish than ordinary rescuers like Bigan would be; they eliminate the "multiple rescuer" problem Levmore discusses later in the chapter since they usually will be the only possible rescuer around (that could have been true in *Yania,* but it would require a judicial inquiry to find out; in cases at sea we more cheaply can assume it). The elements of the Hand formula can be used to sketch the point.

Brosnahan v. Western Air Lines (P hit on head by piece of luggage on D's plane; L)
Boyette v. Trans World Airlines (D's employees chase passenger through airport into trash compactor, where he dies; NL)

Q. What is the distinction between these cases?
A. In *Brosnahan* the plaintiff was on the airplane, so the special relationship between common carrier and passenger was intact. In *Boyette* the relationship had ended because the plaintiff's decedent had left the plane. Once a person leaves an airplane, the costs of imposing a duty on the airline's employees become much higher, and the benefits smaller (he no longer depends on him).

Q. What if the TWA flight attendant in *Boyette* had seen a deactivation switch for the compactor, but malevolently declined to use it? Liability? What about the lack of duty?
A. This apparently would be a case of no liability, since the attendant had no duty to rescue Rutherford. Adding malevolence to a fact pattern often is a useful way of testing a "no duty" claim.

Q.   What if the TWA flight attendant in *Boyette* had bumped into the activation switch for the trash compactor? Liability? What about the lack of duty?
A.   Possible liability. The lack of a duty just means the attendant had no duty to rescue. He still had a duty to refrain from affirmative negligent acts that harmed Rutherford—bumping him into the trash compactor, or bumping into a switch activating the compactor if this was done negligently—in other words, if a reasonable person would have perceived the risk of this and taken care to avoid it.

Charles v. Seigfried (NL for social host)
Kelly v. Gwinnell (L for social host)

Q.   What is the distinction between *Charles v. Seigfried* (NL for social host who lets guest drive drunk) and *Ocotillo West Joint Venture v. Superior Court* (L for defendant who gives car keys to drunken friend)?
A.   In *Ocotillo* the defendant had control over his friend's car keys, and had undertaken to care for him in place of the golf club's attendants. In *Charles,* as in *Cuppy v. Bunch,* the defendant did not have comparable control over the driver. It may be that there would be no liability in *Charles* even if the host in that case had control over the driver's keys. If so, perhaps the difference is just that *Ocotillo* involved a relatively discrete situation where liability could be imposed without raising all of the slippery-slope fears that troubled the court in *Charles* when it considered the consequences of general liability for social hosts.

Q.   Why might some courts impose liability on social hosts when their drunken guests injure others, but not when the guests injure themselves?
A.   The third party is utterly innocent and ought to be able to collect from either the guest or the host, since both are culpable to varying degrees. But the guest himself (or, as in *Charles,* herself) is more culpable than the host, so allowing the guest to collect from the host is less appealing. There is a possible analogy here to *Weirum v. RKO Radio General.*

Q.   What is the difference between the judicial philosophies of the courts in *Charles v. Seigfried* and *Kelly v. Gwinnell*?
A.   The cases present a nice occasion for discussing the pros and cons of using the courts to effect various kinds of social change, New Jersey style, as opposed to leaving such changes to the legislature, as the Illinois court favors.

2. Duties to protect others from third parties

Tarasoff v. Board of Regents (therapist employed by D fails to warn P's decedent that patient plans to kill her; L)
Thompson v. County of Alameda (D fails to warn neighborhood that released inmate plans to kill child in P's neighborhood, which he then does; NL)
Kline v. 1500 Massachusetts Ave. (D apartment building fails to prevent attack on tenant; L)

        Bradshaw v. Daniel and *Hawkins v. Pizarro* are very good cases, but they are the ones to cut if you want to shorten things; some of their policy themes also are discussed in the section of the chapter on the privity doctrine.

From Alan F. Stone, *The Tarasoff Decisions: Suing Psychotherapists to Safeguard Society*, 90 Harv. L. Rev. 358 (1976):

The Tarasoff decisions are the product of a court unwilling to admit the consequences for public safety of the recent general trend, in which it has played a substantial role, toward increasing recognition of the rights of the mentally ill and the resulting change in civil commitment procedures. The California legislature was in the vanguard of these developments. In passing the Lanterman-Petris-Short Act it made civil commitment more difficult to initiate and even more difficult to prolong. Indeed, the Poddar case is an example of these new difficulties of initiating commitment. And on the basis of my understanding of common practice in California, I am willing to speculate that an element in the decision of the campus police not to take Poddar to an L.P.S. detention facility was their experience that someone like him would be back on the street in a few days, resentful of police intervention. These sweeping changes mean that society must tolerate greater disturbance in the community and greater risks of harm to the public. Attempts like that of the *Tarasoff* court to avoid these results by exposing therapists to greater liability are self-defeating for, because of its effect on both therapists and patients, the imposition of a duty to warn third parties will result in a lower level of safety for society. [...]

[T]he imposition of a duty to protect, which may take the form of a duty to warn threatened third parties, will imperil the therapeutic alliance and destroy the patient's expectation of confidentiality, thereby thwarting effective treatment and ultimately reducing public safety. The nature of the illness and treatment of the kind of dangerous person who voluntarily comes to therapy makes the imposition of such a duty particularly destructive. Such a person is typically not a hardened criminal but rather one whose violence is the product of passion or paranoia. The object of that passion or paranoia is most often a person of intense significance to the patient. Such, of course, was the case with Poddar. When a therapist tries to deal with the potential for violence of such patients, he must enter into a therapeutic alliance in which feelings are acknowledged at the same time that the impulses to act them out are discouraged. To maintain this attitude of respect for and acceptance of the patient's feelings while discouraging any violent action is often the central task of the therapist. If all goes well, the patient whose feelings are accepted will come to trust the therapist and be able to explore and understand his violent impulses and consider meaningful alternatives to them. Given the special significance of the potential victim to those whose violence is the product of passion and paranoia, nothing could be more destructive of the tenuous therapeutic alliance than the patient's perception that there exists a significant relationship between the therapist and the potential victim. Nothing is more likely to give a patient the impression that such a significant relationship exists than being told by the therapist that he has a legal duty to protect, and perhaps to warn directly, the potential victim.

Q. What is the distinction between *Tarasoff* and *Yania v. Bigan*? (Why are courts ready to find a duty in the one case but not in the other?)

A. First, it is a useful exercise to be clear about the strand of *Yania* at issue here. When the case being discussed was *Weirum,* the question was whether *Yania* was analogous in the sense that both cases involved claims of liability for goading. The question about *Tarasoff* is how it can be squared with *Yania*'s holding that there was no duty to rescue. Some distinctions: In *Tarasoff* the burden being imposed on the therapist is relatively slight and relatively easy to cabin ("relatively" compared to a general duty on passersby): the therapist is not obliged to put herself at risk, and does not need to use much imagination to decide what to do. There is a simple duty to warn, not a duty to rescue. Further, unlike random members of the public, therapists are trained in part to be able to diagnose dangerous people. So the good likely to be accomplished by a duty on the *Tarasoff* facts is greater than on facts like *Yania*, and the costs seem likely to be smaller.

Q. *Tarasoff* finds liability for the University of California, holding that a psychiatrist has a duty to warn a victim whom her patient has named when the psychiatrist has actually predicted (or, apparently, should

have predicted) that the patient will kill that victim. But *Tarasoff* finds no liability for the actions of University of California police. Why? What is the distinction between the police and the psychiatrist?
A. The police, unlike the psychiatrist, were held not to have a special relationship with the killer. But why? Presumably on the same sorts of policy grounds that drive the rest of the opinion: the benefits of imposing a duty on the police are likely to be lesser, and the costs greater. The police generally may have less ability than psychiatrists to predict violent behavior, and in that case they either will have to spend more resources improving their predictive research or else make more inaccurate predictions; and if they do make lots of inaccurate predictions, the costs of imposing the duty increase and the benefit of imposing the duty goes down. At the same time the police are more likely than psychiatrists to be bombarded with indicators that people they hear about or deal with are threatening others. So imposing a duty to warn on the police might have more far-reaching consequences than the duty imposed here on psychiatrists, which is triggered on a relatively infrequent basis. Finally and relatedly, courts generally may be more willing to impose potentially onerous tort duties on psychiatrists than they are to give comparable orders to the police, which are part of a coequal branch of the government. These are some of the same considerations that lie behind upcoming public duty cases like *Riss*.

Q. What is the distinction between *Tarasoff* and *Thompson v. County of Alameda?*
A. In *Thompson,* unlike in *Tarasoff*, the victim was not individually identified. This would go to the burdensomeness of imposing an obligation: the defendants in *Thompson* would have to notify everyone in the neighborhood, which would be more difficult and also more costly (because more widely stigmatizing) to the released party. That creates costs for the released party and also broader policy costs; hence the court's worry about discouraging an innovative release program. Not knowing who the victim is also would make the warnings less effective because they would be more diffuse. So the costs of imposing a duty here are greater than in *Tarasoff*, and the benefits are smaller.

Incidentally, the plaintiff in *Thompson* did also say that the defendant county had been negligent in releasing James F. at all, but this claim was held to be ruled out by the statute conferring the power to make parole decisions on the county; the court held that the statute "compels immunity from judicial reexamination."

Q. How does the existence of a contract bear on the question of duty in *Kline?*
A. It might be thought to cut against liability, since liability effectively forces a contract term on the parties that they might not have wanted ("apparently did not want" is another way of phrasing it). Obviously the plaintiff, like any tenant, would have liked more protection other things being equal; the question is whether tenants in her position want to pay for it. Are there features of the facts here that support a justifiable distrust of the contract solution to the security problem? (In Thompson there was no contract, making the imposition of tort liability as a sort of substitute potentially appealing on economic grounds.)

In any event, the *Kline* approach has grown steadily in influence. A number of arguments against it are presented in *Goldberg v. Housing Authority of the City of Newark*, 186 A.2d 291 (N.J. 1962), on which the defendant in *Kline* tried to rely. We will excerpt a bit of *Goldberg* here since its arguments can provide a basis for lively classroom discussion of *Kline*. A milkman was attacked on an elevator when he was making a delivery to residents of a public housing project in Newark. He sued the public corporation that operated the project for failing to provide police protection. The jury found for the defendant, and the state supreme court affirmed. The court found that since the corporation operating the project was created by a limited statute that did not give it all the powers of the city government, the corporation's liability should be judged by the standards applicable to private owners of such residential housing. Then:

> The question whether a private party must provide protection for another is not solved merely by recourse to "foreseeability." Everyone can foresee the commission of crime virtually anywhere and at any time. If foreseeability itself gave rise to a duty to provide "police" protection for

others, every residential curtilage, every shop, every store, every manufacturing plant would have to be patrolled by the private arms of the owner. And since hijacking and attack upon occupants of motor vehicles are also foreseeable, it would be the duty of every motorist to provide armed protection for his passengers and the property of others. Of course, none of this is at all palatable. [...]

Subject to modifying legislation, a landlord offers to lease accommodations which a prospective tenant may take or not as he chooses. The landlord may offer sundry services, which of course will be reflected in the rental charge, but in the absence of statute, there is no duty to furnish them. Thus a landlord may offer to provide a doorman during the day or around the clock, but he need not, and we know that such services are available only in the more luxurious apartment houses, beyond the reach of the average citizen. [...]

[W]e should not let our understandable concern for the unfortunate plaintiff obscure the fact that the burden of this duty would fall upon citizens who can hardly afford it. We are not dealing with a risk which can be passed along in an increase in liability insurance premiums. We are talking of the employment of men, perhaps the employment, if something like effective assurance is to be realized, of doormen around the clock to cover each of the entrances to the buildings, here a total of 20 entrances. If the owner must provide that service, every insurance carrier will insist that he do it. The bill will be paid, not by the owner, but by the tenants. And if, as we apprehend, the incidence of crime is greatest in the areas in which the poor must live, they, and they alone, will be singled out to pay for their own police protection. The burden should be upon the whole community and not upon the segment of the citizenry which is least able to bear it.

Hence we believe this most troublesome problem must be left with the duly constituted police forces. The job is theirs to prevent crime and to go wherever need be to that end. It may well be that the owner of multi-family housing may refuse to permit patrol of the common areas by the public police, and if the owner should thus assert his property right, it would indeed be appropriate to visit upon him the losses sustained by those to whom he denied the protection the public authorities were willing to provide. But the duty to provide police protection is and should remain the duty of government and not of the owner of a housing project.

Bradshaw v. Daniel (D doctor fails to tell dying patient's wife that she may be at risk of same disease; L)
Hawkins v. Pizarro (D doctor negligently misinforms patients that she does not have hepatitis; she then meets P and gives him hepatitis; NL)

Q. What is the possible analogy between *Tarasoff* and *Bradshaw v. Daniel*? Is the *Bradshaw* court's reliance on *Tarasoff* persuasive? How might you have distinguished them?
A. In both cases a helping professional with a special relationship to a patient became aware during the course of treatment that a third party was at risk of injury. *Bradshaw* and *Tarasoff* might have been distinguishable because in *Bradshaw* the risk to the third party was not quite a risk caused by the defendant's patient; rather, the risk to the patient and the risk to the third party came from the same independent source (the ticks). Further, a patient's credible statement that he plans to kill a third party is an unmistakable signal to a therapist that the third party may be in danger, whereas it may be less obvious to a doctor that if a patient is suffering from a disease carried by ticks, the patient's spouse may be inor for danger of catching the same disease. Still, the court's statement that the reasons behind *Tarasoff* are "equally compelling" on these facts may not be as far-fetched as it will sound to many students. Here as in *Tarasoff*, the duty imposed is relatively narrow and, if discharged properly, can have important good

consequences. Presumably the extent of the knowledge the doctor had or should have had is a question of fact resolved in favor of the plaintiff here for purposes of summary judgment.

Q. What is the distinction between *Bradshaw v. Daniel* and *Hawkins v. Pizarro*?

A. In *Hawkins* the identity of the potential victim was not clear; indeed, the patient had not yet even met the victim. The case thus might seem analogous to *Thompson*, where the identity of the threatened person likewise was not clear. But *Hawkins* and *Thompson* are potentially distinguishable because in *Hawkins* the doctor could simply have warned his patient that she had hepatitis, whereas in *Thompson* warning the murderous boy was not a useful option. The result in *Hawkins* thus may seem a little hard to understand. Perhaps the concern is that if doctors are potentially liable not only to the families of their infectious patients but also to any new people their patients meet and infect, that potential liability may become unpredictable and immense. The doctor has no way of knowing whether the patient will go on to infect one person or dozens (and then how many more might *they* go on to infect?)—thus making the doctor's liability exposure unwieldy. We see reasoning like this in the privity cases that follow later in this chapter.

A position apparently different from that found in *Hawkins* was taken in *DiMarco v. Lynch Homes*, 583 A.2d 422 (Pa. 1990). The defendant doctor told the patient, who had been exposed to hepatitis in her workplace, that if she was free from symptoms for six weeks she could conclude that she didn't have the disease. After the six weeks had passed, the patient resumed sexual relations with her boyfriend—and gave him hepatitis. The doctors should have advised her to wait six months, not six weeks. The court found liability. The case can be distinguished from *Hawkins* on its facts because the boyfriend's existence was known when the negligence occurred. But the majority suggested that such knowledge was not critical: "The Dissenting Opinion suggests that finding a cause of action in this case and in similar cases will cause professionals to "narrow their inquiries into the client or patient situation, to the detriment of the client or patient, so as to avoid possible liability toward third parties which might come from knowing 'too much.' Such a danger is simply not present here. When treating a patient with a communicable disease, a physician is acutely aware of the possible risk to third persons. Therefore, no such additional inquiry is necessary; nor is it conceivable that any physician, under similar circumstances, would limit his or her treatment of a patient so as to avoid possible liability." But the implications of this were not entirely clear, for the court spoke in the present tense in also holding that "the class of persons whose health is likely to be threatened by the patient includes any one who is physically intimate with the patient."

Q. Suppose a doctor discovers that one of his patients has a venereal disease. Is he obliged to warn the patient's current sexual partners?

A. Probably not. It becomes an especially difficult question in AIDS cases, of course, because the stakes there, as in *Tarasoff*, are life and death. You can build hypotheticals out of the old cases finding liability where doctors fail to warn plaintiffs that a family member or neighbor has a contagious disease—e.g., smallpox; see, e.g., *Edwards v. Lamb*, 45 A. 480 (N.H. 1899); *Skillings v. Allen*, 173 N.W. 663 (1919); *Jones v. Stanko*, 160 N.E. 456 (1928). But in these cases the family member or neighbor typically asks the doctor whether the patient is contagious, is told no, and then gets the disease. So the burden on the doctor was low (nobody was asking the doctor to seek out anyone to issue a warning), and these also were cases where the benefits of the warning might have seemed higher because transmission would have been harder to avoid (no sex was required). The invasiveness of informing someone that their partner has AIDS is greater because it might imply bad things about the behavior in which the patient engaged in the course of contracting the disease. Yes, it also would have been invasive for the therapist in *Tarasoff* to have informed Tarasoff of Poddar's plans, but informing a third party of a patient's intentions to kill them seems less likely to do fresh damage to their relationship than informing a patient's lover of a stigmatizing physical condition. All this might in turn discourage some people from getting tested at all, a worry that probably was less significant in the old disease cases—especially in the cases where the disease might have been curable, since that gave its holder a good reason to want medical attention even if there were side costs associated with it.

3. *The public duty doctrine*

If you want to cut one of these, make it *Wanzer*. *Riss* and *Schuster* alone can take some time to teach.

Riss v. City of New York (P begs D's police for help, doesn't get it, and is attacked; NL)
Schuster v. City of New York (P's decedent identifies crook on "wanted" poster; D fails to protect P's decedent, and he is rubbed out by crook's allies; L)
Wanzer v. District of Columbia (problem: P's decedent calls 911 and is talked out of requesting help; NL)

Q. What is the distinction between *Riss v. City of New York* and *Schuster v. City of New York*?
A. In *Schuster* the parties had a so-called special relationship: the plaintiff's decedent contributed to the cause of law enforcement, and the police therefore owed him a reciprocal duty of care. Riss didn't make such a contribution. Or did she? She did, after all, identify a criminal threat to the police; but perhaps that is just the point. Pugach merely was a *potential* criminal, whereas Willie Sutton was a wanted criminal and the police had asked the public for help in finding him. This might be seen as a matter of fairness: Schuster put himself at risk for the public good, and was entitled to protection as a kind of earned compensation. But the same point can be stated in terms of policy. By fingering Sutton, Schuster was creating an external benefit; if he is not compensated with at least some protection, people in his position can't be expected to cooperate in the long run. Riss was seeking protection for herself, and people in her position can be expected to keep doing so (in furtherance of their own interests) regardless of whether the police are obliged to respond. In any event, Schuster shows one way a special relationship can arise without much of an undertaking by the governmental entity: the decedent gives something to the police, rather than the police undertaking to give something to the plaintiff. (The *Riss* opinion, however, has this to say after the passage quoted in the text: "Quite distinguishable, of course, is the situation where the police authorities undertake responsibilities to particular members of the public and expose them, without adequate protection, to the risks which then materialize into actual losses. *Schuster v. City of New York*.")

Q. What result in *Wanzer v. District of Columbia*?
A. The trial court dismissed the complaint, and the court of appeals affirmed:

> [W]e accept as true appellant's allegations that the EMS dispatcher negligently failed to dispatch an ambulance when Mr. Lee called; that this failure was a departure from accepted EMS protocols and procedures; and that Mr. Lee would have survived his stroke if an ambulance had been sent when first summoned. Whether a special relationship existed between the EMS and Mr. Lee, giving rise to a special duty, is the question we must answer.
>
> A one-time call to 911 for help does not establish a special relationship. It is not enough to allege ineptitude, even shameful and inexcusable ineptitude, by a municipal agency in failing to respond adequately to a call for help. To give rise to a special relationship, the agency's response to the private party must in some demonstrable way exceed the response generally made to other members of the public. Even a series of contacts over a period of time between a public agency and an injured or endangered person is not enough to establish a special relationship, absent some showing that the agency assumed a greater duty to that person than the duty owed to the public at large. If it were otherwise, then the city would be potentially liable for "every oversight, omission, or blunder" of its officials—a liability which potentially could so deplete the resources

necessary to provide police protection, fire protection, and ambulance service as to result in the elimination of those services altogether.

Q. Hypothetical: in *DeLong v. County of Erie*, 469 N.Y.S.2d 611 (1983), the plaintiff's decedent, Amalia DeLong, dialed 911 one evening. The following dialogue occurred:

> Dispatcher: 911.
> Caller: Police, please come, 319 Victoria right away.
> Dispatcher: What's wrong?
> Caller: I heard a burglar; I saw his face in the back; he was trying to break in the house; please come right away.
> Dispatcher: Okay, right away.

The dispatcher miswrote the address as 219 Victoria and mistakenly assumed the caller was referring to Victoria Avenue in Buffalo. In fact she lived on Victoria Street in the nearby town of Kenmore. When the police were unable to find a house at 219 Victoria Avenue in Buffalo, they called the dispatcher; the dispatcher "cleared the call," in effect telling the officers at the scene to disregard it, and took no further action. Eight minutes after the call was cleared, DeLong ran from her house and collapsed on the sidewalk. A neighbor called the police and they arrived one minute later (the police station was a block and a half away). Soon DeLong was pronounced dead from stab wounds she had received from the burglar. Her husband sued Erie County and the City of Buffalo, claiming that her death was caused by their negligent handling of her call for assistance. What result?

A. The jury returned a verdict for the plaintiff, awarding him $600,000 for wrongful death and $200,000 for the conscious pain and suffering Mrs. DeLong endured before her death. The Court of Appeals affirmed, finding the evidence sufficient to support the finding of a duty on the defendant's part:

> The [defendants'] argument is based on the familiar rule that a municipality cannot be held liable for negligence in the performance of a governmental function, including police and fire protection, unless a special relationship existed between the municipality and the injured party.

> This, of course, is not a case in which there was no contact between the victim and the municipality prior to her death. The plaintiff is not seeking to hold the defendants liable as insurers for failing to protect a member of the general public from a criminal act of which they were not aware but should have anticipated and prevented. He is not urging that there should be a police officer on every corner or at every place where a crime is likely to occur. Nor is this a case in which the police refused a plea for assistance or failed to offer assistance when confronted with a situation arguably requiring police intervention. In those instances it has been urged with some force that the proper allocation of public resources and available police services is a matter for the executive and legislative branches to decide.

> In this with case the decision had been made by the municipalities to provide a special emergency service which was intended and proclaimed to be more efficient than normal police services. Those seeking emergency assistance were advised not to attempt to call the general number for the local police, which ironically might have avoided the tragedy encountered in this case, but were encouraged to dial the 911 number to obtain a quicker response. In addition, and most significantly, the victim's plea for assistance was not refused. Indeed she was affirmatively assured that help would be there "right away". Considering the fact that she was merely a block and a half from the local police station, and was not yet at the mercy of the intruder, it cannot be said as a matter of law that this assurance played no part in her decision to remain in her home and not seek other assistance. Unfortunately, it only increased the risk to her life.

Q. What is the superficial similarity between *Wanzer* and *DeLong*? What is the distinction between them?

A. It might seem that in both cases the decedent relied on what they were told by a 911 operator and died as a result. But apparently the claim in *Wanzer* was not so much that the operator's advice was bad; it was that the operator was negligent in not sending an ambulance. Since the operator did not say an ambulance was coming, however, there was no reliance in the sense that DeLong relied. Indeed, the promise plus the rather extensive reliance seems to be the key to liability in *DeLong*; the relationship there was no more "special" than in *Wanzer* (in each of them there was just a one-time call to 911). In *Wanzer* as in *Riss*, the court is worried that liability might result in terrible long-run consequences for the provision of rescue services. The court in *DeLong* is willing to impose a duty when a promise to send help has been made, perhaps because it does not create an open-ended source of liability for the police every time they screw up: they avoid the duty if they just fail to answer the phone, disconnect the caller accidentally, etc.—any time they stop short of making promises. So the burden created by the duty is smaller here than in would have been in *Wanzer*. And the benefits are greater, because the mischief that results is likely to be greater in cases where the police say they are coming and then don't come than in cases where they refuse to come at all.

Q. Might you distinguish *DeLong* from *Riss* on an "undertakings" theory?

A. You might well. Indeed, when courts discuss the special relationship exception to the public duty doctrine, their formulation often includes a requirement that the government have undertaken to assist the plaintiff and that the plaintiff have reasonably relied. Some cases say that such an undertaking creates a special relationship (see, e.g., *Nelson v. Driscoll*, 983 P.2d 972 (Mont. 1999)); other cases treat the undertaking as one of several elements the plaintiff must establish, in addition to showing, e.g., direct contact between the governmental entity and the injured party (as in *Jeffrey v. West Virginia Dept. of Public Safety* (W.V. 1998)).

Still, you can't quite do a direct transplant of the undertakings doctrine to the public arena. *O'Neill v. Montefiore Hospital* was a case of liability for an undertaking, but the undertaking there was not much different from the undertaking in the NL case of *Wanzer v. District of Columbia*. A more substantial undertaking and more compelling reliance is required before the presumption against liability for public rescue services can be overcome, because the costs of imposing a duty on them is perceived to be higher than in private situations. (*Riss*, too, involves an undertaking of sorts: as the dissenter in that case said, the city undertook to provide protection to its residents, and Riss relied in the sense that she forbore from taking other precautions of the self-help variety.)

SECTION D. DUTIES ARISING FROM THE OCCUPATION OF LAND

These materials are pretty concise, but you can make them even more so by dropping *Ehret* and the *Cleveland Electric* case in the first section (on trespassers), and—also from that section—*Keffe* and *Ryan v. Towar*, relying just on the Restatement excerpt after those cases to cover the attractive nuisance doctrine. The problems at the end—*Rhodes* and *Boyd*—aren't essential, but they teach very well (*Boyd* is especially helpful as an exercise in getting students to take notice of incentives).

Category	Example	General rules governing landowner's duty of care
Trespassers	D takes shortcut across P's property	Generally none; but if landowner sees the trespasser or knows (or should know) trespassers are likely, there is a duty of ordinary care in carrying out activities. There may then be a duty to warn of hazardous conditions, too. Some

		jurisdictions say there is just a general duty to avoid inflicting injury by "willful or wanton" conduct (depends on state).
Licensees	**Social guests;** others present with owner's consent	Duty to warn of dangerous hidden conditions of which owner is aware; and duty of ordinary care in undertaking activities. But no duty to inspect premises to make them safe; visitor takes premises in the same condition the owner does.
Invitees	**Business visitors,** or public if premises are open to public	Duty of reasonable care with respect to everything: the condition of the property (there is a duty to inspect the property, and to warn visitors of hazards), and all activities.

1. Duties to trespassers

The general rule is that landowners have no duty of care toward unknown trespassers; they need not make their property safe for them. But once a landowner knows or should know of a trespasser's presence (that he is present, not that he is a trespasser) he has a duty to avoid negligent acts that inflict injury on the trespasser and a duty to warn of artificial hazardous conditions. In some jurisdictions the "no duty" principle is stated as a rule that a landowner simply must refrain from "willful and wanton" behavior toward a trespasser; but the "willful or wanton" standard implies that the owner knows or should know of some likelihood that a trespasser is likely to be present, so this can be understood as fairly consistent with the framework just described. Since the key issue with respect to the duty owed to trespassers is whether they are known to be present, the point of the doctrine seems to involve the burdensomeness of requiring landowners to make themselves aware of who may be trespassing. Before trespassers are discovered, it is asking a lot of the landowner to worry about them, and the trespassers themselves are in the best position to prevent themselves from being injured; after trespassers are discovered, the landowner may well be in the best position to (most cheaply) prevent injurious incidents by carrying out his activities carefully or warning of nonobvious hazards.

Haskins v. Grybko (D shoots trespasser, negligently assuming he is a woodchuck; NL);
Herrick v. Wixom (circus negligently injures trespasser sitting in audience; L)
Ehret v. Village of Scarsdale (gassed trespasser; NL)
Cleveland Electric Illuminating Co. v. Van Benshoten (exploding outhouse; NL)

Q. What if the facts of *Haskins* had arisen not on D's property but in some public woods? What would be the theory of duty?
A. That would be a case of liability for a dangerous affirmative act. The question shows why the writers sometimes frame the no-duty-to-trespassers rule as an immunity more than as a lack of duty: it erases a duty to be careful that otherwise would exist in the world at large. But the no-duty principle also can be stated as part of the background rule: a duty arises only from affirmative acts taken off of the owner's property. Then that formulation would have to be duly qualified regarding licensees, etc.

Q. What if two trespassers had been hunting woodchucks on someone else's property. One of the trespassers negligently shoots the other. Liability?
A. Yes. The question is meant to reinforce that the "no duty" rule is really a privilege that the landowner has to use his property without checking to make sure that there are no trespassers. The point of the rule is not that trespassers are outlaws who generally can be injured by the negligence of others without liability.

Q. What if the defendant in *Haskins* had shot the plaintiff (still a trespasser) deliberately?

A. Then it's a case of liability under the general principle illustrated by *Katko v. Briney* in the chapter on privileges (the section on defense of person and property). Efforts to rid the property of a trespasser have to be calibrated in proportion to the threat he presents.

Q. What is the distinction between *Herrick v. Wixom* and *Haskins v. Grybko*?

A. In *Herrick* the plaintiff was a "discovered trespasser," i.e., recognized as being present, whereas in *Haskins* the trespasser was thought to be a woodchuck.

The most common importance of the general rule about trespassers is in cases where the trespasser is hurt by a dangerous condition on the defendant's land when the defendant is not present. There is no liability for negligence in such cases, but there can be liability if the risks created by the condition are worse than negligent (are "wanton"), or—similarly—if the defendant knows or should know that trespassers are common (the "well-beaten path" cases). *Herrick* is related to this last point: although the defendant doesn't know the plaintiff is a trespasser, he knows he is *there*, and so has to use due care not to injure him by his activities.

Herrick also involved risks created toward trespassers and nontrespassers alike. It was a coincidence that the person injured happened to have trespasser status; the fact that he was a trespasser didn't make it any more likely that he would be in harm's way.

Q. What is the distinction between *Ehret* and *Haskins v. Grybko?*

A. In *Ehret* there was a negligent act in public, with its effects felt where the trespasser happened to be. The cases might have been more analogous if Haskins had shot randomly from the street and the bullet had hit someone on his land (or someone else's land) who happened to be trespassing. It's true that in *Ehret*, unlike in *Herrick*, the trespasser was not "discovered"; but in *Ehret*, as in *Herrick*, the defendant's behavior put trespassers and non-trespassers alike at risk.

Q. What is the distinction between *Ehret* and *Cleveland Electric Illuminating Co. v. Van Benshoten* (exploding outhouse; NL)?

A. The superficial similarity is that in both cases the defendants negligently (by assumption) allowed gas to enter a dwelling; in both cases the plaintiff, who was unknown to the defendants, trespassed and was injured. But in *Ehret* the risk was created to others, too—to members of the public. It merely happened to hurt a trespasser. In *Van Benshoten* the authorized users of the outhouse presumably were aware of the dangers of smoking inside, and they had no reason to expect a trespasser to try to do it.

Q. Suppose defendant finds plaintiff, a trespasser, caught in a bear trap on his land. Assume there is no liability for the injury caused by the bear trap; the defendant had no reason to expect any trespassers would become caught in it. But is there a duty to let the plaintiff out of the trap?

A. No doubt there is; the due care that landowners owe to discovered trespassers has been extended to a duty to rescue them when they get themselves into trouble (see, e.g., *Pridgen v. Boston Housing Authority*, 308 N.E.2d 467 (Mass. 1974)). One can explore this via hypotheticals and ask how a case of the drowning trespasser differs from *Yania v. Bigan*, where the plaintiff's decedent was not a trespasser and yet was owed no duty. The answer presumably is that in the general run of cases, the various downsides of the duty to rescue do not seem as serious in cases involving a trespasser on the defendant's own land: there is no danger of everyone in sight being sued, and perhaps a rescue undertaken by a defendant on his own property is likely to be safer and easier than a compulsory rescue attempt made by a bystander in a public setting. Meanwhile the likelihood of rescue by people other than the property owner is much reduced (cf. the "man overboard" cases). If this sort of reasoning is correct, it tends to put the general no-duty-to-rescue rule on footing that has to do with considerations of utilitarianism, not autonomy. But we'll see in the *Rhodes* problem at the end of the section that some courts limit this rule to cases where the trespasser is in a "place of danger" on the property. If a stranger merely staggers into your yard and collapses there, there may be no duty after all on this view.

Keffe v. Milwaukee & St. Paul R. Co. ("attractive nuisance" doctrine introduced; L)
Ryan v. Towar (attractive nuisance doctrine criticized; NL)

Q. How would the Hand formula apply to attractive nuisance cases?
A. P tends to be high; L tends to be high. B is lower for the landowner than for the parents of the children. The actual balancing of B and PL is required by sec. (d) of the Restatement's test, and indeed (d) seems to subsume the other factors. From Landes and Posner, *The Economic Structure of Tort Law* 95-96:

> Children frequently are attracted to dangerous conditions on land, such as railroad turntables and swimming holes. As trespassers they would under conventional tort principles be barred from recovering damages if injured by one of those conditions, even if the cost of fencing to the landowner was also less than the expected accident cost so that the landowner was negligent too. Since the cost of not trespassing is ordinarily much lower than the landowner's cost of fencing, this might appear to be an alternative care case where the victim's costs of avoidance are lower than those of the injurer, making no liability the appropriate rule. But by virtue of the attractive nuisance doctrine, the landowner's negligence is not excused by the child's status as a trespasser. The costs to the children—more realistically, to their parents—of avoiding the lure of the attractive nuisance are often greater than the costs to the landowner of fencing out the children. [...]

The authors analogize the attractive nuisance doctrine to the rule in many western states that requires farmers to "fence out" straying cattle rather than requiring the owners of the animals to fence them in. *Id.* at 111.

2. Duties to licencees

Davies v. McDowell National Bank (P gassed at house of D's decedent because D let chimney flue become rusted shut; NL)
Lordi v. Spiotta (D negligently fails to turn off gas; deadly explosion results; L)

Q. What is the superficial similarity between *Davies* and *Ehret* (the case of the asphyxiated trespasser in the previous section)? What is the distinction between them?
A. In both cases the plaintiff's decedent was asphyxiated by a gas leak negligently created by the defendant. In neither case did the owner know about the problem. The result might seem strange because there was liability in *Ehret* when the victim was a trespasser, yet no liability in *Davies* where the victims were the defendant's friends. The distinction apparently is that in *Ehret* the defendant's negligence was in public and off the premises, and put many different sorts of people at risk. In *Ehret* as in *Herrick,* it was merely a coincidence that a trespasser was hurt; the fact that the victim was a trespasser bore no causal relationship (in the probabilistic, proximate cause sense) to the injuries suffered.

Negligently allowing gas to seep up from one's *own* premises, as in *Davies,* would not lead to liability whether the plaintiff (or plaintiff's decedent) was a trespasser or licensee. Landowners have a duty to inform their guests of hazards they are aware of and that may not be clear to the guests; but they have no duty to inspect their premises, and cannot be held liable for injuries caused by conditions of which they were unaware. Once such a condition is found, repairs or a warning are in order for the benefit of licensees, but not for the benefit of trespassers, at least if they are unforeseeable.

Q. What is the superficial similarity between *Davies* and *Lordi?* What is the distinction between them?

A. In both cases the injuries the plaintiff is complaining about were caused by negligence with respect to a gas heater. And in both cases the plaintiff (or decedent) was a licensee. But in *Lordi* the defendant committed an *act* of negligence in failing to turn off the gas, whereas in *Davies* there was no affirmative act of negligence: there was merely a condition that Thomas negligently had allowed to exist (the rusty mechanism). A landowner has a duty to refrain from acts of negligence toward licensees (hence liability in *Lordi*) and a duty to warn licensees of known hidden dangers. The facts of *Davies* don't quite fit into either category. In *Davies* there was nothing the plaintiff could point to as a negligent activity (unless it was just owning the heater); there was only an omission.

Why should this distinction between active and passive negligence make any difference? Some courts say it doesn't, and find no liability in either situation—no liability for negligence toward licensees, active or passive, unless it amounts to recklessness. Perhaps the idea behind *Davies* is that you can't find liability on those facts without imposing a general duty on homeowners to inspect their premises. Telling someone to act carefully is less burdensome than requiring them to ensure that there are no dangerous conditions on their property; only the latter requires activities on the owner's part (inspections) that they would not have undertaken anyway.

Q. What if a trespasser had entered the basement of the defendant's bungalow, lit a match so that he could see, and thus ignited the gas from the heater that the defendant negligently had left on? (Or what if a trespasser had been hiding in the shadows when the explosion occurred, and suffered injuries?)
A. It's probably a case of no liability. This is a nice question because every case considered so far can be brought to bear on it. It's similar to *Haskins* because there's an affirmative act (in mishandling the on/off switch for the heater) that harms an unknown trespasser. It's similar to *Cleveland Electric* for similar reasons, and indeed is quite analogous to that case on its facts. Yet it's also similar to *Herrick* and *Ehret* because it was just a coincidence that the person injured was a trespasser; the defendant created risks to others at the same time: perhaps his guests were five minutes away from going downstairs and igniting the guests themselves. Or suppose the explosion injured everyone in the house. Could the social guests upstairs collect, but not the trespasser downstairs? Perhaps so: *Herrick,* after all, can be distinguished because in that case the trespasser had been discovered; and *Ehret* can be distinguished because in that case the negligent act was made in a public place, off the defendant's premises.

3. Duties to invitees

City of Boca Raton v. Mattef (painter falls from water tower before contract is signed; NL)
Jacobsma v. Goldberg's Fashion Forum (customer tries to stop shoplifter and is hurt; L)

Q. In stylizing the facts of *Mattef*, what can we assume about the extent of the town's negligence?
A. We can assume that the town had been negligent in failing to inspect the ladder, just as we can assume that J. Fred Thomas in the *Davies* case had been negligent in failing to inspect his chimney.

Q. Would this be a case of liability if the contract had been signed? Why?
A. It would have been a case of (potential) liability; in other words, there would have been a duty that may have been breached. If the contract had been signed, Mattef would have been an invitee; he would have been on the property of the defendant to confer an economic benefit. Property owners have a duty to invitees to inspect their property for hazards.

Q. What if Mattef had painted the water tower, and had made it to the bottom safely. Might he then have a contract claim or a good claim for restitution? Would this matter? (Might it suggest that he was an invitee after all?)
A. This question is a chance to wade a bit into the relationship between contracts and torts. It's not clear whether Mattef could have collected the $80 for his work on an implied-in-fact contract or on a

quantum meruit theory; he might be found to have been officious in conferring benefits on the defendant. But if he could so collect, that might seem to suggest that he should be understood as an invitee rather than as a "volunteer" after all. On the other hand, allowing this to matter could create an anomaly: if we imagine two parallel universes, each containing a painter named Mattef who climbs a water tower to paint "Boca Raton" on the side of it, it would be odd to say there is no liability for the city in the case where the ladder gives way while he the painter is on the way up, but liability if the ladder gives way while he's on the way down after completing the job (because he then is in possession of a quantum meruit claim).

Q. What is the sense of the outcome in *Mattef*? If he had waited until the contract was finished, does it seem likely that the outcome would have been different?
A. Perhaps not: it seems improbable that the town would have ordered an inspection of the ladder after the contract was signed and before Mattef made it to the tower to perform the work. But you never know; and in any event, it's possible that the contract itself would have contained disclaimers of liability for the condition of the tower. If so, Mattef should not be able to avoid such terms as those by doing the work before the contract had been drafted. Another way to look at it is to imagine what a legislative committee would say if it needed to devise a rule about when a town's (or other entity's) duties to inspect are triggered. A logical place to draw the line might well be with the signing of the contract. The decision seems more difficult here because instead of being made by a legislature it is being made by a court, and the court is obliged to decide the question in the context of a case where a man who had done everything but sign the contract just died.

Q. What is the superficial similarity between *Jacobsma* and *Mattef*? What is the distinction between them?
A. In both cases the plaintiff had no contract (yet) with the defendant, though in a sense a contract was being contemplated in either case; in both cases the plaintiff might be said to have "volunteered" to help. Indeed, the "volunteer" label seems a better fit in *Jacobsma* than in *Mattef*. So why is there liability in the former case but not the latter? Because a customer in a store is almost always going to be considered an invitee (and reasonably expects care to have been taken inside), especially if he is asked by the store's personnel to do something. In *Mattef* there is a reason in policy to want to wait for the contract to be signed, rather than encourage Mattef to bypass that step; but there is nothing to wait for in *Jacobsma* before triggering the invitee status (the plaintiff might as well have slipped on a negligently created puddle of water just inside the store's entryway; it would be an awkward rule that wasn't triggered until the sale was rung up), and no reason to revoke the invitee status on account of his compliance with an unconditional request made by the proprietor. (One can question the meaning of the "Stop thief" utterance, but that's for the jury.) Indeed, the plaintiff in *Jacobsma* was conferring a benefit—and an economic one—on the store by stopping the shoplifter, though there is no reason to think he expected compensation.

Q. Hypothetical: in *Diefenbach v. Great Atlantic & Pacific Tea Co.*, 273 N.W. 783 (Mich. 1937), employees of an A & P grocery were chasing a rat on their premises. The plaintiff, a customer, tried to help them by stepping on the creature; one of the employees then tried to stab the rat with a large fish knife, but mistakenly stabbed the plaintiff in the foot instead. The plaintiff sued the grocery store, alleging negligence by its employees. What result?
A. The jury brought in a verdict for the plaintiff. The Michigan Supreme Court reversed and dismissed the plaintiff's claim on the ground that he was a mere volunteer, "under no obligation to assist the clerks in the performance of their duties. Neither did any emergency exist which would justify him in volunteering his services in behalf of the A. & P. Company. It would be unreasonable to suppose that four or five clerks intent upon destroying the rat could not have accomplished their purpose without the assistance of the plaintiff."

What is the distinction between *Jacobsma* and *Diefenbach*? In *Diefenbach* the plaintiff was a gratuitous helper; he was not responding to a plea for help from the defendant, either explicit or implicit (the latter because there was no emergency that reasonable could cause him to think that his help was needed). The *Diefenbach* case is still a little mysterious, because whether the plaintiff in *Diefenbach* was an invitee, licensee, or discovered trespasser, the defendant normally has a duty not to injure him through negligent affirmative acts. The court, however, says that "[t]he volunteer cannot recover because no duty is owed to him other than not to injure him by willful or wanton acts." Perhaps there are overtones of assumption of risk here that help along the court's decision; it also concluded that even if there had been a duty, there was no negligence.

Q. What is the analogy between *Diefenbach* and *Boyette v. TWA* (from the section of the chapter on special relationships)?
A. In both cases the defendant started out with a duty to the plaintiff, but the duty disappeared when circumstances changed. A customer starts out with an "invitee" hat on, but if he wanders into a part of the store where is not authorized to go, he turns into a licensee at best; and likewise if (as in *Diefenbach*) he engages in acts that have nothing to do with his capacity as customer. The general logic of the point is that we don't want the business to have to lavish expenses on obscure parts of the premises.

Q. Hypothetical: in *Whataburger, Inc., v. Rockwell*, 706 So.2d 1220 (Ala. App. 1997), the plaintiff, Rockwell, made a visit to the defendant's Whataburger restaurant in the town of Chickasaw. As he sat in a booth waiting for his food, Rockwell looked around the restaurant and saw three young men eating at another booth. One of the young men noticed Rockwell looking at them and yelled across the restaurant to Rockwell, asking if he had "a fucking problem." Rockwell replied, improvidently in retrospect, "No, but apparently you do." The verbal threats escalated. The restaurant's manager, one Stringfellow, told the young men and Rockwell that if they were going to fight, they needed to "take it outside." They did so, and in the ensuing melee Rockwell was hit on the head with a brick and sustained various injuries. Rockwell sued Whataburger; his evidence was that several times he had asked Stringfellow to call the police, but that she waited an unreasonably long time to do so. Whataburger contended that it owed no duty to protect Rockwell from the criminal acts of a third party. What result?
A. The trial court entered judgment on a jury verdict in Rockwell's favor. Whataburger appealed the denial of its motion for judgment as a matter of law, and the court of appeals affirmed, relying on language from an earlier case:

> In our opinion the appropriate rule applicable to this case is as follows: There is no duty upon the owners or operators of a shopping center, individually or collectively, or upon merchants and shopkeepers generally, whose mode of operation of their premises does not attract or provide a climate for crime, to guard against the criminal acts of a third party, *unless they know or have reason to know that acts are occurring or [are] about to occur on the premises that pose imminent probability of harm to an invitee;* whereupon a duty of reasonable care to protect against such act arises.

Q. What is the sense of the distinction between licensees and invitees? What's the point of bothering with it?
A. It's easiest to see by focusing on the two core cases where the difference has its most common bite: cases involving homeowners and cases involving businesses. Visitors to homes tend to be licensees; visitors to business tend to be invitees; so the distinction most often amounts simply to a rule that homeowners don't have to inspect their premises for the benefit of their guests (though they do have to warn them of known but nonobvious hazards), and that businesses do have to so inspect. Seen in this light, the rules might be understood as reflecting the reasonable expectations of visitors in the two contexts. A homeowner has to put guests on the same footing as himself, telling them what he knows; what's good enough for him probably is good enough for them, since he and they likely will be using the property in about the same way. That may be less true of commercial invitees. The distinction also might be understood from an economic standpoint: if the burden of having to undertake inspections is imposed

on a business, the business can pass the costs involved along to its customers. Homeowners can't do that, so if they were to react at all to costly obligations to inspect, the most likely response would be to scale back their entertainment of guests. It's true that occasionally a visitor to a home will be considered an invitee (the insurance salesman who visits at night), but these cases are comparatively rare, and in them the duty to inspect usually will not be so great anyway since business visitors to houses, like the meter reader, usually come at predictable times and confine their motions to predictable parts of the defendant's dwelling.

Q. Would a fireman putting out a fire in a house be a licensee or an invitee?
A. Many claims by firefighters are foreclosed by the "fireman's rule," forbidding claims by firemen against people who negligently cause fires to be start and also a number of other types of claims that are considered occupational hazards of rescue workers. But sometimes a fireman is hurt by an incidental condition on the defendant's property, and in that instance the answer to the question of classification—licensee vs. invitee—may matter. Strictly speaking a fireman is conferring a benefit, and he's compensated for it, though not directly by the owner. From a functional standpoint, though, classifying a fireman as an invitee would be inconsistent with the point of classifying most guests in a home as licensees. The point of that approach is that requiring homeowners to constantly inspect their premises is too burdensome. But that is what would be required if firemen, who generally arrive without much notice, were regarded as licensees: a homeowner would have to inspect constantly or else (more likely) take his chances that if a fire comes a firefighter may be hurt by some undiscovered hazard in the house. Meter readers are another story: they and the firefighters similarly are conferring benefits, but inspecting to make sure the meter reader has a safe reception is far less burdensome since the owner knows when they are coming and where they are going. Hence they are more likely to be classified as invitees. We discuss some of these issues further in the section of the book on primary assumption of risk.

Q. Suppose P, a traveling salesman, knocks on D's door and offers to sell him some hairbrushes. D is intrigued and invites D to come in so he can inspect his wares. D is injured when he steps on a loose floorboard of which P was unaware. What result? Is P a licensee or invitee?
A. It's a close case. Door-to-door solicitors are licensees, present with implied permission but not at the owner's behest. The question is whether they become invitees when summoned into the house to transact business. As a practical matter the homeowner has not had a chance to inspect the premises, and the salesman cannot reasonably expect such an inspection to take place (and in the long run, perhaps solicitors are better off with no liability here, since liability would tend to discourage homeowners from letting them come in at all). So it seems like a good case for no liability. For a case finding such a saleman to be a licensee, see *Malatesta v. J. L. Lowry*, 130 So.2d 785 (La. App. 1961).

Rowland v. Christian (Abandonment of categories; P hurts hand on host's faucet; L)
Carter v. Kinney (P slips on ice at D's house; traditional categories retained)

Q. How would *Rowland* have come out if the California supreme court had stuck with the traditional categories?
A. Probably the same way. The plaintiff's evidence was that he was hurt by a non-obvious condition that was known to the occupier of the property. Since the plaintiff was a licensee, it therefore looks like a case of liability—though perhaps not in California, as it is not clear how the courts of that state then regarded obligations to licencees. There was liability for "traps," meaning "a concealed danger known to the defendant, that is, a danger clothed with a deceptive appearance of safety," *Hansen v. Richey*, 46 Cal.Rptr. at 912 (Cal. App. 1965), so the question would have been whether the hazard here satisfied that definition.

Q. What practical difference does it make whether a court uses the *Rowland* approach or the old-fashioned common law categories?

A. The key difference is that the *Rowland* approach causes these cases to go to juries much more often; the most important functional consequence of using duty categories is that they usually are applied by judges, not juries. *Rowland* thus tends to eliminate a useful way for defendants to avoid trials. To be sure, many cases are likely to come out the same way in the end under the two approaches. The common law categories are generalizations about what is reasonable; *Rowland* generally turns reasonableness into a jury question on all the facts. So the jury's answers often may match the common law generalizations: juries may well conclude that a defendant homeowner is not negligent if he fails to look out for trespassers, or fails to inspect the premises for the benefit of social guests. But like any rules, the common law's categories produce some unappetizing results at their boundaries, and those cases (perhaps *Mattef* and *Haskins* is an example; *Haskins* may be another) are likely to go the other way if left to a jury. As for the cost of administration, the California approach trades the difficulty of sorting cases into categories for the difficulty of having to send more cases to juries.

Rhodes v. Illinois Central Gulf Railroad (problem: man lies bleeding in railroad's warming house while railroad's employees make ineffective attempts to summon assistance; NL)

This problem is meant to give the students a chance to try applying duty principles to a fact pattern a bit different from any they have yet seen. In particular the facts raise questions about the duty to rescue a trespasser, which Rhodes may have been. It's also a chance to show how different theories of duty might be brought to bear on the same facts. A jury brought in a verdict for the plaintiff; the Illinois supreme court reversed and remanded for a new trial, finding that the jury had been misinstructed. Below is the text of much of the court's analysis (with most citations omitted); its conclusions, in summary, were as follows:

1. Whether Rhodes was a trespasser or an invitee was a jury question: he might have come into the station to wait for a train, or he might have come in just to sleep. It depends on the facts and the inferences drawn from them. (The court discusses some of the evidence on this late in the excerpt below; this is a good chance to ask students about what facts they might like to have about Rhodes before forming a conclusion about his status.) The defendant does not dispute that if Rhodes was a customer, they owed him a duty of care. The question is whether, if Rhodes was a trespasser, the defendant had any duty toward him. The answer is no.

2. Illinois retains the distinction between the duties owed to trespassers and to others. If Rhodes was a trespasser, the defendant owed him no duty by virtue of its ownership of the property. It might be different if there was evidence that Rhodes was injured by some condition on the defendant's property, but there isn't; and the exception that requires landowners to assist trespassers found injured in a "place of danger" does not apply just because an injured trespasser comes onto the defendant's land and collapses.

3. A duty to rescue Rhodes might have arisen if the parties had a special relationship, but no such relationship came into being if Rhodes was a trespasser.

4. A duty to rescue also can arise from an undertaking, but there was no relevant undertaking here. The defendant had procedures to cover these sorts of situations, but a defendant's internal policies generally cannot be used to argue that the defendant has a duty on an undertaking theory. In a sense the defendant did undertake to help Rhodes, but only by calling the police; and this cannot create a duty to do more. (If it did, people might be discouraged from calling the police.) But query whether there should have been a finding of an undertaking here after all, since the passengers who first reported the problem to the

conductor might have given up on any other avenues of rescue once they believed the railroad was handling it.

And now here are some longish excerpts from the court's opinion for those interested in seeing the reasoning spelled out more elaborately:

> Although the Premises Liability Act abolished the common law distinction between the duties owed by a landowner to an invitee and a licensee, the Act expressly retained the distinction between the duties owed to those lawfully on the premises (invitees and licensees) and those unlawfully on the premises (trespassers). In general, a landowner owes no duty of care to a trespassing adult except to refrain from willfully and wantonly injuring him. […] A number of exceptions to the general rule limiting the landowner's duty to trespassers have been created, however. One such exception imposes upon a landowner or occupier the duty to use ordinary care to avoid injury to a trespasser who has been discovered in a "place of danger" on the premises. The plaintiff argues that Carl comes within this exception because he was a trespasser discovered on the premises in a "place of danger." […]

> The plaintiff does not contend that Carl's head injury was caused by a condition of ICG's premises or by any activities conducted thereon by ICG. Nor does the plaintiff argue that Carl, by virtue of his presence on the premises, was in any danger of being injured by a condition or activity on the premises, such as a moving train or a high voltage rail. Rather, the only basis advanced for a finding that Carl was discovered in a place of danger on ICG's premises is the fact that Carl was discovered on the premises in an injured condition. The place of danger exception does not arise simply because a trespasser is discovered in an injured state on the landowner's premises.

> The place of danger exception is a premises liability concept which defines when a property owner or occupier can be held liable for injuries that a trespasser suffers as a result of a condition or activity on the property. A place of danger thus denotes a place which, by reason of a condition or activity on the premises, risks harm to anyone who is present, whether previously injured or not. It must be the condition or activity on the land that makes it a place of danger, not the mere presence of a person in an injured state. For instance, a trespasser discovered by a railroad on the tracks in the path of the railroad's moving train would properly be considered to be in a place of danger such that the railroad owed him a duty of ordinary care to avoid injury to him.

> To accept the plaintiff's interpretation would render all premises places of danger once an injured trespasser arrives there. Moreover, a place of danger would move wherever the injured trespasser happened to move, regardless of the condition of the premises and the degree of caution taken by the owner to prevent injury to others on the property. An otherwise safe place could alternatively be both a place of danger and not a place of danger as an injured trespasser moves back and forth across the property line.

> Here, Carl was not discovered in a place on ICG's premises where a condition or activity on the premises posed a danger to him. To the contrary, Carl was discovered in what must be considered the relatively safe location (given that the outside temperature was below freezing) of the ICG warming house. We do not agree that this safe location was transformed into a place of danger by the mere fortuity that an injured trespasser came to rest there. […]

Application to Present Case

We further find […] that the duties owed by a landowner under a premises liability theory, though relied upon by the parties, are not implicated in this case. While ICG, as the landowner, owed Carl, as a trespasser, the duty to refrain from willfully and wantonly injuring him, there is no allegation, or evidence, in this case that would support recovery for the plaintiff under that theory. [...] Rather, the plaintiff's only theory of liability against ICG is that ICG had a duty to take some affirmative action to aid Carl because Carl was discovered injured on ICG's premises. The issue we must therefore address is whether, under the facts of this case, a duty arose on the part of ICG to take some affirmative action to aid Carl once he was found injured on ICG's premises. Again, because ICG does not challenge the imposition of this duty upon it if Carl was an invitee, our analysis is limited to determining whether this duty was owed if Carl was a trespasser.

Duty to Rescue

Our common law generally imposes no duty to rescue an injured stranger upon one who did not cause the injury in the first instance. A duty to take some affirmative action to aid another may arise, however, where a special relationship exists between the parties. [...] We must therefore determine whether a special relationship existed between Carl, as a trespasser, and ICG, as a landowner, such that a duty to take some affirmative action to aid Carl should be imposed on ICG. ICG contends that Illinois law does not impose on landowners a duty to take affirmative action to aid injured trespassers. We agree that Illinois law does not support the imposition of such a duty. [...]

The arbitrariness of using an injured trespasser's mere presence on the defendant's premises as justification for imposing a duty to rescue is evident. Employing such a rule, a homeowner who finds an injured, drunken stranger lying on his lawn has a legal duty to rescue, but the homeowner who sees his next-door neighbor drowning is under no such legal obligation. In fact, the duty to take action or not to take action would vary as an injured trespasser staggered back and forth across the homeowner's property line. The imposition of a duty to aid would thus turn on a wholly arbitrary circumstance. [...]

We cannot accept the plaintiff's suggestion that we should be swayed by the fact that ICG was a business, rather than a private, landowner. The rule here sought by the plaintiff, imposing a duty on ICG to rescue Carl simply because he was discovered injured on ICG's property, would apply to all landowners, including private homeowners, because the only required relationship with the landowner is the trespasser's presence on the property. We are not persuaded that we should adopt a rule which could render a homeowner liable to an injured, drunken stranger who comes to rest on the homeowner's lawn.

The plaintiff [cites] a Massachusetts case, *Pridgen v. Boston Housing Authority*, 308 N.E.2d 467 (Mass. 1974), in support of imposing a duty on ICG to rescue an injured trespasser. *Pridgen* involved an 11-year-old trespasser who, after he became trapped in an elevator shaft in the defendant's building, was struck and injured by the moving elevator. The plaintiff charged the defendant with negligence in that, knowing of the child's entrapment, the defendant failed to turn off the power to the elevator. *Pridgen* is factually distinguishable. There, a condition on the defendant's premises, the moving elevator, caused the plaintiff's injury. We note that there is language in the *Pridgen* decision suggesting that Massachusetts should impose an affirmative duty on premises owners and occupiers to rescue a "trapped, imperiled and helpless trespasser." As discussed, however, we do not agree that a legal duty should be imposed on landowners to take affirmative action to rescue injured trespassers. [...]

Accordingly, we hold that, if Carl was a trespasser on ICG's premises, ICG may not be charged with the duty to take affirmative action to obtain aid for him. If Carl was a trespasser, the trial court erred in instructing the jury that ICG could be held liable if it "observed the decedent lying injured * * * but failed to further investigate or to provide assistance or attend to the decedent." Thus, because the trial court's instruction of the jury as to ICG's duty if Carl was a trespasser was incorrect, we reverse the jury's verdict and remand this case for a new trial. On retrial, the jury must decide if Carl was a patron (invitee) or a trespasser on the premises and must be further instructed in accordance with this opinion.

ICG's Procedures

The plaintiff also contends that, even if the law imposed no duty on ICG to take affirmative action to aid Carl, such a duty was created by ICG's own procedures. The plaintiff points to no written policy manual or handbook as the source for this contention, but relies on the trial testimony of ICG employees. Specifically, the plaintiff points to testimony from various ICG employees to the effect that, where a person was reported injured in a warming house, the procedure was to send both the local municipality's police and an ICG patrolman to the scene. As ICG points out, the testimony as to ICG's procedure was far from clear, with some testimony indicating that the procedure was to send an ICG patrolman if he was available and, if he was unavailable, to send the local police. Regardless, even if the plaintiff's interpretation of ICG's procedure is accepted, the plaintiff's contention fails. […]

The only case cited by the plaintiff in support of this contention is *Darling v. Charleston Community Memorial Hospital*, 211 N.E.2d 253 (Ill. 1965). *Darling,* however, does not support the proposition that a legal duty, which does not otherwise exist, may be created by a defendant's internal policies or procedures. Whether a duty was owed by the defendant was not the issue in *Darling,* a medical malpractice case. Rather, the issue was whether evidence in the form of the defendant hospital's bylaws could be introduced on the question of the proper standard of care required to satisfy the duty. It was there held that such evidence was admissible, but not conclusive, on the issue of the appropriate standard of care. *Darling* is therefore inapplicable to this case. […]

Voluntary Undertaking

We briefly dispense with the appellate court's conclusion that, even if the law imposed no duty on ICG to aid Carl, ICG voluntarily undertook that duty and did so negligently by failing to "follow up" on the Chicago police department's response to its calls. […]

ICG here contends, and we agree, that it began no "voluntary undertaking" in this case which could render it liable for Carl's death. Assuming, as we must for this argument, that ICG owed no duty in the first instance to rescue Carl, we find no voluntary undertaking on the part of ICG which gave rise to this duty. At most, ICG undertook to report Carl's presence to the Chicago police department and performed that undertaking by placing several calls to that department. We find nothing to indicate that ICG, by that action, voluntarily undertook to do anything more, such as ensuring that aid would be provided to Carl.

As a matter of public policy, we do not think it appropriate to hold that a party voluntarily undertakes a legal duty to rescue an injured stranger by simply calling the police. Such a holding would discourage citizens from taking even this most basic action to obtain assistance for an injured stranger. We therefore reject the appellate court's voluntary undertaking theory as a basis for ICG's liability in this case.

Carl's Status on Premises

ICG urges us to find that the evidence demonstrated, as a matter of law, that Carl was a trespasser on ICG's premises. According to ICG, the evidence showed that Carl was found intoxicated, surrounded by beer cans and sleeping in the warming house with no money, no ticket, and no apparent intention of boarding a train. There was testimony that access to this warming house, from other than the train tracks, is restricted by turnstiles. To gain entry through the turnstiles, a person must purchase a ticket from a vending machine. However, it is possible, though apparently not authorized by ICG, for a person to enter the warming house without purchasing a ticket, such as by going over or under a turnstile, or by climbing onto the train platform from street level.

The plaintiff points to the trial court's comments that "there is a strong argument that [Carl] was a trespasser," but that his "physical presence in that location [the warming house] I think entitles plaintiff [an] inference that he could have been a patron." The plaintiff further points out that there was no evidence that anyone looked to see if Carl had a passenger ticket in his possession; that, even if Carl had no ticket, ICG allows persons to buy tickets on the train; and, further, Carl could have had a ticket when he entered the warming house but been robbed of that ticket.

We find that the evidence raised a jury question on the issue of Carl's status on ICG's premises.

Boyd v. Racine Currency Exchange (problem: D's teller does not give money to thief, who then shoots P's intestate, a customer in the bank; NL)

This is a great teaching case. Of course it's easy to conclude that the plaintiff's decedent was an invitee of the bank, but the result in almost every case involving this fact pattern is no liability on duty grounds. Grounding the holding in duty rather than breach can be understood as a way of expressing a conclusion on policy grounds that for special reasons there must be no liability here as a matter of law. The basic rationale is that liability creates the wrong incentives. Said the court: "In this particular case the result may appear to be harsh and unjust, but, for the protection of future business invitees, we cannot afford to extend to the criminal another weapon in his arsenal." The same result could be reached by holding the defendant's conduct to be nor breach as a matter of law; apparently courts like the "no duty" holding better because it puts the issue more explicitly into the hands of the judge rather than the jury.

This case is a good opportunity to get students thinking about incentives: how will each of the parties to this case (or parties like them) behave in the future under rules of liability and no liability? If there is liability, the bank presumably will instruct its tellers to hand over the money; and then this will give thieves an incentive to take hostages, a tactic that will have become highly efficacious. To the objection that the thieves won't hear about the legal ruling comes the riposte that they don't have to; they only need to observe that taking threatening customers has become mighty efficacious as a way of getting the money. Naturally there are countervailing considerations one case raise: liability might increase the amount of hostage-taking but decrease the number of fatalities that result from it; liability might give the bank incentives to take other precautions against thieves. And most banks already instruct their tellers to hand over the money—a custom that might be evaluated along the lines discussed in the corresponding section of the casebook. Here the customers had contracts with the bank; can we therefore assume the custom was efficient?

Some students of the case think the incentive arguments are unrealistic, but the cases at least show that such arguments nevertheless can be important to courts and are important for students to learn how to make.

SECTION E. THE PRIVITY LIMITATION

These cases present a good example of a common pattern in tort law: cases with somewhat analogous facts being decided differently, with the results sometimes not very explicable in terms of the glosses that courts use; upon study of the factual distinctions between them, certain principles emerge that make more sense out of both the gloss and the results. The distinctions are economic in a broad sense. The general themes seem to involve the courts' reluctance to saddle defendants with open-ended and unpredictable liability to those affected by their breaches of contract. The existence of the contract itself doesn't mean there can be no liability to others (that would contradict *MacPherson*); but extending liability to those injured by the breach is done very cautiously. One reason is that unpredictable liability is likely to make the defendant a kind of insurer, and it may not be in a very good position to do that. One can also try to distinguish these cases from the preceding ones because here there is time and opportunity for the people involved in these cases to make contracts creating duties and spreading risks. They aren't cases involving strangers, or even brief transactions (as in *Jacobsma*).

For abbreviated treatment, use *Glanzer*, *Moch*, and *Biakanja*, then the problem (*Einhorn*) at the end.

Glanzer v. Shepard (Seller has K w/ D to weigh beans for sale to P; D misweighs them; P sues D. No privity, but liability because P's use of D's certificates was the "end and aim of the transaction" between D and the seller, not a collateral consequence).

Moch v. Rensselaer Water Co. (D water co. has contract with city, but fails to supply water to hydrants; P's warehouse burns down; NL)

Q. What is the distinction between *Moch* and *Glanzer?*
A. It is important for clarity's sake in these privity cases to nail down the superficial similarities—to show that all of them follow a basic pattern in which A makes a contract with B, B performs negligently, C is hurt as a result, and C sues B. To put it differently: in both cases the defendant (the weigher, or the water company) breached a contract with a third party (the seller of the beans in *Glanzer;* the city in *Moch*), with damage then being incurred by the plaintiff. But only in *Glanzer* did the court say the defendant owed any duty to the plaintiff. Why?

The defendant in *Glanzer,* if held liable, can estimate and perhaps also control its likely future liabilities in an orderly way, and so can pass on the costs of insuring against them to its customers in an orderly way as well. If the water company in *Moch* is held to have a duty to those whose property is burned, its resulting liability is likely to be unpredictable (since there's no telling how far the fire will go), and also hard for it to control or insure against (since the water company is not a good position to determine either the value of the properties it is protecting or the precautions the owners of those properties are taking—or should be taking—against fire damage). The liability-spreading point might be loosely analogized to the sense of the distinction between the duties owed to licensees and invitees.

An additional point concerns the content of the contracts involved. The size of the contract in *Moch,* at least, left the court doubtful that the parties to it had imagined that the water company was intended to bear the brunt of liability, and thus act as an insurer, in these situations. That does not mean liability could not be imposed, but it does suggest that in imposing liability the court may just be creating a bothersome default rule around which the parties to these contracts would have to negotiate. Note that contract generally trumps tort; if there had been a disclaimer in the water company's contract with the city that covered this case, we can assume that would end the issue. But if that's true, does it not suggest that part of our thinking here ought to be an attempt to reconstruct what the parties must have intended, or would have said if they could have been asked? We don't know what they would have said, but the contract price perhaps suggests that Moch would have been quite surprised to learn of this sort of liability. Likewise, they can always redo their contracts now if they wish.

Maybe the idea is just that fire insurance companies are better institutions than water works companies to insure against fire damage, even damage from the limited set of cases that involve failures of the water supply. $42.50 per hydrant doesn't give the water company much to work with, and doesn't suggest that such insurance is part of what the citizenry, through its government, was buying. One court (in *Weinberg v. Dinger*, N.J. 1987) abolished the *Moch* immunity just in cases where claims are uninsured or underinsured. What result if insurance contracts are redrafted to provide for no coverage when damage is caused by the negligence of the water company? (For more discussion of the expectations arising from the contract in *Moch*, see the notes on the *Ultramares* case below.)

All of these problems, in any event, seem to be among the reasons why many courts impose a limitation on the duty owed to third parties by *Moch*-type defendants. It is important to make clear that the defendant in *Moch* may well have performed negligent acts, and that the negligence may well have caused harm to the plaintiff; the point is not that there is no duty for "nonfeasance," but rather than the court imposes a kind of immunity here on policy grounds.

Posner suggests that in *Glanzer* a duty was necessary to the efficiency of commercial transactions, since without liability parties like the plaintiffs would have to hire their own weighers. He thus suggests that the decision is supported by "commercial morality," which "is perhaps the same thing as efficiency." *Cardozo: A Study in Reputation* 100.

Q. Why wasn't *Moch* a case where a duty was created by an undertaking, as in *Erie Ry. v. Stewart?*
A. The analogy works tolerably well as a formal matter, though the defendant's representations in *Moch* were made to the city, not to the plaintiff. But the court is simply unwilling to accept the consequences of applying such reasoning to the general run of breached contacts, apparently for the same sorts of reasons described a moment ago: differences in the sort of knowledge the defendant has about the consequences of errors (e.g., the value of the warehouse in *Moch*), and the threat that liability will spread unforeseeably and uncontrollably.

Q. Why didn't the plaintiff sue the *seller* of the beans?
A. Hard to say. It's a common response to these cases to wonder if the plaintiff has a remedy against the unsued party to the contract—the city in *Moch*, or the driver in *Conboy*, infra, or the landlord in *Einhorn v. Seeley*, infra. Often no such suit is possible because that party did nothing negligent. The city made a reasonable decision to hire the water works company, and the driver in *Conboy* made a reasonable decision to rely on her doctor's advice. But in *Glanzer* such a suit does seem possible. Posner's examination of the record for his book on Cardozo turned up no explanation of why Glanzer did not try this; Posner speculates that maybe Glanzer had a relationship with the seller that he did not want to endanger with a lawsuit.

Food Pageant v. Consolidated Edison (Con Ed held liable for food spoiled during blackout)
Lilpan Food Corp. v. Consolidated Edison (Con Ed held not liable for looting during blackout)

Q. What is the distinction between the *Food Pageant* and *Lilpan Food Corp.* cases?
A. In *Food Pageant* the complaint was that Con Ed failed to discharge obligations it owed directly to the plaintiff. In *Lilpan* the complaint was that Con Ed failed to discharge obligations it owed to the city (to supply electricity to light fixtures, etc.), with resultant harm to the plaintiff. The latter facts fit the *Moch* mold. As a matter of policy, if Con Ed is held liable for immediate consequences of its blackout

within a store, the liability is less likely to cascade unpredictably than it is if Con Ed is liable for whatever damage looters may do.

Conboy v. Mogeloff (D doctor negligently advises patient to drive, resulting in injuries to P; NL)
Biakanja v. Irving (D notary botches client's will and P loses inheritance as result; L)
Ultramares Corp. v. Touche (D accounting firm botches audit to third party and P makes bad loans as result; NL)

Q. What is the superficial similarity between *Conboy v. Mogeloff* and *Biakanja v. Irving*? What is the distinction between them?
A. In both cases, a defendant (the doctor/the notary) negligently performed services for someone (the mother/the decedent), and the negligence caused harm to a third party, who then sued. In *Biakanja* this was permitted, but in *Conboy* the court said the doctor owed no duty to the plaintiffs. Why?

In *Conboy,* as in *Moch,* the defendant would find it difficult to know how far his liability might extend if he were held liable. Obviously he has a duty to his patient, and she can sue him for breaching that duty (students sometimes can be a bit confused about this). But if he also can be sued by third parties his patient injures, then there's no telling how far that liability goes: she might injure nobody, or might injure a couple of people a little bit, or might injure a lot of people fatally. It's like the spread of the fire. It's hard to predict, and he's not in a good position to control it, either. This sort of liability is hard (or perhaps just undesirable) for a doctor to pass on in a clear way to patients through higher bills.

In *Biakanja,* as in *Glanzer* but unlike in *Moch* or *Conboy,* the defendant was of a sort that can appreciate fairly precisely the extent of his potential liability exposure. In *Glanzer* it was possible for the defendant to size up the magnitude of the weighing job and the possibility and cost of errors for subsequent parties, and in *Biakanja* it was possible for the defendant to grasp both the amounts at stake in the will and the identities of the people likely to be affected if he erred. In neither case was unpredictable or runaway liability a danger.

Q. What is the distinction between *Biakanja v. Irving* and *Ultramares v. Touche?*
A. In *Biakanja,* again, the defendant was readily able to see the nature and extent of the reliance by others on his work. In *Ultramares,* the defendant did not know what use the client would make of its work, and could not control it; the client's use of the bad audit thus more closely the fire in *Moch* than the a misweighed bag of beans in *Glanzer.* One might ask: Can it really be said that the plaintiff's use of the audit was not the "end and aim" of the transaction in *Ultramares* to the same extent as the seller's use of the weighing certificate in *Glanzer*? Again, however, that formulation may not be very helpful. What we are told is that while Touche knew Stern would use these statements to obtain loans, it did not know from whom (or of what size, etc.). This is important; later New York cases set out the test for liability in accounting cases as follows:

> (1) the accountants must have been aware that the financial reports were to be used for a particular purpose or purposes;
> (2) in the furtherance of which a known party or parties was intended to rely; and (3) there must have been some conduct on the part of the accountants linking them to that party or parties, which evinces the accountants' understanding of that party or parties' reliance.

See *Credit Alliance Corp. v. Arthur Andersen & Co.* (NL for negligent audit by accountant leading to bad loans); *European American Bank & Trust v. Strauhs & Kaye* (L for same).

Also, in *Biakanja* the defendant had all the information he needed to perform his work and estimate the consequences of his errors. In *Ultramares* a duty to non-parties to the contract might be a bit harder to discharge, since the auditor is heavily dependent on the client for its inputs. But perhaps this issue can be handled by careful application of the standard for breach.

To return to the contract angle, maybe it doesn't matter very much what we decide in *Ultramares*; the Coase theorem applies. To think of this as a contract situation, we're trying to figure out who should bear the risk involved. Touche presumably was not compensated for undertaking the kinds of responsibilities that it is being sued on here. The plaintiff can still hire its own auditors; for that matter, if everyone wants the auditors to warranty their work in this way, they can do it by contract. They don't; and if they won't, why should the law insist on doing it for them? Of course even if the law did this, the parties could opt around it. The question is what the default rule should be. If a disclaimer would be effective (as presumably it would be), then tort law becomes just a gap-filler when nobody bothers to make them. Tort duties make most sense where contractual duties are not feasible.

Posner's take on *Ultramares* is that it's hard to distinguish from *MacPherson*—and that "the principle of *Ultramares* has been rejected in most states, yet the sky has not fallen on the accounting profession." He concludes that *Moch* is correct but that *Ultramares* was wrongly decided. H reports that the brief of the water company in *Moch*

> argued that the company's remuneration ($42.50 per year per hydrant, of which there were 197, making a total price of $8,372.50) was too slight to warrant an inference that the company had undertaken to insure the property owners of Rensselaer against the potentially catastrophic consequences of a negligent failure to maintain the pressure in the mains. [...] Touche argued similarly in the suit against it that the fee for the audit (a measly $1,138) was incommensurate with the claims arising from the negligent performance of the audit ($683,000). The difference is that, while the investor may well look to the accountant as a guarantor of the corporation's financial representations, the property owner does not look to the water company as its fire insurer.

Cardozo: A Study in Reputation 112-15. Posner concludes that the inconsistencies between the justifications Cardozo gives for *MacPherson* and *Glanzer* on the one hand and *Moch* and *Ultramares* on the other are "serious defects" in Cardozo's judicial performance, but that all four cases might have been correctly decided on their facts because the extent of the defendants' liability was harder to predict in the first two cases, making it harder in turn for them to know how much care would be optimal to take.

Einhorn v. Seeley (problem; NL for locksmith when sued by tenant for negligence; his K was with the landlord)

Here are some excerpts from the court's opinion affirming summary judgment for the defendant (citations omitted):

> The essential question here is whether the defendant locksmith owed a duty, apart from contract, to plaintiffs. In deciding whether or not there is such liability, as Judge Kaye pointed out in [Strauss v. Belle Realty Co., 65 NY2d 399]: "But while the absence of privity does not foreclose recognition of a duty, it is still the responsibility of courts, in fixing the orbit of duty, 'to limit the legal consequences of wrongs to a controllable degree', and to protect against crushing exposure to liability. 'In fixing the bounds of that duty, not only logic and science, but policy play an important role.' The courts' definition of an orbit of duty based on public policy may at times result in the exclusion of some who might otherwise have recovered for losses or injuries if traditional tort principles had been applied."

> There is no basis in tort for liability in this case. This is not a case in which the defendant locksmith itself injured the plaintiff either by a direct volitional act or even by some negligent act, i.e., leaving a bag of tools in a doorway. Here, the act complained of by plaintiff was perpetrated by an intervening person. There will ordinarily be no duty thrust on a defendant to prevent a third party from causing harm to another. The exception may occur in the case where a special

relationship exists between the defendant and the third person so as to give rise to a duty to control, or alternatively, when a special relationship exists between the defendant and the victim which gives the latter the right to protection (Restatement [Second] of Torts §315). Thus, such special relationships have been held to include employers-employees, owners and occupiers of premises, common carriers and their patrons, and hosts who serve alcoholic beverages to their guests, among others. Although plaintiffs plead such duty on the part of defendant Rem, it is clear that they do not fit into any category which has been held to constitute such a special relationship.

It may be that the landlord is liable to the victim, Lori Einhorn. While there have been a few cases in which the landlord has been held liable to a tenant who has been a victim of crime as a result of a defective lock, none of those cases extends the zone of duty to include a third party who was hired by the landlord to install or repair the lock and who does so improperly. The expansion of the net of obligation to enmesh a landlord in such situation has been a slow process based on discriminating selection and wanton conduct on the part of the landlord. [....]

Applying this analysis to the facts as presented to us, it seems clear that the locksmith, defendant Rem, did not undertake a duty to plaintiff Lori Einhorn when it entered into its relationship with the defendant landlord. Here we are concerned with a possible liability for an injury to a mere guest of a tenant caused by an unlawful act of a third party. Under these circumstances, to hold a locksmith responsible for the alleged consequences of an allegedly defective lock would be to enlarge the obligations of such artisans far beyond the existing law and beyond sound public policy.

Section F. Pure Economic Losses

If you want to lose some cases here, drop *Carbone*, *Henderson*, and *Yarmouth*, all near the beginning. We think the best teaching case in the batch is *532 Madison Avenue Gourmet Foods, Inc. v. Finlandia Center*.

Robins Dry Dock & Repair Co. v. Flint (D, hired by boat's owner to perform repairs, breaks propeller, causing boat to be out of commission for weeks; NL to party who chartered the boat and lost its use)

Q. How would you analyze *Robins* under the privity rules considered in the previous section of the duty chapter?
A. The Robins firm is analogous to the water works company in *Moch* or to the weigher of the beans in *Glanzer*. It had a contract with the owners of the boat to perform repairs upon it. The plaintiffs were not a party to that contract, though they had a strong interest in seeing it performed in a timely fashion because they were renting the boat from the owners and needed it back. Robins acted negligently. The plaintiffs were the ones hurt most by this, like the owners of the warehouse in *Moch*. The court denied recovery here. So one naturally might ask why this case is treated more like *Moch* than like *Glanzer* or *Biakanja*, where recovery was allowed. The idea presumably is that when Robins is carrying out repairs, it generally can't be expected to know what stakes depend on their timely completion. Maybe nobody much cares whether the repairs are done this week or next; or maybe failing to get the repairs done on time will cause a shipment of goods to be lost or ruined with catastrophic consequences. There is an analogy on the contract side to *Hadley v. Baxendale*, the facts of which somewhat resemble those of *Robins*. The crank shaft at the plaintiffs' mill broke, so they sent it out for repair or replacement; the defendants (hired to carry the broken shaft to Greenwich) were late in delivering it. The plaintiffs were not allowed to recover for their lost profits from the delay, as these damages were held unforeseeable. Indirect (or "consequential") damages can be recovered only if they are foreseeable. It's not quite the

same as the operation of the privity or financial loss doctrines in tort, but some of the same policies seem to drive the rules.

Q. How does one read *Robins* to go beyond a mere application of the privity doctrine and establish an "economic loss rule" with other implications?

A. By ignoring the contract between Robins and the boat's owners and focusing instead on a different feature of the facts: Robins committed a negligent act that caused physical damage to property, and the plaintiffs were hurt as a result. The Court said that since the plaintiffs didn't own the property, they had no legal interest entitling them to sue for the inconvenience caused by the damage done to it. The implication, though it is not stated in quite this way, is that pure economic losses unaccompanied by damage inflicted on one's own person or property (but instead caused, as in *Robins*, by a tort committed against someone else) create no right to recover. To bring this point out you can focus on this sentence of *Robins*: "The injury to the propeller was no wrong to the respondents but only to those to whom it belonged." That's the key point, and as a general matter it is separate from (and holds up regardless of) whether there was a contract in the picture between Robins and the boat's owners. But there also are exceptions to it, as we shall see; otherwise it might seem hard to explain those cases from the privity chapter where there *is* liability.

Either here or later (perhaps in connection with the *Madison Avenue* case and its relationship to *Biakanja*) it is worth spending some time on the relationship between the privity doctrine and the economic loss doctrine, since it can be confusing to students. The doctrines have similar rationales and sometimes can affect the same cases, but they function differently. The privity doctrine severs the defendant's duty to the plaintiff when the defendant's negligence occurs in the course of performing a contract with another party. The economic loss doctrine bars a plaintiff from recovering when the defendant's negligence causes the plaintiff economic losses but no damage to person or property. They differ because the privity doctrine can cut off liability even for injuries to person or property, and because the economic loss doctrine can cut off liability even where there is no contract in sight. They can overlap, however, in cases where there is negligence in the performance of a contract *and* pure financial loss.

Notice that even in a case where both doctrines *appear* to apply there still may be liability. The reason is that there are exceptions to both doctrines and the exceptions, too, can apply at the same time. Thus in *Biakanja* the defendant was negligent in writing a will and was held liable to an intended legatee who suffered damages as a result. It looks like a privity case *and* an economic loss case, but recovery is allowed anyway because it fits within exceptions to both rules. The plaintiff wins despite the privity doctrine because the damages were straightforward enough for the defendant to forecast and control. The plaintiff wins despite the economic loss doctrine because there is an exception to the rule for suits against certain types of professionals—perhaps because without such an exception, they never would be held liable for their negligence. More on this under the *Madison Avenue* case.

Carbone v. Ursich (D fouls nets of sardine fishermen; L despite financial loss rule because P fishermen are favorites of admiralty)

Henderson v. Arundel Corp. (P dredge workers thrown out of work when D collides with their vessel; NL)

Yarmouth Sea Products v. Scully (P fishermen allowed to collect again despite *Henderson*)

Q. What is the distinction between *Carbone v. Ursich* and *Robins*?

A. The court says it's that seamen are favorites of admiralty and that their economic interests are entitled to full protection. The interesting question is why this should be so. It's a useful problem for students to think about because you really can't understand why fishermen are treated this way until you first figure out the rationale for the economic loss rule generally; once you do understand the rationale, you then can ask whether it is less present in the case of the seamen. At the end of this section (in the *Barber Lines* case), Breyer offers two rationales for the usual inability to collect for pure financial loss: (a) if recovery were allowed (even if just for those whose financial losses were found foreseeable), the number of suits resulting from a tort would greatly increase, creating a large new set of litigation costs, and (b) if recovery were allowed, you would have runaway ("disproportionate") liability as one tort creates financial ripple effects that are hard to foresee or contain. The costs of the resulting litigation don't seem offset by enough social benefits to justify them. These rationales are similar, of course, to the reasons for the privity limitation considered in cases like *Moch*. In the scenarios where each doctrine applies, the harms at issue often will be open-ended, causing the defendant's liability exposure to become potentially both very large and very unpredictable. And allowing suits in the circumstances forbidden by the two doctrines also would cause a related increase in litigation costs.

But there are exceptions to the privity doctrine, and there are similar rules here. Breyer suggests that the rules for fishermen are just one of many "exceptions seem designed to pick out broad categories of cases where the 'administrative' and 'disproportionality' problems intuitively seem insignificant or where some strong countervailing consideration militates in favor of liability. Thus an award of financial damages to one also caused physical harm does not threaten proliferation of law suits, for the plaintiff could sue anyway (for physical damages). Financial harm awards to family members carry with them an obvious self-limiting principle (as perhaps does awarding such damages to fishermen, as 'favorites' of admiralty)."

There is an analogy not only to cases like *Biakanja* (where liability is imposed because the damages have a self-limiting character) but also more generally to the ways that other duty problems get worked out by the courts. We start with a general rule of no duty to rescue, for example, but then the courts carve out areas (e.g., the sea captain's duty, or *Tarasoff*) where the benefits of such a duty seem unusually great and the costs unusually low when compared with the general run of cases. In those situations duties are imposed after all. In the financial loss area we likewise begin with a background rule of no recovery, sometimes framed as a "no duty" rule—though sometimes not. Breyer puts it this way:

> We note that the courts in the cases we have cited have not always used the same legal terminology to describe their conclusions. One might, for example, use Judge Hand's language in *Sinram*, and say that plaintiffs like those before us are persons to whom appellee owes no "duty of care." Alternatively, one could use the slightly more obscure "proximate cause" terminology, and say that plaintiffs' injuries are too "remote." One could also appeal to historic legal terminology, and describe plaintiffs as suffering damnum absque injuria. Regardless of descriptive terminology, the holdings of these major cases are the same. They refuse to hold a defendant liable for negligently caused financial harm without accompanying physical injury or other special circumstances, none of which is present here.

Those "special circumstances" he mentions are analogous to those in cases like *Tarasoff*: the courts conclude that the rationale for the background rule is weak, and its costs great, in certain classes of situations that can be defined with adequate clarity to permit them to be treated as exceptions.

As for fishermen in particular, the sense of Breyer's claim is that allowing fishermen to recover creates a pretty clearly identifiable set of plaintiffs and interests that a defendant has to worry about; it doesn't create the threat of liability for endless economic repercussions that drives the doctrine. But is this really clear? As the *Henderson* case suggests, negligent acts that leave fishermen out of work can subject a defendant to rather open-ended liability—for while the class of plaintiffs is fixed (the fishermen), the scope of the liability will depend on another factor that is unfixed (how long they are out of work). But maybe the idea is that limiting the number of plaintiffs still produces enough certainty to cabin the defendant's obligations adequately.

And then there is the other side of the equation: the hardship worked by the doctrine. The idea is that fishermen in situations such as these are likely to see their livelihoods wiped out, a harder outcome than seemed likely to result from the delay in completing the repair in *Robins*. The courts seem to care about this (as *Yarmouth* makes clear), though it may be difficult to maintain the point in view of some the NL cases that follow in which plaintiffs likewise seem to suffer large hardships.

Q. What is the distinction between *Yarmouth Sea Products Ltd v. Scully* and *Henderson v. Arundel Corp.*?

A. The court in *Yarmouth* says that fishermen and dredgers are different, and are entitled to different legal treatment, because of the nature of their financial arrangements with the party whose property was damaged. What is it about those arrangements that makes the court want to treat fishermen differently? The fishermen, unlike the dredge workers in *Henderson*, had invested in the voyage and would be paid out of a share of the proceeds. This put them into a kind of "joint venture" with the boat's owners. The court seems to have in mind a couple of different consequences of this arrangement. First, the court in *Yarmouth* says this:

> [W]here the fishermen's wages are dependent on the vessel's catch and that vessel is tortiously incapacitated, their losses are as foreseeable and direct a consequence of the tortfeasor's actions as the shipowner's loss of use. Hence, they are unlike the time charterer in *Robins Dry Dock* [sic] whose contract with the shipowner is impaired "unknown to the doer of the wrong[.]" Cf. *Venore Transp. Co.*, 583 F.2d at 710 ("The principle of *Robins Dry Dock* is perfectly defensible, if pragmatic considerations require the foreclosure of remote damage claims.... There is nothing remote about these damages; the only objection is that they were suffered by the time charterer rather than the owner.").

Again there might seem to be an analogy to the *Hadley v. Baxendale* idea. Here we have a class of cases where there are economic losses inflicted, but where they are unusually likely not only to be capable of being cabined but also where they are unusually capable of being foreseen. If you ram a fishing boat, a big and obvious part of the loss is that you will put a bunch of fishermen out of work for a while. It's not so obvious that if you damage a propeller you will cause any particular type of financial harm to whoever was hoping to use the boat for which it was meant. And maybe the same can be said for ramming a non-fishing boat, such as a dredge: you can't be as sure what the consequences will be.

The other point goes again to the hardship on the fishermen. The court says they "invested" in the voyage. If this means they contributed more than just their time (if they chipped in for equipment, etc.), then the boat did not just deprive them of a chance to work in the future; it wiped out a venture in which they had a different sort of interest than mere expectation. It's also possible that the investment the court has in mind is just the nature of the lay arrangement: the fishermen essentially work for nothing during the initial part of the voyage; they invest this time in hopes of returns later when they get a share of the eventual catch. If the boat is damaged and the catch never gets made, then again the fisherman lose more than just a chance for employment in the future. They end up with nothing to show for the previous months, either. This is a harder result than would be experienced by dredgers who were paid by the hour or week during all phases of their work.

532 Madison Avenue Gourmet Foods, Inc. v. Finlandia Center, Inc. (D negligently causes own building to collapse, putting neighboring deli out of business for weeks; NL)
Newlin v. New England Telephone & Telegraph Co. (D knocks out power to P's mushroom plant, leading to loss of mushrooms; L)
Phoenix Professional Hockey Club, Inc., v. Hirmer (D knocks out P's goalie, requiring P to hire a replacement; NL)
Byrd v. English (problem: D severs power to P's printing shop, causing lost profits; NL)

Q. What is the distinction between *532 Madison Avenue Gourmet Foods, Inc. v. Finlandia Center, Inc.* and *Glanzer v. Shepard* (or *Biakanja v. Irving*)?

A. Start with the superficial similarities. *Glanzer* and *Biakanja*, of course, were cases in the privity section where (to reconsider them from the standpoint of this section) defendants were held liable for pure financial losses the plaintiffs suffered when the defendants negligently performed a contract. In *Glanzer* the defendant misweighed beans that the plaintiff then bought; in *Biakanja* the defendant botched a will he was hired to write. In both cases the result for the defendant was the loss of a sum of money with no accompanying physical damage. Yet in the *Madison Avenue* case the court seemed to say that a plaintiff cannot recover for financial loss without physical harm. Why?

One explanation involves the professional activities in which the *Glanzer* and *Biakanja* were engaged. From *Union Oil Co. v. Oppen*, 501 F.2d 558 (9th Cir. 1974):

> It is but a short step from [*Biakanja*] to a body of law existing both in this country and in the British Commonwealth in which defendants engaged in certain professions, businesses, or trades have been held liable for economic losses resulting from the negligent performance of tasks within the course of their callings. One Commonwealth scholar has stated that 'in a proper case a person may recover economic loss caused by the negligence of persons such as bankers, commission agents, real estate agents, accountants, surveyors, valuers, analysts, insurance brokers, stock brokers, government employees, doctors, architects, car salesmen who undertake to have cars insured, car testers, and drawers of cheques.' Harvey, *Economic Losses and Negligence*, 50 Can.Bar Rev. 580, 603-04 (1972).

> The American cases reflect a similar development. There are numerous cases indicating that economic losses may be recovered for the negligence of pension consultants, accountants, architects, attorneys, notaries public, test hole drillers, title abstractors, termite inspectors, soil engineers, surveyors, real estate brokers, drawers of checks, directors of corporations, trustees, bailees and public weighers.

One way to think about these cases, mentioned in the *Barber Lines* decision that comes at the end of the section, is that they tend to be situations where no recovery by anyone ever will be possible, or at least likely, if recovery for economic harm is not allowed. In *532 Madison Avenue*, the defendant has plenty of reason to worry about liability even if it doesn't have to compensate its neighbors; someone could have been killed (in this sense, the observation by the intermediate appellate court that it was only "fortuitous" that nobody was killed actually cuts against liability). But the drafter of a will may not be disciplined by tort law if the legatees who are made losers by his mistakes cannot sue.

Q. What is the distinction between *Newlin v. New England Telephone & Telegraph Co.* and *532 Madison Avenue Gourmet Foods, Inc. v. Finlandia Center, Inc.*?
A. In *Newlin* the plaintiff suffered property damage (the ruined mushrooms), thus satisfying the gatekeeping rule and allowing recovery for the economic damages that resulted. This is supposed to be an easy point, but some students find it hard to see. The case serves to remind them of the key idea: not that lost profits aren't recoverable, but that they aren't recoverable if they are the *only* damage the plaintiff suffered.

Q. Suppose the owner of the delicatessen in the *Madison Avenue* case sold bananas. Because of the dropoff in customers that resulted from the collapse of the defendant's building, the bananas weren't purchased for a week, turned brown, and were ruined. Could he at least collect for his lost profits on the bananas? Wouldn't they be just like the mushrooms in *Newlin*?
A. Probably not, but it's an interesting question. The analogy would be that just as in *Newlin* the defendant's negligence prevented power from reaching the plaintiff's store and saving the mushrooms, so too did the defendant's negligence in the *Madison Avenue* case prevent customers from reaching the plaintiff's store and saving the bananas. This would not be the same as the recovery the plaintiff sought in the actual case, because he wouldn't be trying to collect for the lost business that never occurred in the weeks after the collapse of the building. In other words, he wouldn't be trying to collect for the bananas he wasn't able to buy and then sell weeks later—and perhaps he shouldn't be, since those bananas probably were just bought and sold by someone else instead. Rather, he would be trying to collect for the actual bananas that he already had bought and that were destroyed. And we know from the *Food Pageant*

case in the previous section that recovery for melted ice cream and the like (as well as lost business) is possible if D negligently cuts off its power.

Still, though, there is a level of remoteness—and a prospect for cascading damages—that would probably cause a court to back away from liability in the banana hypothetical. The defendant didn't directly obstruct the plaintiff's building. It committed negligent acts that caused the street to be closed down, which in turn reduced traffic to the plaintiff's store. What if the collapse of the building caused no customers to reach a bookstore during the two weeks after the big new Harry Potter book were released? Now the bookstore is saddled with copies it can't sell (and let's imagine that they can't be returned). Or the ties in the plaintiff's clothing store go out of style in the interim: when the street reopens, the plaintiff finds that nobody wants to buy his skinny ties any more than they want to buy overripe bananas. Perhaps one could draw a line at perishable food that becomes unfit for human consumption.

Q. What is the distinction between *Phoenix Professional Hockey Club, Inc., v. Hirmer* and *Newlin v. New England Telephone & Telegraph Co.?*
A. They seem similar because in both cases the defendant's negligence imposed costs on the defendant. Again, however, only in *Newlin* did the defendant's negligence cause damage to property owned by the plaintiff. In the hockey case the goalie was not the plaintiff's property. In the old days the common law did recognize a cause of action on facts like *Hirmer*, allowing the master to sue a defendant who injured the master's servant and took him out of commission. Not anymore, though; from the opinion in *Hirmer*:

> Older cases recognized a master's cause of action against a third person tortiously injuring a servant. The action was apparently based upon the particular social status of a master and servant at the time. Just as a father can recover for the loss of services of his child, and a husband can recover for loss sustained by injuries to his wife, a master could recover for the loss of services of his servant, who at that time was a member of the master's household and occupied a quasi-familial relationship with him. *Crab Orchard Improvement Co. v. Chesapeake & Ohio Ry.*, 115 F.2d 277 (4th Cir. 1940). Now that the days of the cottage industry are history, the relation of master and servant no longer represents the close bond it once did and modern courts have refused recovery to the employer. Seavey, *Liability to Master for Negligent Harm to Servant*, 1956 Wash.U.L.Q. 307.

In *Newlin* the plaintiff lost property. The property was not the power that was supposed to be coming to his plant through the wires, as this was a matter of contract. Rather, recovery is allowed in *Newlin* because the plaintiff owned mushrooms that were ruined because of the defendant's negligent act. If the loss of power in *Newlin* had simply caused lost profits, they would not be recoverable; that's *Byrd*—which now follows.

Q. What result in *Byrd v. English?*
A. No liability. From the opinion (which was cited, by the way, in *Robins*):

> It will be borne in mind that this is not an action for an injury to the person or property of the plaintiff. It is not claimed that the defendants have violated any contractual duty owed to the plaintiff. Their duty to the public in performing the work in which they were engaged was to do it in such manner as not to negligently injure the person or property of any one. According to this petition the damage done by them was to the property of the Georgia Electric Light Company, who were under contract to the plaintiff to furnish him with electric power, and the resulting damage done to the plaintiff was that it was rendered impossible for that company to comply with its contract. If the plaintiff can recover of these defendants upon this cause of action, then a customer of his, who was injured by the delay occasioned by the stopping of his work, could also recover from them, and one who had been damaged through his delay could in turn hold them liable, and so on without limit to the number of persons who might recover on account of the

injury done to the property of the company owning the conduits. To state such a proposition is to demonstrate its absurdity. The plaintiff is suing on account of an alleged tort by reason of which he was deprived of a supply of electric power with which to operate his printing establishment. What was his right to that power supply? Solely the right given him by virtue of his contract with the Georgia Electric Light Company, and with that contract the defendants are not even remotely connected. If, under the terms of his contract, he is precluded from recovering from the electric light company, that is a matter between themselves, for which the defendants certainly cannot be held responsible. They are, of course, liable to the company for any wrong that may have been done it, and the damages recoverable on that account might well be held to include any sums which the company was compelled to pay in damages to its customers; but the customers themselves cannot go against the defendants to recover on their own account for the injury done the company. A case in point, which well illustrates the principle governing the one now under consideration, is that of *Dale v. Grant*, 34 N. J. Law, 142, where it was held that "a party who, by contract, is entitled to all the articles to be manufactured by an incorporated company, he (such party) furnishing the raw materials, cannot maintain an action against a wrongdoer, who, by a trespass, stops the machinery of such company, so that it is prevented from furnishing, under said contract, manufactured goods to as great an extent as it otherwise would have done." In the opinion (page 149, 34 N. J. Law) the court say: "The law does not attempt to give full reparation to all parties injured by a wrong committed. If this were so, all parties holding contracts, if such exist, under the plaintiffs, who may have been injuriously affected by the conduct of the defendants, would be entitled to a suit. It is only the proximate injury that the law endeavors to compensate. The more remote comes under the head of damnum absque injuria."

People Express Airlines, Inc., v. Consolidated Rail Corp. (D's negligence causes airline terminal to shut down; L; traditional economic loss rule attacked)
Barber Lines A/S v. M/V Donau Maru (D's oil spill in harbor causes P's ships to be diverted, resulting in economic losses; NL; traditional rule defended)

These cases are offered for their general discussions of the logic of the economic loss doctrine. *People Express* jettisons the usual approach of starting with a background rule and then making isolated exceptions to it; it says instead that there is liability for pure economic losses so long as the class of those injured is "identifiable": foreseeable in number and in the types of economic damages they are likely to suffer. The *Barber Lines* case defends the traditional rule-plus-exceptions approach. Notice that in some respects the two approaches are likely to lead to the same results, since the point of many of the exceptions described in *Barber Lines* is precisely to pick out cases ("favorites of admiralty," etc.) where the plaintiffs and their damages are relatively for a defendant easy to foresee. But the New Jersey court's approach is more likely to create jury questions about foreseeability, whereas the traditional approach creates more room for the judge to decide that the plaintiff has no claim as a matter of law. There is an analogy to the difference between *Rowland v. Christian* and the traditional rules governing landowners' liability to trespassers, licensees, and invitees. The *Rowland* court's replacement of that scheme with a general obligation to be reasonable will produce results similar to the common law rules in many cases, but with some differences at the margins and with a larger role for the jury.

If you like, of course, you can ask someone to try to distinguish *People Express* and *Barber Lines* on their facts. Would the result in *People Express* have been different if the traditional approach had been applied? Would the result in *Barber Lines* have been different if the *People Express* approach had been applied? Probably yes and yes. *People Express* seems similar to *Byrd v. English,* the old case where the power outage shut down the plaintiff's business for a while and no recovery was allowed. It also seems similar to the *Madison Avenue* case, as it involved an evacuation ordered by the city for safety reasons. So if those old cases were followed, there would no liability in *People Express*. And the result in *Barber Lines* probably would have been different under *People Express*, since the harm to other ships in the harbor caused by the defendant's negligence in *Barber Lines* seems no less foreseeable—in type, extent, or any other way—than the harm caused to the plaintiff's airline in *People Express*.

Incidentally, there is a useful passage in the *Barber Lines* case that is omitted from the casebook but that may help guide the discussion. It is indicated by the ellipses in the last paragraph of the excerpt (before "We need not explore..."). Here it is:

> It does not surprise us then that, under these circumstances, courts have neither enforced one clear rule nor considered the matter case by case. Rather, they have spoken of a general principle against liability for negligently caused financial harm, while creating many exceptions. See, e.g., 1) *Newlin v. New England Telephone & Telegraph Co.*, 54 N.E.2d 929 (Mass. 1944) (accompanying physical harm); 2) *Lumley v. Gye*, 2 El. & Bl. 216, 118 Eng.Rep. 749 (1853); *Beekman v. Marsters*, 80 N.E. 817 (Mass. 1907) (intentionally caused harm); 3) *Dalton v. Meister*, 188 N.W.2d 494 (Wis. 1971) (defamation); *Systems Operations, Inc. v. Scientific Games Development Corp.*, 555 F.2d 1131 (3d Cir.1977) (injurious falsehood); 4) *Hitaffer v. Argonne Co.*, 183 F.2d 811 (D.C.Cir. 1950) (loss of consortium); 5) *Chicago, Duluth & Georgia Bay Transit Co. v. Moore*, 259 Fed. 490 (6th Cir.) (medical costs of injured plaintiff paid by a different family member), cert. denied, 251 U.S. 553 (1919); 6) *Hedley Byrne Co. Ltd. v. Heller & Partners Ltd., A.C.* 465 (1964) (negligent misstatements about financial matters); 7) *Jones v. Waterman S.S. Corp.*, 155 F.2d 992 (3d Cir.1946) (master-servant); 8) *Western Union Telegraph Co. v. Mathis*, 110 So. 399 (Ala. 1926) (telegraph-addressee); 9) *Union Oil Co. v. Oppen*, 501 F.2d 558 (9th Cir.1974) (commercial fishermen as special "favorites of admiralty"). These exceptions seem designed to pick out broad categories of cases where the "administrative" and "disproportionality" problems intuitively seem insignificant or where some strong countervailing consideration militates in favor of liability. Thus an award of financial damages to one also caused physical harm does not threaten proliferation of law suits, for the plaintiff could sue anyway (for physical damages). Financial harm awards to family members carry with them an obvious self-limiting principle (as perhaps does awarding such damages to fishermen, as 'favorites' of admiralty). Awarding damages for financial harm caused by negligent misrepresentation is special in that, without such liability, tort law would not exert significant financial pressure to avoid negligence; a negligent accountant lacks physically harmed victims as potential plaintiffs.

Q. Can *People Express* be distinguished from *532 Madison Avenue Gourmet Foods, Inc. v. Finlandia Center, Inc.*?

A. Here is what the New York court said in the latter case:

> Plaintiffs' reliance on *People Express Airlines v. Consolidated Rail Corp.* (100 N.J. 246, 495 A.2d 107) is misplaced. There, a fire started at defendant's commercial freight yard located across the street from plaintiff's airport offices. A tank containing volatile chemicals located in the yard was punctured, emitting the chemicals and requiring closure of the terminal because of fear of an explosion. Allowing the plaintiff to seek damages for purely economic loss, the New Jersey court reasoned that the extent of liability and degree of foreseeability stand in direct proportion to one another: the more particular the foreseeability that economic loss would be suffered as a result of the defendant's negligence, the more just that liability be imposed and recovery permitted. The New Jersey court acknowledged, however, that the presence of members of the public, or invitees at a particular plaintiff's business, or persons traveling nearby, while foreseeable, is nevertheless fortuitous, and the particular type of economic injury that they might suffer would be hopelessly unpredictable. Such plaintiffs, the court recognized, would present circumstances defying any appropriately circumscribed orbit of duty. We see a like danger in the urban disasters at issue here, and decline to follow *People Express*.

Section G. Negligent Infliction of Emotional Distress

These cases can be viewed as a classic series of line-drawing problems. In the old days the courts drew the line at physical contact: there could be no claims for emotional distress unless they were "parasitic" on claims arising from injury to person or property. The line was pretty easy to administer, but the results it produced came to seem harsh, so courts started bending it to find physical contact to which recovery for distress could be attached. Eventually they shed the rule altogether, allowing recovery for negligently inflicted distress without regard to the "impact rule." But now it became necessary to find new places to draw lines to prevent the courts from being inundated with claims that are minor or spurious. The cases in the chapter explore various ways the lines can be drawn.

If cuts are desired, leave out *Potter* and *Lombardo* in the first part of the section.

Robb v. Pennsylvania R. Co. (D negligently causes P's car to become stuck in rut next to railroad tracks; P abandons car at last moment before train hits it; L—at least so long as P was in zone of physical danger and suffered physical harm as a result of the fright)
Lawson v. Management Activities, Inc. (D's airplane crashes near P; NL)
Quill v. Trans World Airlines (D's plane nearly crashes with P on board; L)

Q.   Suppose a fact pattern just like *Robb*, but this time the plaintiff floors the accelerator and manages to get her car to lurch out of the way of the train at the last minute, so that both she and the car escape the impact. Could the railroad still be held liable for her resulting emotional distress?
A.   It shouldn't matter; the court's test doesn't depend on the property damage the plaintiff's property suffered. But it's easy to imagine a court's judgment being influenced by such a fact. The reason is that the destroyed car makes the plaintiff's claim seem more credible: if the car was destroyed, then she's probably telling the truth when she says that she almost got hit as well. A plaintiff who drove away from the crossing with no damage at all might have more trouble convincing a court that she really was in such great trouble.

Q.   Can *Lawson v. Management Activities, Inc.* be distinguished from *Robb v. Pennsylvania Railroad Co.*? The two cases use different legal tests (which is preferable?); but can it be argued that the court in *Lawson* would have reached the same outcome in *Robb* that the court in Delaware did?
A.   Both *Robb* and *Lawson* involved plaintiffs who were afraid they were going to be hit by the defendants' vehicles—but weren't. *Robb* is a case of liability, *Lawson* a case of no liability. Despite their different tests, one can ask whether the court in *Lawson* would have found liability on the facts of *Robb*. It might well have. An earlier California case, *Wooden v. Raveling*, 71 Cal.Rptr.2d 891 (Cal.App. 1998), had found liability for emotional distress when a car accident damaged a house and frightened its occupant. The court in *Lawson* didn't seem to like the *Wooden* decision, but anyway it distinguished that case on grounds that might have some application to *Robb* as well:

> [T]here is a difference between car crashes and airplane crashes as they relate to bystanders. Automobile drivers necessarily must be highly aware of the surrounding area and nearby property through which they drive. Freeways pose different risks than residential streets. Children might dart out into a narrow alley; one must drive slowly to avoid them. No such necessity attaches on a wide stretch of open highway in the desert.

> The risk to bystanders is different in air travel. Most of the time, after all, when a plane is flying, the safety of bystanders on the ground is irrelevant from the point of view of the operators and owners of the plane. It is only relevant when a crash is otherwise inevitable.

One way to interpret these points is to conclude that imposing liability in *Robb* might make more policy sense than imposing it in *Lawson*. In both cases the plaintiffs may have been plenty scared, and reasonably so; and in both cases the fright may have been the result of the defendant's negligence. But in *Robb* there seems to have been solider evidence of injury resulting from the emotional distress. It also seems arguable, on the court's account, that the moral blameworthiness of the defendant in *Robb* was greater than in *Lawson*, though this is not clear. And in *Robb* it seems more plausible that the imposition of liability might make a contribution to public safety at the margin by giving the railroad an incentive it might not otherwise have to be careful in certain respects. A plane crash creates countless huge costs for the airline, and this causes the airline to put great resources into preventing such a result—and this isn't likely to be changed by adding on liability to frightened bystanders on the ground. An incident like the one in *Robb* might not create the same sorts of fixed costs; if the railroad isn't liable for the emotional distress the plaintiff suffered, then it will be liable only for the value of her car, which may not be much. (But there are counterarguments as well. A railroad in a case like *Robb* can't assume that the plaintiff always will make it out of the car.) Finally, perhaps a plane crash is likely to frighten more onlookers than a near-miss caused by a train.

Q. What is the distinction between *Quill* and *Lawson*?
A. There is a lack of moral blameworthiness in both cases, at least as the court sees that issue in *Lawson*. Possibly the injuries of the plaintiffs in *Lawson* were harder to prove than the injuries in *Quill*, but there is no reason to assume that such a distinction will regularly be available in these two types of cases. The key point seems to be that liability in *Lawson* would expand the exposure of airlines in large, unpredictable ways. Liability in *Quill* does not create these problems because the class of plaintiffs is limited to the passengers on the plane. And since they were on the plane rather than being scattered on the ground (like the plaintiffs in *Lawson*), there is less speculation required of courts trying to figure out whether the plaintiff *really* was subjected to a greatly distressing experience.

Another possible argument is that if there is no liability in *Quill*, the airlines might face no threat of liability for the sorts of acts that occurred in that case—the nosedive that almost (but not quite) leads to a crash. Again, though, perhaps no threat of liability is needed to give the airlines fully adequate incentives to avoid such occurrences, since the airline already has to worry that in most such cases the plane *will* crash. But the same general point can also be approached from the standpoint of corrective justice. The airline here has inflicted a large dose of disutility on the plaintiff—an experience the plaintiff undoubtedly would have been willing to pay handsomely to avoid if that option had been available. If this was the result of a failure to use reasonable care, shouldn't the cost of the experience by shouldered by the airline? Against this one can say that the same logic should then apply to *Lawson* as well, but that's not necessarily quite right. One can take the position that in *Lawson* there were other plaintiffs in the picture—the estates of the parties on the plane that crashed—who probably would have held the defendant to account for its negligence. Not so in *Quill*, where there is no reason to think there is any potential plaintiff better situated to recover than the actual plaintiff in that case.

Johnson v. Jamaica Hospital (P's infant abducted from hospital because of D's negligence; NL)
Perry-Rogers v. Obasaju (P's embryo negligently planted in third party; L)

Q. Suppose that in *Johnson* the plaintiffs' baby never had been recovered. Liability?
A. That would resemble a case where a defendant hospital is sued for negligently causing an infant's death. In those cases recovery is governed by wrongful death statutes. It might be possible for the parents to sue for loss of consortium and loss of expected support. But since the infant was returned, none of these theories is applicable.

Q. What is the distinction between *Johnson v. Jamaica Hospital* and *Perry-Rogers v. Obasaju*?
A. In both cases parents were deprived of their child for its first four months of life, and in both cases this resulted from the defendant's negligence. In *Johnson*, however, the court regarded the parents as

bystanders to a tort committed against their daughter. It therefore worried that if liability were found in the case, it also would follow that there is potential liability of nursing homes and hospitals to family members of any patients who are treated negligently, at least if the patients are so old or so young as to be unable to care for themselves (or otherwise be analogous to the plaintiffs' infant). In *Perry-Rogers* it was found that the defendant clinic did owe a duty to the plaintiffs, evidently because they came there for fertilization treatment.

But how satisfactory is the distinction? In both cases the plaintiffs themselves were the ones who chose to come to the defendant's facility for medical assistance. Obviously if the hospital in *Johnson* had committed a negligent act against Mrs. Johnson there would be liability; they did owe her a duty of care in that sense. The court's claim is that the hospital had no duty to the parents to take reasonable care of their infant; the hospital owed that duty only to the infant herself. So perhaps the infant could have sued, but maybe her damages would be hard to prove: no medical expenses, no lost wages, and no demonstrable pain and suffering, though switching mothers at the age of four months (and being in the care of a crook in the meantime) presumably would be unpleasant and perhaps psychologically damaging.

In any event, the question is why the embryo in *Perry-Rogers* wasn't treated the same way as the infant in *Johnson*. After all, the defendants in *Perry-Rogers* didn't injure the mother any more than did the defendant in *Johnson*. Rather, the clinic misplaced the plaintiffs' embryo. Perhaps the idea is that the unimplanted embryo was regarded as the plaintiffs' property, so that misplacing it amounted to a breach to them—whereas the infant in *Johnson* was a person with rights of her own (including a potential right to sue) with respect to whom the hospital owed no tort duty to anyone else. The irony is that the defendant who mistreats the infant person ends up better off than the clinic that mistreats the embryo. But maybe this distinction can be defended on policy grounds: the line between embryo and infant may be uncomfortable but it is plausible to state and feasible to administer. Once hospitals owe duties to parents with respect to their infants, however, it might be hard to find a similar line to separate that case from cases involving other sorts of patients.

Potter v. Firestone Tire and Rubber Co. (Ds dumping puts Ps in fear of getting cancer; NL unless cancer was more likely than not to occur)
Lombardo v. New York University Medical Center (problem: fear of AIDS; L)

Q. Suppose the plaintiff goes to a doctor because he has a cough. The doctor concludes that the cough is the result of a virus. It later turns out that the cough was a symptom of cancer that the plaintiff had contracted, and that the doctor negligently failed to diagnose. The correct diagnosis is made three months after the plaintiff's initial consultation. The cancer is treated and goes into remission. Nevertheless, the plaintiff continues to worry that the cancer will return, and rightly so; his expert witnesses testify that there is a 25% chance that the cancer will recur—and that this chance of recurrence was increased by the delay in diagnosing and treating the disease. The plaintiff sues the doctor for, among other things, negligent infliction of emotional distress; the plaintiff wants compensation for his additional fear of cancer caused by the negligent misdiagnosis. The defendant invokes the *Potter* case. Is it distinguishable?

A. This hypothetical is based on *Boryla v. Pash*, 960 P.2d 123 (Col. 1998), which found liability and concluded that *Potter* was indeed distinguishable:

> In our view, the more probable than not standard articulated in *Potter* is not appropriate in cases where the plaintiff's fear of cancer results from a delayed medical diagnosis. Contrary to toxic exposure cases, where the plaintiff has yet to experience the onset of cancer, fear of cancer cases in the medical setting usually involve a negligent misdiagnosis of a patient's existing cancer. In cases where the plaintiff demonstrates that her cancerous condition physically worsened as a result of the delayed diagnosis, the plaintiff has demonstrated a sufficient physical injury to permit the recovery of emotional distress damages. Thus, the usual reservations courts have

concerning jury speculation and conjecture in cases involving plaintiffs seeking purely emotional damages are inapplicable in a case such as Boryla's.

Additionally, the sweeping policy rationales relevant in a toxic tort case are not present here because the class of potential plaintiffs in a medical malpractice case is "clearly limited" to the parties in dispute.

This hypothetical bears a partial resemblance to the *Herskovits* case in the cause in fact chapter, where a plaintiff is allowed to collect damages for "loss of a c—hance" when her husband's doctor failed to make a timely diagnosis of his cancer. The problem there, similar to the problem here, is that it was not possible to say that the misdiagnosis more likely than not caused the patient's death; he probably would have died even if the diagnosis had been made correctly from the beginning. The court still allows recovery for his lost chance of survival, though, because otherwise a doctor who made such blunders might never be held liable. Is that a danger in *Potter*? Could be. Dumping toxic chemicals in the wrong place could be a practice that tends to increase the risk of cancer in certain areas to a relatively small and uncertain degree, making damages unrecoverable.

But the court in *Potter* did allow recovery of medical monitoring costs, and it also said that its requirement of a "more likely than not" showing wouldn't apply if the defendants were guilty of something worse than negligence—i.e., if the defendant committed *intentional* infliction of emotional distress.

Q. What result in *Lombardo v. New York University Medical Center*?
A. The New York court suggested that recovery would be allowed for the emotional distress reasonably experienced during the "window of anxiety." A number of other courts have used a similar reasonableness test. California's appellate courts, however, apply the same "more likely than not" test to AIDS cases that it used in *Potter*, the fear of cancer case; the following discussion (from *Kerins v. Hartley*, 33 Cal.Rptr.2d 172 (Cal. App. 1994)) can serve as a springboard for an interesting discussion about the policy consequences of compensating for the two types of fears:

All of the policy concerns expressed in *Potter* apply with equal force in the fear of AIDS context. The magnitude of the potential class of plaintiffs seeking emotional distress damages for negligent exposure to HIV or AIDS cannot be overstated. As another division of this court recently observed, "[t]he devastating effects of AIDS and the widespread fear of contamination at home, work, school, healthcare facilities and elsewhere are, sadly, too well known to require further discussion at this point." *Herbert v. Regents of the University of California*, 26 Cal.App.4th 782 (1994). Proliferation of fear of AIDS claims in the absence of meaningful restrictions would run an equal risk of compromising the availability and affordability of medical, dental and malpractice insurance, medical and dental care, prescription drugs, and blood products. Juries deliberating in fear of AIDS lawsuits would be just as likely to reach inconsistent results, discouraging early resolution or settlement of such claims. Last but not least, the coffers of defendants and their insurers would risk being emptied to pay for the emotional suffering of the many plaintiffs uninfected by exposure to HIV or AIDS, possibly leaving inadequate compensation for plaintiffs to whom the fatal AIDS virus was actually transmitted.

Potter demands application of the "more likely than not" threshold to emotional distress claims arising out of negligent exposure to HIV or AIDS. Accordingly, in the absence of physical injury or illness, damages for fear of AIDS may be recovered only if the plaintiff is exposed to HIV or AIDS as a result of the defendant's negligent breach of a duty owed to the plaintiff, and the plaintiff's fear stems from a knowledge, corroborated by reliable medical or scientific opinion, that it is more likely than not he or she will become HIV seropositive and develop AIDS due to the exposure. At the time summary judgment was granted in this case, there remained only the most speculative possibility that appellant would actually develop AIDS at some point in the future. According to *Potter*, no recovery for negligent infliction of emotional distress is permitted.

Notice that in the these settings there is not much danger of defendants repeatedly getting off scot-free when they are negligent, even if recovery for fear is disallowed; sooner or later someone actually will get AIDS as a result of such practices, and will be able to collect their damages.

Marzolf v. Stone (father comes upon accident scene where son is dying after being struck by D; L)
Gain v. Carroll Mill Co. (father sees son's car wreck on television; NL)
Barnhill v. Davis (son sees mother in car accident and reasonably believes she is hurt; she isn't; L)
Barnes v. Geiger (mother sees someone hit by car and thinks it's her son; it isn't; NL)

Q.   What is the distinction between *Marzolf v. Stone* and *Gain v. Carroll Mill Co.*?
A.   The point of the question is to get a discussion going about the work being done by the requirements courts create in these cases. The main purpose of them seems to be to ensure compensation in the core cases where it seems most appealing, but without ending up in a world where the courts are flooded with cases brought by every aggrieved friend and relative of an accident victim. This involves drawing lines that inevitably produce some arbitrary exclusions from recovery. Is watching an accident happen so much worse that coming upon the scene a minute later? Not necessarily as a practical matter; but the California court felt obliged to draw the line there to avoid a slippery slope in which every family member who visits the accident scene (or for that matter the hospital) ends up suing. The Washington court was willing to permit recovery in both cases because it was comfortable with a different line to stem the flood: the bystander has to either see the accident or arrive on the scene before it has been materially altered. The court may have been influenced as well by the fact that the family member came upon the accident scene inadvertently.
        In *Gain* the court holds that there is a want of foreseeability. You can press this a bit, because actually it seems *more* foreseeable that an accident will be shown on the news than it does that the victim's father will coincidentally stumble upon the scene of the accident, as in *Marzolf*. But foreseeability here, like duty, seems to be a mostly conclusory term to express the court's decision not to allow recovery. The policy basis for the decision may have to do with the sense that seeing a horror on television just isn't as affecting as seeing it in person. (Plus it appears that the scene had been materially altered by the time the plaintiff saw it on the broadcast—but this does not seem to be the basis for the court's decision.) Or it may be that the court is determined to cut off liability someplace, and allowing recovery for broadcasts is just too much: when an airplane crashes, every passenger may have a half-dozen family members who watch coverage on television; allowing them to recover for their emotional distress would get out of hand. The set of people who see a family member injured first hand will tend to be inherently limited. So one way to state the distinction between the cases is that the line proposed by the plaintiff in *Marzolf* seemed sturdier and more reassuring than the line proposed by the plaintiff in *Gain*.
        By the way, why *shouldn't* the tortfeasor pay for the distress caused to friends and family who see the victim at the hospital? Aren't those all real costs created by his misconduct? One answer, of course, involves the problem of false claims. An advantage of the approach taken in these cases is that they limit recovery not only to cases where it seems warranted but also to cases where the claims are most likely to be real. Thus the strict requirements for recovery are meant in part to make up for the evidentiary difficulty of sorting the serious claims from the spurious. It may also be that even if we knew the claims were real we would not want to see them compensated. Do we—do the students—want to pay more for cars, insurance, and other products so that if an accident negligently causes harm, everyone who is upset by it will get a payment? Most of us probably would rather forgo our chance at receiving such a payment

in return for lower prices on those goods. (Does the same point apply to those situations where courts *do* allow recovery for emotional distress?)

Q. What is the distinction between *Barnhill v. Davis* and *Barnes v. Geiger*?
A. First get the superficial similarity straight: in both cases the plaintiff may have reasonably but incorrectly believed that a family member had been horribly injured by the defendant. In *Barnhill* the plaintiff recovers despite the apparent mistake, as the court concludes that he had a reasonable basis for his fear (or at least that a jury could so find); in *Barnes* there is no recovery, and this apparently regardless of how reasonable Mrs. Barnes's belief may have been that her child was the one hit by the car. Again, there is a problem regarding the scope of liability that seems to drive the distinction between the cases. If plaintiffs who reasonably but wrongly believe their family members are hurt are correct, at least, about the identity of the victim and the fact of the accident, the door has not been opened too far to bad claims. By assumption, such a claim can only arise in the event of a real accident involving a family member—a situation with real costs for the plaintiff that helps discipline the creation of such claims. But if mistakes about the identity of the victim are allowed to produce recoveries, the consequences may be more substantial. An airplane crashes and a thousand people wrongly think their family members are aboard. Can they sue? Here as in the previous pair cases, the line proposed by the plaintiff in *Barnhill* seems less porous than the line proposed by the plaintiff in *Barnes*.

Johnson v. Douglas (problem: P's dog run over by D; NL)

Q. What result in *Johnson v. Douglas*, the case of the dog run over by the defendant?
A. For analytical purposes let's separate two possible theories the plaintiff might advance. The first is a direct claim by the plaintiff that the defendant's negligence caused her emotional distress by putting her in fear of being hit by his car. In other words, the plaintiff would claim that her position was comparable to that of the plaintiff in *Robb*. Here, as in *Robb*, the plaintiff made it out of the way but her property was demolished—the car in *Robb* and the dog in this case. In neither case would the property damage be formally relevant, but it seems possible that in both instances the plaintiff's claims are lent some credibility by the loss of the property: it suggests that the plaintiff's safety really was a close shave. *Johnson* can be distinguished from *Robb* because, so far as the brief facts reveal, the plaintiff in *Johnson* didn't suffer the kind of physical symptoms as a consequence of the distress that we saw described in *Robb*. But the main reason the plaintiff would lose on this score in *Johnson* is that her claim is brought in New York, where "near miss" claims aren't recognized unless the defendant owes the plaintiff some sort of preexisting duty.

The second theory would be that the plaintiff was a bystander entitled to collect for the death of her dog. This was the actual theory the plaintiff advanced. It failed because most courts, including the courts of New York, will not allow damages for emotional distress to be awarded in claims involving the destruction of property. Dogs may feel like family to their owners, but they are property in the eyes of the law, bringing this case within the same rule that produced no liability in *Lubner*. Said the court:

> [T]he law is clear that pet owners cannot recover for emotional distress based upon an alleged negligent or malicious destruction of a dog, which is deemed to be personal property. The extension of such thinking would permit recovery for mental stress caused by the malicious or negligent destruction of other personal property; i.e., a family heirloom or prized school ring. Although we live in a particularly litigious society, the court is not about to recognize a tortious cause of action to recover for emotional distress due to the death of a family pet. Such an expansion of the law would place an unnecessary burden on the ever burgeoning caseloads of the court in resolving serious tort claims for injuries to individuals. Therefore, defendant's motion for dismissal of the second and third causes of action is granted since both causes of action are insufficient as a matter of law.

Defendant's motion to dismiss the plaintiffs' fifth and sixth causes of action for being in the zone of danger and witnessing the death of their dog is granted. The zone of danger rule has only been applicable to the observance of the death or serious injury of an immediate family member who is a person. As stated by Judge Kaye in the dissent of *Bovsun v. Sanperi*, 461 N.E.2d 843, "While it may seem that there should be a remedy for every wrong, this is an ideal limited perforce by the realities of this world. Every injury has ramifying consequences, like the ripplings of the waters, without end. The problem for the law is to limit the legal consequences of wrongs to a controllable degree." The court is unaware of any recent case law extending the rule to the loss of a family pet.

CHAPTER 5

CAUSE IN FACT

This chapter covers several themes. First is the traditional rule on causation and the exceptions some courts make when they apply the "loss of a chance" doctrine in certain cases. Then come the courts' handlings of various puzzles involving multiple causes and tortfeasors. Everyone covers *Summers v. Tice*; the discretion arises in deciding how much time to spend afterwards on the *Kingston* case and the many variations of it that one can spin out as hypotheticals. Untangling the various permutations can take a good chunk of time—or you can skip them and move from *Summers* to *Sindell* pretty quickly, covering the key points about both cases in a day if you must.

Fully discussing everything here will probably take four days. The first chunk is *Grimstad* up to (but not including) *Herskovits*. Then *Herskovits* up to *Summers*; then *Summers* up to *Sindell*; and finally *Sindell* to the end of the chapter. If this is more time than you want to spend, *Summers* and *Sindell* can be combined and the cases between them omitted (along with some of the stuff after *Sindell*). There are lots of hypothetical variations in the notes below that also can be added and subtracted as time permits. If you want the most abbreviated version that just hits the high points (but why?), perhaps two days can be used to cover *Grimstad*, *Haft*, *Herskovits*, *Summers*, and *Sindell*, with all else used on a hypothetical basis.

SECTION A. BUT-FOR CAUSATION

NY Central Ry v. Grimstad (P's decedent drowns after falling overboard; NL)
Gardner v. National Bulk Carriers (D didn't go back to look for P's decedent when he fell overboard; L)

At some point you will want to explore the meaning of the "more likely than not" standard of proof when one is discussing but-for causation. This is discussed in some detail in the casebook note that follows *Herskovits*, which the students will not yet have read when you discuss this first piece of the chapter—but which they probably will be reading the night afterwards. So you can raise the question now if you like: Suppose the "experts" in the case agree that the lack of a buoy in *Grimstad* raised the decedent's likelihood of death from 40% to 60%. Is this enough to but-for causation on a traditional view? (No, because the defendant only created a third of the risk that Grimstad would die.) What if the absence of a buoy raised his likelihood of death from 10% to 30%—is that enough? (Yes, because the defendant created two-thirds of the risk that Grimstad would die.) These are counterintuitive figures, and it takes some students a while to grasp them. After struggling with them in class for a few minutes, they can read the note after *Herskovits* and hopefully this helps clear it up for them. The other option is to leave the details of these numerical issues to one side until after the lost-chance material is assigned, and to spend the first day focusing just on the policy concerns that distinguish *Grimstad* from *Gardner* (and *Stacy* from *Haft*, etc.).

You may wish to start teaching *Grimstad* with some warm-up questions locating it within the materials already covered: why did a duty exist? Suppose the plaintiff complained that the defendant should have placed nets on the side of the barge to catch anyone who fell overboard. Would the plaintiff have lost on the cause-in-fact issue? On what issue would she have lost? (Probably breach of duty; the nets would have satisfied the cause-in-fact requirement because they would have prevented the accident.)

Q. What is the superficial similarity between *Grimstad* and *Gardner*? What is the distinction between them?

A. In both cases the plaintiff's decedent died after going overboard from a ship, and in neither case did it seem more likely than not that the untaken precautions advocated by the plaintiff would have saved him. Indeed, it seems less likely that the course of action urged by the plaintiff would have made any difference in *Gardner*—yet that is the case of liability. The reason probably involves the worry that without liability in *Gardner,* defendants in such situations would always get off scot-free. In some percentage of cases where men are found to have fallen overboard more than an hour earlier—say 20% of them, just to pick a number—the men will be found if the ship goes back for them. Ideally the boat's owners should be held liable (or at least the cause in fact element should be held satisfied) in those cases. But we'll never know which cases those were. Instead we will have cases that look similar, and where the chance that going back to look for the man overboard would have succeeded is 20%: too little to satisfy the preponderance of the evidence standard. So we need liability to avoid a "recurring miss" problem.

Are these dangers less serious in *Grimstad*? Yes: the defendants will be held liable next time if the decedent is bobbing around in the water for long enough to support an inference that a buoy might have helped. They can't afford to assume that every person who falls overboard will sink right away like the plaintiff's decedent did. Not having buoys will catch up to them eventually, even if it didn't in this case.

A finding for the defendant in *Gardner* also might create an incentive for the defendant to be slow in checking for missing men: the longer the wait before you notice they are gone, the less likely your failure to go searching for them will be to make any difference (and the more likely you therefore will be to win on causation grounds). Think about it like a legislative committee addressing the problem of people drowning when they fall overboard. What is the most critical variable bearing on the likelihood of saving men who fall overboard? Probably how long it takes to notice they are missing. What legal rule will do the most to improve *that* factor? Liability. Though presumably liability will give out after some large number of hours have passed; perhaps the incentive created by liability is to *either* notice the man overboard immediately *or* to make sure you don't notice for at least, say, 48 hours. Or think about how a captain would respond to *Gardner* after being informed of the decision in that case. He might decide that the best thing to do is to keep tabs on his crewmen more often. He knows that if it takes him six hours to notice someone missing, he then has the unhappy and expensive choice of either taking the time to go back and look (and perhaps missing your bonus for being on time), or paying damages—or the owner paying damages—to his estate.

A more direct route to this conclusion would be to focus on whether it was wrong of the captain not to notice the man overboard for six hours; why not base the decision on *that* ground? Perhaps because we really don't know how often we think captains should check for their men. All we know is that we don't want to make a decision that gives captains an incentive to look less often rather than more often; and no liability in *Gardner* might create that bad incentive.

Q. What is the distinction between *The Margharita* and *Gardner v. National Bulk Carriers*? (If *The Margharita* has been read in the chapter in breach of duty.)

A. The *Margharita* found liability when the captain didn't take his maimed sailor to Port Stanley for medical help. But that case involved breach, not duty or causation. The cases make for an interesting contrast, since the B in the two of them may have been fairly similar: the lost time associated with a detour. The cases might be understood as telling a story about the high premium the common law of the seas puts on human life—and the low value it places on avoiding suffering. This point goes to the size of L in the Hand formula (P is large in *The Margharita* and small in *Gardner*; yet there is liability only in *Gardner,* suggesting that L in that case was very much larger indeed).

Stacy v. Knickerbocker Ice Co. (horses fall through ice; NL)
Haft v. Lone Palm Hotel (P's decedents drown in motel swimming pool; L)

Q. What is the superficial similarity between *Stacy v. Knickerbocker Ice Co.* and *Haft v. Lone Palm Hotel*? What is the distinction between them?

A. In both cases the defendant failed to take precautions required by statute, and drownings ensued; in both cases it seems likely that the defendants could have complied with the statutes in ways that would have done little to prevent the accidents. So why is there liability in *Haft*?

One reason is that in *Haft* the harm the plaintiff is complaining about is the kind of harm the statute was meant to prevent, whereas in *Stacy* the statute at issue doesn't seem to have been meant to prevent horses from drowning.

But the cases also can be distinguished on the same sorts of policy grounds just sketched. *Haft* involved a fact pattern that is likely to recur, and in which the statutory precautions sometimes *might* make a difference. Some students might doubt that a sign ever would matter, so take a moment to reflect on this and invite them to think beyond their initial mental picture of the situation, which probably involves a pool with nobody around. Think instead of a case where a mother brings her son to a pool and sees fifteen people there; she lets him go swimming because she assumes one of those present is a lifeguard. A sign might cause her to realize this isn't so. This pattern no doubt would be quite rare, but perhaps it could arise once every hundred or thousand episodes. Yet a finding of no causation in *Haft* probably would prevent anyone from ever being held civilly liable for violating the statute, even though the statutory violation sometimes would have been a factual cause of death.

In *Stacy,* the statutory precautions probably would never make a difference on facts like the plaintiff's, though conceivably the sight of a fence might save a horse every now and then (but can we really expect facts like these to repeat, as we could in *Haft*?). But if the statutory precautions (and the precautions required by due care) in *Stacy* were to be omitted repeatedly, they probably would result in *some* harms for which successful suits could be brought. The court suggests that a suit brought by Clifford, who went into the water while trying to restrain the horses, might have succeeded. So there is not as much danger here that a finding of no liability will mean the defendant can get away with always ignoring the statutes; there are other facts that might well arise that would result in liability and the enforcement of the negligence standard, just as in *Grimstad*.

Q. What is the distinction between *Gardner* and *Stacy v. Knickerbocker Ice Co.*? What is the analogy between *Gardner* and *Haft v. Lone Palm Hotel*?

A. In *Gardner*, as in *Stacy,* the defendant (we may assume) was negligent; and in both cases it seems unlikely that due care would have prevented the accident. But in *Gardner,* as in *Haft,* a finding of no liability on causation would make the due care standard hard to ever enforce as a practical matter—even though in some cases due care might make a difference. So we resolve the doubts against the defendants, holding them liable even though it may be doubtful that due care on their part would have mattered. *Stacy* and *Grimstad* are different because findings of no liability on the facts of those cases do not make the requirements of due care toothless. There are other factual situations where the defendants will lose lawsuits because of their failures to take due care.

Bernard v. Char (P chooses tooth extraction rather than root canal, suffers injuries, and then sues on informed consent grounds; L)
Zalazar v. Vercimak (P has face lift, then sues on informed consent grounds; L)

Q. Which standard—objective or subjective—is more likely to help doctors in these cases the long run?

A. An objective standard. One thing that makes *Bernard v. Char* interesting is that the parties and their interests are reversed from their more usual positions. Normally a subjective approach will be helpful to the patient, because it allows him to make his case by insisting that he would not have gone through with the procedure if he had been informed of the risks. In *Bernard v. Char*, however, the subjective standard might have hurt the plaintiff because he would not have been able to afford the root canal procedure; he might not have been wealthy enough to behave "reasonably."

Note that *Bernard v. Char* arose in Illinois, where state law normally *requries*—rather unusually—expert testimony to support a claim that full disclosure would have caused a reasonable person in the plaintiff's shoes not to undergo the procedure that resulted in the injury.

Q.   What explains the different approaches the courts take in *Bernard* and *Zalazar*?
A.   Both are cases of liability, but they use different legal rules. The reason is that in *Zalazar* it is questionable whether a reasonable person would have gone in for the cosmetic surgery at all, and this adds to the counterfactual features of the question—would a reasonable person *who wanted the cosmetic surgery* have gone through with it if the risks were disclosed?—in ways that make it even more difficult than usual for a jury to answer it intelligently.

Q.   What are the implications of the "framing effects" described in the article by Twerski and Cohen?
A.   Their view:

> Unless the law is prepared to address not only what information the doctor must disclose, but also how and in what manner the information is disclosed, the law cannot honestly answer the decision causation question. An honest answer requires either an unlikely finding of how the doctor would have disclosed the omitted information or imposing an impractical duty to disclose in a particular manner.

Twerski and Cohen, *Informed Decision Making and the Law of Torts: The Myth of Justiciable Causation*, 1988 U.Ill.L.Rev. 607 (1988). In other words, this is just another aspect of the futility of trying to figure out whether a warning would have changed the plaintiff's mind; it depends how the warning would have been presented. They cite this as support for their claim that the law should turn its focus from the counterfactual question (what would the plaintiff have done if better informed?) to an approach that tries to vindicate "process rights" to full information.

Herskovits v. Group Health Cooperative of Puget Sound (D's negligent diagnosis costs P's decedent some chance of survival; L for loss of a chance)
Dumas v. Cooney (rejects loss of chance doctrine as producing inaccurate results in every case)
Wendland v. Sparks (cancer patient has heart attack and is not revived; loss of chance doctrine combined with reduction in damages to reflect plaintiff's uncertain life prospects; L)
Dillon v. Twin State Gas & Electric Co. (boy falls off bridge and is killed when he grabs D's electric cable; NL if he would have fallen to his death if the wire hadn't been there)
Daugert v. Pappas (problem: does loss of a chance doctrine apply to legal malpractice? NL)

This unit of the chapter is relatively long on discussion and light on cases to distinguish. Some students find the conceptual sledding a little rough; the result is that it all takes longer to cover than its practical importance probably warrants, but the result usually is an interesting class session. The most helpful way to organize the discussion is around a firm distinction between the traditional approach and the lost chance doctrine. Under the traditional approach to causation, epitomized by cases like *Grimstad*, the only question is whether due care more likely than not would have prevented the plaintiff's injury. If so, the plaintiff collects a complete damage award. If not, the plaintiff collects nothing. Thus a defendant whose negligence was 75% likely to have caused the harm pays 100% of the plaintiff's damages, while a defendant whose negligence was 25% to have caused the harm pays 0%. Under the lost chance doctrine, the defendant who is responsible for a third of the risk of the bad thing that happened pays a third of the plaintiff's damages (or, in some jurisdictions, might even pay all of them). The general question is when such a departure from the traditional rule is justified. A secondary point that is hard for some students to grasp is the relationship between the loss of a chance doctrine of causation and the role that "lost chance" logic plays in a routine calculation of damages. The *Wendland* case brings this out.

Q. What is the analogy between *Herskovits* and *Gardner v. National Bulk Carriers?*
A. In both cases it seems unlikely that due care by the defendants would have prevented the deaths of the plaintiffs' decedents. In both cases there was a danger that if this point was used to deny liability, the defendants might never be held liable despite repeated acts of negligence—even though due care sometimes (we just won't know when) would have saved lives. In both cases this risk might be restated as a danger that the defendants would end up in a pocket of immunity—an area where they would know it is unlikely that they could be held negligent because causation would be very hard for a plaintiff to prove. Levmore's "recurring miss" idea also works well in both cases.

At this point it may be helpful to go over the general theory of recovery for loss of a chance. Note that while the plaintiff in *Gardner* recovered a complete award of damages, the plaintiff in *Herskovits* was entitled only to a reduced award.

Q. How should damages be measured in a case like *Herskovits?*
A. There are various possibilities; courts don't always use the same approach. One possibility is to award full damages. Another way to think about it is this: the plaintiff should collect a share of damages that reflects the share of the risk of death that the defendant created. So suppose the defendant's negligent misdiagnosis reduces the plaintiff's chance of survival from 40% to 10%. That means the plaintiff ends up with a 90% chance of dying, and the defendant is responsible for 30% of it; thus the plaintiff should collect one-third of his damages from the defendant. This is worth emphasizing because otherwise it's easy to imagine that the percentage of damages awarded should equal the percentage of the plaintiff's chance of survival that the defendant's negligence destroyed. For example, if the plaintiff's chance of survival goes from 39% to 25% (as in *Herskovits*), this represents a 36% reduction (the plaintiff lost fourteen points, and fourteen is 36% of 39). But (on the view sketched here) that doesn't mean that the plaintiff should be awarded 36% of his damages. The correct way to think about it is that the plaintiff ended up with 75 chances to die out of 100, and 14 of those chances were created by the defendant. So the defendant is responsible for about 19% of the total risk the defendant faced, and should pay 19% of the plaintiff's damages if he loses his life to the risk.

Q. Let's make sure we understand the traditional approach to causation—the rule that the plaintiff must prove that the defendant's untaken precaution more likely than not would have prevented the harm from occurring. Suppose a patient goes to a doctor with a serious disease. When the patient walks through the doctor's office door he is 40% likely to die from the disease (assuming he is treated with due care). The doctor negligent misreads the patient's condition; as a result, the patient becomes 60% likely to die from the disease. On a traditional common law view, is the doctor liable?
A. No. The reason was mentioned earlier in these notes and is explained in the casebook text that follows *Herskovits*. Liability seems tempting to many students here because the plaintiff has become more likely than not to die of the disease, and this jump over the 50% mark was the doctor's fault. But the basic point is that we don't look at how likely the plaintiff was to die after the doctor finished with him. We look at the plaintiff's overall risk of death and ask how much of that risk the doctor's negligence created. If the doctor's negligence created less than half of the risk of death, then we can't say there is traditional causation. In the example given here, the patient had a 60% chance of dying; one-third of that risk was created by the doctor's negligence, and two-thirds of it existed already. So if the patient does die, it probably isn't the doctor's fault. For the doctor to be held liable here, his negligence would have to move the plaintiff's likelihood of death from 40% to over 80%. In that case the doctor would be responsible for more than half of the risk. Another way to put the point is that the doctor has to double the plaintiff's risk in order to be responsible for it.

Q. Suppose a doctor is operating on a patient who only has a 10% chance of surviving the operation. The doctor negligently trips over a cord in the operating room, and in doing so pulls the plug on the life support systems sustaining the patient. The patient immediately dies. The patient's administrator sues the doctor. Under the traditional "but for" approach to causation, would the doctor be able to avoid liability because the patient more likely than not would have died anyway?

A. No. It's clear that the decedent's death was caused by the doctor's negligence. The *Herskovits* problem only arises when the risk the doctor creates by his negligence melds with the background risk the decedent already faced, so that it is impossible to tell as a factual matter whether the doctor's negligence made a difference. This is the meaning of the remark in the text note that the example case of medical malpractice would be "easy" if we knew the patient's death resulted from the doctor's negligence. But the damages that could be collected here would have to be reduced to reflect the low likelihood that the plaintiff would have survived anyway—as in *Dillon*. Thus the doctor might be required to pay 10% of the wages the plaintiff would have earned if all went well. This sounds like "loss of a chance" reasoning, but it really isn't. The doctor is liable here without reference to the lost chance doctrine. It's just that the plaintiff's damages have to reflect his short life expectancy, which ends up producing a result similar to a lost chance case.

Q. How should the jury be instructed in *Wendland v. Sparks*?

A. This case is a chance to further explore the point just raised. There are two probabilistic issues here. The first is that the patient might or might not have survived her heart attack if the defendant had administered CPR. The second is that the patient might or might not have then gone on to survive her cancer (and might have suffered various sorts of irreparable damage from the heart attack). The important thing to grasp is that the first uncertainty is relevant to causation (as well as damages), whereas the second uncertainty is relevant to damages alone. Let's walk through it under both the traditional and "lost chance" approaches.

a. Under a traditional approach, the jury should first decide how likely it is that the patient would have been revived by CPR. Everything depends on whether that likelihood was greater than 50%. If not, the doctor wins and we're done. But let's say the jury finds that the CPR was 60% likely to have worked. In that case the defendant is liable and the plaintiff is entitled to collect her damages. Those damages will reflect her lost earnings and whatever other items of recovery are allowed by the state's wrongful death statute; but those sums will have to be discounted to reflect the fact that she might have died of cancer pretty soon anyway. Note, however, that her damages are *not* discounted to reflect the mere 60% likelihood that the CPR would have worked. Since the CPR was more than 50% likely to revive her, she is entitled to a full award of damages—the same award she would get if the doctor had performed surgery on her while drunk and decisively had caused her death.

b. Under a lost chance approach, the jury again starts by deciding how likely it is that the patient would have been revived by CPR. If the answer is that CPR more likely than not would have saved her, we proceed as above and she collects a full damage award. But it's different if the CPR was, say, 20% likely to save her. In that case she becomes entitled to collect 20% of her damages—20%, in other words, of an award that first must be discounted to reflect the fact that she might have died of cancer fairly soon.

Notice that you can use this case to help further illustrate the attractiveness of the lost chance doctrine. Whether to administer CPR to someone who has had a bad heart attack is a good example of a decision that often will be made against a high background likelihood that the patient will die in any event. Maybe juries will bend the causation standard without saying so to find liability in such cases, but the traditional rules of causation, if properly applied, generally would require judgment for the defendant. Is it troubling for doctors' decisions about whether to administer CPR to be undisciplined by the threat of tort liability?

Students sometimes have trouble following this distinction between accounting for probabilities at the causation and damages stages of a case. You can try building up their understanding with simpler cases. You *always* reduce damages to reflect the plaintiff's uncertain life prospects. This has nothing to do with the lost chance doctrine, which is strictly a doctrine of causation. So suppose that the defendant in *Grimstad* had been held liable; perhaps the court determined that the plaintiff's decedent was afloat long enough to catch a buoy if one had been available. The plaintiff's damages would be calculated primarily by forecasting the decedent's lost wages. This is a probabilistic exercise: you have to figure out the different ways his career might have gone, consider whether his cancer (let us imagine) would have killed him, discount all these possibilities to reflect their likelihood, and come up with a figure that fairly expresses the results. If you add a "lost chance" element to the causation side of the case, it just means that you have to take that resulting damage award and discount it further to reflect the fact that the plaintiff isn't being held fully responsible for the plaintiff's death.

Q. What is the distinction between *Herskovits* and *Dillon*?

A. Here is a final chance to play with the preceding points. *Dillon* looks like *Herskovits* because in *Dillon* the defendant was negligent, and the negligence deprived the plaintiff of an uncertain chance of survival that otherwise would have existed. But it's different from *Herskovits* because in *Dillon* we know exactly why the plaintiff died; it's like the hypothetical case where the doctor kicks the plug out of the wall. The lost chance doctrine has no application because cause in fact is completely clear. But damages are another matter. The defendant has to put the plaintiff (or his estate) in the same economic position it would have occupied if due care had been used—i.e., if the wires hadn't been there. In that case the plaintiff would have plummeted to the ground. It's the same principle as described in the previous question: the damage award has to reflect the plaintiff's real life prospects. So his damages will either be very low (because he would have been so badly injured in the fall) or nonexistent (because he would have been killed, leaving him with no lost wages or other items that are recoverable under the wrongful death statute). If the damages were found to be nonexistent because he would have died without the wires to hang onto, then strictly speaking there is no liability at all because there can be no tort without legally recognized damages. This is what it means to say that his probable future bears on liability: not that cause in fact is an issue, but that if he had no future he also had no damages and therefore his estate had no claim.

Q. Why not allow damages for loss of a chance in a case like *Grimstad*? Indeed, why not allow it all the time?

A. It's the same point made earlier to distinguish *Grimstad* from *Gardner*. Recovery for loss of a chance makes most sense in situations where it otherwise may be impossible for people in the plaintiff's position to ever win. *Grimstad*-type plaintiffs can win in cases where their decedents stay at the surface of the water for a while. Liability in those cases, even without liability in *Grimstad* itself, may give defendants adequate incentive to take care without turning every instance of remote causation into a case of liability on loss of a chance grounds. And meanwhile the *Grimstad* rule has the advantage of being cheaper to administer, since disagreements about causation beneath the 50% threshold are of no importance (nor are disputes about what percentage over 50% the defendant is responsible for). All we need to know is whether the more-likely-than-not threshold was crossed.

Q. What is the sense of the *Fennell* court's objection to "loss of a chance" recovery?

A. The usual idea behind recovery for lost chances is that if a plaintiff lost a 10% chance of recovery, the plaintiff should collect 10% of his damages from the defendant; if the plaintiff lost a 40% chance, he should collect 40% from the defendant. But a funny thing happens as soon as the plaintiff gets over the 50% likelihood mark: he collects *all* of his damages from the defendant. Thus a plaintiff whose damages were 60% likely to have been caused by the defendant's negligence collects 100% of his damages, not 60% of them. This asymmetry might well seem unfair to defendants. It might also suggest that they will pay too much in these cases, leading to possible problems of overdeterrence—i.e., of doctors spending more resources on precautions than is cost-effective. If you imagine that doctors are equally likely to be 25% and 75% responsible for deaths in *Herskovits*-type situations, they will pay for a quarter of the damages in the first set of cases and for all of the damages in the second set, even though in many of the cases in the second set their negligence made no real contribution to the plaintiff's injuries. We put up with this latter risk routinely in tort cases; a defendant traditionally loses every time he is found 60% likely to have been responsible, even though we know that in 40% of those cases the defendant's negligence was not a cause in fact of the plaintiff's harm. But this practice can be defended on the ground that those same defendants get off scot free when then are 40% likely to have been responsible. The errors can be thought to cancel out as a matter of both fairness and economics. But if you use the lost chance doctrine to wipe out the second error while retaining the first one, the system ends up lopsided against doctors.

This train of thought is sensitive to its assumptions—i.e., that doctors are equally likely to be 25% and 75% responsible for deaths in *Herskovits*-type situations. If the actual facts of *Herskovits* are actually much more likely to occur—in other words, if doctors in a given situation are much more likely to be 25% likely than 75% likely to contribute to a bad result—then the consequences of applying the lost chance doctrine in those situations won't seem as bothersome.

Q. What is the sense of the *Dumas* court's objection to recovery for loss of a chance?

A. That the doctrine produces errors in every case. For it is never true that a doctor's negligence is 30% responsible for a patient's death. Either the doctor's negligence caused the death or it didn't; in other words, either the plaintiff would have lived if due care had been used or he would not have. So a really accurate resolution of each case would entitle the plaintiff either to full damages from the defendant or to none. The problem is that we can't settle that counterfactual, so jurisdictions following the lost-chance approach award a percentage—calculated to reflect the decrease in probability of survival—as a kind of rough justice. But it's too rough for the California court's liking, because it confesses in every case that the court is awarding incorrect damages. The classic way around this argument is to say that the injury for which the plaintiff is being compensated is not death (in which case the lost chance doctrine would indeed be producing errors); rather, the injury is the loss of a chance *per se*—the loss of a lottery ticket (or the exchange of one ticket for another of less value)—for which the court is trying to compensate quite precisely. A satisfactory argument?

Daugert v. Pappas (problem: attempted application of lost-chance doctrine to legal malpractice; NL)

In *Daugert* it was held, for the defendant Pappas, that the *Herskovits* "substantial factor" test does not apply to legal malpractice suits. The court held that the plaintiff had to prove that in the contract case he more likely than not would have prevailed if his lawyer had filed a timely petition for review. (The court also held that it was error to allow a jury, rather than a judge, to assess the likelihood that the case would have been accepted for appellate review and reversed.) Said the court:

> Despite the *Herskovits* opinion and the questioning by commentators of the use of the "but for" test in legal malpractice claims, we believe it inappropriate at this time to change the test. The primary thrust of *Herskovits* was that a doctor's misdiagnosis of cancer either deprives a decedent of a chance of surviving a potentially fatal condition or reduces that chance. A reduction in one's opportunity to recover (loss of chance) is a very real injury which requires compensation. On the other hand, where the issue is whether the Supreme Court would have accepted review and rendered a decision more favorable to the client, there is no lost chance. The client in a legal malpractice case can eventually have the case reviewed. For example, in the instant case the client's underlying claim was not reviewed by the court initially because of the attorney's negligence. However, in the subsequent malpractice action the trial judge should have decided whether the Supreme Court would have accepted review and held in favor of the client. If the trial judge found review would have been denied, the client could have sought review in the Court of Appeals and ultimately in the Supreme Court. Hence, the client would eventually regain the opportunity to have the claim reviewed by the Supreme Court. On the other hand, in the medical context, when a patient dies all chances of survival are lost. Furthermore, unlike the medical malpractice claim wherein a doctor's misdiagnosis of cancer causes a separate and

distinguishable harm, i.e., diminished chance of survival, in a legal malpractice case there is no separate harm. Rather, the attorney will be liable for all the client's damages if review would have been granted and a more favorable decision rendered, and none if review would have been denied. Thus, clearly the loss of chance analysis articulated in *Herskovits* is inapplicable in a legal malpractice case.

The court then allowed the original appeal to be refiled—sort of: "[R]ather than merely remanding the case for a determination of causation by the trial judge, we believe it appropriate in the interest of judicial economy and fairness to the client to permit the client to file a petition for review in this court pertaining to review of the original action. This court will then decide whether review would have been accepted and whether the client would have received a more favorable decision. Our determination will not, however, change the outcome of the underlying claim. Rather, it will decide the causation issue in the malpractice action."

Q. What is the distinction between *Herskovits* and *Daugert v. Pappas?*
A. Apart from the points raised in the excerpt above, perhaps it is that the lost chance in *Daugert* is not as readily susceptible to statistical testimony as the lost chance in a medical case like *Herskovits.* In *Herskovits,* a medical expert can make reasonably objective assertions about the survival rates of patients whose diseases are detected at various stages. An expert on legal malpractice is unlikely to be able to make a comparably objective assertion about the odds that the state supreme court would have reversed in a contract case. Particular medical situations can arise thousands of times, allowing studies to be conducted and orderly predictions to be made about the likelihood of various outcomes if a disease is caught at state 1, stage 2, etc. But no two appeals are quite alike in this way, so attempts to say just how likely an appeal would have been to succeed are bound to be more conjectural than they are in the medical setting. (A consequence of the rule in *Daugert,* however, is that many legal malpractice cases, especially those arising from litigation decisions, are very hard to win precisely because it's hard to show causation—i.e., that the case would have come out differently if better judgment had been used. Does this create a problem of lawyers who don't worry enough about their malpractice liability?)

Notice too, by the way, that there is a good argument that the lost chance doctrine should have no application to *Daugert* even if the doctrine can be used in legal malpractice cases generally. The reason is that *Daugert* might be said to resemble the hypothetical given a moment ago in which the doctor kicks the cord out of the wall, causing the immediate death of a patient who probably would have died soon anyway. Failing to file the appeal on time, like kicking the cord, was a separable, independent act that was sufficient to cause the resulting injury by itself: the denial of review. On this view, the plaintiff should win on the causation point (easily) and thus be entitled to a full damage award—an award which, however, would have to reflect the plaintiff's small likelihood of success if the appeal had gone forward. (So the trial court got it right in awarding the plaintiff 20% of his damages, setting aside the jury's role in fixing that percentage.) To make *Daugert* truly similar to *Herskovits,* imagine an appeal in which the lawyer negligently fails to make an important argument. The court finds against his client, and it's impossible to tell what difference was made by the failure to offer the argument. In that case we really wouldn't know whether the loss on appeal was caused by the background risk or by the extra risk the court added.

Q. What is the analogy between *Herskovits* and *Ybarra v. Spangard?*
A. They both involve the management of irreducible uncertainties that create policy worries. In *Ybarra* we know (or are certain enough) that someone was negligent and that it mattered, but we don't know who. In *Herskovits* we know that someone was negligent and we know who it was, but we don't know whether it mattered. In both cases the defendant is someone who more likely than not either wasn't negligent or didn't commit negligence that made a difference; and in both cases the defendant nevertheless is held liable. There is a concern in both cases that if liability is not allowed, parties in the plaintiff's position never will be able to win their suits, even though sometimes their suits will have merit.

Q. Suppose a man has a heart attack and his wife calls 911. She can't get through because the local telephone lines are clogged with people trying to buy tickets for a Garth Brooks concert that just went on sale. The man dies. His wife can't prove that it is more likely than not that he would have been saved if her call had gotten through; should she be able to recover from the telephone company for loss of a chance?

A. The court said no on these facts in *Hardy v. Southwestern Bell Telephone Co.*, 910 P.2d 1024 (Okla. 1996):

> The public policy concerns of medical practice which have been held to justify a reduced burden of causation in lost chance cases do not transfer over to ordinary negligence cases. Public policy is not served by extending the causation exception to the "but for" rule to other tortfeasors. Under the decisions discussed and other "loss of chance" medical provider opinions, the physician had the opportunity to perform properly under the terms of the physician-patient special relationship but was alleged to have failed to do so.

> The essence of the doctrine is the special relationship of the physician and the patient. In these cases the duty is clear, the negligence is unquestioned and the resulting harm, the destruction of a chance for a better outcome, has obvious value and is not so speculative as to be beyond being reasonably considered a result of defendant's negligence.

> In *Daugert v. Pappas*, 704 P.2d 600 (Wash. 1985), the Supreme Court of Washington rejected an attempt to apply principles of loss of chance to an action for legal malpractice based on failure to file an appeal. The court found that while the loss of chance to recover from misdiagnosis of cancer such as was present in *Herskovits v. Group Health Coop of Puget Sound*, 664 P.2d 474 (Wash. 1983), resulted in a very real injury with definite value which would require compensation, there is no commensurate harm, no lost chance, in a legal malpractice case as the matter may eventually be reviewed. Neither, held the court, is there in a legal malpractice action a separate and distinguishable harm, a diminished chance.

> Plaintiff presents no convincing arguments regarding application of the loss of chance doctrine to this situation. In *Coker v. Southwestern Bell Telephone Co.*, 580 P.2d 151 (Okla. 1978), we held that plaintiff did not state a cause of action against the telephone company for damages sustained when fire destroyed his place of business with the theory that the defective telephone prevented him from summoning emergency assistance to extinguish the fire. We held that the petition did not assert the requisite causal connection between alleged negligence of the defendant and the resulting damages. We observed that it would be "necessary to heap conclusion upon conclusion as to the course events would have taken had the telephone operated properly" in order to establish the causal connection between the defective telephone and the ultimate destruction of appellant's business. Addressing the issue of causation we found the failure of phone service was too remote from plaintiff's loss to establish grounds for recovery and stated "that the number and character of the random elements which must come together in precisely the correct sequence at exactly the right time in order for it to be established that failure of telephone service was an efficient cause of appellant's loss so far removes appellee's act of negligence from the ultimate consequences as to break any asserted causal connection." [...]

> The trier of fact in the instant case would likewise be forced to heap conclusion upon conclusion as to the course events would have taken if the 911 system had worked properly and have no more than mere conjecture as to what damages plaintiff suffered by reason of defendant's action. Plaintiff's claim of causation is far too speculative and too remote to be sustained here. Plaintiff

presents us with no convincing argument as to why a loss of chance relaxed standard of causation limited by the Court to medical malpractice actions should be applied here to reduce his burden.

We would be remiss in our duty if we failed to observe here that the application of the lost chance of survival doctrine to these facts as urged by plaintiff would cause a fundamental redefinition of the meaning of causation in tort law. While the majority of the Court were persuaded in *McKellips* that the particular facts and circumstances of that case required creating an exception to the "more likely than not" requirement of traditional causation, we refuse to effect a total restructuring of tort law by applying the lost chance doctrine beyond the established boundary of medical malpractice to ordinary negligence actions.

SECTION B. ALTERNATIVE LIABILITY

Summers v. Tice (D hunters negligently fire at P; one of them hits him, but nobody knows which; L)
Kingston v. Chicago & N.W. Ry. Co. (D's fire combines with another to destroy P's property; L if the other fire was negligently set; NL if D can show the other fire was not the result of negligence)
Litzman v. Humboldt County (problem: P hurt by firework left behind by one of two defendants; court says L, but better view probably is NL)

Q. What is the analogy between *Summers v. Tice* and *Haft v. Lone Palm Hotel?*
A. Here is what the court in *Haft* had to say:

> The case of *Summers v. Tice* 199 P.2d 1 (Cal. 1948), provides a close analogy. In *Summers* two hunters (the co-defendants) fired their guns simultaneously; one pellet of shot hit a third hunter (the plaintiff) whom the others should have known to be dangerously near their line of fire. Recognizing the impossibility of plaintiff's task of demonstrating which of the defendants had actually caused his injury, this court declared that, as a matter of fairness and in view of the parties' relative fault, "a requirement that the burden of proof on that subject be shifted to defendants becomes manifest." (33 Cal. 2d at p. 86.) [...]

> Indeed, in some respects the instant action presents a stronger case for shifting the burden of proof to defendants than *Summers*, because the present defendants are in a sense more "culpably" responsible for the uncertainty of proof than were the hunters in *Summers*. Although the difficulty in proof in *Summers* was attributable to the coincidence of the defendants' actions, each hunter was negligent, not because he shot simultaneously with the other defendants, but only because he shot in the direction of the plaintiff. In other words, the uncertainty of proof in that situation, while emanating from defendants' conduct, was not a foreseeable consequence of defendants' negligence. In the instant case, on the other hand, the absence of definite evidence on causation is a direct and foreseeable result of the defendants' negligent failure to provide a lifeguard. Defendants may thus more appropriately be designated at "fault" for the factual deficiencies that are present. [...]

> Without such a shift in the burden of proof in the instant case, the promise of substantial protection held out by our statutory lifeguard requirement will be effectively nullified in a substantial number of cases. One purpose of the statute is to prevent a drowning in a pool where no one else is present to witness it and possibly to prevent it. If the pool owner can disregard the statute and retreat to the sanctuary of the argument that the plaintiff must prove the "cause" of the death which obviously is unknown, he can, without liability, expose his paying patron to the very danger that the statute would avoid. [...]

Q. Suppose that before either defendant had fired, one defendant had shouted to the other, "Shoot!" and by agreement they had both then shot simultaneously. Would that circumstance have made *Summers v. Tice* an easier case?

A. Yes. That would have created a concert of action between the two parties, which would have made them liable as joint tortfeasors under traditional common-law principles.

Q. Hypothetical: In *Garcia v. Joseph Vince Co.*, 148 Cal.Rptr. 843 (Cal.App. 1978), the plaintiff was engaged in a fencing match. His opponent's saber broke through the mask the plaintiff was wearing, injuring his eye. After the accident, one of the fencing coaches present examined the blade of the saber and concluded that it seemed defectively thin. The saber was then put into a bag with other swords and was lost among them; the plaintiff was unable to determine which sword had caused his injury. The swords in the bag were made by two companies: American Fencer Supply and Joseph Vince Co. The plaintiff sued them both. What result under *Summers v. Tice*?

A. No liability:

> Appellant argues that when the evidence is equally balanced as to who supplied the alleged defective product, under the rule of *Summers v. Tice*, the burden of proof should shift to respondent to establish who sold the product. This argument has no merit. In *Summers v. Tice*, the plaintiff established that both defendants had acted negligently by shooting in his direction and thus both violated a legal duty to him. The burden of proof then shifted to the defendants to prove which one's birdshot caused the injury. Here, the appellant has not shown that either respondent has violated a duty to him (i. e., produced the defective product) and seeks wrongly to place on them the burden of proving his case which he himself has found too heavy to bear.

> In the case of *Wetzel v. Eaton Corporation*, 62 F.R.D. 22 (D.C.Minn. 1973), the plaintiff was injured as the result of an accident caused by a faulty tractor part. The part was supplied to the tractor manufacturer by one of two component manufacturers. After the tractor was repaired, the adapter was either discarded or destroyed and so it was unavailable for inspection. Inspection was the only means by which the manufacturer of the part could be identified. The court granted defendant component manufacturers' motion for summary judgment rejecting plaintiff's reference to *Summers v. Tice*, and holding that the facts gave equal support to two inconsistent inferences thus inviting a verdict based purely on conjecture. We find that *Wetzel v. Eaton Corporation* correctly states the appropriate rule applicable to the case at bench.

Q. Hypothetical: in *Burton v. Waller*, 502 F.2d 1261 (5th Cir. 1974), a detachment of Mississippi police officers was sent to Jackson State College to quell a riot on campus. The police were fired upon by a sniper; many of the police then opened fire with shotguns on a building from which the sniper's fire appeared to be coming. A number of students were injured or killed as a result, and suits were brought against the officers to recover damages. The court found that the officers' actions were potentially covered by the privilege of self-defense and an overlapping privilege to use force to put down a riot. The court further found that some thirty-one police officers had fired their weapons appropriately, and were covered by these privileges, while seven other officers had fired too quickly, too carelessly, or too many times for the privileges to apply to their actions. It was impossible to say which officers had fired the shots that caused the plaintiffs' injuries. What result?

A. The court affirmed a jury verdict for the defendant police officers, finding that the plaintiffs were required to carry the burden of showing that their injuries were caused by unprivileged firings and that the jury reasonably could find that the plaintiffs had not carried that burden.

> In the instant case there are many actors potentially the source of harm. There was evidence of sufficient weight to go to a jury tending to show that some defendants firing (at least 31) did not do so negligently and that harm may have resulted from sources other than those acting tortiously.

We are pointed to nothing in Mississippi law indicating that in such a multiple actor situation the courts of that state would hold that as a matter of law actual causation was established with respect to tortious defendants, or to state it differently, that liability attaches to tortious defendants without regard to proof of actual cause of injury. Nor are we cited to any jurisdiction with a rule applicable to like situations that would entitle plaintiffs to directed verdicts with respect to causation.

The State of Mississippi was held to be immune from suit (sovereign immunity), and the question of the command officer's negligence was for the jury to determine. (The court also said that any attempt to recovery using the theory of respondeat superior would fail here, because—again—the plaintiffs couldn't show that their injuries resulted from negligence.)

More notes on joint causation. Why do we make a fuss about distinguishing between those whose negligence causes harm and those whose negligence does no harm? From Judith Jarvis Thomson, *Remarks on Causation and Liability*, 13 Phil. & Pub. Aff. 101, 195-96 (1984):

[D]uring the course of the trial, evidence suddenly becomes available which makes it as certain as empirical matters ever get to be, that the pellet lodged in plaintiff Summers' eye came from the defendant Tice's gun. Tort law being what it is, defendant Simonson is straightway dismissed from the case. And isn't that the right outcome? Don't we feel that Tice alone should be held liable . . .? We do not feel that Simonson should be dismissed with a blessing: he acted very badly indeed. So did Tice act badly. But Tice also caused the harm, and (other things being equal) fairness requires that he pay for it. But why? After all, both defendants acted equally negligently toward Summers in shooting as they did; and it was simple good luck for Simonson that, as things turned out, he did not cause the harm to Summers.

Some interesting replies are offered in Paul Rothstein, *Causation in Torts, Crimes, and Moral Philosophy: A Reply to Professor Thomson*, 76 Geo. L.J. 151 (1987):

Professor Thomson's article brings us into an artificial world where we can assume such things as exactly equal carelessness by two actors. However, we spend most of our time in the real world, where knowledge of exactly how careless an actor was is not available in the vast majority of cases. In the real world, the consequences of an act provide legitimate and valuable data that help us pass moral judgments through the light they shed on the degree of carelessness that the actor probably exhibited. More often than not, an act that produces a bad result is the product of careless conduct.

A vast number of acts or omissions are involved in even the simplest of real world situations. Thus, even when we have substantial result-independent evidence of an actor's conduct, outcome may still be an important clue in deducing how much care an actor most likely took. Consider again Professor Thomson's example of two careless drivers backing out of their driveways. One hits a child, while the other does not only because he is "lucky" and no child is present. Let us presume that eyewitnesses saw both drivers and can testify that neither driver turned around while backing out to look to see if a child was there.

Despite this eyewitness testimony, there are a multitude of steps one driver and not the other may have taken to attempt to avoid hitting a child. One driver may have glanced in the rearview mirror or looked around before getting into the car. One driver may have thought about whether any children lived near his house, while the other may not have. In short, there may have been a reason why the one "careless" driver hit a child and the other "careless" driver did not: the one who did not may have taken one of these steps, or demonstrated more care than the driver who hit a child in one of a myriad of other possible ways. In the absence of completely definitive proof (which is perhaps impossible to acquire) that each driver was equally careless, we are justifiably inclined to believe that the driver who hit the child did not use precisely the same degree of care as the other and therefore is more morally culpable. This judgment, though, should be provisional, subject to change if later received information warrants it. [...]

As stated above, while not a morally relevant factor in itself, outcome is often a good guide to provisional moral judgments in the real world. Furthermore, bad outcomes are often the means by which careless acts come to our attention; we never know of the thousands of drivers who carelessly back down their driveways every day and don't hit children, but we all hear about the one who does hit a child. Finally, since we do not have the time and motivation to investigate the circumstances surrounding the causation of most bad outcomes we become aware of, our provisional moral judgments of condemnation become final.

All of these factors, I believe, combine to create an intuitive association in our minds between bad outcomes and moral culpability. Unless we are somehow reminded of it, we forget that bad outcome is only linked to moral culpability through the careless conduct that bad outcome makes more probable. [...]

Let us carry the analysis a bit further. Suppose that one of our careless drivers backing out of the driveway, the one who, in the last hypothetical, had hit the child, instead narrowly misses the child. This "near misser" would correspond to the hunter in *Summers v. Tice* whose bullet narrowly missed the plaintiff—whose bullet did not do the damage, although we didn't know in *Summers* which of the two hunters hit and which missed. Our thought would be that this "narrowly missing" driver must not have been keeping as careful a lookout as the other (the "widely missing") driver in our same example. Our thought that the near misser must have been less careful than the wide misser is rationally almost but not quite as strongly corroborated by this near miss as by an actual hit. We place the probable degree of inattentiveness (and hence moral badness) of this near misser of the child just next to that ascribed to the driver who hits the child. But a driver who comes nowhere near a child has probably been more careful. This, I believe, explains in part the moral satisfaction we feel with the result in *Summers v. Tice*. In terms of the probability that they engaged in equally risky conduct, the two hunters (the one who hit the plaintiff and the one who nearly missed) are almost indistinguishable and were subject to the same terms of "punishment." Even if in *Summers* we had been able to find out which hunter actually harmed the plaintiff, this analysis explains why we might still equate them morally. [...]

Q. What distinctions can be drawn between the Restatement illustrations that appear before the *Kingston* case?
A. The distinction between #10 and #11 is that in #11 both defendants were negligent, as they were in *Summers*. In #10 only one of the defendants apparently was negligent, so there is a greater reluctance to shift a burden to them; and here, unlike in *Ybarra*, there is no reason to think any of the defendants have useful information that would be pried out of them with a presumption of liability. In illustration 3, the dogs' entry onto the plaintiff's farm is a wrongful act analogous to the negligence of the drivers in illustration 11. It makes the legal system comfortable shifting the burden of disproof onto the defendants.

Q. Which Restatement illustration does *Kingston* most resemble?
A. If you assume that both fires in *Kingston* were caused by negligent actors, then *Kingston* might resemble illustration 11. But it differs because the plaintiff in *Kingston* hasn't managed to get both defendants into the lawsuit. This creates apparent tension with *Summers*, which requires that both defendants be joined as parties (the plaintiff there couldn't have just sued one or the other—why not?). But *Kingston* is distinguishable from *Summers* because the uncertainty is different. The problem isn't

that we don't know who caused the harm. Rather, we know that the harm had two sufficient causes. It would be as if both shooters in *Summers* shot into the same eye of the plaintiff, so that either of them alone would have blinded him. In other words, there is no chance in *Kingston* that the defendant made no contribution to the fire; we know that he did. So we don't need both defendants present.

Q. Isn't *Kingston* wrong as a matter of logic? The case holds that if A negligently starts a fire that burns down Z's house, A is liable—even if the fire combined with another fire started by B that would have burned down the house on its own. The point of "cause in fact" is that the harm wouldn't have occurred if the defendant had used due care; yet obviously in this example the same harm *would* have occurred even if the defendant had used due care. What gives?

A. The problem is that the same logic just described could also be used by *B* to avoid liability; the reasoning would enable A and B both to escape liability by pointing fingers at each other. This unfairly leaves the blameless plaintiff to bear his own losses. But then how should we handle it if the second fire starts naturally? In that case there is no danger that the finger-pointing defense will allow two culprits to get off scot-free. It will allow *one* fire-starting culprit to get away with it; and courts disagree about whether this is a tolerable result. Many courts, unlike *Kingston*, would allow the negligent firestarter to be held liable in this latter case, saying that his negligence was a "substantial factor" contributing to the plaintiff's injuries.

At this point you have the option of working through variations on *Kingston* where the fires arrive at different times. In a sense these problems end up having more to do with damages than causation; but the issues they raise are closely related, so this is the most natural place to treat them. The examples below are adapted, sometimes loosely, from David Fischer, *Successive Causes and the Enigma of Duplicated Harm*, 66 Tenn. L. Rev. 1127 (1999)—an interesting piece.

Q. Suppose A negligently starts a fire that burns toward the plaintiff's house. Before it can get there, another fire—started by natural causes (lightning, perhaps)—arrives at the plaintiff's house and burns it to the ground. The fire started by A arrives twenty minutes later and does no additional damage, though A's fire would have burned down the plaintiff's house if it had arrived first. Liability for A?

A. No. The fire A started didn't actually burn anything belonging to the plaintiff. The plaintiff would collect a windfall if he were able to collect from A, since his house was doomed—was *gone*—for reasons having nothing to do with A's negligence.

Q. Okay, so now reverse it: same facts, but A's fire gets there first. Liability for A?

A. For those into jargon, this is a case of multiple *successive* sufficient causes, whereas *Kingston* is a case of multiple *concurrent* sufficient causes. Doesn't the plaintiff again get a windfall if A is held liable? Maybe in either hypothetical the plaintiff was away from his house the entire time; he simply returns home to find it burned down. Why should his ability to collect from A depend on whether A's fire got there an hour before or an hour after the natural one? Well, one reason is that as a practical matter we generally will have trouble figuring out which cases these are. If the natural fire gets there first and burns the plaintiff's house to the ground, we *know* the defendant's fire made no difference. But if the defendant's fire gets there first and burns the plaintiff's house to the ground, there is some speculation in saying that it would have happened anyway. In occasional cases, like the one described here, our confidence that the same damage would have occurred for innocent reasons anyway may be high. But in most real cases it won't be quite so clear. Perhaps liability for the defendant can be tempered by a reduced award of damages—an issue considered further a couple of questions below. But then suppose a cab driver negligently gets into an accident while driving to the airport, causing his passenger various injuries. Then the plane the plaintiff was supposed to board—but missed—crashes (without negligence, let's assume—we'll save that wrinkle for the next hypothetical). Can it be said that the plaintiff definitely would have died if the cab hadn't crashed, and therefore that the cab driver owes him nothing? No, not quite. But once we admit the logic of "no liability" in the fire hypothetical given above, it becomes messy to figure out where to draw the line in these situations.

Q. Consider another variation. The plaintiff's decedent is killed in a car accident, and the plaintiff sues the driver to collect damages. Assume that under the state's wrongful death statute, the plaintiff is entitled to an award representing the decedent's lost wages. The defendant offers proof that the decedent had terminal cancer. Is this evidence admissible? Typically it is, and the damages are reduced accordingly. *Wendland v. Sparks* is an example from earlier in the chapter; so, really, is the *Dillon* case: they are situations where the defendant's wrong contributes to a death that probably was coming pretty soon anyway, and in these cases we reduce the damages awarded to reflect the relatively small interest of which the plaintiff (or the plaintiff's decedent) was deprived. How are these cases consistent with the preceding discussions of the fire (or the cab driver)?

Joseph King argues that the issue is whether the innocent cause of harm has "attached" before the defendant's negligence does its work. In Fischer's paraphrase, "A cause becomes attached when it is so associated with the value of the plaintiff's interest that the potential harm could not be avoided even if the plaintiff knew about it." So *Dillon* was correctly decided because the plaintiff's decedent had fallen, and his fate was pretty well sealed; there was not much speculation about it. But in the airplane case the innocent cause—the crash of the plane—hadn't "attached" ("vested"?) because it was still too speculative whether the passenger was going to be on board. And in the fire hypothetical the question would be whether the natural fire had become so large, and its progress so inexorable, that there was no doubt but that it would take down the plaintiff's house. (But think of a case where the plaintiff is on an airplane about to take off, but is hurt when a fellow passenger's suitcase falls on him—as in the *Brosnahan* case in the chapter on duties, where the airline was held potentially liable on those facts. The plaintiff gets off the plane to seek medical attention; the plane crashes upon takeoff fifteen minutes later. There would be no real question here that the plaintiff would have died if he hadn't been hit by the falling suitcase. Yet it also seems doubtful that the airline would be able to avoid full liability for his injuries, does it not? Why?)

As Fischer points out, in any event, the "vesting" approach can't explain our practice in wrongful death cases of allowing damages to be reduced on quite speculative grounds—e.g., claims that the plaintiff's decedent was a heavy smoker and that his life expectancy should include some allowance for this. Why do we allow this discount but no discount for the fact that the plaintiff had a ticket for an airplane that went down a week later?

Q. Suppose X negligently starts a fire and it burns the plaintiff's house down. A second fire arrives a couple of hours later; it, too, was started by negligence—the negligence of Y—and it is clear that the second fire would have burned the house down as well. What damages should the plaintiff be able to collect from X?

A. Causation is clear: the house was burned down by the fire X started. The problem is that the plaintiff is entitled, by way of damages from X, only to be put into the position he would have occupied if X had not been negligent; and this would seem to mean that X owes the plaintiff damages only for the lost hour or two of use of the house before it was destined to be destroyed anyway. But everyone seems to agree that the damages available from X should not be discounted to reflect the inevitable destruction of the house. (Should damages be available from Y as well?) From Fischer's article:

> While scholars such as Hart and Honore, Wright, the authors of Prosser and Keeton, and King agree that it is desirable to hold one or both tortfeasors liable for duplicated harm, there is less agreement on the appropriate theory of recovery. For example, they all agree that, in cases like [the hypo just given], X should be liable for all damages without a discount for the harm that fire Y would have duplicated. Thus, Y would be exempt from liability for the duplicated harm. However, they reach the conclusion via different theories. Hart and Honore and Wright subscribe to the theory that X rather than Y destroyed the plaintiff's building. Therefore, X should not be

permitted to set up Y's wrong as an excuse for reducing damages. King and the authors of Prosser and Keeton subscribe to the theory that X deprived the plaintiff of her potential cause of action against Y.

Q. Hypothetical:. in *Glick v. Ballentine Produce, Inc.*, 396 S.W.2d 609 (Mo. 1965), the plaintiffs' complaint alleged that their decedents, three men named Glick, were riding in a car that negligently was struck by one of Ballentine's trucks; that as a direct result of this collision the Glicks were thrown to the pavement of the highway, being "mortally wounded by impact to each and every tissue and cell of their bodies"; that "following in time by a few minutes" several other defendants, all traveling north, collided with the persons of the three Glicks "as they lay on the roadway," and that the negligence of each such driver "contributed to the cause of said collisions" and that as a direct result of the collisions by such subsequent (following) drivers with the three persons "each and every tissue and cell of the bodies of said persons sustained injury which contributed to their respective deaths […]." One of the defendants in the second group—a subsequent driver who hit the Glicks—moved to dismiss the complaint for failing to state a good claim against him. What result?

A. The trial court granted the motion and the plaintiffs appealed. The Missouri supreme court reversed:

> While, from the standpoint of the plaintiff, the use of the term "mortally wounded" would seem to have been very inept, we do not construe it as the equivalent of "dead." We do construe it to mean that these persons had been injured to such an extent that they would eventually die from the injuries; but, even so, if life still existed there remained a right not to be injured further (with an immediate termination of life) by others. In this we do not infer the actual existence of any negligence on the part of the subsequent drivers; but such negligence is alleged. The law recognizes that where "the concurrent or successive negligence of two persons, combined together, results in an injury to a third person, he may recover damages of either or both and neither can interpose the defense that the prior or concurrent negligence of the other contributed to the injury." 1 Thompson on Negligence sec. 75. As stated in [*Brantley v. Couch*, Mo. App., 383 S.W.2d 307]: "* * * According to the great weight of authority, where the concurrent or successive negligent acts or omissions of two or more persons, although acting independently of each other, are, in combination, the direct and proximate cause of a single injury to a third person, and it is impossible to determine in what proportion each contributed to the injury, either is responsible for the whole injury, even though his act alone might not have caused the entire injury, or the same damage might have resulted from the act of the other tortfeasor, and the injured person may at his option or election institute suit for the resulting damages against any one or more of such tort-feasors separately, or against any number or all of them jointly. The injured person is not compelled to elect between the tort-feasors in invoking a remedy to obtain compensation. * * *" In [*Willey v. Fyrogas Co.*, 363 Mo. 406], it is pointed out that liability is not defeated by the fact that the negligence of one defendant may precede or follow that of another in point of time.

Q. What result in *Litzmann v. Humboldt County*?

A. This was a case of liability, though it may have been badly decided; it seems distinguishable from *Ybarra* and *Summers* in a few different ways. Unlike *Summers*, this was a case where, so far as the evidence described by the court reveals, only one of the defendants was negligent. And there was no reason to think that either defendant had information relevant to the culpability of the other. The rationale seems to be that it's more fair to impose liability on two defendants who each are 50% likely to be responsible than to let it rest on the plaintiff. There may be a policy argument here, too: liability here presumably will give the defendants a greater incentive not only to be careful with their bombs, but to be more careful in keeping track of them so that they can exonerate themselves if an accident like this occurs later. The case would have been stronger, however, if both defendants were shown to be negligent in not keeping careful enough track of their wares. At any rate, here are some excerpts from the court's opinion:

Appellants requested the trial court to give an instruction based upon the doctrine of res ipsa loquitur and substantially taken from B.A.J.I. 206, 206-B, 206-C and 206-D. We have concluded that an instruction upon the doctrine ought to have been given. Using the yardstick furnished by *Ybarra v. Spangard,* we think it is apparent from the evidence:

1. That there was evidence sufficient to establish the accident was one which ordinarily does not occur in the absence of someone's negligence;

2. That it was caused by an agency or instrumentality within the exclusive control of one of the two defendants, Golden State or Brooks; and,

3. That it could be found from the evidence it was not due to any legally material voluntary action or contribution on the part of appellant minor. Although there were two defendants, of whom it must be said if one was negligent, the other was not, yet the doctrine was applicable on the authority of Zentz v. Coca Cola Bottling Company, 39 Cal.2d 436, 445, even though appellants were unable to point out from the evidence which of the two was responsible for their injuries. […]

[A]ppellants say that they proved by more evidence than the minimum required by law that the bomb that mained Ralph Litzmann was made accessible to him by the negligence of either the defendant Golden State or the defendant Brooks; they say they have not proved and could not prove that the negligence existed only on the part of one of said two defendants; they say that under the circumstances of this case their burden of proof went no further than that of proving that one or the other of the two last-named defendants was negligent and they did not have to prove that a specified one of said defendants was negligent in order to be entitled to a verdict of the jury. They point to the instructions given which repeatedly told the jury that no defendant could be held responsible unless plaintiffs proved by a preponderance of evidence that that particular defendant was negligent and that such negligence was the proximate cause of the minor's injuries; they say such instructions placed upon them a prejudicial burden which the law did not require them to bear. Specifically, they refer to given instructions such as this: 'If it is just as probable that (a) * * * defendant was not negligent * * * then a case against the defendant has not been established.' […]

Appellants refer to *Summers v. Tice* in support of the position which they take herein. […] Yet it was obvious in that case that if the pellets came from the gun of one appellant only, holding the other was to punish the innocent for the wrong done by the guilty. After discussing the principles involved, the Supreme Court closed by saying: 'We have seen that for the reasons of policy discussed herein, the case is based upon the legal proposition that, under the circumstances here presented, each defendant is liable for the whole damage whether they are deemed to be acting in concert or independently.' We are unable to distinguish *Summers v. Tice* from the case on appeal. Obviously the doctrine of res ipsa loquitur was applicable in that case to each defendant and it followed that the plaintiff had made out a prima facie case against each. […] And if it could be said in *Summers v. Tice* that concert of action was not necessary to holding two where only one was at fault and that such could be done even though the two acted independently, then we think it must be said in this case that if the triers of fact were unable to ascertain which of the two involved was guilty of the actionable negligence which injured the appellants, they should have been told that then in that situation they could hold and should hold both defendants. […]

Incidentally, the court also rejected strict liability:

The risks involved here were: 1. The risk that members of the public might be injured while the actors were discharging fireworks, or, 2. The risk that members of the public might be injured by failure of the actors to keep live fireworks inaccessible. The testimony was generally to the effect that these risks could be eliminated by a degree of care far within the bounds of "utmost care." It goes without saying that ordinary care could and would prevent the leaving of such matter upon the fair grounds through failure of proper custodial care. The testimony showed also that by the method of firing adopted it was a reasonably easy matter to direct the firing so that injury would not arise through misdirection of the missiles; and that observation by those skilled enough to be licensed to explode fireworks was adequate to detect the lack of explosion of the material shot into the air. It appears, therefore, that the activities engaged in and charged to be ultrahazardous were in fact risks which could be and would be eliminated if commensurate care had been exercised. It was the failure of care that caused the injuries and not the nature of the risks involved. Under such circumstances the court was justified in refusing to instruct upon the doctrine of absolute liability.

Sindell v. Abbott Labs (D DES manufacturers sued; mother can't remember whose pills she took; L: market share liability)

Sanderson v. International Flavors and Fragrances, Inc. (attempt to apply market share theory to perfume manufacturers; NL)

Smith v. Cutter Laboratories (problem: application of market share theory to blood products; L)

Q. What is the analogy between *Sindell v. Abbott Labs* and *Summers v. Tice*?

A. In both cases each of the defendants had breached a duty, and only one of the defendants could have been the cause in fact of each individual plaintiff's harm. Given the procedural posture of the case, we should construe the allegations of the complaint in favor of the plaintiffs; we therefore assume that each of the defendants produced defective DES. (Maybe the DES was defective because it was an improper drug for preventing miscarriages, or maybe it was defective for that purpose without a warning of the danger.) Hence all of the defendants were guilty of conduct analogous to a breach of duty. But which manufacturer's DES did her mother take? If a plaintiff's mother took Abbott Labs' DES, then the conduct of Squibb was not the cause in fact of her own illness. This was the same problem as in *Summers v. Tice*.

Q. How did *Sindell* extend *Summers v. Tice*? (Or: why didn't *Summers* provide a complete answer to the problem in *Sindell*?)

A. In *Summers* the odds were 50-50 that each defendant caused the plaintiff's harm, whereas in *Sindell* the odds were substantially less than 50-50 that an individual defendant caused an individual plaintiff's harm. There was liability nevertheless. In either case a defendant may be able to escape liability if it is able to exonerate itself, but *Summers* is a tougher rule for defendants because they are potentially liable for the entire award to the plaintiff. In *Sindell* the liability of each defendant is limited by its market share (discussed below). An additional point is that in *Summers* the court was sure it had the guilty party in front of it. In *Sindell* there was a distinct possibility that the company who caused the plaintiff's injuries was not before the court.

Q. Suppose market share liability is permitted in the suit brought by the *Sindell* plaintiffs, and then next year a new plaintiff shows up with conclusive proof that Lilly's DES caused her ailments. Should she collect 100% of her damages from Lilly, or just collect a share of her damages that corresponds to Lilly's market share?

A. In practice Lilly would have to pay all of the plaintiff's damages. There is an analogy between this question and the objection to "loss of a chance" recovery raised in the *Fennell* excerpt a few pages earlier. The *Fennell* point is this: If defendants are going to pay 20% of a plaintiff's damages in cases where they are responsible for 20% of the risk of the bad thing that happened, then why should they still have to pay for 100% of the damages in cases where they are responsible for 60% of the risk of the bad thing that happened? Likewise, Lilly could say that if it has to pay for (let's say) 10% of the damages of every plaintiff even when it probably wasn't responsible, then it shouldn't also have to pay 100% of the damages in cases where it *is* responsible. Some of this trouble might be relieved if we are *sure* Lilly caused the second plaintiff's damages, because then there is nothing probabilistic about it. But what if the jury is only 60% convinced that the plaintiff's mother took Lilly's pills?

Q. Suppose a plaintiff in a market-share liability case manages to sue defendants constituting 80% of the market for DES; the other 20% are out of business. Should she be able to collect all of her damages from those defendants, so that a defendant who held, say, 40% of the market ends up paying half of her damage award (because they controlled half of the market represented in the lawsuit)? Or should the plaintiff just collect 80% of her damages from those defendants she has assembled, and simply be required to forgo collection of the remaining 20%?

A. The latter approach is the one the California Supreme Court took in *Brown v. Superior Court*, 751 P.2d 470 (Cal. 1988). In that case the Court established that several rather than joint liability should be used; in other words, plaintiffs would be allowed to collect from each defendant only an amount of proportion of damages consistent with that defendant's market share, and could not collect the entire award from any defendant she chose (as would be possible under joint and several liability). The court then addressed the question posed above:

> [P]laintiff proposes an alternate means to apportion liability among defendants. She suggests that if we conclude that joint liability is not appropriate, each defendant's liability should be "inflated" in proportion to its market share in an amount sufficient to assure that plaintiff would recover the entire amount of the judgment. While this ingenious approach would not be as unjust to defendants as joint liability, we decline to adopt the proposal because it would nonetheless represent a retreat from *Sindell's* attempt to achieve as close an approximation as possible between a DES manufacturer's liability for damages and its individual responsibility for the injuries caused by the products it manufactured.

Q. Should the relevant market be the national or local one? And should defendants be able to exonerate themselves in individual cases? Suppose, for example, that in one of the market share cases brought after *Sindell*, the plaintiff's mother remembers only that she took red pills; and suppose that one of the defendants, the Squibb firm, can show that it never made pills of that color. Should Squibb be dismissed from the case or should it still be required to contribute to a share of the plaintiff's damage award in proportion to its share of the market? (Notice that this question is related to the choice between local and national markets; for if a local market is used, some defendants will be able to exonerate themselves because they didn't sell DES there.)

A. From *Hymowitz v. Eli Lilly & Co.*, 539 N.E.2d 1069 (N.Y. 1989):

> [F]or essentially practical reasons, we adopt a market share theory using a national market. We are aware that the adoption of a national market will likely result in a disproportion between the liability of individual manufacturers and the actual injuries each manufacturer caused in this State. Thus our market share theory cannot be founded upon the belief that, over the run of cases, liability will approximate causation in this State (see, *Sindell v. Abbott Labs.*, 607 P.2d 924). Nor does the use of a national market provide a reasonable link between liability and the risk created by a defendant to a particular plaintiff. Instead, we choose to apportion liability so as to correspond to the over-all culpability of each defendant, measured by the amount of risk of injury each defendant created to the public-at-large. Use of a national market is a fair method, we believe, of apportioning defendants' liabilities according to their total culpability in marketing DES for use during pregnancy. Under the circumstances, this is an equitable way to provide

plaintiffs with the relief they deserve, while also rationally distributing the responsibility for plaintiffs' injuries among defendants.

To be sure, a defendant cannot be held liable if it did not participate in the marketing of DES for pregnancy use; if a DES producer satisfies its burden of proof of showing that it was not a member of the market of DES sold for pregnancy use, disallowing exculpation would be unfair and unjust.

Nevertheless, because liability here is based on the over-all risk produced, and not causation in a single case, there should be no exculpation of a defendant who, although a member of the market producing DES for pregnancy use, appears not to have caused a particular plaintiff's injury. It is merely a windfall for a producer to escape liability solely because it manufactured a more identifiable pill, or sold only to certain drugstores. These fortuities in no way diminish the culpability of a defendant for marketing the product, which is the basis of liability here.

From Aaron Twerski, *Market Share—A Tale of Two Centuries*, 55 Brook. L. Rev. 869 (1989):

Sindell, the first of the market share decisions, simply failed to address how the market would be defined. If a defendant was to be held liable for its percentage of the market there was a need to know whether the market was the city of Los Angeles, the state of California, or the United States of America. After years of agonizing, California finally decided that the percentage is to be calculated on the basis of sales in the national market. *Hymowitz* has also wisely opted for the national market.

Why has it taken so long for this issue to be resolved? More important, why have some courts still not seen the light? In *Martin v. Abbott Laboratories*, the Washington Supreme Court opted for the narrowest definable market. Very simply, according to the Washington court, if the DES was purchased from a particular pharmacy (e.g., Joe's Pharmacy), and that pharmacy had purchased its DES from five manufacturers, then the market share would be calculated based on the percentage of sales to a single pharmacy. Why would any rational court choose the Joe's Pharmacy market over a national market? It is obvious that such a narrow definition of the market does violence to the fundamental market share liability theory. A defendant who pays a high percentage on a narrow market today on the happenstance that there is sufficient evidence to link it to a particular pharmacy will be taxed again in a later case where such a narrow definition of the market is impossible. Market share requires that markets be fairly defined for all cases if the theory is to meet even a pretense of even handedness. [...]

Traditionally, causation required the plaintiff to identify the defendant that was the cause of the plaintiff's particular harm. Market share was a radical departure from that traditional norm. Under the new approach, causation would be decided by how much harm was caused in the aggregate in the world at large by three hundred manufacturers. Targeting several manufacturers out of three hundred for liability was most uncomfortable. The chance that the real culprit was made to pay was remote. If the pool was limited to five defendants who sold the drug to a particular pharmacy, plaintiffs were no longer suing the immediate world. The case appears more circumscribed and more traditional. Of course, on reflection, it makes little difference if four non-causal defendants out of a pool of five are made to pay or two hundred ninety-nine out of a pool of three hundred. Logic did not easily emerge the victor over tradition.

Some additional arguments for using a national market were offered in Andrew Nace, *Market Share Liability: A Current Assessment of a Decade-Old Doctrine*, 44 Vand. L. Rev. 395, 425 (1991):

A national marketplace offers a unitary standard that is applicable to all DES cases and, consequently, dispenses with difficult, complicated computations based on smaller geographic units. This unitary standard eases the parties' burdens at trial and should yield more consistent results for both plaintiffs and defendants on a case-by-case basis. Using a national market also reduces litigation costs for plaintiffs and defendants by eliminating the need to reconstruct a new market in each case. Once the national market is established by pooling together the resources of all defendants, courts in all jurisdictions will be able to use it, thus conserving judicial resources. A national marketplace naturally will implicate most or all large DES producers and should result in a more fully informed distribution breakdown. Additionally, many plaintiffs assert that a handful of large drug manufacturers are responsible for ninety percent of the DES distributed nationwide. Hence, a national market should produce an accurate division of overall liability measured by each defendant's contribution of risk to society. At the very least, a national market will capture the general distribution of DES to the American public even though many distributors no longer exist because of insolvency or merger. Finally, a national market is well suited for a state the size of New York in which many plaintiffs likely have been exposed to DES outside the state.

The same article argued against letting makers of DES exonerate themselves in individual cases:

A system of recovery that rewards only those manufacturers fortunate enough to possess exculpatory evidence, while punishing those that do not, merely compounds the problem of deficient information. Market share liability strives to circumvent the information gap in an individual case by using distribution statistics. Courts should not allow defendants to manipulate this information gap, thereby yielding different results for two defendants with the same share of the market merely because one possesses exculpatory evidence and the other does not. The unfortunate result is an uneven distribution of liability among DES manufacturers.

Q. What is the distinction between *Sindell* and *Sanderson v. International Flavors and Fragrances, Inc.?*
A. The defendants in *Sanderson* did not make fungible products, and they did not represent a substantial share of the market. This last point presumably might have been avoidable if the plaintiff had shown that she had collected most or all of the defendants whose products could have caused *her* injuries; but apparently she did not.

Q. Why is it necessary that the defendants' goods be fungible before market-share liability can be used?
A. First, if goods are fungible, it makes it less likely that the plaintiff can trace the product that caused the harm to its source: everybody's is the same. Second, as a matter of fairness, only if the products are fungible can we be confident that each defendant probably caused harm in proportion to its market share. In *Sanderson,* some of the defendants might have been much more likely than others to have been responsible for the plaintiff's injuries, since their perfumes differed in many ways. It therefore is more bothersome to say that the defendants will be held equally liable (per market share). From the *Sanderson* opinion:

The supreme court in *Sindell* emphasized that there was no unfairness in dispensing with individualized proof of causation as among the various potential tortfeasors because their products were identical. Since the DES manufactured by the 200 potential tortfeasors was all produced from the same formula, it is more accurate to speak of a single product, with many manufacturers. [....] [T]he fragrance products which plaintiff contends caused her injuries are not fungible goods made from an identical formula and therefore cannot be equated with the DES at issue in *Sindell*. The only difference between DES manufactured by Eli Lilly and DES manufactured by Abbott was the return address on the package sent by the manufacturer to the pharmacy. Such is not the case here. Plaintiff does not allege that the various defendants' fragrance products are identical; Drakkar Noir and Cool Water and the rest of defendants' perfumes and colognes differ in their composition, not just in the name on the package. What's more, plaintiff's experts acknowledge that different aldehydes have different health effects. Since different fragrance products contain different aldehydes at different concentrations and in different combinations, it cannot be said that plaintiff is targeting a single product made by many manufacturers.

Putting an industry on trial is different than putting on trial a product which happens to have been manufactured by several companies from an identical formula. Courts are ill-equipped to conduct trials of entire industries, and individual plaintiffs in a private action have no right to put entire industries on trial. Private cases and controversies must sweep more narrowly, catching within the litigation net only those persons whom the plaintiff can link to the harm that has befallen her. That application of these principles may leave an injured person without a remedy in tort is no objection, because the tort system is not designed to provide compensation for every injury. Therefore, while the Court is not unsympathetic to plaintiff's injuries, which while not threatening her life have undoubtedly altered her lifestyle, the mere fact (if it be a fact) that plaintiff has been injured by fragrance products is not a basis for holding any particular fragrance product manufacturer responsible. [....] Unfortunately for plaintiff, this is a case that falls through the cracks between traditional, direct causation and burden-shifting causation.

From *Mullen v. Armstrong World Industries*, 246 Cal.Rptr. 32 (Cal. App. 1988), a case declining to hold asbestos manufacturers liable on a market share theory:

One of the predicates for Sindell liability is the absence of discernible distinguishing features or characteristics of the instrumentalities produced by the industry defendants. The court took pains to establish that it was dealing with "fungible goods"—specifically, a drug produced "from an identical formula." Plaintiffs' argument that market share liability should be extended from the DES field of Sindell to the asbestos industry proceeds on the premise that DES and asbestos are simple equivalents. This is far from being the case. [....]

Sindell involved a group of 11 defendants all "engaged in the business of manufacturing, promoting, and marketing" a single product "produced ... from an identical formula." By contrast, asbestos is a generic designation possessing a rainbow-like diversity and a bewildering array of potential uses.

Q. Why is it necessary that the plaintiff have joined a large share of the participants in the market?
A. The larger the percentage of market participants the plaintiff has joined, the smaller the possibility of error in fixing liability on the defendants (i.e., the smaller the danger that the real culprit is not present at all). From the *Sanderson* opinion:

Five years after *Sindell*, the supreme court held that a ten percent market share was insufficient to permit application of the market share liability doctrine. *Murphy v. E.R. Squibb & Sons, Inc.,* 710 P.2d 247 (Cal. 1985). The court explained that "if the plaintiff joined in the action the manufacturers of a substantial share of the DES which her mother might have taken, the injustice of shifting the burden of proof to defendants to exonerate themselves would be significantly diminished." 710 P.2d at 255. Similarly, it was not unjust to require the two defendants in *Summers* to exonerate themselves, since there was a 50 percent chance that each of them was the tortfeasor. The court concluded that a ten percent chance that Squibb was the tortfeasor, compared to a 90 percent chance that a manufacturer not joined as a defendant was the tortfeasor, was not sufficient to meet the substantial market share prong of the doctrine.

Q. What result in *Smith v. Cutter Laboratories*?
A. This case, which allowed market share liability, probably represents the most far-reaching extension of the doctrine to date. Other states have gone the other way. The facts present some interesting problems. Clearly blood is not fungible in the way DES is; blood comes from donors with or without contamination, so there might seem to be no basis for an assumption that the more blood a firm sold, the more harm it did. But what if the firms all committed similar negligent failures to take precautions against contamination? If the failures really were identical, and the firms were obtaining their blood from indistinguishable pools, it might follow that a company's share of the market would indeed track its share of harm caused. From the court's opinion, 823 P.2d 717 (Ha. 1991):

> Appellees take issue with applying theories which were developed, in a large part, for remedies in the field of diethylstilbestrol (DES) drug litigation and the inherent problems associated with those actions. Their strongest argument against using these theories is the lack of comparison of DES to Factor VIII as a fungible product. DES was produced by more than 200 different companies, some of which are defunct, but the identical formula was used universally in a highly regulated industry. With Factor VIII, there are only a handful of manufacturers, and although the product is fungible insofar as it can be used interchangeably, it does not have the constant quality of DES. The reason is obvious—the donor source of the plasma is not a constant. Therefore, Factor VIII is only harmful if the donor was infected; DES is inherently harmful. As we see that the lack of screening of donors and failure to warn are the breaches alleged, appellee's argument for not using DES theories is not convincing. We find consideration of the theories discussed in the DES cases to be helpful, as we strive to find an equitable and fair solution to the case at bar. [...]

> [I]n regard to DES cases, the Illinois Supreme Court refused to adopt the market share theory of liability, in part because "[a]cceptance of market share liability and the concomitant burden placed on the courts and the parties will imprudently bog down the judiciary in an almost futile endeavor." *Smith v. Eli Lilly & Co.*, 137 Ill.2d 222, 253 (1990). In addition, that court criticized the fairness of results in apportioning damage when reliable information on all manufacturers might not be available. Part of that reasoning, of course, is based on the fact that the potential number of defendants in DES cases extends into the hundreds. The numbers here are not nearly so large, and therefore, the harshness of the result, that is, burdening the innocent plaintiff without a remedy, to us seems totally unfair and out of step with current efforts to allow recovery when the proper case is brought. [...]

> Courts differ on their requirements of an assertive effort on the part of plaintiffs to identify the actual manufacturer of the specific product which caused the harm. We take another approach to this concern. Whereas manufacturers here argue that appellant should have kept a log of which manufacturer's product he was using, we fail to see how such failure affects the viability of appellant's suit in view of our adoption of the theory of market share liability.

> Plaintiffs should use due diligence to join all manufacturers, but failure to do so is not a defense. Failure to do so may affect the percentage of recovery, discussed *infra*. However, manufacturers are permitted to implead other manufacturers. But, in this case, all manufacturers are joined, so the issue is not before us. However, we note in passing that the conditions of the [court in *Martin v. Abbott Laboratories*, 689 P.2d 368 (Wash. 1984], which would allow plaintiffs to initiate suit against only one defendant, and of *Sindell*, which would require plaintiffs to join a "substantial"

number of defendants, are immaterial as long as plaintiffs realize their recovery will depend on joining as many manufacturers as they can; plaintiffs will endeavor to join all manufacturers.

We have already discussed our feeling that this action should not be subject to joint liability. We simply reiterate what other courts have said on this point, that "[t]he cornerstone of market share alternate liability is that if a defendant can establish its actual market share, it will not be liable under any circumstances for more than that percentage of the plaintiff's total injuries." Therefore, we advocate several liability.

We define the rules of distribution as to market share for this case as was done in [*Martin*, 689 P.2d 368]:

The defendants that are unable to exculpate themselves from potential liability are designated members of the plaintiffs' ... market[ ].... These defendants are initially presumed to have equal shares of the market and are liable for only the percentage of plaintiff's judgment that represents their presumptive share of the market. These defendants are entitled to rebut this presumption and thereby reduce their potential liability by establishing their respective market share of [Factor VIII] in the ... market.

As to several liability, we adopt the theory that a particular defendant is only liable for its market share. Defendants failing to establish their proportionate share of the market will be liable for the difference in the judgment to 100 percent of the market. However, should plaintiff fail to name all members of the market, the plaintiff will not recover 100 percent of the judgment if the named defendants prove an aggregate share of less than 100 percent.

Moon, J., dissented:

The Sindell court determined that DES was fungible or interchangeable because all DES companies produced the drug from an identical formula; it was usually manufactured as a "generic" drug, without regard to the actual manufacturer. Thus, one manufacturer's DES was equally as likely to have produced the injury as any other manufacturer's DES. In other words, each DES manufacturer's product posed the *same risk of harm* to users.

Unlike DES, Factor VIII is not a generic, fungible drug. Each processor prepares its Factor VIII concentrate by its own proprietary processes using plasma collected from its own sources. Each firm's Factor VIII concentrate is clearly distinguishable by brand name, package color, lot number, and number of units of Factor VIII per vial; each firm's Factor VIII concentrate is separately licensed by the Food and Drug Administration. There is no evidence that all Factor VIII products caused or were equally capable of causing HIV infection. Thus, *the risk posed by the different brands of Factor VIII is not identical.*

Q. Hypothetical: in *Mellon v. Barre-National Drug Co.*, 636 A.2d 187 (Pa. 1993), the plaintiff alleged that his daughter was bulimic; that as a result she repeatedly ingested syrup of ipecac to induce vomiting; that the toxic ingredient in syrup of ipecac, emetine, accumulated in her body; and that at last the emetine caused her to suffer cardiac arrest and die. The plaintiff was unable to determine who manufactured the particular syrup of ipecac that his daughter had taken, so he brought various negligence and strict liability claims against all known manufacturers of it, alleging that all syrup of ipecac always is made the same way and marketed and distributed according to the same federally regulatory specifications. Should he have been allowed to proceed on a market-share liability theory?
A. The court thought not:

We agree with the conclusion of the trial court that the appellants in this case cannot meet their burden of proof by utilizing the market share liability theory in lieu of evidence of the use of a particular defendant's or defendants' products by the decedent, Mrs. Mellon. We reach this conclusion, as did the trial court, on the basis of the inability of the appellants to establish two elements which we believe were essential to the development by the *Sindell* Court of the theory of market share liability—an inability on the part of a plaintiff—*through no fault of his or her own*—to identify the product, and a substantial time lapse—such as that experienced by the children affected in utero by DES—between the use of the product and manifestation of the harm.

As for the element of identification, distribution and labelling of syrup of ipecac is controlled by federal law and while the formula of all of the manufacturers is identical, the one ounce containers, which are available for purchase without prescription, are clearly marked with the name of the manufacturer and a warning that the drug is not to be used without first consulting a physician or poison control center. The inability of the appellants in the instant case to identify the manufacturer of the ipecac allegedly ingested by the decedent was not caused in any way by the appellees but rather was solely a result of the decedent's conduct in purposefully and surreptitiously misusing the product. Thus, one of the essential elements of the *Sindell* analysis is missing.

A further element upon which the development of the market share liability theory was predicated is also absent: there is no substantial time lapse involved between ingestion of syrup of ipecac and manifestation of the effects of emetine poisoning. Thus it is that we are constrained to agree with the conclusion of the learned trial court that, even if market share liability had been adopted in this Commonwealth, application of the doctrine in this case would not be warranted.

Q. What do *Ybarra v. Spangard*, *Herskovits v. Group Health Cooperative*, *Summers v. Tice*, and *Sindell v. Abbott Laboratories* have in common? Compare what we know and what we don't know in each case, and consider how each might be understood as a response to a slightly different problem of uncertainty.
A. All of them are attempts to manage irreducible uncertainties that might raise policy worries of the "recurring miss" variety if they resulted in no liability. Do they also involve suspension of fairness norms to achieve deterrence? In the course of a recent exchange with Ronald Dworkin about the role of theory and philosophy in judicial decisions, Judge Posner made the following provocative claims:

It also helps in doing law to know a great deal of law rather than just a handful of exemplary cases. Law is like a language. It is as difficult to write well about law at the operating level without an intimate knowledge of it as it is to write well about China without knowing Chinese. [...] [Dworkin's] article returns again and again to the DES cases, finally asking challengingly, "Should the judge try to decide whether the drug manufacturers are jointly liable without asking whether it is fair, according to standards embedded in our tradition, to impose liability in the absence of any causal connection?" Any genuine legal insider would consider this a strange question, and not only because the issue was not joint liability in the technical legal sense of the term. [...] In the law of torts, liability is standardly imposed on negligent persons whose acts are merely sufficient and not necessary conditions of harm and so do not fit the usual definitions of cause; is usually imposed on employers of the persons who cause the harm of which the plaintiff is complaining (under the doctrine of respondeat superior); is sometimes imposed on persons who merely fail to avert a harm (as in "crashworthy" products liability cases and cases of attempted but failed rescue); is imposed on persons who conspire with injurers; is imposed on the estates, that is, the heirs, of injurers; and is sometimes imposed (as in "loss of a chance" cases) on an injurer despite the victim's inability to prove causation by a preponderance of the evidence. The question whether it is "fair" to impose liability on a manufacturer of DES who cannot be shown to be the actual "cause" of the plaintiff's injury is thus naive. It is also unhelpful. It will not move us an inch closer to the intelligent evaluation of these cases.

Q. How might the Vioxx litigation have been resolved in an innovative way?
A. This little case study is meant to get students thinking outside the strictures of final judicial resolutions of such problems and to consider as well how they might lead to interesting settlements. Here are some more excerpts from Issacharoff's article:

> The eighteen cases that went to trial established the hurdles confronting other plaintiffs and the damages prospects facing Merck. This was an excellent basis for an informed settlement that would discount the risks faced by all sides and provide for comparable treatment of comparably situated plaintiffs. Indeed, that understanding laid the foundation for a settlement of $4.85 billion to be distributed among plaintiffs who had filed suit before the statute of limitations had run and who could prove certain elements of exposure and harm. The difficult issue was how to create an effective bill of peace that would bring a reasonable (and reasonably certain) end to the litigation, enabling the plaintiffs to be compensated and Merck to obtain closure. A publicly ordered settlement through the use of a class action was too unwieldy because of the elevated burdens on organizing a class after Amchem and Ortiz, as well as the inability to confine the dispute to those individuals who had filed suit in a timely manner before the statute of limitations had run. For all practical purposes, no individual lawsuit could serve as the vehicle for a comprehensive settlement without having a mechanism to coordinate with all potential claimants. . . .

> [O]ne option might have been to wait many years for all claims to work their way through the legal system, a prospect as likely to bring closure as the Philippine appellate procedures. Fortunately in Vioxx, a novel solution could be crafted through private ordering that—like the bankruptcy work-outs under Section 524(g)—would combine private settlement with judicial oversight. The settlement turned centrally on the economic realities of the litigation marketplace for complicated liability claims in mass-harm cases. Cases that involve systemic harms, high fixed costs, and uncertain prospects of recovery, such as Vioxx, simply cannot be handled on a one-off basis under arrangements approximating Justice Souter's ideal of individuals represented privately anticipating their day in court. Rather, the economics of risky pharmaceutical claims meant that even lawyers who were retained by an individual client had to refer the claim up the litigation ladder to firms that could amortize the cost of litigation across a portfolio of cases—in effect, creating cross-subsidies for the prosecution of those claims that might actually reach trial. In the absence of such concentration of claims, plaintiffs could offer no credible threat to litigate and, by extension, could not reasonably hope to secure settlements.

> In Vioxx, plaintiffs' firms who consolidated large numbers of cases took a small number of cases to trial, allowing these to serve as the bellwethers for assessing the likely litigation fortunes of thousands more claims in the pipeline. Following the eighteen cases that were tried to judgment, a settlement was constructed that was structured as an offer from Merck, the manufacturer of Vioxx. Before such an offer was extended, however, the terms had been negotiated with a leading group of plaintiffs' counsel, with the litigated cases serving as the benchmark values for the broad work-out. Having the backing of several of the major representatives of Vioxx plaintiffs, Merck then presented for acceptance or rejection by individual plaintiffs, rather than for court implementation as with a class action. The novel feature of the settlement was that while the offer was made to each Vioxx plaintiff individually, the offer was only valid if accepted by all the clients represented by any particular attorney or law firm. In order to provide closure, however—and to substitute for the inability to use effectively the class action device, as Sprint had asserted in Sprint—the offer required any participating lawyer to certify that all his or her clients had agreed to the terms. In

broad outlines, the offer provided closure with each firm independently (subject to an overall 85 percent acceptance rate to be effective) or it would not become effective. Individual claimants remained free to reject the proposed deal but, assuming court approval and barring exigent circumstances, would have to find other counsel to handle their claims. Participating lawyers or law firms could receive no referral fee nor have any ongoing interest in any case that remained in litigation. The terms of the offer and oversight over withdrawals from nonsettling cases were placed in the hands of the federal and state court judges in whose courts the individual cases had been consolidated.

In effect, the settlement tried to use the forces of market aggregation to realize the sort of consensual closure that the formal rules of procedure could not provide. The settlement then created an ad hoc form of judicial oversight over everything from withdrawal from representation to fees permitted. What Vioxx offered, if accepted, was a novel means of using private ordering to bring sensible closure to common claims, with court supervision, but outside the boundaries of formal procedural law.

Predictably, the Vioxx settlement provoked significant controversy, in large part as a result of the apparent tension between the consolidated nature of the settlement offers and the individual-representation premises of traditional litigation. In this instance it was not the Federal Rules of Civil Procedure that were the issue so much as ethical rules governing representation on matters such as client authority over acceptance of a settlement, the conditions for attorney withdrawal from representation, the duty owed by a lawyer to each client, and even the prohibitions on lawyers entering into agreements restricting future representations. Most of these criticisms have faded in light of the overwhelmingly positive response by plaintiffs (who collectively had not recovered a cent prior to the settlement) to the terms of the offer. But I do not seek here to defend the structure of the settlement against these criticisms and concerns, something I have done in other settings. My argument here is simply that the Vioxx settlement, in order to provide closure to claims premised on the epidemiological risk faced across the cohort of users of the drug, had to devise a private arrangement to overcome the disfunctionality of the formal procedural system. Independent of any considerations of the structure or the ultimate fairness of the settlement terms, the fact remains that there was no way to achieve closure within any of the established pathways of the formal joinder devices available in aggregate litigation.

SECTION C. A NOTE ON APPORTIONMENT

We present this material relatively briefly, preferring to weave in discussion of apportionment possibilities at various other points of the semester—i.e., in cases involving joint tortfeasors. The notes in the casebook suggest some questions to explore if you want to provoke discussion: the relative merits of the approaches taken in the *Gehres* and *Larsen* cases, and the effect on settlement of various rules regarding settlement by one tortfeasor while the other presses on in court.

One issue not discussed in the notes, but which students may find an interesting topic for discussion, involves "Mary Carter" agreements: one defendant secretly settles with the plaintiff; their agreement provides that the settling defendant stays in the case and participates in it, with his liability reduced as the damages awarded against his co-defendants increases. See *Booth v. Mary Carter Paint Co.*, 202 So.2d 8 (Fla. App. 1967). Some jurisdiction ban these sorts of agreements; others allow them but require them to be disclosed. See Annot., 22 A.L.R.5th 483 (1994); Bernstein and Klerman, *AN Economic Analysis of Mary Carter Settlement Agreements*, 83 Geo. L.J. 2215 (1995).

CHAPTER 6

PROXIMATE CAUSATION

SECTION A. REMOTENESS AND FORESEEABILITY

We don't think there is much fat to cut in this section, but the note on *The Wagon Mound (No. 2)* and the material after item 10 (*Pridham*) probably can be omitted without any great loss.

In re Polemis (D's servant bumps plank into hole, unexpectedly causing explosion; L because the harm was the direct result of the negligence)
The Wagon Mound (D spills oil into harbor, which unforeseeably catches fire; NL)
The Wagon Mound No. 2 (L on same facts where fire is found to be foreseeable)
Petition of Kinsman (D's negligence causes boat to come loose, knock loose other boat, wreck bridge, and start flood; L)

Q. What was the negligent act in the *Polemis* case?
A. Allowing the rope to knock the plank into the ship's hold. The important point is that the danger the ship would explode is *not* part of PL; ex ante that risk was not foreseeable. You have to focus instead on the risk that the plank would hit someone on the head, damage the cargo below, etc. The foreseeability of those risks matters; it is the reason that knocking the plank into the hold was negligent.

A fact not explained in the text, and that you may or may not wish to mention, is that the question of the defendant's negligence in *Polemis* was made relevant by the agreement between the defendant (who chartered the boat) and the plaintiffs (the ship's owners). The agreement held the defendants liable for the loss of the ship if it was caused by their negligence. The dispute was tendered to arbitrators chosen by the parties for findings of fact; the arbitrators' rulings were subject to judicial review only as to matters of law.

Note that *Polemis* was not the name of the ship; it was the name of one of the owners of the ship, which was called the *Thrasyvoulos*. The full title of the case is *In re An Arbitration Between Polemis and Another and Furness, Withy and Co., Ltd.* This sometimes is a minor point of confusion for students (and even the occasional commentator), perhaps because the "in re" form of titling sometimes is used in maritime cases to identify the vessel involved.

Q. Given that the risk the plank would cause an explosion was unforeseeable, why was *Polemis* a case of liability?
A. Because the explosion was a direct consequence of the falling plank.

Q. What does "direct" mean? Suppose the plank had fallen onto a barrel of oil, the barrel had broken open, and oil from the barrel had leaked until it came into contact with a lantern at the other end of the hold. A fire starts and the ship is destroyed. Would this have been a sufficiently direct consequence of the falling plank to permit liability? If that would be a case of liability, what *wouldn't* be?
A. The question is meant to highlight the difficulty of making sense out of "directness" as a criterion for causation. It could mean that the consequence was close to the negligent act in time or in space; it could mean that the consequence followed without any further acts, or without any further physical steps. It's a hard term to define in the abstract, and hard for jurors to apply in practice. The hypothetical probably would be a case of no liability. A clearer case of no liability might be a case like *Polemis* where the fire spread to other ships in the harbor.

Q. Suppose an oil truck overturns and spills some of its cargo onto a road. Meanwhile the defendant is driving along a bridge that passes over the road. From where the defendant is driving, the overturned gasoline truck is not visible. The defendant flicks a smoldering cigarette butt out the window. The butt falls over the side of the bridge onto the road below, ignites the oil, and causes a massive explosion that destroys several houses and kills a number of people. Is the plaintiff liable under *Polemis*?

A. Probably. The only question would be whether it's negligent to throw a smoldering cigarette butt out of a car window. Most likely it is—but of course one must decide this by reference only to the foreseeable harm it might cause, which probably wouldn't include the explosion. Assuming that it was negligent to toss out the butt because there is a small chance it could start, say, a grass fire (while the B of disposing of it properly is negligible), D would be on the hook for all the harm it directly caused.

Q. Here is a hypothetical based on *Larrimore v. American National Insurance Co.*, 89 P.2d 340, 342 (Okla. 1939), and made famous in Robert E. Keeton, *Legal Cause in the Law of Torts* (1963). The defendant leaves a tin of rat poison beside a container of flour on a shelf next to a kitchen stove. Placing the rat poison there is negligent because someone could confuse it for the flour and be poisoned. But this doesn't happen; instead, the heat from the stove unexpectedly—indeed, unforeseeably—causes the poison to explode. What result under *Polemis*?

A. Probably a case of liability, since the harm appears to be a fairly direct result of the negligent act.

Q. What was the negligence in the *Wagon Mound* case? *Why* was it negligence?

A. Spilling oil into the harbor. The PL was the high risk that the oil would create a mess—*not* that the oil would catch fire, a risk that was found in this case to be unforeseeable and therefore not part of PL, which is measured as it reasonably appeared *ex ante*.

Q. The oil here caught fire after a substantial amount of time had passed. What if the oil instead had caught fire right away after leaking into the harbor? Suppose, for example, that the oil had drifted up behind a worker who threw a burning cigarette onto it. Would the result be any different?

A. No; since the result was unforeseeable, the closeness in time of the result—the "directness," perhaps—is irrelevant.

Q. What result would the *Wagon Mound* approach produce in the rat poison hypothetical considered a moment ago?

A. No liability. One way to look at the *Wagon Mound* rule is that the set of risks that cause an act to be labeled negligent is the same set that defines the defendant's potential liability as a matter of proximate cause: for purposes of either analysis we confine ourselves to risks that are foreseeable. This doesn't mean that the risk of whatever happened had to be large enough to support a conclusion of negligence by itself; sometimes an act will be negligent because it creates a series of risks, some large and some small, that together cause the act to seem unreasonable; and maybe the act still would seem negligent if one of the smaller risks was subtracted. The point is just that both analyses depend on the question of foreseeability. If it is held unforeseeable that the rat poison could explode, there is no liability for the damage caused by the explosion under *The Wagon Mound*.

Note on the Wagon Mound *cases.* As the casebook text explains, the two *Wagon Mound* cases produced slightly different factual findings concerning the foreseeability that oil spilled into a harbor could catch fire, and the different findings produced different legal results in the Privy Council. The text ascribes this discrepancy to the different incentives the plaintiffs in the two cases had to establish foreseeability—a point made by Lord Reid in his opinion in *Wagon Mound (No. 2)*. In his contribution to the recently published book Torts Stories, Saul Levmore offers a different interpretation. He describes the pair of results in the two cases as strange: a defendant spills oil which results in a fire; the fire first damages one plaintiff's dock and then damages ships belonging to other plaintiffs. The latter plaintiffs, whose injuries were more remote, get to recover from the defendant. The first plaintiffs, who owned the dock that was the fire's first casualty, do not get to recover. You might expect that both could recover if either of them could;—or that if only one of them could recover, it would be the dock owner, whose injuries came first.

Levmore then offers his own way of making sense out of the two cases. His idea is that the law generally tries to assign some legal responsibility to each of the parties that misbehaves in a case in order to deter their misconduct. This is easy enough in a regime of comparative negligence, since then a negligent plaintiff and negligent defendant each can be forced to bear some of the loss produced by their want of due care. In a regime of contributory negligence, though—such as prevailed in the *Wagon Mound* era—it's harder to achieve this effect, because the plaintiff either collects everything or nothing from the defendant. Levmore's thought is that maybe some proximate cause doctrines can be used as tools to accomplish those same ends that he associates with comparative negligence in cases where there are multiple parties involved. As applied to the *Wagon Mound* cases, the point would be that Mort's Dock—the plaintiff in the first suit—was indeed guilty of contributory negligence by welding over a thick oil spill; so the best result as a matter of policy is one where the owners of the Wagon Mound suffer (because they were most negligent), where Mort's Dock also suffers (because they, too, were somewhat negligent), and where the plaintiffs in the second Wagon Mound case recover in full (because they were innocent). The trial court's findings did not support a conclusion of contributory negligence in *Wagon Mound No. 1*, but the Privy Council forced the same result—no liability—by using causation grounds (saying there was no liability because the fire was unforeseeable). Then in the second *Wagon Mound* case the trial court finds no liability—but the Privy Council does, fastening on to the trial court's finding that there was a bit of foreseeability after all. The result is that everyone pays what they should. Levmore speculates that perhaps the Privy Council was ready to let the defendant off in *Wagon Mound (No. 1)* because it knew that there was another plaintiff—this time a quite innocent one—in the queue who would be appearing in the second Wagon Mound case and would give the court a chance to hold the defendant liable without rewarding a plaintiff who contributed to the accident.

This way of thinking also has implications for the *Polemis* case. In that litigation we do not find the multiple parties of cases like *The Wagon Mound*, and thus less need for complex doctrines of causation to try to make sure some liability is distributed to each defendant:

> [P]erhaps we should take the *Polemis* approach, of all but ignoring foreseeability when it comes to damages and in this way limiting foreseeability inquiries to the negligence calculus, as following from the presence of but a single tortfeasor. With just one tortfeasor to deter, the argument goes, judges are more inclined to follow the thinskull rule and to avoid any artificial constructs that limit liability, including the degree/kind distinction.

Torts Stories at 149. Levmore goes on to suggest that with the rise of comparative negligence, the foreseeability limitation may become less important because there is less need for it as a tool to make sure everyone pays what they should in situations with multiple wrongdoers—though "foreseeability may continue to be used as a means of systematic manipulation when some of the relevant wrongdoers are not before the court." *Id.* at 150. Levmore's approach may be questioned on various grounds; it ascribes a level of strategic thinking to judges in general and to the lords on the Privy Council in particular that some may find implausible. But it at least provides an interesting chance to think about how various legal doctrines—e.g., contributory negligence and proximate cause—can be used to further similar policies. We will revisit Levmore's approach in the notes to the *Palsgraf* case later in the chapter.

Q. What was the negligence in *Petition of Kinsman*?
A. Failing to properly secure the deadman to which the *Shiras* was moored. (The owner of the *Shiras*, incidentally, was George Steinbrenner, who would go on to greater fame as the owner of the New York Yankees.)

Q. Why was this negligent? What was the PL?

A. The court's view was that there were a <u>number of foreseeable PLs</u>: a large chance of relatively small harms, such as the barge running into something and receiving damage, or the barge running into another boat or pier and inflicting damage. Then there was a small chance of larger harm of the kind that occurred here. The <u>details of</u> what actually happened <u>might not have been foreseeable at all</u>, but the basic family of results—a <u>calamity</u> when the boat strikes something farther up the river, perhaps bringing down structures and causing damage to property on the shore—was something that <u>could have been foreseen</u> if one paused to think about what might happen if the barge came loose.

Q. Is *Petition of Kinsman* more like the *Wagon Mound* or the *Polemis* case in its approach?
A. It's more like *The Wagon Mound*. It treats <u>foreseeability is a constraint on liability</u> (and notice that the results that followed from the negligence in *Kinsman* <u>weren't very direct</u>). Some room for puzzlement is created because Friendly's opinion makes mention of both foreseeability and directness: "The weight of authority in this country rejects the limitation of damages to consequences foreseeable at the time of the negligent conduct when the consequences are 'direct,' and the damage, although other and greater than expectable, is of the same general sort that was risked." So <u>directness still may do some work in cases where foreseeability is tenuous</u> or occurs at a high level of generality. <u>But in the end there always must be foreseeability</u>—of the forces involved, at least, if not of the precise results: "We go only so far as to hold that where, as here, the damages resulted from the same physical forces whose existence required the exercise of greater care than was displayed and were of the same general sort that was expectable, unforeseeability of the exact developments and of the extent of the loss will not limit liability." *The Wagon Mound* thus is distinguishable because in that case the type of harm that occurred (a fire) was not the type of harm that could have been foreseen (a mess).

Q. In *Petition of Kinsman*, Friendly says that most judges would find no liability if a patient died because his doctor got stuck on the wrong side of the bridge when the defendant's barge demolished it. What is the distinction between that case and the actual *Kinsman* case?
A. The negligence in *Kinsman* gave rise to foreseeable risks of various types of damage to property on the river and on shore. One could imagine the barge running into things and causing water to end up where it shouldn't, etc. That general sort of damage is what occurred, however freakishly. The kind of harm alleged in the case of the delayed doctor, however, is different in kind from anything one would expect to follow from securing a boat too loosely.

Doughty v. Turner (lid slips into cauldron of molten cyanide and causes explosion that injures P; NL)
Colonial Inn Motor Lodge v. Gay (car bumps heater on side of hotel, severing gas line and leading to explosion; L)
DiPonzio v. Riordan (Car rolls when D's patron leaves it running at gas station; NL because hazard that manifested differs from hazard that made it negligent to leave engine running)
United Novelty Co. v. Daniels (problem: flaming rat ignites gas; L)
Steinhauser v. Hertz (problem: negligent driving causes accident that precipitates schizophrenia; L)

This batch of cases is meant to illustrate the principle that so long as the *type* of harm that befalls the plaintiff is foreseeable, liability remains intact even if the extent of the harm or the details of the manner in which it came to pass is unforeseeable—themes introduced in the *Petition of Kinsman* opinion.

Q. What is the distinction between *Doughty v. Turner* and *Petition of Kinsman*?
A. *Doughty* is a hard case because it puts pressure on precisely how one characterizes the legal test and the facts to which it applies. To borrow language from *Kinsman*, *Doughty* might be described as a case where the damage that occurred was of "the same general sort that was risked": it was foreseeable that if the lid fell in the cauldron, molten cyanide would end up leaving the cauldron and hitting bystanders—and that's just what happened. The "exact developments" bearing on how the cyanide escaped (an explosion rather than a splash) were unforeseeable, but that doesn't matter. The

characterization just sketched is the one the court in *Doughty* rejected. It preferred a characterization like this: there were two risks associated with the entry of the lid into the cauldron: the risk of splashing and the risk of explosion. These don't amount to the same general sort of harm, because they involve quite different "forces" (to again borrow from *Kinsman*): in the foreseeable scenario the relevant force was the lid striking the surface of the molten cyanide. In the unforeseeable scenario—the one that played out—the relevant force was the lid sinking and creating an explosion. So the pressure the case puts on the legal test involves just what must have been foreseeable to create liability: the general type of injury that occurred, or the general operation of forces that occurred. *The Wagon Mound* was more straightforward because there differences of both kinds existed: yes, the oil caused harm in both the foreseeable and unforeseeable scenarios, but in the foreseeable one the harm was the creation of a mess from drifting oil, whereas in the unforeseeable scenario the harm was a fire resulting from ignited oil. The types of injuries and what the oil did both were different. In *Doughty* the type of injury that occurred is the same in both scenarios, but the forces involved can be seen as different.

Given the court's way of characterizing *Doughty*, the distinction between that case and *Kinsman* is that in *Kinsman* the general type of harm—and the forces causing it—were foreseeable, even if its probability of occurring was low. Friendly's opinion in *Petition of Kinsman* regarded itself as consistent with *Doughty*: "The risk against which defendant [in *Doughty*] was required to use care—splashing of the molten liquid from dropping the supposedly explosion proof cover—did not materialize, and the defendant was found not to have lacked proper care against the risk that did. As said by Lord Justice Diplock, (1964) 2 W.L.R. at 247, 'The former risk was well known (and so foreseeable) at the time of the accident; but it did not happen. It was the second risk which happened and caused the plaintiff damage by burning.'"

Q. What is the distinction between *Doughty v. Turner* and *Colonial Inn Motor Lodge v. Gay*?
A. The court in *Colonial Inn* in effect thought the case was similar to *Petition of Kinsman* (notice the similarity between the language in the last paragraphs of the excerpts from each of those two cases): *Colonial Inn* involved a general type of harm from a general type of force—destruction of the hotel when the car hit it—that was foreseeable, even if its probability was low; bumping the car into the building was conduct which entailed (to borrow words from *Kinsman*) "a large risk of small damage and a small risk of other and greater damage, of the same general sort, from the same forces, and to the same class of persons[.]" Yes, the harm that occurred was much worse than anyone would have imagined it would be, but that's just a difference in the "extent" of the resulting harm that doesn't affect liability: *Colonial Inn* is an "eggshell skull" case.

But of course this is contestable. One could argue that *Colonial Inn* really is just like *Doughty*. On this view the car hitting the hotel is like the lid falling into the cauldron: either event could cause foreseeable harm. But just as the force unleashed by the sinking lid in *Doughty* was unforeseeable, so too was the force unleashed by the collision in *Colonial Inn*: what was foreseeable was that the car would cause damage upon impact to the part of the building it hit (analogous to the danger of splashing in *Doughty*). It wasn't foreseeable that a fire would end up destroying the building; that's like the explosion in *Doughty*—an entirely different force. Indeed, when looked at in this way *Colonial Inn* might come to seem the weaker case for liability, because the harm that occurred (fire) was so different from what was risked (impact damage)—whereas in *Doughty* the harm was much the same either way: molten cyanide getting on people. So then comes the riposte in *Colonial Inn* that the fire was initiated *by* the physical impact on the building—*by* the foreseeable force; and the harm that resulted was, too, the same *general* sort that was risked: damage to the building.

It can be a nice exercise to appoint students to argue the appeal of *Colonial Inn* based on the assumption that *Doughty* is controlling law. The cases illustrate the room that exists in proximate cause cases for creative characterization of the facts and legal standard.

Notice, by the way, that the *Colonial Inn* opinion also borrows some notions of directness from the *Polemis* tradition: e.g., "the sequence of events that caused the explosion was set in motion with no further action needed to bring about the injury." But it's not clear whether the damage done here would have satisfied the old-fashioned "directness" test of the sort advanced in *Polemis*.

Q. What is the distinction between *Colonial Inn Motor Lodge v. Gay* and *DiPonzio v. Riordan*?
A. *DiPonzio* is a chance to consolidate the points brought out with the prior cases; by now it shouldn't be hard to understand, though precisely distinguishing *Colonial Inn* may take a bit of work. In both of these cases seemingly minor acts of negligence that could have caused obvious, foreseeable harms instead led to surprising results. In *DiPonzio*, we can suppose that if the patron's car had started an explosion, the defendant service station would have been held liable: due care required the station to enforce its rule about turning off the car's engine before fueling. And the exercise of that due care would have prevented this accident as well; so why no liability? *DiPonzio* can be analogized to *Doughty v. Turner*: it was predictable that the car might cause harm if its engine was left on (just as it was foreseeable that the lid in *Doughty* might cause harm if it entered the cauldron), but the foreseeable force involved in *DiPonzio* was combustion, not the physical impact that actually occurred. And in *DiPonzio* the harm that occurred was different from the type of harm that was risked (unless we are to imagine that an explosion would have broken the plaintiff's leg just as the rolling car did). *DiPonzio* also can be viewed as a variation on the rat poison hypothetical given earlier: the bad thing that happened wasn't part of the foreseeable set of risks that caused the defendant's behavior to be considered negligent.

 Colonial Inn might seem similar, only with the facts reversed: physical impact by the car was the foreseeable risk; fire was an unforeseeable risk—yet there was liability for it. The best distinction probably is that there was a close link in *Colonial Inn* between the risk that was foreseeable (physical impact) and the thing that happened (the fire). To make *DiPonzio* analogous you might change its facts so that the car's motor did start a fire, and this led to havoc in which its owner bumped the car into gear (or drove off with it in a panic) and ran over the plaintiff. In that case the specific harm that results might be considered unforeseeable, but it would be an outgrowth of the risk of fire that *was* foreseeable.

Q. What result in *United Novelty Co. v. Daniels*?
A. Liability. The *Daniels* case is a classic example of liability where the basic type of result that occurred was foreseeable, and indeed was the type of harm—and caused by the same sort of force—that made the defendant negligent for sending the employee into the room with gasoline. The fact that it came to pass through a weird chain of "exact developments" (*Kinsman*) does not detract from the defendant's liability. From the opinion:

> The work was being performed in a room eight by ten feet in area, in which there was a gas heater then lighted with an open flame. The cleaning was being done with gasolene. The testimony yields the unique circumstance that the immediate activating cause of a resultant explosion was the escape of a rat from the machine, and its disappointing attempt to seek sanctuary beneath the heater whereat it overexposed itself and its impregnated coat, and returned in haste and flames to its original hideout. Even though such be a fact, it is not a controlling fact, and serves chiefly to ratify the conclusion that the room was permeated with gasolene vapors. Negligence would be predicated of the juxtaposition of the gasolene and the open flame. Under similar circumstances, the particular detonating agency, whether, as here, an animate version of the classic lighted squib, or as in *Johnson v. Kosmos Portland Cement Co.*, 64 F.2d 193 (6th Cir. 1933), a bolt of lightning, was incidental except as illustrating the range of foreseeability.

 The squib case and *Johnson v. Kosmos Portland Cement Co.* both are considered later in the chapter.

From Jack Balkin, *The Rhetoric of Responsibility*, 76 Va. L. Rev. 197 (1990):

Every torts professor has a favorite hypothetical about causal responsibility—some wildly improbable and outrageous chain of events triggered by the defendant that somehow leads inexorably to the plaintiff's injury. I have always been partial to the facts of *United Novelty Co. v. Daniels*. In *Daniels* the defendant negligently set the nineteen-year-old decedent to work cleaning a coin-operated machine with gasoline; the decedent worked in a small room warmed by a gas heater with an open flame. The gasoline vapors surrounding the machine ignited when a rat ran from the machine into the flame, caught fire, and then ran back toward the machine, causing an explosion that killed the decedent. Naturally, the defendant company argued that it was not causally responsible for the freak accident. Nevertheless, the court upheld a jury verdict against the company because it could have foreseen that setting the decedent to work in the room under these conditions was unduly dangerous.

The opinion in *Daniels* takes up barely a page in the reporters, but within this miniature one can find many of the most common structures of argument about human moral responsibility that occur in legal discourse. Consider, for example, the arguments that the defendant company might make (and probably did make) on its behalf:

(1) The explosion was caused by the unpredictable movements of a rat, not by the defendant's negligence.

(2) When the decedent began cleaning the machine with gasoline, it was completely unforeseeable that a rat would jump out of the machine, run headlong toward an open flame, catch fire, and then run back precisely where it could do the most damage.

(3) Decedent was at fault for cleaning the machine with gasoline in the first place. The decedent must have known of the danger when the decedent voluntarily began work.

Next consider the plaintiff's likely responses:

(1) Although the rat was the immediate cause of the explosion, the real cause was the defendant's ordering the decedent to work under unsafe conditions.

(2) It is completely foreseeable that if you set someone to work in a small room filled with gas vapors and an open flame, there is an unacceptable risk of an explosion.

(3) The decedent cannot be held responsible for the explosion, because the decedent was following the orders of the defendant employer and was a minor.

As one would expect, the defendant's arguments are designed to minimize the defendant's causal, legal, and moral responsibility, while the plaintiff's arguments are designed to enhance them. More importantly, however, each side recharacterizes the facts to support its position, emphasizing some details, minimizing or even omitting others—creating a coherent portrait of the situation from the raw materials of experience. Like all pictures, these characterizations are selective; for to record experience is always also to reorder and even to suppress it. In the second argument presented above, for example, the defendant describes the situation in minute detail, while the plaintiff speaks in more general, abstract terms. In this way each side can make plausible its claim about the foreseeability or unforeseeability of the decedent's injuries.

Q. Hypothetical: in *Chase v. Washington Water Power Co.*, 111 P.2d 872 (Idaho 1941), the defendant maintained a series of power lines beside the plaintiff's property. Electricity jumped from the defendant's lines to the plaintiff's barbed wire fence, starting fires on the plaintiff's land and destroying his barn.

Two dead chicken hawks were found at the scene, their talons interlocked and both of them badly singed. The plaintiff's theory (accepted by all the parties) was that the hawks had been engaged in aerial battle, their talons locked, when one of the birds touched one of the defendant's high-voltage lines, and the other bird touched another line—a "guy wire"—that normally did not conduct high voltage. Elsewhere the guy wire contacted the plaintiff's wire fence. The voltage passed from the power line through the two birds to the guy wire, and then traveled from the guy wire to the plaintiff's fence, starting the fires. The plaintiff sued the defendant power company, claiming the fires were caused by its negligence in failing to properly insulate its wires and in allowing its guy wire to come into contact with the plaintiff's fence. What result?
A. Liability; it's the same pattern as *Daniels*. The jury returned a verdict for the plaintiff and the defendant appealed; the Idaho Supreme Court affirmed:

> The record shows that hawks abound in the territory through which appellant's power line passes, and that upon other occasions birds caused disturbances in the transmission of electricity by way of these wires. While, from an anticipatory point of view, the exact manner in which these hawks interfered with the wires upon this occasion may seem unusual or extraordinary, viewed in retrospect it can not be said to have been unforeseeable.

Q. What is the distinction between *Chase v. Washington Water Power Co.* and *Doughty v. Turner*?
A. Many students find these cases hard to distinguish. *Chase* is a case where a foreseeable result, produced by foreseeable forces, came to pass through an unexpected agency—viz., the birds. As we have seen, much rides on how one characterizes what happened in *Doughty*. It could easily enough be described as a case where a bad result that was foreseeable (molten cyanide leaving the cauldron and ending up burning a bystander) occurred, but through unexpected means. On that view the case seems inconsistent with *Chase*. But the Lords in *Doughty* thought about the case in other terms—not as a particular injury (a burned plaintiff) but rather as an *explosion*, which was a different *type* of result (or a result arising from a different force or risk) than a splash. Whether or not this distinction is a successful or determinate one, the lawyering point repeats: students need to see that these cases and their parts—the "result" and the "means by which the result was reached"—are open to interpretation and characterization. You could also point out that the court in *Chase* said the general hazards posed by birds were understood, even if this particular scenario (aerial combat) could not have been imagined; in *Doughty* the risk of explosion was totally unknown.

Q. What result in *Steinhauser v. Hertz Corp.*?
A. Liability. It's a leading "eggshell skull" case, and so is most analogous to *Colonial Inn v. Gay*. In *Steinhauser* the plaintiff lost at trial because the judge insisted on instructing the jury to find liability only if the defendant's negligence caused the daughter's schizophrenia, not if the negligence precipitated the onset of a disease to which she had a pre-existing susceptibility. The plaintiff argued on appeal that the latter finding should have been enough to support liability, and the court (per Friendly, J.) agreed:

> It is unnecessary to engage in exhaustive citation of authority sustaining the legal validity of plaintiffs' theory of the case. Since New York law governs, the oft-cited decision in *McCahill v. New York Transportation Co.*, 201 N.Y. 221 (1911), which plaintiffs' appellate counsel has discovered, would alone suffice. There the defendant's taxicab negligently hit McCahill, broke his thigh and injured his knee. After being hospitalized, he died two days later of delirium tremens. A physician testified that "the injury precipitated his attack of delirium tremens, and understand I mean precipitated not induced"; he explained that by "precipitated," he meant "hurried up,"—just what plaintiffs' experts testified to be the role of the accident here. The Court of Appeals allowed recovery for wrongful death. In *Champlin Refining Co. v. Thomas*, 93 F.2d 133, 136 (10 Cir. 1937), the court held that "where one who has tubercular germs in his system suffers injuries due to the negligence of another, and the injuries so weaken the resistance of the tissues that as a direct consequence tubercular infection sets up therein, the negligence is the

proximate cause of the tubercular infection and renders the negligent person liable in damages therefor." There was no suggestion that plaintiff was required either to admit that he already "had" tuberculosis or to assert that the accident "caused" the development of the germs. In *Pigney v. Pointer's Transport Services, Ltd.*, (1957) 1 W.L.R. 1121, recovery for wrongful death was allowed where head injuries induced an anxiety neurosis leading to suicide. Our own decision in *Evans v. S. J. Groves & Sons Co.*, 315 F.2d 335, 346-349 (1963) (thrombosis of sinus possibly due in part to ear disease but "triggered" by blow to head) is also quite relevant.

The idea seems to be that if a negligently-inflicted impact on the plaintiff causes an unexpected injury, the defendant's liability for it is intact. But while the rule governing cases like this is well-established (as the court notes), fitting it into the cases so far in the chapter is trickier. It is foreseeable that negligent driving might cause physical injuries. Is it foreseeable that it might precipitate a mental disorder such as schizophrenia? Might the onset of the schizophrenia be analogous to the accident that occurred in *Kinsman*—a low-probability occurrence, but still part of the family of foreseeable risks created by the defendant's negligence, which might be defined to include not only physical harms but also mental disturbances such as emotional distress? Or is the point that schizophrenia and broken bones (or at least mental distress of some sort) are all the same general type of result, and that the distinction between them is just a matter of detail?

Notice, by the way, another important point about *Steinhauser*: the plaintiff's damages would have to be reduced to reflect the possibility that she would have developed schizophrenia sooner or later anyway even if the defendant hadn't caused an accident.

Central of Georgia Ry. v. Price (woman taken to wrong railroad stop is injured in hotel fire; NL)
Pridham v. Cash and Carry Building Center (D injures man who then is killed in ambulance accident on way to hospital; L)
Berry v. Borough of Sugar Notch (problem: tree falls on speeding plaintiff; NL for contributory negligence)

These cases are meant to illustrate the principle that to satisfy the proximate cause requirement, the defendant's negligence must increase the probability of the type of harm the plaintiff suffered. This can be tied into the general discussion of foreseeability: what must be foreseen is that the type of injury the plaintiff suffered became more probable as a result of the defendant's conduct. In a sense these cases are just further illustrations of the idea that (to quote the likely language from the Third Restatement) "An actor is not liable for harm different from the harms whose risks made the actor's conduct tortious." But there's a little more to these "wrong place at the wrong time" decisions; they aren't quite the same as cases like *DiPonzio*. In the latter case the defendant's negligence did make the harm that occurred more likely. In cases like *Price* that we consider here, there is cause in fact but no increase in the probability of the damage that occurred.

Q.   What is the logic of the decision in *Price?*
A.   The plaintiff could just as easily have been burned at her actual destination as at the hotel where she stayed because of the defendant's mistake. That may be a little too strong if taken literally, of course; perhaps at her actual destination some of the risks of fire (lanterns and mosquito nets) were not present. But then again, it's also possible that the risk of fire was greater wherever she was headed, and that in the long run people are in some ways safer in hotels than they are at home; blunders of this sort by the railroad, in other words, may save as many people from fires than they endanger. In any event, on the facts we have here it cannot be said with any confidence that the railroad's negligence made this harm more likely to occur.

A related angle to consider, raised by the Posner excerpt at the end of the chapter, is that next time the railroad's blunder might cause a plaintiff to miss her stop and therefore to not to make it to a hotel that burns down the very same night; in that case the railroad's mistake will have saved the passenger's life, but the railroad will not be compensated by the passenger. So why should the railroad pay here?

Q. Most students will find *Hines v. Garrett*, 108 S.E. 690 (Va. 1921), easy to distinguish from *Price*, but putting the cases side by side helps illuminate their logic. The plaintiff in *Hines* was an 18-year-old woman riding on the defendant's train. Her evidence was that the conductor failed to stop the train at her destination. The conductor told the plaintiff that he couldn't back up the train, but that she could ride on to Richmond and catch another train back. The plaintiff asked to be let off immediately so that she could walk back to her stop, a distance of about a mile. The area along the tracks there was known to locals as "Hoboes' Hollow," and was "habitually frequented and infested by hoboes, tramps, and questionable characters." Another man, dressed in a soldier's uniform, got off the train when the plaintiff did. He caught up with her as she walked, carried her down an embankment, and raped her. As she was trying to rise from the ground, another man came along and raped her again. Neither man was ever found.

The plaintiff sued the railway for damages, and the jury returned a verdict in her favor. The defendant appealed. What result?

A. *Held*, for the plaintiff, that the verdict must be upheld. Said the court:

> No 18 year old girl should be required to set out alone, near nightfall, to walk along an unprotected route, passing a spot which is physically so situated as to lend itself to the perpetration of a criminal assault, and which is infested by worthless, irresponsible and questionable characters known as tramps and hoboes; and no prudent man, charged with her care, would willingly cause her to do so. The very danger to which this unfortunate girl fell a victim is the one which would at once suggest itself to the average and normal mind as a danger liable to overtake her under these circumstances. It is no answer to the proposition to say that the presumption is that crimes of this character will not be committed. The presumption applies under ordinary circumstances, but it is not to be indulged, and ordinarily prudent men do not indulge it, to the extent of regarding it safe to expose a young woman to such a risk as the plaintiff in this case incurred in passing "Hobo Hollow" as the shades of night were approaching.

In both *Hines v. Garrett* and *Central of Georgia Ry. v. Price*, a defendant railroad failed to let the plaintiff off at her intended stop, and in both cases the plaintiff came to grief where she was let off. In both cases this was because (as the *Price* court put it) of the "interposition of a separate, independent agency." The difference, as the court says it, is that it was foreseeable that releasing the plaintiff in *Hines* into "Hoboes' Hollow" would put her at risk of being assaulted. To put the point in probabilistic terms, the *Hines* plaintiff's likelihood of suffering a rape was greatly and foreseeably increased by the defendant's negligence.

Q. What is the distinction between *Central of Georgia Ry. v. Price* and *Pridham v. Cash and Carry Building Center, Inc.*?

A. First pin down the superficial similarities—or perhaps they are more than superficial. In both cases the defendant's negligence caused the plaintiff to end up in the wrong place at the wrong time: in a burning hotel in *Price*, and in the back of an ambulance whose driver had a heart attack in *Pridham*. The distinction between the cases evidently is that injuring someone is thought to make it more likely that they will end up injured during routine efforts to attend to their injuries. This might seem a little odd on the facts of *Pridham*, because it's not clear that the injury to Pridham made it more likely that he would die in a car accident after leaving the defendant's premises.

The best place to start in making sense out of the case probably is with a comparison between *Price* and the hospital illustrations set out by the Restatement. Spending the night in a hotel does not make injury more likely than spending the night at home; this seems to be a lesson of *Price*. But perhaps spending the night in a hospital (for purposes of receiving treatment) does increase your risk of injury relative to what it would be if you had been able to stay home. Of course being in a hospital is *less* risky in certain respects: you will be treated more quickly if you have an unexpected emergency. But once you are receiving treatment, your prospects for injury become considerably higher than they would have been without the accident in the first place. Remember that at the time these rules were devised, medical treatment was riskier than it is today; in some instances a large share of the risk imposed on a plaintiff by a tortfeasor might have arisen from the hazards that attended medical treatment by the local sawbones. So in that sense a negligent injury did (and still does) raise the plaintiff's likelihood of subsequent injury at the hands of a doctor.

That brings us back, however, to the question of the driver in *Pridham*. Is being in the back of an ambulance less safe than being behind the wheel (or in the back of) some other type of car? A cab driver could as easily have had a heart attack. Or Pridham could have been driving himself home and been hit by an ambulance (or any car) driven by someone having a heart attack. Can one argue that ambulances are more dangerous places in which to ride than one's own car? More likely Pridham just loses because there is a general rule about routine efforts to provide aid to the victim of a tort—the rule set out in the Restatement excerpts—and it covers his case even if his case is not among the paradigm situations that caused the rule to be created in the first place. A clear rule to handle injuries sustained during rescue efforts may have administrative advantages even if it sometimes leads to particular results like *Pridham* that seem to be outside its rationale.

Q. How does one know whether negligence at a hospital is "extraordinary" such that the original tortfeasor is off the hook for it?

A. The Restatement excerpts involve intentional misconduct by hospital personnel, but it's easy enough to think of cases of negligence that would seem to qualify as well. I am injured in a car accident; while I'm at the hospital I go a vending machine for a candy bar, the machine eats my money, I shake the machine hard, and it falls over on me. Can I sue the original tortfeasor (setting aside the question of my own possible comparative negligence)? Or suppose a visitor to the hospital spills hot coffee on me. Again, presumably there would be no liability for the original tortfeasor for these injuries. Torts generally do not make it more likely that their victims will end up with vending machines falling onto them or getting coffee spilled on them; those things could have happened in the workplace just as easily, at least in the typical case. The general idea seems to be that the original tortfeasor is on the hook for damages resulting from the foreseeable risks that go along with routine medical transportation and treatment.

A nice hypothetical can be constructed from comment c to section 460 of the Second Restatement:

> In view of the absence of decisions, the [Institute] leaves open the question of the actor's liability for a second injury brought about by the negligence of a third person together with the impaired condition of the plaintiff. It would appear that there will be situations in which such a second injury is a normal consequence of the first, as where the plaintiff, walking on crutches, is knocked down by a third person because of his inability to get out of the way in time, or the third person negligently injures him in an attempt to rescue him from a danger which he has incurred because of his condition.

Q. What result in *Berry v. Borough of Sugar Notch*, and why?

A. No liability (for contributory negligence). This is a case, like *Price*, where a party's negligence put him in the wrong place at the wrong time without making it more likely that his injuries would occur. If the plaintiff had hewed to the legally required speed but left the station a few minutes earlier, the tree might just as easily have fallen on him. Indeed, the driver's high speed may have made it *less* likely that a tree would fall on him because it caused him to spend less time on the road. It would be different, of course, if the claim had been that the plaintiff's high speed prevented him from avoiding an object in the road in *front* of him, or from stopping once he saw the tree starting to collapse, for in those cases the high speed would have increased the probability of the type of accident that occurred.

SECTION B. INTERVENING CAUSES

The challenge in teaching this part of the chapter is to get beyond simple claims that the intervening acts involved were or weren't foreseeable. Push the students to articulate more precisely why one set of factual developments is considered foreseeable while another is not. If you want to make cuts, scale back your coverage of the problems that finish off the section.

Brauer v. N.Y. Central & H.R. R. Co. (D's train hits P's wagon; P's goods then are stolen; L)
Watson v. Kentucky & Indiana Bridge & R.R. (arsonist sets spilled gasoline on fire; NL)

Q. What is the distinction between the fruit stand hypothetical at the end of *Brauer* and the dissenting judge's example where a thief boards a train after it derails and ends up murdering one of the passengers? (*Are* the hypos distinguishable?)
A. Scattering the plaintiff's valuable goods out in the open without protection makes theft quite likely because it offers potential thieves an unusually easy way to turn a profit. Derailing a train does not create a comparable likelihood that it will be boarded and that deaths of passengers will ensue; the opportunity for theft and murder that a derailed train provides isn't much better than lots of other opportunities thieves have to commit those acts.

Q. Suppose I negligently injure you and therefore cause you to spend the night at the hospital. During that evening, thieves see that your house is unattended, break in, and steal your television. Do I owe you a television? What is the difference between this case and *Brauer* (or between this case and the fruit stand hypothetical at the end of *Brauer*)?
A. No liability for the television. If students try just to say that there's foreseeability in *Brauer* but not in the hypo, hone in on the "foreseeability of what" questions. The reasoning that emerges from Grady's paradigms is that *Brauer* is an EFR case, whereas the hypothetical is not: by injuring you I don't create such an unusually tantalizing opportunity for thieves; unattended houses aren't that hard to find, but unattended valuables in the street are another matter. What was foreseeable in the fruit stand case was a greatly increased probability that your goods would be stolen relative to the probability that exists most of the time (when you wouldn't be likely to ever leave them unattended).

Q. What is the superficial similarity between *Brauer and Watson*? If *Watson* is styled as a case where Duerr deliberately tossed a match to the gasoline, what is the distinction between that case and *Brauer*?
A. In both cases negligence by a defendant railroad left a plaintiff vulnerable to harm caused by the intentional misbehavior of a third party. But the railroad in *Brauer*, by scattering the plaintiff's barrels, created an unusually juicy opportunity for thieves. It is foreseeable that if you disable someone who is carrying goods, the goods are at a high risk of being stolen that would not otherwise exist; the incentive to steal them is clear because they have market value. But by spilling gasoline the railroad in *Watson* did not create such an unusual opportunity for someone who likes setting fires; such a person can spill their own gasoline or set fires elsewhere without too much trouble. More to the point, setting gasoline on fire does not obviously benefit the arsonist in the same way that theft benefits a thief. If the taste for arson were as widespread as the taste for cider, maybe it would be different.

Grady considers the difference to be that between an EFR case (*Brauer*) and an IIT case (*Watson*). Often an EFR case involves a certain amount of deliberateness by the defendant (*Weirum v. RKO Radio General*, in the chapter on duty, is a classic example). In *Brauer* there may not seem to be much deliberateness on the railroad's part, but perhaps the railroad's knowing refusal to lend the assistance of its guards can be so characterized.

Q. The reason that spilling gasoline is negligent is that it might catch fire, right? And it *did* catch fire. So the type of harm that occurred in *Watson* is the very type of harm that caused us to label the spill negligent in the first place. This makes it sound like there should be liability under *Petition of Kinsman*. It shouldn't matter precisely what chain of events caused that harm to occur; that's also said in *Kinsman* and it's the lesson of *Daniels v. United Novelty Co.* So there should be liability in *Watson* regardless of whether Duerr acted deliberately or negligently. What's wrong with this argument? (Equivalently: what is the distinction between *Watson* and *Daniels*—the case of the flaming rat?)

A. The basic rule that emerges from *Petition of Kinsman* and the cases afterwards—that there's liability if a foreseeable type of harm occurs, even if in an unexpected manner—does not necessarily control in cases where the "unexpected manner" involves a tortious act by a third party. In those cases we do care how the harm came to occur. To make *Kinsman* analogous, imagine that the defendant didn't fully secure the barge to the deadman, creating some risk that it would go adrift in the way that occurred in that case. But instead a miscreant comes along, unmoors the barge, and sends it on its way. If the latter occurred, there might not be liability under the principle of cases like *Watson*. Likewise, to make *Daniels* analogous to *Watson*, imagine that in *Daniels* some enemy of the plaintiff's decedent deliberately loosed a flaming rat into the room. There might not be liability for Daniels' employer in that case, again on the reasoning of *Watson*.

Q. So everyone agrees that the railroad negligently spilled gasoline and that Duerr set it on fire with a match. But doesn't it seem strange that the railroad's liability for the resulting blaze depends on what was going on inside Duerr's mind? What sense could this make as a matter of policy?

A. Back up a moment. People commit lots of negligent acts from which no harm results and for which no liability is found. We single out for liability those cases where the negligence results in harm—with "results" defined to mean that without the negligence, the harm would not have occurred (the cause in fact requirement) and also that the defendant should have understood that the negligence would make the bad result more likely to occur. In this sense the defendant is required to internalize the costs of its mistakes. But if the defendant has to pay for harm that its negligence didn't make any more likely, it will end up internalizing too many costs. So when a railroad (like the one in *Price*) is deciding how careful to be to let people off at the correct stops, it should take into account the costs created when it fails to do so—but those costs should not include the possibility that passengers like the *Price* plaintiff will end up being burned in fires at the hotels where they stay as a result. A similar point can be made about cases where a third party intervenes. It's not quite the same, because in a case like *Watson* the gasoline spill created *some* elevated risk of arson; but that increase in risk was small. And if it is thought to be enough to result in liability, then defendants like the railroad will have to take precautions on the assumption that third parties will take advantage of their negligence in bizarre ways (such as purposely setting gasoline on fire). We want defendants to think this way if their negligence makes bad behavior by third parties substantially more likely, but not if the increase in this risk is small.

Village of Carterville v. Cook (plaintiff, jostled off of high sidewalk, sues city; L)
Alexander v. Town of New Castle (plaintiff, thrown into pit, sues city; NL)

Q. What is the superficial similarity between *Village of Carterville v. Cook* and *Alexander v. Town of New Castle*? What is the distinction between them?

A. In both cases the defendant was a town that created a dangerous condition; in both cases the plaintiff came to grief only when the dangerous condition was combined with a tortious act by a third party. Yet only *Carterville* was a case of liability. *Carterville* involves mere negligence by the third party, of course, whereas *Alexander* involved intentional misbehavior. But we can say a little more than that. In *Carterville* the town's arrangement of the sidewalk was negligent precisely *because* it left people vulnerable to the negligence of others who might negligently jostle them. Thus the harm that occurred there was within the scope of the risk that made the defendant's act blameworthy. Leaving the pit open in *Alexander* was negligent (assuming it was negligent) not because it created a risk that someone like the plaintiff might deliberately be thrown into it, but presumably because someone might fall or ride into it in the dark. To put the point in policy terms, leaving an open hole near the road does not raise—at least much—the likelihood that people like Alexander will get injured in something like the way he did, because a fellow like Heavenridge will probably be able to find some way to incapacitate his jailer if the hole isn't available. By creating the hole the town didn't create all that tantalizing an opportunity for bad guys. *Alexander* thus is analogous to *Watson* when the latter is stylized as a case of no liability (i.e., the version where we assume Duerr started the fire deliberately). *Carterville* is a classic DCE case, in Grady's terms; *Alexander* is an IIT case.

Q. What if the plaintiff in *Carterville* had been deliberately pushed off the sidewalk by one of his enemies? Still liability for the city?

A. That's probably a case of no liability analogous to *Alexander*, but it depends how common such incidents are. To make the issue easier to visualize, think about the obligations of tall buildings to put high railings around their rooftops. They are obliged to do enough to prevent anyone from slipping off accidentally or being jostled off inadvertently. They generally aren't obliged to do enough to make sure nobody is *thrown* off the roof. What would be the result of holding the owners of buildings liable in such cases? One possible answer is *nothing*: they would take no additional care, since the prospect that it will happen is too remote. This might cut against liability, since it would produce no improvement in safety and would just put the building's owner into the role of an insurer. Another possibility is that the owners would build higher fences around the roof at some cost to those who would have wanted to enjoy the view without throwing their enemies to the ground below. That loss might be worth it if such throwing incidents became common. Accordingly, you would want to know in *Carterville* how common it was for people to deliberately push each other off the sidewalk.

This train of thought illustrates the identity between the risks we think about during the negligence inquiry and the risks we think about during the proximate cause inquiry. If people often are deliberately pushed off of such sidewalks (or if gasoline spills routinely are set on fire by arsonists), then that becomes a foreseeable risk that supports the view that the defendants in those situations are committing a breach of duty—and also supports the plaintiff's proximate cause argumente once one of those things happens. This relationship is made explicit in the Restatement (Third) excerpt at the end of the casebook chapter.

Scott v. Shepherd (D tosses lighted squib into crowd, which is passed on until it explodes in the face of P; L)

The Roman Prince (P waits to get off sinking ship damaged by D, then is injured when shc finally exits; NL)

Thompson v. White (D hires clowns to perform by side of the road; they distract driver, who hits P; L)

Q. In *Phillips v. DeWald*, 7 S.E. 151 (Ga. 1887), the defendant left his horse and buggy unhitched in an Atlanta street. A dray horse loaded with pipes approached the defendant's horse from the rear. The defendant's horse began to walk slowly down the street. The defendant went after the horse to stop him, but could not catch up. Some barbers ran out of their shop and tried to stop the horse, but instead caused him to accelerate into a "sweeping trot." More people on the street threw up their hands to try to stop the horse, but only frightened him and caused him to run still faster. At last the horse ran up onto the sidewalk and struck the plaintiff, wounding his scalp, rupturing a membrane in his ear, and causing various other injuries.

The plaintiff brought suit against the owner of the horse, claiming his injuries were attributable to the defendant's negligence in leaving the horse unhitched. The trial court instructed the jury on negligence, rather than strict liability, because the horse was neither "an individual of a vicious species, or a vicious individual of a harmless species." The jury found the defendant negligent and awarded the plaintiff $500 in damages. The defendant appealed, claiming that the facts did not support a finding of negligence and that his acts had not been the proximate cause of the accident. What result?

A. *Held*, for the plaintiff, that the evidence was sufficient to support the verdict. The court said that the acts of the public in frightening the horse into a run did not absolve the defendant of liability:

> The horse may be regarded as a squib,—slow at first, but likely to become swift and destructive. When a horse attached to a buggy is, through the owner's negligence, loose in the street, and moving at will, persons who see the horse thus going at large are at no fault for trying to stop or capture him; and if, by their rush, throwing up of hands, or other demonstrations, they frighten him, and cause him to run away, invade the sidewalk, and injure a person passing lawfully thereon, the owner will be responsible in damages for the injury.

Q. What is the principle of the "squib case" as these subsequent courts seem to have understood it?

A. In each of the liability cases, the defendant committed an act of negligence and the plaintiff was injured, and between the negligence and the injury there were intervening acts by others; and the intervening acts in all of the cases were viewed by the court as being not only foreseeable but perhaps inevitable or at least reflexive. The squib case seems to stand for the idea that intervening acts won't sever liability when they are quick, unreflective responses to the defendant's negligent acts.

Johnson v. Kosmos Portland Cement Co. (lightning strike problem; L)

There are two ways to look at this problem, and the important thing is for students to see them both. The first is to regard it, as the court evidently did, as a variation on the theme of *United Novelty Co. v. Daniels*: the defendant negligently created a risk; the danger that was risked came to pass, though perhaps through a surprising means. To argue the case this way, you would emphasize that the defendant created a risk of explosion on his ship by allowing the vapors to accumulate there. An explosion is what he then got—though by way of a lightning strike, not a blowtorch. But it also could be argued that there should be no liability because the risk that made the defendant's conduct negligent was not that there would be an explosion, but that there would be an *explosion caused by a blowtorch*. That is not what occurred. On this view the case is like a reverse version of *Larrimore v. American National Insurance Co.*—the rat poison hypothetical. D created a negligent risk of explosion from a particular source, but then harm resulted (also an explosion) that was caused by an unrelated source.

So how do we choose between these characterizations? The correct choice depends on precisely why it was negligent to fail to clean out the gases. The court's view was that it was unsafe to leave the gases on the barge because they might explode in any number of ways, and thus that it was a case of liability:

> The fault of the respondent consisted in its failure to remove gases from the barge. Their explosiveness presented continuous menace to the men working the thereon. Any one of a number of expectable circumstances might have brought about the precise injury which resulted; a lighted match, the flame of the acetylene torch, a heated rivet, a spark produced by friction of a tool or boot, and so on. The danger of the injurious result was over present, even though the manner in which, or the means by which, such result was brought about may have had in it some aspect of unusualness.

But the important thing to see is that the winner of the proximate cause debate in this case will be settled in large part during the argument about negligence: once we know why the defendant was negligent, we also will know about how far his responsibility extends. The defendant would have wanted to argue that the negligence, if any, was just in allowing fumes to accumulate where men with blowtorches were working; no blowtorches, no negligence.

Henry v. Houston Lighting & Power Co. (mosquito fogger problem; L)

The Texas court held that a jury could find proximate cause here, but other courts might reach different results. Again, the important point is to be able to see how each side might best argue the case. The argument for liability again starts by focusing on how we define the risks that made it negligent to split the gas line in the first place. There's a step by step approach to this that might help. (a) One of the major risks of splitting the line was that an explosion would result; the first point to settle is that if a worker sent to repair the line were injured when the gas exploded, the defendant would be liable. Some may doubt this on assumption of risk grounds; and if it's not true, then *a fortiori* there should be no liability in the actual *Henry* case either. But assume that utility workers do have a right to sue in these situations and thus that there would be liability on the facts just described. (b) All right; but what if a worker isn't injured in the explosion, but is hurt *escaping* it? Still liability; for in effect the injury still is caused by the explosion. (c) Now what if the worker is injured because he is fleeing a threatened explosion that doesn't occur? Thus suppose the worker sees a passing driver flick a smoldering cigarette butt in his direction and thinks it will cause the gas to explode; his fear was reasonable, though luckily no such explosion occurs. He is injured in his reasonable to scramble away. Perhaps liability again is secure, since we still are within the scope of the basic risk the defendant created: the possibility of an explosion (as well as the related possibilities of injury by those trying to escape that primary risk). This brings us to (d): the actual *Henry* case, where the plaintiff is hurt as he tries to escape the area because he reasonably believes there is about to be an explosion when in fact there isn't. Liability seems plausible so long as we view the scope of the risk to include not just explosions but also injuries sustained in reasonable attempts to avoid them.

So what is the contrary argument? Again, to make the example interesting we need to start with the assumption that the plaintiff could have sued and won if he had been hurt by an actual explosion in the hole. But we might argue that the scope of the risk that makes the defendant negligent ends there: it's a risk of explosion, not a risk of injury in running away from imagined threats of explosions. Perhaps the idea could be that adding liability for the latter sorts of injuries just adds a speculative burden to the defendant's worries when deciding how many precautions to take; the defendant can control the risk of explosion a bit (by not splicing the line), but whether false alarms are generated is determined by the actions of too many people whose acts are unpredictable—such as the workers with the mosquito fogger here. Anyway, here are some excerpts from the court's rather uninformative opinion:

> Intervention of an unforeseen cause of a plaintiff's injury does not necessarily mean that there is a new and independent cause of such a character as to constitute a superseding cause which will relieve the defendant of liability. *Bell v. Campbell,* 434 S.W.2d 117, 121 (Tex.1968). The intervening cause of the plaintiff's injury, even if unforeseeable, may be a concurring cause if the chain of causation flowing from the defendant's original negligence is continuous and unbroken. The intervening cause, if it is a concurring cause, does not break the chain of causation between the defendant's negligence and the plaintiff's injury simply because the intervening cause was unforeseeable.

We consider *Bell v. Campbell* in a moment.

Clark v. E.I. du Pont de Nemours Powder Co. (pail of glycerine left in graveyard for two years, then explodes when kids find it; L)

The court affirmed judgment on a jury verdict for the plaintiff. The two-year delay between the negligence and the injury is a red herring; it's just an odd feature of the chain of events that produced the final result, which itself was predictable. The harder question is whether DuPont should be off the hook because two parties—Joe McDowell and the boys' uncle (but particularly McDowell)—both had opportunities to prevent the injuries and failed to do so. But McDowell had no special duty to the boys, and the uncle didn't know what the pail contained. The court analyzed McDowell's significance this way:

> No new power of doing mischief was communicated to the solidified glycerine by the acts of young McDowell. The power of doing mischief was inherent in the glycerine all the time. That some terrible accident was likely to happen in letting it out of the close custody of some one skilled in its use was not only natural and probable, but almost inevitable. McDowell had no skill or experience in handling the dangerous article. He did the best he could to prevent the damage impending on account of Van Gray's negligence. That he attempted to prevent its doing damage, but failed on account of lack of sufficient knowledge to dispose of it effectively, does not amount to an unrelated and efficient agency to shift the proximate cause from the delict of the powder company to a new proximate cause of his own making.

Thus the case is most interesting as a study in how liability is (or isn't) affected when intervening parties pass up chances to rectify the defendant's negligence. What *would* McDowell have had to do—or who would he have had to be—to interrupt causation? Maybe if he had been an expert in handling the glycerine the result would have been different; or so the court implies. Well, but why? For in that case it still can be said that the defendant's negligence in leaving behind the glycerine put the plaintiffs at heightened risk, even if only a risk that McDowell would handle the glycerine carelessly. It's like a defendant putting a plaintiff into the hospital and thus putting him at risk that the doctors, however expert, will commit malpractice. Perhaps the idea is that if McDowell had been an expert one could argue that the glycerine came to rest safely in his possession and thus that he was solely responsible for the harm it went on to cause. The problem in the actual case is that the glycerine never did come to rest safely because McDowell really didn't know what to do with it.

Richardson v. Ham (D leaves bulldozer unattended; drunken miscreants drive off with it; L)

A "liability" case; the jury brought in a verdict for the defendants, the trial judge granted a new trial to the plaintiffs, and the California supreme court affirmed. The best analogies are to *Brauer* and to *Hines* (the "Hoboes' Hollow" case discussed earlier in this chapter of the manual); it's a case where the defendant created a fun and unusual opportunity for mischief-makers. But why is the case different from the version of *Watson* where Duerr sets the gasoline on fire deliberately and the railroad is not held liable? Is an unattended bulldozer a more predictable invitation to mischief than a big pool of gasoline? Well, probably, yes.

If the students find this case easy—and many of them probably will—it might be interesting to compare it to a hypothetical based on *Richards v. Stanley,* 271 P.2d 23 (1954). In that case the defendant left his keys in his car. A thief stole the vehicle and then ran over the plaintiff, who was riding a motorcycle. The California Supreme Court rejected liability in that case, finding itself unable to distinguish this scenario from one where a defendant lends his car to a friend who then causes an accident:

> The problem is not answered by pointing out that there is a foreseeable risk of negligent driving on the part of thieves. There is a foreseeable risk of negligent driving whenever anyone drives himself or lends his car to another. That risk has not been considered so unreasonable, however, that an owner is negligent merely because he drives himself, or lends his car to another, in the

absence of knowledge on his part of his own or the other's incompetence. Moreover, by leaving the key in the car the owner does not assure that it will be driven, as he does when he lends it to another. At most he creates a risk that it will be stolen and driven. The risk that it will be negligently driven is thus materially less than in the case in which the owner entrusts his car to another for the very purpose of the latter's use. [...]

Were we to hold that it is for the jury to decide whether Mrs. Stanley was under a duty to plaintiff to protect him from the negligent operation of her automobile by a thief, it would logically follow that in many situations where one person entrusts his car to another, a jury question would arise as to whether or not the owner should have foreseen an unreasonable risk to persons on the highway. It is a matter of common knowledge that drivers under 25 years of age as a class have more accidents than older drivers and that they must pay more for insurance. There may be other classes of drivers with similar accident experience. Nevertheless, an owner is not negligent if he entrusts his automobile to a member of such a class unless he knows or has reason to believe that the driver is incompetent, and in the absence of such knowledge he is under no common-law duty to protect third persons from possible misconduct on the part of the driver.

Of course *Richards v. Stanley* is distinguishable from *Ross v. Hartman*, a problem case in the chapter on negligence per se, because *Ross* involved a statute. But how might *Richards* be distinguished from *Richardson v. Ham*? Here is what the court in *Richardson* had to say:

Defendants contend that there is no substantial evidence that would support a judgment against them. They rely on the recent decision of this court in *Richards v. Stanley,* 43 Cal.2d 60, holding that, in the absence of special circumstances, the duty of an owner of an automobile to exercise reasonable care in the management thereof does not include a duty to remove the ignition key to protect persons on the highway from the negligent driving of a thief. Since, however, the kinds of foreseeable intervening conduct by third parties as well as the risks created by such conduct in this case are materially different from those considered in the *Richards* case, that case is not controlling here.

Automobiles do not arouse curiosity, and ordinarily the only appreciable risk that they will be set in motion if they are left unattended arises from the possibility of their being stolen. The record in the present case, on the other hand, shows that defendants' bulldozers aroused curiosity and attracted spectators, while they were in operation as well as while they were parked for the night. Moreover, curious persons had been known to climb on them, and it could reasonably be inferred that they were attractive to children when left unattended at the end of the working day. The evidence is therefore sufficient to justify the conclusion that there was a reasonably foreseeable risk that defendants' bulldozers might be tampered with when left unattended.

Given this foreseeable risk of intermeddling, the question is presented whether defendants were under a duty to exercise reasonable care to prevent intermeddlers from putting their bulldozers in operation. In the *Richards* case it was concluded that even if theft was reasonably to be foreseen, the owner was under no duty to persons on the highway to exercise reasonable care to keep his car out of the hands of a thief. It was pointed out that the owner will ordinarily have no reason to foresee that a thief will be an incompetent driver, that the risk of negligent driving arising from possible theft is less that the risk that the owner might intentionally create without negligence by lending his car to another, and that it would be anomalous to impose greater liability when the car is being driven by a thief than that provided by statute when the owner voluntarily entrusts his car to another. The risks arising from intermeddling bulldozers, however, are entirely different from those arising from the driving of an automobile by a thief. Bulldozers are relatively uncommon, and curious children or others attracted by them ordinarily will not know how to operate them.

An intermeddler who starts a bulldozer accidentally or otherwise may not be able to stop it, and the potentialities of harm from a 26 ton bulldozer in uncontrolled motion are enormous, particularly when it is left on top of a mesa from which it can escape and injure persons and property located below. The extreme danger created by a bulldozer in uncontrolled motion and the foreseeable risk of intermeddling fully justify imposing a duty on the owner to exercise reasonable care to protect third parties from injuries arising from its operation by intermeddlers.

In the absence of an effective lock the bulldozer engine could be started by pushing in a lever and stepping on the starter. Moreover, the engine could be started with the bulldozer in gear, and if so started, the bulldozer would commence to move immediately. Although this risk could be avoided by the use of a simple but effective lock, there is evidence that no such lock was used. Accordingly, there is substantial evidence that defendants did not exercise reasonable care to prevent intermeddlers from setting their bulldozer in motion.

Farmilant v. Singapore Airlines (food poisoning problem; NL)

No liability. To which case is the *Farmilant* problem most analogous? *Central of Georgia Ry. v. Price.* You can ask whether it was foreseeable that Farmilant might have a bad meal if he were forced to take a train from Bombay to Madras. Maybe; but probably just insofar as he might have had a bad meal anywhere in India. The defendant's negligence did not make it more probable than it otherwise would have been that Farmilant would be poisoned by local cuisine. Said the court:

> If all those facts were recited in a first-year law school examination question (from which they might appear to have been lifted), the most obvious issue for the student to spot would be whether Airline could be liable for any damages associated with Farmilant's illness. Farmilant attributes the illness to food bought from a vendor at a stop on his railroad trip from Bombay to Madras. Obviously that intervening or superseding cause would cut off Airline's liability whether Farmilant were proceeding on a tort or a contract theory. Farmilant embarrasses himself when he says "the possibility of his becoming ill during his transportation to Madras was...reasonably foreseeable by" Airline. Farmilant and his counsel would do well to read any of the host of cases exemplified by *Central of Georgia Ry. Co. v. Price,* 32 S.E. 77 (Ga. 1898).

What allegations could Farmilant have made that would have improved his case? Perhaps that by forcing him to take a train, the airline was condemning him to slow passage through some part of the country with terrible sanitary standards or other reasons to expect a high likelihood of food poisoning. That would make this more like the *Hines* case, where the plaintiff walked back to the railroad depot through "Hoboes' Hollow."

Farmilant's case was thrown out of federal court because he was there under the diversity jurisdiction and the court thought the defects in his case made it clear that he could not satisfy the amount in controversy requirement.

Bell v. Campbell (drunk driver hits rescuers trying to move trailer after accident; rescuers sue D who caused initial accident; NL)

The court found no liability. It's a close case. When negligent driving in a case like *Bell* causes an initial accident, it does seem to create an increased likelihood of the sort of later accident that occurred in *Bell,* and indeed there are plenty of other decisions finding liability when an accident on the highway leads to further harm as other cars plow into the original wreckage. This case might be a little different, however, because the plaintiff is a rescuer who was trying to overturn a trailer, and because the driver who hit him was drunk. Here is what the court in *Bell* had to say:

> It is clear that [the plaintiff] would not have been injured but for respondents' negligence, which created the condition that made the second collision possible. The active and immediate cause of the second collision, however, was an entirely independent agency, Fore. All forces involved in or generated by the first collision had come to rest, and no one was in any real or apparent danger therefrom. No one would have been injured if there had not been a second collision. [....]

> We agree with the Court of Civil Appeals that respondents could not reasonably foresee that the manner in which they operated their vehicles prior to the first collision might lead to the serious injury or deaths of persons not even in the zone of danger as a result of their being struck by another automobile which was some distance away at the time. [....]

> All acts and omissions charged against respondents had run their course and were complete. Their negligence did not actively contribute in any way to the injuries involved in this suit. It simply created a condition which attracted Payton, Bell and Bransford to the scene, where they were injured by a third party. Respondents' negligence was not a concurring cause of their injuries.

> An annotation published in 58 A.L.R.2d 270 deals with the general problem presented by this case. The decisions cited there indicate a division of authority and that a number of courts would probably allow the jury to determine the issue of causation under the present facts. That is to be expected in jurisdictions where liability is not limited to the foreseeable consequences of a wrongful act. As previously indicated, the Texas rule is otherwise.

You can follow up on *Bell v. Campbell* by asking about some later Texas cases:

Q. Hypothetical: in *Lear Siegler, Inc. v. Perez*, 819 S.W.2d 470 (Tex. 1991), the plaintiff's decedent, Perez, drove a truck pulling a flashing arrow sign intended to direct traffic around highway construction. The sign malfunctioned, so Perez stopped the truck and went back to fix the sign by manipulating its wires. A man named Alfonso Lerma, who had fallen asleep at the wheel of his car, drove into the sign. The impact of the crash caused Perez fatal injuries. The plaintiffs sued the sign's manufacturer, claiming that Perez would not have stopped his truck and thus would not have been struck if the sign had not malfunctioned. The trial court granted summary judgment for the defendant on the ground that an insufficient causal connection existed between the defendant's negligence and the accident. The plaintiff appealed. What result?

A. *Held*, for the defendant, that its negligence was too remote from the plaintiff's decedent's injury to sustain an action against it. Said the court:

> It is undisputed that Lerma was asleep, and proper operation of the flashing arrow sign would have had no effect on his conduct. Plaintiffs assert that, had the sign functioned properly, Perez would not have been at the place where the collision occurred at the time it occurred. We conclude that these particular circumstances are too remotely connected with Lear Siegler's conduct to constitute legal cause. If Perez had instead taken the sign back to the highway department office where the roof caved in on him, we likewise would not regard it as a legal cause.

The *Lear Siegler* case might be considered analogous to *Berry v. Sugar Notch Borough*.

Q. Hypothetical: in *J. Wigglesworth Co. v. Peeples*, 985 S.W.2d 659 (Tex. 1999), the defendant's employee, Kirby, was driving a truck carrying a mobile home on an interstate highway in Louisiana. His permit to carry the wide load required him to exit the highway at milepost 30, but he failed to do this and soon reached a bridge that was too narrow to accommodate him. The highway was one lane in each direction and there was no shoulder, so Kirby began trying to back his way toward the exit he had missed. This caused traffic to back up on the highway for almost 300 yards. At the end of the backup, behind forty to fifty other vehicles, was a truck driven by a man named Peeples. Peeples came to a halt, but the driver of an eighteen-wheeler behind Peeples was unable to stop, and ran into Peeples's truck, causing Peeples various injuries. Peeples sued the driver of the eighteen-wheeler; he also sued Kirby, the driver of the wide load, and Kirby's employer, Wigglesworth. The jury brought in a verdict against all of the defendants. Kirby and Wigglesworth appealed, claiming they were entitled to judgment as a matter of law because Kirby's negligence was too remotely connected to Peeples's injuries to be considered their proximate cause. What result?

A. *Held,* for the plaintiff, that the evidence was sufficient to support the verdict. But what is the distinction between *Lear Siegler, Inc. v. Perez* and *J. Wigglesworth Co. v. Peeples?* It's that making a defective sign does not create much increased likelihood that someone will be hit by a sleeping driver; but backing a truck down a highway does create an increased likelihood that someone will be injured, even if the injury occurs relatively far away. The distance between the negligence and the site of the accident is like the lapse of time in *Clark v. DuPont*—the case involving the pail of glycerine. It makes the cause look less "proximate" in a literal sense but doesn't disrupt legal causation because the harm that occurred still is of the same sort that made the defendant's act negligent. The court's analysis in *Wigglesworth*, however, is not terribly helpful:

> Unlike the situations in *Lear Siegler* [and other cases, including *Bell v. Campbell*], Kirby's negligence did not simply create a condition that made Peeples's injuries possible or cause Peeples to be in the wrong place at the wrong time. [....] [T]he connection between Kirby's act and Peeples's injuries was not too attenuated as a matter of law to constitute legal causation. As a result, we hold that the evidence was legally and factually sufficient for a rational juror to find that Kirby's negligence in missing his exit, blocking traffic, and backing up on the highway proximately caused Peeples's injuries.

Then there is the question of how *Bell v. Campbell* can be squared with the *Henry* case considered a moment ago, which also was from Texas; the court in *Henry* found *Bell* distinguishable, but wasn't clear about why.

SECTION C. LIMITATION OF DUTY: AN ALTERNATIVE APPROACH?

Of course you have to decide how much fuss to make over *Palsgraf*. If you want to spend a lot of time on it, the materials below provide plenty of angles to pursue. Either way, the three cases that follow it are discretionary, and can both be cut if you have had enough. But don't overlook the new Restatement language at the end of the chapter, which is useful for students to see.

Palsgraf v. Long Island R.R. (P hurt by consequences of explosion caused when D's employees try to help passenger onto train and knock his package loose; NL)

Q. Did the defendant in *Palsgraf* owe the plaintiff a duty of care?

A. Under the principles from the duty chapter, the defendant owed the plaintiff a duty owed by virtue of the special relationship of common carrier/passenger. This characterization is confusing when combined with Cardozo's analysis, however; for he characterizes the apparent absence of proximate cause as the absence of a duty to the plaintiff.

Q. What was the defendant's breach of duty/untaken precaution?

A. It is not especially clear from Cardozo's opinion. It seems that the defendant's railroad guards should have either stopped the passenger from boarding or more carefully helped the passenger board. Cardozo nevertheless admitted, perhaps grudgingly, that the record bound him to conclude that plaintiff had proved a breach of duty. Cardozo stressed the possibility of damage to the package that the guards could see that the passenger was carrying, which seems odd, because the passenger himself was also endangered by the guards' lack of care in helping him board the train. In any event, Cardozo premised his decision upon a finding below, supported by substantial evidence, that the defendant had committed a breach of duty.

Q. Would the facts satisfy the doctrines of foreseeability considered so far in this chapter?

A. Perhaps not; perhaps the type of harm that the plaintiff sustained was not the type that one would imagine could follow from the untaken precaution that was the defendant's breach of duty. The guards helping the passenger onto the train could not have anticipated that more care on their part would help reduce the risk of an injury from a scales to a passenger standing some distance away; it is hard to see a significant probabilistic relationship between carelessly helping a boarding passenger and an accident involving falling scales some distance away.

Q. If we view the case as Andrews did, what is the best analogy to it from the cases we already have considered?

A. Andrews would have allowed the jury to bring in a verdict for the plaintiff because the harm to her followed directly enough from the defendant's negligence, and because in seemed to Andrews foreseeable that knocking a package onto the tracks might cause an injury of some sort to those other passengers nearby, even if the details of this particular injury could not have been foreseen. The best analogy to support this argument might be to a case like *Henry* where the plaintiff hurt his shoulder after running out of a hole where he thought gas might explode and colliding with a telephone pole. In either case the defendant's original negligent act created a risk of eventual harm to others, though the details of the harm that occurred (the falling scales, or the shoulder injury) were not foreseeable in any detail.

Q. What is the practical difference between Cardozo's approach and the approach taken by Andrews?

A. The modern practical significance of the *Palsgraf* approach is not clear; the case frequently is cited sloppily by courts for the simple notion that foreseeability matters. Cardozo's framing of the issue as one of duty, however, would seem more likely than the Andrews approach to make the issue a question of law for the judge, rather than a question of fact for the jury. "Duty" questions under the *Palsgraf* can be sent to a jury if they are found to depend on close judgments about foreseeability, and questions of proximate cause can of course be answered by courts as a matter of law. But Cardozo's approach nevertheless would seem to tend—and sometimes has tended—toward questions of remoteness being more often decided by judges than is the case under the traditional "proximate cause" approach. The Third *Restatement* notes this in the excerpt at the end of the chapter. Cardozo's remains the minority approach.

Q. Suppose the man trying to board the train in *Palsgraf* had been carrying a Ming vase in his bag, and it had been smashed when it fell on account of the defendants' negligence. Liability for the value of the vase?

A. Calabresi thinks not, at any rate:

> [T]he defendant probably would not have been held liable for the extraordinary damages caused by the breakage, despite the basic common law rule imposing liability and despite the fact that the risk that made the defendant's behavior faulty in the first place was precisely the risk of damage to the package. Some courts would have found contributory negligence in this situation, others assumption of risk; whatever the terminology, the result appears foreordained and in accord with

market deterrence goals. Conversely, the person with the thin skull generally recovers for all his injuries even though his knowledge of the condition must be vastly superior to the defendant's. Knowledge without alternatives (adequate helmets do not exist; if they did, the cases might well be different) does not make a category of actor a cheap cost avoider. And placing liability on the plaintiff as a market deterrence incentive to *inform* potential defendants of the particular risk seems relatively useless in such cases since the defendant, by and large, will be a driver who could no readily receive the information. In contrast there are cases in which information *can* be given, as where signs are erected informing drivers that a nursing home is nearby or, to use the reverse case, where *adequate* warning of potential harms from the use of a product is given and the burden of making the cost-benefit analysis is thereby shifted to the plaintiff, who can no longer successfully claim that the harm resulted from a product defect.

Guido Calabresi, *Concerning Cause and the Law of Torts: An Essay for Harry Kalven, Jr.,* 43 U. Chi. L. Rev. 69 (1975).

Notes on the Palsgraf *case.* Instructors will differ in what they want to do with *Palsgraf.* The case is of course widely regarded as a theoretical landmark, so you may wish to talk about different scholarly views of its significance. Here is a somewhat lengthy look at a few notable attempts to assess *Palsgraf* that may provide fodder for classroom discussion, including longer excerpts from the same sources excerpted more briefly in the casebook:

a. G. Edward White, *Tort Law in America: An Intellectual History* 100-101 (2003), argues that both the majority and dissenting opinions in *Palsgraf* implicitly conceded that the case could not be solved by use of formal notions of causation inherited from the nineteenth century:

> Cardozo found causation inapposite as an analytic framework, and Andrews, while employing causation analysis, admitted that "proximate cause" was not doctrine, merely "practical politics." Cardozo's "duty-risk-relation" rationale, while suggesting that the use of doctrines in negligence was still a viable enterprise, abandoned the scientists' formulation of a universal civil duty that had been at the very core of orthodox negligence theory. Andrews's "universal duty" rationale appeared to be meaningless without consideration of the limits on "duties," which seemed, at least in the area of causation, to reduce themselves to the equitable claims of the parties in discrete fact situations.

> *Palsgraf* thus marked the end of conceptions of causation as a generalized legal doctrine and the emergence of conceptions of causation as an issue of public policy.

b. An economic defense of Cardozo's opinion was offered in Guido Calabresi, *Concerning Cause and the Law of Torts: An Essay for Harry Kalven, Jr.,* 43 U.Chi.L.Rev. 69 (1975). Calabresi's view is that Cardozo's approach in *Palsgraf* may not seem to make much sense from the standpoint of "collective" deterrence—in other words, from the standpoint of enforcing decisions made by the community about which acts should be avoided; for once such a prohibited deed has been done, why should anyone care *who* was hurt by it? But focusing on whether the plaintiff was foreseeable makes more sense to the extent that tort law engaged in "market deterrence"—in other words, to the extent the law tries to assign liability to the cheapest cost avoiders of harm so that *they* (rather than the community) can decide whether it's better to avoid the harm or pay for it. For in that case the unforeseeable plaintiff puts potential defendants in a hard spot: the defendant can't tell whether he himself is in a better position to prevent the harm than the plaintiff is, because he doesn't foresee the plaintiff at all. Courts in such cases should inquire into the parties' relative abilities to avoid the accident, and perhaps the manipulability of Cardozo's approach allows this. Well, but then why doesn't this view call for liability in *Palsgraf* itself, where the defendant was a cheaper cost avoider than the plaintiff? Maybe the answer is that Cardozo did care a bit about collective deterrence, one aspect of which is trying to ensure a rough proportionality between the defendant's wrong and the penalty for it. The flexibility of the "foreseeable plaintiff" test allows these worries to be given some effect, too.

c. In the earlier notes on the *Wagon Mound* cases, we saw Saul Levmore sketch a theory in which proximate cause rules can be used to put pressure on each of several tortfeasors. He applies the theory to the *Palsgraf* case as well:

> [A] novel and attractive way to think about [*Palsgraf*] is as another substitute for, or precursor to, comparative negligence. Arguably, there are two wrongdoers, the railroad and the fellow who carries around fireworks in a bag in a crowded public place. Cardozo might have liked to make both pay, perhaps by dividing the damages between these tortfeasors. But in a system where only one is to pay—and where it is plain that the railroad (if it continues to push and pull passengers aboard) will pay another day because the usual portfolio of bruised knees and broken limbs will come about—it is ingenious to let the railroad go free and to encourage Mrs. Palsgraf, or future plaintiffs like her, to sue the carrier of explosive fireworks. In this way, both tortfeasors will be penalized and deterred when all is said and done. Here we must look not to two cases decided by a single court, but rather to the single case before a court along with another that it contemplates (to be brought by a party yet unknown). The talk of the case may be about foreseeability, but that factor is more of a tool than the main point of the exercise.

Levmore, *The Wagon Mound Cases: Foreseeability, Causation, and Mrs. Palsgraf*, in Rabin and Sugarman, eds., Torts Stories 148 (2003).

d. In *Cardozo: A Study in Reputation* 37-46 (1993), Posner suggests that much of the fame of *Palsgraf* is attributable to Andrews' "inept" dissent, as it "conceded the legal high ground" to Cardozo with its talk of "practical politics"; it failed to challenge Cardozo's version of the facts; and it went on at great length, thus magnifying the importance of the difference between the two sides.

e. *Palsgraf* received fairly comprehensive condemnation in Gary Schwartz, *Cardozo as Tort Lawmaker*, 49 DePaul L. Rev. 305 (1999); Schwartz agrees with Cardozo's decision to deny liability, but records many misgivings about the opinion:

> One [complaint] concerns the finding of negligence. In the case, two employees had helped a passenger who was attempting to board a moving train. The passenger dropped a package—which turned out to contain explosives. The resulting explosion knocked over a scale some distance away, injuring the plaintiff who was standing near the scale. The jury found the railroad negligent, and the Appellate Division affirmed this finding. In doing so, the Appellate Division assumed that the railroad's negligence consisted of unreasonably endangering the passenger's own safety by shoving him towards the train when the railroad should instead have been discouraging him from boarding a moving train. For whatever reason, the Cardozo opinion rejects the Appellate Division's understanding. According to Cardozo, there was no risk at all to the passenger; the railroad's negligence consisted merely of unreasonably endangering the contents of the passenger's package. Yet so characterized, the negligence of the railroad is so peculiar, so artificial, and so unreal as to render *Palsgraf* a terrible vehicle for discussing the limitations on the liability of any genuinely negligent defendant.
>
> Secondly, the Cardozo opinion, having hinted at a theory that would exclude liability for unforeseeable outcomes, then limits that theory to the particular problem of the unforeseeable plaintiff. Indeed, the Cardozo opinion explicitly assumes, if only for the sake of argument, that if a foreseeable plaintiff suffers an altogether unforeseeable injury, the plaintiff can secure a

recovery. This arguendo assumption would apply to plaintiffs' claims in many important proximate cause cases. [Schwartz suggests that Cardozo's approach yields liability in Keeton's rat poison hypothetical.] [...]

Also, the Cardozo opinion, having narrowed the issue to that of the unforeseeable plaintiff, then indicates that the doctrine of proximate cause has nothing to do with the case. That doctrine is indeed "foreign" to the case—which instead turns exclusively on the issue of duty. All of this invites further criticism. By introducing a duty concept that is supposedly quite separate from a proximate cause concept, the Cardozo opinion prompts a long dissent by Andrews that discusses duty before it turns to proximate cause. Andrews' broad definition of duty makes it seem as though he is very strongly pro-liability. But when (and if) attention is finally focused on Andrews' treatment of proximate cause, his version of proximate cause turns out to be much less pro-liability than one might have assumed. [...] If, as Andrews states, proximate cause depends not on "logic" but rather on "expediency," "practical politics," "convenience," and "a rough sense of justice," then how in the world does a trial judge instruct the jury? Likewise, how does an appellate court determine whether a trial judge has ruled correctly? In any event, the analytic deficiencies and the anti-liability implications in Andrews' account of proximate cause are obscured by his more dramatic and unambiguous pro-liability pronouncements on the duty issue. These are pronouncements that could have been avoided altogether had Cardozo defined the issue properly as one of proximate cause rather than of duty—and had the case been fully debated in proximate cause terms. In fact, the two opinions join issue on the duty issue, a question which I regard as an irrelevancy. Worse yet, given Cardozo's emphasis on duty, there is simply no joinder on the issue of proximate cause.

To make a bad situation worse, the Cardozo opinion is replete with grandiloquent quasi-philosophical rhetoric that captures but also confounds the reader. There is not a word in the opinion that counts as genuine legal philosophy—that deals with the purpose or functions of the tort system. In his review of the Kaufman biography, Professor Goldberg calls Cardozo "conceptual," and applies this evaluation to the *Palsgraf* opinion. I think he is right in this. But Goldberg is wrong in referring to a "pragmatic conceptualism." Rather, the Cardozo conceptualism is pretentious and essentially arid.

f. Cardozo's opinion received a vigorous defense, however, in Benjamin Zipursky, *Rights, Wrongs, and Recourse in the Law of Torts*, 51 Vand. L. Rev. 1 (1998). He makes sense out of the foreseeable plaintiff doctrine by pointing to notions of rightful "recourse":

[O]ur institution of private rights of action embodies a "principle of civil recourse." According to this principle, an individual is entitled to an avenue of civil recourse—or redress—against one who has committed a legal wrong against her. This principle is a civilized transformation of what is often considered a quite primitive "instinct" of retributive justice, the instinct that I am entitled to "settle a score" or to "get even" with one who has wronged me. In a civilized society, we are not permitted to "get even"—we are entitled to a private right of action in place of getting even. But the quasi-retributive nature of recourse explains why there is a substantive standing requirement. A private right of action against another person is essentially a response to having been legally wronged by that person, and therefore exists only where the defendant has committed a legal wrong against the plaintiff and thus violated her legal right. [...]

Zipursky considers *Palsgraf* a key expression of this idea:

Palsgraf suggests the following question: Why is it not sufficient that [the plaintiff] has been tortiously harmed by the other? [...] Why is it not sufficient that the plaintiff has been foreseeably tortiously harmed by the defendant?

We can get an intuitive grasp of the answer to this question by returning to an earlier characterization of the substantive rule: A plaintiff may not recover unless the defendant's conduct was wrong relative to her. In short, she may not recover unless the defendant breached a tort duty to her or wronged her (relative to the set of wrongs designated under the tort law). If the defendant wronged a third party, but not the plaintiff, then that plaintiff has no right to recover. Why should this be so? The answer is that entitlement to recourse does not spring from the need precipitated by injury. It springs from the affront of being wronged by another. Because one should not have to suffer that affront passively, without response, fairness requires that one have recourse against the wrongdoer. Substantive standing cases are ones in which the plaintiff is injured, but she has not suffered the affront of being wronged by defendant. Thus, while she may have the need for compensation, she does not have a right to act against the defendant.

Behind Cardozo's adherence to the substantive standing rule in *Palsgraf* lies the idea of civil recourse. "One who seeks redress at law does not make out a cause of action by showing without more that there has been damage to his person;" to be entitled to redress, reasoned Cardozo, one must show not just a harm to oneself, but an "[a]ffront to personality." Such an affront is "the keynote of the wrong." Noting that the medieval trespass action is the historical basis of negligence, he wrote that, originally, "trespass did not lie in the absence of aggression, and that direct and personal." Cardozo clearly viewed a plaintiff's right of action as an opportunity to redress, and thereby to vindicate, the violation of rights she has endured, and not as an opportunity to gain compensation for the harm she has suffered. And that is precisely what he says as he concludes his analysis in *Palsgraf*: "The victim does not sue derivatively, or by right of subrogation, to vindicate an interest invaded in the person of another. Thus to view his cause of action is to ignore the fundamental difference between tort and crime. He sues for breach of a duty owing to himself."

Cardozo's mention of the distinction between tort and crime provides another clue as to why his opinion often seems odd to modern scholars. In his insistence that Mrs. Palsgraf lacks standing to sue for a wrong to another, Cardozo appears to display a rejection of torts as an arena of public law, and this apparent rejection seems especially counterintuitive on the facts of *Palsgraf*: If the trainman acted wrongly, why not sanction him? And if Mrs. Palsgraf needed compensation, why not compensate her? When we picture tort law as a form of social insurance funded by sanctions imposed upon wrongdoers, or when we picture it as a form of regulation whose proceeds are used to compensate the injured, the case seems wrongly decided. As I have argued above, however, such an instrumental perspective is incapable of taking into account huge areas of tort doctrine, not just *Palsgraf*. What is so striking about Palsgraf, however, is the explicit recognition, by this highly esteemed common law judge, that tort law is not just about deterrence and compensation. Cardozo seems to be rejecting one of the most widely accepted of Holmes's insights; he seems to be denying that tort law is really a form of public law.

The model I have offered suggests that this conclusion misses the mark. For Cardozo, tort law was both more public and more private than Holmes recognized. Insofar as tort law is about enforcement—rights of action—it is indeed more of a private matter than instrumentalists maintain. In recognizing a private cause of action against a defendant, the state is not necessarily endorsing the view that justice or efficiency or avoidance of social harm will be better served if the defendant is required to pay the plaintiff compensatory damages under these circumstances. While these considerations undoubtedly play important roles within our system, the root justification for a private right of action is the idea that the plaintiff whose legal rights were invaded by the defendant is entitled to act against the defendant through the state, by having the state enforce a judgment against the defendant on her behalf. The justice in the enforcement of private law lies in recognizing in those who are aggrieved a right to recourse against those who wronged them. It does not lie in the justice of bringing about a state of affairs that is optimal from a social point of view, whether corrective, distributive, or economic considerations provide the criteria of optimality.

Zipursky thus disapproves treatment of *Palsgraf* as a case about proximate cause:

[O]ur scholarly tradition's treatment of *Palsgraf* is profoundly ironic. It has accepted the dissent's characterization of the issue in the case as one of proximate cause, and then it has read that issue back into the opinion of the court and understood the court to have resolved the issue in the opposite way from the dissent. In other words, scholars accept that *Palsgraf* is a proximate cause case, as Andrews said, but plaintiff loses, so Cardozo must be merely denying the existence of proximate cause in this particular instance. This is an odd way to read any case, especially a central case of our torts canon. While the traditional "proximate cause" reading of *Palsgraf* may be consistent with the outcome of the case, it is the reasoning of the case that imbues it with general importance in torts, not its outcome. The standard interpretation completely misses this reasoning. Cardozo had nothing to say about proximate cause; for him, this was crucially not a proximate cause case, and he was willing to assume arguendo that Andrews was correct about proximate cause. Thus, neither of the famous opinions in the case agrees with—or even presents—the argument most commonly attributed to it.

Some scholars and courts have essentially retained the traditional interpretation of the opinion, but avoided the awkwardness of calling *Palsgraf* a proximate cause case by instead using the label "duty." According to this view, Cardozo believed that injuries not reasonably foreseeable should not generally be recoverable, but he knew that they were frequently tolerated as part of consequential damages. However, where the plaintiff is in a category of persons whose sole injury is unforeseeable, a floodgates rationale applies fully, and the plaintiff should therefore be denied a right of action entirely. This conclusion is put by saying that the defendant has no duty to this plaintiff.

This relabeled proximate cause argument is problematic for the same reasons as was the proximate cause argument by its proper name: It attributes to Cardozo a view of the central issue of the case that he explicitly rejected, that the dissent recognized that Cardozo rejected, and that the dissent did embrace. It adds insult to injury by suggesting that Cardozo's denials are subterfuge, and the label of "duty" is brought in to cover his work. And it fails to address Cardozo's central propositions pertaining to the relational nature of negligence and the need for a "relational wrong" in order to have a right of action.

For more discussion in a similar vein, see John C.P. Goldberg, *The Life of the Law*, 51 Stan. L Rev. 1419 (1999); and also Ernest Weinrib, *The Passing of Palsgraf?* 54 Vand. L. Rev. 803 (2001), and Weinrib, *The Idea of Private Law* 159-67 (1995). Weinrib's defense is based on notions of corrective justice that are congenial to, though distinct from, the approaches taken by Zipursky and Goldberg.

Edwards v. Honeywell, Inc. (fireman falls through floor of burning house because D delayed in reporting the fire to the fire station; NL)

Widlowski v. Durkee Foods (D's employee becomes delirious and bites off P's finger; NL)

Wagner v. International Ry. Co. (P falls and injures himself while trying to rescue his cousin, who was injured by D; L)

Q. Is there any reason why the policy goals the court describes in *Edwards* would be better advanced by holding that the defendant had no duty to the plaintiff than by saying that the defendant's conduct was not the proximate cause of the plaintiff's injuries?

A. Treating it as a question of duty makes it more likely to be decided by the judge as a matter of law and thus probably makes advancement of the policy goals more certain. Whether it affects the outcome in *Edwards* is unclear; even if the issue there had been regarded as one of proximate cause, it still might have been disposed of by the court without use of a jury.

Q. Does it make any practical difference in *Edwards* whether the court uses the *Palsgraf* approach or a more traditional proximate cause approach?

A. Probably not, as just suggested; this would almost certainly be a case of no liability even in a jurisdiction that didn't follow *Palsgraf*. Partly this is for reasons separate from the *Palsgraf* issues: there were doubts about factual causation; the privity doctrine might have doomed the plaintiff's case from the start; and then the court also mentions arguable extensions of the "fireman's rule." Cases of this general factual type usually fail for one of those reasons—most often factual causation. The more common version of the fact pattern arose in old cases where the phone company failed to promptly put through a plaintiff's call to a fire department; the resulting suits against the phone company frequently fail for multiple reasons described both as failures of proximate cause and failures to show that more timely action would have prevented the damage—resulting in conclusions that the plaintiff's claims are too "remote and speculative." There is a roundup of much of the old case law in *Foss v. Pac. Telephone & Telegraph Co.*, 173 P.2d 144 (Wash. 1946).

  Edwards differs from the pattern just described because this was a specialized alarm company, not a phone company (a difference that would seem to cut in favor of liability here), but also because the party hurt was not the party requesting help but rather the party attempting a rescue (which might cut against liability).   If we assume away all issues except proximate causation, the outcome on that score thus isn't entirely clear. The defendant's negligence did make it more likely that the floor would be weakened and that someone—perhaps a fireman—would be hurt. Is this case thus a little like *Petition of Kinsman*? The immediately foreseeable result of the negligence would be harm to the burning building and those who live there, and one could try to limit liability to those results, treating the fireman's injury here like the hypothetical injury described in *Kinsman* when the doctor can't reach his patient when the bridge over the Buffalo River went down. But this case is a little different because the fireman was foreseeable as a rescuer. After all, the fire was burning when Honeywell screwed up (unless it screwed up earlier by recording the wrong phone number in its records—but since it was an alarm company, the consequences of its screw-ups for firefighters might have been foreseeable enough even then). Still, proximate cause requirements often are used to implement doubts courts have about the policy consequences of allowing liability in certain circumstances, and that's probably how they would be used here as well—much as Posner uses the duty requirement in *Edwards*.

Q. What does the *Widlowski* decision owe to Cardozo's opinion in *Palsgraf*?

A. It seems like a case that cites *Palsgraf* and follows its language ("no duty" to the plaintiff; negligence in the air won't do; etc.) without necessarily owing much to it. First of all, the same result might as well have been reached on the ground that it was not foreseeable that failing to clean the tank and equip the employee would have led to a raised likelihood of someone suffering an injury like the nurse did. If you make the issue one of whether there was a duty *to her*, then the implication is (isn't it?) that there might well be liability if Wells had bitten off the finger of a colleague whose existence and presence was entirely foreseeable. But perhaps the real reason there's no liability isn't that the nurse was unforeseeable. It's that the idea that Wells would bite *anyone's* finger off was an unforeseeable consequence of failing to clean the tank. In any event, despite its attention to *Palsgraf* the court seems to focus on the fact that the result here might be classified as "freakish" and "fantastic," and on the "public policy" problem that would arise if Durkee were held liable to medical personnel over whom it had no control. These are concerns that probably equally could be given effect through an ordinary foreseeability analysis not keyed to the relationship between the plaintiff and defendant. But again, maybe styling it a question of duty makes it easier for the court to decide the issue for itself and order the dismissal of the complaint.

Q. Is Cardozo's decision in *Wagner v. International Ry. Co.* consistent with his opinion in *Palsgraf*? What is the distinction between *Wagner v. International Ry. Co.* and *Edwards v. Honeywell, Inc.*?

A. Cardozo considers rescuers to be foreseeable plaintiffs as a categorical matter; so if Herbert's injury was foreseeable, so was the plaintiff's. Posner's view is that the case is similar to *Eckert* in the chapter on the negligence standard: the rescue was in the best interests of the railroad, since it stood to be held liable for unrescued victims of its negligence.

Putting *Palsgraf* to one side, Grady would classify *Wagner* as a "DCE" case where a defendant's negligence creates opportunities for additional negligence or emergency responses for which the defendant remains liable. But the rescue attempt has to be reasonable; if the plaintiff was reckless, this would end the railroad's liability ("Rescue could not charge the company with liability if rescue was condemned by reason"). The theory would be that when an original wrongdoer's original act of negligence is compounded by *extraordinary* negligence, the original wrongdoer generally is off the hook.

You also can view this is a case where contributory negligence may be forgiven in an emergency. But the emergency doctrine itself doesn't really apply here; there was time here for reflection, as the court said, and the railroad's liability remains intact nevertheless.

CHAPTER 7

STRICT LIABILITY

SECTION A. LIABILITY FOR ANIMALS

The chapter starts with a few cases illustrating how courts distinguish between animals *ferae naturae* (for which liability is strict) and *mansuetae naturae* (liability only with scienter—i.e., knowledge of the animal's vicious tendencies, similar to liability for negligence). *Behrens* covers this, and then *Earl* and *Candler* offer additional examples of how the sorting rules work. Next come two cases (*Smith* and *Banks*) on the law's handling of domestic animals—the one bite rule, etc. *Vaughan* is meant to pursue the question of the theory behind strict liability and its possible influence on activity levels. Last are three cases (*Bostock-Ferari, Baker,* and *Opelt*) on the limits (or non-limits) of liability once an animal is found to be in the strict liability category—a theme that can be tied back into *Behrens*. Last is a problem involving a traveling salesman that ties some of those limits together. If you want intricacies, you can explore how and why the law gives different treatment to the two different types of animals in the strict-liability category: those belonging to a vicious species and those who have shown themselves to be individually vicious (another theme introduced by *Behrens*). All these doctrines are of some interest in themselves, but the greatest value of these materials is that they provide a nice way to introduce the logic of strict liability. At the end of this part of the manual there are some hypotheticals that allow you to explore some of the doctrinal issues in more detail.

This section can fill a class day, particularly when the hypotheticals below are used. For shortened coverage, you can just go with *Behrens*; most of the interesting issues can be gradually derived from it.

Behrens v. Bertram Mills Circus, Ltd. (D's elephant tramples P's booth at circus; L)

There are two issues in the case, and they can be used to anchor the discussion of much of the rest of the section. The first issue is whether elephants, and especially *this* elephant, should be classified as *ferae naturae*. The second issue is how far liability extends once an animal is placed in that category.

Q. *Why* does the court say there is strict liability for damage done by elephants? Why isn't negligence an adequate and appropriate rule to cover such damage?
A. This is meant to provoke general discussion. Consider various possible rationales: that it is negligent or at least suspect to decide to own an elephant (or other potentially dangerous animals; the more common case is the dog known to be a biter); that unlike many activities, owning an elephant can't be made safe by the use of due care (true? what does this really mean?); that, relatedly, we may want to put pressure not only on decisions about how carefully to conduct the activity of ownership, but also on decisions to engage in the activity at all rather than a safer substitute. In connection with these points you can point out that in Burma an elephant is (was) regarded as a domestic animal, liability for which is not strict. *Maung Kyan Dun v. Ma Kyian*, 2 Upper Burma Rulings, Civ. 570 (1900). This can be understood as reflecting the greater practical value the animals have there because of the ways they are used—as opposed to England, where they are kept strictly for their entertainment value. But then why denigrate the entertainment value of elephants, which can be such great fun? Perhaps because there are simpler substitutes for that entertainment value (there are lots of ways to put on a circus) than there are for the services provided by farm animals.

General notes. The Third Restatement seems ready to take a slightly more liberal approach than *Behrens* did in defining the categories into which animals are sorted. From §22:

> *Comment c.* [...] So long as a category of animals is wild, there is no requirement that the plaintiff prove the defendant's knowledge of the danger posed by the particular animal. Indeed, in some instances the defendant may understandably believe that a particular animal (for example, a monkey or chimpanzee) has been rendered tame by having lived in a particular household for many years. This belief does not defeat strict liability under this section. If a category of animal is wild, there is an ongoing risk that a particular animal, though seemingly tamed, will revert to the characteristics of the category itself. A "category" of animal is ordinarily a "species" of animal, as that term is commonly employed. Thus, a particular species of the genus of snakes, such as rattlesnakes and boa constrictors, may be wild, while other species of snakes—such as garter snakes—are not. "Category" however, should be sensibly defined, and at times permits distinctions among sub-species. For example, there may be a clear line, for purposes of the likelihood of causing physical injury, between male bucks and female does.

From the Reporter's Notes:

> *Comment b. Wild animals.* [...] The Restatement Second of Torts (§507, Comment c) accepts the idea that, if a category of animals is undomesticated and wild, the fact that a particular animal has lived with a household over a period of years in a way that has seemingly tamed the animal does not create an exception to the strict-liability rule. The defendant "may reasonably believe that [the animal] has been so tamed as to have lost all those [dangerous] propensities; nevertheless he takes the risk that at any moment the animal may revert to and exhibit them." Strict liability remains even if the particular animal's departure from its own ordinary tameness is "sudden and unexpected." [...] Section 22 follows the Second Restatement in not recognizing any exception for particular wild animals that allegedly have become tamed. Certain recent cases suggest that some wild animals—but not others—are capable of being rendered tame in a way that would defeat strict liability. However, the line between wild and non-wild animals seems complicated enough; it would be undesirable to introduce a third and intermediate classification.

> *Comment d. Rationale.* Professor George Fletcher identifies the reciprocity of risktaking as an important criterion for strict liability; strict liability makes sense when one group imposes risks on the public at large, without being subjected to similar risks in return. George T. Fletcher, *Fairness and Utility in Tort Theory*, 85 Harv. L. Rev. 537 (1972). Fletcher then explains the wild-animal strict-liability rule as stemming from the nonreciprocity criterion. Judge Posner explains the strict-liability rule by using the example of the person who keeps a tiger in the back yard; the purpose of strict liability is to give this person "an incentive to . . . consider seriously the possibility of getting rid of the tiger altogether." *G.J. Leasing Co. v. Union Elec. Co.*, 54 F.3d 379, 386 (7th Cir. 1995). This example relies on the perception that while courts routinely rule on the reasonableness of the precautions that parties should adopt, in negligence cases the issue of the defendant's decision to engage in an activity in the first place often eludes the attention of courts.

Earl v. Van Alstine (bees classified as mansuetae naturae)
Candler v. Smith (baboons classified as ferae naturae)

These cases are meant to illustrate the logic of the line between *ferae naturae* (wild animals whose owners are strictly liable for damage they cause) and *mansuetae naturae* (domesticated animals whose owners are liable if they are on notice that an individual animal has a mischievous disposition). It may help to draw a line on the chalkboard with one of those categories on each side; as you discuss various animals you can add them to one side or another. The different theories the courts use to sort animals into these categories—danger, usefulness—create a nice springboard for discussion of the underlying logic of strict liability; if an activity (e.g., beekeeping) is sufficiently useful, we don't want to pressure the owner to substitute to some other activity. Instead we expect plaintiffs to subsidize the costs created by the activity so long as it done with reasonable care.

Q. What is the distinction between *Earl v. Van Alstine* and *Candler v. Smith*? Why is there strict liability for baboons but not for bees? Which are more dangerous? Which are more useful?
A. Bees are much more useful than baboons: they serve important agricultural purposes. As to danger, naturally one has to consider the dangers not of individual bees but of hives of them; and in head-to-head combat, one might suppose the bees would have the edge over the baboon. But the important question, Hand formula style, is not just how much damage the animal can do but how likely it is to act up. Bees, as the court emphasizes, are very safe in the sense that they are unlikely to attack anyone when handled with due care.

Bees—or honeybees, at least—die after they sting; so there would be no occasion to decide whether the defendant in *Earl* would be held liable if these bees stung again. Whether he would be liable if his replacement bees stung another horse to death is a nice question; presumably so, since the dangerous decision seems to have been to keep the bees near the road.

Q. Hypothetical (or additional illustration): in *McQuaker v. Goddard*, 1 K.B. 687 (1940), the plaintiff had fed the defendant's camel three apples. When he tried to feed it a fourth, the camel bit and crushed his hand. The defendant presented several witnesses who had spent a great deal of time around camels; one of them testified that he had never heard of such a thing a wild camel, and went on to assert that the camel is so domesticated that it cannot copulate without the assistance of man. In affirming a judgment for the defendant, the court said:

> It was quite clearly established by the defendant's witnesses in my view that camels do not exist anywhere in the world today as wild animals. There is no race of wild camels which could be captured and tamed like elephants. [...] In every country where they exist they are domestic animals used for carrying either people or loads on their backs, or for draught purposes. [...] If an animal does not exist in a wild state in any part of the world, it has ceased altogether to be a wild animal, whether in England or in any other country.

Smith v. Pelah (L for dog owner when dog bites for the second time)
Banks v. Maxwell (bull gores farmhand; NL)
Vaughan v. Miller Bros. "101" Ranch Wild West Show (NL for injury inflicted by ape kept with due care)

Q. What theory of strict liability is implied by *Smith* and *Vaughan*? What is the distinction between them?
A. Both cases involve injuries inflicted by animals for which liability traditionally is strict, though the animals are in that category for different reasons—the dog in *Smith* because it has bitten before, and the ape in *Vaughan* because it is *ferae naturae*. In both cases, as well as in *Banks* and the excerpt from Exodus that it quotes, there is a sense that the imposition of strict liability implies a wrongful act on the defendant's part—not hanging the dog after the first bite, or (though the court in *Vaughan* rejected the argument) exhibiting apes and the like. Indeed, in some jurisdictions the rule governing animals has been described as a regime of negligence; it's just that the negligence is presumed in cases where the defendant owns a wild or vicious animal. This particular formulation has mostly been rejected—but why?

In any event, the distinction between the cases is that the court in *Vaughan* finds nothing wrong with exhibiting wild animals, whereas the court in *Smith* thinks there is something blameworthy in keeping a vicious dog. Perhaps the difference is that exhibitions of wild animals are regulated and in that sense condoned by the government. Or that zoos and circuses are safe if managed carefully. Or (a point related to both of the previous two) that strict liability puts pressure on people to consider changes in their activities—which we want owners of vicious dogs to do, but which we don't want owners of zoos to do; there is no presumptive social judgment in favor of replacing zoos with museums. But a majority of jurisdictions, notwithstanding *Vaughan*, still appear to hold zoos and circuses strictly liable for damage done by their wild animals.

The activity-level point allows the *Vaughan* case (and *Smith v. Pelah* as well) to be used to explore the economic theory of strict liability. When liability for an activity is governed by a rule of negligence, the usual assumption is that the activity is safe if it is done carefully—i.e., without negligence. But some activities, such as keeping a ferocious animal, may be dangerous to others even if undertaken carefully. In that case the best way to reduce the amount of harm done by the activity may be to do less of it, or do it elsewhere, or not do it at all. Economists refer to these as changes in activity levels, as opposed to changes in the level of care used in carrying out an activity. Strict liability pressures people to consider changing their activity levels because it requires them to pay for any damage the activity causes regardless of how much care they used to prevent it. If they find that their activities are causing damage despite their efforts to be careful, and grow tired of paying the resulting bills, they can scale back the activity altogether or conduct it someplace else. The application of the point to *Smith v. Pelah*:

> [O]nce a dog is known to be dangerous, the perceived probability of its biting people and hence the expected accident costs associated with the dog rise sharply. Yet as any dog owner knows, it is difficult to restrain a dog at all times. Because care alone may not suffice to avoid an accident, we want the owner of the animal to consider whether the animal is worth keeping—a point about activity level. If vicious dogs were so valuable that the prospect of having to pay repeated damages to victims of dog bites would never deter an owner from keeping such a dog, no allocative purpose would be served by imposing liability for a bite that could not have been prevented by greater care. But because a gentle dog is ordinarily a good substitute for a vicious one, imposing strict liability on the owner of a dangerous dog and thereby forcing him to consider whether the benefits of having such a dog exceed the full social costs may yield substantial allocative benefits.

Landes and Posner, The Economic Structure of Tort Law 108-109 (1987). Since strict liability gives people reason to think twice about whether to carry on an activity at all (even carefully), it also follows that the doctrine may not be well-suited for activities that have great utility or that create external benefits (i.e., benefits not wholly captured by the actor himself): we may not want people who carry out such activities to find something safer to do. Thus the result in Vaughan; see also *City and County of Denver v. Kennedy*, 476 P.2d 762 (Col. App. 1970).

Q. The court in *Banks* says that "The familiar rule of liability for injuries inflicted by cattle has remained approximately constant for more than 3,000 years." Is that true? (What work is done by the word "approximately"?)

A. The truth in the statement is that the law has always been hard on owners of animals who have shown themselves to be threats to humans. Nowadays, though, the owner would be held liable in tort, not put to death, and the animal would not be killed, either—unless the governing animal control ordinances called for its destruction. The rest of the relevant chapter of Exodus also makes for interesting reading: "If the ox shall push a manservant or maidservant; he shall give unto their master thirty shekels of silver, and the ox shall be stoned. [....] And if one man's ox hurt another's, that he die; then they shall sell the live ox, and divide the money of it; and the dead ox also they shall divide. Or if it be known that the ox hath used to push in time past, and his owner hath not kept him in; he shall surely pay ox for ox; and the dead shall be his own." Ex. 21: 31-32, 35-36.

As the *Behrens* opinion suggests, the strict liability that comes into play when a domestic animal is shown to be vicious may be more limited than the strict liability that applies to the owner of a wild animal such as an elephant or tiger. A dog owner's strict liability tends to apply just to damage the dog does that resembles whatever damage it previously has done. An owner of a tiger is more likely to be held strictly liable for *any* damage the animal does—subject to the limits in cases like *Bostock-Ferari*.

Bostock-Ferari Amusements v. Brocksmith (bear frightens horse; NL)
Baker v. Snell ("Go it, Bob"; L)
Opelt v. Al G. Barnes Co. (Leopard scratches boy who comes close to its cage; NL)
Gomes v. Byrne (dog bites Fuller brush salesman; NL)

Q. Why is there no liability in *Bostock-Ferari Amusements v. Brocksmithi*?
A. We are looking now at additional wrinkles that complicate a case once the background rule of strict liability is in place. The classification of bears as ferae naturae requires their owners to keep them secure or pay damages. Here the owner did keep the animal secure; it seemed important to the court that the owner had done everything practicable to keep the bear from threatening anyone—and had been effective. Thus liability here might not result in more care by the bear's owner. It more likely would result in the activity-level change of keeping the bear off the streets (this is the point of the court's concern that a finding of liability would mean that the bear's owner is not allowed to walk the animal down the street at all), or else getting rid of it altogether. The court does not favor this. Notice, therefore, the different rationales behind strict liability that we see here and in the dog cases. Though there is strict liability for damage done by bears, nobody is faulting the defendant for owning one; it is not a "wrongful act," in the sense that owning a vicious dog might be considered wrongful. (A possibility not discussed is that walking the bear down a public street might itself have been negligent. Why consider this a part of the defendant's "activity level" rather than just a decision which ought to be measured against the usual reasonableness standard?)

The other point the court emphasizes, which resembles the reasoning used in proximate cause cases considered elsewhere in the book, is that it was merely a coincidence that the horse was scared by a bear rather than by a bull (bulls being considered mansuetae naturae). Granted, something similar could have been said in *Behrens*: a bull might have been provoked just as easily as the elephant in that case, with the same factual result yet without liability. But whereas in *Bostock-Ferari* the defendant was the owner of the animal causing fright, in *Behrens* the defendant was the owner of the animal that was frightened. If a wild animal causes someone to be scared or shocked, liability has the downside of making it hard to display such animals. But if a wild animal is itself scared or shocked, as in *Behrens*, liability has the more positive effect of requiring the animal's owners to keep it away from situation where it may become frightened.

To put the point in *Brocksmith* differently, the harm caused by the bear has nothing to do with the reasons for treating it as ferae naturae and imposing strict liability. (But cf. Devlin's suggestion in *Behrens* that owners of wild animals are likely to be held liable for all harm their animals cause, including harm by fright—at least if it's a tiger frightening a person.)

Q. What is the analogy between *Baker v. Snell* and *Behrens v. Bertram Mills Circus, Ltd.*?
A. In both cases the bad behavior by the animal was triggered by someone other than its owner—the plaintiffs' manager in *Behrens*, and the potman in *Baker*. Elsewhere in the *Behrens* opinion (in a portion not printed in the casebook), Lord Devlin considered the argument that P (via Whitehead's dog, Simba) had provoked the elephant; he rejected this claim because the dog that snapped at Bullu did not belong to the plaintiffs. It belonged to their manager, over whom they had no control. Devlin took the view that

under *Baker v. Snell,* the provocation of the elephant by a third party could not relieve the elephant's owner from liability.

Q.   What is the superficial similarity between *Opelt v. Al G. Barnes Co.* and *Behrens v. Bertram Mills Circus, Ltd.?* What is the distinction between them?
A.   In both cases the plaintiffs knowingly put themselves near wild circus animals. But in *Behrens* the assumption of risk defense was rejected, mostly because the plaintiffs had not requested that their booth be placed near the elephants' path. Granted, the plaintiffs stayed there once they saw the elephants walking by, but they remained at a distance that reasonably appeared safe. In *Opelt* the plaintiff went too close to where the leopard was; the leopard was where it was supposed to be. In *Behrens,* the plaintiffs were where they were supposed to be, at least so far as the defendant had indicated, and the elephant came to them.

Q.   What if the child in *Opelt* had opened the gate to the leopard's cage, and the leopard had exited and hurt another patron? What result in a suit against the circus?
A.   It's probably a case of liability. The assumption of risk defense available against the child doesn't carry over to others. Again, the obvious authority here is *Baker* or perhaps *Behrens,* where the elephants were excited by a dog under the control of neither the plaintiffs nor the defendant; liability was intact anyway. There is an analogy to other situations where the law only allows a third party to collect from a defendant—e.g., states where a social host can be sued if a drunken guest runs over a third party in his car, but cannot be sued by the drunken guest himself. Our greatest disapproval is for the guest (or at the patron who approaches the cage), and so they collect nothing; but an innocent third party can collect from either the guest or the host (or either from the boy or from the circus in the hypothetical considered here).

  Opelt is intended to illustrate the exception to strict liability for cases involving assumption of risk. The intersection of these doctrines is interesting, and the materials below provide some more questions and hypotheticals you can use to explore it if you have time. If you are going to cover the chapter on assumption of risk, you will find another case there (*Cohen*) illustrating the same point in a slightly different context: no liability for the owner of a dog when it bites a veterinarian inspecting the animal preparatory to neutering it.

Q.   What result in *Gomes v. Byrne?*
A.   No liability. Said the court:

> Under these circumstances, the risk was obvious. Notwithstanding the dog's display of hostility, plaintiff elected to leave his place of safety upon the public sidewalk and to enter upon defendant's enclosed private property. In so doing, he voluntarily exposed himself to the obvious hazard. It was a calculated risk on plaintiff's part, or, as he expressed it, one of the "hazards of the game." We therefore conclude that the trial court's finding that plaintiff assumed that risk is amply supported by the evidence.

Carter, J., dissented, and added some interesting facts:

> The dog was a small dog about a foot high and was not one of the breeds known to be either vicious by nature or normally thought to be vicious or dangerous. Throughout the trial, in fact, defendant's counsel, apparently attempting to underplay the fact that the dog bit the plaintiff, referred to it as 'the little dog.' Also, no signs had been posted warning of the dog. As has been pointed out above, the only evidence upon which the finding of actual knowledge is based is that the dog barked at the plaintiff.

In *Gomes,* as in most such cases, the court also held that the dog-bite statute did not abrogate common-law defenses to such claims, such as assumption of risk. There is an analogy to cases like *Tedla v. Ellman* (in the section of the casebook covering negligence per se), where a statute that displaces a common law rule is not read to abrogate the common law exceptions and other doctrines that went along with it.

You can follow up on *Gomes* with some of the related hypotheticals that follow.

Q. What if a dog known to be vicious bites a trespasser?

A. This is a common and important exception to strict liability for vicious animals. *Woodbridge v. Marks,* in the chapter on the privileges to defend one's property, is an example that might bear revisitation if you have covered it. For the general point see sec. 511 of the Restatement (Second): "A possessor of land is not subject to strict liability to one who intentionally or negligently trespasses upon the land, for harm done to him by . . . an abnormally dangerous domestic animal that the possessor keeps on the land, even though the trespasser has no reason to know that the animal is kept there." Not all jurisdictions go along with this; some of them condition the exception on the dog being suitably restrained, and even then some others remain unforgiving. See Annotation, Liability of owner of dog known by him to be vicious for injuries to trespasser, 64 A.L.R.3d 1039 (1975).

Q. What if a dog known to be vicious bites someone who is not a trespasser—a licensee, let us assume (if you have covered that distinction)—but who saw a "Beware of Dog" (or "Trespassers Will Be Eaten") sign at the front of the defendant's property?

A. These tend to be cases of no liability on the same reasoning as *Gomes*, but the treatment of the classic traveling salesman bitten by a dog depends on the details. Thus from *Burke v. Fischer*, 182 S.W.2d 638 (Ky. App. 1944):

> The rule generally is that there is no liability where a wrongful act of the injured person contributed to the injury. Even where warning signs are posted on the place, the owner of the known bad dog is not to be exempted from liability to one who is rightfully on the premises. If, however, a person with knowledge of the propensities of the dog, wantonly excites him, or voluntarily and unnecessarily places himself in position to be attacked, he will be held to have brought on the injury and ought not to be entitled to recover. "The correct rule of liability therefore seems to be that the owner cannot be relieved from it by any act of the person injured, unless it be one from which it can be affirmed that he caused the injury himself, with a full knowledge of its probable consequences." 2 Am.Jur. 743, §

But see also *Jones v. Manhart*, 585 P.2d 1250 (Ariz. App. 1978). In that case the plaintiff was a door-to-door solicitor who visited the defendant's house to survey the "female head of the household" for her views of a chicken coating product. On the way onto the property she saw a sign depicting a dog's head with teeth bared saying "Trespassers will be eaten." After determining that the female head of the household was not home, the plaintiff started to leave, but she was overtaken and bitten by the defendant's dog. She was held entitled to recover because the sign reasonably could have been interpreted as a joke.

The facts and result were instructively different in *Benton v. Aquarium, Inc.,* 489 A.2d 549 (Md. App. 1985), where the plaintiff was bitten by the defendant's German Sherpherd while making a delivery to the defendant's warehouse:

> Posted on the door to the warehouse was a sign with a drawing of a bulldog with its mouth wide open as it sneeringly displayed a grid of sharp, large canines. The sign boldly proclaimed "TRESPASSERS WILL BE EATEN." Posted on the door of the office was another sign with a drawing of a bulldog wearing a guard's hat. The sign advised, "GUARD DOG ON DUTY." [...] Mr. Benton admitted that while in the waiting area, he had observed the signs on each of the doors. Not truly believing the signs, however, he knocked on the warehouse door, heard muffled voices, opened the door, walked inside, and was attacked by the dog. Just before the dog rushed at Mr. Benton, foreman Brad Lieberman, Barbara Spinks, Mr. Cohen and his father, yelled in

unison, "Get out! There's a dog in here!" The dog's canines pierced the center of Norman Benton's left hand and caused profuse bleeding and progressive pain. [...]

The court held that the plaintiff might have been excused for disregarding the "Trespassers Will Be Eaten" sign—but not the other one:

> Objectively evaluating Mr. Benton's conduct, we believe that it was unreasonable for him to conclude that the posted warnings were not to be taken seriously. In fact, he admitted that the sign that read, "GUARD DOG ON DUTY," which was posted on the office door, was not intended as a joke. Indeed, Mr. Benton testified, "That would be kind of dumb of me if I saw a sign that said, 'GUARD DOG ON DUTY,' not to think it was put there for a reason." Had Mr. Benton equally heeded the sign on the warehouse door, which he must as a normal intelligent person be held to have understood and appreciated, there would not have been a risk of injury. We conclude that, under the facts and circumstances of this case, Mr. Benton voluntarily left his place of safety and crossed the threshold of danger that he should have known and appreciated. We hold that the trial court properly granted appellees' motion for a directed verdict on the theory that Mr. Benton had assumed the risk of being injured.

Q. Hypothetical (regarding provocation): in *Van Bergen v. Eulberg*, 82 N.W. 483 (Iowa 1900), the plaintiff threw sticks and stones at a dog—then was bitten by the animal a few months later. Liability for the owner?
A. The court thought so: "A dog has no right to brood over its wrongs, and remember in malice. The only defense available to the dog's master is the doing of an unlawful act, at the time of the attack, by the person injured." Actively antagonizing a dog, even a vicious one, thus can leave the owner free from liability for the result if it follows soon enough.

Q. Hypothetical (regarding owned and unowned animals): in *Nicholson v. Smith*, 986 S.W.2d 54 (Tex. App. 1999), a man named Nicholson was staying in his trailer at an RV camp in rural Texas. The plaintiff's evidence was that while Nicholson was working under the trailer, he was attacked by fire ants and stung more than 1,000 times, leading to his death. Liability for the camp?
A. The point of the hypo is that this is a negligence case—at least so long as the ants had not been reduced to the possession and control of the landowner. The rules about strict liability only apply to animals intentionally owned by the defendant; when it comes to unwelcome animals, including the insects here, the property owner's obligations are matters of due care—at most. Here was the court's analysis in this case (affirming summary judgment for the defendants):

> The law with regard to *ferae naturae* under a strict liability cause of action is well-settled: a landowner can only be held liable for the acts of wild animals against invitees upon its lands if the landowner has reduced the animal to his or her possession and control, or introduced a non-indigenous animal into the area. With regard to a negligence claim, however, the law is slightly more nebulous. Although most courts which have considered the issue recognize the possibility that a claim for negligence may not be precluded by ferae naturae per se, the majority of cases, including all of the Texas cases, have refused to find that the landowner owed the invitee a duty with regard to the acts of wild animals on its premises. Even though courts generally agree that they may impose a duty on a premises owner, few have actually done so. [...]
>
> Nicholson was attacked by indigenous wild animals in their natural habitat, in the normal course of their existence. The [defendants] did nothing to cause the fire ants to act outside of their expected and normal behavior. Nicholson was not injured while in an artificial structure, nor was he injured where fire ants would not normally be found, nor was the presence of the fire ants due to any affirmative or negligent act of the Smiths bringing them upon the property or drawing

them to the area where Nicholson was parked. In fact, Smith testified that he regularly attempted to kill or drive away the fire ants. Presumably Nicholson chose to stay at the Choke Canyon RV park, as opposed to a hotel, in rural South Texas because he wanted to enjoy the natural environment. His injury, although tragic, was incident to his enjoyment of the natural land. Nature, in Texas, is a rich mixture. A great deal of it is compatible with human happiness and safety. But some is not. Nature is not tamed in Texas and those who seek the outdoors are exposed to its dangers. A good deal of the vegetation in Texas stings, sticks or stinks. Any number of insects and animals can hurt, or even kill you.

We do not say a landowner can never be negligent with regard to the indigenous wild animals found on its property. A premises owner could be negligent with regard to wild animals found in artificial structures or places where they are not normally found; that is, stores, hotels, apartment houses, or billboards, if the landowner knows or should know of the unreasonable risk of harm posed by an animal on its premises, and cannot expect patrons to realize the danger or guard against it. See, e.g., *DeLuce v. Fort Wayne Hotel*, 311 F.2d 853, 857 (6th Cir. 1962) (remanding for new trial where presence of rats in the alley adjoining hotel and on sidewalk in front of created fact question on hotel operator's duty to protect guests from foreseeable event that such rats might enter hotel through its doors); *Carlson v. State*, 598 P.2d 969, 974-75 (Alaska 1979) (reversing summary judgment and remanding for trial on fact issues of State's knowledge of bears' presence, danger posed by them, and foreseeability of attack in location where trash was left uncollected); *CeBuzz, Inc. v. Sniderman*, 171 Colo. 246, 466 P.2d 457, 459 (Colo.1970) (finding that defendant's knowledge of presence of banana tarantulas in last shipment of bananas delivered to store gave rise to liability for bite to shopper)[. ...]

Under ordinary circumstances, Texas landowners do not have a duty to warn their guests about the presence and behavior patterns of every species of indigenous wild animals and plants which pose a potential threat to a person's safety, as well as the extent of that threat. If a landowner was required to affirmatively disclose all risks caused by plants, animals, and insects on his or her property, the burden on the landowner would be enormous and would border on establishing an absolute liability. We do not say that there never can be such a case. But this case fits within the rule, not the exception.

Fire ants, by legal definition, are indigenous wild animals, and, without more, they do not pose an unreasonable risk of harm in their natural habitat. Nicholson was not injured while in an artificial structure, nor was he injured where fire ants would not normally be found. The presence of the fire ants was not caused by any affirmative or negligent act of the Smiths. Indeed, Smith tried to control them, and there was uncontroverted summary judgment evidence that Nicholson was aware of their presence.

SECTION B. RYLANDS V. FLETCHER

These materials can be approached on several levels. First is the challenge of grasping the various meanings that courts in England and America have assigned to *Rylands v. Fletcher*. Another is to use the cases to think about various rationales for strict liability: situations where victims have weak or no precautions available to prevent the harm; situations involving non-reciprocal risks (i.e., risks imposed by the defendant on the plaintiff but not vice versa); activities that are dangerous even when conducted carefully; activities conducted in inappropriate places, making it seem desirable to put pressure on the actor to consider an activity-level change (i.e., moving it elsewhere). These rationales can then be traced into Restatement §520 in the subsequent section of the chapter.

The first batch of cases illustrates how *Rylands* was interpreted by English courts; the second batch offers examples of its reception and interpretation in the United States. At the end of this section of the manual are some excerpts from Brian Simpson's interesting work on the background and consequences of *Rylands*.

For abbreviated coverage, you can go straight from *Rylands* to the American cases discussing it.

Rylands v. Fletcher (exploding reservoir; L)
Crowhurst v. Burial Board of Amersham (poisonous yew grows from D's property within reach of P's horse; L)
Rickards v. Lothian (trespasser stops up sinks, which overflow; tenant sues owner; NL)
Musgrove v. Pandleis (L for fire in car garage when automobiles still were new technology)
Balfour v. Barty-King (blowlamp starts fire that spread to P's property; L)

Q. What is the difference between the Blackburn and Cairns opinions in *Rylands*?
A. Blackburn's is a simpler rule that holds landowners liable if they bring things onto their land for their own purposes that may cause mischief if they escape. Cairns adds the idea that strict liability applies to non-natural uses of land—a contextual inquiry with unclear dimensions.

Q. What does "non-natural" mean?
A. There is no single answer to this question, of course; it's intended to get the students to put forward some candidates that can be explored in the subsequent cases: man-made? Uncommon? Inappropriate to the place where the activity is being conducted?

Q. Does strict liability make sense on the facts of *Rylands*? If so, why?
A. A good discussion here will begin to raise some of the factors that end up being used in Restatement §520 (explored in the next section of the chapter). You can also introduce the idea of reciprocal risks and the presence of absence of good victim precautions.

Q. So far as the court in *Crowhurst* is concerned, whose statement of *Rylands* authoritative: the Blackburn version or the Cairns version?
A. Blackburn's. This is clear from the court's citation of the Exchequer Chamber's (i.e., Blackburn's) decision in *Rylands*; perhaps it also follows from the application of the rule to these facts, for it might be hard to consider planting a yew to be a "non-natural use" of the defendant's property. This case seems to treat *Rylands* pretty much as resting on the "sic utere" maxim.

Q. What is the logic of strict liability in *Crowhurst*?
A. Maybe it's that the case amounted to a kind of trespass. Still, if the defendant was using reasonable care to keep the yew under control, why should liability be strict? Maybe because the defendant is the only one in a position to know that the plant is poisonous; thus he will generally be in position to most cheaply prevent incidents of this sort.

Q. What is the distinction between *Rylands v. Fletcher* and *Rickards v. Lothian*?
A. Both cases involved accumulations of water on the defendant's property that subsequently escaped. But in *Rickards* the accumulation was a matter (as the Restatement later would say) of "common usage"—perhaps making it "natural" under *Rylands*. A policy point might be that we have no desire to put pressure on the defendant in *Rickards* to consider a change in activity levels. (We might want him to take more precautions against miscreants, but that sort of pressure can be created with a suit for negligence.) The water in the lavatory also was supplied in part for the plaintiff's benefit, so the "for his own purposes" part of Blackburn's formulation may not be satisfied; this was not a case where the defendant was imposing risks on a hapless and uncompensated defendant. Finally, here a third party

intervened deliberately; that was not so in *Rylands*. Does this matter? Cf. *Baker v. Snell* in the previous section of the chapter.

Q. What is the distinction between *Musgrove v. Pandelis* and *Rickards v. Lothian*?

A. The accumulation in the defendant's garage in *Musgrove* was for the benefit of the defendant, not the plaintiff. *Musgrove* also involved a new technology, and one not in common use—at least to the extent that it is today. New technologies might be considered good candidates for strict liability because they are unlikely to yet be matters of common usage, so the risks they impose are unlikely to be reciprocal. And when technology is young, its dangers may not be fully understood and care in using it thus may be no guarantee of safety.

Q. Which approach to understanding *Rylands* does the court appear to take in the *Balfour* case: the Blackburn approach or the Cairns approach?

A. The Cairns approach—though the case presumably comes out the same way under either formulation. The court focuses on the inappropriateness of using a blow-lamp in this place and under these circumstances.

Q. What is the superficial similarity between *Balfour v. Barty-King* and *Rickards v. Lothian?* What is the distinction between them?

A. In both cases the defendant was sued when something spread from his property to his neighbor's (fire/water); and in both cases the defendants themselves were not to blame for the spread: the direct causes of the spread were the actions of a third party (the contractor in *Balfour* and the miscreant in *Rickards*). But in *Balfour* the activity involved—use of the blowtorch to thaw the pipes—apparently was for the benefit of the defendant alone, whereas in *Rickards* the activity involved was partially for the benefit of the plaintiff. Nor was using a blow-lamp for this purpose a matter of common usage. As noted earlier, we don't want the defendant in *Rickards* to consider a change in activity levels; we want him to continue to have lavatories so long as he is careful about it. But we might well want the defendant in *Balfour* to consider the activity level change of substituting some other method of thawing pipes. (On the other hand, the decision to use a blowtorch here might seem a suspect candidate for status as an "activity" that we need strict liability to discourage; why not just bring a negligence claim for choosing to use a blowtorch in this setting? And if that claim fails, why conclude that we want the defendant to consider switching to other methods?)

As for the intervention by the third party, some students may be surprised that the Barty-Kings can be held strictly liable for their contractor's decision to use a blow-lamp. The court concluded on this point that there is no requirement in a *Rylands* case that the defendant *know* that he has a potentially mischievous escapee on his property:

> The next point taken by counsel for the defendants was that there was an onus on the plaintiff to prove that the defendants knew that Mr. Brown and Mr. Rogers were bringing the blow-lamp on to their premises, and that as this was not proved, the rule in *Rylands v. Fletcher* had no application. [...] [I]t would seem to me that I am constrained by authority to find against him on this point. The point arose in *West v. Bristol Tramways Co.* (25) ([1908] 2 K.B. 14). [...] Lord Alverstone, C.J., who gave the leading judgment in the Court of Appeal, cites the statement in Garrett on Nuisances (2nd Edn.) at p. 129:

> "'Where the owner of land uses his land for any purpose for which it may in the ordinary course of enjoyment of land be used, he will not, in the absence of negligence on his part, be liable, though damage result to his neighbour in the ordinary enjoyment by the latter of his property; for it lies with the latter to protect himself from the operation of natural laws. But, if the owner of land uses it for any purpose which from its character may be called non-natural or extraordinary user, such as, for example, the introduction on to the land of something which in the natural

condition of the land is not upon it, he does so at his peril, and is liable if sensible damage results to his neighbour's land from its escape, or if the latter's legitimate enjoyment of his land is thereby materially curtailed.' If the contention of the defendants' counsel in this case is correct, this last proposition is stated much too widely; for they contend that the owner of land who has so acted has not done so at his peril, and is not liable, unless the plaintiff shows that the thing introduced on to the land was, to the knowledge of the defendant, likely to escape and cause damage. The authorities do not, in my opinion, support the suggestion that this onus is cast on the party injured."

Q. Hypothetical: in *Read v. J. Lyons & Co., Ltd.*, [1947] A.C. 156, [1946] 2 All E.R. 471, the defendants had a contract with the Ministry of Supply to fill shell casings with high explosives. The plaintiff, an employee of the ministry, went to the defendant's ordnance factory to perform an inspection. While she was there a shell exploded, causing her various injuries. She brought a lawsuit alleging that the defendants were strictly liable for harm resulting from their operation under *Rylands v. Fletcher*; she did not allege that the defendants were negligent in any way. What result?
A. The trial court gave judgment to the plaintiff, holding that it was controlled by *Rylands*; the House of Lords thought otherwise. Said Viscount Simon:

> It is not every use to which land is put that brings into play [the principle of *Rylands v. Fletcher*]. It must be some special use bringing with it increased danger to others, and must not merely be the ordinary use of the land or such a use as is proper for the general benefit of the community. [….] It is not necessary to analyse this second condition on the present occasion, for in the case now before us the first essential condition of "escape" does not seem to me to be present at all. "Escape," for the purpose of applying the proposition in *Rylands v. Fletcher* means escape from a place which the defendant has occupation of, or control over, to a place which is outside his occupation or control.

So the distinction between *Read v. J. Lyons & Co.* and *Rylands v. Fletcher* is that in *Read* nothing escaped from the defendant's property. Why would a court put so much weight on the formal requirement of an "escape"? This might be understood as just a variety of formalism, but there are possible policy justifications for it. Only when there is a bona fide escape are some of the *Rylands* rationales most likely to be fully present: the difficulty the victim has in taking precautions, and the idea that the plaintiff enjoys no benefits from the activity. These points might justify taking a hard line on the "escape" requirement even if they don't apply in every case; do they apply on the facts of *Lyons* itself?

Q. Another hypothetical can be built from *Bolton v. Stone*, the case of the cricket ball that hit the plaintiff on the head. It probably will be familiar to the students from the negligence chapter. The plaintiff asserted a strict liability theory as well as a claim of negligence; this claim, too, failed. What is the distinction between *Bolton v. Stone* and *Rylands v. Fletcher*?
A. *Bolton* did not involve a non-natural use of land, so far as the English were concerned; it involved an activity thought to have great social value, and the activity was being conducted in a place considered as appropriate as any. The judges didn't want any change in the defendant's activity levels. And in *Bolton* the PL, in Hand formula terms, was much smaller than in *Rylands*. As we see when we consider the Restatement's provisions on abnormally dangerous activities, P and L continue to be important in defining those activities to which strict liability applies. From the opinion in *Bolton v. Stone*:

> It was argued that this case comes within the principle in *Rylands v. Fletcher*, but I agree with your Lordships that there is no substance in this argument. In my judgment, the test to be applied here is whether the risk of damage to a person on the road was so small that a reasonable man in

the position of the appellants, considering the matter from the point of view of safety, would have thought it right to refrain from taking steps to prevent the danger. [...]

At the Manchester Assizes (the trial level), Oliver, J. had said: "I hope it will never be said of cricket in this country that it is a non-natural use of land." *Stone v. Bolton*, [1949] 1 All E.R. 237.

Q. What is the distinction between *Bolton v. Stone* and *Crowhurst v. Burial Board of Amersham?*
A. Both cases involve harm to the plaintiff when something that looks innocent escapes from the plaintiff's property onto the defendant's. The sic utere maxim is violated in either case. But by the time *Bolton v. Stone* comes along, the non-naturalness question has come to the fore of the *Rylands* inquiry. Also, a poisonous tree climbing toward a neighbor's property probably involves a higher PL than a cricket ball heading toward the fence of a park.

Losee v. Buchanan (D's boiler explodes; *Rylands* rejected)
Turner v. Big Lake Oil Co. (D's salt water reservoir overflows; *Rylands* rejected)

Q. What does the court in *Losee* think is the meaning of *Rylands v. Fletcher?* What is the court's objection to it?
A. The court's interpretation of *Rylands* isn't entirely clear, but it understands the case to call for strict liability at least some of the time, which is too often given the court's adherence to the idea that liability must always be attached to a showing of fault. The court cites the opinion of the "Exchequer Chamber," which is Bramwell's, so it may have have viewed the case as requiring enforcement of the sic utere maxim. The objection to this understanding of *Rylands*—and to strict liability broadly—is that it would stifle progress. "We must have factories, machinery, dams, canals and railroads," and so long as these are operated carefully their owners should have nothing to fear. The rest of the public receives compensation in kind when they enjoy the benefits of such technology, directly or indirectly.

Q. Every schoolboy knows that liability for damage done by wild animals has been regarded as strict for centuries. So how could the court in *Losee* say that there are "no exceptions" to the rule that "no one can be made liable for injuries to the person or property of another without some fault or negligence on his part"?
A. The court was aware of the rule; indeed, it was used by the plaintiff as a source of analogy. But the court thought that even the rules governing animals can be described as involving fault:

> We are also cited to a class of cases holding the owners of animals responsible for injuries done by them. There is supposed to be a difference as to responsibility between animals mansuetae naturae and ferae naturae. As to the former, in which there can be an absolute right of property, the owner is bound at common law to take care that they do not stray upon the lands of another, and he is liable for any trespass they may commit, and it is altogether immaterial whether their escape is purely accidental or due to negligence. As to the latter, which are of a fierce nature, the owner is bound to take care of them and keep them under control, so that they can do no injury. But the liability in each case is upon the same principle. The former have a known, natural disposition to stray, and hence the owner knowing this disposition is supposed to be in fault if he do not restrain them and keep them under control. The latter are known to be fierce, savage and dangerous, and their nature is known to their owner, and hence the owner for the same reason is bound to keep them under control. As to the former, the owner is not responsible for such injuries as they are not accustomed to do, by the exercise of vicious propensities which they do not usually have, unless it can be shown that he has knowledge of the vicious habit and propensity. As to all animals, the owner can usually restrain and keep them under control, and if he will keep them he must do so. If he does not, he is responsible for any damage which their well-known disposition leads them to commit. I believe the liability to be based upon the fault

which the law attributes to him, and no further actual negligence need be proved than the fact that they are at large unrestrained. But if I am mistaken as to the true basis of liability in such cases, the body of laws in reference to live animals, which is supposed to be just and wise, considering the nature of the animals and the mutual rights and interests of the owners and others, does not furnish analogies absolutely controlling in reference to inanimate property.

Q. What is the objection to *Rylands* made in *Turner v. Big Lake Oil Co.?*
A. It's similar to *Losee,* but the court provides an interesting discussion of the different circumstances in England and Texas that might justify a different rule. In England water is plentiful; in Texas it is scarce, and needs to be stored in artificial accumulations in order to support livestock. In England there are no oil wells. The oil wells of Texas produce salt water as a by-product, which has to be put someplace. The challenge is to articulate why these differences might justify different legal regimes: what do they have to do with the choice between strict liability and negligence?

The court in *Turner* emphasizes the differences in the reasonable expectations involved in the two cases: the use in *Rylands* was outside the contemplation of the parties to the original grants of property involved. But the land grants from the State of Texas must be understood as including, as property rights, the right to accumulate water. From a policy standpoint the cases can be distinguished by reference to the activity level point. Reservoirs in Texas are as important as the lavatories in *Rickards:* we don't want their owners to consider changing their activity levels; we want them to keep doing what they are doing. So there is no reason to apply strict liability and the pressure it creates to consider substitutes.

Lubin v. Iowa City (strict liability for pipes left underground until they break)
Walker Shoe Store v. Howard's Hobby Shop (problem: D's oil tanks leak, starting fire that spreads to P's property next door; NL—no strict liability)

Q. Why does the court in *Lubin* find strict liability more appealing than did the courts in *Losee* and *Turner?*
A. Time had passed and *Rylands* had come to be understood as representing a less exacting principle that those earlier courts apparently understood it to signify. As to the facts, while the activity here might seem somewhat similar to the activity in a case like *Rickards* (i.e., using underground water pipes), the key point is that the city was deliberately waiting for damage to be caused by its pipes before replacing them. This case thus presents several features that make strict liability appealing: risks are being imposed on the plaintiffs at least somewhat unilaterally (the in kind compensation they receive by enjoying water in their faucets doesn't seem quite proportionate to the risks these poorly positioned plaintiffs are being called upon to endure); the PL involved is quite high; and there are substitute policies that seem worth considering (replacing the pipes before they break), and the choice between them might not be reachable by an inquiry into negligence. The court also thought that times had changed, so that the impulse toward subsidizing industry through the use of a negligence standard has been replaced at least in some cases by an inclination to make industries pay their way when they cause damage.

Students may wonder why the defendant's liability wouldn't be clear on negligence grounds; perhaps the answer is that the city's practice was capable of being judged reasonable, or in any event consistent with the Hand formula.

Q. What result in *Walker Shoe Store v. Howard's Hobby Shop?*
A. No liability—or at least no *strict* liability. The key distinctions the court drew between this case and *Lubin* were that in *Walker* the activity involved was not *necessarily* dangerous, and might have been made safe through inspections and other forms of due care; and the loss-spreading rationale mentioned in *Lubin* didn't apply here, since the defendant was a private entity. Here are some excerpts from the court's opinion in *Walker* reversing summary judgment for the plaintiffs:

In *Lubin* the plaintiffs sued Iowa City for damages sustained when a city water main broke, flooding their basement and damaging merchandise which was stored there. The water pipe, which had an estimated life of one hundred years, had been in the ground eighty years at the time of the rupture. There was no evidence of any previous break in that part of the system. There was no possibility of inspecting the pipe, once it was installed, unless it was exposed for other purposes. These are circumstances not present in the case now under consideration.

We believe the decisive holding of *Lubin* is reflected in the following quotation: "It is neither just nor reasonable that the city engaged in a proprietary activity can deliberately and intentionally plan to leave a water main underground beyond inspection and maintenance until a break occurs and escape liability. A city or corporation so operating knows that eventually a break will occur, water will escape and in all probability flow onto the premises of another with the resulting damage.... The risks from such a method of operation should be borne by the water supplier who is in a position to spread the cost among the consumers who are in fact the true beneficiaries of this practice and of the resulting savings in inspection and maintenance costs. When the expected and the inevitable occurs, they should bear the loss and not the unfortunate individual whose property is damaged without fault of his own."

The emphasized language highlights the difference in that case and this one. The tanks in which oil was stored in the case now before us were not beyond inspection and repair. They were, indeed, periodically inspected and, if necessary, repaired. Unlike the water in the *Lubin* case, the escape of oil was neither expected nor inevitable; nor was there any reason that a break was certain to occur. Furthermore, the parties here do not occupy the relative positions of the parties in *Lubin,* where we held the loss should be borne by the city partially on the ground it was in a "position to spread the cost among the consumers who are in fact the true beneficiaries of this practice and of the resulting savings in inspections and maintenance costs." No such equitable consideration is present here.

Q. Hypothetical: in *Golden v. Amory*, 109 N.E.2d 131 (Mass. 1952), the defendants owned a hydroelectric plant in Ludlow. A hurricane caused the defendants' dam on the Chicopee River to overflow, with resultant damage to the plaintiffs' property. The evidence at trial was that the torrential rains and flood that accompanied the hurricane were without precedent in Massachusetts; the defendants hired 24 workers to sandbag the dam, but to no avail. What result?
A. After the jury returned a verdict for the plaintiffs, the trial court granted the defendants' motion for judgment notwithstanding the verdict on the ground that the plaintiffs had to prove negligence on the defendants' part and had failed to do so. The plaintiffs appealed, and it was held that the trial court did not err in granting judgment n.o.v. to the defendants. Said the court:

The plaintiffs rely upon the rule stated in [*Rylands v. Fletcher*], that "the person who for his own purposes brings on his lands and collects and keeps there anything likely to do mischief if it escapes, must keep it in at his peril, and, if he does not do so, is prima facie answerable for all the damage which is the natural consequence of its escape." That rule is the law of this Commonwealth. But that rule does not apply where the injury results from "vis major, the act of God * * *, which the owner had no reason to anticipate." In the present case the flood, as disclosed by the evidence, was plainly beyond the capacity of any one to anticipate, and was clearly an act of God. For this reason the rule under discussion does not apply, and the defendants cannot be held liable for injury caused by the flood waters.

Also, was the water in this case brought into the enclosure for the "own purpose" of the defendant?

Some background on the Rylands *case.*   A.W. Brian Simpson, *Legal Liability for Bursting Reservoirs: The Historical Context of Rylands v. Fletcher*, 13 J. Leg. Stud. 209 (1984), provides some informative background materials on *Rylands v. Fletcher*. Simpson suggests that the decision in the case may have been influenced by some recent English disasters involving exploding reservoirs.

> [I]n nineteenth-century Britain there occurred two sensational reservoir disasters, and to appreciate the significance of these incidents it is important to appreciate the menacing character of a large dam once anxiety as to its security becomes current. Those who live or work in the area thought to be endangered by failure can conceive of themselves as permanently and continuously threatened; and depending on the state of the law, they may be, or at least think themselves to be, impotent in the facing of the ever present threat. Nuclear power stations possess this menacing character for many people today, and it is not a product of the frequency of accidents at all. Major killers such as ships and railways lacked this quality; indeed they seemed to be essentially benevolent artifacts, though a ship voyage was viewed by contemporaries as a hazardous undertaking. But what was feared was the sea, not the ship.

The first of the disasters was the collapse of a dam at Holmfirth in 1852; it was estimated that "4,986 adults and 2,142 children had been put out of work and in consequence faced destitution." The other dam failure involved the Dale Dyke in Sheffield in 1863, during the *Rylands* litigation. More than 200 people were killed.

> All those involved in the case must have realized that the litigation raised issues of considerable general importance. Furthermore, the two major disasters, coupled with the general fear and anxiety they inevitably generated in a country liberally provided with reservoirs of all shapes, sizes, and ages, must have brought home to them, as to the public generally, the menacing power of these bodies of water, capable at any moment of unleashing death and destruction on an enormous scale. [...] [W]hen [Henry] Manisty, arguing for the plaintiff, opened with the remark: "A large collection of water is a thing pregnant with danger, and it behoves anyone who makes a collection for his profit, to beware how he may prejudice his neighbours by mismanaging it," the court could hardly have failed to have been reminded of the recent major disasters. [...] The three judges who took part in the decision [in the Court of Exchequer] disagreed in the result; Chief Baron Pollock and Baron Martin ruled for the defendants[;] both opinions can be read as attempting to distinguish the facts of the case not so much from some earlier precedent (for there was none directly in point) as from the Dale Dyke disaster, whose mention legal convention forbade.

Meanwhile Parliament was passing a series of Acts regulating reservoirs and dams, a process that continued into the twentieth century and that came to greatly limit the application of *Rylands* to actual dam failures; and at the same time bursting dams have become less common:

> Since 1930 there have been no serious reservoir disasters in Britain, [...] and in the whole long curious story the only individual in Britain who ever seems actually to have employed the rule in *Rylands v. Fletcher* to recover damages for a burst reservoir is Thomas Fletcher himself.

Simpson has this to offer on the theoretical context of the decision:

> *Rylands v. Fletcher* has long been viewed as an anomalous decision; it is only in very recent times that any sustained attempt has been made to develop an intellectually coherent case in favor of the principle of strict liability. A commonly held is that the old common law proceeded on the basis that a man acted at his peril; this harsh doctrine was progressively relaxed in the nineteenth century with the reception of the principle of liability for fault only. The law was thus moralized,

and *Rylands v. Fletcher* appears as an atavistic decision, a throwback or a survival from more primitive times. The various qualifications to the principle fo strict liability that have been developed since represent the process of getting the ship back on course; some indeed have seen this process beginning at once, when Lord Cairns in the House of Lords state the principle as governing liability only where there was "non-natural" use of property. The case appears as an aberration, out of line with the general development of this branch of the law.

I suspect that many legal historians would today doubt this picture of the historical evolution of tort law. Yet the alternative story still leaves much to be explained. It goes like this. Before the nineteenth century, questions of fault, contributory fault, assumption of risk, standards of appropriate behavior, causation, and so forth, certainly arose in litigation, and this is in the nature of things. But they were treated as jury questions, to be handled in the main by lay common sense, and insofar as judicial guidance was given to the jury about how they should be handled, such guidance was not regularly a subject of review. There was in consequence little or no law on these matters, and what jappened in the nineteenth century was not the substitution of new law for old law, but the creation of law where there had been none before. But on this hypothesis, *Rylands v. Fletcher* still appears puzzling, for it comes at the end of a period of legal development in which the fault principle had been steadily gaining ground through the extension of the tort of negligence and through the injection of notions of reasonableness into the old tort of nuisance. And Blackburn's idea that strict liability is the norm is more surprising still. [...]

Simpson had a bit more to say about this in his book *Leading Cases in the Common Law*:

The numerous judges who were involved in the case must have been aware that, if tort law was to incorporate two different principles of liability, there was a need to explain the relationship between them. Only two of them attempted to do so. One was Bramwell B, who favoured strict liability in his dissenting opinion in the Court of Exchequer, and the other was Blackburn J, speaking for his colleagues in the Court of Exchequer Chamber. By the 1860s it was quite clear that fault liability reigned in some areas, typically in collision cases. Bramwell B dealt with the problem very briefly, but thought that in collision cases the negligence principle had to apply as a matter of logic, and this because of a problem over causation: "where two carriages come into collision, if there is no negligence in either it is as much the act of the one driver as of the other that they meet." Only by deciding who was at fault could you decide who collided with whom. Blackburn J, the judge most closely identified with the so-called rule in *Rylands v. Fletcher*, offered a much more radical theory. It was that the *primary* principle of tort law was that of strict liability. The negligence principle applied only as an exception in situations in which people had, by implication, agreed that it should—the theory of assumption of risk.

Here Simpson cited the language from Blackburn's opinion stating that "Traffic on the highways, whether by land or sea, cannot be conducted without exposing those whose persons or property are near it to some inevitable risk; and that being so, those who go on the highway, or have their property adjacent to it, may well be held to do so subject to their taking upon themselves the risk of injury from that inevitable danger." Simpson concludes that Blackburn's theory "was not very convincing, but his contention that strict liability was the norm was stated in an opinion agreed by [five colleagues][. ...] This, viewed at least from a modern perspective, seems to reverse the natural order of things, and certainly nothing of the sort had ever been said in the nineteenth century before this."

SECTION C. ABNORMALLY DANGEROUS ACTIVITIES

If you want to shorten this section, your best bet probably is to just leave out everything after the *Madsen* case except the excerpt from the Third Restatement (item 9).

Indiana Harbor Belt Ry. v. American Cyanamid Co. (D ships chemicals that spill from tank car; NL)
Siegler v. Kuhlman (D's gasoline trucks overturns, spills, explodes; L)

Q. How did the court apply the factors from Restatement §520 in *Indiana Harbor Belt Ry. v. American Cyanamid Co.*?

A. The court thought the most important factor (in this case, and in such inquiries generally) was (c): whether the risks involved in the activity—here, shipping acrylonitrile though a metropolitan area—can be eliminated by due care. The court thought, first, that the accident here seemed likely to have been caused by carelessness on someone's part, which (if true) can be deterred by liability for negligence. Second, the issue underlying factor (c) is whether the best way to avoid the accident is by changing whether or where the activity is conducted (as opposed to doing it more carefully); and such an "activity level" change by the *shipper* of the goods (the defendant here) probably would not make sense. The shipper does not generally have any direct control over the route the shipping car follows; the shipping company controls that. And even if it were reasonable to expect the defendant to control the route its shipments follow, it seems unlikely that there is any better way to send acrylonitrile across the country. (This goes to factors (e) and (f)). To route the shipments away from metropolitan areas might, aside from being expensive, increase the total expected accident costs involved, since it would lengthen the journeys and might send them over inferior lines of track. It's possible that the true change in activity levels that we want is for the defendant to stop making and shipping acrylonitrile and to substitute some other chemical for the same uses. But there is no evidence that this is feasible. The court suggests that the most useful change in activity levels here (i.e., the cheapest way to avoid the problem of contamination disasters if due care alone isn't enough) might be for the people who live near the Blue Island yard to move elsewhere.

Good general questions to bring out these points: why didn't the court find strict liability here? The chemical escaped from a tank car, and was prone to cause mischief, was it not? (Yes, but this wasn't a *Rylands* case.) What did the court mean by suggesting that the people who live near Blue Island should perhaps move away? It is treating strict liability as a way of putting pressure on activity levels to achieve the cheapest overall solution to the problem of contamination near residences. Moving the residents elsewhere might be cheaper and more effective than trying to route the chemicals elsewhere. Note the indifference to the distributional issue characteristic of economic analysis.

Q. What is the superficial similarity between *Indiana Harbor Belt Ry. v. American Cyanamid Co.* and *Siegler v. Kuhlman?* What are the distinctions between them?

A. In both cases an inflammable substance escaped from the tank in which it was being transported, causing damage. But (a) *Siegler* involved a risk that the evidence would be destroyed if an accident occurred, creating a possible pocket of immunity if a negligence regime applied; the *Cyanamid* case did not involve such a risk (but could this problem not have been overcome in *Siegler* by the use of res ipsa loquitur?). (b) *Siegler* involved a suit against the transporter; *Cyanamid* involved a suit against the shipper. (But can we assume *Cyanamid* might have come out differently if the suit had been brought against the shipper? Probably not, since the court seemed so doubtful that a change in activity levels by the transporter would make sense.) (c) Finally, perhaps transporting gasoline in a truck really is more irreducibly dangerous than transporting dangerous chemicals on a train, since roads contain more hazards than railway tracks.

Here is how Judge Posner distinguished *Siegler* elsewhere in the *Cyanamid* opinion:

> *Siegler v. Kuhlman*, 502 P.2d 1181 (Wash. 1972), also imposed strict liability on a transporter of hazardous materials, but the circumstances were again rather special. A gasoline truck blew up, obliterating the plaintiff's decedent and her car. The court emphasized that the explosion had

destroyed the evidence necessary to establish whether the accident had been due to negligence; so, unless liability was strict, there would be no liability—and this as the very consequence of the defendant's hazardous activity. But when the Supreme Court of Washington came to decide [New Meadows Holding Co. v. Washington Power Co., 687 P.2d 212 (Wash. 1984)—no strict liability for gas that leaks from damaged underground gas line], it did not distinguish *Siegler* on this ground, perhaps realizing that the plaintiff in *Siegler* could have overcome the destruction of the evidence by basing a negligence claim on the doctrine of res ipsa loquitur. Instead it stressed that the transmission of natural gas through underground pipes, the activity in *New Meadows,* is less dangerous than the transportation of gasoline by highway, where the risk of an accident is omnipresent. We shall see that a further distinction of great importance between the present case and Siegler is that the defendant there was the transporter, and here it is the shipper. [....]

There are so many highway hazards that the transportation of gasoline by truck is, or at least might plausibly be thought, inherently dangerous in the sense that a serious danger of accident would remain even if the truck driver used all due care (though *Hawkins v. Evans Cooperage Co.,* 766 F.2d 904, 907 (5th Cir.1985), and other cases are *contra*). Which in turn means, contrary to our earlier suggestion, that the plaintiff really might have difficulty invoking res ipsa loquitur, because a gasoline truck might well blow up without negligence on the part of the driver. The plaintiff in this case has not shown that the danger of a comparable disaster to a tank car filled with acrylonitrile is as great and might have similar consequences for proof of negligence. And to repeat a previous point, if the reason for strict liability is fear that an accident might destroy the critical evidence of negligence we should wait to impose such liability until such a case appears.

This discussion provides a nice chance to review res ipsa loquitur; Posner's discussion contains some parallels to *Haasman* and *Walston,* the cases from the res ipsa section involving airplanes and boats that vanish. Indeed, there is a nice point that can be made here about the relationships between res ipsa loquitur and strict liability. Think back to *Judson v. Giant Powder Co.* in the section of the negligence chapter covering res ipsa loquitur. Under the modern doctrines governing abnormally dangerous activities, a dynamite factory might be subject to strict liability for any explosions that occur. One of the things a plaintiff would say in making the case for strict liability is that making dynamite is inevitably dangerous even if done carefully. If the defendant tries to argue against this by saying that making dynamite *is* safe if done carefully, then notice that he walks into a res ipsa trap: if making dynamite is safe if due care is used, and an explosion in fact resulted, then the implication is that due care was not used. The first prong of the res ipsa test therefore is satisfied.

Klein v. Pyrodyne Corp. (fireworks injure P; strict liability)
Miller v. Civil Constructors, Inc. (stray bullet injures P; no strict liability)

Q. What is the superficial similarity between these cases? What is the distinction between them?
A. In both cases the plaintiff was injured by a stray projectile from an instrument operated by the defendant. The distinctions apparently are these: (a) Due care can "virtually" eliminate the risks involved in using guns, but not the risks involved in using fireworks. The idea presumably is that guns are more precise than aerial bombs, and that when guns are used carefully they fire projectiles at absorbent surfaces, whereas fireworks are explosives deliberately fired into the open. (b) The use of firearms is more a matter of common usage than displays of fireworks, and (relatedly) involves greater social benefits. This point might most easily be understood by considering the costs of switching away from the activity to substitutes. If people stop putting on fireworks displays, it is not an enormous loss; there are fairly good substitutes for the entertainment value fireworks provide. But if the police can't practice firing their weapons, the social loss seems potentially higher and harder to replace. Since they were practicing in an out-of-the-way place, no further activity level change seems desirable; firing the

guns was an appropriate activity for the place where it was carried out. Thus liability for negligence is enough to regulate that activity.

Sullivan v. Dunham (blasting hurls tree stump onto P's decedent; L)
Madsen v. East Jordan Irrigation Co. (blasting frightens mink into killing their young; NL)

Q. What is the analogy between *Sullivan v. Dunham* and *Siegler v. Kuhlman?*
A. In both cases the defendants were involved in activities that present some dangers even if conducted carefully; and perhaps in both cases there was at least some risk that evidence of negligence in carrying on activity would be destroyed by the activity itself—though strict liability for blasting is not, of course, conditioned on that danger.

   The even more snug analogy to *Sullivan* is the *Pyrodyne* case (fireworks): both involve the use of dangerous explosives in situations where alternative ways of locating or accomplishing the same ends (amusement/uprooting trees) are feasible.

Q. What is the superficial similarity between *Sullivan v. Dunham* and *Madsen v. East Jordan Irrigation Co.?* What is the distinction between them?
A. In both cases the defendant's blasting led to freakish injuries. (Blasting, of course, is a quintessential strict liability activity; you can talk through the factors in Restatement §520 to show why, and also refer to how blasting interacts with whatever theoretical explanations for strict liability you have been discussing.) But in *Madsen*, the damage that occurred was not (in the words of Rest. §519(2)) "the kind of harm, the possibility of which makes the activity abnormally dangerous." It's useful to compare this phrasing to the similar language used by the Third Restatement to explain the general rule of proximate cause in negligence cases (it's contained in the casebook at the very end of the proximate cause chapter). The rules are quite similar; they ask whether the bad thing that happened was within the scope of the risk that caused us to label the conduct negligent or to impose strict liability on it.

Q. What is the analogy between *Madsen* and *Bostock-Ferari Amusements v. Brocksmith* (from the section on liability for animals)?
A. In both cases the defendant was engaged in an activity to which strict liability generally attaches; in both cases the harm the plaintiff suffered was of a variety that could have pretty easily occurred by other means (the court in *Brocksmith* thought the horse could as easily have been frightened by a large domesticated animal, and the minks in *Madsen* could as easily have been frightened by other loud noises). In *Madsen,* however, there were not many ways other than blasting for a tree to be flung at the plaintiff's decedent.

Q. Hypothetical: in *Yukon Equipment v. Fireman's Fund Ins. Co.*, 585 P.2d 1206 (Alaska 1978), the defendants owned a storage facility near Anchorage that contained 80,000 pounds of explosives. Four young men stole some of the explosives; then they returned a day later, hoping to cover the evidence of their theft by blowing up the magazine. They set up a charge, then fled. The resulting explosion caused damage to buildings two miles away, and registered 1.8 on a richter scale 30 miles away. Those whose property was damaged sued the owners of the magazine on a theory of strict liability. What result?
A. Liability; the trial court gave summary judgment to the plaintiffs on the liability issue, and the Alaska Supreme Court affirmed:

> Based in large part on the Restatement (Second), petitioners argue that their use was not abnormally dangerous. Specifically they contend that their use of the magazine for the storage of explosives was a normal and appropriate use of the area in question since the storage magazine was situated on lands set aside by the United States for such purposes and was apparently located in compliance with applicable federal regulations. They point out that the storage served a

legitimate community need for an accessible source of explosives for various purposes. They contend that before absolute liability can be imposed in any circumstance a preliminary finding must be made as to whether or not the defendant's activity is abnormally dangerous, that such a determination involves the weighing of the six factors set out in section 520 of the Restatement (Second) of Torts, and that an evaluation of those factors in this case could not appropriately be done on motion for summary judgment.

The factors specified by section 520 of the Restatement (Second) of Torts are for consideration of the court, not the jury. [...] The first three factors, involving the degree of risk, harm, and difficulty of eliminating the risk, are obviously present in the storage of 80,000 pounds of explosives in a suburban area. The fourth factor, that the activity not be a matter of common usage, is also met. [...] The fifth factor, inappropriateness of the activity, is arguably not present, for the storage did take place on land designated by the United States government for that purpose. However, the designation took place at a time when the area was less densely populated than it was at the time of the explosion. Likewise, the storage reserve was not entirely appropriate to the quantity of explosives stored because the explosion caused damage well beyond the boundaries of the reserve. The sixth factor, value to the community, relates primarily to situations where the dangerous activity is the primary economic activity of the community in question. Thus comment (k) states that such factor applies particularly when the community is largely devoted to the dangerous enterprise and its prosperity largely depends upon it. Thus the interests of a particular town whose livelihood depends upon such an activity as manufacturing cement may be such that cement plants will be regarded as a normal activity for that community notwithstanding the risk of serious harm from the emission of cement dust. [...]

Since five of the six factors required by section 520 of the Restatement (Second) are met and the sixth is debatable, we would impose absolute liability here if we were to use that approach.

However, we do not believe that the Restatement (Second) approach should be used in cases involving the use or storage of explosives. Instead, we adhere to the rule [...] imposing absolute liability in such cases. The Restatement (Second) approach requires an analysis of degrees of risk and harm, difficulty of eliminating risk, and appropriateness of place, before absolute liability may be imposed. Such factors suggest a negligence standard. The six factor analysis may well be necessary where damage is caused by unique hazards and the question is whether the general rule of absolute liability applies, but in cases involving the storage and use of explosives we take that question to have been resolved by more than a century of judicial decisions.

The reasons for imposing absolute liability on those who have created a grave risk of harm to others by storing or using explosives are largely independent of considerations of locational appropriateness. We see no reason for making a distinction between the right of a homesteader to recover when his property has been damaged by a blast set off in a remote corner of the state, and the right to compensation of an urban resident whose home is destroyed by an explosion originating in a settled area. In each case, the loss is properly to be regarded as a cost of the business of storing or using explosives. Every incentive remains to conduct such activities in locations which are as safe as possible, because there the damages resulting from an accident will be kept to a minimum.

The next question is whether the intentional detonation of the storage magazine was a superseding cause relieving petitioners from liability. [...] The incendiary destruction of premises by thieves to cover evidence of theft is not so uncommon an occurrence that it can be regarded as highly extraordinary. Moreover, the particular kind of result threatened by the defendant's conduct, the storage of explosives, was an explosion at the storage site. [...]

Absolute liability is imposed on those who store or use explosives because they have created an unusual risk to others. As between those who have created the risk for the benefit of their own enterprise and those whose only connection with the enterprise is to have suffered damage because of it, the law places the risk of loss on the former. When the risk created causes damage in fact, insistence that the precise details of the intervening cause be foreseeable would subvert the purpose of that rule of law.

Luthringer v. Moore (insecticide problem: L)

This problem can be used to discuss the activity-level idea: here as in cases like *Sullivan v. Dunham,* there are different ways to accomplish the defendant's goals; and like using dynamite, using hydrocyanic gas may be an inevitably dangerous technique for which there are socially preferable substitutes. If there were liability only for negligence, there might be no liability in cases like this and so no incentive to substitute other, less dangerous chemicals (unless the plaintiff were able to base the negligence claim on the mere decision to use hydrocyanic gas in the first place, rather than the care with which the gas was applied). *Luthringer* can be distinguished from the *Cyanamid* case because the reconsideration of activity levels called for by strict liability seems less burdensome here, and because here it seems clear that even if the gas is used carefully it is quite dangerous. From the opinion in *Luthringer*:

> Defendant Moore introduced a written notice which he claims was attached to the door of the pharmacy directing that he be contacted before entering the building because of possible gas leakage, indicating that he believed a leakage possible although he testified that he took every precaution to seal the basement before he released the gas. This evidence, as above discussed, clearly points to the conclusion that the gas escaped from the basement into the pharmacy although great care to prevent it was exercised by Moore. As before seen, the activity in releasing the gas was carried on the basement of commercial buildings where there are a great many tenants. Under these circumstances we have a case which calls for liability without fault a case failing within the category of what has been defined as the miscarriage of an ultra-hazardous activity. [....]

> The above quoted evidence [in the casebook] shows that the use of gas under the circumstances presented is a hazardous activity; that it is perilous and likely to cause injury even though the utmost care is used; that defendant Moore knew or should have known that injury might result; and that the use of it under these circumstances is not a matter of 'common usage' within the meaning of the term. In regard to the last feature it may be used commonly by fumigators, but they are relatively few in number and are engaged in a specialized activity. It is not carried on generally by the public, especially under circumstances where many people are present, thus enhancing the hazard, nor is its use a common everyday practice. It is not a common usage within the definition: 'An activity may be ultrahazardous because of the instrumentality which is used in carrying it on, the nature of the subject matter with which it deals or the condition which it creates.' Rest., Torts, sec. 520(b), com. Cl. (b). And in this connection the instruction advising the jury that the usage was not common, was proper.

Crosby v. Cox Aircraft Co. (falling airplane problem: NL)

The Washington supreme court held that liability for ground damage caused by airplanes is governed by a rule of negligence:

In the early days of aviation, the cases and treatises were replete with references to the hazards of "aeroplanes". The following assessment is typical:

> [E]ven the best constructed and maintained aeroplane is so incapable of complete control that flying creates a risk that the plane even though carefully constructed, maintained and operated, may crash to the injury of persons, structures and chattels on the land over which the flight is made.

Restatement (First) of Torts, §520, Comment b (1938). [...]

The court then considered Restatement (Second) of Torts §520, and concluded that as applied to aviation at present, all six factors (with the possible exception of (b)) militate against strict liability:

> Factor (a) of § 520 requires that the activity in question contain a "high degree of risk of some harm to the person, land or chattels of others." No such showing has been made. Indeed, statistics indicate that air transportation is far safer than automobile transportation. Factor (b) speaks to the gravity of the harm—that is, in the unlikely event that an airplane accident occurs, whether there is a "likelihood that the [resulting harm] will be great." It is apparent that this possibility is present. However, this must be further evaluated in light of factor (c), which speaks of the "inability to eliminate the risk by the exercise of reasonable care." Given the extensive governmental regulation of aviation, and the continuing technological improvements in aircraft manufacture, maintenance and operation, we conclude that the overall risk of serious injury from ground damage can be sufficiently reduced by the exercise of due care. Finally, factors (d), (e), and (f) do not favor the imposition of strict liability. Aviation is an activity of "common usage", it is appropriately conducted over populated areas, and its value to the community outweighs its dangerous attributes. Indeed, aviation is an integral part of modern society.

Brachtenbach, J., dissented:

> In this case we have a totally innocent, non-acting homeowner whose property is suddenly invaded and damaged by an airplane—operated by the person who voluntarily chose to fly that airplane, for his own purpose and benefit. The result of the majority is that the wholly innocent, non-active, non-benefited, but damaged person must shoulder the burden of proving that the person who set in motion the forces which caused the damage was negligent.

SECTION D. RESPONDEAT SUPERIOR

We don't recommend cuts here, but if you just want a quick look at respondeat superior you might try using the *Bushey* case, *Konradi v. United States*, *Miami Herald Publishing Co. v. Kendall*, and item 10 afterwards.

Ira S. Bushey & Sons v. United States (drunken sailor opens valves that flood drydock; L for government)
Miller v. Reiman-Wuerth Co. (employee runs over P while on his way to work after depositing paycheck; NL for employer)
Konradi v. United States (postman hits P with his car while commuting to work; L for employer)
Roth v. First Nat'l. State Bank of New Jersey (bank teller tips off thief to customer's habits; NL for bank)
Forster v. Red Top Sedan Service (bus driver hits P because P was delaying him; L for bus line)
Reina v. Metropolitan Dade County (bus driver hits P because P made obscene gesture at him; NL for bus line)

Like the previous materials on strict liability, this section provides a good chance to emphasize the levels on which legal arguments take place: doctrinal rules and the policies behind them. *Bushey* is a nice teaching case because it presents a well-written discussion of some possible underlying rationales for respondeat superior, the conclusions of which can be contrasted with the different approach taken in the *Konradi* case that follows. The caveat that needs to be added, of course, is that most judges would not feel themselves comfortable thinking out cases like these from scratch, as it were; they would be more likely than Friendly and Posner to invoke conventional rules and tests—and might well find no liability for the government in *Bushey* on the ground that the sailor was not on the job and was in no perceptible sense out to further his employer's interests.

Q. What is the distinction between *Miller v. Reiman-Wuerth Co.* and *Ira S. Bushey & Sons v. United States*?

A. The cases seem similar because in both of them the employee commits a wrongful act while off duty. One distinction between them is that in *Bushey*, the L case, the sailor committed his wrongful acts while in the "closed-off area where his ship lay," and thus within the area where his employer should expect to be held responsible for his negligence. In *Miller* the negligence occurred away from the worksite. Stated in terms of the criterion favored by the court in the *Bushey* case, the difference is that the misconduct in *Miller* was less foreseeable because it occurred elsewhere. Though Friendly doesn't mention it, another rationale for the distinction is that within the area where the employee is was performing work, the employer has the potential to control his conduct fairly readily. Still another rationale is a matter of line-drawing. The court in *Miller* worried that if Grandpre had been found to be acting within the scope of his employment, it might be hard to avoid liability when he is on his lunch break or on weekends. The sailor in *Bushey* wasn't on his master's business, either, but this could be overlooked because he was making trouble at the worksite. A related point is that the sailor didn't just work on the ship; he lived there. This gives the employer an unusual measure of involvement in control in the sailor's "off duty" life (compared to the typical employee in a case like *Miller*, who really leaves his work behind when he goes home). Perhaps this fact should make us more inclined to find liability for his employer when he commits bad acts that are technically "off duty" but still in the area the employer has established for him as a place to live.

Q. Is there a satisfactory distinction between *Konradi v. United States* and *Miller v. Reiman-Wuerth Co.* (the NL case where the employee was in an accident while returning to work from the bank)?

A. In each case the plaintiff was hit by a driver who was on his way to work; in *Miller* he was driving back to work after depositing a check, and in *Konradi* he was on his way to work to start the day. The distinction is that in *Konradi* the accident occurred during driving that the employer more or less required the employee to do—"more or less" because the employer required the employees to furnish their own cars for their mail delivery, and this made it very likely that they would drive to work. There is nothing necessarily wrong with this, but it suggests (in Posner's view) that respondeat superior makes sense because it will force the employer—here, the government—to internalize the costs of this decision and perhaps reconsider it if it results in accidents that make the policy inefficient. In *Miller* the employee's choice to drive to the bank had a random quality; it seems to have been his own, and not encouraged by the employer, as the employee had written checks that he was afraid would bounce. Stated the *Konradi* way, there is not much reason to think that holding the employer liable in *Miller* could lead to any policy change that would be likely to make the world any safer.

Q. What other rationales for respondeat superior are available (besides the economic one suggested in *Konradi*)?

A. One classic justification, mentioned in the introduction to the section, is ensuring that the plaintiff is able to collect from *someone*. But why should it be important that the plaintiff collect from anyone? Perhaps the typical employer is considered better able to stand the loss by buying insurance and/or spreading out the cost among its customers. There also is the justification offered in *Bushey*: that the issue is not one of policy (in the sense of shaping incentives) but more "that a business enterprise cannot justly disclaim responsibility for accidents which may fairly be said to be characteristic of its activities"—with "characteristic" then defined as "foreseeable." But perhaps this can be linked to policy justifications after all: precisely by holding employers liable for foreseeable costs created by their activities, respondeat superior forces enterprises to internalize more of the costs of doing business and to respond in any number of ways—e.g., by investing in safer procedures, by training or screening employees more carefully, or by scaling back or simply closing.

Notice that neither *Bushey* nor *Konradi* relies on the straightforward test of making liability depend on whether the employee was motivated by a purpose to serve the master. Here, however, are some additional excerpts from the *Konradi* opinion that help explain its relationship to the traditional analytical categories:

> Not only may the imposition of liability on the Postal Service be consistent with most of the Indiana cases [...]; it is consistent with all three of the formulas that courts in Indiana and elsewhere intone when they are trying to generalize about scope of employment. By driving to and from work Farringer conferred a *benefit* on his employer because he was bringing an essential instrumentality of the employer's business. (True, the employer would not have cared if Farringer had left his truck in the post office parking lot and thumbed a ride to work, but few employees would thus forgo all personal use of their vehicle.) The employer exerted substantial *control* over the employee's commuting, as shown by the regulations discussed earlier. And finally the employee while commuting was in the *service* of the employer because he was keeping and maintaining the instrumentality.

> These "tests" should not be thought conclusive. Tests divorced from purposes tend not to be useful, let alone conclusive, and the linkage between the tests and what the discussion in this opinion conjectures is the underlying purpose of the scope of employment concept is obscure. The law has drawn a line between at work and at home but treats commuting as an intermediate zone that can be placed within or outside the scope of employment depending on circumstances, though the presumption is in favor of outside. The purpose of a doctrine determines what circumstances are relevant. The purpose of this doctrine may be to induce the employer to consider activity changes that might reduce the number of accidents. One possible change might be to substitute a fleet of postal vans for the employees' personal vehicles driven to and from work daily perhaps over substantial distances.

Q. Why is it that employers are strictly liable for the negligence of their employees, while parents generally are not liable for the negligence of their children?

A. You can neither pick your children nor fire them. This repeats a point made in the chapter on intentional torts (in the section on the intent requirement for battery).

Q. What is the distinction between *Roth v. First Nat'l. State Bank of New Jersey* and *Ira S. Bushey & Sons v. United States*?

A. Since *Bushey* states the test for "scope of employment" in terms of foreseeability, this question invites consideration of whether the crooked acts of the teller were foreseeable. In neither case was the employee in fact acting to serve the master's interests, but in *Roth* the misconduct was more calculated and seems more plainly to be have been in fairly direct opposition to the employer's interests. (The sailor's acts in *Bushey* hurt the employer, too, but it's not as clear there that the hurt was understood by the sailor to be a likely consequence of what he did.)

Q. What is the distinction between *Roth* and *Konradi v. United States* (the L case of the plaintiff hit by a mailman on his way to work)?

A. *Konradi* states the test for "scope of employment" in terms of whether holding the employer liable would create any useful pressure on the employer to reconsider its activity levels. Distinguish this from the question of whether we want the bank to supervise or choose its tellers more carefully. These latter steps are examples of the bank changing its level of *care*, not its level of *activity*; the practical point is that the bank already can be held liable for those failures even without respondeat superior. It's always possible to claim that the employer should be held liable for the employee's torts not because the employee was acting within the scope of employment but because the employer was negligent in hiring or supervising the wrongdoer—a claim of "direct" negligence. The question is whether there are other steps we should want the bank to consider that might be hard or awkward to use as a basis for negligence liability but that it might consider on its own if it had to pay for misdeeds like those of the teller here. Perhaps not. An example might be a switch from tellers to greater automation, which in turn would create fewer chances for tellers to betray customers to their thieving friends. It might not be feasible to hold a bank negligent for failing to automate (the decision involves so many disparate costs and benefits that it would be hard for a jury to second-guess either way), but strict liability might cause the bank to consider such steps on its own. On the other hand, at the time the case was decided (1979), and still today, automating doesn't sound like a particularly useful answer to the problem presented in this case. The plaintiff was exiting the bank with $72,000 in cash, which he would be unlikely to get out of an ATM under any circumstances.

Q. What is the distinction between *Reina v. Metropolitan Dade County* and *Forster v. Red Top Sedan Service*?

A. In *Forster* the bus driver was arguably motivated by a wish to advance his employer's interests when he attacked the plaintiff; he was trying to get to the beach on time. In *Reina* the driver appears just to have been satisfying a private wish to settle a score with the plaintiff, perhaps at the expense of the employer (since he slowed the progress of his other passengers). Does drawing the line in this way make any sense as a policy matter? Perhaps the idea is that if a bus driver beats up a stranger because he is in a hurry to fulfill his assigned tasks, this may be because his employer has put pressure on him. Thus behavior like that found in *Forster* may be something the employer can address by adopting different policies—different schedules, or different consequences if the driver is late. To this list one might be tempted to add that liability in *Forster* will also encourage the company to punish the driver for doing stupid things like punching strangers in the face—but *that* notion doesn't distinguish *Forster* from *Reina*, where we might likewise like to see the employer have an incentive to discipline the employee. But there is no liability in *Reina*, and the reason on the theory of policy just sketched would be that the driver probably was not responding to any policy of the company's that needs adjustment. He was just a jerk. (As for the bus company's incentive to discipline the driver, it may be worth stressing that if the driver in *Reina* did this a second time, the company might end up being held liable for negligently retaining him after his first outburst.)

Reina may seem hard to distinguish from the *Bushey* case, since here the misconduct occurred near the workplace (outside the bus) and so might seem foreseeable. But maybe beatings of passengers just can't be said to be a "characteristic" feature of the activity of running a bus line in the same way that foolishness by drunken sailors may be considered a characteristic side-effect of running a ship.

Q. As a follow up to the bus driver cases, you might enjoy using the following provision from the Restatement (Second) of Agency (1958) as a source for a hypothetical:

§236. Conduct Actuated By Dual Purpose

Conduct may be within the scope of employment, although done in part to serve the purposes of the servant or of a third person.

Illustration 1. A, servant of P, in order to get to his destination ahead of a rival coach driver, and also to revenge a personal insult from him, strikes the horses of the rival in passing him upon the road, causing the horses to run away. This evidence will support a verdict that the act of A was within the scope of employment.

Q. Hypothetical: in *Thompson v. United States*, 504 F.Supp. 1087 (D.S.D. 1980), a man named Kitteaux was employed as a trainee in the Bureau of Indian Affairs; he was working as a police officer for the Crow Creek Sioux Tribe. One day he entered a BIA police station and performed a "fast draw" with his pistol, aiming it a bystander, one Thompson. Kitteaux intended the fast draw to be a simulation, but by mistake he fired the weapon and killed Thompson. Kitteaux pled guilty to involuntary manslaughter. Thompson's estate sued the United States under the Federal Tort Claims Act on a respondeat superior theory. The government argued that Kitteaux violated its rules by employing the quick draw maneuver in these circumstances. Assume (a) that Kitteaux was practicing "quick draw" techniques that were part of his training, but (b) that practicing the techniques in this way (e.g., away from the firing range) was strictly forbidden by his employer. What result?

A. After a bench trial (there are no juries in FTCA cases, of course), the court found for the plaintiff:

> Can it be said that Kitteaux was acting within the scope of his employment when Thompson was killed? Kitteaux was on duty at the time, within the confines of the BIA police station, armed with his BIA-issued gun. This leaves the question of his motive in leveling his gun at Thompson, which Skow indicates is particularly one for the finder of fact. To reach a determination of this matter, one must consider the context in which the act took place.

> Kitteaux was a recently hired police trainee. As a part of his training as a policeman, he was given firearms training by a Special Agent of the FBI, David Powers. This training includes, as Powers testified, extensive instruction of "quick draw." Given this background, and the circumstances with which Kitteaux was surrounded on the day the shooting occurred, the Court must draw the inference that, though tragically misguided, Kitteaux's motive in pulling his gun up and pointing it at Thompson was to practice and perfect his police firearms techniques. In this unfortunate way, Kitteaux evidently intended to improve himself as a policeman, and to thereby carry out his employer's business. It could not be contended that if a similar accident had occurred on a firearms range, in the course of firearms practice by a government employee, the United States would not be liable. Simply because the situs of the practice is moved from a range to the interior of a BIA police station, the result is not changed.

> Defendant complains that such behavior was strictly forbidden. Whether it was forbidden or not does not allow defendant to escape liability, for the law is plain that an "act may be within the scope of employment even though forbidden or done in a forbidden manner...." *Alberts v. Mutual Service Casualty Insurance Co.*, 123 N.W.2d 96, 99 (S.D. 1963), citing Restatement, Agency 2d §230. As Prosser said, if a master could escape liability by ordering his servant to act carefully, few employers could ever be held liable. "If the other factors involved indicate that the forbidden conduct is merely the servant's own way of accomplishing an authorized purpose, the master cannot escape responsibility no matter how specific, detailed and emphatic his orders may have been to the contrary." Prosser, Torts, 461 (4th ed. 1971).

Q. In sec. 265 of the Second Restatement of Agency, what is the distinction between the third illustration and the first two?

A. In Illustration 3, the person who was run over was not relying on a belief that the person behind the wheel of the car was working for the defendant. Why is this so important? It might seem to be partly a question of causation: the apparent authority in Illustration 3 didn't increase the driver's ability to run someone over, whereas the apparent authority in the other illustrations did increase the agent's ability to cause the timber to be cut or the defamation to be spread. The lesson is that if an agent is stripped of actual authority, the master loses control over him and thus won't be held responsible for the agent's actions—but with this comes an obligation to say so to anyone who might trust the agent precisely because they understand him to be under the control of the master.

Miami Herald Publishing Co. v. Kendall (paper boy runs over P; NL for newspaper)
Yazoo & Mississippi Valley Railroad Co. v. Gordon (railroad's independent contractor negligently allows steer to escape and gore P; L for railroad because duty was nondelegable)
Wilton v. City of Spokane (city's independent contractors negligently leave dynamite behind; NL for the city when it explodes because negligence was "collateral" to the contrator's work rather than "incident" to it)

Q. What is the distinction between *Miami Herald Publishing Co. v. Kendall* and *Konradi v. United States*?
A. In both cases the agent hit someone with his vehicle. In *Konradi* this was on the way to work, while in the *Miami Herald* case it was *during* the performance of the work—yet *Miami Herald* is the case of no liability for the employer. And in *Miami Herald* the defendant's manager seems to have had a closer relationship with Molesworth than any manager did over the plaintiff in *Konradi*: in *Miami Herald*, the manager would rout Molesworth out of bed if he was late and specified (to an extent) how the newspapers were to be folded. It seems doubtful that the mailman in *Konradi* was subject to such close supervision—and yet, again, *Miami Herald* is the case of no liability.

The reason for all this seems to involve the employer's control over the employee, and especially over the feature of the work that caused the accident. In *Konradi*, the postal service's rule (that rural mailmen supply their own cars) made it very likely that they would drive to work, and the court thought this policy should be subject to the pressures of respondeat superior. In *Miami Herald* the employer had, by contract, disclaimed any say over the means by which the papers were delivered. Thus the facts of the *Miami Herald* case might seem to suggest that while a policy change might be desirable—perhaps substituting from motorcycles to the time-honored bicycle—the defendant was not in a position to require this.

(You have to a be a little careful in comparing *Konradi* and *Miami* Herald because in *Konradi* the issue was not whether the driver was an employee; it was whether he was acting within the scope of his employment. If the question in *Konradi* had been the driver's status as an employee or independent contractor, the "employee" status would have been an easier call for reasons besides the pressure on him to drive his own car to work. Mailmen work regular hours for a steady wage and their performance is governed by many regulations. Some of the policy considerations at stake in the two cases nevertheless seem to overlap, since the principal's ability to affect the agent's likelihood of causing harm figures both into whether the agent is considered an employee and whether he is considered to be acting within the scope of the employment.)

It's potentially troubling, of course, to rely on the contract between the *Herald* and the paper boy, because the newspaper *could* put itself into a position to require its employees to use bicycles; why should it be able to elimimnate its liability—to so affect the rights of third parties—by simply writing a contract that assigns the choice of vehicle to its paper boy? Maybe the idea in general is that if an employer gives up control over some aspect of its agents' performance, it probably has business reasons for doing so (it might be in a bad position to know whether a bicycle or motorcycle makes more sense for any given route; what if there are steep hills?), and also will find that decision subject to other costs and pressures (relinquisihing control over how the work is done means the employer has to suffer through bad decisions the contractor makes on that subject). So in the general run of cases it may be doubtful that the decision to make a agent a "contractor" rather than an "employee" will be driven by the wish to avoid liability for their mistakes. But this is only a generalization, and it certainly leaves room for counterexamples where the choice is made precisely on liability-avoiding grounds. The following hypothetical provides a chance to explore this a bit further.

Q. Suppose plaintiff is run over by a driver for Domino's Pizza on his way to make a delivery. Is Domino's liable? Is the driver an employee or an independent contractor? Imagine that Domino's requires its delivery people to supply their own cars, and then pays them a small base salary plus a dollar per pizza delivered; the rest of their income comes in tips.

A. To some students it might seem that the driver is a contractor because he supplies his own car. But the employer still controls the key point, which is that the delivery driver has to use *some* car or other motorized vehicle. (Cf. *Konradi*.) Domino's also controls where the driver goes and can exert a certain amount of control over the rest of his conduct (route, time allowed for the trip, etc.). Thus the driver is likely to be considered an employee. See, e.g., *Toyota Motor Sales v. Superior Court*, 269 Cal.Rptr. 647 (Cal. App. 1990). In principle maybe Domino's could avoid liability by turning their drivers into "independent contractors," but in practice the firm would have to relinquish so much control over the drivers that their business would be adversely affected. If they convincingly told the drivers to use any means they like to get the pizza delivered, they no longer could promise that delivery would be fast. If the circumstances were such that all drivers would naturally be expected to use cars even if not required to do so, then Domino's is back to being liable on a theory like the one in *Konradi*.

Actually, though, in real life this fact pattern would be even a bit more complicated than appears. The driver might be held to work not for Domino's, Inc., but for the franchisee who runs the local Domino's outlet under a licensing agreement with the company's headquarters. This in turn raises another layer of questions: Does Domino's exercise enough control over its franchises to be liable when the franchisee's driver gets into an accident? An affirmative answer was permitted in *Parker v. Domino's Pizza*, 629 So.2d 1026 (Fla. App. 1993). The court relied on two pieces of evidence. The first was the franchise agreement, which contained a long list of requirements (including a requirement "that delivery service zones may not extend to areas where pizza could not feasibly be delivered within 30 minutes"); the second the operations manual Domino's furnished to the franchisee:

> The manual which Domino's provides to its franchisees is a veritable bible for overseeing a Domino's operation. It contains prescriptions for every conceivable facet of the business: from the elements of preparing the perfect pizza to maintaining accurate books; from advertising and promotional ideas to routing and delivery guidelines; from order-taking instructions to oven- tending rules; from organization to sanitation. The manual even offers a wide array of techniques for "boxing and cutting" the pizza, as well as tips on running the franchise to achieve an optimum profit. The manual literally leaves nothing to chance. The complexity behind every element of the operation gives new meaning to the familiar slogan that delivery is to be, "Fast, Hot and Free."

> The foregoing leads us to the self-evident conclusion that it was error to determine as a matter of law that Domino's does not retain the right to control the means to be used by its franchisee to accomplish the required tasks. At the very least a genuine and material question of fact is raised by the documentation.

Q. Is *Miami Herald Publishing Co. v. Kendall* consistent with the test offered in section 220 of the Second Restatement of Agency?

A. Well, the court thought so. Keep in mind that even among courts that go for the Restatement's ten-factor test, the right of the principal to control the agent's manner of performance tends to be treated as most important. With that said, here is the relevant excerpt from the opinion in the *Miami Herald* case:

> We have studied the 'matters of fact' listed in the Restatement of the Law of Agency, supra, that are to be considered in 'determining whether one acting for another is a servant or an independent contractor.' In this consideration we have not found that every element is so clearly present as to establish beyond argument that the arrangement between the appellant and Molesworth was one of independent contractorship, but when all elements are taken together, we think the conclusion

is sound. We have already written our view about 'the extent of control' exercised by the publisher over the details of the work, Sec. 220(2)(a). We have the definite opinion that newspaper boys as they perform their work generally in this country have a place in the pattern of American life that constitutes a 'distinct occupation,' Sec. 220(2)(b), and that the provisions of the contract in this case are harmonious with this idea. True, there was some supervision by the publisher's representative but while the newsboy was actually making his deliveries, he was acting alone and was a specialist, at least to the extent of following his route, remembering the addresses of subscribers who were in good standing, and collecting and properly accounting for funds coming into his hands, Sec. 220(c) and (d). The newscarrier furnished his own instrumentality, a motorcycle, Sec. 220(2)(e). The length of the engagement, or rather the condition for termination of the engagement, was specified in the contract, Sec. 220(2)(f). The method of payment, that is by the subscriber to the newsboy, was the compensation received under the contract, and the newsboy became indebted for papers delivered to him by the publisher whether or not he collected from the subscriber, Sec. 220(2)(g). We do not doubt that distribution of newspapers is a part of the regular business of the publisher but there is no reason that this cannot be done by independent contract, Sec. 220(2)(h). From the contract it is clear to us that the parties believed they were making Molesworth an independent contractor, Sec. 220(2)(i).

Q. What is the distinction between *Yazoo & Mississippi Valley Railroad Co. v. Gordon* and *Miami Herald Publishing Co. v. Kendall* (the NL case of the paper boy)?
A. A principal generally is not held liable for torts committed by an agent if the agent is an independent contractor (notice that a worker can be an *agent* without being a *servant*), but there are exceptions to this rule for "nondelegable duties" considered important to the public at large and for activities that are "inherently dangerous" (these categories can overlap; some regard the latter category as a subset of the former). As the *Yazoo* case shows, an activity need not be "abnormally dangerous" in the sense familiar from Restatment §520 for the exception to apply; there was no strict liability for the injuries inflicted by the steer in that case, but there was a nondelegable duty nevertheless. Indeed, courts have extended the exception to activities that aren't at all "ultrahazardous" but that involve "peculiar" risks that threaten great harm if particular precautions aren't taken. As suggested by the Restatement excerpt in the text, examples include the transportation of logs that require special efforts at fastening so that they don't fall into the road and many kinds of construction projects that are especially dangerous if not done carefully.

Turning, then, to these two cases: the idea evidently is that transporting animals that can gore people is too dangerous to the public to allow the transporter to escape liability by hiring a contractor to carry out the job; but delivering newspapers is not generally so risky. Maybe the idea, along economic lines, is that there are good activity-level alternatives to shipping cows by train (cf. the *Indiana Harbor Belt Ry.* case), but there aren't good activity-level alternatives to delivering newspapers as the defendant was. But is that right? In the *Miami Herald* case, Molesworth was using a motorcycle rather than the more familiar bicycle to deliver the papers; would it not be desirable to cause the publisher to worry about whether this is the right way to make the deliveries?

Q. What is the distinction between *Wilton v. City of Spokane* and *Yazoo & Mississippi Valley Railroad Co. v. Gordon* (the L case of the escaped steer)?
A. This is a nice pair of cases because *Wilton* looks on its face like the more attractive candidate for expanded liability: it involved blasting, the prototypical strict-liability activity that one would expect to amount to a non-delegable duty. But there is an exception to the exception described above. The principal is off the hook if the harm is caused by "collateral" negligence: the occurrence of harm that is not among the risks that one would expect from the activity and that cause us to label it "inherently dangerous." There is a natural analogy to strict liability cases where the plaintiff loses because the harm that occurred was outside the scope of the risk that caused the activity to be labeled "abnormally dangerous" (e.g., *Madsen*, where the minks devour their young when the defendant's airplane makes a loud noise). But there are differences between this collateral negligence doctrine and the causation

principles familiar from other chapters—differences revealed by these cases. In the *Yazoo* case the harm that occurred was just what one worries about: someone got gored. In the *Wilton* case—well, the *harm* that occurred is what one might expect (personal injuries from an explosion), but the *manner* in which it came about seemed freakish and not something the city could have addressed by requiring (or providing) different general precautions. We might not expect to see such a distinction in the proximate cause chapter, but we find it here.

Q. Here is a hypothetical to illustrate the "peculiar risk" doctrine described in Restatement 416: Suppose plaintiff is walking down Broadway in New York when a window washer drops a brush on her, causing her various injuries. She sues the principal who hired the window washer—the building's owner—who in turn is able to show that the window washer was an independent contractor. What result? **A.** The questions are (a) whether window washing involves "peculiar risks," responsibility for which is nondelegable; and, if so, (b) whether the dropping of the brush was one of them, or was "collateral." The court in *Lockowitz v. Melnyk*, 148 N.Y.S.2d 232 (App. Div. 1956), treated these as triable matters of fact:

> Following a nonjury trial, a decision was handed down dismissing the complaint, the court stating that '[t]his court feels that the proper procedure would be a cause of action against the independent contractor, the [window cleaner].' Upon appeal, the Appellate Term reversed and ordered a new trial in an opinion in which it was stated that since the work of the window cleaner as an independent contractor was inherently dangerous, in that danger to the traveling public was reasonably to be anticipated from its performance, the defendant was liable for the negligence of the contractor. We agree that a new trial is required because of the failure of the trial court to pass upon the factual issues, but, upon this record it cannot be said, as a matter of law, that the work of the window cleaner was so inherently dangerous as to cast upon the appellant liability for the negligence of the independent contractor.

> The general rule is recognized that one is not liable for the negligence of an independent contractor unless danger is inherent in the work; but, '[w]hether danger is inherent in the work contracted for and should be reasonably anticipated is a question dependent on the facts of each case.' *Wright v. Tudor City Twelfth Unit, Inc.*, 276 N.Y. 303, 307.

> Upon the new trial, it would seem to be a minimal requirement to have some evidence as to the location of the building with reference to the street line, the height of the building, the time of day when the windows were customarily cleaned and the surrounding conditions at such times. It is upon such evidence or the absence of it that the trier of the facts may determine whether there was 'a high degree of risk in relation to the particular surroundings, or some rather specific danger to those in the vicinity, recognizable in advance as calling for definite precautions.' Prosser on Torts, 2nd Ed., p. 361.

> Moreover, in a case such as this, consideration should be given as to whether the danger was inherent in the work to be done or had its origin in an act of negligence 'collateral' to the work. For such collateral negligence only the independent contractor is liable. The distinction is that '[w]here the particular risk is involved in the work to be done itself, as where the sign is to be painted over the sidewalk, the fact that the harm materializes through the incidental negligence of the servant in dropping the paint bucket will not relieve the [owner] of liability. The distinction is thus one between risks inherent in the normal performance of the work and those which arise from the abnormal and unusual misconduct of the workmen; and it is the latter only which are to be regarded as 'collateral', and for which the [owner] will not be held responsible.' Prosser on Torts, 2nd Ed., p. 362.

Q. A related hypo to pursue the issues further: Suppose the defendant hires two contractors to wash his windows. One of the contractors attempts to remove an anchor from his ladder, but mistakenly—and negligently—instead removes the anchor from his colleague's ladder, causing his colleague to fall four stories and suffer various injuries. The window washer who fell sues the defendant, claiming that window washing is inherently dangerous and that the principal therefore should be liable for the agent's negligence even though he was an independent contractor. What result?

A. The court found no liability on these facts in *Salinero v. Pons*, 177 Cal.Rptr. 204 (Cal. App. 1981):

> We acknowledge certain special and identifiable risks associated with washing windows on tall buildings. Among these are the danger that window washers not adequately protected by means of safety devices or adequate attaching mechanisms would fall while working. However, such "peculiar risks" do not include the dangers associated with the negligence of a fellow worker in removing the window washer's means of attachment to the building. A risk of this sort cannot be reasonably foreseen by the landowner, and is outside the scope of those dangers intimately associated with window washing. It is collateral to the risks that normally arise out of that activity.

Q. Is *Miami Herald Publishing Co. v. Kendall* consistent with section 429 of the Second Restatement of Torts?

A. An interesting tension arises here because we saw that the basic rule for sorting out independent contractors and employees depends heavily on the expectations of the principal and agent—not on the expectations of third parties. Yet this Restatement provision suggests that the victim's expectations matter, too. Wouldn't a person seeing Molesworth on his motorcycle reasonably assume that he is an employee of the *Herald* and that his manner of transportation is approved by the newspaper, if not selected by it? An answer can be derived by analogy to the rules seen earlier in the chapter regarding apparent authority. Maybe an onlooker *would* think Molesworth was an employee, but if so, this only becomes relevant if the onlooker relied on that impression in some way. The plaintiff in *Miami Herald*, who was run over by Molesworth, probably wasn't relying on a belief that Molesworth was a servant (rather than a mere *agent*) of the newspaper.

Q. Is there an economic explanation for the law's distinction between employees and independent contractors, and the notion of nondelegable duties when contractors are used—an explanation consistent with the general rationale for *respondeat superior* offered in the *Konradi* case earlier in this section?

A. From *Anderson v. Marathon Petroleum Co.*, 801 F.2d 936 (7th Cir. 1986) (Posner, J.):

> The reason for distinguishing the independent contractor from the employee is that, by definition of the relationship between a principal and an independent contractor, the principal does not supervise the details of the independent contractor's work and therefore is not in a good position to prevent negligent performance, whereas the essence of the contractual relationship known as employment is that the employee surrenders to the employer the right to direct the details of his work, in exchange for receiving a wage. The independent contractor commits himself to providing a specified output, and the principal monitors the contractor's performance not by monitoring inputs—i.e., supervising the contractor—but by inspecting the contractually specified output to make sure it conforms to the specifications. This method of monitoring works fine if it is feasible for the principal to specify and monitor output, but sometimes it is not feasible, particularly if the output consists of the joint product of many separate producers whose specific contributions are difficult (sometimes impossible) to disentangle. In such a case it may be more efficient for the principal to monitor inputs rather than output—the producers rather than the product. By becoming an employee a producer in effect submits himself to that kind of monitoring, receiving payment for the work he puts in rather than for the output he produces.

Since an essential element of the employment relationship is thus the employer's monitoring of the employee's work, a principal who is not knowledgeable about the details of some task is likely to delegate it to an independent contractor. Hence in general, though of course not in every case, the principal who uses an independent contractor will not be as well placed as an employer would be to monitor the work and make sure it is done safely. This is the reason as we have said for not making the principal vicariously liable for the torts of his independent contractors. See Calabresi, Some Thoughts on Risk Distribution and the Law of Torts, 70 Yale L.J. 499, 545 (1961).

The rule is not applied, however, when the activity for which the independent contractor was hired is "abnormally dangerous," see Restatement (Second) of Torts § 427A (1964), or in an older terminology "ultrahazardous," see, e.g., Cities Service Co. v. State, 312 So.2d 799, 802 (Fla. Dist. Ct.App. 1975)—i.e., if the activity might very well result in injury even if conducted with all due skill and caution. When an activity is abnormally dangerous, it is important not only that the people engaged in it use the highest practicable degree of skill and caution, but also—since even if they do so, accidents may well result—that the people who have authorized the activity consider the possibility of preventing some accidents by curtailing the activity or even eliminating it altogether. See Bethlehem Steel Corp. v. EPA, 782 F.2d 645, 652 (7th Cir.1986); Shavell, Strict Liability versus Negligence, 9 J. Legal Stud. 1 (1980). On both scores there is an argument for making the principal as well as the independent contractor liable if an accident occurs that is due to the hazardous character of the performance called for by the contract. The fact that a very high degree of care is cost-justified implies that the principal should be induced to wrack his brain, as well as the independent contractor his own brain, for ways of minimizing the danger posed by the activity. And the fact that the only feasible method of accident prevention may be to reduce the amount of the activity or substitute another activity argues for placing liability on the principal, who makes the decision whether to undertake the activity in the first place. The electrical utility that has to decide whether to transport nuclear waste materials by motor or rail may be influenced in its choice by the relative safety of the modes—if it is liable for the consequences of an accident.

True, the principal would in any event be liable indirectly if the price it paid the independent contractor fully reflected the dangers of the undertaking; but this condition would be fulfilled only if the contractor were fully answerable for an accident if one occurred. And though fully liable in law, the independent contractor would not be fully liable in fact if a damage judgment would exceed his net assets. The likelihood of the independent contractor's insolvency is greater the more hazardous the activity; by definition, expected accident costs are greater. Another thing making them greater is that the contractor will be strictly liable for accidents caused by the abnormally dangerous character of his activity, see Restatement, supra, §427A, comment a, and therefore his expected legal-judgment costs will be higher than those of a contractor liable only for negligence. With the exposure of the independent contractor to liability so great, it may be necessary to make the principal liable as well in order to ensure that there is a solvent defendant. This is important not only to provide compensation for accident victims but also to reduce the number of accidents. Without such liability a principal might hire judgment-proof independent contractors to do his dangerous jobs, knowing that the contractors would have an incentive to cut corners on protecting safety and health and that this would reduce the cost of the contract to him. See Sykes, *The Economics of Vicarious Liability*, 93 Yale L.J. 1231, 1241-42, 1272 (1984).

CHAPTER 8

PRODUCTS LIABILITY

SECTION A. HISTORICAL DEVELOPMENT

Instructors will vary in how they want to teach the cases in this section; so far as this manual is concerned, the cases do not lend themselves to suggested questions and answers. We think it will be most useful here to instead present some of the interesting scholarly commentaries on the cases that put them into fuller context. Instructors can decide for themselves which contextual features to bring into their class discussions and how best to do it

MacPherson v. Buick Motor Co. (exception swallows privity rule for products cases)

a. Posner, *Cardozo: A Study in Reputation* 108-09 (1993), notes that most of Cardozo's opinion is spent discussing the precedents; the opinion turns "practical" only in saying that "The dealer was indeed the one person of whom it might be said with some approach to certainly that by him the car would not be used. Yet the defendant would have us say that he was the one person whom it was under a legal duty to protect." But Posner suggests that this might could make more sense that Cardozo acknowledges:

> The dealer warrants the safety of the automobile to the consumer but cannot warrant its safety to himself. The injured consumer can sue the dealer under the warranty; the dealer in turn can try to shift the ultimate burden of liability to the manufacturer through the doctrine of indemnity or through an express contract; and the manufacturer can try to shift the liability to the maker of the defective part, also through either the doctrine of indemnity or an express contract. The pragmatic issue in *MacPherson*, which Cardozo does not discuss, is whether the allocation of liability for product injuries should be left to contract (or to the doctrine, loosely contractual, of implied indemnity) or made a task for tort law. There are practical reasons for the second choice—for example, the possibility that the dealer will lack sufficient assets to pay a judgment and will therefore not be fully deterrable by a suit for damages, and the desirability of avoiding circuitous litigation (consumer versus dealer, followed by dealer versus manufacturer, rather than consumer versus manufacturer).

Posner notes that while those these latter issues were not discussed in Cardozo's opinion, they were emphasized in MacPherson's brief.

b. From Gary T. Schwartz, *New Products, Old Products, Evolving Law, Retroactive Law*, 58 N.Y.U. L. Rev. 796 (1983):

> Prior to *MacPherson v. Buick Motor Co.*, the common law was not nearly so hostile to injured consumers as standard accounts tend to indicate. Nor, for that matter, was the case law very dense; before the advent of the automobile—to which *MacPherson* was a prompt response—there simply were not large numbers of product-related lawsuits. *Winterbottom v. Wright* itself involved not a manufacturer but a serviceman; moreover, the latter's negligence evidently took the form of a mere omission, a point on which one of the *Winterbottom* judges relied. *Huset v. J. I. Case Threshing Machine Co.* is generally regarded as the leading synthesis of the privity-based rule negating manufacturer liability. Yet the *Huset* opinion also recognized important exceptions

to this rule, the first of which seemed to cover those cases in which 'the natural and probable result' of the manufacturer's negligence was an injury to the ultimate consumer rather than to the intermediate retailer. The 1898 edition of the Shearman & Redfield treatise on negligence regarded manufacturers' liability as a minor corner of the law, and the treatise's exposition of that law clearly conveyed a pro-plaintiff tenor. In California, only five suits brought by injured consumers reached the appellate courts prior to that state's acceptance of *MacPherson* in 1933; plaintiffs secured recoveries in four of the five. Edward Levi's throughtful book discusses thirteen product-related cases decided in England and New York prior to 1915; in eight of these, the plaintiffs emerged victorious.

There is every reason, then, for accepting Cardozo's own later characterization of *MacPherson*: in its treatment of the privity issue, *MacPherson* did not transform the law, but rather resolved the ambivalences that preexisting law exhibited. In any event, in the decades following *MacPherson* (and its sequelae), manufacturers became subject to broad liability, under a negligence theory, for what the law now refers to as "manufacturing defects." Observe in this regard the expansive interpretation that *MacPherson* conferred on the negligence standard: even when a manufacturer buys component parts from a reputable supplier with a perfect safety record, negligence law still imposes an obligation to inspect. In many cases, however, the plaintiff's inability to reconstruct what went wrong inside the manufacturer's plant would inhibit his ability to recover, unless he were allowed to rely on the doctrine of res ipsa loquitur. Traditionally, res ipsa had required that the harm-causing instrument be within the 'exclusive control' of the defendant at the time of the accident. Yet in product cases, the exclusive control test could seem obtuse, since it would not serve its characteristic function of identifying who was probably the negligent party.

c. From Richard A. Epstein, *The Unintended Revolution in Product Liability Law*, 10 Cardozo L. Rev. 2193 (1989):

In practice, the level of product liability litigation did not increase substantially on account of *MacPherson*. One measure of the consequences of that case is the flat level of insurance premiums for product liability that held firm in the decades that followed. All through the 1940s and 1950s, premiums remained very low, whether measured in absolute dollars or percentage of insurance sold. In some instances, product liability insurance was quite literally given away, as an added inducement to get more substantial lines of business, such as general liability, premise liability or workers' compensation programs. The simplest explanation for the stable condition of product liability insurance premiums is probably the best. While plaintiffs could freely sue, their recovery was effectively hedged in by a broad range of substantive requirements that survived the demise of privity. Negligence itself could be difficult on occasion to prove, even with res ipsa loquitur; the causal connection between defendant and plaintiff had to be close—and most importantly, the conception of product defect was quite narrow, and the scope of defenses based upon plaintiff misconduct or assumption of risk was very broad. Several restrictive doctrines operating in tandem could do most of the work of the single privity limitation—which, it should be added, was far from watertight even before *MacPherson*. The earlier law had allowed some suits against manufacturers. *MacPherson* allowed a few more. Recasting the prior exceptions into a new rule was a conceptual tour de force, which changed the outcome in some small percentage of cases, but did not amount to any sea change in the law.

d. John Goldberg and Benjamin Zipursky have made it their project to challenge the most common ways that tort scholars think about duties. We saw an example in the section of this manual on the *Palsgraf* case; another example, relevant to our current material, is their piece *The Moral of MacPherson*, 146 U. Pa. L. Rev. 1733 (1998). It's a long piece, well worth checking out if their approach is to your taste; in this space it will be possible just to suggest the flavor of their thinking by excerpting some portions of the piece discussing *MacPherson* and its interpretation:

> [In the view of most modern scholars], *MacPherson* marks the rejection by one of our greatest jurists of the most egregious instance of conceptually muddled and politically regressive duty-talk. Conversely, the decision constitutes Cardozo's clear-eyed embrace of the Holmes-Prosser model of negligence, combining a simple, non-relational state directive to act reasonably with judicially-crafted immunities from liability where necessary to further public policy.

As the story is told by Prosser, *MacPherson* "struck through the fog" created by Winterbottom's no-duty holding by identifying clearly that the question in the case was not whether the manufacturer owed a duty of reasonable care to the plaintiff, a question which in turn rested on the subsidiary doctrinal issue of whether a car constituted an inherently dangerous product. Those questions needed no answer. Under the Holmes-Prosser model, Buick, like any other person or entity, was subject to the generic directive to act reasonably; thus, any product could serve as the basis for negligence liability if it posed a risk of harm. For the same reasons, Buick's liability did not turn on evidence as to the existence of some relationship between Buick and MacPherson. Indeed, as Prosser read *MacPherson*, it held that a manufacturer like Buick was subject to liability "based upon nothing more than the sufficient fact that [it] ha[d] so dealt with the goods [in question] that they [we]re likely to come into the hands of another, and to do harm if they [we]re defective."

Moreover, because *MacPherson* came to the Court of Appeals with the unreasonableness of Buick's actions assumed, Prosser maintained that Cardozo, being a good Holmesian, must have recognized that the only real question before the court was whether *Winterbottom* had properly granted manufacturers a policy- driven waiver of the compensation sanction that negligence law ordinarily imposes for harms caused by unreasonable acts. Even if the *Winterbottom* decision was justified in 1842, it could not be sustained in 1916. The intervening years had seen a "definite change" in both "social philosophy" and economic reality. Accordingly, Cardozo properly revoked the privilege to act unreasonably that *Winterbottom* had granted to Buick and other manufacturers.

Prominent contemporary scholars, notably Professors Rabin and White, even more explicitly attribute to *MacPherson* the embrace of modern, Holmesian negligence. In his important analysis of the rise of the "fault principle," Rabin sought to trace the historical transition from pre-Holmesian notions of negligence liability, in which duties of care were thought to be relational, to the modern Holmesian fault principle—the notion of a comprehensive liability principle founded on a "general" duty of due care. Pointing to the continued vitality of no-duty cases like *Winterbottom* into this century, Rabin argued that previous scholars had misdated this transition by claiming that it had already occurred when Holmes was writing in the late nineteenth century. As was clear from the privity cases and other "no-duty" decisions, negligence law continued to retain "doctrinal barriers that served to vitiate the fault principle" well into this century. Thus, according to Rabin, it was only after Cardozo "artfully manipulated" the privity rule and its exceptions that the Holmesian fault principle was established in the critical area of products liability.

Even though it is one of Rabin's targets, Professor White's intellectual history of American tort law provides a similar account of *MacPherson*. According to White, although Cardozo may not have been the first to embrace Holmes's notion of "universal duty"—the idea "that the negligence principle . . . was not tied to status or vocation or contract, but was a reflection of generalized civil obligations"—his rejection of Buick's privity argument constituted a seminal instance of

Holmesian thinking. Thus, "*MacPherson* appears as a classic modern negligence case, where a broad universal duty of care is substituted for particularized obligations owed only by certain persons."

Finally, Judge Posner expresses much the same view of *MacPherson* in his recent study of Cardozo. According to Posner, the hallmark of Cardozo's decisions was his overriding concern to "mak[e] law more pragmatic," that is, to enact intelligent social policy through his decisions. While noting that Cardozo's *MacPherson* opinion is devoted to an analysis of cases, Posner nevertheless argues that the decision was driven by Cardozo's assessment that *Winterbottom's* waiver of liability amounted to bad policy, and that liability was in fact most efficiently placed upon manufacturers like Buick. That Cardozo chose not to justify his decision in these terms is seen by Posner as a testament to Cardozo's tactical wisdom. Rather than writing a policy tract, he wrote what appeared to be a traditional judicial opinion in order to increase the likelihood that his judicial brethren would embrace it.

Thus, from Prosser to Posner, mainstream tort scholars have maintained a near-consensus on the moral of *MacPherson*. They believe that it represents a seminal decision marking the judicial embrace of the Holmes-Prosser model of negligence. That model rejects the notion that a question exists as to whether a given defendant owes a given plaintiff a duty of care. There is always such a duty because the tort of negligence imposes a generic standard of reasonable care owed by all to all. The only questions that require consideration under the model are: the jury question of whether that generic standard of care was breached in a manner that proximately caused the plaintiff harm, and the judicial question of whether there is any public policy reason to override the default sanction that ordinarily requires a defendant to compensate the plaintiff for that harm. By refusing to rely on the distinction between inherently dangerous and not-inherently-dangerous products, Cardozo embraced the generic, or universal, duty of care. All products, he argued, might pose unreasonable risks of danger, and hence all manufacturers were potentially subject to liability for injuries caused by those products. Likewise, by rejecting the privity limitation, Cardozo signaled his progressive assessment that, as a class, manufacturers no longer were entitled to the immunity from negligence liability that *Winterbottom* had afforded them.

The authors then set out their alternative view:

[T]extual evidence against the Prosserian reconstruction is found in the [*MacPherson*] opinion's repeated return to the issue of whether the defendant was obligated to conduct itself in a certain way. According to Prosser's account, the issue in the case was the policy question as to whether negligent product manufacturers should be required to compensate non-purchasers injured by their products. For Cardozo, however, the resolution of that question turned on the duty issue; the issue itself had meaning for him apart from the question of liability. Moreover, its meaning did not concern whether a manufacturer does, or should, have a duty to compensate such a plaintiff. The questions, according to the court, were whether Buick had a "duty of vigilance," whether it bore an "obligation to inspect," how great was the "need of caution," and how "strict[ ]" was the duty to which Buick had to conform its conduct. In its grandest passage, quoted earlier, Cardozo's opinion announces that he and his brethren have "put aside the notion that the duty to safeguard life and limb, when the consequences of negligence may be foreseen, grows out of contract and nothing else. We have put the source of the obligation where it ought to be. We have put its source in the law." It would be hard to find a more emphatic announcement stating that manufacturers owe a duty to conduct themselves so as to attend to the safety of product users. [...]

[M]ost importantly, our reading of *MacPherson* makes sense of Cardozo's legal argument in a way that Prosserian readings cannot. [...] Within the inherently dangerous product cases, Cardozo found the principle that, where the nature of the product provides notice that due care in manufacture is necessary to avoid probable physical harm to a class of persons who cannot be expected to inspect the product, a duty of care runs to that class of persons, regardless of privity. As such, his reading of the cases does not adopt Holmes's notion of the duty to the world. The obligation to take care described by Cardozo is not grounded in a general or generic duty to the public. Rather, it derives from a set of obligations, owed by certain classes of defendants to certain classes of plaintiffs, that Cardozo found implicit in the common law of torts, including the "thing of danger" precedents. [...]

One might ask what point is served by describing Cardozo's approach as articulating a relational theory of duty, given that the theory treats even strangers as having "relationships." The short answer is that, from a relational view, the question of liability to the plaintiff does not turn on whether liability is morally permissible or socially desirable, but rather turns on whether defendant's conduct breached an obligation to the plaintiff. Hence, in both *MacPherson* and *Palsgraf*, Cardozo held that the critical question was not (as Holmes and Prosser would suppose) whether the imposition of liability made for good policy or was fair, but whether the defendant was obligated to use ordinary care to protect the physical well-being of the plaintiff, and whether the negligent conduct alleged by the plaintiff was a breach of that duty. This "short answer" in fact contains several distinct ideas [explained elsewhere in the article]: that duty is to be understood deontologically, not consequentially; that standing is to be understood relationally, not instrumentally; and that the concept of duty in negligence is relationship-sensitive, rather than generic. For the moment, our point is simply that, as a conceptual matter, a relational, but universalistic, conception of duty is in important ways different from a non-relational conception.

Escola v. Coca-Cola Bottling Co.
Greenman v. Yuba Power Products, Inc.

a. G. Edward White, *Tort Law in America: An Intellectual History* 198-200 (2003), details how Traynor's opinion in *Escola* borrowed heavily from Prosser; not only the ideas but much of the language Traynor uses can be matched with nearly identical phrases in Prosser's 1941 treatise. White remarks that Traynor's concurring opinion in *Escola*

came at a time when strict liability theory was in an embryonic state; he gave it a model for practical application. Like *MacPherson*, *Escola* was one of those cases that helped recast thinking about an entire area of tort law. Traynor's opinion shifted inquiries from the proper theory of liability in the defective products area—the logic of strict liability in tort overwhelmed that of negligence or warranty—to inquiries about the limits of the strict liability principle.

b. From George Priest, *The Invention of Enterprise Liability: A Critical History of the Intellectual Foundations of Modern Tort Law*, 14 J. Leg. Stud. 461 (1985):

There had been battles within tort law scholarship since the 1910s over the privity issue. Through the 1950s, however, defeat of privity in tort law allowed a plaintiff no more than an opportunity to prove negligence. Similarly, none of the Code drafters to my knowledge seriously proposed the prohibition of disclaimers of liability or limitations of warranties. Thus the effective gain to the nonbuyer victim from the elimination of the privity requirement may easily have been illusory.

More striking evidence of the conceptual constraints of the time is the apparent inability of even the most distinguished of scholars to appreciate the broader relevance of risk distribution. [...] [T]he most prominent antecedent of our modern regime is Justice Traynor's 1944 concurring opinion in *Escola v. Coca Cola Bottling Co.* Traynor's opinion sets forth the grounds for the strict liability standard for product defects that later was adopted by the California Supreme Court (and the large majority of U.S. jurisdictions) nearly two decades later. Perhaps the best measure of the exceptional character of Traynor's vision, however, is that the opinion received very little attention by scholars at the time. Levi's 1948 history does not discuss or cite it. Prosser, in a 1949 article, regards Traynor's approach in *Escola* as specific to food cases. Charles O. Gregory's celebrated 1951 history, "Trespass to Negligence to Absolute Liability," documents the progressive decline of the fault system and the rise of absolute liability, but does not cite *Escola*. [...] It is a measure of the strength of the conceptual barriers that remained intact in the early 1950s that Traynor's brilliant anticipation of the modern theory of enterprise liability could be so largely ignored.

c.   From Gary Schwartz, *The Beginning and Possible End of the Rise of Modern American Tort Law*, 26 Ga. L. Rev. 601 (1992):

In the products liability context, Justice Traynor's famous concurring opinion in *Escola v. Coca Cola Bottling Co.*—appropriated by courts in the 1960s—reasoned that "[t]he cost of an injury . . . may be an overwhelming misfortune to the person injured, and a needless one, for the risk of injury can be insured by the manufacturer and distributed among the public as the cost of doing business." Traynor certainly seemed to be assuming that for manufacturers and consumers the aggregate expenses of liability would be no more than moderate—substantial enough to induce some safety efforts by the manufacturer, but not so large as to seriously inflate the price of products, let alone to occasion any significant economic dislocations. By the 1980s, however, it had become clear that at least for certain service providers and product manufacturers, the costs of liability had become quite high. Then, during the tort crisis that began in late 1984, liability costs proceeded to soar. While the official mid-1980s tort crisis has by now receded, the price of liability insurance remains high even while the extent of its coverage has been considerably reduced.

We are hence left with a tort system that entails financial consequences that were very poorly anticipated 30 years ago. To gain a sense of the significance of the increased cost of liability, assume that you are a judge who is asked to rule on the extent of liability of a community health center serving a low-income community. In 1970, your understanding might well have been that the price of liability insurance is typically low, and this understanding would have enabled you to establish liability at the broad level that you deemed otherwise appropriate. Assume now, however, that you today read in a reliable journal that the high cost of liability insurance is requiring these centers to give up on certain medical services that the centers themselves regard as quite important to patients' welfare. You may well suspect that these cost increases are due to some malfunction in the liability insurance mechanism. Even so, faced with the reality of the clinics' new situation, you would be inhibited from issuing a ruling that might broadly define these clinics' tort liability.

Turn now to tort liability of more ordinary commercial enterprises. In the corporate context, by the 1980s high tort costs seemed to matter in quite a new way. Major American corporations—such as the Big Three automakers—which had appeared so dominant in the 1960s were now being perceived as fragile, buffeted by consumer resistance and foreign competition. Moreover, by the 1980s it had become clear that imposing liability on corporations could produce results that go beyond mere reductions in corporate profits. Consider *Brown v. Superior Court*, the 1988 California case that remained with the negligence standard in cases involving prescription drugs and declined to adopt hindsight strict liability. Justice Mosk's opinion for the court expressed his awareness that the application of products liability to drug companies had already induced the tripling of the price of one drug, the decision by one company not to introduce at all another apparently valuable new drug, the unwillingness (absent federal support) of companies to supply a flu vaccine, the withdrawal from the market of most of the producers of the DPT vaccine, and the increase in the price of a dose of this vaccine from eleven cents to eleven dollars. As Justice Mosk noted, these were consequences that had ensued merely because of other courts' application of the negligence standard. Faced with these social consequences, one can understand why Mosk and his California colleagues would be quite unwilling to extend liability, by virtue of the hindsight idea, well beyond the boundaries of negligence. Similarly, one can understand why the New York Court of Appeals would worry about the over-deterrence of drug companies in deciding to adopt its two-generation duty-like limitation on the scope of those companies' liability. One can likewise appreciate that court's opinion in *McDougald v. Garber*. As noted above, the size of the average tort award has increased dramatically during the modern era; more-over, the portions of awards attributable to general damages such as pain and suffering have apparently gone up even more sharply than the portions due to out-of-pocket special damages. The New York court's undoubted awareness of these modern tendencies in tort verdicts certainly helps explain its unwillingness in *McDougald* to create a special heading of general damages for lost life enjoyments.

d. From Robert A. Rabin, *Tort Law in Transition: Tracing the Patterns of Sociolegal Change*, 23 Val. U. L. Rev. 1 (1988):

Tort liability for defective products has been twice transformed in this century—the second major shift coming in the present tort revival of the past twenty-five years. Before 1900, however, product harm was an area hardly worth mentioning. Under the nineteenth century approach, the requirement that the victim of a product injury be in contractual privity with the defendant served as an effective damper on litigation against product manufacturers. Although the privity bar was undermined by judicially-created exceptions during the latter part of the century, particularly for a category of 'imminently dangerous' products, there was no generally recognized duty of due care until the landmark case of *MacPherson v. Buick Motor Co.*, decided in 1916.

MacPherson represented the initial transformation of products liability law. Defective products were brought into the mainstream of doctrinal liability for accidental harm under the fault principle. But there is nothing to suggest that product injuries were, as a consequence, singled out as a particularly critical social problem. On this score, a comparative look at some of the other roughly contemporaneous leading sources of accidental harm is revealing. Study commission reports and legislative activity were devoted to workers' injuries, auto accidents, and grade-crossing collisions. By contrast, product defect claims, even after *MacPherson*, seem to have made modest demands on the legal system and to have gone unnoticed in the political forum.

Perhaps this low-visibility phenomenon is the principal explanation for the remarkable fact that for more than forty years after MacPherson was decided the theory of enterprise liability, which had served as the ideological foundation for the demise of common law negligence in cases of workers' injuries, made virtually no headway in the consumer injury setting. This state of affairs came to pass despite the clearly apparent argument that product injuries, like industrial accidents, could be viewed as a cost of production properly assigned to the manufacturing enterprise in order to better achieve both injury prevention and risk spreading objectives.

Indeed, when the frontal assault on the established law of negligence in products cases (*MacPherson*) began, it appeared for the moment that enterprise liability theory—and tort law, more generally—would be left by the wayside. In *Henningsen v. Bloomfield Motors*, the New Jersey Supreme Court took the major step of enunciating a strict liability approach in product injury cases on a theory of implied warranty of merchantable quality. Instead of relying on a tort/enterprise liability nexus, the court adopted a contract/inequality of bargaining power perspective to displace negligence.

But even this false start (as it turned out) did not occur until 1960. The post-*MacPherson* decades had been consonant with the generally tranquil world of tort in which the risk-generating behavior of professionals, business establishments, homeowners, and government officials, let alone product manufacturers, was taken seriously only when it constituted a departure from ordinary standards of conduct. At the time, there was no disposition to view such behavior as an inevitable consequence of routine activities.

Then, in the early 1960s, a notable doctrinal development took place. In *Greenman v. Yuba Power Products, Inc.*, the California Supreme Court adopted strict liability for defective products, and, shortly thereafter, the American Law Institute took a similar position by adding Section 402A to the Restatement Second of Torts. These developments triggered a nationwide movement in which a second paradigm shift in liability for defective products, rejection of negligence in favor of strict liability, was widely adopted. In fact, paralleling the malpractice experience, a turbulent era in products law was ushered in that continues to the present. Since the mid-1960s, judicial ingenuity has been stretched to the limit by the necessity of articulating intelligible standards for design defect cases, establishing judicial guidelines for failure to warn controversies, and defining meaningful defenses and causal limitations in a wide variety of product cases. The movement to strict liability brought products law to center stage, initially as a focal point of scholarly analysis, but before long as the lightning rod for criticism and debate over the efficacy of tort law. [...]

Thus, the parameters marking out what constituted a colorable claim were widened by the advent of strict liability. This landmark development, and the concomitant across-the-board rise in product claims and award levels, call for some sort of explanation. Just as highway accidents have been decided for two centuries by reference to the fault principle, product injuries might have remained under the sway of *MacPherson* through the end of the twentieth century and beyond. There was nothing inevitable about the liberalization of defective products law, not to speak of the corresponding growth in claims and award levels.

How is the expansion of products law to be explained then? George Priest has argued that the erosion of *MacPherson* was a consequence of the convergence of two schools of influential legal scholarship in the 1950s and early 1960s: the work of Friedrich Kessler, on the contracts side, emphasizing the inequality of bargaining power between manufacturers and consumers, and the writings of Fleming James, on the tort side, highlighting the risk-spreading potential of liability insurance. Eventually, in Priest's view, James' enterprise liability theory prevailed in the form of strict liability for defective products. Witness the rejection of *Henningsen* in favor of *Greenman*, mentioned above.

Without denigrating the influence of legal scholarship, I would suggest that the transformation of products liability law over the past quarter century, and particularly the rapid growth in claims and award levels in recent years, requires a broader focus. In terms of tort doctrine, the enduring contribution of *MacPherson* was to substitute a generalized duty of due care for the traditional status-based paradigm of responsibility for tortious harm. In doing so, Cardozo had the breadth of vision to weave products liability deftly into the dynamic pattern of tort law development generally over the past two centuries.

However, as far as the moral basis of tort responsibility was concerned, Judge Cardozo's approach in *MacPherson* remained firmly rooted in the nineteenth century. Product manufacturers might owe a general duty of care to consumers in Cardozo's view, but his vision of tort liability remained grounded in an individualized determination of carelessness. Cardozo was a creature of his time. Accident law retained its two-party focus.

The significance of *Greenman* and its progeny was in rejecting wrongful behavior as an adequate guide to liability for accidental harm. The central thrust of enterprise liability—the underpinning for strict liability doctrine—is its singular indifference to conventional moral-based, corrective justice notions of assigning responsibility for harm. The constant (albeit rather misleading) litany that these cases focus "upon the safety of the product, rather than the reasonableness of the manufacturer's conduct" is precisely the expression of this point: strict liability for products abandons the search for careless behavior in favor of an impersonal mechanism for distributing and responding to risk. Insurance was surely a factor; it highlighted the risk-spreading potential of enterprise liability and almost certainly was the dominant influence in the initial adoption of strict liability. But from all appearances, the real growth in products cases did not begin until almost a decade after *Greenman*. Indeed, like medical malpractice, there appears to have been a period of turbulence in products cases in the early 1970s followed by an even sharper disturbance in the mid-1980s. While doctrinal development, as discussed, preceded the growing demands on the tort system, it offers only a partial explanation of the groundswell that developed in the succeeding two decades.

Throughout the 1960s, the consequences of post-World War II economic growth became more apparent. An increasingly affluent society created a market for a wife array of technologically sophisticated new products, ranging from drugs and medications to power tools and lawnmowers--products that generated significant risks to health and safety along with their readily apparent utility. Similarly, new affluence, suburban life styles, and the network of interstate highways promoted new levels of use of the automobile—and soon exacerbated longstanding concerns about auto safety.

Still, a catalyst was necessary to alter the climate of claims and award levels in product cases. The Interagency Task Force on Product Liability, established in 1976 as a response to the first wave of concern about products claims, documented, as best it could with limited data, rapid growth in claims and award levels in the period between 1970 and 1975. But the explanatory mechanism remained uncertain.

Like medical malpractice, a satisfying explanation necessitates reference to exogenous circumstances, rather than exccessive preoccupation with internal developments in the tort system. The growing turbulence in tort law was only a single aspect of deeper stirrings in the surrounding legal environment. Health and safety concerns had become paramount in the public mind by the early 1970s. Just a few year earlier, Ralph Nader's campaign for auto safety had ignited long latent consumerist impulses that soon spilled over into regulatory reform on a wide variety of fronts in the name of product safety. The Consumer Product Safety Commission was established, amidst considerable media attention, and a well-publicized system of monitoring and 'prioritizing' consumer injuries was soon in place. The Federal Trade Commission was revitalized. Congress adopted a bevy of product-specific regulatory schemes, and local consumer complaints offices flourished.

For present purposes, it is especially important to note that Nader's prominence in the early 1970s rested not just on consumer safety issues, but on a broader questioning of the legitimacy and responsibility of existing institutions, particularly the responsibilities of corporate America to the ordinary citizen. These sentiments were reflected, in my view, in the removal of intangible barriers to claims consciousness—not unlike the erosion of the professional mystique of physicians. The technological prowess that yielded a steadily growing output of consumer products was no longer viewed as an unmixed blessing. Moreover, the contemporaneous public concern about the environment, focused initially on air and water pollution, and soon afterwards on toxic harms, almost certainly contributed to the erosion of deference. Here the public's ambivalence was manifest. Everything that corporate America promised seemed to bear a hidden cost--unseen risks to health and safety that necessitated accountability. In tandem, the demand for regulation and compensation expanded, and the characterization and valuation of personal harms took on a more expansive aspect.

In sum, doctrinal changes in the products area were the surface indications of a new social vision of the functions of tort law. The ideology of enterprise liability was the driving force that initiated these changes. But even deeper stirrings were taking place. There came to be a radical loss of faith in the old view that personal injury was the result of isolated failures on the assembly line. In its stead, a heightened sensitivity arose to the latent risks in standardized products that appeared to be the ubiquitous consequence of technological and material progress.

e. From Richard A. Epstein, *The Unintended Revolution in Product Liability Law*, 10 Cardozo L. Rev. 2193 (1989):

The first major shifts in received doctrine after *MacPherson* occurred in two cases decided in the early 1960s, *Henningsen v. Bloomfield Motors* and *Greenman v. Yuba Power Products Co.* These two cases stood for two propositions that are closely entwined historically, but nonetheless analytically separable: the rejection of freedom of contract and the adoption of strict liability (or implied warranty) in torts cases.

First, both these cases contain an explicit attack on, and rejection of, the principle of freedom of contract as it applies to product-related injuries. In *Henningsen*, the conclusion followed a detailed discussion about product warranties and the limitations on recovery that they contained. Heavily influenced by the "contract of adhesion" writing that dominated academic circles in the 1940s and 1950s, *Henningsen* concluded that private limitations on warranties served no useful social purpose, and were therefore an attempt by manufacturers to distance themselves from the harmful consequences of the defective products they had placed into the stream of commerce. The analysis was in accordance with the dominant learning of the time, which, in retrospect, is strikingly incomplete. The court focused solely upon the effects of the warranty upon recovery, given that the injury had occurred. At no point did the court ask how warranties could reduce the level of cross-subsidization across consumers, control against the problems of consumer moral hazard, or allow consumers to unbundle their purchases of insurance from that of automobiles. [...] *Henningsen* established an instant judicial consensus. Just two years later in *Greenman*, Justice Traynor could confidently say:

> the recognition that the liability is not assumed by agreement but imposed by law, and the refusal to permit the manufacturer to define the scope of its own responsibility for defective products make clear that the liability is not one governed by the law of contract warranties but by the law of strict liability in tort.

This sentence captures perfectly the dominant view of the law today. With contract rejected, the next question was what standard of liability the law should impose. The answer that was reached in both *Henningsen* and *Greenman* was strict liability. There is no question that this system has advantages over the alternative negligence view of the subject. One factual issue is removed from consideration at trial, and the defendant has a clearer sense of the net expenses that it could incur from the product in question. Indeed in the context of both *Henningsen* and *Greenman*, as well as the pre-Restatement (Second) of Torts cases, the strict liability rule looks quite effective. Both cases involved relatively new products with latent defects that failed in ordinary use. The strict liability standard thus did not appear to open any floodgates, or to pose any major threats in the underlying integrity of tort law. The relative want of any short-term institutional response shows that the immediate consequences of both cases were essentially benign.

Nonetheless, the anticontractual bias of both *Henningsen* and *Greenman* has proved to have devastating long-term consequences for the soundness of the product liability system. The system of product liability was stripped of its powers of self-correction. In essence, *Henningsen*, *Greenman*, and the Restatement (Second) of Torts reserved to the courts a legal monopoly to fashion the relevant terms and conditions on which all products should be sold in all relevant markets. The centralization of power has the same consequences here that it has in other areas of government regulation. It leads to a legal regime that is unresponsive to changes in demand or technology. The judicial standard form becomes a Procrustean bed into which all private transactions have to fit at their peril. It may well be the case that certain uniform provisions are appropriate for the full range of product liability cases. But if the optimal solution is one that cuts off the tort liability for consequential damages, then a judicial rule that renders tort liability nonwaivable will not only be uniform, but also wrong in every case. More likely, in practice there may be important variations in the kinds of terms that are appropriate for certain classes of products and defects. Strict liability on manufacturers for contamination of products sold in sealed containers may make good sense, but far more complex allocation of risks may be appropriate in design and warning cases, especially when third party intermediaries—employees or physicians—have special, and varying, roles to play. Yet here, too, all efforts to find better ways to sell and market products are cut off before they are born, so that new information about product liability terms cannot be generated by voluntary transactions. Today all doctrinal innovation has to come from the courts, where the technical lags and information deficits are at their highest. Yet there is no alternative forum, save legislation, in which to override judgments when they have proved mistaken; indeed, there is no way to find out whether they are mistaken at all. [...]

The elimination of the negligence requirement in product liability cases brought to the fore the question of what counted as a product defect. In *Greenman*, Justice Traynor relied upon a conception of product defect that stressed the misrepresentation to the product user based on the product appearance, its accompanying literature, and the circumstances of its sale. "Implicit in the machine's presence on the market, however, was a representation that it would safely do the jobs for which it was built." As such, the law of product defect bore a close affinity with the law of "traps" that had always been of such importance in, say, occupiers' liability cases. Once the negligence limitation on recovery had been removed, this conception of defect (oftentimes styled "the consumer expectations" model) set the threshold for liability. But in retrospect, it seems clear that it could not survive the anticontractual bias of the courts. The theory of implied misrepresentation was articulated as part of the attack on freedom of contract in *Greenman*. But given that individual consumers could not sign disclaimers of liability, there was no reason to expect that they could sensibly evaluate all the options associated with the use of complex products, even with knowledge of the risks. The law had to do that for them. Toward this end, the definition of product defect was expanded to facilitate the necessary substitution of collective for individual judgment.

The tools that were available for that transition were, however, quite limited. It became clear that the standard of customary practice, itself discredited in ordinary negligence cases, could not possibly be revived in the new product liability environment. The dictates of custom and contract converge so closely that each is considered some variant upon the market standard. "Real" strict liability, of the sort which allows no cost/benefit analysis at all, could not be adopted either. While it may be sensible to make a polluter pay for pollution damage inflicted upon a stranger, no matter how great his level of precautions, it simply makes no sense to say that whenever a product is "involved" in an injury, it has necessarily been defective. Some collisions are too devastating even for the strongest cars to withstand; and the only machine tool that is completely safe is also completely inoperative. The complex duties between product maker and product user cannot be set by the simple "keep off" type of tests which characterize actions for trespass to land and nuisance.

By process of elimination, there was only one standard to invoke: cost/benefit. Oddly enough, the standard itself rings of the Hand formula and thus seems to invoke the very standards of negligence which the earlier strict liability cases such as *Henningsen* and *Greenman* had repudiated. There was a wide range of variations on the basic cost/benefit standard, and which should be adopted was an open question. The early cases, such as *Larsen v. General Motors*, all relied upon "general" negligence principles, as they applied to the new circumstances of automobile crashes. Thereafter, Professor Wade's risk/utility standard gave a more complicated version of the cost/benefit calculations that incorporated some explicit mention of the plaintiff's knowledge. Finally, such cases as *Barker v. Lull Engineering Co.*, held firm to some version of cost/benefit analysis while shifting to the defendant the burden of proof on product defect. Any continuity with pre-1960 cases is something of a mirage. Defendants would have obtained directed verdicts in the vast bulk of machine tool and automobile cases under the narrower standards of liability prior to *Larsen*, and even under the tests for design defects set out in Dix Noel's 1962 article on the subject.

f. From Richard A. Epstein, *The Risks of Risk/Utility*, originally published at 48 Ohio St. L. J. 469 (1987):

[I]f one had to summarize the traditional law before, say, 1968 in a couple of propositions, these are the two I would choose: First, ordinarily no liability for products with patent defects, and second, liability for latent defects only if the product caused damage in ordinary use. The application of these two tests was designed to make sure that liability existed only when (1) there was differential knowledge or access to knowledge between the parties, and (2) no misconduct of the plaintiff (who typically is using the product at the time of injury and well able to prevent the loss) helped bring about the loss in question.

This system of liability may give the wrong answer in some cases. Still as a rule of thumb it gives a clear, cheap, and correct answer in most cases. The distribution of cases along the latent/patent axis is such that there are few cases when the line between latent and patent is in doubt. By working to insure the easy transmission of information, this account strengthens market institutions by helping consumers make informed choices. Private contracts work fitfully at best before individual consumers have purchased or used a wide variety of goods, and the prohibition against latent defect spares producers from having to devise ways of providing independent guarantees that the product sold meets its promised quality standards. What seller of foodstuffs is able to provide warranties to all the people who eat its products? The utter want of any concern about 'contracting out' of products liability rules, and the complete disinterest in undoing them through legislation is pretty strong evidence of how close the common law rules once adhered to the social optimum.

The risk/utility formulas are a very different kettle of fish, as a bare listing of the Wade factors shows. While Professor Wade wrote as if his factor analysis offered a convenient rationalization of existing tort law, he was an unwitting firebrand. Risk/utility represents nothing less than a totally revolutionary way of looking at products liability. The latent defect tests reinforce market disciplines. The risk/utility test is a massive, if unintended, assault on markets and private ordering, for defendants are now required to justify independently every decision that they and their customers have made with respect to a product's use. No longer is it sufficient to say that the defendant informed the plaintiff of the hazards involved. Instead it becomes necessary to go behind the consent of consumers by finding expert testimony to reconstruct their past decisions from the ground up. And for what end?

Surely it is not to control administrative costs. The traditional rules have massive administrative efficiencies that are frittered away under Wade's risk/utility test. Substantive certainty is sacrificed as well. Risk/utility opens up every machine tool and every generic product to case-by-case attack within the judicial system: after all, the mere fact that the risk was assumed can no longer be treated as decisive on the reasonableness of the risk in question, even if relevant in some attenuated sense. But for all the intrusiveness of his test, Wade never explains why ex post collective judgments are superior to the ex ante judgments people make on their own. Yet surely the obviousness of the danger (which surely conveys something of its seriousness as well) is protection against both ordinary mistake and manufacturer misrepresentation or deceit, both of which harken back to the traditional concern with latent defects. And when the defect is patent, the ability to sell the product in the first instance is surely diminished, so that there is a powerful market check against systematic product abuse, one which the risk/utility test wholly ignores.

To see both the magnitude and the weakness of this entire risk/utility approach, it is instructive to ask the questions: Where does the application of the risk/utility test end, and why? If it can be used to decide whether certain features of a machine tool should be replaced, why cannot it be used to answer the question of whether entire classes of products, from handguns to convertible automobiles to alcohol should be marketed at all? There is nothing in the disorganized array of relevant factors that prevents a single headstrong jury from making fundamental decisions about what may be marketed and what may not be sold at all. Indeed, whenever the defendant has obtained a directed verdict or summary judgment, the judicial decision sooner or later returns to the 'open and obvious' test whose supposed inadequacy ushered in the risk/utility test in the first instance. In truth, it is no principled way to identify one domain where open and obvious dominates and another where risk/utility prevails. While we have been largely spared risk/utility in generic product cases, the risk/utility test continues to work its mischief by undermining countless standardized product warnings and designs.

There is, moreover, nothing about the parade of utilitarian factors that justifies the risk/utility test on any utilitarian grounds. Quite the opposite, its cost and unreliability suggest that it should be banished from the legal system. The older view, which said, let us control force and fraud, does have application to products liability. It explains why the latent/patent distinction, while widely rejected today, has far more intellectual staying power than the voguish, complex, multifactored test that has replaced it. The latent/patent distinction can yield the clean yes/no answer necessary on the issue of liability. In contrast, the Wade factors are utterly untranslatable into yes/no inquiry. We are asked, for example, to take a wide range of variables with continuous distributions, but without preassigned weights, and to meld them into a single yes/no judgment on the question of product defect.

A cursory inspection of the text shows how difficult that task is to execute. Who can decide what the total levels of social utility are, as set out in factor #1? Nor is there any single 'substitute product' against which the challenged product can be compared, as factor #3 might suggest. There are in reality a large number of different products (all of which can be configured in different ways) which may be the baseline on comparative analysis. These alternative products may not 'eliminate' the risk, as suggested in factor #4. They may reduce it by an uncertain amount. Alternatively they may increase the probability of injury but reduce the anticipated severity of the injuries that do occur. Nor must a substitute product meet the 'same' need. It could only meet some portion of the need and perhaps at some greater, or different, cost. And the ability to respond to changes in liability rules may be met only in part by changes in price or insurance coverage, as noted in factor #7.

With variables so numerous, the ingenuity of lawyers should never be doubted when the stakes in litigation are very high and discovery underregulated. The test is couched in an offhand way that makes difficult matters of degree look as though they involved simple distinctions in kind. It is a utilitarian nightmare. What starts out as a faithful application of the utilitarian calculus ends up as an unprincipled battle of the experts. Everything is admissible; nothing is quantifiable; nothing is dispositive. The degree of freedom left to the trier of fact after trial is as great as it was before. All too often, anything from a plaintiff's verdict for punitive damages to a defendant's verdict of no liability is consistent with the evidence. And it is all quite unnecessary; 'awareness' in factor #6 points to the key element of knowledge, and usually gives more useful information than everything else taken together.

Nonetheless, once courts are committed to risk/utility, it quickly becomes clear that they no formal test of liability equal to the task of sorting out the cases they must decide. Courts have quite naturally been most reluctant to grant any defendant (or plaintiff) a summary judgment, which is likely to be reversed on appeal in any event. Instead, judges are encouraged to hide behind the verdict, which decides without reasoning. The rise of the jury in modern law is no accident. It is an inevitable consequence of the present level of doctrinal poverty. Error costs and administrative costs continue to rise, and only the lawyers and experts, whose skills are necessary to navigate the morass, are able to turn a profit. For in these times the best legal and professional talent is strictly necessary to handle any complex case.

g. From Gary T. Schwartz, *New Products, Old Products, Evolving Law, Retroactive Law*, 58 N.Y.U. L. Rev. 796 (1983):

Those in the vanguard of the product liability movement seemed to have been of two minds respecting the implications of the strict liability rule. On the one hand, Prosser regarded the fall of the "citadel of privity" as 'the most rapid and altogether spectacular overturn of an established rule in the entire history of the law of torts.' Yet Prosser also recognized from an early date that 'an honest estimate might very well be that there is not one case in one hundred brought against manufacturers in which strict liability would result in recovery where negligence does not.' Justice Traynor's concurring opinion in *Escola* and his opinion for the full court in *Greenman v. Yuba Power Products, Inc.*, are rich with rhetoric that suggests the novelty of the strict liability doctrine. Yet much of his *Escola* and *Greenman* opinions are dedicated to showing why strict liability is a limited and sensible extension of modern negligence and warranty law.

Indeed, it may be that the most important changes in product law during the last twenty years have had relatively little to do with the formal strict liability doctine. The defense of assumption of risk, for example, clearly has declined in product liability actions; but this has been largely a consequence of the retreat of that defense in tort law overall. This retreat had been recommended by Harper and James in 1956 and accelerated by the New Jersey Supreme Court in a 1959 negligence opinion. In addition, prior to 1960, the traditional rule of contributory negligence was still recognized in tort law generally and hence in product cases in particular. A few states, however, had already adopted comparative negligence, and the comparative negligence idea clearly was on the table. Since then, comparative negligence has largely replaced the traditional defense in negligence law proper, and most courts have been willing to extend the comparative negligence rule into the product liability setting. The second Restatement had stipulated that in a product liability action ordinary contributory negligence would serve as no defense at all. The judicial abandonment of this district product liability position in favor of more general tort doctrine plainly has advantaged manufacturers in an important way.

Prior to 1960, the factors of patent hazard and unintended use counted substantially in favor of manufacturers. In some instances, the obviousness of a product's danger properly eliminated any obligation to warn. In other cases, the obviousness of the danger or the plaintiff's unintended use of the product served to raise the defenses of contributory negligence and assumption of risk. Moreover, both factors could bear on the general negligence issue of foreseeability of injury—since a particular product misuse may be unpredictable and since a patent hazard is most commonly avoided. In addition, unintended use sometimes provided an explanation for the product-related accident that all but excluded any claim of manufacturer negligence. Drawing on (but extending) all these points, a few courts established unintended use as a formal defense in product liability actions, while several courts seemingly recognized a special liability limitation for 'open and obvious' hazards. Many courts rejected the first of these defenses, however, thereby requiring manufacturers to construct and design products and provide product warnings in light of foreseeable uses generally, without much regard for the niceties of whether the use was intended. Also, a few judges declined to acknowledge the obvious hazard defense; they were joined by leading commentators, who argued that a firm obvious hazard rule would depart from more general negligence principles, with their emphasis on the reasonableness of risks.

Since 1960, the significance of obvious hazards and unintended uses has plainly diminished. Insofar as these factors were associated with the defenses of contributory negligence and assumption of risk, their diminution is basically a consequence of those defenses' decline in tort law generally. In addition, by the late 1960's, courts were strongly confirming the tentative pre-1960 view that the foreseeability of a product's (mis)use is the relevant consideration. And in 1966, courts began to deemphasize the obvious hazard factor, relying on both the scholarship of the 1950's and the pro-consumer impetus provided by the initial strict liability opinions of immediately previous years.

With these restrictions on liability modified, courts have increasingly relied on negligence law's traditional risk-benefit liability test in assessing manufacturers' trade-off design choices. Those who oppose these modern design defect cases have made clear that the uninhibited application of the negligence standard is what provokes their opposition. Actually, in most instances, the alternative design recommended by the plaintiff is already in use by one or more manufacturers—a circumstance that limits the reach of design defect findings. While in a few cases courts have boldly assessed as defective a fully customary design, these courts have conservatively relied on negligence law doctrine espoused by Judge Hand back in 1932.

Our current "defect" liability rule can be better appreciated by contrasting it with what could be called a rule of genuine strict liability. Resembling workers' compensation, the latter rule would subject manufacturers to liability for all harms resulting from the use of their products, whether or not those products contain anything resembling a defect. It suffices to say that courts have responded to the prospect of such a rule with dismay: it is a rule that 'no one wants' and whose consequences 'are beyond the ability of a court to know or comprehend.' This judicial antagonism to genuine strict liability, in combination with the extensive pre-1960 application of negligence and warranty principles, leads me to the view that our existing rule of product liability is a moderate rather than a radical doctrine, a doctrine that has developed in an evolutionary rather than a revolutionary manner. What seems fundamental to that rule is the high correlation between product defect and manufacturer negligence, making the issue of negligence not worth the costs and uncertainties of litigation.

h. From George Priest, *The Invention of Enterprise Liability: A Critical History of the Intellectual Foundations of Modern Tort Law*, 14 J. Leg. Stud. 461 (1985):

Our modern tort law regime is built on three basic concepts:

1. *Manufacturer Power.* Manufacturers possess vastly greater power than consumers with respect to all relevant aspects of the product defect problem. Manufacturers are able to control the rate of product-related accidents by investments in product safety features or in quality control, while consumers, generally, are powerless to avoid accidents from product use. Consumers have little influence over product quality through buying behavior, in part because of low levels of consumer information about product quality. It follows that manufacturers, if allowed to do so, will exploit the inferior bargaining position of consumers.

2. *The Benefits of Manufacturer-provided Insurance.* It is advantageous to spread the risks of product injuries broadly through insurance in order to reduce the incidence of loss to any specific individual. Risk spreading can best be provided by manufacturers, rather than by consumers in private insurance markets, because manufacturers can easily collect a small insurance premium in the price charged for the product.

3. *Internalization of Injury Costs to Manufacturers.* Society will benefit from internalizing the costs of operation to product manufacturers, including losses resulting from product-related injuries. Although the principal benefits from internalization are greater manufacturer investments to prevent losses and to provide insurance, other less tangible benefits may also accrue. Manufacturers, if forced to internalize costs, may make greater research investments into the sources of product-related injuries. At the minimum, an internalization policy will introduce an appropriate control on the level of manufacturing activities, in general and with respect to individual products. As the losses generated by a particular industry increase, the industry's costs of operation will increase.

SECTION B. MANUFACTURING DEFECTS

Welge illustrates the problems of proof that often accompany litigation over manufacturing defects; it also introduces the meaning of strict liability and explains the impact of the doctrine on seller and those earlier in the product's chain of distribution. The note cases afterwards focus largely on these latter issues: how to think define the "products" and "sellers" to whom these rules apply. If you want to shorten the section, omit *Winter* and *Saloomey*, which are very interesting but of less practical importance than the other cases.

Welge v. Planters Lifesavers Co. (D, injured when peanut jar breaks, sues retailer and manufacturer; L)

Q. What was the plaintiff's theory of liability in this case? Was it res ipsa loquitur? (Or: What is the relationship between res ipsa loquitur and the court's decision in this case?)

A. Not exactly. The theory was strict liability. But for the strict liability to apply, it must be shown that the product contained a defect—a deviation from its design specifications—at least by the time it left the hands of the last defendant (K-Mart). This is a question of fact. It is not a question of negligence. The court's reference to res ipsa is just an analogy; it is making the point that the fact of an accident can itself give rise to inferences. In the case of res ipsa, the inference is that the party controlling the instrument of harm was negligent. In the case of a peanut jar that collapses, the inference is that the jar must have contained a defect, i.e. some feature that was not part of its specifications.

The next question is when that defect entered the product. If the plaintiff's evidence is credited, it seems unlikely that the defect entered the product after purchase. Neither of these inferences—that the product contained a defect, or that the defect entered the product before sale—is required. The point is just that they permissibly could be drawn by a jury, even if the plaintiff hasn't offered proof to rule out other explanations for the collapse of the jar.

Q. Suppose the evidence at trial shows that the defect was introduced by a K-Mart employee; in trying to set up the bottles in a pyramid for display, he caused them all to fall down and one of them apparently cracked. He didn't see the crack, however, and put the jar back on top of the pyramid; the plaintiff selected it the next day, and the crack led to the injuries described in the case. Liability for Planters? (If not, why not, given the application of strict liability?)

A. No liability for Planters; strict liability here means that anyone who handles the product after the defect is introduced is liable regardless of fault, not that anyone who *ever* handled it is liable.

Q. Suppose the evidence at trial shows that a miscreant at the Planters factory carved weaknesses into the jar, then hid it with the others in a box. The K-Mart employees use all due care in handling and inspecting the jars, but do not catch the bad one. Liability for K-Mart?

A. Yes; see above.

Q. Suppose the jury found that the jar did collapse because Godfrey weakened it with her Exacto knife. Liability in whole or in part for the defendants?

A. Liability for K-Mart apparently would be complete because it participated in inviting the misuse, which caused it not to be misuse after all—at least vis a vis K-Mart. As for the other defendants, the most they probably could hope for is to have their liability reduced to reflect Godfrey's responsibility for the accident. They would have to show that they were not parties to the invitation to take the knife to the jar, and that taking the knife to the jar was "misuse."

Winter v. Putnam & Sons (Ps are injured when they rely on misinformation in D's *Encyclopedia of Mushrooms*; NL)
Saloomey v. Jeppesen (pilot and passengers killed in plane crash resulting from defective flight map; L)

Q. What is the superficial similarity between *Winter v. Putnam & Sons* and *Saloomey v. Jeppesen*? What is the distinction between them?

A. Both cases involved harm caused when someone relied on misinformation in a publication. Some possible distinctions: the Hand formula works out differently in the two situations. The PL of misinformation on a flight map may be higher than in a book about mushrooms (though it could well be pretty high in both cases). The B involved—the costs likely to follow from an imposition of strict liability—may be more tolerable in the case of the mapmaker; perhaps the result here is just to make maps more expensive, rather than to chill the creation of them (the demand for flight maps probably is not very elastic), whereas a general rule of strict liability for misinformation in books might well deter the creation of some books at the margin. Maps also are an exception to that rule easy to define and cabin. It's also possible to argue that opportunities for victim precautions may be unusually bad with respect to flight maps, because sometimes a pilot's need for information in them will arise suddenly and there will be no time for him to do anything but rely—whereas with most books, including an *Encyclopedia of Mushrooms*, there is usually a chance for victims to take other measures to protect themselves. Finally, perhaps consumer expectations regarding maps are higher than they are regarding books—though one would expect them to be pretty high in the case of the *Encyclopedia of Mushrooms*.

One might suggest that liability should be strict in *Winter* (the mushroom case) because picking mushrooms is an activity we don't mind seeing discouraged by high prices, employing some of the logic that might help distinguish the next two cases, *Magrine* and *Newmark*. But then courts would often have to make judgments about whether a particular book serves a socially important purpose. We don't mind seeing courts make judgments like that in some circumstances (e.g., in deciding whether a beekeeper is strictly liable for damage done by his charges), but we balk when it comes to courts making the same judgments about books and the ideas in them. The values behind the First Amendment come into play, and perhaps the First Amendment itself.

Here was what the court in *Winter* had to say in distinguishing its facts from cases involving flight maps:

> Aeronautical charts are highly technical tools. They are graphic depictions of technical, mechanical data. The best analogy to an aeronautical chart is a compass. Both may be used to guide an individual who is engaged in an activity requiring certain knowledge of natural features. Computer software that fails to yield the result for which it was designed may be another. In contrast, *The Encyclopedia of Mushrooms* is like a book on how to use a compass or an aeronautical chart. The chart itself is like a physical "product" while the "How to Use" book is pure thought and expression.

Q. Hypothetical: in *Birmingham v. Fodor's Travel Publications*, 833 P.2d 70 (Ha. 1992), the plaintiffs vacationed on the Hawaiian island of Kauai. They alleged that they were led by a book the defendants published, *Fodor's Hawaii 1988*, to visit the area known as Kekaha Beach and to go body-surfing there. The sustained various injuries in the process, and brought a suit claiming that Kekaha Beach was dangerous to swimmers and that Fodor's was negligent in recommending it for that purpose. What result?

A. No liability, of course. As is usual in these cases, all theories failed—negligent misrepresentation, failure to warn, and strict products liability. From the opinion affirming summary judgment for the defendants:

> [T]here are compelling policy reasons, apparently recognized by all jurisdictions addressing the issue, that militate against imposing a duty on a publisher to warn of the accuracy of its publication, absent authorship or warranty of the publication's contents. Therefore, we hold that a publisher of a work of general circulation, that neither authors nor expressly guarantees the contents of its publication, has no duty to warn the reading public of the accuracy of the contents of its publication.

> Because the *Guide* was a work of general circulation, and Fodor's neither authored nor expressly guaranteed the contents of the *Guide*, Fodor's had no duty to warn the Birminghams of the accuracy of the information contained in the *Guide*. Therefore, the trial court was correct in granting summary judgment in favor of Fodor's on the Birminghams' negligence claim against it.

The court also affirmed the dismissal of the products liability claim, citing the *Winter* case approvingly.

The courts' treatment of flight maps as "products" seems to be unique; claims of that sort about all other publications apper to fail.

Magrine v. Krasnica (NL for dentist who uses defective needle in plaintiff's mouth)
Newmark v. Gimbel's, Inc. (L for hairdresser who sells plaintiff defective treatment)

Q. What is the superficial similarity between *Magrine v. Krasnica* and *Newmark v. Gimbel's, Inc.*? What is the distinction between them?
A. In both cases a product used by a professional on a client caused injury to the client. Only in *Newmark* did this result in strict liability for the professional.

In *Magrine* the court found NL because the doctor was not in a better position than the plaintiff to discover and correct latent defects in his instruments, because the dentist was not a large enough enterprise to be able to spread the loss over large numbers of consumers, and (relatedly) because strict liability would significantly drive up the price of dental and medical care, which already is expensive. In *Newmark* the court found strict liability because it thought it formalistic to distinguish between a case where the hairdresser sells the client the product for home use (clear strict liability if it's defective) and the case where the hairdresser applies the product to the plaintiff in the ship. (To this it might be added, however, that many of the products used to create a "permanent" are not sold for home use.)

Perhaps the dental case can be distinguished because the needle was not something that plausibly could have been sold to the plaintiff as an ordinary product. (What result if the dentist gives away a free toothbrush at the end of the cleaning, and the toothbrush contains a defect that causes harm to the patient at home?) The court also relies on the idea that medicine and beautification are fundamentally different activities. Perhaps the idea is that the kind of activity-level pressures strict liability can create are more tolerable with respect to less important services like hairdressing.

Q. Hypothetical: in *Royer v. Catholic Medical Center*, 741 A.2d 74 (1999), the plaintiff had his knee replaced with an implanted prosthesis at the defendant's hospital. The pain in his knee became worse after the operation than it was beforehand. His doctors determined that the prosthesis was defective. They performed another operation to remove it and install a new one. The plaintiff initially brought suit against the manufacturer of the prosthesis, Dow Corning, to recover his damages. When Dow went bankrupt, he sued the hospital, alleging that it should be held strictly liable as the seller of the prosthesis. What result?
A. No liability. Said the court, affirming dismissal of the claim:

> Although a defendant may both provide a service and sell a product within the same transaction for purposes of strict liability, see Restatement (Second) of Torts § 402A, comment f at 350; cf. Bolduc v. Herbert Schneider Corp., 117 N.H. 566, 570, 374 A.2d 1187, 1189 (1977), the dispositive issue in this case is not whether the defendant "sold" or transferred a prosthetic knee, but whether the defendant was an entity "engaged in the business of selling" prosthetic knees so as to warrant the imposition of liability without proof of legal fault. [...]

> That the hospital charges a fee for the prosthesis and transfers possession does not transform the character of the hospital-patient relationship. "The thrust of the inquiry is thus not on whether a separate consideration is charged for the physical material used in the exercise of medical skill, but what service is performed to restore or maintain the patient's health." [Citations omitted, here and elsewhere.] We cannot agree that this distinction is merely a legal fiction. "[T]he essence of the transaction between the retail seller and the consumer relates to the article sold. The seller is in the business of supplying the product to the consumer. It is that, and that alone, for which he is paid." Hoff v. Zimmer, Inc., 746 F.Supp. 872, 875 (W.D.Wis.1990). A patient, by contrast, does not enter a hospital to "purchase" a prosthesis, "but to obtain a course of treatment in the hope of

being cured of what ails him." Indeed, "to ignore the ancillary nature of the association of product with activity is to posit surgery, or ... any medical service requiring the use of a physical object, as a marketing device for the incorporated object."

We decline to ignore the reality of the relationship between Ira Royer and CMC, and to treat any services provided by CMC as ancillary to a primary purpose of selling a prosthetic knee. Rather, the record indicates that in addition to the prosthesis, Royer was billed for a hospital room, operating room services, physical therapy, a recovery room, pathology laboratory work, an EKG or ECG, X rays, and anesthesia. Thus, it is evident that Ira Royer entered CMC not to purchase a prosthesis, but to obtain health care services that included the implantation of the knee, with the overall objective of restoring his health. Necessary to the restoration of his health, in the judgment of his physicians, was the implantation of the prosthesis. We do not find this scenario, as the plaintiffs urge, analogous to one in which a plaintiff purchases a defective tire from a retail tire distributor and has the distributor install the tire.

Moreover, the policy rationale underlying strict liability [...] does not support extension of the doctrine under the facts of this case. With respect to the inherent difficulty of proving negligence in many products liability cases, this rationale fails in the context of non-manufacturer cases alleging a design defect. Because "ordinarily there is no possibility that a distributor other than the manufacturer created a design defect[,] ... strict liability would impose liability when there is no possibility of negligence." The plaintiffs do not allege in this case that the defendant altered the prosthesis in any way. Further, holding health care providers strictly liable for defects in prosthetic devices necessary to the provision of health care would likely result in higher health care costs borne ultimately by all patients, and "place an unrealistic burden on the physicians and hospitals of this state to test or guarantee the tens of thousands of products used in hospitals by doctors." Additionally, "research and innovation in medical equipment and treatment would be inhibited." We find that the "peculiar characteristics of medical services[,] ... [which] include the tendency to be experimental, ... a dependence on factors beyond the control of the professional[,] and a lack of certainty or assurance of the desired result," outweigh any reasons that might support the imposition of strict liability in this context.

"In short, medical services are distinguished by factors which make them significantly different in kind from the retail marketing enterprise at which 402A is directed." We conclude that where, as here, a health care provider in the course of rendering health care services supplies a prosthetic device to be implanted into a patient, the health care provider is not "engaged in the business of selling" prostheses for purposes of strict products liability. Accordingly, the trial court did not err in granting the defendant's motion to dismiss.

Sellers and non-sellers (problems)

Q. What result in *Keen v. Dominick's Finer Foods, Inc.*?

A. The trial court dismissed the strict liability count, and the court of appeals affirmed:

In the present case, plaintiff concedes that Dominick's is not in the business of either selling or renting shopping carts. She maintains, however, that although Dominick's gratuitously furnishes the carts to its customers, such is done as an incident of the sale of the items which constitutes Dominick's business. [...] In the present case, plaintiff's use of the allegedly defective shopping cart could only be considered as a use of a convenience furnished by Dominick's to facilitate its customers' shopping. Any mishap which might occur from availing oneself of such a convenience does not render the store liable under the principles of strict products liability. In this case, the allegedly defective shopping cart was placed into the stream of commerce by the parties responsible for its distribution to Dominick's. The store, like its customer, is merely a user of the shopping cart.

Public policy considerations do not demand that the duty of a storekeeper to keep its premises in a safe condition be elevated beyond the traditional standard of reasonable care. Plaintiff is not denied a cause of action in negligence nor is she precluded from establishing a cause of action in strict products liability against the manufacturer of the shopping cart and others who placed the shopping cart into the stream of commerce and reaped the profits therefrom. We simply hold that Dominick's cannot be considered to be part of the distributive chain within the ambit of the principles of strict products liability.

Simon, J., dissented:

> Although, as the majority points out, Dominick's neither sells nor rents shopping carts, it does supply them for its customers. It would be virtually impossible for a customer to make substantial purchases at Dominick's supermarts without the use of a cart. The customer may be regarded as paying for this use because the cart is a cost of doing business which no doubt is reflected in the charge Dominick's makes for its merchandise. The cart not only provides a convenience for Dominick's customers, but also increases Dominick's sales and profits. As the majority states, one of the reasons for imposing strict liability is to ensure that losses are borne by those who reap the profit of marketing an allegedly defective product. By supplying the carts, Dominick's fits within this rationale.

Q. What result in *Peterson v. Lou Bachrodt Chevrolet Co.*?
A. The trial court struck the strict liability counts in the plaintiff's complaint, and the Illinois Supreme Court affirmed:

> One of the basic grounds supporting the imposition of strict liability upon manufacturers is that losses should be borne by those 'who have created the risk and reaped the profit by placing the product in the stream of commerce.' Imposition of liability upon wholesalers and retailers is justified on the ground that their position in the marketing process enables them to exert pressure on the manufacturer to enhance the safety of the product. A wholesaler or retailer who neither creates nor assumes the risk is entitled to indemnity. Therefore, although liability is imposed upon anyone who is engaged in the business of selling the product (Restatement (Second) of Torts sec. 402A (1965)), the loss will ordinarily be ultimaterly borne by the party that created the risk.

> There is no allegation that the defects existed when the product left the control of the manufacturer. Nor is there any allegation that the defects were created by the used car dealer. If strict liability is imposed upon the facts alleged here, the used car dealer would in effect become an insurer against defects which had come into existence after the chain of distribution was completed, and while the product was under the control of one or more consumers.

Goldenhersh, J., dissented:

> In *Galluccio v. Hertz Corp.*, 1 Ill.App.3d 272, the appellate court held strict liability applicable to the lessor of a motor vehicle. No reason presents itself for not applying the principle to a used car dealer who places in the stream of commerce a vehicle rendered unreasonably dangerous by reason of a defect discoverable upon reasonable inspection.

I am aware of the argument made by defendant and *amici curiae* that many vehicles are sold 'as is' and that the cost of repairs in some instances might exceed the value of the vehicle. These pleadings present no such issues, and assuming, *arguendo*, that in some future case they will arise, there is precedent for weighing the cost of remedying the dangerous condition against the nature and extent of the risk which it creates.

Q. What result in *Nutting v. Ford Motor Co.*?

A. The court rejected Hewlett Packard's attempt to have the strict liability claims dismissed:

> Strict products liability should not be imposed upon a party whose role in placing the product in the stream of commerce is so peripheral to the manufacture and marketing of the product that it would not further the policy considerations which are the foundation for the imposition of this onerous liability on certain sellers. These policy considerations include the ability of the seller, because of its continuing relationship with the manufacturer, "to exert pressure for the improved safety of products and [to] recover increased costs within their commercial dealings, or through contribution or indemnification in litigation; additionally, by marketing the products as a regular part of their business such sellers may be said to have assumed a special responsibility to the public, which has come to expect them to stand behind their goods."

> We are of the view that these policy considerations will be furthered by the imposition of strict products liability upon HP for its role in the regular distribution of used vehicles. HP itself has recognized the leverage generated by its purchases of large numbers of vehicles directly from the manufacturer, leverage which can be used to encourage improved safety as well as to obtain financial advantages. Additionally, HP can recover from the manufacturer for any strict products liability imposed on HP which is not the result of any active wrongdoing by HP. It is also reasonable for the public to assume that vehicles which are used in HP's large fleet of vehicles and regularly disposed of at auctions to used car dealers for resale to the public after approximately one year of service will be well maintained and in good working condition. Based upon all of the relevant facts and circumstances which are undisputed, we conclude that HP is in the regular business of a used car dealer for the purpose of imposing strict products liability.

Q. Hypothetical: in *Musser v. Vilsmeier Auction Co.*, 562 A.2d 279 (Pa. 1989), a company called Wenger's Farm Machinery was going out of business and hired the Vilsmeier Company to auction off its assets. The plaintiff attended the auction and bought a tractor. The tractor ran him over when he tried to start it, causing him various injuries. He sued the auction house on theories of strict liability. What result?

A. No liability. From the court's decision affirming summary judgment for the auction company:

> The basis of [strict seller's liability] is the ancient one of the special responsibility for the safety of the public undertaken by one who enters into the business of supplying human beings with products which may endanger the safety of their persons and property, and the forced reliance upon that undertaking on the part of those who purchase such goods. This basis is lacking in the case of the ordinary individual who makes the isolated sale, and he is not liable to a third person or even to his buyer in the absence of his negligence. [...] We note however that the broadened concept of "supplier," for purposes of predicating strict liability, is not without practical limits. The limits obtain in the purposes of the policy. When those purposes will not be served, persons whose implication in supplying products is tangential to that undertaking will not be subjected to strict liability for the harms caused by defects in the products.

> The auction company merely provided a market as the agent of the seller. It had no role in the selection of the goods to be sold, in relation to which its momentary control was merely fortuitous

and not undertaken specifically. Selection of the products bought was accomplished by the bidders, on their own initiative and without warranties by the auction company. [...] [T]he auctioneer is not equipped to pass upon the quality of the myriad of products he is called upon to auction and with which his contact is impromptu. Nor does he have direct impact upon the manufacture of the products he exposes to bids, such as would result from continuous relationships with their producers and which would be expected to provide him with influence over the latter in acting to make products safer.

Secondly, Appellee is not in the business of designing and/or manufacturing any particular product or products. We fail to see how the imposition of strict liability would be more that a futile gesture in promoting the manufacture and distribution of safer products, the purpose of the underlying policy. Nor do we perceive that the auctioneer would be in any better position than the consumer to prevent the circulation of defective products. This factor implies the existence of some ongoing relationship with the manufacturer from which some financial advantage inures to the benefit of the latter and which confers some degree of influence on the auctioneer. But, as pointed out above, there is no such relationship between the auctioneer and the manufacturer which might equip the auctioneer to influence the manufacturing process. We fail to see how the imposition of strict liability on the auctioneer would confer on him any influence in the manufacture of safer products.

The New York courts say that "a business which disposes of surplus equipment in an occasional sale has, at most, the duty to warn the purchaser of known defects that are not obvious or readily discernible." *Sukljian v. Ross & Son Co.*, 503 N.E.2d 1358 (N.Y. 1986).

Notes on sellers of used products. From the Restatement (Third) of Products Liability:

§8. Liability Of Commercial Seller Or Distributor Of Defective Used Products

One engaged in the business of selling or otherwise distributing used products who sells or distributes a defective used product is subject to liability for harm to persons or property caused by the defect if the defect:

(a) arises from the seller's failure to exercise reasonable care; or

(b) is a manufacturing defect under §2(a) or a defect that may be inferred under §3 and the seller's marketing of the product would cause a reasonable person in the position of the buyer to expect the used product to present no greater risk of defect than if the product were new; or

(c) is a defect under §2 or §3 in a used product remanufactured by the seller or a predecessor in the commercial chain of distribution of the used product; or

(d) arises from a used product's noncompliance under §4 with a product safety statute or regulation applicable to the used product.

A used product is a product that, prior to the time of sale or other distribution referred to in this Section, is commercially sold or otherwise distributed to a buyer not in the commercial chain of distribution and used for some period of time.

Comment b. Rationale. [...] Subsections (b) and (c) subject commercial sellers of used products to liability without fault only under special circumstances. Consumers of most used products sold in obviously used condition typically do not, and should not, expect those products to perform as safely, with respect to the possibility of mechanical defects, as when those products were new. Many factors affect consumer expectations in this regard. For example, the age and condition of used products and the commensurate lower prices paid for such products alert reasonable buyers to the possibility of defects and the need to monitor the safety aspects of such products over time according to their age and condition. Given the awareness of buyers generally regarding the risks of harm presented by used products in varying stages of physical deterioration, primary responsibility for allocating these risks may, in the absence of fault on the part of the used-product seller or some special circumstance that justifies strict liability, be delegated to commercial markets for used products, in which the terms of sale vary widely depending on the apparent condition of such products at the time of sale.

When a used product is sold commercially under circumstances in which a reasonable buyer would expect the risk of defect to be substantially the same as with a new product, a different judicial response is justified. Thus, under the circumstances described in Subsection (b), many of the same rationales that support strict liability for harm caused by mechanical defects in new products support strict liability for mechanical defects in like-new used products. [...]

It will be observed that, in contrast with Subsection (c), Subsection (b) imposes liability without proof of fault only for harm caused by manufacturing defects as defined in § 2(a) and defects whose existence may be inferred under §3, even in connection with used products sold in such good condition that reasonable buyers would expect the risk of defects to be substantially the same as if the products were new. The factual difference between the circumstances described in Subsection (b) and those described in Subsection (c) is that in the latter the used-product seller (or a predecessor in the chain of distribution of the used product) has somehow introduced or chosen not to eliminate the design defect during remanufacture, whereas under Subsection (b) the design defect originates with the manufacturer in the original, new-product chain of distribution and the used-product seller is in no position to change the design.

Commercial sellers of like-new used products occupy a different position from that occupied by retailers of new products. Retailers of new products are part of the original chain of distribution and in fairness should be liable for harm caused by defects, even design defects, that exist when products are sold new. See §1, Comment e. Retailers of new products have opportunities, as used-product sellers generally do not, to contract with those above them in the chain of distribution regarding who should ultimately bear the costs of defending design claims in court and paying successful claimants. Holding new-product retailers liable for defective designs originating at manufacture encourages them to apply pressure on manufacturers within the distributive chains, directly and indirectly, to produce safe products and to adopt reasonable designs. In contrast, sellers of like-new used products are not, except coincidentally, members of the original distributive chain. Typically they exercise little if any control over original design choices or decisions regarding indemnity for costs of liability.

Mexicali Rose v. Superior Court (bone in enchilada; NL)
Doyle v. Pillsbury Co. (problem: insect in can of peas; NL for injury suffered when P recoiled in horror)
Klages v. General Ordnance Equipment Corp. (problem: mace pen doesn't work; L)

Q. Suppose a mouse is found in a Coke bottle. Liability under *Mexicali Rose*?
A. Yes—for the retailer as well as for Coke, if the mouse got into the bottle at the bottling stage. A consumer would not reasonably expect such a thing, and it wouldn't be natural to the beverage.

Q. What about a bone in a hamburger?
A. Strict liability on the dissent's view, but probably not under the majority's rule.

Q. What result in *Doyle v. Pillsbury Corp.*?

A. The trial court gave summary judgment to Pillsbury, and the Florida Supreme Court affirmed:

> A producer or retailer of food should foresee that a person may well become physically or mentally ill after consuming part of a food product and then discovering a deleterious foreign object, such as an insect or rodent, in presumably wholesome food or drink. The manufacturer or retailer must expect to bear the costs of the resulting injuries. [...] The same foreseeability is lacking where a person simply observes the foreign object and suffers injury after the observation. The mere observance of unwholesome food cannot be equated to consuming a portion of the same. We should not impose virtually unlimited liability in such cases. When a claim is based on an inert foreign object in a food product, we continue to require ingestion of a portion of the food before liability arises.

The ingestion rule is followed in most jurisdictions. The result might best be explained not by appeals to foreseeability but on policy grounds: if a plaintiff ingests food that contained a foreign object, this helps guarantee that the claim for distress arising from the incident is genuine. Otherwise we worry about the plaintiff triumphantly holding up a coke bottle with a mouse still sealed inside and claiming that the distress he has suffered from the spectacle of it entitles him to a large award of damages, even though it really didn't really upset him all that much (but how can this be proved?). But this worry might seem relatively minor on the facts of *Doyle*, where the plaintiff apparently suffered substantial injuries (let's assume she broke her leg). Is the issue then more a question of reasonableness? Maybe we expect people to be able to keep their composure when confronted with bugs in their food. Or maybe it's another of those cases where the value of a clear rule (in this case a rule that the plaintiff must ingest at least a bit of the contaminated food or beverage) is great enough to justify the occasional case like *Doyle* that the rule just gets wrong.

Q. What result in *Klages v. General Ordnance Equipment Corp.*, 367 A.2d 304 (Pa. Sup. 1976)?

A. We put this case here to introduce the problem of causation in products cases. The result was liability: a jury awarded the plaintiff $42,000, and the court of appeals affirmed:

> In the instant case [...] the appellant manufactured a product designed for use in situations involving criminal attacks. The appellant clearly recognized, or should have recognized, the possibility of harm resulting to a purchaser if this weapon did not perform as represented. While the intervening criminal act of a third party can satisfy the requirements of a superseding cause, it does not do so where the criminal act is reasonably foreseeable. Had the mace weapon in the instant case immediately, instantaneously, and completely disabled the assailant, the appellee would not have been shot. Failure of the weapon to conform to the appellant's representations is not only a 'factual' cause, but is also a 'substantial' cause of the appellee's injuries. Here, the issue of proximate cause was submitted to the jury in a clear, comprehensive charge. The lower court acted properly in submitting the issue to the jury.

Q. Hypothetical: in *Williams v. RCA Corp.*, 376 N.E.2d 37 (Ill. App. 1978), the plaintiff was a security guard who used a two-way radio made by the defendant to report a robbery he saw occurring at the restaurant where he worked. The radio malfunctioned and did not transmit his request for help; he alleged that he was injured as a result when he tried to stop the thieves himself. What result?

A. No liability; the court affirmed dismissal of the complaint:

> While it might be said that the manufacturer of the two-way receiver could have foreseen that the shooting might conceivably occur, we do not believe its occurrence was objectively reasonable to expect, for the following reasons: (1) Under ordinary circumstances, the manufacturer may reasonably assume that no one will violate the criminal law; (2) the portable two-way receiver is a

product designed for short-range, out-of-presence communication between individuals possessing such units and not the prevention of criminal attack; and (3) it cannot fairly be said, under the circumstances here, that the manufacturer should reasonably foresee that the security guard would approach the armed robber before he became aware of the presence of his support whether or not he had knowledge of the malfunctioning of the receiver.

SECTION C. DESIGN DEFECTS

If greater brevity is desired, cut the causation cases at the end (*Price* and *Rodriguez*).

It probably will be helpful at this point to go back to the earlier Restatement (Third) provisions setting out the rules of liability for design defects. Notice the use of the word "reasonable" twice in the Restatment's standard, which is redolent of negligence law and the reasonable person test; and indeed, the most common test for liability for design defects is a risk-utility balancing that resembles the Hand formula. (The "untaken precaution" in an ordinary tort case corresponds to the "reasonable alternative design" in a design defect case.) So why is liability for design defects called "strict"? There is some discussion of this in the Restatement comments at the beginning of the design defect materials. Liability does remain strict in the sense that retailers can be held liable even if they had nothing to do with the choices that went into the design of a product. Also, it is irrelevant how much effort the defendant put into designing the product; the only question is how the design compared to feasible alternatives.

Dawson v. Chrysler Corp. (P, hurt in auto accident, sues maker of car on ground that it isn't crashworthy; L)
Wyeth v. Levine (recent S.Ct. case; tort liability possible despite compliance with federal regulations)
Green v. Smith & Nephew (example of liability based on consumer expectations test)

Q. What risk-utility tradeoff was at stake in *Dawson*?
A. The automobile was built to allow objects it struck to deform the body of the car and enter the passenger space; this had the advantage of reducing "deceleration on the occupants of the vehicle"—i.e., the passengers would be less likely to be thrown through the windshield, etc., because the car would not be suddenly stopped when it ran into something. On the other hand, this design feature allowed the utility pole in this case to crush the driver, Dawson. There also is a price and weight tradeoff: making the car more resilient would have made it a little more expensive ($300).

Q. What are the pros and cons of tort liability as a means of regulating product designs?
A. The question invites general discussion of direct regulation administered by agencies ex ante and compensation in tort administered by juries ex post. First, you can discuss the idea of letting juries—panels of six laypeople ignorant of the relevant technology—pass judgment on designs of complex products after receiving a brief and abridged crash course (pardon the expression) from the parties' experts. What could justify such an approach? Perhaps some notion that the jurors are serving as stand-ins for super-well-informed consumers. Next you can ask whether it makes sense to allow product manufacturers to be whipsawed in the way suggested by the court in *Dawson*: i.e., potentially held liable no matter which design they choose. You can use this point to draw out again the various functions of products liability law. To the extent it is meant to create incentives to design safer products, the whipsawing possibility is counterproductive; it just turns the defendant into an insurer. But to the extent the point of products law is to spread losses—i.e., to provide a kind of insurance—maybe it's not so crazy after all. If that is the rationale, however, it cuts beyond cases like *Dawson* and suggests very wide liability of manufacturers for products even if there really was no better way to design them. What one must then do is compare the tort system to alternative institutions that can serve the purposes in question. If the purpose of the system is to generate safer (or more optimally safe products), the question is how it

compares to, say, direct regulation; if the purpose of the system is to spread losses, the question is how it compares to various more direct forms of insurance that generally involve far lower administrative costs.

Q. Consider the tests courts use: reasonable expectations vs. risk/utility vs. safe for its intended use. When would you expect a difference in the results produced by these tests? Which do you favor?
A. This is another situation where we think the most useful thing this manual can offer are a few interesting excerpts from the scholarly work on the subject.

a. From Abraham, Rabin, and Weiler, *Enterprise Responsibility for Personal Injury: Further Reflections*, 30 San Diego L. Rev. 333 (1993):

> In our view, risk/utility analysis, coupled with a requirement that a reasonably feasible, safer alternative design is available, is an appropriate test for design defect. Theoretically, risk/utility creates the appropriate incentives for safe design. Conceptually, risk/utility meshes well with the defenses of consumer fault, product misuse, and alteration. Pragmatically, the requirement that a reasonably feasible alternative must exist focuses the risk/utility inquiry, making it concrete to the jury, and avoids global speculation about whether a product—for example, all-terrain vehicles or above-ground swimming pools—is "essential" or "inessential" in cases where a generic product line is under attack.
>
> Our critics protest the elimination of consumer expectations as an alternative basis for liability. In response, we would suggest that our approach eliminates a test that suffers from a number of flaws. In patent defect cases, a consumer expectations test may be used as a broad defense against liability for harm caused by "open and obvious risks"—a bar that many courts have considered excessively generous to the makers of dangerous products. By contrast, in latent defect cases the test may be easily used in a conclusory sense to avoid inquiry into the optimal level of design safety to be expected from product manufacturers. More specifically, the consumer's expectation in any particular case is, quite simply, that the product will not cause harm. Moreover, when consumer expectations do arguably deserve some independent weight—consider, in this regard, Professor Shapo's product promotion rationale for manufacturer liability—no reason exists why consumer expectations cannot be factored into the "risk" term in a risk/utility test. For example, the actual risk of a product is actually increased when product promotion creates justifiable expectations by consumers that the product is safe for use without consumers having to take special precautions.

b. The Ford Pinto case makes an appearance at the end of the casebook's treatment of the Hand formula, and then reappears in the section on punitive damages. But this is a good place to bring it up as well. From Gary Schwartz, *The Myth of the Ford Pinto Case*, 43 Rutgers L. Rev. 1013 (1991):

> [T]he consumer expectations theme in product liability currently seems to be somewhat on the wane. In most cases, design defect liability hinges on the risk-benefit standard. This standard, while frequently presented as an aspect of strict liability, is now commonly understood as an application of ideas that are essentially drawn from the law and jurisprudence of negligence; and I will refer to that standard hereinafter as a negligence standard of manufacturer design liability.
>
> In considering how that standard might play out in *Grimshaw*, one can take note of a point repeatedly made by the court of appeal: that the Pinto's safety could have been improved for a per-car cost that would have been "inexpensive," "minimal," and even "nominal." Indeed, Ford's willingness to tolerate a design hazard when the hazard could have been eliminated in such an inexpensive way is clearly part of the overall myth of the Pinto case. But what is the actual analytic significance of say a $10 safety figure? In ascertaining its significance, a relevant issue

relates to the incidence of the costs of safety modifications. The court of appeal's rhetoric about Ford "balancing human lives and limbs against corporate profits" tends to presuppose that these costs, had they been incurred, would have remained with Ford rather than been passed forward to consumers. On this issue of incidence the *Grimshaw* jury may have been enticed by the evidence into making somewhat inconsistent assumptions.

If, for one reason or another, the costs of safety modifications would have been borne by Ford, then the fact that these costs can be expressed in terms of a low per-car figure would seem largely irrelevant; for risk-benefit purposes, the meaningful data would remain the overall cost to Ford and the number of lives that would have been saved if those costs had been incurred. If, however, consumers would have borne the incidence of the costs of safety improvements, then there is some appeal in the idea that all consumers would or should be willing to spend $10 each so that death to a few consumers might be avoided. Indeed, this idea seems to be part of the larger set of public beliefs that surrounds the Pinto case.

On closer inspection, however, this turns out to be one instance in which the public's basic attitude seems analytically weak. About ten million cars are sold in the United States each year; an added $10 per car would hence cost consumers $100 million per year. If the safety improvements from this expenditure save 500 lives over the duration of the cars' lives, then it can easily be said that almost all consumers would be delighted with the $10 expenditure.   If, however, only five lives are saved by that design improvement, then that improvement is worthwhile only if life can be valued at more than $20 million. This figure is, however, much in excess of the highest current estimate of life value. Accordingly, unless consumers are extremely risk averse, one would expect them to be unhappy with that expenditure.

Expressing the cost of safety improvements in a "nominal" per-car way does not rescue us, therefore, from the need to consider the magnitude of the safety gain. And even the analysis set forth above is, in a basic way, too simple. For it can be assumed that the $10 cost for improving fuel-tank safety is only one of a large number of individually low cost design modifications that could improve the safety of a car such as the Pinto; and at some point, the aggregate of these $10 items can no longer be downplayed as "minimal." Consider, for example, all those auto design improvements that have been required by the NHTSA program. While no one of these is especially expensive, in their aggregate by 1984 they had added $491 to the price of the average car. Of course, these price increases might well be justified. But the justification in question comes from the very substantial safety benefits that the NIITSA standards actually provide, and not from any mere claim that the overall cost of all of these standards can be deprecated as minimal.

The ability, therefore, to characterize the cost of individual design improvements as "nominal" does not enable us to escape from the rigors of a full risk-benefit analysis in order to determine design defectiveness. The Ford Pinto case can now be reconsidered from the perspective of Ford's liability under the negligence-oriented risk-benefit liability standards. As noted, a $9 package of design changes could have somewhat improved the safety of the Pinto. Over 2,200,000 Pintos were sold during the 1971-1976 model years. The aggregate cost that Ford would therefore have incurred had it incorporated these design changes would have been almost $20 million. In order to determine whether the absence of these design features rendered the Pinto defective, a jury, considering all the evidence, would need to render correct judgments as to the number of the casualties that these design changes would have averted and the appropriate monetary valuation for injuries and loss of life.

At this point in the assessment, however, we re-encounter the apparent crisis in the administration of the risk-benefit test. So long as my composite lawyers' statement is assumed correct, the typical jury's distrust of corporate risk-benefit analysis will lead that jury to neglect correct judgments and instead rule almost automatically in the plaintiff's favor whenever the manufacturer argues that its design was justified by the monetary costs of a design alternative. In these cases, therefore, the limitation on liability that seems like an essential part of the risk-benefit test is being disregarded. For that matter, as that test is applied, there are additional factors that might well bias the jury in the plaintiff's favor. The test apparently calls on the jury to appraise the risk entailed by the product's design in an ex ante way: the smaller the ex ante possibility of an accident, the more likely should be a jury's finding that the manufacturer's design indeed satisfies the risk-benefit test. In any tort case, however, the accident has indeed happened, and the victim is sitting there in the courtroom, his injuries apparent to all. Given the way in which the victim's presence vividly dramatizes whatever risks may have inhered in the product's design, any fact-finder, whether judge or jury, is likely to lack the discipline that would prevent it from overestimating the ex ante possibility of injury. In addition, even if affording compensation to accident victims is assumed not to be an actual purpose of tort liability rules, the presence in the courtroom of the badly injured and financially strapped victim might well incline the fact-finder—even a judge, and especially a lay jury—to resolve doubts in a way that would provide compensation to the victim.

In many cases, then, the risk-benefit standard is apparently applied in a way that highlights and even enlarges the relevant risk while all but excluding consideration of one quite relevant benefit. In these applications, a standard that is justified in negligence terms devolves into something like strict liability.

This is an administrative reality that defenders of the risk-benefit standard are likely to find seriously disturbing. In further assessing, however, exactly how disturbing this de facto practice of strict liability is, it is worth noting that over the years scholarly attention has frequently been given to the strict design liability idea; I myself looked at that idea in a 1979 article. A rule of strict design liability would render manufacturers liable, without regard to any showing of defect, for all harms resulting from their products' use. Such a rule would, among other things, give manufacturers the most ample incentives to consider all possible risk-reducing design alternatives and to adopt whichever of those alternatives seem, on balance, intelligent; and this objective could be achieved without the need for any intervention by an expensive trial and an ad hoc amateur jury. My 1979 article in no way endorsed strict design liability, but did suggest that the idea was useful, at least as a heuristic.

c. Douglas Kysar, *The Expectations of Consumers*, 103 Colum. L. Rev. 1700 (2003), begins by noting the resistance of some courts to the Third Restatement's endorsement of risk/utility balancing in design defect cases. He finds that "judicial opinions that purport to apply the consumer expectations doctrine generally fail in practice to articulate and apply anything other than a veiled risk-utility standard or a simple res ipsa loquitur-like exception thereunder." But he also believes the reasonable expectations test should be rehabilitated in different form. He begins with a useful rehearsal of criticisms of the traditional consumer expectations test:

> Most fundamentally, scholars repeatedly have complained that the expectations of consumers provide too amorphous a basis on which to assess manufacturer liability. As Deans Prosser and Keeton note in their treatise, "The meaning is ambiguous and the test is very difficult of application to discrete problems.... [As a result, t]he test can be utilized to explain most any result that a court or jury chooses to reach." In a particularly memorable critique of the doctrine's arbitrariness, Professor Gary Schwartz recites a series of ever-shifting automobile marketing

messages, querying whether the extent of a manufacturer's liability really should hinge on the particular message that happens to entice an injured consumer. These commentators encapsulate the widely held view that consumer expectations provide only the most meager and insufficient guidance to factfinders charged with the difficult task of assessing the adequacy of a product design. Indeed, to many observers, the test simply "is so vague as to be lawless."

Scholars also have made more narrow attacks on the consumer expectations test. For instance, several commentators have pointed out that the test provides little or no guidance in cases where product-caused harm befalls bystanders who have neither purchased nor consumed the product. In such a case, the factfinder is directed to evaluate the product in light of expectations that are likely to be nonexistent. Similarly, for a great variety of technologically complex products, consumers may not have formed specific expectations at all with regard to the relevant product features. As Professors Montgomery and Owen observe, in such cases "the consumer may have at most only a generalized expectancy—perhaps more accurately only an unconscious hope—that the product will not harm him if he treats it with a reasonable amount of care." To the extent that consumer attitudes do take this simplistic form ("I expect not to be harmed by a product"), then the consumer expectations test threatens to become in practice the very standard of absolute manufacturer liability that no American jurisdiction has appeared ready to accept.

An altogether different objection to the consumer expectations test is that the doctrine too easily can work against plaintiffs under circumstances in which defendant liability might further the instrumental goals of products liability law. For instance, because consumer expectations generally derive from impressions of the existing state of the product marketplace, safety demands of consumers may lag behind technological improvements in product design whose absence under risk-utility balancing would subject a manufacturer to liability. Similarly, manufacturers under a consumer expectations test may escape liability for product-caused harm whenever consumers can be said to "expect" the possibility that such harm will occur. Thus, whenever a product-imposed danger may be characterized as "open and obvious" to the typical consumer, plaintiffs may be unable to recover irrespective of whether the manufacturer could have eliminated the risk cost-effectively. [...]

Kysar argues, however, that the consumer expectations test usefully can be reconstructed by incorporating insights from cognitive science:

> A great deal of human judgment and decisionmaking research focuses on the manner in which individuals perceive and process information regarding risks. As it turns out, the notion of "risk" for most individuals is not a purely actuarial concept involving probabilistic estimates of harm. Rather, according to proponents of the "psychometric paradigm" view of risk perception, risk is a complex, textured assessment of numerous variables that surround a given environmental, health, or safety hazard. In addition to the likelihood and severity of a harm, individuals also appear to care about a variety of qualitative attributes, such as whether a risk is voluntarily confronted by the victim, whether its potential harm is equitably distributed among the population, whether it poses a particularly dreaded form of death or illness, whether it threatens future generations, and whether the perceived source of the risk is believed to be a trustworthy actor. Such factors do not appear within the basic model of cost-benefit analysis, which tends to abstract away from qualitative characteristics in order to provide a uniform basis for assessing a wide range of health and safety risks. Thus, as cognitive psychologist Paul Slovic has put it, lay individuals' "basic conceptualization of risk is much richer than that of the experts and reflects legitimate concerns that are typically omitted from expert risk assessments."

> Some analysts have argued against legal or regulatory acknowledgment of these perceptual

differences. Professors Nichols and Zeckhauser, for instance, recognize the standard "rationale . . . that the simultaneous death of 1,000 people in the same incident is somehow worse than the isolated deaths of 1,000 otherwise identical people in separate incidents," but explain that they "are extremely skeptical of such views." Such a conclusion reflects the impact of a methodological individualism in which death only matters to the dead. Risks and harms undeniably connote social meanings, however, some of which demand more attention than others, irrespective of whether purely numeric body counts reach similar results. Consider, for instance, a contrast between the tragic and the tragically mundane: 2,800 people lost their lives in the collapse of the World Trade Center on September 11, 2001. By approximately 7:30 p.m. that day, the same number of people were expected to die worldwide in traffic accidents. Although both figures may be cause for concern, failure to see a distinction between these two categories of harm for purposes of regulatory decisionmaking would be, as Professor Sunstein puts it, "genuinely obtuse." It would fail to acknowledge the myriad ways in which "social amplification of risk" can result in enormous secondary emotional, physical, and economic costs, separate and apart from the direct tolls that figure exclusively in Nichols and Zeckhauser's calculus. [...]

In light of findings such as those described in this subsection, divergences between lay and expert observations of risk should not be written off as the result of mere ignorance or error on the part of lay observers. Instead, lay and expert approaches to risk reflect rival rationalities in which "[e]ach side, expert and public, has something valid to contribute" to decisions about the regulation of risk. Significantly, because expert assessments utilize thinner notions of risk and relevant detail, they often understate the desirability of avoiding or preventing the imposition of a risk. That is, expert assessments typically measure only the expected quantitative level of death or bodily harm from a risk, without considering the lessons of the psychometric paradigm or other findings from the risk perception literature. As the World Trade Center example demonstrates, however, qualitative aspects of danger matter tremendously to our shared vision of what risks signify and how strenuously they should be avoided. [...]

Consider a concrete example. In a series of cases arising out of injuries and deaths caused by the Black Talon hollow-point bullet—which was allegedly designed with "razor sharp edges" so that it would "severely rip through and mutilate body parts of the individual shot by such bullets"—courts rather reflexively rejected design defect claims against the bullet manufacturer on the ground that such products "are designed to cause injuries and are thus not unfit for their intended purpose." Such reasoning resembles the expert mode of risk analysis, in which all deaths from guns are treated as equal, thereby eliminating any basis on which to distinguish the hollow-point bullet from other types of ammunition. Lay individuals, on the other hand, care a great deal about the manner in which a death occurs, particularly when it is accompanied by pain and suffering, terror, or some other dread-inducing characteristic. Accordingly, factfinders employing a newly sensitized consumer expectations test might reasonably conclude that the hollow-point bullet was in fact defectively designed.

Consider also a hypothetical manufacturer faced with a choice of two automobile air bag designs: Design A, which will save 3,000 lives over a given time period but induce the death of 100 others who would have survived in the absence of the device; and Design B, which also will save 3,000 lives while only costing the lives of 90 others. A "macro-balancing" risk-utility test clearly approves of either design. Equally as clear, a "micro-balancing" test favors Design B over Design A, assuming that any increased production costs associated with Design B yield a "reasonable" value per life saved. Suppose, though, that the 100 lives lost by Design A are divided equally among adult men and women, while the 90 lives lost by Design B consist primarily of women. From the more nuanced risk perspective of cognitive and social psychology, it is no longer clear that Design B is preferable to Design A, given its disparate gender impacts.

Indeed, there is strong reason to suppose that a majority of consumers would be willing to accept the increased risk of death associated with Design A in order to impose a more equitable distribution of risk. Again, a properly attuned consumer expectations standard for design defect may be capable of capturing important psychological variables such as these, which tend to be left out of the standard risk-utility approach. [...]

To be sure, application of the consumer expectations doctrine must not consist of the type of largely unguided, formless judgment that commentators to date have associated with it. Rather, juries should be charged with the task of determining specifically, as a factual matter, what level of safety the ordinary consumer expects, taking into account the types of factors that cognitive psychologists and other observers of human judgment and decisionmaking have identified as pertinent to public understanding and beliefs about risk. Expert testimony therefore should be admissible for those aspects of a product's design, manufacture, or marketing that raise issues relating to lay risk perception. More specifically, to survive a summary judgment motion, plaintiffs must demonstrate the existence of a triable question of fact concerning the extent to which consumer risk perceptions and safety expectations of the product in question differ in legitimate and significant ways from the standards derived under risk-utility analysis. In this manner, despite the longstanding complaint of products liability scholars that consumer expectations fail to provide a coherent and workable basis for design defect liability, and despite the failure of courts generally to articulate such a basis, the doctrine will provide an important complement to the spare instrumentalist balancing of risk-utility analysis. [...]

By allowing plaintiffs to establish design defectiveness based either on traditional risk-utility analysis or on a brand of consumer expectations analysis that is sensitive to the research regarding lay risk perceptions, courts can promote both maximization of utility and respect for qualitative nuances that might be missed in purely technical analysis of product attributes. Under the risk-utility test, product manufacturers will be held liable whenever an alternative design might cost- effectively have eliminated or reduced a threat of death or bodily injury, regardless of whether consumers expected less safety from the product. On the other hand, whenever risk-utility analysis would ignore significant areas of concern to consumers—such as the distributive impact of a product risk or its perceived involuntariness—the consumer expectations test will be available to give effect to such legitimate concerns. Employment of both risk-utility and consumer expectations tests in this manner reflects the sensible view that, as Professor Moran has noted more generally in regard to risk regulation, "[t]echnocratic and populist decision-making [should] become complementary ways of balancing distinctive values, rather than mutually exclusive, antagonistic perspectives on risk." [...]

The Reporters speculate that "[p]erhaps the lure of [the consumer expectations] doctrine is that it awakens in all of us nostalgia for a world in which technology was not dominant." Their musing, however, presupposes the answer to one of the most significant questions facing products liability law today: whether and under what conditions the value structure implied by risk-utility analysis should trump the value structure inherent in the expectations of ordinary consumers. Is technology really "dominant" or, instead, do consumers retain, and should products liability laws reflect, a contrary set of attitudes and beliefs about the proper roles of technology and risk in an advanced society? This Article has argued that allowing design defect liability to rest on the frustrated expectations of consumers provides an avenue for judicial expression of legitimate public values that are not readily captured by risk-utility analysis. Ours is "a world of incredible technological sophistication," as the Reporters note, but it is not yet a world of technocratic domination.

d. Kysar's article drew a response from the reporters for the Third Restatement in Henderson and Twerski, *Consumer Expectations' Last Hope: A Reply to Professor Kysar*, 103 Colum. L. Rev. 1791 (2003). They begin by saying that "Any open-minded observer who finds Kysar's analysis persuasive can reach but one conclusion: The consumer expectations test as it is currently advocated by a handful of academics and most of the plaintiffs' bar is an unprincipled, intellectually bankrupt approach to design-based liability that only a proponent of unrestricted liability could knowingly embrace." But they also reject Kysar's proposal to rehabilitate the test: "In our view, Kysar's proposal to substitute soft, behavioral science for hard, physical science as a solution to what he sees as technological dominance under the Restatement would seriously undermine the integrity of design litigation and would send that branch of products liability law in the same lawless direction that the failure-to-warn branch seems destined to travel." They continue:

> Our concern is that, under his plan, as long as an expert psychologist can convince a jury that consumers are willing to accept less overall automobile safety in exchange, say, for better gas mileage (an environmental consideration), a plaintiff injured by a safer but less fuel-efficient automobile might be allowed to recover damages based on proof that consumers disapprove of the manufacturer's decision to adopt a safer but less fuel-efficient alternative—assuming, of course, that the plaintiff can satisfy Professor Kysar's proximate cause requirements. We anticipate that Professor Kysar would argue that the air bag example pits safety-to-women against safety-to-men in the context of treating men and women equally and, unlike increased fuel efficiency, raises a "safety" issue. But regardless of how one frames the issue, the simple fact is this: Relying on what expert psychologists say about actual consumer expectations, Kysar would condone harming one victim class in order to help another victim class, even when overall safety is thereby reduced, all in the name of social interests such as gender neutrality or environmentally-motivated fuel efficiency.

> It is not the notion of tradeoffs among classes of consumers, as such, that bothers us—that is what risk-utility is all about, and we would allow the jury in the first air bag variation to deny plaintiff's recovery on that ground. Rather, it is the proposition that such tradeoffs may condemn a design as defective even when the alternative design proposed by the plaintiff would diminish the aggregate safety of all accident victims. We reject the idea of trying to accommodate a more sensitive, politically acceptable outcome in that admittedly unusual case by allowing courts in the run of cases to redefine "safety" in ways that actually increase overall product risks. Kysar's proposal strikes us as highly susceptible to manipulation across the run of cases, and would open every product design to attack on what are, from a safety standpoint, tangential policy grounds. We believe that the "overall safety" approach in the Restatement will lead to a better mix of outcomes in the long run, even if it seems to sacrifice some worthwhile interests in the short run.

Dreisonstok v. Volkswagenwerk (suit against maker of VW microbus; NL)
McCarthy v. Olin Corp. (suit against maker of Black Talon bullets; NL)

Q. What is the distinction between *Dreisonstok* and *Dawson*? How does one draw the line between features of a car to which no liability can attach and features a court is willing to measure with a risk-utility balancing test?
A. The cases are similar because in each of them the product presented a risk that could only be eliminated by reducing some other attractive feature of the product—the ability of the car to absorb impact in *Dawson*, and the ability of the car to carry lots of cargo in *Dreisenstok*. This is a good time to survey some of the different types of "costs" that can be plugged into a proper cost-benefit analysis. An alternative design can be costly in the sense of improving safety in some ways but sacrificing it in others (*Dawson* is an example; drugs provide other illustrations, since designing a drug to avoid one hazard

often creates others that may be less likely but more severe). Or it can be costly in the sense of being uglier or less useful. Are all of these types of costs entitled to weight? How is a jury supposed to think about the assignment of values to them? In *Dreisenstok*, safety was traded away for convenience and the court said there could be no liability; in *Dawson*, one kind of safety was traded away for another kind of safety—and the court said there *could* be liability. Is this backwards?

The distinction between the cases seems to be that in *Dreisenstok* the feature that would have to be traded away for greater safety is the main attractive feature of the vehicle, not just a safety feature of a slightly different variety. Another possible distinction is that the trade-off in *Dreisenstok* is just much more obvious. Someone who buys a VW bus can plainly see that it affords more storage space by pushing the driver up to the front. If a buyer can see this tradeoff and likes it, why should the law second-guess his decision? But in *Dawson* there might be a paternalistic sense that car buyers are less likely to understand the trade-offs between the two different types of crashworthiness at issue there, so there is less reason for a court to defer to the consumer's choice. A final point is that the utility of a microbus's design (or, more obviously, the design of a convertible) is more a matter of idiosyncratic taste than the utility of a stronger cage around the passenger compartment of a car. The preference for a convertible is hard to quantify; it's a little like the preference for riding on the Flopper in the *Murphy* case (in the chapter on assumption of risk). So courts are more inclined to leave it alone.

A natural question to raise is why liability ever should be imposed for the design of a product if the pros and cons of it were obvious to the consumer; for in that case the benefits might seem to clearly have exceeded the costs (otherwise the consumer would not have made the purchase). One answer is the paternalistic one; another is that some of the costs (and perhaps benefits) of a product may be visited on others besides the purchaser. SUVs are a possible example: the benefits may exceed the costs for the purchaser but not socially.

In any event, it is unusual for courts to rule that a design feature cannot be attacked because it is too obvious or too central to the product. Convertibles and Volkswagens are the classic cases where such things are said; one can analogize to the related problem (considered next) of liability for products that are unsafe no matter how they are designed because that is their purpose—e.g., Black Talon bullets.

Q. Should liability be possible because a product itself flunks the risk-utility test?

A. This is the question raised by the *Olin* case (Black Talon bullets). Again, an interesting question to focus on is the institutional one: why should (or shouldn't) *juries* be able to make general judgments that a given product's overall costs outweigh its benefits, given that they already can make such judgments about a product's specific features? Allowing such determinations may cause people who can't succeed in getting products banned by a legislature to turn to the courts as another tool for achieving the same result (the legislature may not have the wherewithal to reverse a court's decision that a product is unreasonably dangerous, even if the legislature was not ready to make any such decision itself).

The Kysar article excerpted a few pages ago included some thoughts about the Black Talon case. The Reporters replied with the institutional objection: "[T]he reason the Restatement would reject category liability on these facts is not that hollow-point bullets are socially acceptable. Clearly they are not, and courts do not need expert psychologists to tell them that. Instead, the Restatement rejects category liability because it is believed to be beyond the proper bounds of judicial competence to make such categorical risk-utility decisions."

More on dangerous products. If you want to spend more time on the question of "inherently unsafe" products, here are notes on a couple of other cases you can use as a basis for discussion or hypotheticals; both of them involve some back-and-forth between courts and legislatures, making them useful vehicles for discussing the institutional issues at stake in this section:

a. In *Kelley v. R.G. Industries*, 497 A.2d 1143 (Md. 1985), the plaintiff worked at a grocery store. He was shot and injured during a robbery. The gun used in the shooting was a revolver made by the defendant. The plaintiff claimed that the gun was unreasonably dangerous in design. The state court of appeals, on certification from the federal district court where the case was litigated, rejected most of the plaintiff's claim:

> [A] handgun is not defective merely because it is capable of being used during criminal activity to inflict harm. A consumer would expect a handgun to be dangerous, by its very nature, and to have the capacity to fire a bullet with deadly force. Kelley confuses a product's *normal function,* which may very well be dangerous, with a defect in a product's design or construction. For example, an automobile is a dangerous product, if used to run down pedestrians. In such a situation, injury would result from the nature of the product—its ability to be propelled at a great speed with great force. But that same automobile might also be defective in its design or construction, *e.g.,* if the gasoline tank were placed in such position that it could easily explode in a rear-end collision. Only in the second instance, regarding the placement of the gasoline tank, would the design of the product be defective, exposing the product's manufacturer to liability[.]

The court did, however, leave open one possible theory for the plaintiff: the defendant could be held liable if the guns it manufactured were found to be "Saturday Night Specials," which the court defined as guns characterized by short barrels, light weight, easy concealability, low cost, use of cheap quality materials, poor manufacture, inaccuracy and unreliability. The court noted that importation of such guns is restricted under federal law and said that they are of little use for the legitimate purposes authorized by the state's gun control laws. This result has not been followed elsewhere, however, and was later repudiated in Maryland by statute. See Md. Ann. Code Art. 27, §36-I(h)(1) ("A person or entity may not be held strictly liable for damages of any kind resulting from injuries to another person sustained as a result of the criminal use of any firearm by a third person, unless the person or entity conspired with the third person to commit, or willfully aided, abetted, or caused the commission of the criminal act in which the firearm was used.").

    b. In *O'Brien v. Muskin Corp.,* 463 A.2d 298 (N.J. 1983), the plaintiff dove into an above-ground swimming pool made by the defendant. When his hands hit the vinyl floor of the pool, they slid apart; he hit his head on the bottom and sustained various injuries. His theory of liability was that the pool was defectively designed because the bottom of it should have been made of a less slippery material. The trial court gave judgment as a matter of law to the defendants; the court of appeals reversed, and the state supreme court agreed that there must be a new trial:

> Although the appropriate standard [for judging a claim of a design defect] might be variously defined, one definition, based on a comparison of the utility of the product with the risk of injury that it poses to the public, has gained prominence. [...] A critical issue at trial was whether the design of the pool, calling for a vinyl bottom in a pool four feet deep, was defective. In removing that issue from consideration by the jury, the trial court erred. To establish sufficient proof to compel submission of the issue to the jury for appropriate fact-finding under risk-utility analysis, it was not necessary for plaintiff to prove the existence of alternative, safer designs. Viewing the evidence in the light most favorable to plaintiff, even if there are no alternative methods of making bottoms for above-ground pools, the jury might have found that the risk posed by the pool outweighed its utility.

Schreiber, J., dissented in part; he agreed that the jury might reasonably have concluded that there was a better way to design the sort of pool the defendant manufactured, but disagreed with the majority's claim that the plaintiff could prevail by showing that the product generally created more costs than benefits:

> The majority holds that the jury should have been permitted to decide whether the risks of above-ground swimming pools with vinyl bottoms exceed their usefulness despite adequate warnings and despite unavailability of any other design. The plaintiff had the burden of proving this proposition. Yet he adduced no evidence on many of the factors bearing on the risk-utility

analysis.   There was no evidence on the extent that these pools are used and enjoyed throughout the country; how many families obtain the recreational benefits of swimming and play during a summer; how many accidents occur in the same period of time; the nature of the injuries and how many result from diving.   There was no evidence of the feasibility of risk spreading or of the availability of liability insurance or its cost.   There was no evidence introduced to enable one to gauge the effect on the price of the product, with or without insurance.   The liability exposures, particularly if today's decision is given retroactive effect, could be financially devastating.

These factors should be given some consideration when deciding the policy question of whether pool manufacturers and, in the final analysis, consumers should bear the costs of accidents arising out of the use of pools when no fault can be attributed to the manufacturer because of a flaw in the pool, unavailability of a better design, or inadequate warning. If this Court wishes to make absolute liability available in product cases and not leave such decisions to the Legislature, it should require that trial courts determine in the first instance as a matter of law what products should be subject to absolute liability. In that event the court would consider all relevant factors including those utilized in the risk-utility analysis.

The difference between absolute and strict liability is not one of semantics.   Significantly different elements are evaluated by different entities with different standards of review. As used in this opinion, "strict liability" and "absolute liability" signify distinct and separate concepts. Strict liability is imposed where there is a defect in a product due to an individual product flaw, an improper design or an inadequate warning. Irrespective of strict liability, a manufacturer or other seller may nevertheless be liable in an appropriate case under *absolute* liability. Absolute liability is imposed where, on the basis of policy considerations including risk-spreading, it is determined that a manufacturer or other seller should bear the cost of injuries he causes to foreseeable users, regardless of the presence or absence of any defect. In some circumstances a manufacturer may be liable though a product is free from defects.

The majority's view of "strict liability" encompasses both strict liability and absolute liability. Although the majority and I adopt the same formulaic statement that strict liability is imposed only where there is a "defect," the majority uses the term to include not only individual product flaw, improper design and inadequate warning cases, but also a fourth category of cases in which the jury decides that the risks outweigh the utility of the product. It follows from the majority's rationale that a jury may be permitted to find that there is a "defect" whenever there is an accident involving a product.

   The New Jersey legislature responded to *O'Brien* with a statute providing for no liability in product cases if "there was not a practical and technically feasible alternative design that would have prevented the harm without substantially impairing the reasonably anticipated or intended function of the product." But the statute makes an exception where "(a) the product is egregiously unsafe or ultrahazardous; (2) the ordinary user or consumer of the product cannot reasonably be expected to have knowledge of the product's risks, or the product poses a risk of serious injury to persons other than the user or consumer; and (3) the product has little or no usefulness." N.J. Stat. Ann. §2A:58C-3.

   The Third Restatement likewise generally requires that a plaintiff demonstrate the existence of a "reasonable alternative design," and takes the dissenter's side in *O'Brien;* but it leaves open the possibility that liability may be found without an alternative design if a product's costs may so outweigh its "negligible social utility" that no rational person would choose to use it. The example offered is an exploding cigar purchased from a novelty shop that sets the plaintiff's beard on fire. §2, Illus. 5.

Price v. Blaine Kern Artista, Inc. (oversized mask made by D hurts P's neck when he is pushed down; L)
Rodriguez v. Glock, Inc. (P's decedent shot in struggle over gun made by D with no safety; NL)

Q. Is there a satisfactory distinction between *Price v. Blaine Kern Artista, Inc.* and *Rodriguez v. Glock, Inc.*?

A. The cases seem similar because in both of them a product without a safety feature caused harm when it became the focus of a violent encounter. Indeed, *Rodriguez* might seem the more obvious case for liability because violence surrounding a gun seems more foreseeable than violence provoked by a mask. One possible distinction between the cases is that in *Price* there was no indication that the lack of a harness provided benefits (other than perhaps a reduced price for the mask). In the *Glock* case there was an advantage to having a short trigger-pull; remember that we are dealing here with an off-duty police officer and his service revolver, so making the gun easy to fire might be important, and in any event was a core property of the product, a little like the dangerous properties of the Black Talon bullets. The absence of a safety is a little harder to explain in this way. Perhaps one wants a gun that's always ready to be fired; you would think this could be achieved by having a safety on the gun that the user always leaves in the off position, but conceivably there is a risk that the safety would be flipped on by accident and cause the gun not to fire at first when the officer needs it. But this doesn't quite go to causation, which is the court's concern. A different sort of causation point might be urged: if Bedoya or his police department wanted guns without safeties, then perhaps it's reasonable to assume that if the gun did have a safety it would not have been turned on—a failure of causation in fact. But the court evidently did not conclude that the case raised problems of this sort.

SECTION D. FAILURE TO WARN

If you want to cut material, consider dropping *Liriano* and perhaps the cases on the learned intermediary doctrine (*Brooks* and *Perez*). You also could cut the coffee cases at the end; they take a little longer (especially if you play the oral argument tape), but they invariably produce good discussions.

Again, at the outset you may wish to refer the students back to the basic Restatement (Third) language regarding warnings at the end of the first section of the casebook chapter.

From George Priest, *The Invention of Enterprise Liability: A Critical History of the Intellectual Foundations of Modern Tort Law*, 14 J. Leg. Stud. 461 (1985):

> During the 1970s the defective warning field erupted, and the liability of manufacturers was expanded dramatically. Recovery was easier on a defective warning allegation, in my view not primarily because of reduced reliance on technical production judgments, but because the implications of enterprise liability theory are clearer for allegations of a defective warning than for a defective design. The insurance and internalization preferences are no different. But the relatively superior power of manufacturers to consumers is strikingly obvious in the context of potential warnings. A manufacturer is likely always to have information superior to a consumer about inherent product characteristics.

American Tobacco Co. v. Grinnell (P sues cigarette maker for not warning him of the danger of addiction; L)
Graves v. Church and Dwight (P sues baking soda maker for not issuing adequate warnings with product; NL—jury verdict for D affirmed)
Brown v. McDonald's Corp. (P sues when McLean contained seafood without warning; L—goes to jury)

Q.   One question in *Grinnell* is whether the warning Grinnell says should have been given would have made any difference. Is this a question that should be answered using a subjective or objective standard? What is the relationship between the duty to warn in products cases and the informed consent doctrine in medical cases (considered in the chapter on cause in fact)?

A.   In the medical cases the plaintiffs complain that they should have received warnings of possible bad consequences of medical procedures that were performed on them; the question was whether the warning would have caused them to make a different decision. The parallel to Grinnell's case is obvious; Grinnell's claim was that if he had been warned about the addictive dangers of cigarettes (think of it as a type of informed consent), he would not have started smoking them. So now let's consider some differences.

In a medical case we usually are concerned with risks that many people would agree to tolerate for the sake of having the medical procedure. It therefore is meaningful to speak of a reasonable decision to go forward with the procedure despite the risks, and thus the majority view in the usual informed consent case is that the standard is objective: one asks whether a reasonable person's judgment would have been affected by the information not given. This approach is hard on the autonomy of the idiosyncratic plaintiff whose judgment would have been affected (even if a reasonable person's judgment would not have been), but a subjective standard creates other problems: it's hard to prove what a plaintiff's "risk preference" profile is, and thus to figure out how the plaintiff would have responded to more information in advance; and more generally it's hard to accurately assess a person's claim, made after something bad has happened to him, that better information would have caused him to behave differently. What he says about this may be strongly colored by wishful or strategic thinking.

In a products case those last dangers of a subjective inquiry also are present. Grinnell may be sure in retrospect that he wouldn't have started smoking if he had been told of the risks—but he may be wrong. But in other respects the problem presented in the products cases is a little different than in the medical setting. In a products case we usually are concerned with a kind of misuse of the product that nobody would choose to engage in if they understood it ("keep hands and feet from under mower"). We're typically not asking what the product user's *choice* or *preference* would have been; we're asking whether he would have obeyed warnings. An objective test would be awkward in such a case, because it would always lead to the same result: we assume that no reasonable person would misuse a product once warned of its dangers. So we use a kind of subjective test after all, asking whether the warning would have made a difference to this plaintiff or whether he was the type to ignore warnings. Maybe it's easier to figure out whether a plaintiff was an attentive and obedient sort in a products setting than it is to determine what a plaintiff would have decided in a medical case if he had known more about the costs and benefits of a procedure.

The difficulty with all this when applied to Grinnell's case is that his facts are not typical of a failure to warn case. The warning he wanted is not one that we can assume a reasonable person would have "obeyed" in the sense of avoiding cigarettes; reasonable people (in the tort sense) start smoking every day despite knowing of the danger of addiction. So Grinnell's case bears an unusually strong resemblance to a medical informed-consent case: we have to ask not whether he obeyed warnings but what sort of balance he would have struck between the pleasures of smoking and the risk of addiction and death as a result. Perhaps the best analogy is from *Grinnell* to those informed consent cases that involve elective medical procedures such as the cosmetic surgery discussed in *Zalazar v. Vercimak* (again in the cause in fact chapter). In that case as in Grinnell's, subjective inquiries are difficult; but it is even harder to speak intelligently about how a reasonable person would have responded to warnings, since a reasonable person might well have had no interest in the activity in the first place. Idiosyncratic tastes play a large part in the decision to smoke or get plastic surgery, so attempts to figure out how a reasonable (usually an average) person would have balanced the risks and benefits aren't of much use.

For more discussion of different types of warnings ("risk reduction" warnings vs. "informed choice" warnings), see Twerski and Cohen, *Informed Decision Making and the Law of Torts: The Myth of Justiciable Causation*, 1988 U.Ill.L.Rev. 607 (1988).

Q. In *Graves v. Church & Dwight*, the court thought the fact that the plaintiff was a smoker was enough evidence to permit a jury to conclude that he didn't follow warnings—and thus that a warning on the baking soda wouldn't have made a difference. What's the strongest argument one can make against that position?

A. Not all warnings have same implications. A warning that smoking is addictive and causes cancer is not the same as an instruction not to smoke. But a warning that using an excessive dose of baking soda could cause a stomach rupture is more like a straightforward instruction not to use too large a dose; it's hard to imagine a reasonable person doing so deliberately in spite of the warnings. So evidence that the *Graves* plaintiff smoked despite warnings to the contrary seems like dubious evidence that he wouldn't have noticed or heeded a more prominent warning on the box of baking soda. It goes back to the point just discussed. His choice to smoke may just reflect his attitude toward pleasure and risk, not any general failure to read or obey instructions. What the case really shows is that the heeding presumption tends to be fragile, and that courts are ready to use slight evidence to dissolve it and leave the issue to a jury.

Q. Why give the plaintiff the benefit of a "heeding presumption"?

A. One of the arguments for the presumption is similar to the reasoning behind causation cases like *Haft v. Lone Palm Hotel*. Many of the warnings that plaintiffs say should have been given would not have been heeded if provided. But if juries make losers out of all plaintiffs on this ground (i.e., the ground that the plaintiff was less than 50% likely to have changed his behavior because of the warning), then there will be no liability even in those cases, perhaps a minority, where the warning *would* have made a difference—and the manufacturer will repeatedly escape liability despite being responsible for some of the bad outcomes. It's another "recurring miss" of the type Levmore discusses in his article in the cause in fact chapter. In this case we deal with it by creating a weak presumption that helps plaintiffs a bit and will make winners out of a few of them who would otherwise lose. It's a crude mechanism, but helps preserve some tort pressure against the manufacturer.

Q. Is there tension between *Brown v. McDonald's Corp.* and *Graves v. Church & Dwight*?

A. No, and this for two reasons. In *Graves* there was evidence, missing from the *McDonald's* case, that the plaintiff was bad about heeding warnings. But there's also a procedural point. In both cases the court decided that whether the warning would have been heeded was fit for resolution by a jury, and probably would have affirmed a jury verdict either way. *Graves* thus is a "no liability" case in a weaker sense than is usual in the casebook: it's not a decision that liability would not be permitted, as in a case where a summary judgment is affirmed; it's just a decision that a finding of no liability *is* permitted—just as a finding of liability no doubt would have been permitted as well.

Q. In *Brown v. McDonald's Corp.*, McDonald's is unable to avoid liability for failing to put warnings on its McLean Deluxe sandwiches indicating that they contain seafood products. Does this decision cause the rule on warnings to more resemble negligence or strict liability?

A. It's a negligence standard. The court makes clear that the manufacturer's duty depends on the likelihood of injury (P in the Hand formula) and the seriousness of injury (L). Liability might seem strict just because a finding for the plaintiff on these facts seems harsh to most students, but that is only because it is so easy to create jury questions about B, P, and L and so correspondingly difficult to obtain summary judgment in warning cases. When it comes time for a jury to actually decide the case, it will be balancing those considerations. If they seem as lopsided in the defendant's favor as most students imagine, then presumably the jury will bring in a verdict against the plaintiff. The Ohio standard used in *Brown* is statutory, but the common law rule runs along the same lines.

Q. If liability for failure to warn essentially involves applying the Hand formula, why don't defendants like McDonald's in the *Brown* case always lose on the ground that adding a warning would have been cheap? Wouldn't the expense of putting warnings about seafood into the side of the McLean container have been trivial, and more than offset by the cost of even a few injuries like the plaintiff's?

A.   The cost is not necessarily trivial; you have to take a broad view of what to count as a cost. If the risk of a reaction like the plaintiff's was tiny but still called for a warning, then liability here presumably would mean that McDonald's would be obliged to include warnings on all of its products regarding every reaction a consumer might have with a "PL" as high as the allergic reaction the plaintiff suffered. That could amount to a lot of warnings, and a fair amount of expense learning about such low-level risks in order to figure out what warnings are required. And once lots of warnings are included they may tend to dilute each others' force, as the *McMahon* opinion suggests later in the section.

Liriano v. Hobart Corp. (P's hand is caught in meat grinder, the guard on which had been removed by the supermarket; L for manufacturer)

Q.   What result if Hobart decides simply to dispense with the guard on its grinder—and still not to put a warning on the machine?
A.   There might be no liability. This was the worry behind Newman's concurring opinion in the case. The failure to warn claim might then fail on the ground that the danger associated with getting one's hand caught in a meat grinder is too obvious to require a warning; and now there would be no need to warn about the missing guard, since no such guard would exist. Newman thinks that Hobart would therefore be tempted by "rationality" to omit guards from the machine, but hopes humanitarian considerations will cause it to do so anyway. But Newman may be laboring under too narrow a sense of what it means for Hobart to be rational. Even apart from its possible liability on a design defect theory, Hobart might find that the market rewards safer products. Tort law is not the only source of incentives to make products that don't cut the users' hands off. (There is a little more food for thought on this in *Kopczick* case in the casebook's section on punitive damages.)

Q.   The court in *Liriano* notes that the plaintiff was 17 years old, had recently immigrated to the United States, and had been on the job for only a week. Is any of this relevant to the legal issues in the case?
A.   Not directly. The test is not whether this particular plaintiff knew of the dangers; it is whether the dangers were matters of common knowledge, and presumably it is possible for someone to lack knowledge that is common in others. So proving that Liriano had less knowledge than most people, without more, is no help to him. The court's point, however, is that the plaintiff's circumstances may have been likely enough to oblige the manufacturer to take them into account in deciding what warnings to give. In other words, we have to define the relevant community in which to determine what knowledge was common; and possibly within the community of people likely to be pressed into service as meat grinders the risks weren't obvious here. Possibly to most grinders the dangers of what Lirano did are obvious—but not to beginning grinders, and beginners comprise a large enough share of the population of grinders that the manufacturer might be required to offer warnings for their benefit. But the court does not quite settle this. It says that even if most ordinary users understand the dangers of using grinders without guards, a smaller number (small enough to trigger a duty to warn) may not understand that guards are available if requested to make the process safer.

Students sometimes are perplexed by the idea that Hobart could be held liable when a purchaser of its product removes a guard and someone is injured as a result; wasn't this a misuse of the product? It may well have been, but then again it may have been foreseeable misuse for which the manufacturer should have provided in some way. This is a point mentioned back in the *Welge* case in the section on manufacturing defects.

Note on post-sale duties to warn. Students may wonder about manufacturers' duties to warn about a product if they become aware of its dangers after it is sold. Space didn't permit the casebook text to treat that issue, but in case it does come up here is sec. 10 of the Third Restatement, which folds the issue into the usual reasonableness inquiry:

(a) One engaged in the business of selling or otherwise distributing products is subject to liability for harm to persons or property caused by the seller's failure to provide a warning after the time of sale or distribution of a product if a reasonable person in the seller's position would provide such a warning.

(b) A reasonable person in the seller's position would provide a warning after the time of sale if:

> (1) the seller knows or reasonably should know that the product poses a substantial risk of harm to persons or property; and
> (2) those to whom a warning might be provided can be identified and can reasonably be assumed to be unaware of the risk of harm; and
> (3) a warning can be effectively communicated to and acted on by those to whom a warning might be provided; and
> (4) the risk of harm is sufficiently great to justify the burden of providing a warning.

Note on prescription drugs. The casebook text sets out section 6(c) of the Third Restatement, which has occasioned a bit of controversy as indicated by the case excerpt that follows it. For a bit more on the subject, here is an excerpt from George W. Conk, *Is There a Design Defect in the Restatement (Third) of Torts: Products Liability?* 109 Yale L.J. 1087 (2000); the arguments he makes, and the response from the reporters that follows it, can form the basis of an in-class exercise in interpretation of the Restatement's language:

> In section 6(c), the ALI, virtually without debate, adopted a rule that exempts sellers of prescription drugs and medical devices from the alternative-safer-design standard applied to all other products. Under the ALI's new rule, designers and manufacturers of drugs and medical devices will not be held liable even if their products reasonably could have been made safer. The manufacturer need persuade the factfinder only that, on balance, the product does more good than harm for at least one class of users, so that a reasonable physician would prescribe it. The alternative-safer-design standard is rejected not only for drugs, but also for vaccines and mechanical devices such as cardiac pacemakers. Blood products, although regulated as drugs by the Food and Drug Administration (FDA), are excluded entirely from the Restatement, which acquiesces in the wide legislative ban on strict or warranty liability for blood products. The Restatement (Third) thus carves out a special, protective standard for a uniquely favored industry. [...] Section 6(c) mirrors the "manifestly unreasonable" design standard recognized (somewhat grudgingly) in section 2, which states that some product designs have such low social utility and are so dangerous that liability should attach even absent proof of a reasonable alternative design. Section 6(c) is also notable in that it represents a "product category" approach to liability rules even though the ALI elsewhere rejected the categorical approach. [...]

> The net benefit rule is a standard under which liability rarely will be imposed. Indeed, a design-defect claim will not survive even the summary judgment stage unless the court determines that a reasonable person could conclude that the product was defective under this narrow standard. While it is true that for most prescription drugs there is no alternative safer design, this is not always the case. Moreover, that fact does not logically compel a categorical doctrinal exception for all such drugs, vaccines, and medical devices—a group of products that has in common only the fact that they are prescribed or administered by a licensed health care provider. By any measure, section 6(c) is an aberration, and an unjustifiable one. [...]

> The choice between the Sabin live-attenuated-virus oral polio vaccine (OPV) and the Salk killed-virus injected polio vaccine (IPV) presents a concrete case in which the reasonableness of a design choice can be tested using the alternative-safer-design test. OPV virtually eradicated the

polio epidemic in the United States within a few years of its introduction. However, because it contains live polio viruses, OPV sometimes caused vaccinees to develop Vaccine Associated Paralytic Polio (VAPP). Persons who are immunocompromised are particularly susceptible to developing VAPP. The virus can infect not only vaccinees, but also persons in close contact with them. Of the 133 reported cases of polio in the United States in the 1980-1994 period, 125 were VAPP cases. At present, the risk of contracting VAPP from an OPV vaccination is about one case in 2.4 million doses distributed. This risk translates into eight or nine OPV cases per year.

Enhanced-potency IPV, an alternative design of the polio vaccine that does not use live polio virus, was developed in 1978. Enhanced IPV is as effective as OPV in preventing polio but cannot itself cause the disease. France, Finland, Sweden, and the Netherlands have eliminated polio by relying exclusively on IPV. The United States has been slow to change, but in 1999 the Centers for Disease Control recommended complete reliance on IPV.

The question for products-liability law is whether the risk associated with OPV can be justified in light of the availability of an alternative safer design, the enhanced-potency IPV. In making this determination, both the reduction of VAPP risk achievable through IPV and the relative effectiveness of the two vaccine designs in preventing polio should be considered. Since research has demonstrated conclusively that IPV and OPV are equally effective in preventing the disease, the clear choice under this test is IPV. There is thus a strong argument that the availability of IPV has rendered OPV unreasonably unsafe, despite the enormous social utility of OPV.

In urging that the United States move toward an IPV-only vaccination regime, the Centers for Disease Control sought an optimal product design. The risk-benefit analysis it undertook closely tracked the analysis of tort law, weighing the benefits, costs, and risks of the proposed heightened safety precaution. However, the regulators and vaccine manufacturers might justly be faulted by a person infected with VAPP for waiting to recommend the exclusive use of IPV until sixteen years after France made that change.

Under a section 2 alternative-safer-design analysis, OPV would be deemed a defective product and the manufacturers of OPV thus could be held liable for VAPP injuries caused by their product. But under a section 6(c) analysis, these manufacturers would not be held liable. Although IPV is an entirely reasonable and much safer alternative design, the section 6(c) defect test would deem the use of OPV reasonable because the OPV vaccine has a net benefit for its users. Because it is effective in preventing polio in the population and causes the disease in only a small percentage of cases, in the aggregate the vaccine does more good than harm. However, the existence of an equally effective safer alternative design makes the risk of serious injury, however small, an unreasonable risk. That OPV has a high social utility should be irrelevant to the question of whether it was unreasonable not to move more quickly to the safer alternative design. Application of the section 2 defect standard would achieve the more just result in adjudicating VAPP claims.

The reporters replied in Henderson and Twerski, *Drug Designs are Different*, 111 Yale L.J. 151 (2001):

We emphatically disagree with Conk's insistence that section 6(c) does not allow any alleged RAD to be considered by the court in determining whether a prescription product's design is defective. The key to understanding the meaning of section 6(c) on this point lies in its explicit reliance on the construct of whether "reasonable health-care providers" would knowingly "prescribe the drug or medical device for any class of patients." Obviously, such a reasonable provider should consider available alternative drugs in deciding which drug, if any, to prescribe. Indeed, that may be said to be the essence of the healer's craft—assessing and comparing all available courses of medical treatment. Conk's suggestion that the new Restatement requires the hypothetical prescribing physician to focus exclusively on the risks and benefits of a given drug in isolation, wearing blinders that prevent consideration of other readily available drugs, attributes a meaning to section 6(c) that would require that physician to violate her Hippocratic oath.

Admittedly, section 6(c)'s description of the risks of harm that would support a finding of defectiveness as "great in relation to [the drug's] therapeutic benefits" might lead, at first blush, to Conk's conclusion. That is, this language might suggest that the drug is to be judged on its own bottom, in isolation from all other possible alternatives. And comment f appears to reinforce this reading with its first sentence: "Subsection (c) reflects the judgment that, as long as a given drug or device provides net benefits for a class of patients, it should be available to them . . . ." But the admittedly ambiguous phrase "provides net benefits" must, in fairness, be read to refer to "net benefits in light of available alternatives." This reading is made clear by the second sentence in comment f: "Learned intermediaries must generally be relied upon to see that the right drugs and devices reach the right patients." This second sentence conjures the appropriate image of responsible prescribing physicians deciding what is best for their patients among available alternatives--not the distorted image that Conk reads into section 6(c) of a health-care provider acting with blinders firmly in place.

Our reading of section 6(c) is bolstered by the reality that, if Conk's contrary reading were correct—if the design standard under section 6(c) were whether, judged in isolation, a given drug benefited any class of patients—then there would be no reason to couch the standard in terms of what a reasonable physician would do for her patients. Section 6(c) could just as easily have said "a prescription drug or medical device is defective if, on balance, it benefits no class of patients." In fact, section 6(c) must have been intended to allow reasonable alternatives to be considered by the hypothetical prescribing physicians, because the blinders Conk reads into section 6(c), by forcing those physicians needlessly to harm many of their hypothetical patients, would otherwise constitute a gratuitous insult to the medical profession. [...]

Why, then, does the rule in section 6(c) of the Restatement refuse to hold liable a manufacturer for not developing a safer alternative drug that would have prevented the plaintiff's injury? Such refusal rests not on deference to the FDA but on an understandable reluctance to allow courts to determine whether a proposed alternative drug would have received FDA approval. Development by a manufacturer of a safer alternative drug does not, by itself, help anyone. For physicians to prescribe such a safer drug, it must reach the market. To reach the market, a prescription drug must be approved by the FDA. Thus, the question of whether a new alternative drug should have been developed by the defendant must be recast as whether the proposed alternative drug would have won FDA approval in time to help the plaintiff. No court can answer that question without seeking, in some manner, to replicate the FDA approval process. [...] No expert could honestly opine that approval would have been granted without engaging in rank speculation. The approval process is accompanied by countless opportunities to decline or delay further progress. The data required to be developed for drug approval are beyond the capabilities of the litigants to replicate in a trial setting. Trials are compressed in time and scope; they do not allow for the expansive multi-year analysis and interaction between the manufacturer and the FDA that characterize the American drug regulatory process. Even if comparing a defendant's drugs with drugs that might have been developed made sense substantively (it does not), from the standpoint of legal process it could never be accomplished fairly or sensibly.

Brooks v. Medtronic, Inc. (P injured by pacemaker; NL because although D didn't warn P of danger, D did warn his doctor: the learned intermediary doctrine)

Perez v. Wyeth Laboratories (learned intermediary doctrine inapplicable to D's aggressively marketed drugs)

Q. What is the rationale for the learned intermediary doctrine? Why does it apply to doctors but not to car salesmen?

A. The most forceful rationale seems to be that there are lots of risks created by medicines; rather than inundate the patient with information about all those risks, it is better to leave the transmission of warnings to a doctor who has information about which specific risks are most relevant to the patient. If notification of all risks were delivered directly to the patient, figuring out which of them (if any) might be applicable to his own case might be such a nuisance that he doesn't bother to study them at all. Car salesmen are different, first, because they do not have the same duty of care to their customers that physicians have to their patients (why?), so it does not make sense to rely on them to tell their customers everything they need to know. Another distinction is that safety warnings about cars need not be tailored to their individual users. They are pretty much the same for everyone, so they might as well be passed on directly. Finally, to anticipate a point of the *Perez* case, automobile manufacturers, unlike some drug manufacturers (especially in times past), have direct relationships with consumers: they market their cars directly to them. So perhaps there are obligations to warn that go along with this, whereas in the medical case the patient's only interaction with the pharmaceutical industry establishment may be through his physician.

Q. In *Brooks*, the relevant risk was the possibility that the leads of the pacemaker might come dislodged from his heart and cause him various injuries. It was undisputed that this risk is common to all pacemakers and their users. Given this uniformity, why wasn't a warning of such risks required to be given to all purchasers of the defendant's pacemakers? Why wasn't the pacemaker like a car at least with respect to this risk?

A. It may just be that the administrative convenience of having a clear rule for medical devices outweighs the benefits of making exceptions for those cases determined (after much argument, no doubt) to involve risks uniform to everyone. Another distinction, though, is that while the risk that the leads would come loose may have been the same for all patients, the cost of passing that information on was not the same for all patients. The court's view was that giving Brooks full warnings about this risk might have caused him stress that he could not handle; he was better off making his choice in the dark, even though (indeed, *because*) the relevant risk applied to him. This suggests an additional and quite paternalistic rationale for the learned intermediary doctrine: medical patients may have bad reactions to information about risk, and in that case the most cost-beneficial decision may be not to tell them. Their doctor is in the best position to make this judgment. Evidently there are no comparable circumstances involving car salesmen.

Q. What is the distinction between *Brooks* and *Perez*? Why treat medical products differently if they are advertised on television?

A. Part of the idea here is that leaving warnings in the hands of doctors made sense when consumers had virtually no contact with drug manufacturers, but doctors did; now those manufacturers are trying to reach consumers directly, and with this change in communication strategy should come a change in the duty to warn: it should run directly to consumers. But what does this mean? Are television commercials supposed to contain references to all the risks such a product creates? The list would have been long in the *Perez* case, at least if the plaintiffs' complaint is assumed to be accurate. Well, apparently that isn't quite the point. You can put it, rather, in terms of where the locus of the patient's decision is. A patient deciding whether to use a drug formerly based the choice entirely on what the doctor said about it; now a patient is more likely to base the decision on direct information from the manufacturer in advertisements of various sorts. The doctor still has to write the prescription, but if the maker has directly helped to induce the patient to make the decision, the maker should likewise accept some responsibility for making sure the information the patient receives—at some point before taking the drug—is complete. The warnings may not be in the advertisements (though some commercials now contain a quickly-spoken laundry list of warnings at their tail end), but they have to be supplied to the consumer at some point.

And it's not just that consumers and drug manufacturers have different relationships now than in the old days; it's also that patients and their doctors have different relationships, causing courts to put less trust in them. Doctors now may operate under constraints or conflicts of interest that didn't exist before, or weren't as powerful. The drugs available to them to prescribe may be limited by the managed care organization that has contracts with the patient and physician; and pharmaceutical companies push hard to get physicians to promote their products, both though aggressive pressing of free samples and professional associations between companies and doctors

McMahon v. Bunn-O-Matic Corp. (coffee spill case; NL)
Liebeck v. McDonald's Corp. (the fabled McDonald's coffee case; L)

Q. What is the distinction between *McMahon v. Bunn-O-Matic Corp.* and *Liebeck v. McDonald's Corp.*?
A. In *Liebeck* the plaintiff had evidence that the plaintiff in *McMahon* was missing: evidence that the coffee produced by the defendant was hotter than the coffee produced elsewhere. This didn't mean the defendant necessarily was liable, but it is relevant to what the plaintiff should have expected as a consumer and therefore to what obligation the defendant had to issue a warning. It's worth emphasizing that we don't *know* the coffee in the McDonald's case was hotter than all the other coffee served nearby. We only know that the plaintiff managed to get some evidence to that effect into the record; and once this is done, the weighing of the evidence is up to the jury.

Students like talking about the coffee cases, both because most of them have heard about the *McDonald's* case and because most of them drink coffee. Some of them find that after reading more about Liebeck's case they find the result more agreeable than they expected. (Others don't.) Just asking them about that is usually enough to get a good discussion rolling, which then can go in many different directions and can be used to explore, one last time, the rationales for product liability law. One of us (Farnsworth) has a tape of the oral argument in the *McMahon* case. It's fun to play in class; contact him if you would like a copy.

CHAPTER 9

DAMAGES

SECTION A. COMPENSATORY DAMAGES

1. Damage to Property

There really is nothing to cut here once you have decided to teach the section at all; the best way to achieve brevity is with swift treatment of the problems at the end of the section. But we suppose you could also just teach *Hatahley* as a general introduction to compensatory damages without touching the rest of the materials.

United States v. Hatahley (United States destroys tribe's horses and donkeys; L; analysis of various types of damages)

Q. The opinion contains a paradox, does it not? It starts by saying that the fundamental goal of a damage award "is to restore the injured party, as nearly as possible, to the position he would have been in had it not been for the wrong of the other party." But then it says that the plaintiffs should be awarded the "replacement cost" of their animals, when it seems obvious that the plaintiffs would not have sold the animals for that amount. What is the meaning of this?

A. The law resorts to market measures of damages where it can. This does violate the "make whole" principle in the sense that few plaintiffs will be as happy with a payment of the market value of their goods as they were before the goods were destroyed. Even setting litigation costs to one side, most people value their property at some amount more than the market does; that's what it usually means to say that something is "not for sale." We commit errors of undercompensation every time we award such plaintiffs the market value of their destroyed goods. The reason for the practice is that attempts to determine the true value of the goods to the owner would be an error-prone exercise as well—and would have the additional problem of making cases much harder to settle out of court, since the parties wouldn't be able to repair to a clear, objective source of guidance (of the sort that markets frequently provide) to determine how much the defendant owes the plaintiff. If the result seems unfair, notice that many owners of animals and other goods who are compensated too little when their things are lost may be more or less equally likely to accidentally destroy the goods of others and thus benefit from the rule.

Q. What were the elements of the damages that the court said could properly be awarded to the plaintiffs? How did the trial court blunder with respect to each of them?

A. There were three elements:

i. Replacement cost. First, the plaintiffs were entitled to the replacement cost of the horses and other animals: the price of comparable animals, including the cost of training them. Sentimental value does not figure into it, nor does the fact that the plaintiffs probably would not have been willing to sell the animals for that price, as noted above. Normally market value and replacement cost will be the same; this is a point brought out by some of the problems that follow later in the section. In this case, however, the plaintiffs' testimony evidently was not limited to the animals' market value, but also consisted of testimony from the owners about the animals' value to them. In addition, the market the trial court used was just the community of Indians and the value of the sheep and other animals that they would have given in trade for the stolen horses. Apparently the court of appeals wanted a larger market used as a benchmark for the stolen animals' value. It also wanted more care used in calculating the cost of new animals and the separate cost of training them.

ii. Loss of use. Second, the plaintiffs were entitled to damages for loss of use. Here that would include the extent to which the plaintiffs' herds of other animals (sheep, goats, and cattle) had to be reduced because they had fewer horses or donkeys to use to facilitate looking after them. But while the plaintiffs' herds did decrease in size after the seizure of the horses and donkeys, the trial court did not do an adequate job of figuring out how much of the reduction was attributable to the defendants' acts and how much of the reduction was attributable to other factors such as the ages of the donkeys and goats. The court also says that "No consideration was given to the disposition of the livestock by the plaintiffs in reducing the herds," perhaps suggesting that the trial court failed to take into account the returns the plaintiffs got when they liquidated some of those animals that they no longer were able to contain. The court notes as well that the plaintiffs can collect for damages they suffered in not being able to ride their horses to obtain medical care, attend ceremonies, etc. But all of these rights to recover are limited to damages suffered only up until the time when a prudent person would have replaced the horses—the doctrine of avoidable consequences.

iii. Suffering. Finally, and unusually in a property case, the plaintiffs were eligible to receive damages for pain and suffering; but these amounts had to be assessed individually.

Property damage problems

These problems are intended to get students thinking creatively about different ways of measuring lost value. Here are a few thoughts on each of them.

a. *The crushed bicycle.* Hopefully a student will start by suggesting that defendant owes plaintiff a new bicycle. Then you can bring out that this doesn't make much sense, since the bicycle that was destroyed was not (let us imagine) brand new. So maybe the defendant should just give the plaintiff forty dollars. The plaintiff might complain that this leaves her with forty dollars and no bicycle; but if forty dollars is the correct amount, the implication is that she can buy a used bike for that price—which is what she lost. This is the general approach when damages is done to cars or other property in which there is a thick market.

Another way to come at the problem is to ask for a list of possible measures of damages. They can be assessed by reference to the repair cost (but assume the damage was irreparable), the cost of a new bicycle, or the reduction in the bicycle's market value. The last measure is the right one, and in a it's the same as replacement cost: the replacement measure should entitle the owner not to a new bicycle, but to a used bicycle of similar value to the old one. .

Then there is the possibility of lost use. As *Hatahley* and Rest. §918 show, the plaintiff cannot collect damages that easily could have been avoided with precautions afterwards (but notice the tension between this principle—*zero* recovery for non-mitigated damages—and the rise of comparative fault). Whether the plaintiff also has to take more expensive measures—e.g., replacing a destroyed car promptly so he can continue work as a traveling salesman—depends on his circumstances, as comment e to Rest. §918 discusses.

b. *The telephone pole.* The previous problem illustrates the simple use of market measures of damages. This problem introduces the complications that can arise when there is no such thick market to use as a reference point: here there is no market for used telephone poles that we can use to figure out how much the defendant should pay. This means that market value and replacement cost aren't symmetrical, as they were in the previous problem. The opinion in the case on which this problem is based, *Portland General Electric Co. v. Taber*, 934 P.2d 538 (Or. App. 1997), thus finds replacement cost too generous to the plaintiff, since it amounts to making the defendant buy a new pole to replace a demolished one that may have been 30 years old and due for replacement soon anyway. Yet by this logic perhaps the defendant should owe *nothing* to the plaintiff if the pole already had outlasted its life expectancy when the defendant knocked it over. The court is troubled by this possibility, but uses such an approach anyway: we find out what the expected life of a pole is by checking the number of years over which the plaintiff depreciated it (wrote off its cost on its taxes); and we make the defendant pay a sum that reflects the number of years of use the pole still was expected to have. If that number happens to be zero, the defendant owes nothing.

The court finds appealing an additional possibility: one could calculate the expected remaining life of a pole *given* that it had reached an advanced age. The analogy is to an old person who has outlived her life expectancy. We don't expect such a person to die momentarily. We say: given the fact that she has made it to age X, her expectancy now is Y. We could do the same thing with telephone poles, but apparently the argument was not made clearly enough by the parties for the court to rely on it.

c. *Lost film.* Here's an introduction to the even more difficult problems that arise when neither market value nor any form of replacement cost is available as a measure of damages. The film itself has a market value, of course, and that was the basis of the defendant's suggestion about the proper size of the award: reimburse for the blank film. The plaintiff counters that the film that was lost was not blank, but had pictures on it; that was the main source of its value. Yet the pictures have no market value. Restatement §911, in the excerpts that appear in the casebook before these problems, has some discussion on point; notice the text struggling with the problem of property damage when the property can't be replaced and has trivial market value. We are told that "value to the owner" can be awarded, but not "sentimental value." Evidently the idea is to glean the owner's value from side measures such as the original purchase price (if any) or the value of the time put into the creation of the property (if it can be determined). But of course these measures are not of any great help in the case of the lost film. From the court's opinion in *Mieske v. Bartell Drug Co.*, 593 P.2d 1308 (Wash. 1979), from which this problem was drawn (affirming a jury award of $7,500):

> The standard of recovery for destruction of personal property was summarized in *McCurdy v. Union Pac. R.R.*, 413 P.2d 617 (Wash. 1966). We recognized in *McCurdy* that (1) personal property which is destroyed may have a market value, in which case that market value is the measure of damages; (2) if destroyed property has no market value but can be replaced or reproduced, then the measure is the cost of replacement or reproduction; (3) if the destroyed property has no market value and cannot be replaced or reproduced, then the value to the owner is to be the proper measure of damages. However, while not stated in *McCurdy*, we have held that in the third *McCurdy* situation, damages are not recoverable for the sentimental value which the owner places on the property. [...]

> Necessarily the measure of damages in [the third situation, applicable here] is the most imprecise of the three categories. Yet difficulty of assessment is not cause to deny damages to a plaintiff whose property has no market value and cannot be replaced or reproduced. [...] The problem is to establish the value to the owner. Market and replacement values are relatively ascertainable by appropriate proof. Recognizing that value to the owner encompasses a subjective element, the rule has been established that compensation for sentimental or fanciful values will not be allowed. That restriction was placed upon the jury in this case by the court's damages instruction.

> What is sentimental value? The broad dictionary definition is that sentimental refers to being "governed by feeling, sensibility or emotional idealism. . . ." Webster's Third New International Dictionary (1963). Obviously that is not the exclusion contemplated by the statement that sentimental value is not to be compensated. If it were, no one would recover for the wrongful death of a spouse or a child. Rather, the type of sentiment which is not compensable is that which

relates to "indulging in feeling to an unwarranted extent" or being "affectedly or mawkishly emotional..." Webster's Third New International Dictionary (1963).

Under these rules, the court's damages instruction was correct. In essence it allowed recovery for the actual or intrinsic value to the plaintiffs but denied recovery for any unusual sentimental value of the film to the plaintiffs or a fanciful price which plaintiffs, for their own special reasons, might place thereon.

Some students are surprised by this result, since receipts from photo developing stores usually contain language limiting the store's liability if the film is lost. Such language was present on the receipt here, and it would indeed have prevented such a large recovery in many jurisdictions. But in this case the provision on the receipt was held unconscionable. (What are the likely consequences of such a ruling for the price of having film developed?)

Q. If I run over your dog with my car, most courts will allow you to collect only the dog's market value from me, which usually will be a very small amount (imagine that it's a beloved mutt). Isn't that like awarding the plaintiff in the photo shop case just the price of a few new rolls of film? Why do we treat the plaintiff in the photography case so much more generously than a dog owner?

A. The answer probably has to do with the possible policy consequences of using the "value to the owner" approach in the two situations. The defendant in *Mieske* (the film case) was a repeat actor who constantly developed film. If the measure of its damages was limited to the price of replacement rolls of film, arguably it would have an inadequate incentive to take care (setting aside the contractual setting of the case, as the court did). But usually when a pet is killed, it's in a random accident caused by someone who is unlikely to do it again (and, as noted before, who may be as likely in the future to be turned into a plaintiff under similar circumstances). Since the risks created by the rule are reciprocal, and since there are no systematic incentive problems, we forgo the attempt to determine the value to the owner in the dog case. It might be different if there was a repeating problem with veterinary malpractice that accounted for a large share of pet deaths; in that case maybe the *Mieske* approach would seem more warranted in the animal setting after all.

d. *The sinkhole.* The law's usual response in the situations like this is to award the plaintiff the reduction in value that had occurred immediately after the defendant caused the damage. The logic of this is that the plaintiff could have sold the house right away after the damage occurred, and thus have felt the damage inflicted by the defendant in full regardless of the sinkhole. Attempts to differentiate between cases where the plaintiff would or wouldn't have attempted such a sale are likely to be cumbersome and expensive swearing contests we would prefer to avoid. (Is there an additional danger that a different rule might in some cases create odd incentives to sell property promptly after it is damaged, lest it be wiped out so that no recovery is possible at all?) It's different if the property was not transferable, since then this logic no longer applies: the plaintiff couldn't have sold it after all. The discussion and illustrations after Restatement §912 (just before these problems) make this point. Illustrations 17 and 18 are instructive points of comparison; they differ because in Illustration 17 the goods were transferable. This enables us to presume that the plaintiff might have sold them before they were destroyed. No such possibility exists in Illustration 18.

An additional consideration, of course, is that we would want to know whether the risk that the house would be swallowed up by the sinkhole was known and impounded in its price. In that case the defendant should simply pay the full market value of the house—which might be meager, given the risk that it would vanish soon.

e. *The unexpected raise.* You can use this problem to raise issues discussed in the excerpts from Rest. §920. Judge Posner argues in *Rice v. Nova Biomedical*, 38 F.3d 909, 910-911 (7th Cir. 1994), that the plaintiff's damages should not be reduced to reflect the ways in which the wrongful discharge turns out to have made him better off:

> The defendants were allowed, all unavailingly, to argue to the jury that Rice's serendipitous gains from being fired should be offset against the loss of income that he incurred during his brief period of unemployment. It is true that this argument, despite its appeal to common sense, was not relevant to damages, and in fact the evidence on which it was based was admitted only to rebut evidence that Rice had experienced a loss of self-esteem as a result of being fired. He could not have recovered for losses that, though they would not have occurred but for the discharge, were not the sort of loss made more likely by it; it would be as if he had been injured as a result of slipping on a banana peel on his way from the meeting at which [the defendants] fired him. It follows that he should not be denied serendipitous gains—gains that while they would not have accrued had it not been for the discharge were not made more likely by it. Otherwise tort damages would be systematically underestimated. Still, having suffered in fact, if not in the contemplation of law, no pecuniary injury from being discharged (and presumably only a transient diminution in self-esteem), Rice might have been expected to use his time to better advantage than litigating. The suit is four years old and after paying his lawyers Rice is unlikely to have obtained a compensatory rate of return on the investment of time and emotion that he must have made in the suit. It is not only his own time and emotional tranquillity that he has spent bounteously. Beset by swollen dockets, judges cannot be expected to look with favor upon lawsuits brought not to recoup losses but to vent indignation or generate windfall gains.

2. Lost Earnings

If you're going to teach this section at all, there probably is no point in making cuts. But the most interesting cases here are the first two.

Landers v. Ghosh (P, wife of carpenter killed through D's negligence, receives $400,000 in damages)
Pescatore v. Pan Am Airlines (P, wife of oil executive killed through D's negligence, receives $14,000,000 in damages) (fyi, it's pronounced Pescator, not Pescatoray)

Q. What justification can there be for the gigantic disparity between the amounts for lost support awarded to the plaintiffs in these cases?
A. This is a question without a clear-cut answer, of course; it is meant to provoke discussion. The only ways to equalize the situation would be to either award much more to Landers's wife, which is problematic because it might make him worth much more dead than alive from an economic standpoint; or to award much less to Pescatore's wife, which would be a possibility if a uniform schedule of compensation awards were used in cases like these. But in the latter case the tortfeasor would indeed be leaving Pescatore's wife much worse off than she had been when he was alive, which rankles from the standpoint of corrective justice. In the long run the approach used in these cases has some administrative advantages, since it creates a standard (lost wages) that everyone can understand. But then so would fixed schedules for compensation.

Is there also a broader social argument for the larger compensation award—an argument that Pescatore was in fact a more productive member of society than Landers, and that his pay reflected this? This argument is not easy for many to swallow in the case of an oil executive vs. a carpenter, but it may be that the superb oil executive has a very rare set of skills that make great indirect contributions to the happiness of everyone who consumes oil—which is to say, everyone. Good carpenters are easier to find or create. Another comparison for the sake of discussion would be the spouse of an aging mobster and the spouse of an industrial giant or a young medical researcher well on her way to discovering a cure for cancer. Do we want different damage awards in those cases? (In which of those cases would we expect higher actual awards?) Is it conceivable that different awards in those cases would lead to different behaviors by any potential tortfeasors in the world? (Should they? Should a surgeon use just a little extra care in working on a patient who holds a position of public responsibility?) Really there are two questions here: whether some people are more "valuable" than others in any sense the law ought to recognize, and then, if so, the extent to which the size of their salaries reflects this.

Contrary to what some students may suggest, the logic of the damage awards in these cases is not that one person's life is worth more than another's. The suit is being brought by the spouse, and the claim is that the spouse's standard of living should not be reduced on account of the defendant's negligence; the defendant should be responsible for keeping Mrs. Pescatore right where she was before she lost her husband's support. It may or may not be fair, but courts are pretty emphatic in saying that they are not engaged in a general exercise of setting a value on the lost life.

Q. How might we explain the differences between the awards in these cases for loss of consortium? Pescatore's wife got $5,000,000; Landers's wife got an amount for loss of consortium that is impossible to pin down from the general verdict in that case, but was no more than $400,000 and probably was much less than that.

A. This discrepancy seems hard to explain. It is difficult to believe that the court in *Landers* would have permitted the spouse in that case to be awarded $5,000,000 for loss of society; it would seem strange to most people if the carpenter's wife came away from the case a multimillionaire when it seems so unlikely that she ever would have been in such a financial position if he had lived—though of course it's possible that she considered herself "wealthier" with her husband than she would with the cash.

The point for the students to see is that lost earnings and loss of society differ because there is a market usable to measure the former but not the latter. Juries therefore are left to rather arbitrarily fix damage awards for loss of society, and perhaps they do it in part by using the market measures that *are* available in the case (e.g., lost earnings) as some sort of starting-point or benchmark—perhaps an "anchoring" fallacy: in *Pescatore* the jurors already were thinking in millions. Thus they might make the award for loss of society a fraction of the award for lost earnings, which is why the award was so much larger in *Pescatore* than it was in *Landers*. But this seems a strange way to think about loss of consortium. There is no reason to assume a rich man is better company than a poor one, and some reason to suppose he may be worse: the unemployed decedent in *Landers* might well have spent more time with his wife than the highly ambitious decedent in *Pescatore*.

Haddigan v. Harkins (illustrates use of hourly rates to value wife's labor)
Benwell v. Dean (evidence of remarriage inadmissible to reduce damages)
Louisville & Nashville Ry. v. Creighton (illustrates attempt to value child's lost earnings)

Q. If a person dies as a result of a defendant's negligence and the plaintiff (the decedent's spouse) remarries, should the plaintiff's damages for loss of support be reduced? Suppose that after Michael Pescatore dies, his wife marries his boss, whose earning potential is even greater than Michael Pescatore's was. Should she still be entitled to collect $14,000,000 from Pan Am?

A. The difficulties with allowing damages to be reduced on this ground seem to be largely based on administrative and other policy concerns. If damages are to be reduced because the plaintiff remarried, then why not also reduce them in any event to reflect the *chance* that she will remarry? But here the figuring becomes impossibly speculative and unpredictable. Who knows whether she will remarry another oil executive or a carpenter? One could distinguish between cases of actual and expected remarriage, but that would create a perverse incentive to stay unmarried until the litigation is over. Another possible rationale is that the defendant should pay over the full amount even if the plaintiff doesn't need it because otherwise the defendant isn't internalizing the social cost of eradicating a valuable oil executive (or whatever the decedent was). Still, it does seem troubling that a plaintiff can collect twice, as it were; at least one of the rationales of the collateral source cases the court mentions—namely, that the plaintiff has paid in advance for the insurance policy, so that its benefits should not now be counted against her—is not present here.

By the way, notice that one might want a separate analysis of this question with respect to damages for lost support and lost society. With respect to which of those items is the case stronger for taking into account the remarriage?

Q. Is there any distinction between the logic of the "opportunity cost" approach as applied to a housewife and as applied to an executive who quits his job to become an oil painter?

A. The assumption behind the theory in either case is that the plaintiff was the beneficiary of the decedent's activities, whether the activity is conventional employment or something different. But that may be less clearly true in the case of the painter than in the case of the housewife. In other words, an executive who becomes an oil painter may be deciding to support his family *less,* rather than deciding to support them to the same or greater extent but in a different form. (Maybe his wife sees just as little of him as she ever did before.) In theory the same could be true of woman who quits her job at a firm to become a housewife, but a housewife's work more obviously consists of services provided directly to the rest of the family. For some discussion of the opportunity-cost approach, see Richard A. Posner, *Conservative Feminism*, 1989 U. Chi. Legal F. 191. The example points up some general difficulties with the idea of using opportunity cost in cases involving a housewife. It's hard to figure out how much of the forgone income was essentially transferred to her family and how much was in effect consumed by her because she was happier there. Opportunity cost is theoretically appealing but administratively hair-raising. The temp-agency approach shown in *Haddigan v. Harkins* is less theoretically appealing but more easily manageable.

Suppose someone leaves a job at a big, hard-driving firm in favor of a government job with tamer hours—then dies as a result of some defendant's negligence. Should damages for the survivors be set by reference to the well-paying job? The same problems arise again: we don't know how much of the decision to change jobs amounted to a transfer of wealth (time, attention, etc.) to his family and how much of it was just a rearrangement of his own utility.

An interesting problem with the opportunity cost approach involves the party who becomes a zen master—or, more plausibly, a housewife—without ever bothering to go to law school; perhaps she says she knew all along what some people learn only after getting an advanced degree and then going into the workforce: she likes raising a family better. Why should her family make out worse than the family of the lawyer-turned-homemaker if both of them are killed by a defendant's negligence? Well, it would have to be a question of proof: anyone can *say* that they could have made a million dollars if they hadn't stayed home raising kids; but we would want to reserve the legal finding to that effect (in a world where this theory was used!) to cases where there is strong reason to think it's really true.

Q. Should a person have to pay more for negligently causing the death of a child with a high IQ than a child with a low IQ?

A. That is one possible implication, occasionally accepted by courts, of allowing recovery for the loss of expected support from a person now a child and not earning anything. In such a case the jury has to find some way of projecting the child's eventual earning power, and evidence of the child's extraordinary abilities may be admissible to try to prove this. Parents who can produce no such evidence thus are made worse off than those who can. The whole idea of awarding damages to parents for lost support from their children may be easier for students to understand if they realize that these rules were devised in an era when it was more common for children to contribute to the household economy—e.g., the family farm—as they grew, so that children were important financial assets for their parents. That is less widely true today, though many parents still expect to receive some benefits from their children in old age.

By the way, the $10,500 awarded by the jury in *Louisville & Nashville Ry. v. Creighton* is the equivalent of about $200,000 in inflation-adjusted dollars in the year 2002.

Q. Why do some jurisdictions *not* take taxes into account when calculating awards for lost wages?

A.   They think it's all too speculative: it's hard to predict what the tax rates will be years from now, or what the plaintiff's tax returns would have looked like. Thus Judge Friendly's worry in *McWeeney v. N.Y., N.H. & Hartford RR Co.*, 282 F.2d 34 (2d Cir. 1960):

> The instruction here requested and refused illustrates the delusive simplicity with which the subject has been invested. Defendant wished the jury to be told merely that 'If your verdict is in favor of plaintiff, you must calculate any past or future loss of earnings on the basis of his net income after deduction of income taxes.' All of us agree the jury needs more guidance than that. But what is the alternative? The trial court could begin by instructing that under the optional tax provided in §3 of the Internal Revenue Code, which McWeeney was entitled to elect, the tax on a bachelor's income of $4,800 would have been $773. This is still simple enough but the jury must determine not what McWeeney's tax on $4,800 now is but what it would be over his expectancy. In these lower brackets the amount of the tax and its percentage relation to earnings are enormously affected by the number of exemptions. The simple act of matrimony, coupled with the filing of a joint return, would reduce McWeeney's tax from $773 to $620. Is the jury to consider the likelihood of this not unusual occurrence? If the lady brought two children with her, or if these were produced in the ordinary way, the tax would be cut in half, to $380. Each additional child would bring a further tax saving of $110, so that a total of five would make the tax nominal. While such fecundity might be unlikely in a plaintiff of 39 the rule here framed for McWeeney must apply to men who evidence greater interest in marriage and parenthood, and the rise in the birth rate is a phenomenon of our age. Is the jury in each case to speculate, or hear testimony, on the procreative proclivities and potentialities of the plaintiff and his spouse? Moreover, children are by no means the only source of exemptions; §152 of the Code lists nine other categories. Nor will it do to say that this is over-refinement. If a defendant claims that a plaintiff in these brackets would have had to pay 20% of his income in taxes, the court cannot deprive the plaintiff of an opportunity of showing that he would not have paid anything of the kind, and once the rule were adopted, we see no way of eliminating the question of potential babies and the exemptions they trail with them.

Q.   Should prejudgment interest be awarded with tort damages?
A.   The traditional custom has been to allow prejudgment interest only where the amount at stake was clearly defined—not on "unliquidated" damages where it was unclear to the defendant how much would actually be owed if the plaintiff won. At present it is more common for interest to be ordered on the amount even where it wasn't clear in advance. You can invite students to ask what incentive is created by defendants under one rule or the other: if no prejudgment interest will be due and the amount is large, defendants may be better off delaying and prolonging litigation to obtain interest on the sum before parting with it. This explains the Ohio statute reprinted in the text, which allows prejudgment interest in tort cases only if the defendant has resisted good-faith attempts to negotiate a settlement.

3. Pain and Suffering; Emotional Distress; Hedonic Damages

   This section can take more than one class session to cover; there's a lot to discuss here. If you want to shorten it, you might cut some or all of items 8-12 ("Recovery for Humiliation" through the *Hogan* case), and item 14 (notes on hedonic damages).

From W. Kip Viscusi, *Pain and Suffering: Damages in Search of a Sounder Rationale*, 1 Mich. L. Pol'y Rev. 141 (1996):

> There are a variety of approaches one could take to pain and suffering damages. The reason for this diversity of viewpoints is that the manner in which one should quantify the pain and suffering

damages depends in large part on the rationale for these damages. One possibility is to establish damages that would provide appropriate incentives for the injurer to avoid injuring the plaintiff in such accident contexts. A possibly related objective is to make the plaintiff whole and restore the plaintiff to the same level of welfare as would be experienced if there had been no injury. Alternatively, is the objective of these damages to provide the victim with the same level of insurance that the victim would have chosen had pain and suffering insurance been available? Whereas these three approaches may lead to identical compensation levels for monetary losses, they usually will have quite different implications for pain and suffering for personal injuries. This article will be concerned with these and other possible rationales for pain and suffering damages and their differing implications for how damages awards should be set. [...]

One possible approach for justifying full insurance [for pain and suffering] is to appeal to a Rawlsian approach. Perhaps individuals would choose to set up a pain and suffering compensation regime that equalized utility irrespective of an accident, based on their assessment of what would happen behind a Rawlsian "veil of ignorance." This Rawlsian construct is frequently used to assess social decisions. If one applied this approach to thinking about how prospective accident victims might set up a compensation scheme, one might ask how people would structure insurance if they did not know their future medical condition following an accident. Would they choose to equalize utility across states of nature or, in a strict Rawlsian sense, maximize the utility in the state in which one's welfare was lowest?

What is missing from this approach is appropriate recognition of the probabilities that the different pain and suffering events would occur and the implications these probabilities and payoffs have for the costs of purchasing insurance. The thought experiment of asking people how they would structure pain and suffering compensation if they could purchase such insurance on an actuarially fair basis is identical to what one might hope to achieve through the Rawlsian veil of ignorance. The only difference is that there might be some person-specific characteristics influencing the insurance decision, such as the choice of consumption patterns. However, even if we purge the optimal insurance problem of these person-specific aspects, the fundamental economic result that expected utility maximizers will purchase actuarially fair insurance to equalize the marginal utility in different health states remains true. This is not mere intuition. It is a well established theorem of how individuals would behave if they are rational. To the extent that the accident impedes one's ability to derive welfare from additional expenditures, thus lowering the marginal utility for any given income level, it will be desirable to transfer less income to the post-accident state once the physical or mental impairment has occurred.

It is also possible to appeal to the actual structure of observed insurance policies, which appear to be consistent with these empirical findings regarding the shape of individual preferences. For example, people do not generally purchase pain and suffering insurance for their accidents. The fact that we do not observe such insurance purchases in the market is consistent with the stronger empirical evidence with respect to the structure of utility functions. However, it is not fully conclusive because of the possible insurance market imperfections. Insurers may, for example, not be able to readily monitor the severity of the pain and suffering loss. It should be noted, however, that even market imperfections do not prevent the provision of some minimal pain and suffering amounts even though full compensation of all losses may involve problems in monitoring the extent of the loss. [...]

Unfortunately, it is not possible to structure the optimal pain and suffering amounts to simultaneously promote the objectives of optimal insurance and optimal deterrence. If we provide pain and suffering compensation equivalent to the optimal deterrence amounts, then this coverage will provide excessive insurance. Similarly, if courts only provide plaintiffs with pain and suffering amounts that are optimal from an insurance context, then the court awards will not generate adequate incentives for deterrence. The task for any award is to strike a balance between these competing objectives. To the extent that deterrence objectives are more salient, the higher deterrence values are more pertinent, whereas if insurance is the dominant goal then the rationale for pain and suffering awards becomes substantially weakened.

It should be noted with respect to the insurance objective, however, that tort liability is not the only source of insurance. Some victims can and often do have first party insurance to cover the losses they have experienced. To the extent that these insurance needs have been met through their own purchases, the main concern should not be with insurance but rather with the deterrence role of tort liability.

One possibility is to impose a tort fine that would penalize injurers for the pain and suffering damages but would not transfer resources to the injured party. Thus, this segment of the award would go to the state and would not provide excessive insurance. The difficulty with any such proposal is that at the settlement stage the plaintiff could capture some of the expected cost to the injurer associated with the tort fine since it would be in the injurer's financial self interest to bargain for only the economic loss component as well as any residual amount that was necessary to provide an economic inducement for the plaintiff to avoid seeking a court verdict that would trigger payment to the state. [...]

It may be the case that many current pain and suffering awards are currently in the appropriate range in the sense that they are above the optimal insurance amount and below the optimal deterrence amount. However, the current rationale for pain and suffering awards typically stems from the size of the injury in terms of the magnitude of the financial loss and the character of the injury experience rather than the character of the behavior of the injurer. To the extent that the intent of the pain and suffering award is to simply restore welfare of the victim to the pre-accident level, one might well question whether these awards are on sound footing. Restoring the individual's utility is not an appropriate objective of pain and suffering compensation if one were to ask how this compensation would be structured by the plaintiff if faced with the prospect of purchasing an insurance policy to cover these losses in the event of an injury. [...] The main consequence of injuries that lead to substantial pain and suffering is that there is also an associated limitation on the ability of the injured to derive additional well-being from consumption expenditures. Juries should consider not only how much pain and suffering reduces welfare but also how effective compensation will be in enhancing welfare. This phenomenon will tend to reduce the optimal amount of compensation that is pertinent.

The problems in the casebook involving closing arguments are intended to provoke discussion of whether and how damages for pain and suffering ought to be measured and awarded.

1. *Per diem arguments.* There is a division of authority on the admissibility of "per diem" arguments; for the rundown, see 3 A.L.R.4th 940. Many courts allow them in one form or another. The "dentist hypothetical" argument was disallowed in a case holding that it violated *Botta v. Brunner*, a leading case from New Jersey forbidding both *per diem* and "golden rule" arguments. The rule in *Botta* was modified in N.J. Court Rule, R. 1:7-1[b], as shown in the casebook:

> Closing statement.... In civil cases any party may suggest to the trier of fact, with respect to any element of damages, that unliquidated damages be calculated on a time-unit basis without reference to a specific sum. In the event such comments are made to a jury, the judge shall instruct the jury that they are argumentative only and do not constitute evidence.

The comment to the Rule explains that

> the compromise effected by the rule is to continue the ban on the suggestion of specific monetary amounts either on a lump sum or time-unit basis but to permit counsel to argue to the trier of fact the appropriateness of employing a time-unit calculation technique for fixing any element of unliquidated damages.... The so-called "golden-rule" argument, that is, asking the jury to award an amount it would want for itself in similar circumstances, remains interdicted.

Here are some excerpts from *Botta* laying out the court's rationale in that case:

> For hundreds of years, the measure of damages for pain and suffering following in the wake of a personal injury has been "fair and reasonable compensation." This general standard was adopted because of universal acknowledgment that a more specific or definitive one is impossible. [S]ince the nature of the subject matter admits only of the broad concept of reasonable compensation, may counsel for the plaintiff or the defendant state to the jury, in opening or closing, his belief as to the pecuniary value or price of pain and suffering per hour or day or week, and ask that such figure be used as part of a mathematical formula for calculating the damages to be awarded? Without expressing a personal opinion, may he suggest that the valuation be based on so much per hour or day or week, or ask the jurors if they do not think the pain and suffering are fairly worth so much per hour or day or week—and then demonstrate, by employing such rate as a factor in his computation, that a verdict of a fixed amount of money would be warranted or could be justified? [...]

> In our neighboring state of Pennsylvania the rule assigning the admeasurement of damages for injuries to the jury has been adhered to over the years with the utmost fidelity. No suggestion of the character made in the present case either by court or counsel is tolerated; nor is reference to the *ad damnum* clause of the complaint permitted. Speaking on the subject in a fairly early opinion, the Supreme Court said:

>> 'Pain and suffering are not capable of being exactly measured by an equivalent in money, and we have repeatedly said that they have no market price. The question in any given case is not what it would cost to hire someone to undergo the measure of pain alleged to have been suffered by the plaintiff, but what, under all the circumstances, should be allowed the plaintiff in addition to the other items of damage to which he is entitled, in consideration of suffering necessarily endured. * * * This should not be estimated by a sentimental or fanciful standard * * *.

>> 'But let us further assume that these days of enforced idleness have been days of severe bodily suffering. The question then presented for the consideration of the jury would be: What is it reasonable to add to the value of the lost time in view of the fact that the days were filled with pain, instead of being devoted to labor? Some allowance has been held to be proper; but, in answer to the question, 'How much?' the only reply yet made is that it should be reasonable in amount. Pain cannot be measured in money. * * * The word 'compensation,' in the phrase 'compensation for pain and suffering,' is not to be understood as meaning price or value, but as describing an allowance looking towards recompense for or made because of the suffering consequent upon the injury.' *Goodhart v. Pennsylvania* R. Co., supra (177 Pa. 1, 35 A. 192).

> [...] There can be no doubt that the prime purpose of suggestions, direct or indirect, in the opening or closing statements of counsel of per hour or per diem sums as the value of or as compensation for pain, suffering and kindred elements associated with injury and disability is to

instill in the minds of the jurors impressions, figures and amounts not founded or appearing in the evidence. An outspoken exponent of the approach described its aim in this fashion:

> 'When you break down pain and suffering into seconds and minutes and do it as objectively as this (on a blackboard), then you begin to make a jury realize what permanent pain and suffering is and that $60,000 at five dollars a day isn't an adequate award. (Insertion ours.)

> 'So let's put on the board $60,000 for pain and suffering. Of course in your opening statement you are only privileged to say that you are going to explain to the jury and ask for $60,000 as pain and suffering in order to make up your total figure. It would be improper to argue, this must be reserved for the final summation.

> 'The jurors must start thinking in days, minutes and seconds and in five dollars, three dollars and two dollars, so that they can multiply to the absolute figure. Maybe your juror will feel that $5 a day is not enough, that it should be $10 per day. They may feel that it should be $4 or $3 a day. At least you have started them thinking; and when they follow the mechanics of multiplication they must by this procedure come to some substantial figure if they are fair. A jury always tries to be fair. Never forget this.' Belli, 'The Use of Demonstrative Evidence in Achieving the More Adequate Award,' Address before the Mississippi State Bar Association (1954); Belli, Modern Trials, p. 1632 (1954).

Aside from the aspect of speculation involved and the circumstance that the suggestion of a precise valuation of pain and suffering by the hour or day introduces into the case in terms of fact that which is not susceptible of proof, another difficulty is presented, consideration of which cannot be avoided by an appellate tribunal concerned with the fair and orderly administration of justice. If plaintiff's counsel is permitted to make such valuation suggestions to the jury, justice cannot be administered fairly in the trial of this type of case. Can defense counsel argue that pain and suffering are worth only $2.50 per day or $1 or any lesser sum?   If he attempts to do so, he must necessarily inject as further factual suggestions valuations which again are incapable of proof. By doing so, he fortifies his adversary's implication that the law recognizes pain and suffering as having been evaluated and as capable of being evaluated on such basis. [...]

And now here are some excerpts from *Cox v. Valley Fair Corp.*, disallowing the "dentist hypothetical" in particular:

We conclude that counsel's summation violated *Botta v. Brunner* in two regards. First, there are suggestions that the members of the jury consider the few extra dollars they would be willing to spend to avoid the pain of a tooth extraction and to think what it means to suffer on a daily basis. This is a subtle appeal to the "golden rule," i.e., that the members of the jury consider what one day of pain and suffering or, conversely, its avoidance, would be worth to them. Second, the summation plainly suggests a per diem formula for calculating plaintiff's damages for pain and suffering. The reference to plaintiff's daily pain for the rest of her life, to the few dollars persons would pay to avoid the pain of one visit to the dentist's office, together with the later reference to plaintiff's life expectancy of about 11,000 days and the comment that she was entitled to fair compensation for each and every one of those days, could only serve to suggest a per diem formula for the jury to apply. This is a patent violation of *Botta v. Brunner*.

Counsel's comments during summation, if considered separately, arguably do not violate the *Botta v. Brunner* rule. However, when the summation is taken as a whole, as it must be, the suggestion of a per diem formula is clear. […] In this connection, the amount of the award in light of the proof of damages is of some relevance. Here plaintiff's medicals were $672.25 and her loss of wages approximately $500. Additional claims of damages involved subjective complaints as to pain, suffering and so-called permanent disability. The jury awarded Mrs. Cox $51,200, apparently representing the estimated $1,200 in specials and $50,000 for her subjective complaints. The trial judge said he disagreed with the award but could not say it was manifestly unjust. This would be correct if the sole issue were excessiveness of verdict. The size of the verdict, however, supports defendant's contention that counsel's per diem formula argument impermissibly influenced the jury and refutes any contention that the error was harmless.

2. *The Golden Rule.* "Golden Rule" arguments are generally not allowed, as noted in the comments on the previous problem. Here is the reasoning from the *Red Top Cab* case:

This argument, in effect, affirms as a correct principle that a man may properly sit in judgment on his own case-an idea abhorrent to all who love justice. Nor is such argument given a cloak of respectability by association it with the Golden Rule. Such Rule is perfect but it applies in favor of the defendant as well as the plaintiff. To hold that the type of argument made here is not, as a matter of law, reversible error in any case and regardless of how vicious it may be, unless the trial judge fails, upon request, to do his obvious duty and instruct the jury not to consider it is but to invite counsel to indulge in this kind of improper argument.

3. *The job offer.* This argument was rejected in *Faught v. Washam:*

The objection of defendant's counsel 'to this highly improper, prejudicial and inflammatory argument' was, in effect, overruled by the court's comment that 'the jury will regard these arguments purely as arguments, and not as evidence in this case' [Hancock v. Crouch, Mo.App., 267 S.W.2d 36, 44(12)]; and, with this argument thus approved, plaintiff's counsel in substance repeated it. The quoted 'job offer' was a tandem plea (a) that the jurors put themselves in plaintiff's place and (b) that they employ a so-called mathematical formula in assessing his damages for pain and suffering. Standing alone, an appeal to jurors to put themselves in plaintiff's place does not always constitute reversible error, particularly where the trial court has taken effective action with respect thereto or where there is no complaint on appeal that the verdict was excessive, but this character of plea is consistently condemned and uniformly branded as improper, the rationale of rejection being that a juror 'doing that would be no fairer judge of the case than would plaintiff' himself[.]

From time immemorial, the judicial measure of damages for pain and suffering has been fair and reasonable compensation, because there is and can be no established standard, fixed basis, or mathematical rule by which such damages may be calculated. Only within the past few years have resourceful and ingenious counsel developed the 'trial technique' of appealing to the jury to follow a mathematical formula in admeasuring damages for pain and suffering. Cases in this jurisdiction have gone no further than to hold that counsel's 'mere argumentative suggestion' of a lump sum does not constitute reversible error, and no Missouri case discussing the so-called mathematical formula technique has been cited or found. Among other appellate courts, by whom this technique has been considered, there is a sharp cleavage, some approving and some disapproving, with no strong preponderance either way.

Q. Should damages for future pain and suffering be reduced to present value?
A. Jurisdictions vary in their treatment of this question. It might seem odd to order such a reduction since it treats the damages as a more literal sort of compensation than may be intended or plausible: in ordering compensation at a rate of, say, $10 per day for the plaintiff's suffering, is the idea really that the

plaintiff should get $10 each day, or is it more just that the "daily rate" is a way to conceptualize the proper size of the award? Posner took the literal view in *Abernathy v. Superior Hardwoods, Inc.* 704 F.2d 963 (1983); the case can serve as a good basis for testing the students' intuitions about present value:

> We said earlier that the plaintiffs' counsel suggested to the jury that $10 a day would not be unreasonable compensation for Mr. Abernathy's pain and suffering. No figure was suggested for Mrs. Abernathy's loss of consortium but it could not be so great, and suppose it was $5 a day. Then the maximum verdict the jury could have awarded the Abernathys on their counsel's own theory would have been $219,000. But even this would be too much. In gauging the reasonableness of an award of damages for a future loss, the court must consider the present discounted value of that loss. If $15 a day would compensate the Abernathys for the damage (apart from medical expenses) that they can expect to suffer over the next 40 years, and they are awarded $15 today for each day of future suffering, then assuming as we must that they will invest the money, however conservatively, they will have more than $15 when each of those future days rolls round—dramatically more, for the last days. (The present value at a 2 percent discount rate of $15 to be received in 40 years is $6.79.). Assuming that the plaintiffs' counsel was speaking in "real" (that is, inflation-free) terms—a reasonable assumption since he named a constant figure rather than one rising over time—the proper discount rate would have been the real, that is, the inflation-free, discount rate for riskless investments. That rate is usually estimated at 1-3 percent. The present value of $219,000 to be received over 40 years, discounted at 2 percent, is $149,771.36. We cannot understand how an award of damages greater than the sum of this amount and the stipulated medical expenses of $3,333.25—$153,104.61 in total—could have been made consistently with the evidence, the instructions, and the closing argument of the plaintiffs' counsel (compare Barker v. Cole, 396 N.E.2d 964, 969 (Ind.App.1979), upholding a $50,000 verdict for much more serious orthopedic injuries)—especially when we consider how likely it is that Mr. Abernathy's pre-existing disc disease would eventually have caused him pain even if he had not had an accident but instead had continued doing heavy work.

Olin Corp. v. Smith ($5,000,000 award for loss of leg)
Williams v. United States ($500,000 award for loss of leg)

There is a mistake in the text: *Olin Corp.* involved a bench trial, not a jury trial.

Q. What is the distinction between *Olin Corp. v. Smith* and *Williams v. United States*?
A. The most obvious is that the plaintiff in *Olin Corp.* was much younger—16 years old, rather than 48. So he had more expected years of discomfort ahead of him (55, as opposed to 24), and the years involved might be considered the prime of his life. But what are we to make of the discussion in *Williams* of the plaintiff's past—his prison record, his drug and alcohol abuse? Is this relevant to the question of his suffering? This might be a case like *Pescatore* appears to be where the factfinder, in measuring values that are hard to quantify (loss of society in *Pescatore*, suffering in *Williams*), is influenced by those features of the case—earning power and the like—that *can* be measured by reference to a market. Just as in *Landers* (the case of the carpenter's wife who received a modest award of damages for loss of society), it might have similarly seemed perverse to the court in *Williams* to award the plaintiff millions of dollars when it seems clear that this would suddenly make him wealthier in pecuniary terms than he ever could have been otherwise. The cases differ in other ways, though; in *Williams* the plaintiff put in no proof of damages for lost earning power, but sought recovery only for pain and suffering. So the idea of anchoring suggested by the *Pescatore* case does not precisely apply here, though the general point might still be valid.

An additional point to notice, though not mentioned by the court, is that in *Williams* it might be possible to argue that some portion of the plaintiff's suffering would have occurred regardless of the defendant's negligence. It's not entirely clear from the facts, which do suggest that with due care he might have had his problems diagnosed early and cured without much trouble; but to the extent that some agony was unavoidable even with reasonable treatment, the defendant should not have to pay for that.

Beynon v. Montgomery Cablevision (damages for pre-impact fright)

Q. Does it follow from *Beynon* that if the plaintiff had been able to stop his car, he still would have been entitled to $350,000?
A. Probably not as a practical matter; his death no doubt drives up the amount the court will tolerate as an award by providing a kind of guarantee of genuineness concerning the fright he must have experienced. Whether recovery is allowed at all would depend on the jurisdiction's rules concerning recovery for the negligent infliction of emotional distress, an issue treated in the casebook's chapter on duties. The common law restricted the availability of such suits, generally requiring that psychic distress be accompanied by physical harm before it could be made the basis for a damage award. From this standpoint the novelty of the pre-impact fright cases like *Beynon* is just that they allow the distress to precede the physical injury rather than (as is more common and traditional) the injury coming first and the distress second. In cases where an act causes distress but no physical injury, states vary in their reactions but tend to limit recovery in various ways to reduce the risk of spurious claims. Those states that do not require physical harm will tend to require other indicia that the claim is legitimate—e.g., egregious behavior by the defendant, or evidence that the emotional distress manifested in objectively identifiable symptoms.

Q. If damages for pre-impact fright are to be awarded, how should they be quantified?
A. This invites discussion of the per-minute or per-second sums that juries may (in effect) award in these cases. Should juries be told to calculate a value for each second or minute, and then add up the resulting figures? Or should they be told to name a lump sum amount that seems right? In pain and suffering cases the per diem approach typically is helpful to the plaintiff, often generating a larger sum than would a general invitation to the jury to determine a reasonable amount of damages. Here the opposite tendency seems likely: a jury would probably not conclude that $400,000 per second is a sensible figure, though this is the implication of its verdict in *Beynon*.

Q. What are the economic implications of liability for pre-impact fright?
A. It might be easier to discuss this point by using a hypothetical on top of *Beynon*. A good one is *Haley v. Pan Am World Airways*, 746 F.2d 311 (5th Cir. 1984). In that case the plaintiffs' decedent, Michael Haley, was a passenger aboard a Pan Am airplane that crashed in Kenner, Louisiana, disintegrating upon impact and killing the 138 passengers and seven crew members on board. Pan Am conceded liability; the case proceeded to trial on damages. A jury awarded the Haleys $350,000 for the loss of their son's society, and $15,000 for the mental anguish he suffered during the airplane's descent. Pan Am appealed, arguing that there was no basis for concluding that Michael Haley had suffered anguish before his death, and that in any event $15,000 was excessive compensation for any anguish he did suffer. The court of appeals affirmed:

> Plaintiffs' expert, a psychiatrist who had treated survivors of aircraft accidents and was familiar with the physiological effects of stress, explained the five levels of anxiety that culminate in panic. He then rendered his opinion that "most of the people [aboard Flight 759], if not all, would be in an absolute state of pandemonium, panic and extreme state of stress," at least from the time the plane hit the tree, if not from the beginning of its descent and roll, until impact seconds later. Defendant's expert expressed uncertainty as to whether "any of the passengers, in

fact realized that they were about to die." He conceded, however, that when the passengers experienced a "violent change in the plane, the last couple of seconds," they "certainly would have been thrown about and *fighting for their lives* and experienced a whole different situation." (emphasis added). [...] The jury could have reasonably inferred [...] that Michael Haley experienced the mental anguish commonly associated with anticipation of one's own death. [...]

One consequence of a decision like *Haley* is that the possibility of having to pay such damages becomes a cost of doing business for the airline, and so gets impounded in the cost of flying. In effect the passenger buys compulsory insurance so that if the plane goes down his survivors will be able to collect something for his frightful last seconds. Would the students want to buy this insurance if given the choice, or would they just as soon save whatever small amount of money is involved and waive any right of their estate to be paid for this?

This hypothetical is a helpful addition to *Beynon* because it involves institutional actors—the airlines—that have to confront the possibility of paying these sorts of damages on a repeating basis (anytime there is a crash), and that are in a position to pass the cost of such damages on to consumers of their services. But query whether it is important to award damages in these cases so that the airline, in planning how much precaution to take against crashes, is fully internalizing the entire costs of a crash that its victims and their kin would pay to avoid. Another point here, which gets repeated almost anytime damages for the suffering of someone now dead are awarded in a survivorship action, is that it might seem perverse for the defendant to escape liability if the victim dies if it would be on the hook for pain and suffering damages if the victim miraculously had survived. Tortfeasors should not be made better off by the deaths of their victims; this is the part of the logic of wrongful death statutes, as well as of other doctrines under consideration here. Cases like *Quill* in the duty chapter (in the section on the negligent infliction of emotional distress) suggest that damages for distress might have been recoverable if the plane had avoided crashing at the last minute. Should that aspect of the airline's liability be erased when the plane crashes?

Douglass v. Hustler Magazine ($300,000 award for emotional distress reversed as "absurd")
Weller v. American Broadcasting Companies ($1,000,000 award for emotional distress affirmed)

Q. What is the distinction between *Douglass v. Hustler Magazine* and *Weller v. American Broadcasting Companies*?
A. The recitals of the facts suggest that Weller may in fact have suffered more misery than Douglass did, but then that may just be because the court in *Douglass* (per Posner, J.) is not so inclined to give weight to the types of unhappiness discussed in *Weller*. One can also point out that all of Weller's miseries were due to the defendant's acts in that case, whereas in *Douglass* it's hard to shake the sense that if the plaintiff was ready to appear nude in one magazine she can't have suffered so very much marginal emotional distress at seeing the photographs turn up elsewhere. But one must resist this train of thought and accept the factual predicate of the case, i.e., that in fact there is a big difference between appearing in *Playboy* and in *Hustler*. If so, then the difference between the cases seems to involve not so much the facts as the legal approaches the courts use to reviewing damage awards.

One way to review them, illustrated by *Douglass*, is to study awards in other cases and use them as rough benchmarks; even if we don't know how to put dollar figures on emotional distress, we may have some confidence in our ability to make *relative* judgments: if the first case produces an award of X, we can talk about whether the second case justifies a similar award. Of course there are problems with this approach. If the decision in the early case is too low, it can put downward pressure on later cases; if the decision in the earlier case is too high, it creates an unreasonably high ceiling for review. The latter is more likely, as the actual tendency in these types of cases is for the size of an allowable award to rise in the fashion of a one-way ratchet: the new award is affirmed if it's only a little higher than the previous maximum, but then it creates a new benchmark; eventually it is exceeded by a little bit, and this too is allowed; gradually the size of an allowable award rises considerably.

Another way to review damage awards, illustrated by *Weller*, is to put comparisons to one side and just ask if the award seems to suggest that the jury was carried away by passion and prejudice. This is a more impressionistic judgment, and thus its outcome depends heavily on who is performing it. It seems unlikely that the Seventh Circuit would have affirmed the million dollar award for emotional distress in *Weller*. Combining this method with the ratcheting method described in the previous paragraph creates a potent engine for increasing the average size of permissible damage awards.

Daugherty v. Erie Ry. Co. (P loses sense of taste; L)
Hogan v. Santa Fe Trail Transportation Co. (P loses ability to play violin; NL (later reversed))

Q. Are there any respects in which calculating hedonic damages (for loss of pleasure) is harder or more problematic than calculating damages for the presence of pain?
A. One additional difficulty is that plaintiffs' capacities for pleasure may vary more than their capacities for pain. Anyone with a back injury will suffer, and there may not be much difference between the suffering of two people with the same such injury. But the hedonic damages caused by a broken pinky finger will vary enormously depending on whether the plaintiff was a violinist. Likewise, should the damages in a case like *Daugherty* vary depending on whether the plaintiff had a taste for fine dining and good wine, or was content with tofu anyway? So it would seem; but of course this adds another layer of speculativeness to the process of valuation. On the other hand, in some cases the loss of the ability to seek pleasure may be the major component of the damage the defendant has caused, and in those cases the argument may be strong that some award should be made so that future defendants will figure in this type of risk (in some very broad sense) when thinking about the precautions to take.

At the end of the casebook's discussion of "willingness to pay" studies, it mentions that some further objections to their use are raised in McClurg, *It's a Wonderful Life: The Case for Hedonic Damages in Wrongful Death Cases*, 66 Notre Dame L.Rev. 57 (1990). Here are some excerpts from the article in case you are interested in pursuing the issues in class discussion:

> [T]he validity of the willingness-to-pay theory depends upon assumptions that people have freedom of choice in deciding whether to confront risks, and that they perceive those risks accurately. Unfortunately, both of these assumptions are probably false.

> Most willingness-to-pay studies attempt to value human life by looking at the relationship between risky jobs and the wages paid to workers in those jobs. These studies necessarily assume that workers in high-risk industries choose to be exposed to those risks in order to receive a wage premium. This, in turn, requires the broader assumption that people accept particular jobs out of freely choice, rather than because of external factors. This is a dubious proposition. Diverse barriers—geographic, educational, language and racial, to name but a few—preclude free choice in employment decisions for many groups of people. For example, we cannot say that residents of Appalachian coal mining regions freely choose to be exposed to the risks of coal mining in return for a wage risk-premium. For many, coal mining is the only choice because of their lack of mobility.

> Even if one were to assume that workers have the mobility necessary to make truly voluntary job choices, the willingness-to-pay theory still fails unless it can also be shown that the workers fully understand the hazards involved. This is also true of willingness-to-pay studies that focus upon consumptive behavior. One cannot express a preference to be exposed to a particular risk unless one knows and appreciates the risk. This requires that one accurately perceive both the

probability that the risk will materialize and the losses that will occur if it does. This is rarely the case.

Professors Gillette and Hopkins note that appreciation of the risk is particularly unlikely for "single-or infrequent-play players," that is, individuals who will not confront the risk on a regular basis. Consumers are unlikely to exert the effort necessary to acquire information about the risks involved with many kinds of products because the search for that information is too costly given the infrequent use of the product. Repeat players—usually workers—are more likely to acquire information regarding risks that they will regularly encounter, but they may not acquire this information until after spending some time on the job. By then, other practicalities may influence the worker's decision to stay in that occupation. This calls into question whether the worker is exposing herself to the risk as a matter of preference. The worker may have moved her family to the location to take the job; her financial obligations may have grown commensurate to her higher earnings, locking the worker into the job; or the worker may not want to admit to herself that she made a bad decision.

The most basic flaw in the willingness-to-pay theory, however, is that it simply does not comport with the reality of how people behave. The truth is that we often fail to avoid risks even when they involve little cost. This is probably because we believe in our own immortality, sharing a kind of "that only happens to other people" mentality. Presumably, most drivers know that the failure to wear a seatbelt substantially increases their chances of dying in a serious auto accident, yet most drivers still do not wear seatbelts. Does their failure to accept a small inconvenience to avoid a significant risk of death mean that people do not value their lives highly, or does it mean only that, regardless of the existence of the risk, they do not think it will happen to them?

People accept risks not because they are willing to gamble on losing their lives in order to save or make a little money, but because they do not think the risk will ever materialize. To permit a realistic appraisal of a person's willingness to trade risk for wealth, we would have to confront the person with a known, substantial and imminent risk of death. For example, how much would a person demand to play Russian Roulette with a six-chamber revolver loaded with one bullet? The risk is easily computed as a one-in-six chance of death. To know the amount people would demand to confront this risk would allow us to calculate with accuracy the value people attach to their lives. We can predict with confidence that the amounts would be tremendous, and that they probably would not vary widely between those who wear seat belts and those who do not.

The 9/11 Fund
Workers' Compensation Damage Schedules

Q. What trade-offs are involved in the use of fixed schedules to set damages?
A. From Bovbjerg et al., *Valuing Life and Limb in Tort: Scheduling 'Pain and Suffering,'* 83 Nw. U. L. Rev. 908 (1989):

Which type of scheduling model should a jurisdiction prefer? Policy decisions will be influenced by policymakers' judgments along many dimensions, but their answers to two questions are central. First, to what extent do legitimate factors not captured by objective analysis cause the observed variation in awards in the existing tort regime? Those who believe that most of the current variability in awards is legitimate will seek to maintain maximum jury discretion—if they support reform at all—by supporting such proposals as floors and caps to deal with extreme outliners, perhaps advisory scenarios as aids to juries, and possibly matrices containing ranges of values. Those who see award variability as caused mostly by illegitimate factors or random jury error are more likely to support the more standardizing approaches, like point-value matrices and more rigorous scenarios.

A second significant policy decision is the relative importance of doing justice in individual cases versus arriving at fair results across cases. The strongest attribute of a matrix-based regime is the ability to achieve equal dollar results in equal cases of all types and severities, especially when the point-value format is used. A point-value matrix may, however, insufficiently respond to unusually worthy (and unworthy) cases, a weakness that may necessitate the adoption of a process to handle outliers. In sharp contrast, a flexible range of floors and caps addresses only the outliers, maintaining jury discretion in the vast majority of cases, but also likely maintaining the current wide, inconsistent, and unexplained disparity among cases. Any individual method, while arguably meant to achieve fairness in each case, will most likely fail to achieve fairness across cases-continuing past failures in this regard. The ability to discriminate can readily yield inconsistent and inappropriate results, whether or not intended by a particular jury.

Q. Why don't the uniform awards of damages that people accept in the 9/11 situation cause the legal system to move towad uniform awards generally?
A. An interesting speculation is offered in Sanders, *Why Do Proposals to Control Variability in General Damages (Generally) Fall on Deaf Ears? (And Why This is Too Bad)*, 55 DePaul L. Rev. 489 (2006):

Part of the answer, strangely, may be that similar procedures have been widely used in one very important corner of tort law. In the area of mass torts, procedures designed to produce greater horizontal equity are commonplace. If we set aside those mass torts that arise from a single catastrophic event such as an airplane crash and the few medical device, drug, or toxic mass torts that have resulted in substantial defense victories on the merits, a substantial percentage of other mass torts result in defendant bankruptcy or mass settlement, often through the use of a claims facility. This small but highly visible portion of the tort docket is resolved by using such procedures, which systematically impose substantial horizontal equity when paying claims. Horizontal equity was also an important consideration in the resolution of claims under the statute established to compensate victims of the September 11, 2001 terrorist attacks on New York and Washington, D.C.

Several factors militate toward placing greater emphasis on horizontal equity in these cases. In ordinary litigation, the arguable injustice of horizontal inequity is largely invisible. When two similarly situated parties receive different general damage awards in separate lawsuits, the plaintiff receiving the lesser amount is unlikely to even know of this inequity. His or her lawyer has little incentive in making a point about this unfortunate outcome that after all could be blamed, at least in part, on the advocacy skills of counsel. Even if the lawyer were to seek redress, achieving any relief by way of an additur or a new trial on damages is remarkably unlikely. And from the court's point of view, the outcome may be rationalized as the result of some unique facts and the inevitable give and take that occurs within the black box of jury deliberations.

Many of the factors that render inequity invisible in ordinary litigation disappear in the mass tort, class action settlement context. In these cases it is often far more difficult to argue that substantial substantive differences exist between the parties. Attorneys are much more likely to object if their clients are treated differently from other, similarly injured individuals. Moreover, judges, masters, or others in charge of settlement processes or claims facilities are, inevitably, pushed toward a bureaucratic justice model in which standards are set by external bodies (not the jury), each case is evaluated in terms of only a limited number of weighted factors, and the standards are based, at least in part, on aggregative and averaging processes. As McGovern noted, in many settlement processes a number of variables, generally between five and twenty, may be considered and applied to individual cases by the use of an algorithm or formula. Within such systems, horizontal equity, especially with respect to general damages, becomes an important criterion of fairness.

The existence of now routine aggregation procedures in the mass-tort context underscores the point that the tort system's general failure to adopt proposals such as those discussed above is not due to any fundamental inability to implement such schemes. The explanation for the failure to adopt such schemes lies elsewhere. In my judgment, two factors seem most important: the relative superiority of damage caps in achieving defendant objectives, and the organizational and normative structure of the plaintiff's bar that causes the bar to treat such proposals with little more than benign neglect.

Q.   Can you think of any approaches to damages that might have some of the advantages of fixed schedules without the precise numbers?
A. Some interesting suggestions are offered in the Bovjberg et al. article cited a moment ago. Here is a relevant excerpt:

Instead of a numerical matrix, a second form of damages scheduling might be to give juries a limited number of standardized injury "scenarios," with associated dollar values of non-economic loss for each. These descriptions of prototypical circumstances of injury would help jurors assess the non-economic damages in a given case, relative to the approved values in the scenarios. For each lawsuit, a relevant spectrum of scenarios would be provided, ranging from less severe to more severe injury. In effect, a set of scenarios would constitute a relative-value scale in readily grasped, qualitative terms. These scenarios would be best promulgated by legislatures or judiciaries, based upon the types of data reviewed for Table 5, with appropriate normative adjustments.

The scenarios would resemble the legal "hypotheticals" so beloved by law professors, but would focus on the circumstances of injury, rather than on the law. A small number of them, perhaps up to ten, would be included as jury instructions, preferably given in writing and allowed into the jury room. The jury would be instructed that no single scenario is expected to fit their own case perfectly, but that the scenario values are approved benchmarks by which to assess their case. They should decide which scenarios most nearly resemble the injury in the case they are deciding, then make the appropriate level of award somewhere near those values. The scenario values would thus be advisory rather than mandatory. Even so, while juries would retain discretion to choose intermediate amounts between the scenario levels, their choices would be subject to more active judicial review to maintain consistency of valuation across cases.

The scenario approach reflect the normal mental response of people to difficult valuation problems outside the jury room-that is, making comparisons to other cases. A person looking to buy or sell a house wants to know the selling price of other three-bedroom, two-bath houses in the neighborhood. Certainly, every house is unique, and small variations in location or features make a difference. Nonetheless, having a quantitative benchmark is essential to reasonable valuation-and it also helps buyer and seller agree more rapidly than they otherwise might. Similarly, when psychological researchers have asked people to consider how they value certain states of injury, it has proven helpful to present scenarios about the extent of disability and pain. Moreover, trial and appellate judges use a very similar approach when reviewing a jury award for excessiveness or inadequacy-that is, they consider prior awards, drawing upon their personal experience, relying on the parties' briefs, or consulting published listings of awards. In contrast, adoption of the scenario approach would require a legislature to review and incorporate a complete body of information into the standardized scenarios and their valuations. . . .

Valuation scenarios must offer descriptions that are vivid enough to be comprehensible and offer a practical guide. They must not, however, consist of cases that are memorable for being unusual, but rather ones truly typical of each level of injury represented. As with any scheduling approach, it is vital to keep matters simple. The most important factors to reflect in a scenario are the physical severity of the injury, the victim's age or life expectancy, the extent of pain endured, the extent of incapacity to engage in normal activities, and the duration of each factor. Physical injury and age are relatively unambiguous and so help "anchor" the scenario objectively. The importance of duration (even if only given as temporary versus permanent) is obvious. These objective factors alone considerably help distinguish among injuries, as shown by the sample matrix and supporting data discussed previously.

Pain and inability to function, though highly subjective, are also intuitively important. Moreover, they correspond to the two main types of intangible harm previously noted-newly imposed suffering and loss of former enjoyment of life. For them, one might use fairly simple descriptors, such as the strength of drug needed to control pain and the type of activities curtailed. These are subjective measures, so plaintiffs will tend to exaggerate their suffering while defendants try to minimize it; but the situation will be no worse than at present.

In general, the scenarios should describe only circumstances of injury relative to damages, not to responsibility or causation. The degree of "color" to provide in a scenario must still be determined. One could give only neutral descriptors, as in the nine-point severity scale; alternatively, the scenarios could offer more engrossing depictions of the injury. Particularized details make a scenario seem more real, but may also make it overly case-specific and difficult to generalize to other cases. A typical neutral scenario might read:

> Permanent minor injury (level 5). Life expectancy 25 years. Mild persistent*955 pain, usually controllable with aspirin. Unable to engage in more than light housework.

A more colorful version might explain:

> Plaintiff Peters has completely and permanently lost the use of her left arm. Her life expectancy is 25 years, according to standard life insurance tables. Her arm throbs painfully most of the time, but the pain can usually be controlled with aspirin. She cannot do more than light housework.

Another issue is the handling of death cases. One could maintain the traditional restrictive approach to nonpecuniary losses, limiting the description to conscious pain and suffering endured by the decedent. Alternatively, in the interest of greater deterrence, one could describe the emotional losses of survivors and perhaps also the enjoyment of life lost by the decedent. This choice is a matter of substantive law, however, and not strictly a problem of constructing scenarios.

SECTION B. PUNITIVE DAMAGES

The first two cases in this section present general arguments for and against allowing punitive damages in civil cases. The note cases then appear in pairs that explore particular issues: how courts decide whether a defendant is eligible for punitive damages at all (*Kopczick v. Hobart Corp., Grimshaw v. Ford Motor Co.*); how courts assess the correct size of an award of punitive damages (*Moskowitz v. Mt. Sinai Medical Center; Rufo v. Simpson*); and the liability of an employer for punitive damages when an employee commits a tort (*Kennan v. Checker Cab Co., In re Exxon Valdez*). There are brief notes at the end of the section on statutory activity in this area and on the due process clause.

If you want shortened treatment, any one of those pairs just described can be cut; it's a question of which issues you find most interesting. The *Grimshaw* case, involving the Ford Pinto, always produces a good discussion, but you if you have touched on it already you might want to leave it out here.

Q. Why are punitive damages awarded to the plaintiff rather than being payable to the state?
A. The classic justification is mentioned in *Kemezy*: they serve as a kind of bounty that gives a plaintiff an incentive to act as a private attorney general, seeking punitive damages for the sake of deterrence that will redound to the benefit of the public at large. At the end of the chapter there is a note mentioning an example of a state (Georgia) that causes part of a punitive damage award to be paid to the state. In a recent Ohio Supreme Court case—*Dardinger v. Anthem Blue Cross Blue Shield*, 98 Ohio St. 3d 77 (2002)—the court took a more exotic route, finding that it had a common law power to order an "alternative distribution" of a punitive damage award where appropriate. In that case a $49 million punitive damage award was made against a health insurer for bad-faith denial of claims for therapy to treat an insured's brain tumor. The court reduced the award to $30 million by remittitur, ordering $10 million to go to the plaintiff (the insured's executor) with the remainder to go to the creation of a cancer research fund at Ohio State University.

Query: in a regime where punitive damage awards were destined to go to the state, what would settlement negotiations between the plaintiff and defendant sound like?

Kopczick v. Hobart Corp. (NL for punitive damages for meat slicer that repeatedly injures users)
Grimshaw v. Ford Motor Co. (L for punitive damages for car that repeatedly injures users)

Q. What is the distinction between *Kopczick* and *Grimshaw*?
A. First, it is important to make sure the students grasp the precise issue these cases involve: a defendant's *eligibility* for liability for punitive damages, which has to be formally settled by the trial court before such damages can be awarded by a jury. An initial difference between the cases involves the point in time when the defendant was alleged to have had the critical knowledge. In *Grimshaw* the plaintiff had evidence that the defendant knew that deaths were virtually certain to result from its design, and chose not to use a relatively inexpensive method of fixing the problem—a violation of the Hand formula. In *Kopczick* the plaintiff also had evidence that the defendant knew its machines caused problems—not at the design stage, however, but subsequently on account of the prior accidents. The court nevertheless dismisses the plaintiff's evidence as establishing only a small probability of accidents. But of course only a small percentage of Pintos were involved in fiery collisions; maybe the saw in *Kopczick* was the "Pinto" of meat slicers. Perhaps the idea is that the defendant in *Kopczick* did not so clearly violate the Hand formula (though notice that design defects were found, and compensatory damages awarded, in both cases); or perhaps it is that the plaintiff in *Kopczick* did not establish clearly enough that the number of accidents caused by the defendant's machine was greater than the baseline number of accidents to be expected from a properly designed machine.

Moskovitz v. Mt. Sinai Medical Center (court reduces punitive damage award as excessive because it threatents to take too large a share of D's net worth)
Rufo v. Simpson (court approves massive punitive damage award)

These cases present opportunities to discuss the relationship between punitive damage awards and the defendant's wealth, a theme that can be continued with discussion of the *Exxon* case later in the section.

Q. What is the distinction between *Moskovitz v. Mt. Sinai Medical Center* and *Rufo v. Simpson*?

A. A distinction is needed because in *Moskovitz* the court restrains an award of punitive damages that would threaten to consume the defendant's net worth; in *Simpson* the court allows an award that exceeds the defendant's net worth. It's easy enough to explain on multiple grounds. There is the heinousness of Simpson's conduct, and then Simpson has a pension that the damages can't reach (you can ask why this should be so) and that will provide him with an income stream regardless of the size of the award; and he also had a sufficiently large expected earnings stream regardless of the pension.

Another question, related to the one mentioned above: why *shouldn't* the award of punitive damages in a case like Simpson's be ruinous to him? Maybe the reason has to do with spillover from our lower confidence in the correctness of civil verdicts as compared with verdicts delivered under the standard of proof on the criminal side. A defendant shouldn't be entirely ruined on the basis of a jury's decision that he is 55% likely to have committed a killing.

Q. Is it just to award more punitive damages against a rich defendant than against a poor one?
A. There is an interesting discussion of the theory on this issue in the *Kemezy* case. One way to pursue this question is by pointing out that we don't generally scale *criminal* punishments according to the defendant's wealth. A rich man might be as deterred by the thought of one night at Riker's Island as a poor one would be by the thought of a month there, but we don't sentence them differently. Why should tort damages be different?

Here are some thoughts on a possible answer. The reason we impose punishment—whether in the form of criminal sentences or punitive damages in tort—is to inflict disutility on the defendant. That's just the *immediate* reason, of course; that imposition of disutility in turn is supposed to serve larger purposes like retribution or deterrence, which we think are more likely to be advanced by sending prisoners to Riker's Island than to Coney Island. Now suppose we had a device—a helmet, perhaps a "utilometer"—that could measure precisely how much subjective unhappiness a punishment would cause to a person. If we did, could there be any objection to using it to measure punishments? We could say: the punishment for crime X is a punishment that will bring you to -100 on the utilometer. If in your case that amounts to one night in prison, so be it; if it amounts to a thousand nights in prison, so be it. Why would this be unjust? It would not ensure equality of factual treatment, but it would ensure equality in that which we are trying to achieve: disutility.

Now of course we don't have utilometers, or anything resembling them; we generally are in the opposite position of profound ignorance of the difference between defendants' utility schedules. Any attempt to guess at things like the size of a defendant's aversion to a night in prison is likely to be fraught with huge errors and result in terrible incentives and injustices. So we don't invite a jury or sentencing judge to speculate about that. This results in real injustices and inequities of its own: the same prison sentence may be applied to two people even if it hurts one of them much more than the other. That's the lesser evil, given the difficulty of trying to scale the punishment to the offender more precisely, but it might not be considered a necessary feature of good corrective justice.

In the world of tort damages, however, we are dealing in a different medium: money, rather than loss of liberty. While we don't have utilometers even with respect to money, we do have some fairly well-established economic ideas about how people value dollars and the loss of them. The most important is the diminishing marginal utility of wealth: the loss of a dollar means less to you if you have a hundred million of them than it does if you only have ten. In recognition of this idea, we award larger sums of punitive damages against people with large fortunes than against people with less wealth. Notice that the legitimacy of this practice does not necessarily depend on a commitment to deterrence as a purpose of punishment. Even if the purpose is retribution or some other notion of corrective justice, the point is the same: we want the defendant to experience a particular punishment; and the punishment—the disutility—experienced by a defendant when $100,000 is awarded just isn't the same if the defendant's net worth is $100,000,000 as it is if his net worth is $100,000.

Against this one might riposte that even criminal *fines*, unlike punitive damages, aren't scaled according to wealth. To the extent this is true, perhaps it is for the sake of providing the extra measure of clear notice we expect in criminal matters. But maybe a defendant's wealth should be (and indeed sometimes will be) relevant when a judge in a criminal case selects a fine from a range of possibilities. (In Finland, incidentally, fines for speeding are scaled to the defendant's wealth; in 2002 an executive was fined fourteen days' worth of income for his speeding offense, which amounted to tens of thousands of dollars. Query whether rich people speed more than poor people.)

Might one also argue for larger awards of punitive damages against rich people because they have better lawyers, making their expected chances of being caught (held liable) smaller than those of poor people? Or do rich people fear judgments against them more because they have more to lose in the way of reputation and professional opportunities if they are found guilty/held liable?

Q. Is it just to subject Simpson to civil liability after he has been acquitted in a criminal court?
A. This is an issue on which one can refer back to some of the arguments in *Murphy v. Hobbs*. The civil suit serves different purposes than the criminal suit in that it provides compensation for the victims or (here) their kin. The superficial tension lies in the award of punitive damages in the teeth of the criminal acquittal, and based on a lesser standard of proof than would have been required there.

There is, of course, a crucial procedural point you can raise if you have the appetite for it. If Simpson had been found guilty in the criminal case, collateral estoppel might well have caused nearly automatic liability to be imposed on the civil side, so long as the issues in the criminal and civil cases really could be shown to be identical; yet he gets no benefit on the civil side from being acquitted. In defense of this state of affairs, one must remember that the plaintiffs in the civil case did not have their "day in court" in the criminal case, and were entitled to a chance to make the case against Simpson (perhaps with better lawyers than the state had been able to provide in the criminal prosecution); and also that the legal issue in the criminal case was whether Simpson's guilt was established beyond a reasonable doubt, not (as in the tort case) by a lesser standard: the preponderance of the evidence. Thus the civil and criminal verdicts were not inconsistent. If he was 60% likely to have been the killer, both were correct.

Kennan v. Checker Cab Co. (punitive damages against employer unavailable for driver's bad acts)
In re Exxon Valdez (punitive damages against employer available for captain's bad acts)

These cases introduce the relationship between punitive damages and the doctrine of respondeat superior. If you haven't covered respondeat superior (in the chapter on strict liability), you will want to review the essentials of the doctrine. The facts of *Kennan* raise the problem not only of whether punitive damages can be assessed against an employer for an employee's misconduct, but also of whether an employer can be held liable even in compensatory damages for an employee's intentional torts. The common law rule was that employers were liable for intentional torts only if committed in furtherance (misguided or actual) of the employer's business. (The bus driver cases in the respondeat superior chapter illustrate the idea in a factual setting close to *Kennan*.) Though it's a little hard to see how the cab driver's beating of the plaintiff in *Kennan* was furthering the cab company's interests, the employer was held liable for the plaintiff's compensatory damages on a respondeat superior theory; maybe the idea was that the cab driver understood himself to be enforcing a company rule or protecting company property. The court of appeals in *Kennan* did not address this issue.

With respect to the punitive damages, Posner had this thought to offer on the choice of regimes in a diversity case from Illinois, where *Kennan* arose:

> If free to do so we would follow what apparently is still the majority rule that punitive damages can be awarded against an employer for an employee's wrongdoing without proof of fault on the employer's part. Unless a corporation that profits from the wrongdoing of its agents is made to bear the cost of that wrongdoing, the corporation will have an incentive to conduct its affairs through judgment-proof employees, and will escape punishment for wrongdoing that it condones and profits from. But the question is no longer an open one for a federal court in a diversity case governed by Illinois law. [The Illinois cases] adopt the complicity rule.

Q. What is the distinction between *In re Exxon Valdez* and *Kennan v. Checker Cab Co.*?

A. In the *Valdez* case the ship's captain was found to be acting in a managerial capacity, which is one of the justifications offered by the Agency Restatement for assessing punitive damages against an employer. The jury in the *Valdez* case was instructed as follows:

> An employee of a corporation is employed in a managerial capacity if the employee supervises other employees and has responsibility for, and authority over, a particular aspect of the corporation's business.

Said the court:

> Exxon's argument assumes that Hazelwood's scope of employment was strictly circumscribed by company policy to the effect that Hazelwood should have been on the bridge when the grounding occurred. Yet a managerial employee's scope of employment is not circumscribed by company policy to the extent Exxon suggests and a managerial employee, particularly a supertanker master, can interpret policy and engage in policy-making decisions as part of the scope of employment. [...]
>
> Exxon next argues that the jury was entitled to attribute Hazelwood's leaving the bridge to Exxon only if leaving the bridge was within the scope of Hazelwood's employment. Exxon's argument does not accurately reflect the law. "An act, although forbidden, or done in a forbidden manner, may be within the scope of employment." *Restatement (Second) of Agency* § 230 (1958). Thus, even if Hazelwood's leaving the bridge was a violation of company policy, that does not mean that his action was outside the scope of employment.

What is the difference between being captain of a tanker and captain of a taxicab? The existence of underlings (as well as the sheer amount of mischief the agent can cause).

CHAPTER 10

DEFENSES

SECTION A. CONTRIBUTORY AND COMPARATIVE NEGLIGENCE

The first chunk of this section of the chapter is mostly informative; it illustrates how contributory negligence worked and sketches the turn to comparative negligence. There are no cases to distinguish here, so the most productive use of class time usually lies in clarifying how the doctrines work and asking students about which they prefer and why. For brief treatment, you can just assign *McIntyre v. Balentine*. It may not be necessary to assign this section at all if you have spent time on contributory vs. comparative negligence elsewhere in the course and don't want to go into more detail.

Q. What is the best that can be said for contributory negligence?
A. This is an open-ended question, of course; it's easy for students to conclude that contributory negligence is a barbaric artifact of old times without seriously asking why it ever might have seemed appealing. You can bat around the question of whether it created better deterrence of negligence by potential victims, since it warned them that if they failed to use due care their recovery would be not merely reduced but eliminated. Against this there is Prosser's riposte that few victims in any setting are sufficiently aware of these rules to be affected by them (were any of the students aware of them before coming to law school?), and that in the meantime potential victims already have excellent incentives to use due care to avoid hurting themselves. The usual comeback to arguments of this sort is that tort law may deter at the margin—if not in the case of the usual automobile driver, then maybe in institutional settings where firms have lawyers who do understand these rules and give their advice accordingly. The problem with the argument here is that most of those institutional actors are far more likely to be defendants than plaintiffs in tort suits.

Another point to discuss is the administrative cost of contributory and comparative negligence. The costs take two forms: the time and trouble required to make the inquiry and the rate of error it produces. Contributory negligence naturally is easier to use, as it requires only a binary determination of whether each side used due care (at least in the ordinary case; sometimes questions of last clear chance and the like may complicate the inquiry). Comparative negligence requires a more fine-grained determination of just how much negligence each side displayed. This will take longer and be more uncertain. You can show this by taking the facts of any case and asking the students to jot down their own sense of how the negligence should be apportioned between the two sides. A good example for the purpose is the *Davis* case used as a problem at the end of the casebook's section on the Hand formula. The plaintiff's leg was severed when a train he was inspecting pulled away. He was negligent for failing to put a blue flag on the train; the railroad's agents were negligent for failing to blow the train's horn. Of course a real jury would hear more about the case than this, but maybe not too much more. The students' assessments are likely to be pretty widely distributed, with many making a 50/50 allocation, others 60/40 one way or the other, and some others still more extreme.

A little exercise like this helps the students see how much room for error the inquiry creates (assuming there is a "right" answer someplace) and how much uncertainty. The range of possible outcomes creates more room for different predictions by the lawyers and thus makes settlements harder to reach. Thus comparative negligence is more expensive than contributory negligence; perhaps we bear the expense to buy what we believe is more fairness, though this, too, can be questioned: the different reactions to cases like *Davis* suggest that the same case may produce different results when placed in front of juries, creating a fairness problem of a different kind: like cases won't be treated alike.

To facilitate the discussion of the large questions about these doctrines, here are a few interesting passages about them from the writings of Gary Schwartz:

a. Schwartz, *Contributory and Comparative Negligence*, 87 Yale L.J. 697 (1978):

> The justification that the new law-and-economics literature offers for a contributory negligence defense is not at all esoteric or highly technical; it is easy enough to understand and indeed had been anticipated by traditional tort writings. By denying recovery, in whole or in part, to the victim who has been contributorily negligent, the law can discourage people from engaging in conduct that involves an unreasonable risk to their own safety. Such "dysfunctional" victim conduct is a significant cause of accidents in virtually every major category of personal injuries with which the law is concerned. (The interesting exception is injuries resulting from medical malpractice.) Any legal rule that holds the potential of reducing the incidence of that conduct deserves our closest attention.

> When given such attention, however, the safety-incentive rationale for contributory negligence becomes problematic. This is so for four reasons. The first reason is concerned with the difficulty of formulating an optimal contributory negligence rule; the second, with the limited effects of such a rule, no matter how formulated; the third, with the psychological complexities of the conduct that the law criticizes as unreasonably risky; and the fourth, with the opportunities of some defendants to prevent contributorily negligent conduct by potential plaintiffs. [...]

> [T]he plaintiff is the biological victim of the accident. Hence the plaintiff has a strong "first-party" incentive to prevent the accident without regard to tort liability rules. Of course, to the extent that the injured victim can secure a recovery from a negligent defendant, he can transfer to another his original accident costs. It can therefore be argued that absent a contributory negligence defense, the victim's opportunity to collect in tort eliminates his original incentive to behave in a reasonably safe way. This argument, however, rests on several assumptions that are valid only in part.

> To be deterred by a contributory negligence rule, the victim must first of all know and understand both the general rule and its relevant applications. Yet studies have shown that a substantial portion of the public lacks such an understanding. Since victims tend to be private citizens who have never before been in a tort situation, this lack of understanding is not surprising.

> Second, the original incentive to act carefully can be affected by tort rules only to the extent that the potential victim can predict that his injury will occur in circumstances indicating the tort liability of some other party. In some cases, this knowledge exists or can easily be obtained. Thus, the employer considering on-the-job carelessness knows or should know that his employer will be liable for an accident. But consider the pedestrian who jaywalks. This pedestrian may be hit by a car that is being driven negligently or that has been defectively designed. But for all the pedestrian knows, the colliding driver and car will be free of any basis for tort liability. To the

extent that the victim cannot predict that his accident will involve the tort liability of another party, his original incentive for careful conduct remains fully in effect.

Now let us assume that the victim's injury is caused by the negligence of the defendant. Even if, despite his contributory negligence, the victim is given all the damages that the law allows, those damages will usually fall considerably short of compensating him for the full cost of his accident. [Schwartz discusses legal fees, the "miseries of litigation," and the fact that a damage award rarely leaves the victim indifferent to the fact of the original accident—particularly when the accident is fatal.] [...]

Schwartz suggests that "psychology rather than economics may best help us to understand contributorily negligent conduct," and continues:

[T]here is a misfortune to report: the question of how to *prevent* unreasonably self-risky conduct is one that applied psychologists have until now largely overlooked. In an effort to think about the question of prevention in a psychologically realistic way (though without much help from the psychological literature), it seems helpful to break up the whole of contributorily negligent conduct into two categories.

The first of these covers situations in which the individual is aware of the risk. But merely to describe such a category raises the question of why anyone would choose to engage in conduct of this sort. At least three reasons are identifiable. First, on the basis of the facts as he perceives them, the person may have concluded that the risk involved in his conduct is reasonable. He is wrong in his judgment because his facts are wrong; he has either undercalculated the risk or overcalculated the cost of abjuring the risky conduct. Second, on the basis of the values that the individual holds, he may conclude that his conduct is reasonable. If the law deems his behavior negligent, it does so because the community (*viz.*, the jury) adheres to a different set of values. Consider [...] the risk-preferring victim who is willing to jaywalk partly because he does not really mind (or even enjoys) dodging cars. Third, the victim may be one of those persons who are psychologically inclined to believe that accidents happen only to the "other guy," and who, in the face of known risks, are therefore likely to make decisions that are not genuinely consistently with their own real interests.

What happens when a contributory negligence defense is imposed on unreasonably and deliberately risky conduct that can be explained in any of these ways? For the victim with the wrong facts, it is not clear, as a matter of law, that his conduct entails contributory negligence at all. Even if the victim's factual perceptions are objectively incorrect, so long as they fall within the bounds of "reasonableness" the victim will perhaps be regarded as having heaved as a "reasonable man" and hence as not guilty of contributory negligence. Next, in the case of the victim with atypical values, it is hardly clear that his is conduct that society should really want to prevent. [...] Economics is keen on leaving to each individual the right to define and determine his goals; the economic assumption of rationality relates to choices that the person makes in pursuing his goals. Finally, for conduct occasioned by psychological deficiencies, there is at least a possibility that an individual's knowledge of the contributory negligence implications of his behavior might reinforce his lagging self-discipline. The problem is that the magnitude of this possibility is very difficult to figure out; the incentive afforded by a contributory negligence rule may well be effective occasionally, but more than this one cannot say.

The second category of contributorily negligent conduct includes instances in which the victim, because of inattention or inadvertence, is not conscious of the risk. In some of these situations, the victim's conduct is barely even deliberate: consider the worker whose hand finds its way into a dangerous machine and who is utterly unable to explain how this came to pass. [...] Starting with this fact of mindlessness, the conclusion easily follows that liability rules like contributory negligence, which themselves appeal to the mind, will have little effect. [...]

[Another] reason for doubting the safety-incentive rationale is this: at least in some situations, the plaintiff's unreasonable conduct may effectively be prevented by the *defendant*. [...] [B]y imaginative management and supervision, the employer can eliminate a large percentage of its employees' careless acts. [Schwartz also discusses the application of the point to warnings in product liability cases.] [...] [I]f the plaintiff's contributory negligence is often beyond his own control and is sometimes within the defendant's control, then the traditional rule seems less capable of achieving tort law's safety purposes than a direct, unencumbered rule of the defendant's negligence liability.

Schwartz also examines defenses of contributory negligence based on fairness and finds them lacking. He concludes that the negligence of a tort defendant is ethically worse that the negligence of the plaintiff, because the defendant's negligence is "egoistic" conduct that invades the rights of someone else (i.e., the plaintiff), while the plaintiff's own negligence is merely foolish.

b. Gary T. Schwartz, *Reality in the Economic Analysis of Tort Law: Does Tort Law Really Deter?* 42 UCLA L. Rev. 377 (1994), distinguishes between the "strong" form of the deterrence argument—which assumes that tort law does in fact deter as thoroughly as economic models suggest—and the more "moderate" form of the argument—which assumes that tort law provides a significant amount of deterrence, yet considerably less than the economists' formulae tend to predict." Schwartz favors the moderate form and offers this discussion of its implications:

> this intermediate verdict, by suggesting that the realistic objections have more force in some contexts than in others, enables readers to appreciate that economic reasoning—if it cares about social impacts—should learn to be somewhat selective in the problems it addresses. In an earlier article, I looked at defenses such as contributory and comparative negligence. Relying on several factors, such as the inattentiveness of much of the conduct that the law calls contributory negligence, I criticized the economists' conventional treatment of contributory negligence defenses. Indeed, the article has sometimes been read as claiming that such defenses have no impact on the conduct of victims. Yet I acknowledged that "it would be groundless to contend that a contributory negligence rule can have no effect on [victim] conduct." My point was that "there is good reason to conclude that this effect is partial and erratic." In line with this assessment, assume that the impact of rules of negligence liability on the conduct of potential defendants is twenty-five percent greater than the impact of rules of contributory negligence on the conduct of potential victims. In considering the deterrence wisdom of various alternative rules of contributory and comparative negligence, this twenty-five percent differential in real-world effectiveness almost certainly subordinates most of the other variables that economists have identified in their discussions of the contributory negligence problem.

> Moreover, if one can be selective in distinguishing between defendants and plaintiffs, one can be even more selective in distinguishing between various kinds of plaintiffs. Consider the farmer who stacks crops close to the railroad tracks, thereby exposing those crops to the risk of being set afire by railroad-engine sparks. This farmer, whether an individual or a firm, is faced with a continuing choice as to the appropriate method of operations. One of the choices entails over time a very high probability of harm; moreover, this is harm which, when it occurs, will predictably give rise to a lawsuit. Consider next the pedestrian whose careless conduct on one occasion exposes him to a risk of injury on a highway, or on railroad tracks. It might well be unrealistic to believe that this pedestrian's behavior would be significantly affected by doctrines

of contributory negligence. Even so, it is very plausible to assume that the conduct of the farmer would be influenced by liability rules. Scholars such as Coase and Grady have thus been quite shrewd in utilizing the railroad-farmer problem as a vehicle for exploring complex issues of contributory negligence.

Manning v. Brown (P allowed to collect nothing from accomplice for injuries sustained during joy ride)
Fritts v. McKinne (P collects in full for medical malpractice despite being put in need of treatment by his own negligence)
Ouellette v. Carde (P collects in full from D for injuries sustained in effort to rescue him—despite P's possible negligence during rescue)
Alami v. Volkswagen of America, Inc. (problem: P's decedent, a drunk driver, dies in car accident; estate sues car manufacturer; comparative negligence applies).
Van Vacter v. Hierholzer (problem: P disobeys doctor's instructions, suffers heart attack, then is victim of malpractice; P collects in full)

These cases explore the doctrinal issues surrounding comparative negligence that probably are most interesting: when should it not apply? Sometimes, as in *Fritts*, the plaintiff collects in full despite committing negligence that contributed to his own fix; sometimes, as in *Manning*, the plaintiff's own conduct causes her to collect nothing despite being the victim of undisputed negligence. Why does the law sometimes go to these extremes—and why does it usually take a middle route between them? Three cases, two problems, and a couple of hypotheticals at the end if you want them.

Q. What is the distinction between *Fritts v. McKinne* and *Manning v. Brown*?
A. First, be careful about how different the results are in these cases. In *Fritts* the defendant doctor just wanted the jury to be able to balance the plaintiff's negligence (in getting into an accident) against his own (in committing malpractice). The court said that no such balancing is allowed, and that the plaintiff should recover in full. In *Manning* the defendant driver went farther, asking that the plaintiff be forbidden to recover *at all*—and the request was granted. Both rulings might be understood as extreme. The moderate alternative would be to allow the plaintiffs in each case to obtain partial recoveries but to reduce them a bit to reflect the fact that they contributed to their own injuries—the classic comparative negligence approach. Instead the plaintiff in *Manning* collects nothing while the plaintiff in *Fritts* collects everything.

So let's compare the cases. In both of them a plaintiff was injured while engaged in, and as a result of, conduct that was not only negligent but criminal (at least assuming that Fritts was driving the pickup truck); indeed, the misconduct in *Fritts*—driving drunk at 70 miles per hour—seems more dangerous and thus more culpable than the joy-riding in *Manning*. One distinction involves the relationship between the injury and the wrongful act. In *Manning* the injury arose from the very sorts of risks that cause us to condemn the plaintiff's behavior in the first place. In *Fritts* the injury arose later, in the course of medical treatment that the plaintiff *could* have needed for any reason. In *Manning* we can say to the plaintiff: this never would have happened if you hadn't decided to do the wrong thing in the first place. We can't quite say that in *Fritts*, because people like Fritts are at the mercy of doctors for lots of reasons. The snug relationship between wrong and injury probably supports the intuition that the plaintiff has no business complaining about her injury. It also helps as a policy matter because denying recovery feels like a partial penalty against the plaintiff for engaging in the wrongful act. But this rationale may be fact-sensitive. What if Amidon had swerved into a wall and caused no injuries to herself but horrible injuries to Manning? Maybe the outcome would be the same; or maybe the court would find less rough justice in denying liability altogether, and would allow Manning's recovery merely to be reduced.

A related and more critical distinction involves the policy implications of allowing the defendant's proposed argument in the two cases. We don't want the obligations of doctors to use care to vary with the reason why the patient comes through the doors of the hospital. It seems unfair to the patient, and in some cases it might lead to bothersome incentives (a little like *Herskovits* in the chapter on cause in fact). A problem with not allowing the defense is that someone like Fritts ends up recovering just as much from the doctor as an entirely innocent victim of an accident. This might seem unjust, and also might seem to reflect a failure to preserve good incentives against drunk driving. But perhaps the thought is that the natural incentives against such self-endangering conduct already are pretty high; if they aren't strong enough to be effective, it's hard to imagine that they will be made usefully stronger by adding the additional threat that drunk plaintiffs won't get to recover in full if they become victims of malpractice when their resulting injuries are treated.

In *Manning* there aren't any worries that are quite comparable—are there? The principle would seem to be that accomplices in crime can't sue each other for negligently-inflicted injuries. Almost. Evidently the injuries have to arise quite directly from the bad act. So suppose two thieves are in the same car and on their way home from a robbery. The driver negligently takes a turn too tightly and skids off the road into a telephone pole. The passenger—his accomplice—suffers various injuries. Can he sue the driver? Maybe it depends on whether the crooks were being chased by the police and making a getaway, with the passenger urging on the driver. If so, then the plaintiff's injuries arose directly from the wrongful act; to be more precise, we might be able to say in a fairly strong sense that the plaintiff wouldn't have had these injuries without the wrongful act. But now suppose the police weren't in sight. Indeed, the thieves had gone undetected, and were on their way to a restaurant to toast their success. In that case maybe the passenger gets to recover after all. The rule isn't that thieves can't collect from each other, and thus that they have license to mistreat each other at will; for that would create bad incentives for them to do so. A rule confined to the "direct" consequences of wrongdoing avoids those incentives; it discourages the wrongful conduct in which the plaintiff was engaged, without creating a bad incentive for gratuitous carelessness.

But all this runs into trouble in *Alami*, considered below.

Q. How can *Fritts* be squared with cases like *Pridham v. Cash and Carry Building Center* in the chapter on proximate cause? *Pridham* and cases like it hold that if my negligence puts you in the hospital and you're injured by the doctor in the normal course of treatment, I'm legally responsible. So if you negligently put *yourself* into the hospital, shouldn't *you* be legally responsible for the injuries the doctor inflicts on you—contrary to *Fritts*? The way out of the conundrum is to observe that under *Pridham* the plaintiff still can collect in full from the doctor (or the ambulance driver); the doctor's liability isn't reduced by the liability of the person who initially injured the plaintiff. The plaintiff simply gets two tortfeasors to sue instead of one. But if the doctor in *Fritts* tries to invoke *Pridham*, he is doing so precisely in order to reduce his own liability, which is not a result *Pridham* supports.

Q. What principles arise from *Ouellette v. Carde* and *Fritts v. McKinne*? (Is the rule that we sometimes don't compare negligence a rule about defendants or about plaintiffs?)
A. Both are cases where we forbid comparisons of the parties' behavior, but for different reasons. The plaintiff in *Ouellette* was engaged in conduct we want to encourage: trying to rescue her friend. So in *Ouellette* we give the plaintiff a deliberate reward, allowing her to recover in full despite being negligent, though this comes at the expense of a defendant who we have no special reason to want to treat severely. In *Fritts* we want to discourage the defendant fully, so we impose a tough rule that gives the plaintiff an incidental windfall.

Closer analysis of the facts of *Ouellette* is a little difficult because the opinion doesn't specify what Ouellette's alleged negligence was; we have to speculate. Maybe she didn't give enough thought to the large accumulation of gasoline on the floor. Incidentally, Ouellette won a jury verdict that was affirmed on the following basis:

> The rescue doctrine assigns the party who negligently creates a dangerous situation with responsibility for any rescuer injured in a reasonable rescue attempt. The party creating the

danger is by law charged with foreseeing all nonreckless rescue attempts; therefore, the trial justice did not err in denying the defendant's motions for directed verdict and the defendant's motion for new trial.

This anticipates some questions raised later in the chapter (in the section on primary assumption of risk) concerning the fireman's rule and its limits.

Q. How can *Ouellette* be squared with *United States v. Lawter* from the chapter on duties?
A. If you haven't studied *Lawter* you can make the relevant point from that case more generally: rescuers are obliged to use due care toward the people they are trying to save. Yet here Ouellette is excused from her failure to use due care. Why? The difference is that the usual rescue doctrine requires the rescuers to use due care toward others, not toward themselves. The first rule is needed to avoid a policy problem of rescuers having too few incentives to be careful not to hurt others. A similarly tough rule probably is not needed to prevent them from hurting themselves. The same logic can be turned into a fairness argument along the lines Schwartz had in mind: negligence toward others is egoistic; negligence toward oneself is merely foolish.

Q. What result in *Alami v. Volkswagen of America, Inc.*?
A. This is a nice problem because it tests the limits of *Manning* and *Fritts*. It involves a plaintiff who was a drunk driver, as did *Fritts*; but it involves alleged negligence by the defendant in advance of the accident, and before the defendant had any way of knowing its liability might be reduced on comparative negligence grounds, so the policy worry involved in giving doctors a free pass might seem absent. There are three options: (a) forbid the plaintiff to collect anything, following *Manning* (his conduct was worse than the plaintiff's there, and the defendant's conduct here wasn't as bad as the defendant's conduct there); (b) allow the plaintiff's recovery to be reduced in part to reflect his own negligent (or worse) contribution to the situation; or (c) allow the plaintiff to recover in full, forbidding any reduction in accord with *Fritts* (he's entitled to a crashworthy car regardless of how he gets into the crash; he could have been sober and been hit by someone else who was drunk, so why should VW get a windfall?).

The Court of Appeals took the middle route, concluding that comparative fault principles applied and entitled the plaintiff to a reduced but still partial recovery. *Manning v. Brown* was said to be distinguishable:

> Plaintiff does not contest Volkswagen's assertion that Alami's intoxication was the cause of the vehicle's *collision* with the utility pole. Moreover, plaintiff has not identified any other cause of the crash[. …] She has sued only Volkswagen and argues that her husband's *injuries* were caused by design defects in the vehicle that rendered it unsafe. Thus, plaintiff asserts that under these circumstances, her claim is not precluded on public policy grounds because the injuries upon which the claim is based do not have the necessary causal link to the decedent's serious violation of the law.

> While we might quarrel with the dissent over whether a plaintiff's illegal conduct must be *a* direct cause or *the* direct cause to raise the bar of preclusion, our conclusion in this case is based on more than semantics. The *Barker/Manning* rule is premised on public policy. "It extends the basic principle that one may not profit from his own wrong to tort actions seeking compensation for injuries resulting from the plaintiff's own criminal activities of a serious nature." […] The *Barker/Manning* rule is based on the sound premise that a plaintiff cannot rely upon an *illegal act* or *relationship* to define the defendant's duty. We refuse to extend its application beyond claims where the parties to the suit were involved in the underlying criminal conduct, or where the criminal plaintiff seeks to impose a duty arising out of an illegal act.

If Volkswagen did defectively design the Jetta as asserted by plaintiff's expert, it breached a duty to any driver of a Jetta involved in a crash regardless of the initial cause. Plaintiff does not seek to "profit" from her husband's intoxication—she asks only that Volkswagen honor its well-recognized duty to produce a product that does not unreasonably enhance or aggravate a user's injuries. The duty she seeks to impose on Volkswagen originates not from her husband's act, but from Volkswagen's obligation to design, manufacture and market a safe vehicle.

That same reasoning, however, would deny a burglar injured on a defective staircase from asserting a claim against his victim. Although landowners do have a general duty to the public to maintain their premises in a reasonably safe condition, this duty does not exist in the abstract. It takes form when someone enters the premises and is injured. Thus, the injured burglar is not entitled to benefit from his burglary because he cannot invoke a duty triggered by his unlawful entry. […]

Rosenblatt, J., dissented:

Under the majority's unwarranted contraction of the preclusion doctrine, suits prosecuted by plaintiffs injured as a result of their own serious violations of law may now more easily avoid dismissal. A plaintiff who commits a serious violation of law and sues for damages need only invoke a duty on the part of the defendant that does not "arise out of" the illegality (for example, the landowner's duty to keep the premises safe for *everyone*). That duty is thus converted into a defense against preclusion. As a result, despite the express prohibition of *Barker* and the majority's reaffirmation that the hypothetical burglar cannot sue, today's opinion validates a contrary result.

Moreover, the Court's analysis overlooks the premise that preclusion has always considered only the conduct of the plaintiff—the seeker of damages—not the conduct of the defendant. When invoking the preclusion doctrine, we bar suit "at the very threshold of the plaintiff's application for judicial relief" (*Manning*, 91 N.Y.2d at 120) before the plaintiff can ever argue the nature of the defendant's duty or when it "arises." In both *Barker* and *Manning* we precluded the suits *only* because of the plaintiffs' seriously unlawful conduct, and in spite of the defendants' acknowledged breach of their legal duties. By inquiring into the nature and origin of the defendant's duty, the majority debilitates the preclusion doctrine itself. […]

In the case before us, plaintiff's suit should be dismissed because it fits the *Barker-Manning* rule and in some ways makes an even stronger case for preclusion. This is so for two reasons. First, while Manning did not cause her accident in any but the remotest sense, decedent undeniably caused his collision. Although Manning was complicit in the crime of joyriding and had taken a turn at the wheel, her accomplice drove the car into a pole, resulting in Manning's injuries. Here, however, decedent's drunk driving was the sole cause of his accident. If Manning (a passenger not directly responsible for her accident) was precluded, then surely plaintiff should be precluded where decedent's intoxicated driving was the *sole* cause of his collision.

Second, the hazards posed by drunk drivers are at least as great as those posed by joyriders. In concluding that joyriding is precisely the "serious violation of the law" that *Barker* contemplated, we noted in *Manning* that automobiles are "inherently dangerous" instruments and that joyriding "is typically characterized by more than mere unauthorized use. The unauthorized use is usually accompanied by reckless or excessively fast driving, posing a threat to innocent third parties." Drunk driving deserves at least comparable treatment.

Plaintiff seeks to distinguish between the accident and decedent's injuries, asking us to allow a jury to apportion fault between decedent and Volkswagen for enhanced injuries resulting from Volkswagen's alleged failure to design a crashworthy car. Put differently, plaintiff seeks compensation only for the difference between decedent's actual injuries and those he claims he would have received had he not been driving a vehicle plaintiff alleges was improperly designed. While not without appeal, this argument is ultimately flawed.

The dissent added in a footnote: "Contrary to the majority's assertion, precluding this suit would not relieve Volkswagen of its obligation to manufacture safe cars. If a car manufacturer breaches its duty to design a safe automobile, that duty is (and should be) eminently enforceable by the universe of deserving plaintiffs. This Court did not 'relieve' Manning and Barker of their respective duties to drive safely or refrain from helping to make a bomb. Preclusion operates not to extinguish a duty, but to prohibit a *particular* criminal plaintiff (or here, decedent's estate) from profiting by enforcing that duty." […]

Q. What result in *Van Vacter v. Hierholzer*?

A. The court's treatment of the issue was brief: "The [disobedience of his doctor's instructions] was not a proximate cause of Van Vacter's injury, except to the extent it described Van Vacter's failure to obey Hierholzer's and Coltharp's treatment instructions [on the night of his death]. Rather, it gave rise to his condition and the occasion for Hierholzer's and Coltharp's negligence."

The result in *Van Vacter* is pretty easy to guess, especially after *Fritts* and *Alami*, but it's interesting to talk about the reasoning. The court held that it was error to allow Van Vacter's disobedience to be treated as a type of negligence that could be balanced against the defendant's conduct. The differences between this case and *Fritts* are that here the plaintiff's negligence seems less egregious but also was different in kind: disobedience of instructions from his doctors. (He wasn't now suing the same doctors who gave him the advice—but suppose he were, to make it more interesting. Same result.)

Some of the practical objections to the trial court's approach in *Van Vacter* (allowing the jury to reduce the plaintiff's recovery to reflect his role in the accident) are the same as found in *Fritts*: a great many cases of medical malpractice might end up involving such defenses. People often hurt themselves through obvious negligence and even more frequently fail to do all that their doctors say that they should (whether to call this "negligence" is more controversial; a jury would have to decide that). Those claims would be hard to sort out intelligently, and probably would amount to a pretty wide reduction of awards against doctors. On the other hand, might the holding on appeal give an inadequate incentive to the Van Vacters of the world to obey their doctors' instructions? We *want* someone in his position to worry that if he never gets any exercise he will bear some of the costs. But as with *Fritts*, perhaps the idea is that guys like Van Vacter already have a pretty good incentive to do what their doctors say—viz., the threat of death. If that isn't enough, shaving down their recovery in tort seems unlikely to matter, either.

The new issue the case raises involves the question of comparative fault when a patient disregards a doctor's orders, and thus commits negligence not quite as independent from the doctor's malpractice as was the car accident in *Fritts*. To turn it around: it was pretty clear in *Fritts* that the patient died because of a slip of the doctor's knife; the patient's own negligence provided an occasion for the slip, but the slip nevertheless was a distinct cause of the death. In *Van Vacter* it's a little harder to say this: evidently the doctor should have done more, but in the end the patient died of a heart attack that he largely brought on himself.

Q. Hypothetical: in *Wyatt v. United States*, 939 F.Supp. 1402 (E.D.Mo. 1996), the plaintiff was an Army veteran who had lost the use of his legs during the Vietnam war. One of the problems created by his disability was pressure sores on his legs. His practice was to to relieve them by sitting on cushions. In 1991 he went on a long car trip without a cushion and thus developed pressure sores. He went to a VA hospital for treatment. Treatment with antibiotics was indicated, but this was not done; as a result, the plaintiff's condition deteriorated: he developed osteomyelitis in both legs, and both ended up being amputated. He sued the United States to collect for his injuries. The government's defense included two claims that Wyatt had be contributorily negligent: that he had failed to use his cushion during the car trip, and that once in the hospital he disobeyed his doctors' instructions not to smoke cigarettes. (The point of the latter claim was that smoking worsens circulation and thus slows healing.) What result?

A. The court accepted both of the government's theories and reduced the plaintiff's recovery by 5% on the basis of each of them. The result on the claim about his failure to use a cushion—based in part on his admission that he showed bad judgment—seems wrong, or at least impossible to square with cases like *Fritts*, *Van Vacter*, and the many others holding that a doctor takes the plaintiff as he finds him and cannot have his liability reduced by any feature of the plaintiff's negligence before he showed up for treatment. We wonder whether the fact that the United States was the defendant exerted any influence on the decision here. Then again, if it's obvious that his own negligence helped get him into this mess, why shouldn't his claim be reduced as a result? If someone else had treated him as negligently as he treated himself, and then he had received negligent treatment from the doctor, he would have good claims against both the original tortfeasor and the hospital. So why shouldn't he bear some ongoing responsibility when his wound instead is self-inflicted?

And then what about the reduction based on his failure to stop smoking? How is that distinguishable from *Van Vacter*? In both cases the patient disobeyed his doctors' orders. The difference is that in *Van Vacter* the disobedience came before the malpractice, while in *Wyatt* it came afterwards. Most courts hew to that distinction in deciding cases like these. One advantage of such an approach is that at the moment a physican acts, he always is under the full pressure of the law to be careful; he can't imagine that any negligence that already has occurred will get him off the hook.

Q. Hypothetical: in *Guice v. City of New York*, 748 N.Y.S.2d 723 (App. Div. 2002), the plaintiff's decedent was being chased by police in New York City. He tried to swallow a plastic bag he was carrying that contained cocaine. He soon collapsed and was taken to the hospital. He died there seven hours later of asphyxiation caused by the plastic bag, which remained in his throat the entire time. (It had not broken.) The plaintiff sued the city, claiming that its medical employees had been negligent in failing to remove the bag. The city sought summary judgment on the theory of *Manning v. Brown*—i.e., that the defendant's death resulted from criminal behavior on his part and that they city should not be held liable for any portion of the financial consequences. The trial court denied the motion and the city appealed. What result?

A. The Appellate Division affirmed:

> The motion was properly denied. Unlike the plaintiffs in *Barker v. Kallash* and *Manning v. Brown*, whose injuries were incurred "in the course of committing a serious criminal act" (*Barker*), this plaintiff's death occurred seven hours after he allegedly attempted to swallow the plastic bag as the result, according to the complaint, of defendants' negligence and malpractice. In addition, because this is not a case "where the parties to the suit were involved in the underlying criminal conduct, or where the criminal plaintiff seeks to impose a duty arising out of an illegal act" (*Alami v. Volkswagen of America, Inc.*), the public policy rule to deny judicial relief to persons injured in the course of committing serious criminal acts is not applicable.

Okay, but then should the plaintiff's damages be reduced at all? Or is this basically a rerun of *Fritts*?

SECTION B. EXPRESS ASSUMPTION OF RISK

These materials teach fine in about one class day, depending how long you draw out treatment of the problems in the text. If you want a more cursory pass at them that gives the students quick exposure to the issues at stake, the key things to assign probably are *Tunkl* and the summarizing materials right afterwards.

Van Tuyn v. Zurich American Ins. Co. (P thrown from mechanical bull; L)

Manning v. Brannon (P hurt when parachute is improperly packed; NL)

Q. If the release in *Van Tuyn* didn't cover the facts of that case, what *did* it cover?
A. It covered the risk that the plaintiff would fall off the bull and suffer injuries even if the defendant used due care. The release might seem to have little utility if limited to such cases, since by assumption they seem to involve no negligence by the defendant. But the release may still serve a purpose in preventing claims that the defendant was negligent in offering the activity at all, or in barring claims of strict liability. The release also could rule out claims that the defendant failed to warn the plaintiff of the bull's dangers.

Q. What is the distinction between *Van Tuyn v. Zurich American Ins. Co.* and *Manning v. Brannon?*
A. The key distinction, of course, is that the *Manning* release explicitly provided that the defendant could not be held liable for its own negligence.

Q. Can we assume that the defendants in *Manning* were negligent? Can we assume the result would have been the same if they had packed Manning no parachute at all?
A. The answer to the first question is yes. The answer to the second question is not necessarily. That might be a case of gross negligence that the release would be held not to excuse—either because "gross negligence" was not mentioned in the release or more likely because a release absolving the defendant of responsibility for gross negligence is against public policy. See, e.g., *Smith v. Golden Triangle Raceway,* 708 S.W.2d 574 (Tex. App. 1986). (In this respect the dissenter in *Manning* is speaking too strongly when he suggests that the majority's holding would relieve the defendants from liability for their willful disregard of the safety of others.)

Q. What are the differences between how courts handle assumption of risk agreements and ordinary contracts? Why are many courts so much more skeptical about the former? In some of the Restatement illustrations in this section we see suggestions that courts care whether the party who signed the agreement actually read it. Would "I signed it but didn't read it" generally be a useful defense in a contract case? (No.) So why is it sometimes a valid argument in a tort case?
A. With assumption of risk agreements, unlike ordinary contracts, courts are likely to insist on exaggerated clarity rather than just finding for the defendant if the ordinary meaning of the document cuts that way. Courts also are likely to ask whether the plaintiff really read and understood the contract, which is not a question normally asked in contract cases. Perhaps it is because most contract cases involve the provision of goods and services, whereas these contracts involve responsibility for personal safety. The consequences of a release in the latter situation can be devastating in ways different from an ill-considered commercial contract, and maybe harder for the party making the release to fully appreciate in advance (why? Cognitive hazards?). So the courts show an extra measure of solicitude in making sure that the bargain was one that the party understood. (We see a parallel in the UCC, which holds "prima facie unconscionable" provisions attempting to waive the right to sue for personal injuries caused by goods.) And maybe personal injuries are more than breaches of commercial agreements likely to create costs for third parties that the parties may not internalize.

Q. Should a defendant be able to obtain an enforceable release absolving itself from responsibility for its negligence (or for that matter its gross negligence) when the activity involved is very dangerous?
A. This is the question raised by the dissent in *Manning*. It is a good discussion topic; like *Tunkl* (which soon follows), it raises interesting questions about the relationship between free markets, collective standards, and moral hazards. If releases like the one in *Manning* are not allowed, the natural consequence will be to make the activities involved more expensive: the parachuting school would have to charge enough to cover its expected litigation and liability costs when someone gets hurt (or more precisely to cover its insurance for those occasions). This will cause some people to be priced out of the market for such schools, and may cause the schools to close altogether. This might seem like a shame,

since by assumption we have two parties here with they power to make each other better off by their own lights if they can enter into a legally binding agreement—yet they can't (if we decide not to enforce them). Why override the parties' preferences about these things? Is there good ground for doubt about the information on which the customer's decision is based?

From here you can explore a bit the relationship between contract and tort. Contract traditionally is a realm of private agreement, tort a realm of communitarian standards (the reasonable person, etc.). Sometimes it is possible to view them harmoniously by styling tort cases as attempts to reconstruct the contract the parties would have made if transactions costs between them had not been prohibitive. But the courts' handling of express assumption of risk does not quite lend itself to that explanation. Transaction costs may be as low as you please, but courts often will refuse to enforce waivers of the right to sue for gross negligence and worse. The reason seems to be paternalism. We also find occasional paternalism in contract law, as with the doctrine of unconscionability; but the disparity of bargaining power associated with unconscionability is not necessary to provoke the the law's disdain for the waiver in *Van Tuyn* or waivers of the right to sue for extreme misconduct.

Anderson v. Erie Ry. Co. (Release on back of reduced-fare train ticket held enforceable; NL)
Tunkl v. Regents of the Univ. of California (P signs waiver of negligence claims on way into hospital; L)

Q. The usual common law rule, as *Anderson* implies, was that a passenger's release was void if it promised not to sue a common carrier for injuries suffered as a result of the carrier's negligence. What is the sense of that rule—and of the exception to it recognized by *Anderson*?
A. As for the background rule making releases generally unenforceable by common carriers, the rationale was put this way (in the admiralty context) in *Railroad Co. v. Lockwood*, 84 U.S. 357 (1873):

> Under the admiralty law of the United States, a common carrier by sea cannot by any contract it makes exempt itself from all responsibility for loss or damage by perils of the sea arising from the negligence of its officers or crew. It is a fundamental principle of that law that common carriers are bound to exercise the utmost care and diligence in the performance of their duties.

> The courts of the United States recognize the fact that a common carrier and his customer do not stand upon a footing of equality, and that the individual customer has no real freedom of choice. "He cannot afford to higgle or stand out." He prefers to accept any bill of lading the carrier tenders him, for in many cases he has no alternative; and it is against the policy of the law to allow a public carrier to abandon its obligations to the public by stipulating for exemptions which are unreasonable, and which excuse it from negligence in the performance of its duty. That such contracts are illegal and void under our law is well settled.

For a slightly different rationale, see the *Rogow* case described next: the passenger has little ability to protect himself once he is in the hands of the carrier. But the main idea behind the background rule is protection of the party who must have transportation. Remember that there were no cars when these rules were devised; 98% of intercity travel was by railroad, with the remainder driven by horses. This put the common carrier into a powerful position: if it were to demand a release from liability it would be hard for a passenger to turn down (unless a competing rail line were offering better terms, which might not be so in many locations). In this sense the railway can be analogized to the modern hospital that is the subject of *Tunkl*. So the rule was that a passenger could force the carrier to take him, and to use due care, by presenting the full fare.

But then why the exception to the rule in *Anderson*? The idea seems to be that the parties there, unlike the ones envisioned in the excerpt from *Lockwood* above, *were* "higgling"; Anderson was getting a reduced rate. A passenger who pays the full fare has an unwaivable right to due care, but a passenger who has managed to bargain his way out of the full fare evidently has some bargaining power—so the rules against waiver are relaxed.

Q. Suppose Tunkl had been a clergyman and had been offered a "clerical discount" upon his admission to the hospital, in exchange for which he would be obliged to forfeit his right to sue for negligence; imagine, in other words, the precise pattern of the *Anderson* case recurring in *Tunkl*'s factual setting. What result? What is the distinction between this hypothetical and *Anderson*?

A. The waiver would not be enforced. The court's view in *Anderson* was that the waiver created no policy worries because "free passengers are not so many as to induce negligence on [the railroad's] part." The same presumably goes for passengers using clerical tickets. The distinction is that unlike a hospital, most precautions a railroad provides will affect a whole trainload of people, not just one patient at a time. So long as most of the passengers have a right to due care enforceable in tort, the railroad will have adequate incentives to behave itself. In a hospital, where patients are cared for one at a time, presenting a doctor with a patient who has no right to sue could create policy problems unrelieved by the logic of the train case.

The basic ideas in *Anderson* remain good law on the subject of common carriers, at least where it hasn't been changed by statute—as occasionally is done. Thus Cal. Civ. Code sec. 2174 provides that "The obligations of a common carrier cannot be limited by general notice on his part, but may be limited by special contract"; and then sec. 2175 says, "A common carrier cannot be exonerated, by any agreement made in anticipation thereof, from liability for the gross negligence, fraud, or willful wrong of himself or his servants." The latter provision has been held by implication (*expressio unius*) to allow releases of liability for mere negligence—as was done in *Platzer v. Mammoth Mountain Ski Area*, 128 Cal.Rptr.2d 885 (Cal. App. 2003). The plaintiff fell off of a chair lift at the defendant ski resort. The court thought that supplying the chair lift made the defendant a "common carrier" (seems odd, but another statute provided that "Every one who offers to the public to carry persons, property, or messages, excepting only telegraphic messages, is a common carrier of whatever he thus offers to carry"); but a release barred the claim.

Q. Hypothetical: in *Rogow v. United States*, 173 F.Supp. 547 (S.D.N.Y. 1959), Leon Rogow was a freelance writer hired by the Air Force to write the script for a recruiting film. Rogow arranged to visit several Air Force bases for the purpose and to ride between them on military aircraft. Before boarding his first flight, Rogow signed a release that read in part as follows:

> [I]n consideration of the permission extended to me by the United States, through its officers and agents to take said flight or flights, I do hereby, for myself, my heirs, executors and administrators, remise, release and forever discharge the Government of the United States and all its officers, agents, and employees, acting officially or otherwise, from any and all claims, demands, actions, or causes of action, on account of my death or on account of any injury to me or my property which may occur from any cause during said flight or flights or continuances thereof, as well as all ground and flight operations incident thereto.

After signing the release, Rogow boarded a B-25 aircraft headed to Ohio from Long Island. The plane crashed soon after takeoff. Rogow and all others aboard the plane were killed in the accident. His executor sued the United States for damages, claiming the crash was caused by negligence. The government interposed Rogow's release as a defense. What result?

A. The court found the release unenforceable:

> The rationale behind the numerous decisions invalidating releases of the kind involved here is based upon the policy of encouraging the exercise of care. The courts seek, also, to protect individuals from the effects of agreements which are rarely considered by the signer with the

thoughtfulness and care appropriate to the catastrophic consequences which may result to him and his family. Where the plaintiff has either paid full fare for his passage or where a pass has been issued as part of a contract of employment, releases have not been upheld. [...]

The release can stand only if the plane trip was a gratuitous benefit to Mr. Rogow. On the basis of the testimony bearing on the circumstances leading to the signing of the release, it is quite clear to me that the flight was not provided gratuitously. [...] [T]he main benefits resulting from the flight were those flowing to the Air Force. Rogow benefited only incidentally. As a writer of considerable repute, he had an interest in producing the best possible script. But, in the main, there can be little doubt that the principal beneficiary of Rogow's military travel was the Air Force, because the trip would enable Rogow to give them a more meaningful script at an earlier date. It can hardly be said that an individual (1) traveling in furtherance of an Air Force project; (2) in a manner suggested by the Air Force and (3) whom the Air Force is in any event obligated to reimburse for his travel costs, is nevertheless the recipient of Air Force largess in the form of a "free ride." [...]

The defendant has attempted to distinguish some of the cases invalidating releases on the ground that they involve common carriers. The decisions of the New York courts in this area are founded on broad public policy considerations. I do not believe that the courts would deprive these precedents of much of their force by limiting their applicability in the manner urged by the defendant. Releases of the kind involved here are unenforceable in New York where the defendant has not conferred a gratuitous benefit on the plaintiff.

Furthermore, in attempting to distinguish the common carrier cases, defendant loses sight of their most important factor. What was significant was not the defendant's technical status as a common carrier. Rather, the key to those cases lies in the fact that, once having placed himself in defendant's hands, the plaintiff was no longer able to take any steps to provide for his own safety.

The reasoning underlying cases involving railways and such instrumentalities as elevators is especially apt here. From the moment the decedent stepped aboard the defendant's aircraft his survival depended upon the skill of defendant's pilots and maintenance personnel. As a layman, he could hardly inspect the aircraft himself or even detect the most blatant operational negligence. Thus, this case must be distinguished from those instances where the signer of the release is in a position to protect himself through the exercise of care.

Q. In one of the Restatement illustrations, a driver is not bound by the language on the ticket from a parking garage because he is in a hurry and hasn't been able to find parking for several blocks. What possible sense can this make? Obviously the defendant had no way knowing these things; shouldn't that count for something?

A. There is a possible analogy to the common carrier cases considered a moment ago. The type of case on which this illustration evidently is based is typified by *Miller's Mut. Fire Ins. Ass'n. v. Parker*, 65 S.E.2d 341 (N.C. 1951), where the court explained its decision this way:

The obligation to use due care in contracts of this type arises from the relation created by the contract and is independent, rather than a part of it. That the obligation arises from the relation and not as an implied term of the contract is shown by the refusal of the law under certain circumstances to give effect to provisions in the contract undertaking to nullify the effect of the obligation.

It is a well-recognized rule of law that in an ordinary mutual benefit bailment, where there is no great disparity of bargaining power, the bailee may relieve himself from the liability imposed on him by the common law so long as the provisions of such contract do not run counter to the public interest. [...] Respecting other types of bailment, there are various shades of opinion. Many courts hold that where the bailee makes it his business to act as bailee for hire, on a uniform and not an individual basis, it is against the public interest to permit him to exculpate himself from his own negligence. And the decided trend of modern decisions is against the validity of such exculpatory clauses or provisions in behalf of proprietors of parking lots, garages, parcel check rooms, and warehouses, who undertake to protect themselves against their own negligence by posting signs or printing limitations on the receipts or identification tokens delivered to the bailor-owner at the time of the bailment. In such cases, the difference is the difference between ordinary bailees, on the one hand, and what may be called professional bailees, on the other. They hold themselves out to the public as being possessed of convenient means and special facilities to furnish the service offered for a price. They deal with the public on a uniform basis and at the same time impose or seek to impose predetermined conditions which rob the customer of any equality of bargaining power. [...]

The complexity of today's commercial relations and the constantly increasing number of automobiles render the question of parking a matter of public concern which is taxing the ingenuity of our municipal officials. People who work in the business sections of our cities and towns and who rely on automobiles for transportation find it difficult—sometimes impossible—to locate a place on the public streets where daily parking is permitted. They are driven to seek accommodation in some parking lot maintained for the service of the public. There they are met by predetermined conditions which create a marked disparity of bargaining power and place them in the position where they must either accede to the conditions or else forego the desired service.

Such was the case here. The defendant was engaged in the business of accepting automobiles for parking for hire, both on a daily and a monthly basis. He required the owner-bailor to surrender the keys to his automobile so that he or his employee could park it at any place of his choosing and move it from time to time during the day as occasion might require. He had 'a pretty good-sized sign', 'very prominently displayed' saying 'Not responsible for loss by fire or theft.' He told Mrs. Jenkins 'we would not be responsible for loss by fire or theft.' 'I told her if there was any loss from fire or theft, it would be her responsibility. She left the car. She did not make any statement.' This same provision was printed on the identification tokens furnished those who parked by the day only. Under these circumstances it is against the public interest to give force and effect to the exculpatory agreement which would relieve defendant from all liability for his own negligence.

The court stressed that this was the rule for bailments, but not necessarily for other sorts of arrangements the parties might make—a lease, for example.

Shorter v Drury (Jehovah's Witness signs release for consequences of refusing blood transfusion, then dies when transfusion is required because of D's negligence; mixed result)
Vodopest v. MacGregor (P goes on Himalayan trek for medical research; release held unenforceable)

Q. What result in *Shorter v. Drury*?
A. This is a good problem because it raises hard questions about how to honor the release without falling into *Tunkl*-type difficulties. The jury found the defendant doctor negligent, but reduced the plaintiff's wrongful death damages by 75% because of the release Mrs. Shorter had signed. The Washington Supreme Court affirmed:

> Defendant concedes a survival action filed on behalf of Mrs. Shorter for her negligently inflicted injuries would not be barred by the refusal since enforcement would violate public policy.

Defendant argues, however, the refusal does not release the doctor for his negligence but only for the consequences arising out of Mrs. Shorter's voluntary refusal to accept blood, which in this case was death. [...]

Plaintiff argues the purpose of the refusal was only to release the defendant doctor from liability for not transfusing blood into Mrs. Shorter had she required blood during the course of a nonnegligently performed operation. He further asserts the refusal as it applies to the present case violates public policy since it would release Dr. Drury from the consequences of his negligence. [...] He claims that if it is a release of liability for negligence it is void as against public policy and if it is a release of liability where a transfusion is required because of nonnegligent treatment then it is irrelevant. [...]

The document is more, however, than a simple declaration that the signer would refuse blood only if there was no negligence by Dr. Drury. It is a specific request that no blood or blood derivatives be administered to Mrs. Shorter. The attending physician is released from "*any responsibility whatever* for unfavorable reactions or *any untoward results* due to my refusal to permit the use of blood or its derivatives." (Italics ours.) The release signed by the Shorters further stated: "I fully understand the possible consequences of such refusal on my part." [...]

We also hold the release was not against public policy. We emphasize again the release did not exculpate Dr. Drury from his negligence in performing the surgery. Rather, it was an agreement that Mrs. Shorter should receive no blood or blood derivatives. The cases cited by defendant [including *Tunkl v. Regents of Univ. of Cal.*] all refer to exculpatory clauses which release a physician or hospital from all liability for negligence. The Shorters specifically accepted the risk which might flow from a refusal to accept blood. Given the particular problems faced when a patient on religious grounds refuses to permit necessary or advisable blood transfusions, we believe the use of a release such as signed here is appropriate. Requiring physicians or hospitals to obtain a court order would be cumbersome and impractical. [...] The alternative of physicians or hospitals refusing to care for Jehovah's Witnesses is repugnant in a society which attempts to make medical care available to all its members. [...]

If the refusal is held valid, defendant asserts it acts as a complete bar to plaintiff's wrongful death claim. We disagree. While Mrs. Shorter accepted the consequences resulting from a refusal to receive a blood transfusion, she did not accept the consequences of Dr. Drury's negligence which was, as the jury found, a proximate cause of Mrs. Shorter's death. Defendant was not released from his negligence. We next consider the impact of the doctrine of assumption of the risk on this negligence. [...]

The defendants do not argue, nor do we hold, that the Shorters assumed the risk of the "direct consequences" of Dr. Drury's negligence. Those "consequences" would be recoverable in a survival action under RCW 4.20.046, .050, and .060. Defendant argues, however, and we agree, that the Shorters could be found by the jury to have assumed the risk of death from an operation which had to be performed without blood transfusions and where blood could not be administered under any circumstances including where the doctor made what would otherwise have been correctable surgical mistake. The risk of death from a failure to receive a transfusion to which the Shorters exposed themselves was created by, and must be allocated to, the Shorters themselves.

Q.   What result in *Vodopest v. MacGregor?*
A.   The court found the agreement unenforceable. Here are some excerpts from the court's opinion, applying *Tunkl* and Washington's variation on it, *Wagenblast v. Odessa Sch. Dist*, 110 Wash.2d 845 (1988):

[M]edical research is the kind of endeavor which is generally thought suitable for public regulation and is, in fact, highly regulated. It is also of great importance to society. In this case, Defendant's invitation to participate as a research subject was open to the public and the allegation here is that the influence and control the Defendant had over the Plaintiff was the cause of Plaintiff's injuries. Generally, medical researchers have significant control over the safety of their human research subjects. In spite of the fact that this was not an adhesion contract, in that there was no particular unequal bargaining strength, we conclude there are critical public policy reasons to maintain the usual standard of care in settings where one person is using another as a medical research subject. Medical research using human subjects is one of those settings where public policy reasons for preserving an obligation of care owed by the researcher to the subject outweighs our traditional regard for freedom of contract.

An important inquiry in deciding if a release for negligence should be upheld is whether the agreement concerns an endeavor of a type which is generally thought suitable for public regulation. [...] Medical research is highly regulated. There are extensive federal regulations for the protection of human research subjects [which] explicitly prohibit the use of exculpatory agreements in any human subjects research. [...]

One of the important characteristics that Washington cases have identified when deciding if exculpatory clauses violate public policy is the practical importance of the activity in question. One author suggests that a survey of cases assessing exculpatory clauses reveals that the common determinative factor for Washington courts has been the services' or activities' importance to the public. [...] The fact that a given disease is not commonly encountered by members of the public does not make medical research into its cure of little public importance. Dr. Schoene's declaration emphasizes the seriousness of high altitude sickness and that it progresses from cerebral edema to coma and death. [...] We conclude that medical research, including research involved with attempts to find a way to avoid the onset of high altitude sickness, is a matter of public importance.

Another important consideration in deciding if an exculpatory clause violates public policy is whether the person who signs the release will be under the control of the person seeking exculpation for negligence and subject to the risk of that person's carelessness. The element of a researcher's control over a subject is common to most medical research projects and is one of the reasons why such strict regulations are imposed. Scholars on the subject of the ethics of medical research describe the relationship between investigator and subject as a fiduciary relationship.

In this case, the Defendant designed the research protocol, had the Plaintiff chart her symptoms twice daily, and had her test her oxygen saturation levels using an oximeter. Furthermore, the Defendant allegedly instructed the Plaintiff to use the breathing techniques the Defendant had taught her and to continue to ascend after the Plaintiff began exhibiting symptoms of high altitude sickness. Dr. Schoene's declaration explains that one of the known symptoms of altitude sickness is mental confusion and lack of judgment and that this made the Plaintiff particularly dependent on the leader of the research to inform her of the need to descend. Defendant MacGregor admitted she was the leader of the research, and it is reasonable to assume that one doing research on this illness would know of these symptoms. [...]

We wish to be very clear that it is only negligent conduct which cannot be the subject of a preinjury release. With proper informed consent, an ill patient may wish to consent to a highly experimental treatment which might otherwise not be generally accepted. [...] We conclude that a preinjury agreement, which releases a medical researcher for liability for negligent conduct which occurs in the course of medical research, violates public policy.

SECTION C. PRIMARY ASSUMPTION OF RISK

Cases to cut if you don't want to assign everything: *Hendricks* and perhaps *Cohen*.

Murphy v. Steeplechase Amusement Co. (P injured on "Flopper"; NL)
Woodall v. Wayne Steffner Productions ("Human Kite" injured when car goes too fast; L)
Cohen v. McIntyre (dog bites veterinarian; NL)
Neighbarger v. Irwin Industries (safety workers at petroleum plant burned trying to stop spill; L, as firefighter's rule doesn't apply to them)
Hendricks v. Broderick (one turkey hunter injured by another in woods; L)

Q. Was the defendant in *Murphy* negligent? If not, why bother with the doctrine of assumption of risk?
A. It is possible to argue, as Professor Sugarman does in *Assumption of Risk*, 31 Val.U.L.Rev. 833 (1997), that the doctrine of primary assumption of risk serves no really useful purpose; every case where it applies can more accurately be described as a case where the defendant had no duty, or where the duty wasn't breached, or where the breach didn't cause the plaintiff's harm. Thus Sugarman says that in *Murphy* the real reason the plaintiff loses is that there was no negligence on the part of the amusement park. Yet perhaps *Murphy* helps to illustrate the value of the assumption of risk doctrine after all, for on reflection it is not so easy to say whether the defendant was negligent. True, there wasn't much evidence that the defendant was operating the ride in an unintended or obviously defective manner (the case didn't go the jury on that theory, at any rate), but it still is possible to argue that it was negligent to offer a ride such as the Flopper with all its dangers. A safer ride, perhaps slower or more stable, should have been offered instead. But this argument would be hard to evaluate. The "B" of making the ride safer would not just be the out-of-pocket cost of doing so; it would also include the diminution in pleasure that thrill-seekers take from the attraction, and it would be hard to know how to compare these losses to the gains in safety. Stating the issue as a "reasonableness" test would be unhelpful, because a reasonable person might have little taste for a ride on the Flopper in the first place.

The assumption of risk doctrine helps sidestep these problems. We don't need to assess whether it was negligent to offer the Flopper. We only need to know that the plaintiff understood the risks involved and decided that for *him*, at least, the benefits seemed to outweigh the costs. The objective inquiry into whether the ride satisfied community standards is replaced by a more subjective inquiry into whether the plaintiff's private balance of costs and benefits was satisfied. There is a possible analogy to *Zalazar v. Vercimak*, the case in the chapter on factual causation where the plaintiff was injured when she sought to have the bags under her eyes removed and the procedure went badly. Applying an objective test—in other words, asking a jury to decide whether a reasonable person would have gone through with the procedure if informed of the risks—was impractical, because a reasonable person might have had no interest in having the surgery in the first place. So instead the inquiry was made subjective: we ask whether *this* plaintiff would have gone through with it if fully informed. In *Murphy* the issue might be considered similar. Maybe we aren't sure we can confidently say whether the defendant was negligent—and maybe we don't have to, since this wasn't a "stranger" case where one party hurt another out of the blue. It was a case where the plaintiff had a chance to think about whether the risks of the defendant's offering were outweighed by the fun of it. He decided they were. There is no reason to try to replace this judgment the plaintiff made for himself with a collective determination to the contrary.

Granted, primary assumption of risk is not usually dependent on particular findings about the plaintiff's subjective awareness of the risks involved; it is more often said to be a conclusion of law drawn from the parties' relationship. Still, it can serve a useful purpose in situations where the private conclusion the plaintiff drew about the costs and benefits of an activity seems a better basis for decision than a speculative attempt to make a collective judgment on the same points.

We offer some excerpts from Sugarman's article below.

Q. What is the difference between assumption of risk and comparative negligence? In either of the first two cases in this section are we saying that the plaintiff was negligent?
A. No. The plaintiffs were not (or at least not necessarily) negligent. Their behavior, including their decisions to participate in the dangerous activities involved, may well have been justified from either a reasonableness or a cost-benefit standpoint. This is an important point, because it is why assumption of risk in its primary sense bars recovery altogether, rather than just causing the plaintiff's damages to be reduced. Secondary assumption of risk is different: it applies when the defendant has indeed been negligent, and the negligence has harmed the plaintiff; it means the plaintiff is partly responsible for the harm caused to him by the plaintiff's negligence. Nowadays such a finding is likely just to cause a reduction in the plaintiff's damage award, operating much like comparative negligence (and indeed it has been subsumed into the doctrine of comparative negligence in many jurisdictions).

Q. What is the distinction between *Murphy v. Steeplechase Amusements* and *Woodall v. Wayne Steffner Productions?*
A. The cases might seem similar because of Cardozo's remark in *Murphy*: "Whether the movement of the belt was uniform or irregular, the risk at greatest was a fall. This was the very hazard that was invited and foreseen." But in *Woodall* the plaintiff was hurt by a danger that was not among those to which he consented: that the driver would go too fast; and this made his harm far more likely to occur. Indeed, Woodall was not supposed to come diving down to the ground, but Murphy was. And Woodall, unlike Murphy, had particular evidence that the machinery at issue (in his case, the car) wasn't operated properly. The general point is that one can assume the risks standardly involved in some activity without assuming the risk of every injury that can result from it. The cases would be more similar if the theory of liability in *Murphy* had been that the Flopper was operated at an unusually high speed. If Cardozo's language seems to the contrary, it's probably best considered incautious.

Q. What is the distinction between *Cohen v. McIntyre* and *Woodall v. Wayne Steffner Productions?*
A. In *Cohen* there were no misrepresentations made, and as a result the court thought it fair to assume that the risks the plaintiff assumed included what happened—the dog bite.

Q. What is the distinction between *Neighbarger v. Irwin Industries* and *Cohen v. McIntyre* (the NL case of the dog bite)?
A. The court in *Neighbarger* distinguished *Cohen* as follows:

> As defendant notes, the firefighter's rule, or more accurately, the doctrine of assumption of risk, has been held generally to exempt those who contract with veterinarians to treat their dogs from liability should the dog bite the veterinarian during treatment. Although the elements of public service and public compensation are missing, the "defendant's ordinary duty of care is *negated* due to the nature of the activity and the relationship of the defendant to the plaintiff." *Cohen v. McIntyre,* 16 Cal.App.4th at p. 655. Further, the court pointed out that "the risk of being attacked or bitten in the course of veterinary treatment is an occupational hazard which veterinarians accept by undertaking their employment and are in the best position to guard against by taking the necessary precautions. 'The risk of dog bites during treatment is a specific known hazard endemic to the very occupation in which plaintiff voluntarily engaged." [...]

> If the [veterinarian's] rule is based [...] on the defendant's relationship with the veterinarian, and the defendant's conduct in entrusting the animal to the professional care and control of the veterinarian, it may be sound. But like the classic firefighter's rule, it does not provide support for the application of the doctrine of assumption of risk when the defendant is a third party who has not secured the services of the plaintiff or otherwise entered into any relationship with the

plaintiff. In fact, the defendant in this case is not in the position of the dog owner who secures the services of a veterinarian. Rather, the defendant is more comparable to a person delivering dog food to a veterinarian's office—presumably such a person would be under a duty of care not to negligently cause the clientele to bite the veterinarian.

Q. What is the analogy between *Hendricks v. Broderick* and *Woodall v. Wayne Steffner Productions*?
A. In both cases the plaintiffs engaged in dangerous activities, but did not assume the risk that someone else involved in the activities would act negligently.

Q. What is the distinction between *Hendricks v. Broderick* and *Murphy v. Steeplechase Amusement Co.*?
A. In *Hendricks* the defendant was negligent, and in being negligent exposed the plaintiff to risks beyond those he had assumed. In *Murphy* the defendants were not negligent, and (equivalently) exposed the plaintiffs involved only to the risks they knowingly assumed.

Q. Hypothetical: in *Herrle v. Marshall*, 53 Cal.Rptr.2d 713 (Cal. App. 1996), the plaintiff worked at a convalescent hospital as a nurse's aide. The hospital had many patients suffering from Alzheimer's disease, one of whom was a woman named Marshall. One day the plaintiff saw a nurse trying move Marshall from a chair to a bed. Marshall had become combative, and the plaintiff was worried that she would fall to the floor; when the plaintiff entered the room to help, however, Marshall struck her about the head several times, injuring her jaw. The plaintiff sued Marshall's estate to recover for her injuries. The trial court found for the defendant after a bench trial. The court of appeals affirmed:

> Plaintiff was engaged as an aide in a convalescent hospital to assume responsibility to care for mentally incompetent patients, many of whom are occasionally violent. Marshall was placed specifically in the hospital's care in part to protect her from injuring herself and others because of her violent tendencies. In the words of [*Knight v. Jewett*, 834 P.2d 696], "the nature of the activity" was the protection of the patient from doing harm to herself or others; "the parties' relationship to the activity" was plaintiff's professional responsibility to provide this protection, the "particular risk of harm that caused the injury" was the very risk plaintiff and her employer were hired to prevent.

From the dissent:

> Public policy supports finding liability in this case. As the California Psychiatric Association states in its amicus brief supporting Herrle, "[H]ad Ms. Herrle known that the trial court would apply the doctrine of primary assumption of the risk to rule categorically that she could not recover from the patient's liability insurer for any injuries she suffered in coming to the patient's aid, she might have taken the safer course of not intervening to protect the patient and the other health care provider who was endangered by the patient. As a result of the trial court's [and the majority's] ruling, it will be much more likely that caregivers will use impersonal mechanisms, such as seclusion and restraint, to control patients and, thereby protect themselves at the expense of more humane treatment for the patients. This result is antithetical to good patient care."]

Q. Another hypothetical—or perhaps it's better offered just as an illustration during class discussion—can be built from *Powell v. Metropolitan Entertainment Co.*, 762 N.Y.S.2d 782 (N.Y.S.Ct. 2003), the plaintiff was a 51-year-old attorney who claimed that his hearing was damaged by the loud music played at a concert staged by John Fogerty, the former singer and guitarist for Creedance Clearwater Revival. The plaintiff sued Fogerty, his management company, and the concert hall to recover for his injuries. The trial court gave summary judgment to the defendants:

> This Court finds that the "primary assumption of risk" doctrine is appropriate in concert cases and

is applicable here. That "loud music" can cause hearing impairment is "perfectly obvious" and "commonly appreciated." In making this determination, this Court finds that an objective, reasonable person standard applies, and that an objective, reasonable, 51-year-old lawyer, particularly one who has experienced ringing in his ears after prior concerts, would know that loud music can cause hearing impairment.

Plaintiff argues that the conditions were not as safe as they appeared to be because the Ballroom had recently been stripped of some drapes and, thus, as one of defendants' employees testified, the room was "vibrant." However, even assuming defendants did not simply compensate for this by rotating their knobs a notch or two counterclockwise during the de rigeur sound checks that precede every concert, plaintiff was in a position to hear exactly how loud the music was. Indeed, plaintiff had noticed that the opening act, apparently an a capella singing group, was rather loud. He elected to stay for the headliner, complete with guitars, bass, and drums, obviously aware that the volume would only rise. […]

This Court is well aware of the suffering that a hearing loss and related conditions such as tinnitus can cause. However, in the final analysis, whether concerts are "too loud" should be decided by the legislature or the marketplace, not by the courts. Litigation by an "eggshell ear" plaintiff is not an appropriate means to impose an unlegislated noise code upon performers who want to perform a certain way, and their legions of screaming fans, who want them to do just that. Lawyers learn in law school that a plaintiff with an "eggshell skull" can collect from an assailant who inflicts a slight blow to the head. However, the instant plaintiff is in the position of an "eggshell skull plaintiff" who chose to stand in a thunderous hailstorm, and who, unfortunately, cannot now be heard to complain.

Lowe v. California League of Professional Baseball (P hit by foul ball when distracted by mascot during baseball game; L)
Hackbart v. Cincinnati Bengals, Inc. (one football player strikes another after play is dead; L)

Q. What result in *Lowe v. California League of Professional Baseball?*
A. The trial court gave summary judgment to the defendants. The court of appeals reversed. It's a fun problem because most students have been to baseball games and can think about the scope of the risks they assumed. You also can spin off interesting hypotheticals based on the other cases the *Lowe* court describes in its opinion (and considered distinguishable):

Defendants were able to persuade the trial court, under the doctrine of primary assumption of the risk, that defendants owed no duty to plaintiff, as a spectator, to protect him from foul balls. Such rationalization was faulty. […] [D]efendants had a duty *not to increase* the inherent risks to which spectators at professional baseball games are regularly exposed and which they assume. As a result, a triable issue of fact remained, namely whether the Quakes' mascot cavorting in the stands and distracting plaintiff's attention, *while the game was in progress,* constituted a breach of that duty, i.e., constituted negligence in the form of increasing the inherent risk to plaintiff of being struck by a foul ball. […]

[U]nder the holding in *Neinstein v. Los Angeles Dodgers,* 185 Cal.App.3d 176, 229, *absent any distraction by the mascot,* that plaintiff could have assumed the risk. Justice Compton, writing in *Neinstein,* observed that the plaintiff "voluntarily elected to sit in a seat which was clearly unprotected by any form of screening.... She was sufficiently warned of the risk by common knowledge of the nature of the sport.... The Dodgers were under no duty to do anything further to protect her from the hazard." However, in *Neinstein,* there was no mascot bothering the plaintiff and thus distracting her attention from the playing field.   Thus, *Neinstein* is readily distinguishable.

The same can be said of [*Clapman v. City of New York,* 468 N.E.2d 697] decided by the Court of Appeals of New York. In that case, a spectator at Yankee Stadium was struck by a foul ball. He contended that a vendor moving in front of him obscured his view. As to this contention, the court said that "respondents had no duty to insure that vendors moving about the stadium did not interfere with Clapman's view." That is not this case. In *Clapman,* the plaintiff at all times was facing the field of play. Here, plaintiff, because of the distraction, had turned away. This presents a substantially different set of facts, recognized at once by anyone who has ever attended a professional baseball game.

Incidentally, the Quakes are a Class A minor league affiliate of the Anaheim Angels. The "Epicenter," where the Quakes play, was named Best Class A Ballpark in the country by *Baseball America* magazine in 2003.

From Sugarman, *Assumption of Risk*, 31 Val.U.L.Rev. 833 (1997):

Many cases in which the courts talk about "assumption of risk" are best understood as ones in which there simply has been no negligence, or more precisely, "no breach" of the duty to exercise due care. Although the Flopper case, which I already discussed, is a prime example, I will focus now on a different, very familiar situation. Suppose you are a spectator at a baseball game and you are struck by a foul ball while seated in an area of the stadium that is not protected from such balls by a screen. Although this sort of injury is often said to be governed by the principle of "assumption of risk," that is a mistake. The reason you lose the case is that the defendant's conduct was reasonable.

Surely it cannot be negligent merely to promote the national pastime. Obviously, we want to attend live baseball games, we don't want baseballs constructed of soft material, and arming each fan with some sort of individual protective shield seems silly as well. Moreover, despite the slight danger, we don't want all the stadium seats fenced, just as we don't want the seats all moved so far back from the game to be out of reach of foul balls. Either of those precautions would deprive the fans of an important pleasure they ought to be able to enjoy—seeing the game relatively up-close without the annoyance of having to look through a screen. Rather, we only want the seats to be screened where the risk from foul balls is especially great, a precaution that I assume was taken in the stadium where you were injured. That is, I assume you were struck in a location where no case for screening could reasonably be made.

In short, while spectator foul ball injuries are a regrettable by-product of baseball, they are generally not injuries that we should blame on the stadium operators because there was nothing careless about their behavior. Hence "assumption of risk" is beside the point.

Indeed, the "no breach" analysis explains why, for example, even very young children in attendance at the game, who do not really know anything about baseball or the danger of being hit by a foul ball, also properly lose their cases. In the leading California case on the subject, Judge Wood gets into trouble when he writes, "by voluntarily entering into the sport as a spectator he knowingly accepts the reasonable risks and hazards inherent in and incident to the game." Fans struck by foul balls do indeed lose because the risks created are reasonable, but not because they knowingly accepted them. In the case before the court the plaintiff alleged that since she was ignorant of baseball, had never been to a ball park before, and was paying no attention to the game at the time, she "cannot be said to have knowingly assumed the risk." The opinion tries to escape from this seemingly telling point (given the court's analysis) by evading it—talking about the risks being "common knowledge," and that they are "imputed to her," and that they "should have been observed by her" (piling on yet more confusion by suggesting, quite wrongly I believe, that first-time adult spectators at baseball games are somehow at fault if they choose to spend the afternoon talking with a friend rather than watching the action).

Rather, to repeat, for both the first-time fan and the five-year-old fan, just as for the experienced fan, being hit by a foul ball is just bad luck—because there is just nothing more that should reasonably have been done to protect the victim from the danger. Obviously, if foul ball injuries were much more common and much more harmful, we might well think differently about the precautions that stadium operators should take.

Q. What result in *Hackbart v. Cincinnati Bengals, Inc.?*
A. The trial court gave judgment to the defendant after a bench trial, as the text shows. The decision was reversed on appeal. Said the court:

> The evidence at the trial uniformly supported the proposition that the intentional striking of a player in the head from the rear is not an accepted part of either the playing rules or the general customs of the game of professional football. [...] The [trial] judge compared football to coal mining and railroading insofar as all are inherently hazardous. Judge Matsch said that in the case of football it was questionable whether social values would be improved by limiting the violence. [...]

> Contrary to the position of the [trial] court [...] there are no principles of law which allow a court to rule out certain tortious conduct by reason of general roughness of the game or difficulty of administering it.

> Indeed, the evidence shows that there are rules of the game which prohibit the intentional striking of blows. Thus, Article 1, Item 1, Subsection C, provides that:

> > All players are prohibited from striking on the head, face or neck with the heel, back or side of the hand, wrist, forearm, elbow or clasped hands.

> Thus the very conduct which was present here is expressly prohibited by the rule which is quoted above.

> The general customs of football do not approve the intentional punching or striking of others. That this is prohibited was supported by the testimony of all of the witnesses. They testified that the intentional striking of a player in the face or from the rear is prohibited by the playing rules as well as the general customs of the game. Punching or hitting with the arms is prohibited. Undoubtedly these restraints are intended to establish reasonable boundaries so that one football player cannot intentionally inflict a serious injury on another. Therefore, the notion is not correct that all reason has been abandoned, whereby the only possible remedy for the person who has been the victim of an unlawful blow is retaliation.

You can spin out many interesting hypothetical variations on *Hackbart*: is an assumption of risk defense if a football player is hurt when he is "speared" during a play? (Spearing means hitting another player with your head down, so that your helmet becomes a weapon; it can seriously injure a player, and is punished with a 15-yard penalty. Which way does the existence of the penalty cut in the tort suit?) Is there an assumption of risk defense to the battery claim that might arise if a baseball player is hurt when an opposing pitcher throws at his head, or when a player is hurt when a bench-clearing brawl follows such an "headhunting" incident, or when hockey players get into fights (as they very frequently do), or when Mike Tyson bites off part of Evander Holyfield's ear during a boxing match?

From Sugarman, *Assumption of Risk*, 31 Val.U.L.Rev. 833 (1997):

[T]here may well be good policy reasons generally to prevent lawsuits by professional athletes for injuries suffered as part of the game through the fault of other participants. The broad argument here is […] that courts should keep out of the business of resolving disputes within professional athletics because the social objectives that tort law might serve by providing a remedy are already effectively dealt with through parallel institutions.

Specifically, professional sports have their own special rules (and rule-making bodies), their own umpires and referees, and their own penalty structure (both during the game and afterwards when higher-up officials can impose even stronger sanctions). Hence, in most professional sports there already exists, outside the formal legal system, an elaborate structure to deal with goals of deterrence, punishment and justice. Moreover, professional athletes (and their leagues) typically (although not always) have reasonably generous injury insurance schemes that go well beyond what workers' compensation would provide, thereby, arguably, eclipsing tort law's compensatory function. Finally, as an administrative matter, were tort law to try to offer a remedy for ordinary negligence, there might be considerable uncertainty and inconsistency in deciding whether certain conduct was fairly treated as negligence. Examples here include a wild pitch or throw in baseball, or tackling to break up the flow of the game in soccer—conduct which, on the one hand, may be undesired by the injurer but perhaps not reasonably avoidable in the heat of play, or, on the other hand, conduct which, although "penalized" by the officials, is generally treated by the players as a legitimate "part of the sport."

In sum, it is perhaps well justified to deny recovery in tort to a professional athlete for an injury arising from what would otherwise be viewed by the jury in a specific case as the negligence of another competitor. Nonetheless, the ["volenti non fit injuria"] principle is not the persuasive justification[.] […] Rather, the explanation I have put forward is of the sort classically used to justify a "no duty" rule.

Notice further that, if the sporting behavior in question (or perhaps I should say, the "unsportsmanlike conduct" in question) goes too far beyond the bounds of routine misconduct within the sport, or perhaps if the game's officials are seen by the courts as having lost control of the sport, then the judges may well conclude that tort law has a role to play after all, and they achieve this result by recognizing a legal duty of care. […] Yet this line, if and when it is crossed, does not have anything to do with the point at which the risk of physical injury, in any real sense, ceases to be assumed, since athletes voluntarily compete knowing that they are at risk of flagrant infractions as well. Put differently, for the participants, it is not any more "all right" for opponents to carelessly injure them than it is for opponents to recklessly or intentionally injure them. Rather, the courts probably sensibly draw that line on grounds that, once the defendant's conduct has become flagrant, the policy reasons that free an athlete from liability for injuring an opponent no longer apply.

SECTION D. SECONDARY ASSUMPTION OF RISK

This section is pretty brief as is, so there isn't much room for cutting. *Fagan v. Atnalta* is probably the best teaching case if you're just looking for one that gives students a sense of the issue.

Marshall v. Ranne (P bitten by D's boar on his own property; L)
Kennedy v. Rhode Island Hockey Club (P hit by puck while in audience at hockey game; NL)
Hennessey v. Pyne (P hit by ball from golf course next to her residence; L)
Fagan v. Atnalta (P tries to break up bar fight and gets beaten; NL: he assumed the risk)

Q. Ranne could have just shot the hog. Why didn't *that* alternative, and his failure to use it, mean that he assumed the risk of attack?
A. Here is what the court had to say about that possibility:

> Defendant Ranne argues also that the plaintiff Marshall had yet another alternative,*261 that of shooting the hog. The proof showed that Marshall was an expert marksman and had a gun in his house with which he could have killed the hog. Plaintiff Marshall testified that he was reluctant to destroy his neighbor's animal because he did not know how Ranne would react. We do not regard the slaughter of the animal as a reasonable alternative, because plaintiff would have subjected himself arguably to charges under the provision of two criminal statutes.

The criminal statutes the court has in mind are mentioned in a footnote:

> Whoever shall wilfully maim, wound or disfigure any horse, ass, mule, cattle, sheep, goat, swine, dog or other domesticated animal, or whoever shall wilfully kill, maim, wound, poison, or disfigure any dog, domesticated bird or fowl of another with intent to injure the owner thereof, shall be fined not less than Ten Dollars ($10) nor more than Two Hundred Dollars ($200). In prosecutions under this Article the intent to injure may be presumed from the perpetration of the act.' Art. 1373, Texas Penal Code.'Whoever knowingly kills any unmarked or unbranded animal of the cattle species, or any unmarked hog, sheep or goat, not his own, shall be fined not less than twenty-five nor more than one hundred dollars. It shall only be necessary to allege and prove that the animal killed was not the property of the accused, without stating or proving the true owner.' Art. 1462, Texas Penal Code.

Q. What is the superficial similarity between *Marshall v. Ranne* and *Kennedy v. Rhode Island Hockey Club*? What is the distinction between them?
A. In both cases the plaintiff was put to an unwelcome set of alternatives: stay inside or brave the hog (in *Marshall*), or go home or take the seat near the ice (in *Kennedy*). But in *Kennedy* the bad alternative was undesirable because it was expensive, not because it was dangerous or because it put the plaintiff to a choice that the defendant had no right to impose.

Q. What is the distinction between *Hennessey v. Pyne* and *Kennedy v. Rhode Island Hockey Club* (the NL case where the plaintiff was hit by a hockey puck)?
A. The court in *Hennessey* did not hold that the plaintiff *didn't* assume the risk; it just held that summary judgment was inappropriate. It offered three distinctions of *Kennedy*, where summary judgment was granted:

1. Even if Hennessey was aware of the risk, it does not necessarily follow that she voluntarily accepted it. She may have had no reasonable alternative course of conduct. "[B]y pleading assumption of the risk as a defense, Pyne should not have been allowed via summary judgment to condemn Hennessey, whenever the golf course was playable, to the Hobson's choice of home confinement in her Plexiglas bunker or of venturing outside subject to being suddenly stoned by a mishit golf ball." "The 'alternatives' open to Hennessey—moving away, avoiding all going out of doors during daylight hours when golfers are on the course, or the wearing of some type of protective armor when she ventures forth during playing hours—do not strike us as options that are so reasonable on their face as to convert Hennessey's alleged assumption of the risk into a summary judgment question." (Citing *Marshall v. Ranne* and the Restatement (Second) provision that appears later in the chapter.)

2. Unlike the plaintiff in *Kennedy*, Hennessey was neither a participant in the game being played nor a spectator of it. (Perhaps the idea is that Hennessey was not receiving the kind of benefits from the risky activity that make the assumption of risk doctrine a more comfortable fit in cases like *Kennedy*.)

3. Hennessey apparently lived in her condominium *before* golf started to be played on the adjacent property. This again ties into the relationship between assumption of risk and various benefits that the plaintiff may enjoy from it; here she had not received compensation for the risk ex ante, as she might have if she had moved in after the hazard had been established. The court thus distinguished this case from a New York decision that contained this language: "one who deliberately decides to reside in the suburbs on very desirable lots adjoining golf clubs and thus receive the social benefits and other not inconsiderable advantages of country club surroundings must accept the occasional, concomitant annoyances."

Q. What is the distinction between *Fagan v. Atnalta* and *Marshall v. Ranne?*
A. In *Marshall* the plaintiff did not voluntarily confront the risk. Granted, the confrontation was voluntary in that Marshall could have shot the boar earlier. But for policy reasons the court is loath to impose such an expectation on people in the plaintiff's position. The plaintiff also could have stayed inside, but in defining "voluntary" we treat the plaintiff's full enjoyment of his property rights as a baseline of neutrality rather than regarding it as an assumption of any risk of harm that might be inflicted there by the defendant or its animals (cf. *Hull v. Scruggs*—the "egg sucking dog" case in the chapter on privileges to commit prima facie intentional torts).
In *Fagan* the plaintiff could have declined to subject himself to the danger caused by the defendant's negligence, and in making that decision he would not have been forfeiting any baseline rights he was thought to have; he could have sat at the bar nursing his drink, which is what the common law entitles him to do.

Q. What is the distinction between *Fagan* and *Woodall* (the L case of the human kite)?
A. The superficial similarity is that in both cases the plaintiff deliberately did something dangerous and came to grief because of the defendant's negligence. In *Fagan,* however, the plaintiff saw the manifestations of the defendant's negligence but proceeded anyway. In *Woodall* the plaintiff expected certain dangers to exist in connection with his stunt, but negligence by the defendant was not one of them. *Woodall* would be similar to *Fagan* if the plaintiff—the Human Kite—had learned that the driver the defendants provided was inexperienced, but went ahead with the stunt anyway.

Q. What is the distinction between *Fagan* and *Wagner v. Int'l Ry. Co.* ("danger invites rescue"?).
A. The point of *Wagner* was that an initial act of negligence can be the proximate cause of subsequent rescue efforts and injuries that they produce. The plaintiff's claim in *Fagan* did not fail for want of proximate cause; it foundered on the affirmative defense of assumption of risk, an issue on which the court in *Wagner* did not pass; it was left to the jury in *Wagner* to determine whether the plaintiff's rescue efforts were unreasonable. But perhaps this is not a complete answer, because the court in *Fagan* does not say that the plaintiff necessarily was *unreasonable;* it just says that he assumed the risks of involvement. Why can't *this* much at least be said of the plaintiff in *Wagner*? The defendant there was described as arguing, after all, that the plaintiff "had time to reflect and weigh; impulse had been followed by choice; and choice, in the defendant's view, intercepts and breaks the sequence." This sounds like the stuff that arguments for assumption of risk are made of. Perhaps the distinction between the cases has to do with the intervening intentionality of the conduct by the belligerent bar patrons.

From Sugarman, *Assumption of Risk*, 31 Val.U.L.Rev. 833 (1997):

Suppose you go out dancing at a nightclub. You meet someone who offers to drive you to a second club. Your new friend clearly has been drinking too much, although you have not. But you are in a carefree mood and agree to go along. You see just how unsteady your friend is both while walking to the car and as your friend drives through the parking lot toward the street. Yet you remain in the car and say nothing. Sure enough, about two blocks away your friend smashes the car into a tree, and you are hurt. Assuming your state has neither an automobile guest statute (now a rarity) nor a comprehensive auto no-fault plan (which currently exists in North America only in Quebec), what happens when you sue the car's driver in tort? Volenti non fit injuria—you clearly assumed the risk. Do you lose? My sense is that the clear majority, if not universal rule, is "no," and properly so. [...]

[T]he attitude of tort law today towards my example of you riding with your drunk driver friend is "a plague on both of your houses." The driver was clearly negligent in driving while seriously inebriated; you, too, were negligent, however, by accepting a ride in those circumstances. The way we punish you both for your combined foolishness is by making the defendant pay something, but at the same time by denying you full recovery. To be sure, the timorous would have stayed at the first club. But going for the ride is not the same as signing away your right to sue. To be sure, in this instance, even the venturous would have refused the ride. But, as I have just said, your contributory negligence, almost everywhere, is no longer a complete bar; instead, you will obtain a partial recovery, something like, say, three-quarters of your damages.

One more thing. A person might well ask why does tort law consider the drunk driver negligent when the passenger was willing to go along for the ride? The paradigm case for the application of the modern notion of comparative negligence, after all, is one in which both parties are carelessly inattentive—for example, one motorist is talking to a passenger and not paying attention to his speed or the road ahead while the other motorist pulls away from the curb without checking for traffic from the rear. [...] But not all careless conduct is inattentive or oblivious, or the product of misjudgment or poor application of skill. That is to say, sometimes actors may be said to be "knowingly" or perhaps even "deliberately" negligent. That was certainly the case in the drunk driving example before us. A fundamental policy issue therefore is whether this latter sort of conduct by plaintiffs—about which it may be said "assumption of risk"—should be treated in a different way from inattentive negligence. On the whole, the answer has been to treat the two the same.

In order to understand why that is so, the first thing to note is that this is tort law, not contract law. The community sets standards of behavior in tort law, not the parties themselves. Still, one might press, if the parties are willing to run the danger, why does the community demand more of them? Why does it, in effect, paternalize them, telling them to act safer than they apparently felt was necessary? In short, why doesn't it treat the car ride like the Flopper? This actually is a very difficult question about which I will have more to say later. For now, however, let me offer at least three reasons that together seem reasonably compelling in this situation.

First, the drunk driver endangered not just the passenger, but others on the road as well, and since we are eager to discourage and punish drunk driving generally, we are not about to let the driver off completely just because, as it happens, only the passenger was hurt.

Second, the drunk driver was far more dangerous to the passenger than the Flopper was to its participants. And so, even if the passenger and the drunk driver want to get their kicks like this, we, the rest of society, simply do not approve of that in the way we do approve of people running some other risks. After all, if someone is hurt, which is all too likely in this situation, the rest of us are probably going to have to pick up some or all of the tab through public or private insurance arrangements, but we are not eager to do that. This is in contrast to the Flopper situation where we think of the plaintiff as merely a victim of fate, like someone who happens to be hit by lightning and now needs medical care.

Third, even though the passenger willingly got in the car at the time, this is probably the sort of risk that the passenger would candidly acknowledge, in the light of day, that he should not have run. This is unlike the Flopper situation, which presumably continued to draw its patrons, even those in line when the plaintiff in that case was hurt. Indeed, the very victim of the Flopper would probably like to try the ride again, at least if his knee were up to it.

A needful doctrine? (Problems)

The most interesting question about secondary assumption of risk is whether it can and should survive the rise of comparative negligence. If a plaintiff makes a foolish or otherwise unreasonable decision to assume some risk created by the defendant, the doctrine of assumption of risk is not needed to provide at least some accounting for this; the plaintiff's damages will be reduced under comparative negligence (though recovery will not be altogether denied, as secondary assumption of risk would hold; which penalty for the plaintiff is preferable?). But secondary assumption of risk still could have distinctive bite in cases where the plaintiff made a *reasonable,* cost-justified decision to confront some hazard created by the defendant, and then was hurt. Under principles of comparative negligence such a plaintiff would collect all resulting damages from the defendant, but under secondary assumption of risk such a plaintiff would not collect anything. The reason the latter result troubles some people is that by assumption the defendant was acting unreasonably and the plaintiff was acting reasonably—yet the plaintiff still collects nothing. Why should this be? These problems are an invitation to explore those questions. They raise hard, fundamental issues regarding the purpose of tort liability.

As an additional hypothetical, you can offer the facts of the old *Meistrich* case. I operate a skating rink, and you come to the grand opening. When you arrive I explain that I negligently failed to freeze the ice properly, so the rink is too slippery. I give you the choice of proceeding anyway or not. You enter the rink and slip and hurt yourself. Under comparative negligence the question is whether you acted reasonably in deciding to try to skate on the extra-slippery ice. Under secondary assumption of risk the question is just whether you fully appreciated the danger.

Maybe it seems obvious that someone who chooses to skate on ice that was negligently frozen is acting at least somewhat unreasonably, but that isn't necessarily so. Suppose you (a somewhat clumsy, amateur skater) enter the rink without notice of its excessive slipperiness. You slip and fall. You collect in full from the defendant, because the defendant was negligent and you were not. Now suppose that Bobby Orr (the hockey player—but insert your own professional skater of choice here) enters the rink from another angle and does receive notice of the slipperiness. He decides to skate anyway, because he needs the practice and is confident—reasonably so, let's assume—that with his high level of skill he can navigate it without hurting himself. Alas, he does slip and suffers various injuries. Perhaps he, too, will collect in full from the defendant. But does it make sense to treat you and Orr the same way here? It is true that you both acted reasonably while in either case the defendant did not; yet there is a difference: Orr knew what he was getting into. Shouldn't that count for something? Perhaps the answer depends in part on whether the purpose of tort liability is regarding as being to create incentives for people to behave in a cost-justified manner or to vindicate notions of autonomy.

CHAPTER 11

DEFAMATION

SECTION A. INTRODUCTION

We don't discuss this at any length.

SECTION B. DEFINING "DEFAMATORY."

Cuttable cases: *Wildstein, Oles, Louisville Times v. Stivers, Gross v. Cantor*. If the latter two cases are omitted, be sure to keep the Restatement excerpt after *Gross v. Cantor*.

Grant v. Reader's Digest Association (P accused of association with Communist Party; L)
Stevens v. Tillman (P called "racist"; NL)
Dilworth v. Dudley (P called "crank"; NL)
Wildstein v. New York Post Corp. (P said to be "associated" with man not her husband; L)

Q. What is the distinction between *Stevens v. Tillman* and *Grant v. Reader's Digest Association*?
A. The irony of the cases is that many people—most?—nowadays would consider it worse to be thought a racist than to be thought a Communist; yet calling someone the latter name is held defamatory while the former is not. The reason is that calling someone a racist, at least today, can mean many different things, or almost nothing. It does not necessarily imply any embarrassing factual state of affairs; often it may just be the defendant's way of saying that the plaintiff's thought processes are infected with stereotypes or prejudices, which generally will be impossible to prove or disprove. Calling someone a Communist usually, though not necessarily, has clearer factual implications. More from the *Stevens* opinion, fyi:

> Formerly a "racist" was a believer in the superiority of one's own race, often a supporter of slavery or segregation, or a fomenter of hatred among the races. Stevens, the principal of a largely-black school in a large city, obviously does not believe that blacks should be enslaved or that Jim Crow should come to Illinois; no one would have inferred these things from the accusation. Politicians sometimes use the term much more loosely, as referring to anyone (not of the speaker's race) who opposes the speaker's political goals—on the "rationale" that the speaker espouses only what is good for the jurisdiction (or the audience), and since one's opponents have no cause to oppose what is beneficial, their opposition must be based on race. The term used this way means only: "He is neither for me nor of our race; and I invite you to vote your race." When Stevens called Tillman a "racist", Stevens was accusing Tillman of playing racial politics in this way rather than of believing in segregation or racial superiority. That may be an unfortunate brand of politics, but it also drains the term of its former, decidedly opprobrious, meaning. The term has acquired intermediate meanings too. The speaker may use "she is a racist" to mean "she is condescending to me, which must be because of my race because there is no other reason to condescend"—a reaction that attaches racial connotations to what may be an inflated opinion of one's self—or to mean "she thinks all black mothers are on welfare, which is stereotypical". Meanings of this sort fit comfortably within the immunity for name-calling.

Q. Hypothetical: in *Buckley v. Littell*, 539 F.2d 882 (2d Cir. 1976), the defendant wrote a book called *Wild Tongues: A Handbook of Social Pathology* that purported to discuss political extremism on the right and left. The book described Buckley as a "fellow traveler" of "fascism," and said that Buckley acted as a "deceiver" and used his journalistic position to spread materials from "openly fascist journals" under the guise of responsible conservatism. Buckley sued for libel. What result?

A. No liability. The trial court found for Buckley: "(W)hen Littell speaks of Buckley as a fellow traveler of fascism, indicating that he sympathizes with and promotes conspiracy and subversion . . . we are surely dealing with questions of fact, and not merely ideas." The Second Circuit reversed:

> We find, to the contrary, that the use of "fascist," "fellow traveler" and "radical right" as political labels in *Wild Tongues* cannot be regarded as having been proved to be statements of fact, among other reasons, because of the tremendous imprecision of the meaning and usage of these terms in the realm of political debate, an imprecision which is simply echoed in the book. This is not a case such as *Greenbelt Cooperative Publishing Ass'n v. Bresler*, 398 U.S. at 22, 23, relied on by the district court, where a word is used which has only two precisely articulable meanings. There, for example, the word "blackmail" was found in context to refer to hard or unfair bargaining rather than to an allegation of the commission of a punishable crime. The concept "fellow traveler" of "fascism" by contrast is referable to a whole range of meanings and characteristics. The search for the precisely articulable meaning of the statements about Buckley to the ordinary reader could only be, in a sense, an arbitrary one because of the ambiguous and sometimes even contradictory content of the terminology necessarily utilized in Littell's polemical tract. This is not a case where a person is being accused of being a member of the Communist Party, or a legislative representative of the Communist Party, as in the New York cases relied upon by the district court, all of which incidentally predate *New York Times Co. v. Sullivan*, e. g., *Toomey v. Farley*, 138 N.E.2d 221 (N.Y. 1956); *Grant v. Readers Digest Ass'n, Inc.*, 151 F.2d 733 (2d Cir. 1945) (Learned Hand, J.). Such allegations of membership or well-defined political affiliation are readily perceivable as allegations of fact susceptible to proof or disproof of falsity. They are quite dissimilar to the terms "fellow traveler," "fascism" and "radical right" which, whether as used by Littell or as perceived by a reader, are concepts whose content is so debatable, loose and varying, that they are insusceptible to proof of truth or falsity. The use of these terms in the present context is in short within the realm of protected opinion and idea under *Gertz*. [...]

> We find further that there was nothing libelous in the statement as it appears in Wild Tongues that the National Review and "On the Right" frequently "print 'news items' and interpretations picked up from the openly fascist journals." The issue of what constitutes an "openly fascist" journal is as much a matter of opinion or idea as is the question what constitutes " fascism" or the "radical right" in *Wild Tongues*. See note 5, supra. Buckley himself admitted that he or the National Review had occasionally printed items and interpretations picked up from openly fascist journals even as he defined them, although "for the purpose of denouncing them." Surely the difference of opinion between Buckley and Littell regarding what is "approval" of what one calls "fascist" and the other calls "radical right" or "denunciation" of the same highly debatable categories cannot give rise to recovery by the one against the other in this case.

Q. What is the distinction between *Dilworth v. Dudley* and *Grant v. Reader's Digest Association*?

A. Again, part of the distinction is that "Communist" has harder factual implications than "crank." As a practical matter it would be hard to have a trial to determine whether the plaintiff is a crank; this administrative problem by itself cuts against finding it defamatory, but it also suggests that the word "crank" doesn't conjure up as clear (and thus as clearly defamatory) a factual meaning as "Communist." An additional and related point is that to call someone a crank is to express a judgment about their ideas. The free expression of those judgments is valuable, as it aids the reader's attempts to determine which ideas are sound and unsound; so we don't want such remarks chilled by worries that they have to be supportable in court. There is no similar value to being able to mislabel someone a Communist or member of any other movement.

Q. What is the distinction between *Wildstein v. New York Post Corp.* and *Stevens v. Tillman* (the NL case where the plaintiff was called a "racist")? What is the distinction between *Wildstein* and *Dilworth v. Dudley*?
A. The cases might seem similar because in all of them the defendant used vague language with negative implications to talk about the plaintiff. The distinction is that in *Wildstein*, the word "associated" with scare quotes around it implied particular facts about the plaintiff's conduct. Saying that a woman had an extramarital affair is defamatory, so it's also defamatory to convey that meaning more elliptically. "Racist" and "crank" were not thought to be conveying any comparably precise factual claim, even elliptically.

Saunders v. Board of Directors, WHYY-TV (P, a prison inmate, said to be an informant; NL)
Braun v. Armour & Co. (P, a kosher deli, said to sell bacon; L)
Oles v. Pittsburg Times (D recites suggestion that P is a witch; L)

Q. What is the distinction between *Saunders v. Board of Directors* and *Grant v. Reader's Digest Association*? What is the distinction between *Saunders* and *Braun v. Armour & Co.*?
A. In *Braun* and *Grant*, the statements at issue discredited the plaintiff in the eyes of a respectable portion of the community. In *Saunders* the plaintiff was discredited only in the eyes of fellow inmates and perhaps crooks at large—not a respectable segment of society, or so the courts say. In a case that had facts similar to *Saunders* and reached a similar outcome, the court put the point this way:

> This result is compelled by the rule that, in order to be libelous, a false communication must hold the plaintiff up to scorn or ridicule in the eyes of a *significant* element of the community. The criminal element, albeit the milieu within which plaintiff's misdeeds have placed him, is simply not such an element:

> "A communication to be defamatory need not tend to prejudice the other in the eyes of everyone in the community or all of his associates, nor even in the eyes of a majority of them. It is enough that the communication would tend to prejudice him in the eyes of a substantial *and* respectable minority of them . . . . The fact that a communication tends to prejudice another in the eyes of even a substantial group is not enough if the group is one whose standards are so anti-social that it is not proper for the courts to recognize them . . . ." Restatement (Second) of Torts s 559, Comment e (1977) (Emphasis added).

Burrascano v. Levi, 452 F.Supp. 1066 (D.Md. 1978). An economic way to view the distinction might be that in *Braun* the defendant's words, assuming of course that they were false, could have misled the public into missing out on beneficial transactions. In *Saunders* that wasn't true—or was it? Now no inmates are likely to talk to Saunders and give him any juicy information, but that's not a cost if Saunders really *isn't* an informant; and his denial of informant status is a necessary part of his claim. So maybe the real cost is that nobody will want to become an informant anymore if they can be "outed" with impunity. And yet that can't quite be the point, either, because if someone really *is* an informant they have no possible claim for defamation on facts like these: the statements would be true, and truth is a good defense to a defamation claim. (The case is thus a good chance to drill students on the importance of remembering that in all these cases the statements must be assumed to be false.)

The strong criticism of *Saunders* is simpler. The defendants said something false about him and as a result may have caused him severe injuries at the hands of his fellow inmates. But maybe this result can be defended as an outlier consequence of a more general rule that usually makes better sense. Courts don't want defamation suits arising from statements that generally would be considered praise just because the statements make criminals mad. But the general rule works better when the plaintiff isn't locked into a building full of members of the "bad" community. The result in *Saunders* thus strikes us as dubious as a matter of policy.

Q. Imagine a variation on *Saunders* in which the plaintiff, Saunders, is embroiled in a long-standing feud with a neighbor of his regarding the erection of an ugly fence Saunders built along the edge of his yard. Saunders is imprisoned for some reason—perhaps a drug bust. Now his neighbor, who is a journalist or who knows one, maliciously announces that Saunders is an FBI informant just to get him in trouble inside the prison. As a result, Saunders is viciously attacked by his fellow inmates. Liability?
A. No liability, at least for defamation. The point of the question is that the decision about whether statements are defamatory is independent of questions about why the statements were made; if they aren't defamatory, the motive for making them is irrelevant. On facts like these a court might well work to find liability on some other ground, though—perhaps intentional infliction of emotional distress? (Some states recognize a creature known as a "prima facie tort", by which they mean a malicious attempt to make the plaintiff worse off.)

Q. What result in *Oles v. Pittsburg Times*?
A. Liability. From the opinion (we have inserted a paragraph break):

> Were it not for the testimony in this case we might hesitate to believe that the article in question could, by any possibility, tend or be calculated to make the plaintiff infamous or odious, for the reason that it seems incredible that a belief in witchcraft should be entertained by any one in this age. But the fact being established that such belief is still prevalent, to some extent at least, amongst that class of people to which the plaintiff belonged, a publication like the one in question would be quite as injurious in a legal sense as if it had charged, in the same way, any common dereliction. The defamatory accusation need not be one which every one would credit. We cannot state what we mean any more clearly than by quoting from the charge of the learned judge who presided at the trial: "Now, when you come to that you have got to take the world as you find it, and people who publish newspapers have got to take the people as they know them, or are bound to know them to be. If this was an article read in some society of learned men who did not believe in such things as witchcraft, or that there were such things as witches, probably it would have no effect at all; they would not believe it, and therefore it would do no harm. But you have heard the testimony, and you have your own knowledge on that point—a knowledge of the superstitions of the masses of the people, and if with that knowledge you are led to believe that being called a witch would be calculated to injure the reputation of another and injure his standing in society, then it becomes libelous and becomes the foundation for damages."
>
> This was a correct and plain statement of the law applicable to the case; for, strange as it may seem, there was ample evidence to warrant the jury in finding specially the following facts, if they had been requested so to do. *First.* There is and was a considerable number of persons living in the community where the plaintiff resides, and where the newspaper containing this alleged defamatory article had a large circulation, who believe in witchcraft. *Second.* The publication had a tendency to produce and assisted in producing in the minds of persons entertaining such belief the further belief that Irena Oles, the plaintiff, was a witch, and to produce in the minds of some such the belief that the malady from which the Newman boy was suffering was a possession of devils for which the plaintiff was responsible. *Third.* In consequence of this belief she was subjected to insults and assaults, was hooted at, called witch, and stoned upon the streets, was shunned by her neighbors, and suffered loss in her business and occupation. There being testimony that these things occurred afterwards and not before, it was for the jury to say how far

the publication had a tendency to produce and did produce the false and injurious opinion entertained of her.

Q. You can build a nice hypothetical out of *Cox v. Hatch*, 761 P.2d 556 (Utah 1988), which appears in the casebook chapter on invasion of privacy. The plaintiffs were postal workers in Utah. In 1982 one of the state's Senators, Orrin Hatch, visited the plaintiffs' post office and they posed for pictures with him. One of the resulting photographs was printed in an eight-page political flier Hatch later distributed, the "Senator Orrin Hatch Labor Letter." The photograph was not captioned. The plaintiffs were shown smiling at Senator Hatch, who was looking at their work. The accompanying article presented claims that the Republican Party was committed to creating a better life for union members. The plaintiff brought a suit alleging that the photograph reasonably could be construed as an implicit endorsement of Hatch on their part. They denied having endorsed him; indeed, because they were postal employees they were forbidden by federal law to publicly approve or endorse any political candidate or actively participate in a political campaign. They claimed that that after the publication of the photograph, they were investigated by their employer and the union as to the extent of their involvement in Hatch's campaign. What result?
A. The trial court dismissed the plaintiffs' claims, and the Utah Supreme Court affirmed. The court first held that the pictures and their use was not defamatory:

> The tort of defamation protects only reputation. A publication is not defamatory simply because it is nettlesome or embarrassing to a plaintiff, or even because it makes a false statement about the plaintiff. Thus, an embarrassing, even though false, statement that does not damage one's reputation is not actionable as libel or slander. If no defamatory meaning can reasonably be inferred by reasonable persons from the communication, the action must be dismissed for failure to state a claim.

> Here, the photograph shows the plaintiffs with Senator Hatch in a work setting, and it appears in a political advertisement dealing with labor issues. At most, the photograph can be construed to imply that the plaintiffs are members of the Republican Party or that they supported Hatch's reelection. However, attribution of membership in a political party in the United States that is a mainstream party and not at odds with the fundamental social order is not defamatory, nor is attribution of support for a candidate from one of those parties.

This then can lead to a question such as the following:

Q. What is the distinction between *Cox v. Hatch* and *Oles v. Pittsburg Times*?
A. The similarity is that in both cases the plaintiff was said to have attributes that may have caused others to treat her worse. In *Cox* the court evidently thought that being considered a Republican couldn't subject a person to great opprobrium. What if the plaintiff in *Cox* had been stoned in the streets like the plaintiff in *Oles*? In principle it might seem that such facts shouldn't make a difference to the anterior decision about whether the words were defamatory, but in practice judges need some way to determine how the community regards the words that were used about the plaintiff, and the actual reaction of the community may have to be relevant for that purpose. Thus calling someone a witch nowadays, if it provoked no serious reaction, might not be considered defamatory after all.

Q. Hypothetical: in *Zbyszko v. New York American*, 239 N.Y.S. 411 (App.Div. 1930), the defendant newspaper published an article titled "How Science Proves Its Theory of Evolution." The article discussed Darwin's theory of evolution, calling special attention to the structural resemblances between humans and gorillas; the article said that "the general physique of the Gorilla is closely similar to an athletic man of today, and the mind of a young gorilla is much like the mind of a human baby." Near the top of the page was a photograph of a famous wrestler, Stanislaus Zbyszko, in an athletic pose, with this caption: "Stanislaus Zbyszko, the Wrestler, Not Fundamentally Different from the Gorilla in Physique."

Nearby ran a picture of a gorilla with this caption: "A mounted specimen of the Great Kivu Gorilla in Lord Rothschild's private museum at Tring, Hertsfordshire, England." The text of the article did not mention Zbyszko.

Zbyszko brought suit for defamation. He alleged, as the court recounted it, "that the two pictures were so placed and so arranged in design and pose as to create in the minds of readers an association of ideas which would result in the judgment that the said gorilla and the plaintiff were akin to and not different from one another in most important respects." He further alleged that the defendant had "held up the plaintiff to public contempt, disgrace, hatred, infamy, and reproach, caused him to be shunned and avoided and to be treated as an outcast by his wife, relatives, neighbors, friends, and business associates, and injured him in his professional calling and deprived him of his standing among good and worthy people." What result?

A. The trial court dismissed the complaint; the appellate court reversed:

> We think that the publication is libelous per se, because its tendency is to disgrace plaintiff and bring him into ridicule and contempt, and that therefore it is actionable without alleging special damages. The rule is that any written article is actionable without alleging special damages if it tends to expose the plaintiff to public contempt, ridicule, aversion, or disagrace, or induce an evil opinion of him in the minds of others and deprives him of their society. It is not necessary that words impute disgraceful conduct to the plaintiff. If they render him contemptible or ridiculous, he is equally entitled to redress.

Q. Hypothetical: in *Cowan v. Time, Inc.*, 245 N.Y.S.2d 723 (Sup.Ct. 1963), *Life* magazine published a pictorial article titled "Some Idiots Afloat." It consisted of eight pictures of people using boats, commentary about each of them, and a brief statement to the effect that many people who use boats take insufficient care. One of the pictures featured the plaintiff at the tiller of a small boat containing four other people. The picture's caption read "Rub-a-dub-dub, too many in a tub"; the plaintiff's name was not given. The plaintiff brought suit for defamation. What result?

A. The trial court dismissed the complaint, and the appellate court affirmed:

> At most the plaintiff, together with some of the others whose pictures are shown, are charged with acts of carelessness. To charge even a professional man with "ignorance or mistake on a single occasion only and not accusing him of general ignorance or lack of skill cannot be considered defamatory on its face." November v. Time, Inc., 244 N.Y.S.2d 309. [...] While the word "idiot" may have the meaning ascribed to it by the plaintiff, in the context in which it is used, it may only be considered as a charge of lack of care. Moreover, as the complaint does not allege in what respect the picture in the article showing the plaintiff in the small boat was not true or accurate, and as the matter involves a subject of public interest, it must be held that the commentary, whether or not all agree with it, is fair comment. "A comment is fair when it is based on facts truly stated and free from imputations of corrupt or dishonorable motives on the part of the person whose conduct is criticized, and is an honest expression of the writer's real opinion or belief. *Mere exaggeration, slight irony, or wit, or all those delightful touches of style which go to make an article readable, do not push beyond the limitations of fair comment. Facts do not cease to be facts because they are mixed with the fair and expectant comment of the story teller, who adds to the recital a little touch by his piquant pen.*" Briarcliff Lodge Hotel v. Citizen-Sentinel Publishers, 260 N.Y. 106 (emphasis supplied).

One difference between *Cowan v. Time, Inc.* and *Zbyszko v. New York American* is that the court in *Cowan* thought the speech at issue was protected by the "fair comment" privilege, a defense we will consider in more detail later (at first blush can you see any distinction between the cases in this respect?). But the court in *Cowan*, unlike the court in *Zbyszko*, did not consider the speech in question to be defamatory in the first place. What is the distinction between the two cases on this point?

Louisville Times v. Stivers (D makes claims damaging to "Stivers clan"; NL)
Gross v. Cantor (D disparages radio editors; L)
Neiman-Marcus v. Lait (D maligns various groups of Neiman-Marcus employees; L for some of the statements but not others)

Q. What is the distinction between *Gross v. Cantor* and *Louisville Times v. Stivers*?
A. In *Gross v. Cantor*, but not in *Stivers*, the plaintiff was able to allege the existence of a closed and reasonably compact set of people to whom the defendant's words must have referred—and could have been understood by readers to have referred. *Gross v. Cantor* would have been a case of no liability—and more like *Stivers*—if the complaint were simply that Cantor had insulted "New York journalists" generally as being incompetent. It's possible that in *Stivers* the "clan" at issue was about as clearly defined as the radio editors involved in *Gross v. Cantor*, but the plaintiff evidently didn't make this clear.

A different issue in the two cases involves the content of the claims made about the plaintiffs. In discussing *Stivers* case, it may be helpful to clarify the reason the plaintiffs thought the defendant's speech was defamatory. The complaint included this passage:

> We submit that the words of that libel, which is admitted, charge the plaintiff with:
>
> a. Assault and Battery—for what else can fist-fights be?
> b. Assault with a deadly weapon, firearms—for how else may a gun-battle be held?
> c. Attempt to do murder, added to conspiracy to murder since gun-battles by a family against a family amount to local war, or, as is alleged, 'vindictive strife and guerilla warfare.'
> d. Murder—how else can the Baker family have become reduced to a sole survivor?

This might well seem more clearly defamatory than the speech in *Gross v. Cantor*. In *Gross*, it is true, the accusations were more direct. On the other hand, in *Stivers* we have elliptical accusations of real wrongdoing (somewhat analogous to those in *Wildstein*—the scare quotes case); whereas in *Gross v. Cantor* the defendant accused the plaintiffs of "logrolling" and disgracing the newspaper profession, which might seem to be judgments like "racist" or "crank" that have no provably false factual connotations. But perhaps the "logrolling" claim does imply real, potential provable wrongdoing, as opposed to the "disgrace" claim, which would not be concrete enough to support liability, at least today.

Q. Why do courts decline to allow defamation claims when false factual statements are made about members of large groups?
A. Often it's the case that as the group gets larger, it becomes less likely that the audience for the words will believe they really are accusations against each member of the group personally; the words become diluted by having their force spread among so many people. The dilution could occur because the large size of the class would cause the audience to conclude that the words are being used loosely or figuratively (to say that "all lawyers are crooks" might be understood to imply a very loose definition of "crook"); or it could occur because the reference to the group makes clear that the speaker is exaggerating ("all mechanics are crooks" could be understood to mean that the speaker really just thinks that a troubling number of mechanics are crooks). Either way, the result is that no one could be expected to think any less of the individual plaintiff as a result of the defendant's utterances. That is what these rules are trying to address: their goal is to catch the cases where a plaintiff's actual reputation is damaged by the defendant's utterances, and not the cases where the plaintiff is indignant because the defendant said something bad about or about a group of which he is a member.

From the opinion in *Stivers*:

> We find analogous rules regarding other questions. In the case of a public nuisance, everyone is affected by it, but an individual cannot sue where the injury done him by the nuisance differs in

no respect from that suffered by the public generally. [...] All taxpayers are affected by the ineligibility of public officers, yet a taxpayer cannot sue to enjoin payment of salary to an officer on ground the officer is ineligible. Any obstruction of a street in a city interferes to some extent with the rights of any resident of that city, yet, unless a resident can show some damage or inconvenience to himself greater than and different from that suffered by the public generally, he cannot maintain an action for its removal.

Q. What result in *Neiman-Marcus v. Lait*?

A. Apparently there was no effort made to dismiss the claims of the models, so we can assume those are legally sound. As to the other plaintiffs, the court allowed the claims of the salesmen to go forward, but not the saleswomen.

Of course one interesting issue for possible discussion—though it may be too sensitive for some instructors to want to treat in any detail—involves the defamatory content of the claims. Those interested in pursuing the issue can check out the annotation at 3 A.L.R.4th 752 as a starting point. Calling someone a prostitute clearly is defamatory; but how do we decide whether it's defamatory to call someone a homosexual? In any event, the motion to dismiss in this case, and thus the court's opinion, focused on the question of the size of the plaintiff classes:

> An examination of the case and text law of libel reveals that the following propositions are rather widely accepted:
>
> > (1) Where the group or class libelled is large, none can sue even though the language used is inclusive.
> >
> > (2) Where the group or class libelled is small, and each and every member of the group or class is referred to, then any individual member can sue.
>
> Conflict arises when the publication complained of libels some or less than all of a designated small group. Some courts say no cause of action exists in any individual of the group. Other courts in other states would apparently allow such an action. While no choice of law is made at this time, it appears from the complaint that Texas or New York law will be of greatest importance at the trial because of the many contacts with these states; not of small significance is the fact that the individual plaintiffs' community and place of livelihood is in Texas.
>
> The courts of Texas do not seem to have spoken on the 'some' allegation of libel. A reading of the New York cases indicates a trend towards submitting to the jury the question as to whether the "charge against several individuals, under some general description or general name * * * has the personal application averred by the plaintiff."' Gross v. Cantor, 200 N.E. 592, 593 (N.Y. 1936).
>
> The Court of Appeals for this Circuit has referred to the Restatement of Torts for the "general law". If we do so in this instance, we find that Illustration 2 of § 564, Comment (c) reads as follows:
>
> "A newspaper publishes the statement that some member of B's household has committed murder. In the absence of any circumstances indicating that some particular member of B's household was referred to, the newspaper has defamed each member of B's household."
>
> Thus the Restatement of Torts would authorize suit by each member of a small group where the defamatory publication refers to but a portion of the group. This result seems to find support in

logic and justice, as well as the case law mentioned above. An imputation of gross immorality to some of a small group casts suspicion upon all, where no attempt is made to exclude the innocent.

Applying the above principles to the case at bar, it is the opinion of this Court that the plaintiff salesmen, of whom it is alleged that 'most * * * are fairies' have a cause of action in New York and most likely other states; where the courts have specifically held to the contrary, a fortiori no cause exists. Defendants' motion to dismiss as to the salesmen for failure to state a claim upon which relief can be granted is denied.

The plaintiff saleswomen are in a different category. The alleged defamatory statement in defendants' book speaks of the saleswomen generally. While it does not use the word 'all' or similar terminology, yet it stands unqualified. However, the group of saleswomen is extremely large, consisting of 382 members at the time of publication. No specific individual is named in the alleged libellous statement. I am not cited to a single case which would support a cause of action by an individual member of any group of such magnitude. The courts have allowed suit where the group consisted of four coroners, twelve doctors composing the residential staff of a hospital, a posse, twelve radio editors, and in similar cases involving small groups.

But where the group or class disparaged is a large one, absent circumstances pointing to a particular plaintiff as the person defamed, no individual member of the group or class has a cause of action. Thus actions for libel have failed where the groups libelled consisted of all officials of a state-wide union, all the taxicab drivers in Washington, D. C., the parking lot owners in downtown Washington, D. C., or the members of a clan, Louisville Times v. Stivers, 68 S.W.2d 411 (Ky. 1934).

Giving the plaintiff saleswomen the benefit of all legitimate favorable inferences, the defendants' alleged libel cannot reasonably be said to concern more than the saleswomen as a class. There is no language referring to some ascertained or ascertainable person. Nor is the class so small that it follows that defamation of the class infects the individual of the class. This Court so holds as a matter of law since it is of the opinion that no reasonable man would take the writers seriously and conclude from the publication a reference to any individual saleswoman.

While it is generally recognized that even where the group is large, a member of the group may have a cause of action if some particular circumstances point to the plaintiff as the person defamed, no such circumstances are alleged in the amended complaint. This further exception is designed to apply only where a plaintiff can satisfy a jury that the words referred solely or especially to himself. The plaintiffs' general allegation that the alleged libellous and defamatory matter was written 'of and concerning * * * each of them' is insufficient to satisfy this requirement. Accordingly it is the opinion of this Court that as a matter of law the individual saleswomen do not state a claim for libel upon which relief can be granted and the motion to dismiss their cause of action is granted.

SECTION C. PUBLICATION

If you want to skip some cases, cut the first two (*Gambrill* and *Chalkley*). In a pinch the next two cases (*Scott v. Hull* and *Hellar v. Bianco*) can go, too.

Gambrill v. Schooley (liability for publishing to a stenographer)
Chalkley v. Atlantic Coast Line Railroad Co. (no liability for publishing to a stenographer)

Q. Can you articulate the sense of the distinction between *Chalkley v. Atlantic Coast Line Railroad Co.* and *Gambrill v. Schooley*?

A. The distinction seems to us to be messy. *Chalkley* distinguishes *Gambrill* on grounds of privilege, libel *per se*, and duty, and thus invites some confusion between all of these concepts. Begin with the distinction between publication and privilege. In *Chalkley* the communication was the subject of a conditional privilege because it was a notice of dismissal from employer to employee. In *Gambrill* the communication evidently was subject to no privilege; it was simply a defamatory letter. This in itself might seem a reasonable basis for distinction—though the consequence of it would be that the defendant in *Chalkley* still could lose if he was shown to act with malice (for then the privilege is lost), whereas a defense of no-publication ends the case entirely. In any event, it's hard to see why the presence or absence of the privilege should bear on whether there was publication, unless the point is simply that the reasons for recognizing a privilege in the employment situation are also reasons for cutting off liability entirely by denying that the statement was published. But if the statement was made with express malice, why should the defendant avoid liability for damage done by relaying it to his secretary?

The relevance of whether the statement was libelous *per se* also is not quite clear. It does shed some light on a puzzle in these cases: the plaintiff's damages. How badly hurt is a plaintiff likely to be by the transmission of a defamatory statement from the defendant to the defendant's secretary? Perhaps not much. But if the statement is "actionable per se," damages can be presumed without a showing of particulars; so in such a case it is easier to understand a suit based on publication to a stenographer. If the statement is not actionable per se, the usual plaintiff would appear to have a tough row to hoe in proving damages. But it's still difficult to understand why this should result in a finding of no *publication*, rather than simply a finding that the plaintiff has to do the hard work of proving damages. Nominal damages would be available in any event—and maybe punitive damages as well.

This leaves the question of the stenographer's "duty" and the relationship between the corporation and the people who carry out its work. This is indeed the most common ground for exception to the usual rule, which is that defamatory statements are indeed published when spoken to a stenographer. In cases where a corporation is sued, courts sometimes say that anything said or heard by the corporation's agents—whether by its officers or secretaries—may be considered instances of the corporation talking to itself, as it were, and thus not amount to publication. To us this distinction, too, seems difficult to understand. The law of defamation is meant to protect the defendant's interest in his reputation, which may be sullied when others hear damaging things about him. Whether those others hear the damaging things because they were carrying out corporate responsibilities or because they were simply taking orders from the non-corporate boss does not seem germane to the law's purposes. Perhaps there should be no liability in either case; it's the distinction between them that is puzzling.

Scott v. Hull (graffiti on defendant's building; NL)
Hellar v. Bianco (graffiti on bathroom wall of defendant's bar; L)

Q. What is the distinction between *Scott v. Hull* and *Hellar v. Bianco*?

A. Here is what the court in *Scott v. Hull* had to say about it:

> In *Hellar v. Bianco*, the graffiti were on the walls of a restroom inside the business establishment of the defendant, were with little doubt placed there by invitees of the defendant, and were open to view by other invitees. The court held that "persons who *invite* the public to their premises owe a duty to others not to knowingly permit their walls to be occupied with defamatory matter." (Emphasis added.) [...] It may thus be observed from these cases that where liability is found to exist it is predicated upon actual publication by the defendant or on the defendant's ratification of a publication by another, the ratification in *Hellar v. Bianco* [...] consisting of at least the positive acts of the defendants in continuing to invite the public into their premises where the defamatory matter was on view after the defendants had knowledge of the existence of same.

Q. Hypothetical: in *Tacket v. General Motors Corp.*, 836 F.2d 1042 (7th Cir. 1987), Thomas Tacket was the night supervisor at one of GM's manufacturing plants. The plant needed to buy some crates. Tacket helped steer a contract for the purchase of them to a friend and subordinate of his doing business by the name "S & T Specialties." The union representing the plant's workers protested that the work should have been done by GM's workers rather than being subcontracted out; a controversy then arose surrounding the propriety of Tacket's actions. The firm suspected that Tacket may have been the "T" in "S & T", and it was clear that he had acted beyond his authority in arranging for the order of the crates. Tacket was suspended but finally retained by GM, but was moved to another department of the plant because the controversy had soured his relations with the workers in his accustomed area. Sometime during Tacket's suspension, someone painted the following words on a wall inside the plant: TACKET TACKET WHAT A RACKET. GM painted over those words seven to eight months later. Tacket brought a suit against GM claiming that he had been defamed during the months the words remained on the wall. What result?

A. The trial court gave a directed verdict to GM. The court of appeals, per Easterbrook, J., reversed:

> GM's liability [...] depends on its publication of the libel by failure to remove the message. [...] Indiana has neither embraced nor rejected [the Restatement's] approach. Adoption of another's publication is an old basis of liability, however, and a speaker can adopt implicitly as well as explicitly. Failing to remove a libel from your building, after notice and opportunity to do so, is a form of adoption. We predict that Indiana will follow §577(2) when the time comes, as have other states.

> The principle can be overdrawn. The *Restatement* suggests that a tavern owner would be liable if defamatory graffiti remained in a bathroom stall a single hour after their discovery. Section 577 Illustration 15, derived from *Hellar v. Bianco,* 244 P.2d 757 (1952). The common law of washrooms is otherwise, given the steep discount that readers apply to such statements and the high cost of hourly repaintings of bathroom stalls. The burden of constant vigilance greatly exceeds the benefits to be had. A person is responsible for statements he makes or adopts, so the question is whether a reader may infer adoption from the presence of a statement. That inference may be unreasonable for a bathroom wall or the interior of a subway car in New York City but appropriate for the interior walls of a manufacturing plant, over which supervisory personnel exercise greater supervision and control. The costs of vigilance are small (most will be incurred anyway), and the benefits potentially large (because employees may attribute the statements to their employer more readily than patrons attribute graffiti to barkeeps).

> Tacket testified that shortly after his reinstatement he complained about the sign to John Swan, the maintenance superintendent of Plant 17, and asked Swan to have the sign removed. [...] John Huffman, who worked at [GM] for 24 years and had never seen another sign stenciled on a wall, said that the sign was at eye level in one of the plant's main thoroughfares, an area visited daily by management. Another employee, who verified the uniqueness of the sign, opined that it could not have lasted for eight months without management's acquiescence and approval—which, he inferred, it had. Tacket testified that he saw Lyle Crouse, the general superintendent of Plant 17, standing next to the sign months before the sign was painted over, and one may infer that Crouse saw the sign. A reasonable person could conclude that Delco "intentionally and unreasonably fail[ed] to remove" this sign and thereby published its contents.

Overcast v. Billings Mutual Insurance Co. (D sends P letter denying insurance coverage on damning grounds, which P shows to other insurers; L)
Sullivan v. Baptist Memorial Hospital (problem: D fires P for damning reasons, which P tells to other potential employers; NL).

Q.   What result in *Sullivan v. Baptist Memorial Hospital?*   Can it be distinguished from *Overcast v. Billings Mutual Insurance Co.?*

A.   The court in *Sullivan* found no liability, which is the result reached in a majority of jurisdictions (not all) when confronted with ex-employees like the plaintiff there.   The analogy to cases like *Overcast* is clear, which is why some courts do find liability in cases like Sullivan's; the case might be distinguished from *Overcast*, however, on the ground that the policy issues at stake in the two situations are different. Insurance companies are obliged to give good reasons for refusing coverage, but the normal rule governing employment relations is employment at will: the employer can fire the employee for any reason, good or bad.   That regime may in effect be modified if claims for defamation are allowed based on the employee's later repetition of the given reason.   That was the objection Posner raised to the idea of self-defamation in the employment setting in *Rice v. Nova Biomedical Corp.*, 38 F.3d 909 (7th Cir. 1995): "The combination of the doctrines of defamation per se and self-defamation gives employees who regret not having negotiated an employment contract a tort surrogate for it.   [...]   [I]]t makes it impossible for an employer to communicate his grounds for discharging an employee to the employee even confidentially without incurring a grave risk of being sued for defamation."   The reference to "defamation per se" is an allusion to the doctrine that words calling into doubt a person's competence in his profession are considered defamatory on their face and entitle the plaintiff to general damages.

The court in *Sullivan* raised some related objections.   The threat of a defamation suit would seem to discourage employers from telling employees why they are being fired.   In at-will relationships no reason *need* be given; and that is the safer route if a stated reason can result in a defamation suit (even granting that liability would be unlikely in such cases unless malice could be shown; again, there is a privilege to consider).   The consequences are discussed in Eble, *Self-Publication Defamation: Employee Right or Employee Burden?* 47 Baylor L.Rev. 745, 779-80 (1995):

> A shutdown of communication would hurt both employees and employers.   Employees falsely accused of misconduct may be wrongfully terminated because they would never have a chance to rebut the false accusations.   Employees who may be able to improve substandard job performances may fail to do so because needed feedback is withheld[....]   It seems that both employees and employers stand to lose if employers adopt a policy of silence[. ...] Unfortunately, employees will bear the costs of such a policy without a corresponding benefit.

It is also possible, as the court in *Sullivan* worried, that the self-defamation doctrine might create problems for employees who believe they have been fired for discriminatory reasons.   Again from the Eble article:

> Normally, a factfinder would be justifiably suspicious if an employer fired an employee in a protected group and refused to explain the reason for the termination at the time of discharge. Certainly, a judge or juror would question why the employer did not tell the employee the "legitimate" reason for the discharge prior to the commencement of litigation.   As one commentator noted, "Indeed, the fact that an employer is unwilling to state the reason for its actions is itself compelling."   [...]

> [But as] discussed above, it would not be unreasonable for an employer to withhold the reason for employee terminations from all employees in order to avoid being subjected to the costs of defending a self-publication claim.   [A court that recognizes] the self-publication theory [...] will give all employers a convenient excuse for withholding reasons for employee terminations. Avoiding litigation costs is a valid reason and one with which many jurors and judges can sympathize.   Because [the doctrine] will legitimize employers' silence if they recognize the self-publication theory, the Title VII plaintiff will have an extra obstacle to overcome.

If the self-publication theory is adopted, often the first time a Title VII plaintiff will learn the reason for her termination will be after the commencement of litigation or the filing of a complaint with the Equal Employment Opportunity Commission (EEOC). The employer will be given additional time to come up with a "legitimate" reason for the employee's termination and the reason will usually be screened by an employment lawyer before it is released. No longer will an employer's silence during the discharge be viewed suspiciously. Further, because the employer will not give a reason for the discharge at the time of termination, the plaintiff will be unable to show that the employer's reason at the time of trial is inconsistent with the reason given at the time of discharge.

Once more the *Overcast* case is a little different because the insurance company is obliged to justify its denials of coverage and can already be sued if the reason is a bad one. Allowing a suit for defamation in those circumstances thus may not put the insured in a fundamentally different position than he already occupied, nor should it alter so significantly the incentives of the insurer. It adds pressure on the insurer not to turn down a claim, since a mistaken decision to that effect can now be penalized heavily in more than one way: not only with a suit for breach of contract or bad faith, but sometimes also in a defamation suit. One can debate whether this added pressure is a good thing, but the point is that it's on top of similar pressures that already existed.

One answer to some of these concerns is to apply a qualified privilege to the employer's reasons for the dismissal—as the courts recognizing the self-publication doctrine generally do. Thus from *Lewis v. Equitable Life Assurance Soc'y*, 389 N.W.2d 876, 886-88 (Minn.1986) (a leading case for the minority position recognizing these claims):

> A former employer in a compelled self-publication case may be held liable as if it had actually published the defamatory statement directly to prospective employers. Where an employer would be entitled to a privilege if it had actually published the statement, it makes little sense to deny the privilege where the identical communication is made to identical third parties with the only difference being the mode of publication. Finally, recognition of a qualified privilege seems to be the only effective means of addressing the concern that every time an employer states the reason for discharging an employee it will subject itself to potential liability for defamation. It is in the public interest that information regarding an employee's discharge be readily available to the discharged employee and to prospective employers, and we are concerned that, unless a significant privilege is recognized by the courts, employers will decline to inform employees of reasons for discharges. We conclude that an employer's communication to an employee of the reason for discharge may present a proper occasion upon which to recognize a qualified privilege.

A qualified privilege can be defeated, of course, if it is abused. Courts sometimes differ in how they define "abuse," but the term generally refers to either "actual" or "express" malice. This issue is treated in more detail in the next section of the chapter.

Q. Is there a problem in these self-publication cases regarding the plaintiff's incentive to mitigate damages? Every time the plaintiff repeats the defamation, his claim for damages against his former employer becomes larger.

A. The majority in *Lewis v. Equitable Life Assurance Society*, *supra*, wasn't worried about this:

> [Mitigation] does not appear to be a problem, however, if liability for self-publication of defamatory statements is imposed *only* where the plaintiff was in some significant way compelled to repeat the defamatory statement and such compulsion was, or should have been, foreseeable to the defendant. Also, the duty to mitigate can be further protected by requiring plaintiffs when they encounter a situation in which they are compelled to repeat a defamatory statement to take all reasonable steps to attempt to explain the true nature of the situation and to contradict the

defamatory statement. In such circumstances, there would be no voluntary act on the part of a plaintiff that would constitute a failure to mitigate.

But the dissenter to the *Lewis* decision disagreed:

> Recognition of the so-called "doctrine" of "self publication" under circumstances similar to this case discourages plaintiffs from mitigating damages[.] For example, respondents here originally sought to have "gross insubordination" expunged from their records as part of declaratory relief. Obviously, such an expungement would work against their self interest because, if granted, would mitigate, if not eliminate, the basis of recovery of future damages. Predictably, therefore, respondents chose to dismiss this claim for declaratory relief because expungement would lower, if not eliminate, recovery of future defamation damages.
>
> In my view, the majority opinion gives insufficient attention to the ramifications of the mitigation problem. The opinion asserts the nonexistence of such a problem "if liability * * * is imposed *only* where the plaintiff was in some significant way compelled to repeat the defamatory statement and such compulsion was, or should have been, foreseeable to the defendant." In claims brought by ex-employees against employers for defamation when the employment was terminated for "incompetence," "dishonesty," "insubordination" or for any other reason carrying a connotation of immorality, ineptness, or improbity, "compulsion" will almost automatically be found in connection with future job applications by the discharged employee. Such "compulsion" would, with certainty, be foreseeable by the ex-employer.

Said Forsberg, J., also dissenting (in the court of appeals below):

> The first remedy of any victim of defamation is self-help—using available opportunities to contradict the lie or correct the error and thereby to minimize its adverse impact on reputation. The terminated employee has the best conceivable opportunity to lessen the damage caused by his reason for discharge, since he or she may accompany the statement with an explanation.
>
> If the doctrine of self-publication is to be adopted, it should be limited to compelling fact situations, to avoid making a defamation case of every termination. In some cases, such as a charge of embezzlement or employee theft, there may be a strong compulsion to republish the charge without a real opportunity for explanation. In general, however, an employee is only obligated to state the true reason for his termination. It is apparent that the further from the truth the former employer's allegation is, the less the employee is under a duty to "republish" it in a damaging form. In this case, a less damaging characterization than "gross insubordination" would have been fully justified.

Emmens v. Pottle (D sells newspaper containing defamation of P; NL)
Coffey v. Midland Broadcasting Co. (D broadcasts radio show containing defamation of P; L)
Zeran v. American Online (D internet service provider leaves defamatory content online; NL)

Q. What is the superficial similarity between *Coffey v. Midland Broadcasting Co.* and *Emmens v. Pottle*? What is the distinction between them?
A. In both cases the defendant took defamatory statements uttered by someone else and passed them on to others, apparently without knowing that they were doing so; but there was liability for this only in *Coffey*. The court in *Coffey* analogizes the local radio station there to a newspaper publisher: either could be burned if someone unexpectedly snuck something defamatory into their newspaper or broadcast. This is no defense for a newspaper or other "primary publisher," and so shouldn't be a defense for the radio station either. This argument is open to criticism because a radio station like the defendant's in *Coffey*

has no direct control over the speech uttered on the radio show; it just sends along to its listeners whatever comes over the line from the CBS studios in New York. It's true that a newspaper *can* be burned unexpectedly despite taking all due care to prevent anything defamatory from getting into its pages, but holding the newspaper publisher strictly liable for defamation it prints creates a useful incentive for vigilance. There may be no comparably useful incentive created by the decision in *Coffey*. Even if Midland had screened the broadcast as it came over the wire from New York, it probably wouldn't have been able to determine whether the defamatory statement here—that the plaintiff had been in prison—was false and defamatory.

On the other hand, maybe local stations like the defendant in *Midland* can put contractual pressure on companies like CBS to be more careful in screening the scripts for its shows before they go out in the first place. This would tend to diminish the potential for spontaneous utterances, making a radio show more like written expression. But maybe that's not a bad thing.

There was a nice discussion of the strengths and weaknesses of the analogies offered in this area in *Summit Hotel Co. v. National Broadcasting*, 8 A.2d 302 (Penn. 1939), which more or less rejected the *Coffey* approach. We hope the interest of the passage excuses the length at which we present it here; it can provide many useful ideas for class discussion:

> The speaker here was an employee of a third party to whom the broadcasting company had leased its facilities. He was not under the broadcasting company's control, authority or command. The script used was examined and rehearsed exactly as written. It contained nothing offensive, and appellant, in renting its facilities, had no reason to believe anyone would utter a defamatory statement. There was no power or means possessed by the broadcasting company that enabled it to prevent the transmission of the defamatory remark. It was physically impossible for the monitor or program director to have intervened, as the performer, without notice, interjected his terse defamatory remark so quickly that no one in appellant's employ was able to prevent its transmission.
>
> In these circumstances the analogy between the radio broadcaster and the newspaper publisher is demonstrably weak, considering not only the practical differences between the two media of communication but the different conditions under which the industries operate. Newspaper matter is prepared in advance, reviewed by members of the various staffs, set into type, printed, proof read and then 'run off' by employes of the publisher; at all times opportunity is afforded the owner to prevent the publication of the defamatory statement up to the time of the delivery of the paper to the news-vendor. The defamation thus may be said to be an intentional publication, or at least one published without due care.
>
> Similarly, the broadcaster may, as it did here, require the submission of the script in advance for editing; it may require rehearsals and its production director may prevent the transmission of doubtful matter. But where the circumstances like those now presented are such that the defamation occurs beyond the control of the broadcaster, it is perfectly clear that the analogy between newspapers and broadcasting companies collapses completely. The superior control of the newspaper publisher is self-evident.
>
> Other analogies have been suggested which, when first mentioned, may be thought of assistance, but when analyzed possess inherent weaknesses. In communications by telegraph the rule of due care has been invoked. We know of no case where a telephone company has been held for defamation for the use of its lines, but its duty should rise no higher than that of a telegraph company. Both activities are public utilities, and cannot select the users of their facilities. Radio companies are not in that category. They may select their performers and choose between applicants for the use of their facilities, which are designed, not for private communications from one individual to another, but for those to the public generally.

It has been suggested that the dissemination of matter by radio may be likened to dissemination by newsvendors and booksellers, who merely republish original utterances. The rule of absolute liability does not apply to such vendors. While this is possibly a close analogy and has the support of eminent legal writers, its weakness is in the fact that the sound which is transmitted to radio listeners is carried directly by the facilities of the broadcaster, though the activating impulse may have been the spoken word at the microphone. It is a trifle more than the mere delivery of a newspaper to the purchaser. It has been held that it is the reproduction of the spoken word from the broadcasting room. The combination of the voice and the transmitting apparatus is necessary to effect the broadcast. The speaking and publication of a defamation are simultaneous.

The closest analogy suggested is the loud-speaking device installed in public halls, owned, maintained and operated, very much like the radio, by the owner of the premises. The halls are rented for public addresses, and may be equipped with outside amplifiers or loudspeakers, increasing the size of the audience. The only practical difference here is in the number of persons who hear the remarks. If the newspaper analogy is to be carried to its logical conclusion, the owners of the loud-speaking devices should be liable for the defamatory utterances of those leasing or using these devices.

The real difficulty arises from attempting to adapt to the new tort of radio defamation, rules of liability applicable in other fields of kindred, but not identical, types of wrong. Defamation in the law, until the radio appeared, was either libel or slander. Now, it is urged by some that the law of libel should be extended to defamation by radio because of the number of persons that hear it, others indicate that it should be treated as slander. [...]

That part of the Roman law of defamation taken into the English law of libel was applicable to more serious cases. The strict rules of libel were originally directed at the printing press, which provided a wider means of publication. The differences between libel and slander, and the comparative ease of recovery in libel as against the more restricted and less stringent liability in slander, are well known. Some authors dispute these formal distinctions, asserting there is no sound reason to support them. Among the factors to be considered in reaching a rule of liability for defamation is the extent of the publication; but that is not the only, or the main, reason for the distinction between libel and slander. The more serious consideration is the permanence of the printed libel, and its capacity for continuous future harm over a wide area. Slander, or the spoken word, is not bound to any set form; it is easily fabricated and made to appear much worse than actually spoken; it offers opportunity for fraudulent and fictitious claims; it is usually uttered in the presence of a few. The law has, therefore, encased it in most rigid rules.

When the radio sound reaches the human ear it is the spoken word. It is urged that the radio gives to it a power for harm even greater than the printing press gives to the printed word, but this conclusion does not consider the factor of permanency just mentioned, or the traditional belief in the veracity of the printed word, particularly important in the community where the injured person resides. Newspaper defamations possess possibilities for real harm far greater than defamations by radio, as they constitute permanent, continuing records, which, through circulation, are constantly republished. The radio word is quickly spoken and, generally, as quickly forgotten. Because of the differences in power of the stations from which it is sent, it may receive widely varying circulation.

The radio is, admittedly, a powerful agency for advertising and the conveyance of important public matters, as well as the promotion of religion and politics. It also affords its listeners a measure of entertainment, and brings to them the reports of many occurrences more quickly than the newspaper could possibly do. It does, to a certain extent, compete with the newspaper. But these factors, standing alone, should not be sufficient to cast upon the radio the cloak of liability without fault for defamatory publications, as libels, by extension of the law applicable in some States to newspapers. The Restatement has taken the position that when the words broadcast are read from script it is libel, but has expressed no specific conclusion as to extemporaneous remarks. [...]

Radio broadcasting presents a new problem, so new that it may be said to be still in a state of development and experimentation. It was not conceived nor dreamed of when the law of libel and slander was being formulated. Publication by radio has physical aspects entirely different from those attending the publication of a libel or a slander as the law understands them. The danger of attempting to apply the fixed principles of law governing either libel or slander to this new medium of communication is obvious. But the law is not so firmly and rigidly cast that it is incapable of meeting a new wrong as the demands of progress and change require. In this State our tort actions are in trespass; the pleader need not lay his cause either in slander or in libel, and, as defamation by radio possesses many attributes of both libel and slander, but differs from each, it might be regarded as a distinct form of action. Certainly, there is no necessity of extending to this situation a so-called rule of absolute liability without fault, particularly when our law of libel merely creates a high standard of care. A rule should be applied which will not impose too heavy a burden on the industry, and yet will secure a high measure of protection to the public or those who may be injured.

That a rule of this nature should be adopted becomes increasingly apparent when it is considered that in the field of its operation radio broadcasting is subjected to many restrictions which are not imposed upon newspapers. Any person, firm, or corporation may publish a newspaper without asking the government's consent. Newspapers are the freest medium of communication in this country today. They are protected by the Constitution, by statutes, and by the liberal decisions of many courts. They determine their own policies, print as they desire, unrestricted and unlimited, except by criminal statutes for libel and by the possibility of civil action. The rule of civil liability for libel applicable to them is just and fair, considering the opportunities of correction or control.

On the other hand, a broadcasting company cannot operate without a license from the Federal Government, which must be renewed from time to time. No license may be granted unless the licensee serves the public interest. Radio is a governmentally-regulated industry. The number of stations, their locations and wavelengths, the hours in which they may broadcast, and their transmitting power, are all subject to regulation. In this manner their effective range of communication and the number of their listeners may be controlled. The power of Congress in this respect has been upheld as essential. [...] [T]he Federal Radio Communications Commission is given broad powers to formulate rules for the conduct of radio stations; severe penalties are imposed for violations. A broadcasting company that oversteps these rules may have its license revoked and lose the value of its entire plant; this, in the realm of radio, is capital punishment. And, the publication by a broadcasting station of defamatory matter, as also the transmission of certain forms of false and fraudulent advertising, may, if persisted in, result in the revocation of the license of the station or its deletion. But, even here, 'It seems inherently unreasonable to suppose that a station should be deleted by the Commission for the dissemination of defamation without knowledge or fault of the licensee.' [...]

All of these considerations cause the newspaper analogy to utterly fail, and no consideration of public policy could in any sense cause a broadcaster to be punished by a rule of absolute liability such as that invoked by the court below. If, as has been suggested, the imposition of such liability on newspapers was originally desirable as a matter of public policy because of the frequency of defamatory publications, and because no other means of discouraging the practice was available , these reasons do not exist in the case of radio broadcasting. Radio defamations have been infrequent, and governmental regulation affords a potent check. [...]

We therefore conclude that a broadcasting company that leases its time and facilities to another, whose agents carry on the program, is not liable for an interjected defamatory remark where it appears that it exercised due care in the selection of the lessee, and, having inspected and edited the script, had no reason to believe an extemporaneous defamatory remark would be made. Where the broadcasting station's employe or agent makes the defamatory remark, it is liable, unless the remarks are privileged and there is no malice.

The First Restatement, §577, comment g, said this:

Caveat: The Institute expresses no opinion as to whether the proprietors of a radio broadcasting station are relieved from liability for a defamatory broadcast by a person not in their employ if they could not have prevented the publication by the exercise of reasonable care, or whether, as an original publisher, they are liable irrespective of the precautions taken to prevent the defamatory publication.

But the comments to Restatement (Second) §581 (1977) went farther:

Comment g. Radio and television broadcasting. Although radio and television broadcasting companies are engaged in the transmission of the human voice and likeness and must to a great extent rely upon matter prepared for them by others, they are publishers more nearly analogous to a newspaper or the publisher of a book than to a telegraph company. They are not engaged solely in rendering the service of transmission to those who seek it. For their own business purposes they initiate, select and put upon the air their own programs; or by contract they permit others to make use of their facilities to do so, and they cooperate actively in the publication. Their activity is similar to that of a newspaper, which employs its own reporters or writers to prepare matter to be published, or by contract agrees to publish matter, such as advertisements, prepared and controlled by others.

The broadcasting company is therefore not to be regarded as engaged solely in the transmission of messages. As in the case of a newspaper, it is an original and primary publisher and is not subject to the exceptional rule stated in Subsection (1). It is therefore subject to liability for the broadcast of defamatory matter in accordance with the provisions of §§580A and 580B.

The reference to the rule of "Subsection (1)" is to the text of §581, included in the casebook text.

Q. How does the logic of *Emmens* and the radio cases apply to the situation in *Zeran*?
A. Obviously *Zeran* is a statutory case, and instructors will vary in what they want to do with it in class. One interesting angle to explore is the distinction the plaintiff presses (but that the court rejects) between publishers and distributors. *Emmens* involved a claim of liability for a distributor; the question in *Coffee* in effect was whether to regard the radio station there as a publisher (and thus liable) or distributor (not liable), with the resulting arguments both ways that we have just reviewed. *Zeran's* argument was that the statute says AOL cannot be held liable as a publisher, but it doesn't say anything about AOL being held liable as a distributor. *Zeran* wanted AOL to be treated like the bookseller in *Emmens* or in the Restatement examples who becomes liable once put on notice that it is making defamatory statements available through its internet services.

One way to look at the confusion in the *Zeran* case is that the word "publisher" can have two different meanings: it can mean one who produces a defamatory statement, such as a newspaper, and thus can be held liable for damages without fault; or it can mean anyone who passes on ("publishes") a defamatory statement. The court essentially interprets "publisher" in the statute to have the second meaning, so that the statute's immunity is very broad and the defendant cannot be held liable for transmitting a defamatory statement no matter how much notice it had. Another way to look at it is that the court really did consider AOL to be a classic publisher in the first sense just described, that AOL had immunity in that capacity, and that its role can't be changed into that of unprotected "distributor" by anything the plaintiff does, such as giving notice of the defamatory statements. Either way, matters of policy seem to provide the impetus for the court's reading of the statute. Liability for ISPs would lead either to unrealistic burdens on them in trying to police what is said by their users, or to drastic and undesirable attempts by the ISPs to limit their users' speech. The purpose of the statute was to avoid these problems, and it shouldn't be circumvented by quarrels about whether the "distributor" label applies to companies like AOL.

You can have an interesting time exploring analogies between radio stations and internet service providers. The latter have no control—or anyway we don't want them to exert too much control—over their members' speech, so the case for treating them like a radio station, much less like a newspaper, seems weak. The hard question is whether at least holding them liable after they have notice of the defamation, as in *Zeran*, would really be as burdensome and damaging as the court says. Perhaps it would be, since companies fearing liability might be likely to err on the side of silencing any speech that provokes a complaint.

Intent. This is as good a place as any to talk about the intent required to make out a defamation claim, since the issue doesn't receive independent treatment in the chapter. As the publication cases and Restatement provisions show, the intent required at common law was minimal; there had to be an intent to publish the defamatory statement, but otherwise it was regarded as a strict liability tort. (So it was a possible defense to say that one published a statement accidentally, but not a possible defense to say that one accidentally named the plaintiff in a document published deliberately.) A vivid example is *Jones v. E. Hulton & Co.*, [1910] A.C. 20. The defendant newspaper printed an article in its *Sunday Chronicle* that read, "'Whist! There is Artemus Jones with a woman who is not his wife, who must be, you know—the other thing!' whispers a fair neighbor of mine excitedly to her bosom friend's ear. Really, is it not surprising how certain of our fellow-countrymen behave when they come abroad?" The plaintiff was a man named Artemus Jones who was a barrister in North Wales. He conceded that the defendant's never had heard of him and meant to use "Artemus Jones" as a fictitious name in the story; but he produced witnesses who thought the article was referring to him. The jury gave judgment to the plaintiff, and the House of Lords affirmed. Said Loreborn, L.C.:

> Libel is a tortious act. What does the tort consist in? It consists in using language which others knowing the circumstances would reasonably think to be defamatory of the person complaining of and injured by it. A person charged with libel cannot defend himself by shewing that he intended in his own breast not to defame, or that he intended not to defame the plaintiff, if in fact he did both. He has non the less imputed something disgraceful and has non the less injured the plaintiff. A man in good faith may publish a libel believing it to be true, and it may be found by the jury that he acted in food faith believing it to be true, and reasonably believing it to be true, but that in fact the statement was false. Under those circumstances he has no defence to the action, however excellent his intentions. If the intention of the writer be immaterial in considering whether the matter written is defamatory, I do not see why it need be relevant in considering whether it is defamatory of the plaintiff.

The result in the *Jones* case was controversial, and the potential field for strict liability in defamation cases seems to have been eliminated by *New York Times v. Sullivan* and *Gertz v. Robert Welch, Inc.*—as we see later in the chapter.

SECTION D. DEFENSES

Looking for ballast? This is a hard place to find it, but the *Sternberg* case probably can go if something needs to be cut. You also could drop one of the cases at the end of the section on truth as a defense.

1. *Conditional privileges.*

Watt v. Longsdon (D hears that colleague, P, has had extramarital affair, etc., and tells P's wife and board of directors; L for telling wife (no privilege at all) and potential L for telling board of directors if there was malice (so that conditionally privilege was destroyed).
Flowers v. Smith (D agent for electrical utility tells P's wife that P has been stealing electricity; NL)

Q. Why is there a privilege that covers Longsdon telling the board of directors about Watt, but not one that covers telling Watt's wife?
A. The idea might be that if the marriage contains dishonesties, there are no obvious consequences for anyone but Mr. and Mrs. Watt; whereas if people in a business can't report the misfeasance of their colleagues, there might be serious commercial consequences.

Q. What is the distinction between *Flowers v. Smith* and *Watt v. Longsdon* (a case that the court in *Flowers v. Smith* cited with approval)?
A. From the opinion in *Flowers*:

> The difficulty here, as always, is not in ascertaining general legal principles, but in making application of these. In discussing a similar situation, the court in *Watt v. Longsdon*, 69 A. L. R. 1022, in substance, says that such question cannot be answered by any fixed test or rule, but each case must be determined upon its own particular facts. This case quotes the following with approval: "If fairly warranted by any reasonable occasion or exigency and honestly made, such communications are protected for the common convenience and welfare of society."

> [W]e have here a case where the husband sues for a slanderous statement made to his wife at her special instance and request, concerning a matter in which she was as much interested as her husband. It pertained to the household which she presumably managed. An electric light bill in modern times, we think, may be properly classed with "necessaries" for which her interest in the community property is liable. Such bill contracted during marriage is prima facie a community debt. With certain limitations, even her separate property may be liable for such bill. Any recovery in this case is community property. She had a right to make inquiry respecting a matter affecting her household. Plainly it was the duty of Smith to protect the interest of his company; and that the communication was made in furtherance of such duty is not denied.

So one distinction is that in *Flowers* the wife asked for the information. To pursue the point you can ask whether the outcome in *Longsdon* have been any different if Mrs. Watt had gone to Longsdon and asked him if he knew anything about possible infidelity by Mr. Watt. It's interesting to discuss the significance of a request: why should so much turn on it? The Restatement regards this as important, as astute students will notice in the illustration to §595 that follows in the casebook. From §595, comment j:

The circumstances of each case are important in determining whether the publication to the particular recipient is within current standards of socially desirable or at least permissible conduct. Thus while it is not always necessary that the defamatory matter be published in response to a request by the person whose interest is concerned, the fact that the request has been made is an important one. The fact that the recipient has made the request is an indication that he, at least, regards the matter in respect to which information is desired as sufficiently important to justify the publication of any defamatory matter that may be involved in response to the request. In that case, the person requested to give information is not required nicely to evaluate the interest that the person making the request seeks to protect, nor to make that comparison otherwise required of him, between the harm likely to be done to the other's reputation if the defamatory matter is false and the harm likely to be done to the third person's interest if it should prove true. Even in those cases, if the request or other circumstances indicate that the interest sought to be furthered by the person making the request is altogether trivial, the response is not privileged unless the harm likely to be done to the person defamed in the event that the defamatory matter proves false is correspondingly slight. On the other hand, one may not, unasked, intermeddle with the affairs of another by volunteering information merely because he reasonably believes that the recipient would ask for it if he knew that it were available. If he chooses to do so, the person thus offering gratuitous information must himself determine whether the harm likely to be done if his information proves false is substantially less than the good that it is likely to accomplish if it should prove true, that is, that the likelihood of advantage to the one person clearly offsets the risk of harm to the other.

The second big distinction between *Watt* and *Flowers* is that in *Flowers* the request was supported by a legitimate interest in the answer; the defendant's act had financial implications for the plaintiff's wife (evidently it was going to cause the household's bill to rise), so she had a right to ask why it was done—and a right to an answer uninhibited by fear of a defamation suit, so long as it was given in good faith. And since that was so, Smith had a correlative interest: in principle, his company could have been sued by Mrs. Flowers if he didn't have a good explanation for his behavior. In the Watt case, Longsdon had no interest comparable to Smith's, at least vis a vis Mrs. Watt. Longsdon did have an interest a little like Smith's when he communicated the letter to the chairman of the board, which is why that communication *was* privileged. To turn the point around, Mrs. Flowers might be considered more analogous to the chairman of the board in *Watt* than to Watt's wife; her interest in the issue was economic in the strict sense, not social.

To state the distinction from the standpoint of policy, it's clear that discouraging open communication between utilities and their customers could create costs in an unambiguous sense: the result might be inappropriate overcharges or needless litigation. The costs created by silence about Mr. Watt's conduct are more ambiguous. Perhaps Mrs. Watt was better off knowing the truth; perhaps she wasn't. Reasonable people might disagree about this. This leads to yet another question: would the outcome in *Watt* have been different if Browne's letter had reported that Mr. Watt had contracted a vicious venereal disease from his mistress? In that case the costs to Mrs. Watt of her ignorance might become higher and less ambiguous, and thus the moral duty of Longsdon to tell her about it would have been in sharper focus.

Q. Were the privileges at issue in *Watt v. Longsdon* and *Flowers v. Smith* the same?
A. Not quite. Remember that in *Watt* there were three different acts of publication at issue. The communication of the letter to the chairman of the board can be understood in modern terms as cloaked in the common interest privilege, as can the statements in *Flowers v. Smith*. The publication of Watt's letter to his wife resulted in liability (or can be stylized as resulting in liability—obviously we don't know what the real outcome was) because there was no such common interest. The best that Longsdon could say was that the transmission was needed to protect the interest of the recipient. But for that privilege to

apply there has to be a duty, formal or informal, to convey the information. That was the hard issue in the case.

Israel v. Portland News Pub. Co. (after D defames P, P defames D; NL for latter)
Sternberg Mfg. Co. v. Miller, DuBrul & Peters Mfg. Co. (P circulated document suggesting D was infringing P's patents; D firm replies by defaming P; L)

Q. Is there a satisfactory distinction between *Sternberg Mfg. Co. v. Miller, DuBrul & Peters Mfg. Co.* and *Israel v. Portland News Pub. Co.*?

A. The cases do seem to take different positions on the legal issue, with *Sternberg* declining to acknowledge (as most courts would) the potential availability of a self-defense privilege. But even if the court in *Sternberg* had acknowledged that privilege it might not have applied here; the cases may be distinguishable on their facts. Notice the little analogy the court in *Sternberg* draws to retaliation for assaults. The analogy can be developed further, as is done in Newell on Slander and Libel:

> The law does not allow independent wrongs, of the nature treated of in this work, to be set off against each other and a balance found in favor of the less culpable party. The principle which allows proof of provocation in mitigation of damages is the same as that which is applicable in the case of a provoked assault; and if there has been time and opportunity for hot blood to cool and calm reason to resume its ordinary control, a mere provocation not connected with the wrong cannot be shown. If in this respect there is any distinction between the cases of personal encounter and assault and written defamation, it would seem that the rule should be applied with at least as great strictness in the latter class as in the former, since the composition and publication of a libel in general involves necessarily some degree of deliberation and opportunity for reflection. There are plain reasons of public policy for this limitation of the right to reply in extenuation of such wrongs, upon remote provoking inducements not connected with the matter in issue. If the law were less strict there would be less self-restraint from acts of violence and wrong calculated to disturb the peace of society. Men would be too ready to take it upon themselves to avenge their personal grievances; and again, in the trial of causes for alleged wrongs, the principal issue would be embarrassed and confused, if not overwhelmed, by numerous collateral issues.'

Here, then, is a possible distinction between *Miller* and *Israel*: in the *Israel* case the allegedly libelous reply followed on the same day as the statements that provoked it. In *Miller* there evidently was a greater cooling period. But the distinction probably won't bear much weight for several reasons. We don't know quite how much time elapsed in *Miller*; nothing in *Israel* suggests that the result there would have been different if Mrs. Akin had delayed in making her reply; and courts generally do not indicate that the passage of time is an important factor in determining whether the self-defense privilege applies. Yet conceivably it is true that courts are more receptive the privilege when invoked by people whose reputations have been freshly attacked than when invoked by firms like those in *Miller*.

A different possible distinction is that in *Israel* the original, provocative statement was more clearly libelous than it was in *Miller*. Whether the original circulars described by the court in *Miller* were defamatory is not clear; we aren't given their full text, but the idea presumably would be that if Miller said it had exclusive rights to do X, this necessarily was defamatory of someone else who also was doing X. But while the trial court found that the Miller firm did have some good patents, the appellate court's decision in *Miller* seems to say that even if the original notices were defamatory, this did not enlarge the defendant's rights by way of reply.

If there is no good distinction between the cases, and maybe there isn't, then perhaps it's best just to consider which rule is better. You can explore the logic offered in the Newell excerpts above and in the book's excerpt from *Israel*, and also this passage from Wilkes, J., in *Huntley v. Ward*, 6 C. B. (N. S.)

514: 'There are, however, certain excepted cases where a communication is privileged, though prima facie libelous. But these are cases where the matter is written in the assertion of some legal or moral duty, or in self-defense, and the thing is done honestly, and without sinister motive, and in the bona fide belief in the truth of the statement at the time of making it. In such cases, no matter how harsh, hasty, untrue, or libelous the publication would be but for the circumstances, the law declares it privileged, because the amount of public inconvenience from the restriction of freedom of speech or writing would far outbalance that arising from the infliction of a private injury. Therefore, upon principles of public policy, such communications are protected.

2. *Absolute privileges.*

Roush v. Hey (judge appears on television and defames P, a party to a case he decided; L)
Sriberg v. Raymond (lawyer publishes defamatory letter about P in demand letter before lawsuit is filed; NL)
Yoder v. Workman (problem: judge disparages P lawyer in "news release" on court website; L)

Q. What is the distinction between *Sriberg v. Raymond* and *Roush v. Hey*?
A. First get straight the superficial similarities. Both involved participants in the legal process making (let us assume) defamatory statements outside a courtroom. In *Roush*, at least, a case was pending; in *Sriberg* it wasn't. Yet *Roush*, involving a judge rather than a lawyer, is the case of liability. Why?

The simplest point is that the attorney was thought to be performing a socially valuable function: negotiating, even if in hardball fashion. The judge was not performing a socially valuable function in discussing his case on television. One can ask why the courts find no social value in the latter case; clearly the public was interested in what Hey had to say (else he would not have been invited onto the program). Here there is room for a good discussion of why we generally expect judges to confine the expressions of their opinions about their cases to their opinions and courtrooms. The court in *Roush* describes what is expected by litigants, but *why* are those their expectations?

The discussion can bring out the point that privileges generally attach to *functions*, not to people. The point is made clear in these further excerpts from the court's opinion in *Roush v. Hey*:

> Some of the policies that sustain the doctrine [of absolute judicial immunity from defamation suits] are expressed as follows: (1) insuring the finality of judgments; (2) protecting judicial independence; (3) avoiding continual attacks upon judges who may be sincere in their conduct; and (4) protecting the system of justice from falling into disrepute.

> Will the cause of judicial independence be jeopardized if we do not immunize the comments of a judge made during the course of a debate on national television regarding the merits of one of his decisions? We think not. Judge Hey was not exercising any judicial prerogative or discretion. He was attempting to publicly defend to a national television audience an order, the basis of which was to condemn a single parent for cohabiting with a person to whom she was not married. Judicial immunity is justified and defined by the functions it protects and serves, not by the person to whom it attaches. Granting Judge Hey immunity under the facts and circumstances of this case would be protecting Judge Hey only because he is a judge and not because of the function that he was performing. [...]

> The only rational explanation why Judge Hey chose to be a guest on "Crossfire" and publicly comment about a pending case was that he wanted to justify his opinion to as many people as possible. Comments made in pursuit of personal notoriety and national recognition are not judicial acts and are therefore not protected against civil liability.

Q. Suppose the lawyer for the father in *Roush* had gone onto *Crossfire*, rather than Judge Hey; and suppose he had made the same statements. Absolute immunity?

A. No; statements by lawyers to the press are generally not considered privileged. It's different if the lawyer is reciting or delivering a pleading to the press, but there is no privilege for television appearances. So here is a chance to relate the policies behind the judge's and lawyer's privileges.

Q. What result in *Yoder v. Workman*?

A. It's a case of liability (at least at this writing; an appeal remains possible). It's a nice problem because it raises several issues and thus provides a chance for some review as well as for exploration of the issues under current consideration:

1. An initial issue involves the defamation of the group described as "his stable of lawyers." The court found the plaintiff to be readily enough identified; there were six lawyers in the stable.

2. Second was the question of judicial immunity. Said the court:

> The issue here is whether a judge's publishing a press release on the court's website to explain and elaborate her recusal notice is an act normally performed by a judge. The obvious answer is no. Courts speak through their orders. They do not issue press releases or other "public relations" materials to explain, justify or further inform the public about their decisions. Judicial codes of conduct prohibit judges from making "any public or nonpublic comment about any pending or impending proceeding which might reasonably be expected to affect its outcome or impair its fairness." *Code of Judicial Conduct Canon* 3(B)(9). In this case the public comment accompanied a recusal notice, so the justice herself was no longer involved. Nevertheless, the case continued pending before the court and public comment by a justice about the parties and lawyers involved was inappropriate at best. A press release about the recusal order was not a judicial act and, as such, absolute judicial immunity does not apply to shield its author.

The court also noted that Workman had the option of issuing a formal order stating her decision—and that she did so.

3. Next, Workman argued that even if judicial immunity did not apply she nevertheless was entitled to a qualified privilege based on "common interest." Again the court rejected the argument:

> As [Workman] reports, it is well-settled that a "qualified privilege exists when a person publishes a subject in good faith about a subject in which he has an interest or duty and limits the publication of the statement to those persons who have a legitimate interest in the subject matter." Workman's press release was published on the state Supreme Court's website, however, and not limited to those with an interest in the matter, but made available to the general world- wide public via the Internet. Accordingly, no qualified privilege is available to her publication.

And then this footnote:

> Similarly, the privilege for defamatory statements concerning future litigation is available only where the matter is published "*only* to persons with an interest in the prospective judicial proceedings." Defendant misstates the test, by leaving out the crucial word "only". Again, the publication audience of Defendant's press release was unlimited.

4. Finally, Workman claimed that her statements were not defamatory because they were "rhetorical hyperbole." The court disagreed:

[I]t is not immediately apparent to a reasonable reader that "vitriolic campaign of judge shopping," "spurious and unethical legal actions and false allegations," and "campaign ... designed to stalk, harass and defame me" are used in a loose, figurative or imaginative sense. These phrases could, in fact, be reasonably interpreted as stating actual facts about Yoder as well as Chafin's other lawyers.

Beggarly v. Craft (D calls P a whore; L, with evidence that P *later* engaged in prostitution held inadmissible)

Guccione v. Hustler Magazine, Inc. (D describes P as adulterer, but P no longer was married; P had, however, been unfaithful during his marriage; NL)

Buckner v. Spaulding (D accuses P of adultery with one man; in fact P had adulterous relationship with different man; L)

Q. What is the distinction between *Beggarly v. Craft* and *Guccione v. Hustler Magazine, Inc.*?
A. In both cases the statement made about the plaintiff was false when it was made but was (we can assume) true at some other time—very soon afterwards in the case of *Beggarly*. But in *Beggarly* the court detects a policy worry: if evidence of *later* prostitution can be used to prove the truth of the defamatory statement, then the defendant who makes such a statement will have an incentive to induce the plaintiff to commit such acts in order to make the statement come true and create a defense for himself. This isn't a problem if the evidence of substantial truth is limited to acts that already were committed. (What if P wants to introduce the evidence to support the theory that D's claim left her with such a bad reputation that she had no economic recourse but to *become* a prostitute?)

Q. What is the distinction between *Guccione v. Hustler Magazine, Inc.* and *Buckner v. Spaulding*?
A. In *Guccione* the allegedly defamatory statement was wrong only in its timing: Guccione had, in fact, been having an affair with Keeton during his marriage; the marriage merely had ended by the time the defendant's statement was made. In *Buckner* the statement was correct in its timing—correct (we can assume) in saying that the plaintiff was having an affair—but incorrect in naming the person with whom the affair was being conducted. The idea evidently is that a significant part of the sting of a claim of adultery lies in who the partner to the adultery is said to have been. Maybe its effect on the plaintiff's reputation will vary depending on whether the partner also was married or was a person of ill repute. In the *Guccione* case the sting of the defendant's charge came almost entirely from features of it that were true; those who were troubled by it would be unlikely to change their minds if told that actually Guccione's 13-year adulterous affair with Keeton had become non-adulterous when he divorced his wife in 1979, four years before the defendant's statement was made.

For a still more ribald study in the operation of the principle (brace yourself), we find this headnote in *Downs v. Hawley*, 112 Mass. 237 (1873): "A defendant in slander cannot justify by proving the plaintiff to have been guilty of another crime of the same kind as that alleged to have been in the accusation. Thus one cannot justify his charge of sodomy with a mare by proof of sodomy with a cow." The opinion in the case, by the felicitously-named Colt, J., is a little more oblique.

Q. Hypothetical: in *Cardillo v. Doubleday, Inc.*, 518 F.2d 638 (2d Cir. 1975), the plaintiff, Robert Cardillo, was an inmate in a federal prison. He alleged that he was defamed in a book published by the defendants called *My Life in the Mafia*. The book was the story of a man named Teresa who was involved in organized crime and became a government informant. Cardillo claimed that Teresa made various false claims in the book about Cardillo's participation in crimes the book described, such as participation in a robbery above a laundromat and fixing a horse race at the Suffolk Downs race track. The defendant countered that Cardillo was serving a sentence of 21 years for a number of uncontested felonies, including convictions for stolen securities and bail-jumping, and had been indicted for fixing other races at the same track. Cardillo also admitted to being "frequently" in Teresa's company during the relevant period, to knowing that Teresa was a petty thief and confidence man, and to being "directly involved" with Teresa "in several minor crimes, none of which were noteworthy or profitable." What result?

A. No liability. This evidently was the first case establishing the idea that the plaintiff could be "libel proof": in possession of such a low reputation that the defendant's misstatements were incapable of doing him real harm. Said the court, affirming summary judgment for the defendants: "we consider as a matter of law that appellant is, for purposes of this case, libel-proof, i. e., so unlikely by virtue of his life as a habitual criminal to be able to recover anything other than nominal damages as to warrant dismissal of the case, involving as it does First Amendment considerations."

The hypo is meant to raise questions about whether a plaintiff ever should be considered "libel proof." Then-Judge Scalia dismissed this is a "fundamentally bad idea" in *Anderson v. Liberty Lobby*, 746 F.2d 1563 (D.C.Cir. 1984):

> [Defendants] claim that the unchallenged portions of these articles attribute to the appellants characteristics so much worse than those attributed in the challenged portions, that the latter cannot conceivably do any incremental damage. This apparently equitable theory loses most of its equity when one realizes that the reason the unchallenged portions are unchallenged may not be that they are true, but only that appellants were unable to assert that they were willfully false. In any event, the theory must be rejected because it rests upon the assumption that one's reputation is a monolith, which stands or falls in its entirety. The law, however, proceeds upon the optimistic premise that there is a little bit of good in all of us—or perhaps upon the pessimistic assumption that no matter how bad someone is, he can always be worse. It is shameful that Benedict Arnold was a traitor; but he was not a shoplifter to boot, and one should not have been able to make that charge while knowing its falsity with impunity. So also here. Even if some of the deficiencies of philosophy or practice which the appellees' articles are lawfully permitted to attribute to the appellants (which is not necessarily to say they are true) are in fact much more derogatory than the statements under challenge, the latter cannot be said to be harmless. Even the public outcast's remaining good reputation, limited in scope though it may be, is not inconsequential. ("He was a liar and a thief, but for all that he was a good family man.")

But he added this:

> There may be validity to the proposition that at some point the erroneous attribution of incremental evidence of a character flaw of a particular type which is in any event amply established by the facts is not derogatory. If, for example, an individual is said to have been convicted of 35 burglaries, when the correct number is 34, it is not likely that the statement is actionable. That is so, however, not because the object of the remarks is "libel-proof," but because, since the essentially derogatory implication of the statement ("he is an habitual burglar") is correct, he has not been libeled.

Q. Hypothetical: in *Ray v. Time, Inc.*, 452 F.Supp. 618 *aff'd.*, 582 F.2d 1280 (6th Cir. 1978), the plaintiff was James Earl Ray, confessed assassin of Martin Luther King, Jr.; he also had been convicted of other felonies The defendants published an article saying that Ray was a "narcotics addict and peddler" and a thief. Ray denied this and sued for libel. The defendants said he was libel proof. What result?

A. The complaint was dismissed: "The Court is persuaded, in the light of all the circumstances in this cause and in the public record involved in the other cases mentioned, that plaintiff, James E. Ray, is libel-proof, as that term was used in *Cardillo v. Doubleday & Co., Inc.*, 518 F.2d 638, 639 (2d Cir. 1975) (Oakes, J.). Ray, as Cardillo, is a convicted habitual criminal and is so unlikely to be able to recover damages to his reputation as to warrant dismissal of his libel claim in the light of First Amendment considerations attendant to publication of material dealing with his background and his criminal activities."

SECTION E. CONSTITUTIONAL DEVELOPMENTS

1. Public plaintiffs

New York Times v. Sullivan (establishing "actual malice" requirement for suits by public officials)
Curtis Publishing Co. v. Butts (extends requirement to public figures)
Hutchinson v. Proxmire (P, winner of "golden fleece" award given by D for bad federally-funded research, not a public figure; L)
Wolston v. Reader's Digest Association (P, found guilty of contempt during espionage investigation, not a public figure; L)
Dameron v. Washington Magazine, Inc. (P, air traffic controller when accident occurred, found to be a public figure; NL)
Clyburn v. News World Communications (problem: P, friend of D.C. bigshots whose girlfriend died at party, held to be a public figure; NL)

The pedagogical approach of this part of the chapter is to present the key Supreme Court cases and then explore their implications with cases from the lower appellate courts. This first batch of cases focuses on how "public figures" are defined. The next batch focuses on the meaning of the "actual malice" requirement. If you want shortened treatment, you could just assign *New York Times v. Sullivan* and then maybe *Hutchinson* and *Dameron* from the first block of materials, and the *Masson* and the *Kaelin* problem from the second batch. If you want to abbreviate the subsequent section (the materials on private plaintiffs), cut the *Phantom Touring* case and the excerpt from *Stevens v. Tillman*.

Instructors will have a range of preferences regarding how much time to spend working through the details of the Court's arguments in *New York Times* and the Court's other leading cases. Most of our focus in this manual will be on the cases that test the applications of the Court's doctrines, but there are a few particular angles on the *New York Times* case worth mentioning. First, you might ask how the case should have been analyzed before the First Amendment enters the picture. Was it clear that the statements in the *Times* were "of and concerning" the plaintiff, who was not named by them? Were the statements in the advertisement substantially true (despite being mistaken in detail)? If not, did the inaccuracies warrant $500,000 in general damages? The Alabama decision seemed vulnerable on all of these traditional grounds, which is worth seeing in itself and also as a basis for wondering whether the strong steps the Court took were necessary.

Second, what of the extension of the *New York Times* rule from public officials to public figures? The former doctrine is easy enough to understand by reference to the need for vigorous political debate, a value everyone understands as central to the First Amendment. But what rationale for the First Amendment justifies such extensive protection for criticism of athletes, entertainers, and artists? Is the idea is that those sorts of figures have ample opportunity to rebut defamatory statements because they can make their voices heard?

From the concurring opinion of Warren, C.J., in *Curtis Publishing Co. v. Butts*:

To me, differentiation between 'public figures' and 'public officials' and adoption of separate standards of proof for each have no basis in law, logic, or First Amendment policy. Increasingly in this country, the distinctions between governmental and private sectors are blurred. Since the depression of the 1930's and World War II there has been a rapid fusion of economic and political power, a merging of science, industry, and government, and a high degree of interaction between the intellectual, governmental, and business worlds. Depression, war, international tensions, national and international markets, and the surging growth of science and technology have precipitated national and international problems that demand national and international solutions. While these trends and events have occasioned a consolidation of governmental power, power has also become much more organized in what we have commonly considered to be the private sector. In many situations, policy determinations which traditionally were channeled through formal political institutions are now originated and implemented through a complex array of boards, committees, commissions, corporations, and associations, some only loosely connected with the Government. This blending of positions and power has also occurred in the case of individuals so that many who do not hold public office at the moment are nevertheless intimately involved in the resolution of important public questions or, by reason of their fame, shape events in areas of concern to society at large.

Viewed in this context, then, it is plain that although they are not subject to the restraints of the political process, 'public figures,' like 'public officials,' often play an influential role in ordering society. And surely as a class these 'public figures' have as ready access as 'public officials' to mass media of communication, both to influence policy and to counter criticism of their views and activities. Our citizenry has a legitimate and substantial interest in the conduct of such persons, and freedom of the press to engage in uninhibited debate about their involvement in public issues and events is as crucial as it is in the case of 'public officials.' The fact that they are not amenable to the restraints of the political process only underscores the legitimate and substantial nature of the interest, since it means that public opinion may be the only instrument by which society can attempt to influence their conduct.

I therefore adhere to the *New York Times* standard in the case of 'public figures' as well as 'public officials.' It is a manageable standard, readily stated and understood, which also balances to a proper degree the legitimate interests traditionally protected by the law of defamation. Its definition of 'actual malice' is not so restrictive that recovery is limited to situations where there is 'knowing falsehood' on the part of the publisher of false and defamatory matter. 'Reckless disregard' for the truth or falsity, measured by the conduct of the publisher, will also expose him to liability for publishing false material which is injurious to reputation. More significantly, however, the *New York Times* standard is an important safeguard for the rights of the press and public to inform and be informed on matters of legitimate interest. Evenly applied to cases involving 'public men'—whether they be 'public officials' or 'public figures'—it will afford the necessary insulation for the fundamental interests which the First Amendment was designed to protect.

Q. What is the distinction between *Dameron v. Washington Magazine, Inc.* and *Wolston v. Reader's Digest Association*? What is the distinction between *Dameron* and *Hutchinson v. Proxmire*?
A. From the *Dameron* opinion:

Dameron was a central figure, however involuntarily, in the discrete and specific public controversy with respect to which he was allegedly defamed—the controversy over the cause of the Mt. Weather crash. Wolston, by contrast, was not defamed with respect to the controversy in which he played a central role—his refusal to testify before a grand jury—but rather with respect to a controversy in which he played a role that was at most tangential—the investigation of Soviet espionage in general. [...]

Paradoxically, the magazine article never mentions Dameron's name or other identifying characteristics. If Dameron had not been previously linked with accounts of the tragedy, no magazine reader could tie the alleged defamation to Dameron. Indeed, it was partly *because* of the defendant's public notoriety that he was identifiable at all from the oblique reference in *The Washingtonian.*

So the implication is that Wolston would have lost (or at least would have been considered a public figure) if he had been defamed in 1958 in an article discussing his failure to respond to the subpoena. This is a useful point to bring out. As for *Hutchinson*, the superficial similarity is that in both that case and *Dameron* someone working for the government came under unexpected and uninvited scrutiny that included defamatory statements about them. But in *Dameron* the plaintiff's profile was elevated by an occurrence other than the defamation itself: the accident. The *Dameron* decision nevertheless is questionable, as the plaintiff seems to lack both of the characteristics that the Court suggested in *Gertz* tend to be most important in a public figure: a voluntary act that amounts to an assumption of the risk of scrutiny, and some heightened ability to take defensive measures by responding in the media to defamatory statements.

Q. What result in *Clyburn v. News World Communications*?
A. Clyburn was held to be a public figure. From the opinion:

> In discussing whether a plaintiff's role in a controversy was central enough to justify imposing the actual malice burden, the Supreme Court has explained that a private individual typically lacks the public figure's ability to use the media for rebuttal, and "[m]ore important," has not run "the risk of closer public scrutiny" that falls on those who, for example, seek public office. *Gertz,* 418 U.S. at 344. Clearly concerned lest the *New York Times* standard be thrust on individuals who chose not to run such risks, the Court declared that though it "may be possible for someone to become a public figure through no purposeful action of his own, ... the instances of truly involuntary public figures must be exceedingly rare." *Id.* Typically, the Court suggested, limited-purpose public figures will be persons who "have thrust themselves to the front of particular public controversies in order to influence the resolution of the issues involved." *Id.* Clyburn denies that he injected himself into the public controversy at all.

> Courts have placed weight on a plaintiff's "trying to influence the outcome" of a controversy. *Waldbaum,* 627 F.2d at 1297; compare *Wolston v. Reader's Digest Ass'n,* 443 U.S. 157 (1979) (plaintiff who "did not in any way seek to arouse public sentiment in his favor" found not to be limited-purpose public figure). Of course, this can not include statements that merely answer the alleged libel itself; if it did, libellers could "create their own defense by making the claimant a public figure." *Hutchinson v. Proxmire,* 443 U.S. 111, 135 (1979). Similarly, we have doubts about placing much weight on purely defensive, truthful statements made when an individual finds himself at the center of a public controversy but before any libel occurs; it is not clear why someone dragged into a controversy should be able to speak publicly only at the expense of foregoing a private person's protection from defamation. Indeed, the cases have suggested that ordinarily something more than a plaintiff's short simple statement of his view of the story is required; he renders himself a public figure only if he voluntarily "draw[s] attention to himself" or uses his position in the controversy "as a fulcrum to create public discussion." *Wolston,* 443 U.S. at 168. Here, Clyburn *falsely* told the Washington Post that he had been alone with Medina and had called 911. We view this cover-up attempt as going beyond an ordinary citizen's response to the eruption of a public fray around him.

> More important, Clyburn's acts *before* any controversy arose put him at its center. His consulting firm had numerous contracts with the District government, he had many social contacts with administration officials, and Medina, at least as one may judge from attendance at her funeral, also enjoyed such ties. Clyburn also spent the night of Medina's collapse in her company. One may hobnob with high officials without becoming a public figure, but one who does so runs the

risk that personal tragedies that for less well-connected people would pass unnoticed may place him at the heart of a public controversy. Clyburn engaged in conduct that he knew markedly raised the chances that he would become embroiled in a public controversy. This conduct, together with his false statements at the controversy's outset, disable him from claiming the protections of a purely "private" person. See, e.g., *Marcone v. Penthouse International Magazine for Men,* 754 F.2d 1072, 1086 (3rd Cir.1985) (plaintiff's "voluntary connection" with widely publicized motorcycle gangs contributed to his public figure status); *Rosanova v. Playboy Enterprises, Inc.,* 580 F.2d 859, 861 (5th Cir.1978) (plaintiff held to be limited-purpose public figure because he "voluntarily engaged in a course that was bound to invite attention and comment").

Finally, the alleged defamatory statement—that Clyburn and his friends delayed calling for help so that other partygoers could first leave—relates directly to Clyburn's role in the controversy with respect to which he became a limited-purpose public figure.

St. Amant v. Thompson (NL because D lacked actual malice; failure to investigate not enough)
Masson v. New Yorker Magazine, Inc. (D changed Ps quotes; NL because this didn't create "knowledge of falsity" unless the meaning of the quotes was materially affected)
Kaelin v. Globe Communications Corp. ("Cops Think Kato Did It" headline implied that P was may be murderer, then D clarified that headline referred to possible perjury; L)
Meisler v. Gannett Co. (D publishes incorrect story about P, overlooking correction that had arrived by wire soon afterwards; NL)
Martin v. Wilson Publishing Co. (D reports rumor that P was involved in arson; L)

We turn to the "actual malice" requirement.

Q.   What result in *Kaelin v. Globe Communications Corp.*?
A.   Liability—in that summary judgment was denied and a verdict for the plaintiff was found permissible on this evidence. This set of problem cases invites review of issues from earlier in the chapter as well as exploration of actual malice. Regarding the basic elements of defamation, the court in *Kaelin* had this to say:

> Globe argues that the "it" refers to perjury. Even assuming that such a reading is reasonably possible, it is not the only reading that is reasonably possible as a matter of law. So long as the publication is reasonably susceptible of a defamatory meaning, a factual question for the jury exists. [...]

> Globe argues that the entirety of the publication, including the story itself, clears up any false and defamatory meaning that could be found on the cover. Whether it does or not is a question of fact for the jury. The Kaelin story was located 17 pages away from the cover. In this respect, the National Examiner's front page headline is unlike a conventional headline that immediately precedes a newspaper story, and nowhere does the cover headline reference the internal page where readers could locate the article. A reasonable juror could conclude that the Kaelin article was too far removed from the cover headline to have the salutary effect that Globe claims. [...]

Regarding actual malice:

> First, Globe editor John Garton testified at his deposition that he saw the headline before it ran and did not think that it "was very accurate to the story." He stated that he was "a bit concerned" that readers might connect the "it" in the headline with the murders. This is direct evidence from which a reasonable juror could find that Globe knew that the headline was factually inaccurate or

that Globe acted with reckless disregard for the truth. It is for a jury to decide whether, as Globe argues, it intended to clarify the sentence "COPS THINK KATO DID IT!" with the sentence that followed, "... he fears they want him for perjury, say pals." The editors' statements of their subjective intention are matters of credibility for a jury.

Second, it is undisputed that Globe ran the headline "COPS THINK KATO DID IT!" *knowing* that it had no reason to believe that Kaelin was a murder suspect. This is not a case where Globe relied in good faith on information that turned out to be false. It is undisputed that Globe never believed Kaelin to be a suspect in the murders. The fact that Globe ran the headlines *anyway* -- "act [ing] with a 'high degree of awareness of ... probable falsity' "—is circumstantial evidence of actual malice. *Masson,* 501 U.S. at 510; *see also Eastwood v. National Enquirer, Inc.,* 123 F.3d at 1253 ("As we have yet to see a defendant who admits to entertaining serious subjective doubt about the authenticity of an article it published, we must be guided by circumstantial evidence. By examining the editors' actions, we try to understand their motives.")).

Alas, soon the case will be just a little less fun as fewer students will have any recollection of who Kato Kaelin was.

Q. What result in *Meisler v. Gannett Co.?*
A. No liability. From the court's opinion:

> "Reckless disregard," for purposes of proving actual malice, is shown if "the defendant entertained serious doubts as to the truth of his publication." *St. Amant v. Thompson,* 390 U.S. 727, 731 (1968). Stated differently, the standard is met by proving that the defendants "actually had a high degree of awareness of [the statement's] probable falsity." *Id.* (quoting *Garrison v. Louisiana,* 379 U.S. 64 (1964)). *St. Amant* reaffirms the rule that "reckless conduct is not measured by whether a reasonably prudent man would have published, or would have investigated before publishing." Both of Meisler's expert witnesses admitted that there was no evidence to indicate that Davis acted with knowledge of the article's falsity, or with serious doubts about the truth of the article, or with a high degree of awareness of the article's probable falsity. At best, the defendants' actions were negligent; negligence is not the appropriate standard for proving actual malice. *See St. Amant,* 390 U.S. at 731-32.

Q. What result in *Martin v. Wilson Publishing Co.?*
A. Below are some long but interesting and useful excerpts from the court's opinion. In brief, the plaintiff was held to be entitled to a trial. He was a public figure, so the question was whether the reprinting of the defamatory rumor was done with actual malice. In a sense the answer obviously is yes: the writer indicates in the text itself that he doubts the rumor is true. So the larger question is whether there can be liability under the Supreme Court's cases for printing a rumor like this. The court says there can indeed be liability, and distinguishes this case from *Edwards v. National Audubon Society,* a Second Circuit case where the publication of a rumor was held constitutionally privileged because the rumor was uttered by a respectable source and thus was legitimately newsworthy. The court begins by pointing out that Martin had been the subject of a number of newspaper stories and thus that he had attained public-figure status by virtue of being known to a substantial portion of the defendant's readership. The court continued:

> In *New York Times,* the doctrine was enunciated and later refined by subsequent United States Supreme Court cases to the effect that a public figure may not recover damages for a published defamatory falsehood about him "unless he proves that *the statement* was made with 'actual malice'—that is, with knowledge that it was false or with reckless disregard of whether it was false or not." *New York Times,* 376 U.S. at 279-80. (Emphasis added.) The critical inquiry in

this case is what is meant by "the statement," as that term is used in the oft-repeated principle articulated in *New York Times.* This is especially so when the case involves the publication of false defamatory rumors. In respect to rumors, there is a statement by the originator of the rumor (who is generally unknown); there then is repetition (further publication) of the statement by others; and finally, as in this case, there may be printed publication of either the statement itself or the fact that others are circulating the statement or even some hybrid version of both in which it is unclear whether the publisher has concurred in the statement, has completely disavowed it, or is in some way impartially trying to distance itself from those who are reported as having made the statement.

The defendants argued at trial, and the trial justice instructed the jury, that defendants would not be liable for the publication of rumors that plaintiff had been guilty of the crime of arson if, in fact, such rumors existed. In essence, the trial justice ruled as a matter of law that if such rumors were current at or before the time of publication, the newspaper could republish such rumors with impunity. Consequently, the trial justice required plaintiff, in order to prevail, to prove that there were no such rumors. With this proposition of law we respectfully disagree.

It has long been recognized in respect to the law of defamation that one who republishes libelous or slanderous material is subject to liability just as if he had published it originally. [...] Although the press is entitled to a number of privileges relating to fair comment, neutral reportage, and the expression of pure opinion, there is no constitutional value in false statements of fact. *See Gertz,* 418 U.S. at 339-40. Consequently, the appropriate inquiry to be submitted to the triers of fact in the instant case was not whether such rumors existed but whether the rumors were based upon fact or whether they were false. If the answer to the first question was that the rumors were false, we would then come to the question posed by *New York Times,* 376 U.S. at 279-80, as made applicable to a public figure pursuant to *Curtis Publishing Co.,* 388 U.S. at 152-54, namely, whether the publication of such rumors was made with knowledge that they were false or with reckless disregard of whether they were false or not.

It seems obvious beyond question that the publication of rumors that the writer of the article stated were based upon the stretching of available facts and "imaginations" would create a jury question concerning whether the publication was made with "actual malice," namely, knowledge that the statement was false or with reckless disregard of whether it was false or not. Even if the reporter or publisher might not have had actual knowledge of the falsity of the rumors, either one certainly had sufficient doubts about their truth to make it a question of fact about whether the statements had been published with reckless disregard of whether they were false or not. [...]

We would be remiss at this point if we did not fully dispose of an argument that is advanced by defendants in this case and which has been asserted elsewhere in situations similar to that in the instant case. What is argued is that there are at least some instances in which a newspaper should not be barred from reporting the existence of defamatory statements, including rumors, if only for the fact that the making of such statements is newsworthy in itself. This argument undoubtedly derives its basis from the common-law privilege of fair report and the more recent doctrine of neutral reportage as suggested in *Edwards v. National Audubon Society, Inc.,* 556 F.2d 113, 120 (2d Cir. 1976).

The common-law privilege of fair report protects the publication of fair and accurate reports of public meetings and judicial proceedings, even when an individual is defamed during the proceeding or action. This privilege does not abrogate the policy of protecting one's reputation but rather subordinates this value to the countervailing public interest in the availability of information about official proceedings and public meetings.

The defendants argue by analogy that the underlying concept of fair report should similarly protect republishing a rumor already in existence, even in the face of knowledge of its falsity. We are of the opinion, however, that there is little merit to this argument, especially in light of the contours of this case. It is important to observe that the fair-report privilege accommodates the important societal interest in facilitating dissemination of information about judicial and governmental proceedings at which identified and identifiable persons may participate in resolving disputes and advancing the progress of government. In a judicial proceeding if one is defamed through cross-examination, opportunity exists for the one defamed to respond to rebut the defamation. With public meetings those susceptible of defamation may attend such gatherings and defend against attacks. We find no similar countervailing policy to protect repetition of rumors. The spreading of rumors does not give the person defamed by them the opportunity to rebut the underlying allegations of the rumor. To attempt to defend against a rumor is not unlike attempting to joust with a cloud. Publication of a rumor further fuels the continued repetition and does so in an especially egregious way by enshrining it in print. Thus there is little room to deny that the opportunity for abuse of the reporting of the existence of a defamatory rumor is great, and as a result a number of courts (and today we join them) have denied the right to report the existence of rumors when the underlying accusation of the rumor is believed to be false.

From a slightly different point of view, defendants argue that a rule precluding reportage of a third person's defamatory remarks would act as a perpetual bar to ever reporting that a third person has made such remarks or that defamatory rumors were circulating in a community. A case that arguably would allow such reportage is *Edwards, supra,* in which a defamation suit arose in the aftermath of a raging controversy between the proponents of the pesticide DDT and the National Audubon Society. The society claimed that the proponents had misinterpreted data relevant to the controversy and accused as "paid liars" certain scientists who used such data to aid the pesticide proponents' cause. A reporter for the New York Times accurately reprinted the accusations, the names of the scientists, and their outraged denials. In the ensuing litigation that reached the United States Court of Appeals for the Second Circuit, Chief Judge Kaufman, writing for the court, held that "when a responsible, prominent organization like the National Audubon Society makes serious charges against a public figure, the First Amendment protects the accurate and disinterested reporting of those charges, regardless of the reporter's private views regarding their validity." Reasoning that "[w]hat is newsworthy about such accusations is that they were made," the court concluded that the reporter should not have been required to suppress the story merely because he may have had serious doubts concerning the truth of the charge.

We are constrained to conclude, however, that there is a remarkably wide gulf between *Edwards* and the case at bar. In *Edwards* the court emphasized the existence of a prominent responsible organization originating the charges. This itself has been argued to have been newsworthy. With rumors, however, any such characteristics are wholly absent. A rumor by definition is anonymously spawned, and those who give it currency, if their identity can be ascertained, certainly do not take any responsibility for its truth. In *Cianci,* 639 F.2d at 69-70, the United States Court of Appeals for the Second Circuit noted that:

"The need for the careful limitation of a constitutional privilege for fair reportage is demonstrated by the breadth of that defense, which confers immunity even for publishing statements believed to be untrue. Absent the qualifications set forth by Chief Judge Kaufman in *Edwards,* all elements of the media would have absolute immunity to espouse and concur in the most unwarranted attacks, at least upon any public official or figure * * * by persons known to be of scant reliability."

We believe that this portion quoted from *Cianci* supports a rule that republication of false defamatory statements about an individual may be printed only in the extremely limited situation in which the publication accurately attributes such statements to an identified and responsible source. Assuming, without deciding, that *Edwards* as limited by *Cianci* is a correct statement of this aspect of the law of libel, we find this principle to be wholly inapplicable to rumors since a responsible source is lacking. Moreover, we discern no public policy which would be served by immunizing the reporting of false or baseless rumors. The need to report judicial and governmental proceedings is not paralleled by any discernible advantage to be secured to the public by the reporting of rumors. Consequently, publication of such rumors makes the publisher responsible under the "actual malice" test of *New York Times* for ascertaining the truth of the underlying defamatory material in such circumstances.

2. *Private plaintiffs*

Gertz v Robert Welch, Inc. (forbidding liability without fault, and requiring actual malice to support presumed or punitive damages, in suits involving private figures)
Dun & Bradstreet, Inc. v. Greenmoss Builders, Inc. (limiting *Gertz* to cases involving speech of public concern)
Philadelphia Newspapers v. Hepps (burden of proving falsity on the P when speech is of public concern)
Milkovich v. Lorain Journal Co. (when speech is of public concern, liability only if speech has provably false factual connotations)
Flamm v. American Assoc. of University Women (problem: P called "ambulance chaser"; L)
Phantom Touring, Inc., v. Affiliated Publications, Inc. (problem: P's production said to be deliberately calculated to confuse people; NL)
Mr. Chow of New York v. Ste. Jour Azur S.A. (problem: P's restaurant receives scathing review; L for some of the statements)

Again, our focus here will be on the cases exploring the application of the Supreme Court's cases; but here, first, are some notes on *Gertz* and its consequences:

First, in the retrial of *Gertz* itself the plaintiff went on to win $100,000 in compensatory damages and $300,000 in punitives—an upgrade over his original award.

Second, most states have responded to *Gertz* by requiring private plaintiffs to show negligence when they sue over statements on matters of public concern; some have gone farther, limiting or forbidding punitive damages in such cases by judicial decision or statute.

Third, how should the negligence of a media defendant be judged? From the Restatement (Second), sec. 580B:

Comment g. The negligence standard. Negligence is conduct that creates an unreasonable risk of harm. The standard of conduct is that of a reasonable person under like circumstances. Insofar as the truth or falsity of the defamatory statement is concerned, the question of negligence has sometimes been expressed in terms of the defendant's state of mind by asking whether he had reasonable grounds for believing that the communication was true. Putting the question in terms of conduct is to ask whether the defendant acted reasonably in checking on the truth or falsity or defamatory character of the communication before publishing it.

The defendant, if a professional disseminator of news, such as a newspaper, a magazine or a broadcasting station, or an employee, such as a reporter, is held to the skill and experience normally possessed by members of that profession. Customs and practices within the profession are relevant in applying the negligence standard, which is, to a substantial degree, set by the profession itself, though a custom is not controlling. If the defendant is an ordinary citizen, customs of the community as a whole may be relevant.

Evidence of custom within the profession of news dissemination would normally come from an expert who has been shown to be qualified on the subject. It may be testimony that the course of conduct followed by the defendant was or was not in accordance with recognized professional practices. It might also be to the effect that publication of the particular false and defamatory communication would not ordinarily have taken place in the absence of negligence. In the absence of expert testimony, however, the court should be cautious in permitting the doctrine of res ipsa loquitur to take the case to the jury and permit the jury, on the basis of its own lay inferences, to decide that the defendant must have been negligent because it published a false and defamatory communication. This could produce a form of strict liability de facto and thus circumvent the constitutional requirement of fault.

Comment h. Factors in applying the negligence standard. In determining whether the defendant acted as a reasonable, prudent person under the circumstances in publishing the defamatory communication on the basis of his check or lack of check as to its accuracy and as to its defamatory character, there are factors to be taken into consideration. The thoroughness of the check that a reasonable person would make before he published the statement may vary with the play of these factors. The standard of care does not change, but its application may vary with the circumstances. One factor is the time element. Was the communication a matter of topical news requiring prompt publication to be useful, or was it one in which time and opportunity were freely available to investigate? In the latter situation, due care may require a more thorough investigation. A second factor is the nature of the interests that the defendant was seeking to promote by publishing the communication. Informing the public as to a matter of public concern is an important interest in a democracy; spreading of mere gossip is of less importance. How necessary was this communication to these recipients in order to protect the interest involved? If there was no substantial interest to protect in publishing the communication to these recipients, then a reasonable person would be hesitant to publish the communication unless he had good reason to believe that it was accurate.

A third factor is the extent of the damage to the plaintiff's reputation or the injury to his sensibilities that would be produced if the communication proves to be false. Was the communication defamatory on its face? Would its defamatory connotation be known only to a few? How extensive was the dissemination? How easily might the plaintiff protect his reputation by means at his own disposal?

What is the source of the pressure created by the "time element" to which the Restatement refers? From Schaefer, *Defamation and the First Amendment*, 52 Col. L. Rev. 1 (1960):

It should not be forgotten [...] that these time constraints are entirely self-imposed. Apparently the media people believe that for competitive reasons it is desirable to be first with a particular news story. My own impression is that the public is massively unconcerned about that question. But if my impression is wrong, deadline pressures afford no more justification for harm caused by negligent attacks upon reputation than for harm caused by a reporter's negligent driving in his haste to cover a story. Both negligent acts are have been insurable.

Q. In *Flamm*, how is the trial court supposed to decide whether the statements at issue were true?
A. From the court of appeals opinion:

Flamm alleges in his complaint that his description in the AAUW directory as an "ambulance chaser" states that he "has engaged in improper activities to solicit and obtain clients." Following *Milkovich*, we must decide whether the description of Flamm as an "ambulance chaser" reasonably implies that he has engaged in unethical solicitation, and if so, whether the accusation of unethical solicitation is capable of being proven false. The second question, however, is conceded by the defendants. They admit that the term "ambulance chaser" is provable as true or false when understood literally to accuse a lawyer of the unethical or criminal behavior of solicitation.

We conclude that the statement challenged by Flamm reasonably implies that he has engaged in unethical solicitation. The directory in all other respects states facts: names, addresses and phone numbers; a note that Ms. R "will not be able to consult with anyone affiliated with the Florida State University system because of a conflict of interest"; the warning that Mr. A "charges a $50.00 initial consultation fee and does not discuss potential cases over the phone"; and so on. Furthermore, the directory has the stated purpose of providing referrals to qualified attorneys and professionals to assist victims of gender discrimination. A reader of the directory, seeing the only negative comment among several hundred entries, would likely turn elsewhere for assistance. Indeed, the note about Flamm is highlighted in italics, suggesting that it warrants special attention and consideration.

Next, the AAUW contends that the phrase "with interest only in 'slam dunk cases'" indicates that the challenged statement cannot be read literally, because "slam dunk" is an imprecise term of slang suggesting that the entire statement amounts to a purely subjective judgment. There is little merit to this argument. Even if the "slam dunk" language might cause a reasonable reader to consider whether the entire statement was merely an informal complaint, we cannot say that it would be unreasonable to conclude otherwise. The description "an 'ambulance chaser' with interest only in 'slam dunk cases'" can reasonably be interpreted to mean an attorney who improperly solicits clients and then takes only easy cases. This reading, which separates to a degree the "ambulance chaser" characterization from the "slam dunk cases" language, is especially plausible because, in the challenged statement as printed, each of those phrases was separately enclosed in quotation marks. It would not be unreasonable to read the "ambulance chaser" excerpt literally, because it could have been unrelated to the "slam dunk cases" reference in whatever passage the AAUW was quoting.

AAUW also argues that "ambulance chaser" cannot be read in the literal sense of a lawyer who "has engaged in improper activities to solicit and obtain clients" because dictionary definitions of "ambulance chaser" typically refer to solicitation of negligence or accident victims. This peculiar argument, challenging the alleged meaning of "ambulance chaser" as overly literal because not literal enough, is without merit. Although "rhetorical hyperbole" and "lusty and imaginative expression" may not be actionable, there is at the same time no requirement that the defamatory meaning of a challenged statement correspond to its literal dictionary definition. It is sufficient, for the purpose of defeating this motion to dismiss, that the challenged statement reasonably implies the alleged defamatory meaning.

We therefore hold that the challenged statement is "reasonably susceptible to the defamatory meaning imputed to it." However, it remains for the jury to decide whether the challenged statement was likely to be understood by the reader in a defamatory sense.

Q.   What result in *Phantom Touring, Inc., v. Affiliated Publications, Inc.*?
A.   The trial court dismissed the plaintiff's defamation complaint. The court of appeals affirmed:

Arguably, the connotation of deliberate deception is sufficiently factual to be proved true or false, and therefore is vulnerable under *Milkovich*. To rebut the implied assertion, appellant might be able to present objective evidence demonstrating longstanding plans to take its "Phantom" on a nationwide tour of the United States, or evidence showing that the "Original London production" language in its advertising was developed before Webber's "Phantom" rose to prominence, and thus was not designed to deceive consumers.

Whether or not the allegation of intentional deception meets the "provable as true or false" criterion, however, we think the context of each article rendered the language not reasonably interpreted as stating "actual facts" about appellant's honesty. The sum effect of the format, tone and entire content of the articles is to make it unmistakably clear that Kelly was expressing a point of view only. As such, the challenged language is immune from liability.

The nonfactual nature of [the] articles is indicated at first glance by the format. Both appeared as a regularly run theater column, a type of article generally known to contain more opinionated writing than the typical news report. The structure and tone of the language reinforced this subjective design. [...] Kelly's snide, exasperated language indicated that his comments represented his personal appraisal of the factual information contained in the article.

Of greatest importance, however, is the breadth of Kelly's articles, which not only discussed all the facts underlying his views but also gave information from which readers might draw contrary conclusions. In effect, the articles offered a self-contained give-and-take, a kind of verbal debate between Kelly and those persons responsible for booking and marketing appellant's "Phantom." Because all sides of the issue, as well as the rationale for Kelly's view, were exposed, the assertion of deceit reasonably could be understood only as Kelly's personal conclusion about the information presented, not as a statement of fact.

Q. What result in *Mr. Chow of New York v. Ste. Jour Azur S.A.?*
A. The district court submitted six of the review's statements to the jury, instructing that if any of the statements were false, defamatory, and made with malice, they would support a verdict for the plaintiff:

(1) "It is impossible to have the basic condiments ... on the table."
(2) "The sweet and sour pork contained more dough ... than meat."
(3) "The green peppers ... remained still frozen on the plate."
(4) The rice was "soaking ... in oil."
(5) The Peking Duck "was made up of only one dish (instead of the traditional three)."
(6) The pancakes were "the thickness of a finger."

The trial court entered judgment on a jury verdict for the plaintiff. The court of appeals reversed:

[A] reasonable reader would not take [statements 1-4 and 6] literally. Read reasonably, the statements are incapable of being proved false. For example, the proper amount of oil in fried rice is clearly a matter of personal taste. What is too oily for one person may be perfect for some other person. The same can be said for the temperature of vegetables, the thickness of pancakes, the amount of dough in sweet and sour pork and the quality of service. Perhaps Mr. Chow could prove that the reviewer's personal tastes are bizarre and his opinions unreasonable, but that does not destroy their entitlement to constitutional protection.

When viewed in the entire context and given a reasonable rather than a literal reading, only the statement that Mr. Chow served Peking Duck in one dish instead of the traditional three can be viewed as an assertion of fact. The statement is not metaphorical or hyperbolic; it clearly is laden with factual content. Moreover, the statement contains allegations that are seemingly capable of being proved true or false.

The court held, however, that even on this last score the plaintiff must lose because he was a limited-purpose public figure and was unable to show actual malice.

CHAPTER 12

INVASION OF PRIVACY

SECTION A. HISTORICAL BACKGROUND

We assign this without conducting much discussion of it.

SECTION B. DISCLOSURE OF EMBARRASSING PRIVATE FACTS

We start with this branch of the privacy tort because it is intuitively very interesting and fairly easy to understand even if its practical significance has been eroded by constitutional developments. If you want to shorten the section, cut *Neff* and *Daily Times Democrat v. Graham*. If you want *very* short treatment, you might just assign the note on *Cox Broadcasting Corp. v. Cohn* and then *Haynes v. Alfred A. Knopf* afterwards.

Briscoe v. Reader's Digest Association (D's article names P and describes his criminal past; L)
Sidis v. F-R Publishing Co. (D's "where are they now" article embarrasses reclusive P; NL)
Doe v. Mills (D abortion protestors name patients outside clinic; L)

Q. What is the distinction between *Briscoe* and *Sidis*?
A. The oddity of the cases from a policy standpoint is that in some senses Briscoe's past may be of greater legitimate interest than Sidis's present. Briscoe once was a criminal; perhaps those who deal with him would find this helpful to know in evaluating his trustworthiness. The article about Sidis seems to have little comparable benefit for anyone who might care to deal with him. It just exposes his life in a way that onlookers might find appealing to their sense of curiosity.

But one also can look at the cases not in terms of the value of the information to those who would deal with the plaintiffs, but from the standpoint of the larger public interest in the point each story was making. The article about Briscoe did not need to identify him to tell its story about the business of hijacking, but the article about Sidis did need to name him for its story to have any real meaning to the reader. The consumers of the Sidis piece may not have learned anything useful about Sidis personally (i.e., nothing that would cause them to revise their dealings with him—they didn't have any), but they did learn something potentially useful about prodigies and their fate. Sidis's father, Boris, put great effort into making his son a prodigy, and perhaps he succeeded (it's hard to know whether there was causation)—but his son's life did not turn out too well, at least by conventional standards, and there may be a public interest in knowing this.

Beyond these points, of course, one can simply apply the Restatement test or the test offered by the court toward the end of the opinion in *Briscoe*. The marginal social value of *naming* the subject of the story was greater in Sidis's case for the reasons just discussed. Sidis's entry into public life was more voluntary than was Briscoe's, setting aside Sidis's youth at the time he became famous. And the knowledge that was exposed about Briscoe would be more offensive to a reasonable person than the information exposed about Sidis.

Q. Consider this hypothetical variation on *Briscoe*: the plaintiff is released from prison after serving a fifteen-year sentence. He moves into a new neighborhood. Others in town who hear about his arrival and know of his past begin distributing leaflets about him; the community newspaper runs a front-page story about his arrival. Any liability for invasion of privacy?

A. Probably not. These facts have some similarities to *Briscoe*, since in both cases the crime had occurred more than a decade earlier and the plaintiff had "paid his debt to society"; but in the hypo the plaintiff had not yet shown that he was rehabilitated and had not yet built a new life for himself. The presence of those factors in *Briscoe* arguably reduced the legitimate value of the story about him because his criminal past no longer seemed to suggest a heightened possibility of a criminal future—as it ordinarily might in the case of a freshly released convict. (Does the answer to the hypothetical depend at all on what the crime was?)

Q. In *Sidis* the court found the story newsworthy. Was the court offering a descriptive or normative judgment?
A. Mostly descriptive: people are interested in the misfortunes of public figures, "regrettably or not." But the court seems to reserve the possibility of making normative judgments if it turns out that the public has an interest in information so intimate that exposure of it would shock the community's sense of decency. (Is there a bit of a contradiction in that standard? If the revelation shocks the community's sense of decency, why is the community interested in it? Is it not inevitable that the court is referring to itse own sensibilities?)

A related question is how "newsworthiness" should be determined: by judge or jury. Notice that there are tensions created by either approach. A jury might conclude that scandalous matter is "newsworthy" just because the jurors' own curiosity is titillated by it; or a jury might conclude that a story is not newsworthy because it offends the jurors' narrow sensibilities. Either risk also is present if a judge makes the decision; but in which decisionmaker's hands are those risks greater? In any event, the usual approach is to treat newsworthiness as a jury question if reasonable minds can differ about it.

Q. On what ground can it be said that the names of the plaintiffs in *Doe v. Mills*, who were about to have abortions, were not matters of public interest?
A. Perhaps the best (most neutral) way to explain the decision is that the revelation of the names of the plaintiffs wasn't necessary for the defendant's purpose if that purpose was just to call attention to the fact that someone was about to have an abortion, just as naming Briscoe wasn't necessary to write a story about former criminals who have turned their lives around. But maybe the purpose was different. From the defendants' standpoint the plaintiffs were committing profoundly immoral acts. Some in the community would agree, though of course others would not; but why shouldn't the defendants be able to make this known and let passersby decide for themselves? Perhaps some of those who saw the signs would not want to associate with the plaintiffs or with anyone else who had an abortion. But then perhaps that wasn't quite the defendants' purpose, either. More probably their real purpose was to pressure the plaintiffs not to have abortions (or to pressure others not to have abortions because they see what happens to people who do) by embarrassing them. Whence comes the embarrassment? It could be because the plaintiffs were ashamed to be getting abortions or fearful of being shunned by others who heard about their plans; or it could just be that they were embarrassed to have intimate facts about their medical lives made public. There are a lot of medical procedures people have that would cause them to feel embarrassed if they were advertised on placards.

Some might want to suggest the relevance of the constitutional right to have an abortion; but the defendants weren't state actors and they weren't preventing abortions from occurring. They were publicizing them. Let's put it this way: it seems unlikely that the result in the case would be different if *Roe v. Wade* were reversed but abortion remained legal.

Q. Suppose a group of people opposing prostitution organizes protests near a brothel. They know that Smithers arrives there for a visit every Friday after work wearing sunglasses and a false beard. So one Friday they stand on a nearby sidewalks with placards saying "DON'T DO IT, SMITHERS!" Liability for invasion of privacy under *Doe v. Mills*?
A. The case might differ from *Doe* if it occurred in a jurisdiction where prostitution is illegal; for then the public interest in knowing that Smithers is a criminal would be reckoned higher: the criminal nature

of the act would make its publication more embarrassing to Smithers but also more valuable, and more *legitimately* valuable, to those in his community. But suppose the case occurs in a county in Nevada where prostitution is legal. Now the issues seem similar to those in *Doe*—though there remains the aforementioned fact that under current case law the right to an abortion has been held "fundamental," whereas the right to consort with a prostitute is not—not yet, anyway.

Neff v. Time, Inc. (D publishes photograph of P at a football game with his fly undone; NL)
Daily Times Democrat v. Graham (D publishes photograph of P at carnival with her skirt in the air; L)

Q. What is the distinction between *Neff* and *Graham*?
A. The obvious doctrinal difference is that Neff was part of a group asking to have their pictures taken, whereas the plaintiff in Graham had no wish to be photographed. Perhaps this isn't completely satisfactory, though, since Neff probably would not have wanted to be photographed if he had known his fly was open (and Graham probably wouldn't have minded being photographed if her dress hadn't been in the air). But the cases also can be distinguished on economic grounds. The photograph of *Graham* did not tell anyone anything useful to know about her; it just showed that she was in the wrong place wearing the wrong thing at the wrong time—a matter of bad luck. The photograph of Neff arguably was a bit more probative of his character, for he had permitted his fly to come undone, which was not quite a matter of bad luck. This point also can be used to distinguish the Restatement illustration in the text from *Graham*: someone with a rip in his pants is not "involuntarily and instantaneously enmeshed in an embarrassing scene," as the court in *Graham* puts it; he is more or less voluntarily enmeshed in embarrassment for so long as he walks around wearing the torn pants. It would help the distinction if it turned out that the plaintiff *knowingly* was walking around with torn pants day after day; the point becomes harder to press if he had torn the pants moments earlier without realizing it, since this might seem as random and unrevealing an occurrence (pardon the expression) as was suffered by the plaintiff in *Graham*.

This general way of thinking about the cases follows the theory of Posner's that is excerpted at the end of the chapter: people shouldn't have a right to privacy in information that would help others decide whether to enter into transactions with them. Revealing that the plaintiff is a slob could be helpful in this way and thus shouldn't be actionable. Revealing something embarrassing about the plaintiff that is just a matter of luck does not contribute to anyone's useful knowledge in this way and therefore can form the basis of a good claim.

Cox Broadcasting Co. v. Cohn (D publishes name of victim of rape and murder; NL)
Haynes v. Alfred A. Knopf (D is subject of social history containing embarrassing stories about him; NL for publisher)

Q. Does *Briscoe* survive *Cox Broadcasting* and *Florida Star*?
A. It seems somewhat doubtful. One might like to distinguish *Briscoe* on the ground that it involved old news—so old that the plaintiff's *name* was of no public interest. But the opinion in *Florida Star* permits liability for the publication of "truthful information which it has lawfully obtained" only if the liability is "narrowly tailored to a state interest of the highest order." It seems unlikely that the Court would say the common law standard used in *Briscoe*—or the result there—satisfies that criterion.

Q. Are *Briscoe* and *Haynes* distinguishable?

A.   The issue in *Briscoe* was whether the plaintiff's name should have been used; the court thought not. In *Haynes* the plaintiffs made the same claim. The court in *Haynes* rejected the argument because it thought that a change of name would not have affected the defendant's liability: Haynes still would have been identifiable from the rest of the story—and notice that this wasn't true in *Briscoe*. So (the court says) Lemann also would have had to change other factual details of the story to prevent Luther Haynes from being identified. Isn't that too strong, though? Telling the story with all the names changed might still have left Haynes identifiable to some people in his life, but not to nearly as many as would have recognized him by name—and maybe not to enough to satisfy the Restatement's publicity requirement (see comment a in the excerpt at the start of the casebook chapter). The court nevertheless treats liability as a binary matter: since there still could have been *some* liability if the plaintiffs' names had been changed, the idea that changing the names should be *required* is a non-starter.

A different way to defend the point is that if you find liability for failing to change the names of people in a story like Lemann's, you have opened the door to a general principle that could require authors of non-fiction to change names and to make other changes as well to protect the identities of the people they write about. This in turn could create pressure to make stories more fictitious, less verifiable, and otherwise less valuable.

Q.   Hypothetical: in *Pemberton v. Bethlehem Steel Corp.*, 502 A.2d 1101 (Md. App. 1986) (also considered in the casebook chapter on outrage, or intentional infliction of emotional distress), the plaintiff, Pemberton, was an official for the union that represented the Bethlehem Steel Corporation's employees. He sued the corporation for invasion of privacy and other torts. Pemberton claimed that Bethlehem, unhappy with his conduct on behalf of the union, hired a private investigator to place him under surveillance; that the investigator obtained evidence that Pemberton was conducting an extramarital affair; and that Bethlehem anonymously sent this evidence to Pemberton's wife, ultimately precipitating their divorce. Bethlehem also obtained mug shots from an arrest of Pemberton that had occurred about fifteen years earlier and circulated the pictures to the members of his unions. The trial court gave summary judgment to the defendant. The court of appeals affirmed. As to the invasion of privacy claim, it said:

> These activities fall within that branch of the tort making actionable the publicizing of matters concerning one's private life. See Restatement, supra, §652D. To come within that branch of the tort, the matter disclosed must be a private fact and it must be made public. With respect to the latter requirement, comment a to §652D makes clear that "it is not an invasion of the right of privacy, within the rule stated in this Section, to communicate a fact concerning the plaintiff's private life to a single person or even to a small group of persons." In light of that requirement, it is clear that there can be no liability with respect to the mailing of the excerpts from the detective reports to appellant's wife; that does not constitute a publicizing of the reports or the information contained therein.

> Appellant's complaint about the circulation of his criminal records fails because of the former requirement; they are not private facts. The requirement that the information publicized be private in nature is both an element of the tort itself and is necessitated by First Amendment principles. In *Cox Broadcasting Corp. v. Cohn*, 420 U.S. 469 (1975), the Supreme Court noted that "even the prevailing law of invasion of privacy generally recognizes that the interests in privacy fade when the information involved already appears on the public record," but that, in addition, the First and Fourteenth amendments prohibit States from imposing sanctions "on the publication of truthful information contained in official court records open to public inspection." [...]

> We need go no further than *Cox Broadcasting Corp.* to hold that the circulation of court records pertaining to appellant's conviction is Constitutionally protected and cannot, therefore, form the

basis of tort liability. Circulation of the "mug shot" presents a somewhat different question, but, unfortunately for appellant, the answer is the same.

An interesting feature of this hypothetical as a basis for discussion is that Pemberton's two privacy claims fail for different reasons: the "mug shot" claim fails under *Cox Broadcasting*, while the claim based on the exposure of the plaintiff's extramarital affair fails because it wasn't publicized to anyone but his wife. This provides another good chance to discuss the Restatement's suggestion (given at the start of this section in the casebook) that there is no actionable invasion when embarrassing private information about the plaintiff is provided only to a small group of people. What sense does this make? It's true that in *Briscoe* the information was disseminated widely, but wasn't the real thrust of the plaintiff's case—and the real basis for anyone's sympathy with it—that it fouled up his relationship with his immediate family and friends? Yet doesn't the Restatement imply that there would be no liability if *only* Briscoe's friends and family were told about his criminal past?

Perhaps the idea is that in the general run of cases, widespread publicity is likely to do significantly more serious harm than the small-scale variety, even if there are particular cases like *Briscoe* where that might not be true. Conversely, in cases where only a few people are told the plaintiff's dark secrets, maybe they are more likely to have a legitimate use for the knowledge. The logic of the point in this case would be that Pemberton has a right to conceal his extramarital affair from people in the world at large because their only real interest in hearing about it is voyeuristic. But he has no particular right to conceal it from his wife, since her interest in hearing about it is legitimate. Or maybe the point is that the cases where a plaintiff's dark secrets are told to only a small number of people, it's harder to imagine that the law can have much useful deterrent effect (since no media outlet is involved that is likely to know much about the law), and easier to imagine the courts getting involved in utterly private messes where the costs and benefits involved are harder to sort out. *Watt v. Longsdon*, in the chapter on defamation, provides an example of such a fact pattern: a private party tells one of his friends that her husband is having an affair. Is this the stuff that invasion of privacy claims should be made of?

You may wish to note that not all courts follow this same approach. In *Johnson v. K-Mart Corp.*, 723 N.E.2d 1192 (Ill. App. 2000), which appears in the next section of the casebook chapter (covering intrusion upon seclusion), K-Mart hired detectives to pose as employees in its warehouses; the detectives' job was to get other employees to tell them things and then pass the information along to management. The Illinois court sustained the plaintiffs' claim for invasion of privacy—not only of the "intrusion" variety (covered in a moment) but also for the public disclosure of embarrassing private facts. The facts had only been passed on to the plaintiffs' employer, but the court thought this was good enough:

> In [*Miller v. Motorola, Inc.*, 560 N.E.2d 900 (Ill. App. 1990)], the plaintiff alleged that her employer had invaded her privacy when, without her authorization, the employer told her coworkers that she had undergone mastectomy surgery. The lower court in *Miller* dismissed the plaintiff's complaint, holding that she failed to state a cause of action for invasion of privacy. However, on appeal, the court held that egregious conduct resulting in disclosure to a limited audience is actionable if "a special relationship exists between the plaintiff and the '*public*' to whom the information has been disclosed." According to *Miller*, if the plaintiff is not a public figure, such a public may be fellow employees, club members, church members, family, or neighbors.

> We adopt the position of the court in *Miller*. We too hold that the public disclosure requirement may be satisfied by proof that the plaintiff has a special relationship with the "public" to whom the information is disclosed. However, we also believe that the rationale in Miller should be extended to include an employer as a member of a particular public with whom a plaintiff may share a special relationship. The evidence shows that personal details about plaintiffs' private lives were disclosed to their employer by the investigators. We find that these facts raise a genuine issue as to whether publicity was given to private facts.

You can renew the *Pemberton* hypothetical when you discuss the next section of the chapter, because another issue in the case was whether the plaintiff's right to seclusion was invaded by the defendant's surveillance of his motel room. The court sent that issue to the jury. More on this in a moment.

Q. Hypothetical: in *Sipple v. Chronicle Publishing Co.*, 201 Cal.Rptr. 665 (Cal. App. 1984), a woman named Sara Jane Moore tried to assassinate President Ford while he was in San Francisco. A man named Oliver Sipple grabbed Moore's arm as she was about to fire her gun, foiling the assassination. Herb Caen (pronounced "Cane"), a famous columnist for the *San Francisco Chronicle*, wrote a piece that ran in part as follows:

> One of the heroes of the day, Oliver "Bill" Sipple, the ex-Marine who grabbed Sara Jane Moore's arm just as her gun was fired and thereby may have saved the President's life, was the center of midnight attention at the Red Lantern, a Golden Gate Ave. bar he favors. The Rev. Ray Broshears, head of Helping Hands, and Gay Politico, Harvey Milk, who claim to be among Sipple's close friends, describe themselves as "proud—maybe this will help break the stereotype." Sipple is among the workers in Milk's campaign for Supervisor.

The column was understood by many readers to imply that Sipple was gay, and other newspapers published articles referring to Caen's column as a basis for reaching that conclusion; some of the articles wondered whether Ford's failure to thank Sipple promptly was attributable to Sipple's sexual orientation. Sipple sued the *Chronicle* and some of the republishers of the story—including the *Los Angeles Times*—for invasion of privacy. Assuming the column was construed to accurately reveal Sipple's homosexuality, what result? (There are some additional facts to consider below.)
A. The court of appeals affirmed summary judgment for the defendants:

> The undisputed facts reveal that prior to the publication of the newspaper articles in question appellant's homosexual orientation and participation in gay community activities had been known by hundreds of people in a variety of cities, including New York, Dallas, Houston, San Diego, Los Angeles and San Francisco. Thus, appellant's deposition shows that prior to the assassination attempt appellant spent a lot of time in "Tenderloin" and "Castro," the well-known gay sections of San Francisco; that he frequented gay bars and other homosexual gatherings in both San Francisco and other cities; that he marched in gay parades on several occasions; [...] that his friendship with Harvey Milk, another prominent gay, was well-known and publicized in gay newspapers; and that his homosexual association and name had been reported in gay magazines (such as *Data Boy*, *Pacific Coast Times*, *Male Express*, etc.) several times before the publications in question. In fact, appellant quite candidly conceded that he did not make a secret of his being a homosexual and that if anyone would ask, he would frankly admit that he was gay. In short, since appellant's sexual orientation was already in public domain and since the articles in question did no more than to give further publicity to matters which appellant left open to the eye of the public, a vital element of the tort was missing rendering it vulnerable to summary disposal.

> Although the conclusion reached above applies with equal force to all respondents, we cannot help observing that respondents *Times Mirror* and its editor are exempt from liability on the additional ground that the *Los Angeles Times* only republished the *Chronicle* article which implied that appellant was gay. It is, of course, axiomatic that no right of privacy attaches to a matter of general interest that has already been publicly released in a periodical or in a newspaper of local or regional circulation. [...]

But even aside from the aforegoing considerations, the summary judgment dismissing the action against respondents was justified on the additional, independent basis that the publication contained in the articles in dispute was newsworthy.

As referred to above, our courts have recognized a broad privilege cloaking the truthful publication of all newsworthy matters. Thus, in *Briscoe v. Reader's Digest Assn., Inc.*, our Supreme Court stated that a truthful publication is protected if (1) it is newsworthy and (2) it does not reveal facts so offensive as to shock the community notions of decency. While it has been said that the general criteria for determining newsworthiness are (a) the social value of the facts published; (b) the depth of the article's intrusion into ostensibly private affairs; and (c) the extent to which the individual voluntarily acceded to a position of public notority, the cases and authorities further explain that the paramount test of newsworthiness is whether the matter is of legitimate public interest which in turn must be determined according to the community mores. As pointed out in *Virgil v. Time, Inc.*, 527 F.2d at p. 1129: "In determining what is a matter of legitimate public interest, account must be taken of the customs and conventions of the community; and in the last analysis what is proper becomes a matter of the community mores. The line is to be drawn when the publicity ceases to be the giving of information to which the public is entitled, and becomes a morbid and sensational prying into private lives for its own sake, with which a reasonable member of the public, with decent standards, would say that he had no concern."

In the case at bench the publication of appellant's homosexual orientation which had already been widely known by many people in a number of communities was not so offensive even at the time of the publication as to shock the community notions of decency. Moreover, and perhaps even more to the point, the record shows that the publications were not motivated by a morbid and sensational prying into appellant's private life but rather were prompted by legitimate political considerations, i.e., to dispel the false public opinion that gays were timid, weak and unheroic figures and to raise the equally important political question whether the President of the United States entertained a discriminatory attitude or bias against a minority group such as homosexuals. Thus appellant's case squarely falls within the language of Kapellas in which the California Supreme Court emphasized that "when, [as here] the legitimate public interest in the published information is substantial, a much greater intrusion into an individual's private life will be sanctioned, especially if the individual willingly entered into the public sphere."

SECTION C. INTRUSION UPON SECLUSION

Things to cut if cuts are needed: *Irvine v. Akron Beacon Journal, Estate of Berthiaume v. Pratt*, and *Froelich v. Werbin*. If you want the briefest useful exposure, just use the first three cases and the problem at the end (*Shulman*).

Nader v. General Motors Corp. (D engages in various acts of surveillance and harassment against P; L for some of it)
Figured v. Paralegal Technical Services (personal injury litigant P is followed around by agents of D who want to see if she really is injured; NL)
Johnson v. K-Mart Corp. (D hires spies to infiltrate workplace and report on P employees; L)

The "intrusion upon seclusion" language, and the Restatement provision attempting to gloss its elements, conjures up images of peeping toms and others who intrude on someone who wants to be left alone. But the cases show that the actual tort the courts have created here is more complicated than that; it can cover situations where information is elicited under false pretenses without any literal intrusion—and it may not cover cases where someone is followed around physically, despite the "intrusiveness" of the behavior. Along with appropriation of name or likeness, this is one of the branches of the privacy tort that seems to be retaining the most vitality.

Q. What is the distinction between the acts in *Nader* that gave rise to liability and the acts that didn't?
A. In *Nader* the court found no liability for interviewing the plaintiff's acquaintances, for hiring women to make lewd proposals to him, or for making threatening phone calls to him at odd hours. It found (potential) liability for wiretapping and eavesdropping and for sending an agent to engage in offensively close surveillance of Nader at his bank and see what sorts of withdrawls he was making. The court's theory of the tort was that liability arose only when a defendant made intrusive attempts to gather private facts. This last criterion drives a wedge between the L and NL claims in Nader's case: the harassing phone calls and interviews with (let us assume) everyone Nader knew may have been intrusive, but they didn't involve attempts to obtain private information (the court takes the position that the information *couldn't* have been private within the meaning of the tort if others knew it). The hired women were an annoyance but don't satisfy the court's test, either.

Q. As noted in the previous section of the manual, you can return here to the *Pemberton* case as a hypothetical. To start from scratch: In *Pemberton v. Bethlehem Steel Corp.*, 502 A.2d 1101 (Md. App. 1986) (considered in the casebook's section on intentional infliction of emotional distress), the plaintiff, Pemberton, was an official for the union that represented the Bethlehem Steel Corporation's employees. He sued the corporation for invasion of privacy and other torts. Pemberton claimed that Bethlehem, unhappy with his conduct on behalf of the union, hired a private investigator to place him under surveillance; that the investigator obtained evidence that Pemberton was conducting an extramarital affair; and that Bethlehem anonymously sent this evidence to Pemberton's wife, ultimately precipitating their divorce. The trial court gave summary judgment to the defendant. The court of appeals reversed on Pemberton's claim for intrusion upon seclusion:

> Restatement of Torts 2d, §652B describes this branch of the tort as the intentional intrusion upon the solitude or seclusion of another or his private affairs or concerns that would be highly offensive to a reasonable person. As pointed out in Comment c to § 652B, the gist of the offense is the intrusion into a private place or the invasion of a private seclusion that the plaintiff has thrown about his person or affairs. There is no liability for observing him in public places, "since he is not then in seclusion."

> Surveillance, depending on how it is conducted, may constitute such an intrusion. See, for example, [...] *Nader v. General Motors Corporation*, 255 N.E.2d 765 (N.Y. 1970).

> There is some dispute in the record as to the exact nature of the surveillance at issue here. In his affidavit, Mr. Skipper stated that actual surveillance was conducted on 12 days[.] He averred that the surveillance consisted of observing appellant from outside his residence, outside what appeared to be his girlfriend's home, outside a shopping center and convenience store, and along public roads. Interstate's reports summarizing the surveillance on 9 of the 12 days are in the record, and they tend to confirm Mr. Skipper's assertions. That evidence, coupled with appellant's concession in his deposition testimony that he was unaware of the surveillance while it was being conducted, would justify judgment in favor of the defendants. That kind of surveillance does not, under the caselaw, constitute an actionable invasion of privacy.

> The problem is that the excerpts received by Mrs. Pemberton show a more extensive intrusion. They reveal that, on at least one occasion, a "detection device" was placed on the door of a motel room where appellant was staying and that surveillance (either on that occasion or another) was maintained from the bottom of a stairwell. The record is not entirely clear as to the nature of the

"detection device," but from other statements in the excerpts, a fair inference can be drawn that it was a listening device of some sort. That kind of surveillance has been held actionable.

In considering a motion for summary judgment, the court is obliged to resolve all inferences against the moving party. It is fairly inferrable from the record before us that a surveillance, not reflected in the nine Interstate reports, was undertaken at a motel and that a listening device was attached to the door in order that the detective could hear what transpired inside the room. Given those inferences, it appears that summary judgment would be inappropriate with respect to the complaint that the surveillance directed or undertaken by these defendants (other than Markakis) constituted an actionable intrusion upon appellant's seclusion or private affairs.

Q. What is the distinction between those parts of *Nader* finding liability (e.g., liability for the surveillance of Nader at his bank) and *Figured v. Paralegal Technical Services* (NL for following P around all the time)?
A. The main point is that whereas the surveillance at the bank in *Nader* allowed the defendant's agents to see things that Nader didn't mean to expose to any member of the public, the surveillance efforts in *Figured* all involved observations of things that anyone could see. Yes, the defendant's attentions to the plaintiff were unusually intense, but in the end the things observed weren't "private." The interesting question is why the law draws a line here—why it makes liability hinge on whether the information sought was confidential when it seems obvious that nobody would want to be pursued in the manner that Figured was. A first answer must have to do with administrative issues. As a practical matter the court's rule requires it to distinguish between information that is publicly observable and information that isn't—not always an easy distinction, but simpler to draw than a line between attentions in the street that are offensive and inoffensive. How much peering at the plaintiff must the defendant do before liability results? The court is able to avoid this inquiry by focusing instead on the nature of the information gained by the peering.

Then there also is the policy point the court mentions: allowing the surveillance in *Figured* serves an important purpose by helping defendants in accident suits gain evidence of whether a plaintiff really is injured. Finding liability here might chill those efforts in a way that ends up facilitating corrupt claims. There was no similar justification—and no similar danger of overdeterring useful conduct—with respect to the nosiness at the bank exhibited by the defendant's agent in *Nader*.

Q. Can doggedly following someone around in public ever amount to an invasion of privacy?
A. Presumably a court would find its way to a remedy in an extreme case. In real life, cases like this tend to result in liability because they usually end up accompanied by a bit more than just "watching" the plaintiff in public; there is obstruction and harassment, which ends up forming a basis for relief. A partial study on point that makes for a nice discussion is *Galella v. Onassis*, 487 F.2d 986 (2d Cir. 1973), where Jacqueline Onassis sued a freelance photographer for invasion of privacy (among other things). The court affirmed the entry of a modified injunction against the defendant's conduct:

> Galella fancies himself as a "paparazzo" (literally a kind of annoying insect, perhaps roughly equivalent to the English gadfly.) Paparazzi make themselves as visible to the public and obnoxious to their photographic subjects as possible to aid in the advertisement and wide sale of their works.

> Some examples of Galella's conduct brought out at trial are illustrative. Galella took pictures of John Kennedy [Jr.] riding his bicycle in Central Park across the way from his home. He jumped out into the boy's path, causing the agents concern for John's safety. The agents' reaction and interrogation of Galella led to Galella's arrest and his action against the agents; Galella on other occasions interrupted Caroline at tennis, and invaded the children's private schools. At one time he came uncomfortably close in a power boat to Mrs. Onassis swimming. He often jumped and

postured around while taking pictures of her party[,] notably at a theater opening but also on numerous other occasions. He followed a practice of bribing apartment house, restaurant and nightclub doormen as well as romancing a family servant to keep him advised of the movements of the family.

Galella's action went far beyond the reasonable bounds of news gathering. When weighed against the de minimis public importance of the daily activities of the defendant, Galella's constant surveillance, his obtrusive and intruding presence, was unwarranted and unreasonable. If there were any doubt in our minds, Galella's inexcusable conduct toward defendant's minor children would resolve it.

Relief must be tailored to protect Mrs. Onassis from the "paparazzo" attack which distinguishes Galella's behavior from that of other photographers; it should not unnecessarily infringe on reasonable efforts to "cover" defendant. Therefore, we modify the [trial] court's order to prohibit only (1) any approach within twenty-five (25) feet of defendant or any touching of the person of the defendant Jacqueline Onassis; (2) any blocking of her movement in public places and thoroughfares; (3) any act foreseeably or reasonably calculated to place the life and safety of defendant in jeopardy; and (4) any conduct which would reasonably be foreseen to harass, alarm or frighten the defendant.

Any further restriction on Galella's taking and selling pictures of defendant for news coverage is, however, improper and unwarranted by the evidence.

Q. What is the distinction between *Johnson v. K-Mart Corp.* and those parts of *Nader v. General Motors Corp.* finding no liability?

A. The cases call for a distinction because in *Nader* there was no liability when the defendant contacted people the plaintiff knew to try to get them to reveal embarrassing facts about him; the idea was that if Nader voluntarily had chosen to reveal embarrassing things to others, there could be no liability when those same things found their way into the hands of people Nader didn't foresee. Yet there was liability in *Johnson* when the defendant got the plaintiffs to voluntarily disclose embarrassing things about themselves that likewise found their way into the hands of unexpected listeners. One distinction is that in *Johnson* the investigative efforts by the defendant's agents were meant to extract private information from the plaintiffs—i.e., information they hadn't necessarily shared with anyone else. In *Nader* the NL acts were attempts to learn things the plaintiff already had chosen to reveal to others. In other words, *Nader* had at least made his own initial decision to reveal the information and send it off into the world, whereas in *Johnson* that initial decision was influenced by the misrepresentations from the defendant's agents. Maybe control over that first line of revelation is important because it gives the plaintiff a large measure of control over how far the information goes: if he is thinking about whether to tell X some embarrassing facts, he can make an assessment of X's discretion and reliability and decide whether the risks outweigh the benefits. But if the spies contaminate that initial decision to reveal the information, as in *Johnson*, they are undermining the plaintiff's ability to make that analysis in the first place.

Johnson rounds off a key point of these first cases: "intrusion upon seclusion" sounds like an effort to penetrate the plaintiff's private physical space, and sometimes it is. But courts also read into the tort a separate interest in keeping personal information private. In other words, the tort often has an informational as well as a spatial dimension—and sometimes, as in *Johnson*, the informational dimension is the only one at stake. Next we will see some cases where the spatial dimension is more prominent.

Q. What is the distinction between *Johnson v. K-Mart Corp.* and *Figured v. Paralegal Technical Services*?

A. The cases might seem to be in slight tension because the surveillance in *Figured* was so much more annoying when it occurred than the spying in *Johnson*. *Figured* involved an irritating and somewhat offensive invasion of the plaintiff's "space" by following her closely, whereas *Johnson* didn't involve an invasion of the plaintiffs' space at all. The point, of course—by now familiar—is that the information the defendants gained by their acts in *Johnson* was private. In *Figured* the information extracted was visible to the public. To this one might riposte that in both cases the plaintiff's disclosures were voluntary; but as just discussed, the voluntary disclosures in *Johnson* were contaminated by fraud.

As mentioned at the end of the notes to the prior section, in *Johnson* liability also was found on a different theory of invasion of privacy: the public disclosure of private facts. This raised an interesting issue concerning the publicity requirement of the disclosure tort. See those earlier notes for more on this if you haven't covered it and want more to work with on *Johnson*.

Dietemann v. Time, Inc. (D investigative reporters pose as patients, visit P's house, and record results; L)
Desnick v. American Broadcasting Co. (D investigative reporters post as patients, visit P's offices, and record results; NL)
Irvine v. Akron Beacon Journal (telemarketers call repeatedly at all hours of the night; L)

Q. What is the analogy between *Dietemann v. Time, Inc.* and those portions of *Nader v. General Motors Corp.* that find potential liability?
A. In both cases the defendants made surreptitious recordings of the plaintiff. It's tempting to add that both defendants were recorded in their homes, but the opinion in *Nader* doesn't settle that the wiretapping was of his home phone; maybe it was his business phone. In any event, both plaintiffs had a right to expect no such recordings to be made. At this point the cases separate a bit. The act of recording was important to the court in *Dietemann* because it meant that what the plaintiff did in his home could be exposed to the millions outside. Presumably no recording was necessary in *Nader*, though; simple eavesdropping would be enough. The difference, of course, is that in *Dietemann* the plaintiff consented to the defendants' presence. Despite the fraud that gave rise to the consent, the court regards it as a kind of waiver of the plaintiff's right to seclusion as to those individual defendants—but not as to all those who later would see and hear the defendants' story.

Picking up on this last point, you can ask for a distinction between *Johnson* and the court's statement in *Dietemann* that there would be no liability if the defendants merely had tricked the plaintiff into talking with them without making recordings. Both of those situations would involve disclosures induced by fraud. But in *Dietemann* the plaintiff wouldn't be revealing anything personal about himself; he would just be showing his methods to the plaintiffs, which (unlike the plaintiffs in *Johnson*) he was perfectly prepared to show to many others as well.

Q. What is the distinction between *Dietemann* and those portions of the *Nader* case that find no liability?
A. This takes us into territory that by now may be too familiar to warrant more discussion. In *Dietemann* the defendants entered the plaintiff's home and exposed his conduct there to the world. In the NL parts of *Nader* the defendant's agents did not see or expose anything about Nader that he hadn't already chosen to reveal to people outside his home. The hardest part of the distinction probably involves the defendant's questioning of people that Nader knew. When Nader chose to tell things to those people, he might not have been intending to let the whole world hear about them—just as the plaintiff in *Dietemann* didn't intend his voluntary communications with the defendants' agents to be broadcast to the world. Yet in *Nader* the plaintiff's voluntary communication of things to third parties is treated as a waiver of his right to complain when the third parties pass on the information to the defendant's agents. Why weren't Dietemann's voluntary communications to the defendants a waiver of his right to complain when they transmitted his statements and conduct to others? Well, we have seen that it *was* a waiver of his right to complain if the defendants went off and told others what they saw and heard. It just wasn't a waiver of his right to complain about secret electronic recording. You assume the risks that are visible to you, not the ones that are invisible. The risk that a visitor is lying about his motive evidently is considered visible, or evident (but cf. *Johnson*), whereas the risk that the visitor is carrying a tape recorder

is not visible or evident. One reason to draw the line there is the administrative difficulty of handling cases where a plaintiff complains that a defendant had false motives for visiting. Another reason to draw the line there is that mechanical recordings tend to expose the plaintiff's private doings in a way different from, and more intrusive than, mere recollections.

A related puzzle is that there still would be liability in *Nader* if the defendant eavesdropped on conversations between Nader and people Nader knows (indeed, that is one of the claims the court explicitly sustains); how come there's liability for that, but not for going to Nader's conversational partners later and asking them what he said? The answer is that when the defendant listens in on a conversation, nobody in the conversation is consenting. Nader takes his chances that his friends will consent to repeat what he tells them, but he doesn't assume the risk that others will be listening in to his conversations without consent from either side.

Q. What is the distinction between the *Desnick* case and *Johnson v. K-Mart Corp.*?
A. First the superficial similarities: in both cases the defendants' agents managed to get the plaintiffs to talk with them by lying about their reason for wanting the conversation. In both cases this occurred in a workplace. Indeed, *Desnick* might seem the worse case because in *Desnick* there were recordings made, and we have seen that courts care about this; and in *Johnson* the employer had a legitimate immediate interest in finding out whether its employees were stealing, whereas in *Desnick* the defendant had no immediate interest in gaining the information other than its desire to get exciting copy for one of its TV shows. So why is there liability in *Johnson* but not in *Desnick*?

First, in *Johnson* the information obtained was personal; in *Desnick* (as in the NL variant of *Dietemann* where no recordings are made) the plaintiff's employees evidently just revealed to the defendant the same processes they revealed to any member of the public who sought treatment. Second, the defendant's agents in *Johnson* obtained information about K-Mart's employees that was outside the scope of the possibly legitimate purposes that motivated the surveillance program. The opinion in *Johnson* doesn't make clear whether the potential liability in the case extends to everything the spies told management or only just to information about the employees' personal lives. Meanwhile in *Desnick* there was a legitimate interest in the picture, even if it didn't belong to the defendant per se: the public's interest in knowing about corrupt eye doctors. The defendant's efforts didn't seem to stray outside the service of this interest.

Q. Is *Desnick* distinguishable from *Dietemann v. Time, Inc.*?
A. The court in *Desnick* thought so. It said: "*Dietemann* involved a home. True, the portion invaded was an office, where the plaintiff performed quack healing of nonexistent ailments. The parallel to this case is plain enough, but there is a difference. Dietemann was not in business, and did not advertise his services or charge for them. His quackery was private." That was in the court's discussion of the plaintiff's trespass claim, but the court said that its discussion of trespass "largely disposes" of the invasion of privacy claim as well. The court added that "The right of privacy embraces several distinct interests, but the only ones conceivably involved here are the closely related interests in concealing intimate personal facts and in preventing intrusion into legitimately private activities, such as phone conversations. As we have said already, no intimate personal facts concerning the two individual plaintiffs (remember that Dr. Desnick himself is not a plaintiff) were revealed; and the only conversations that were recorded were conversations with the testers themselves."

Desnick is a hard case—but probably harder from the standpoint of trespass law than as a matter of invasion of privacy. Under trespass law the nature of the consent the plaintiff gave the defendant, and whether it was induced by fraud, is critical. Although that point repeats in *Dietemann* and in the *Johnson* case considered above, a privacy claim based on "intrusion upon seclusion" does not typically depend on fraud; it focuses in a way that trespass law does not on the location and nature of the invasion. Thus in *Desnick* the defendant's agents entered a business open to the public and received counseling; this seems like less of an "intrusion upon seclusion" than the entry of the defendants into the plaintiff's house in *Dietemann*. And notice that in *Dietemann* the court didn't regard it as enough that the defendants had entered the plaintiff's house under false pretenses (think of the NL variant again), which again suggest that fraud in the inducement of the consent isn't the pivotal issue. (See the section of the casebook on trespass law, and the corresponding parts of this manual, for more on *Desnick*.)

Q. What is the distinction between *Irvine v. Akron Beacon Journal* and *Figured v. Paralegal Technical Services*?

A. The superficial similarities are that both cases involved repeated harassment of the plaintiff; in both cases the harassment may have seemed frightening, at least at first; and in neither case did the defendant obtain any private information about the plaintiff. The distinction must involve the time and place of the harassment. In *Figured* it all occurred in public during the day. In *Irvine* the harassment occurred inside the plaintiff's house, and late at night. The *Irvine* case shows that the "intrusion upon seclusion" tort does have an aspect directed at preventing disruption of the plaintiff's quarters even without any attempt to pry into personal information. As for the difference between the annoying phone calls in *Irvine* (L) and the annoying phone calls in *Nader* (NL), it's presumably a matter of degree.

Estate of Berthiaume v. Pratt (P is photographed in hospital bed against his wishes; L)
Froelich v. Werbin (samples of P's hair are stolen from his hospital wastebasket; NL)
Harkey v. Abate (D put spying device in ice rink restrooms; L)
Elmore v. Atlantic Zayre, Inc. (D spies on P in restroom and catches P in homosexual act; NL)
Shulman v. Group W Productions (problem: D records and broadcasts rescue of P from auto accident; L in part)

Q. What is the distinction between *Estate of Berthiaume v. Pratt* and *Figured v. Paralegal Technical Services*?

A. The point isn't that one case involved photography and the other didn't, despite the court's broad language about photographs in *Estate of Berthiaume*. We really don't know whether any pictures were taken by the defendant's agents in the *Figured* case, but it wouldn't have mattered if they were; the court in *Figured* took the position, with the Restatement, that there could be no liability for taking someone's picture in public because they have no interest in seclusion there. (Various *uses* of such photographs may become actionable under a different branch of the tort covered in the next section of the book: appropriation of likeness.) The distinction, rather, is that the photograph of the plaintiff's decedent in *Estate of Berthiaume* was taken in a place—a hospital room—where the plaintiff had a greater right to control his exposure than he did in public. In this sense the *Estate of Berthiaume* case is analogous to *Dietemann*: you can't record somebody without their consent in their home, or (here) in their hospital room.

Q. What is the distinction between *Froelich v. Werbin* and *Estate of Berthiaume v. Pratt*?

A. The first distinction is that the invasion in *Froelich* didn't involve entry into the plaintiff's hospital room, at least so far as the evidence in the record showed. A second distinction is that in *Estate of Berthiaume* the plaintiff's decedent was upset about the intrusion as it was occurring. Both of these distinctions seem a bit rickety. On the first, can it really be right that anything leaving in the plaintiff's trash is fair game for others to inspect? Perhaps there is some oblique support for this idea in cases like *California v. Greenwood*, 486 U.S. 35 (1988), which holds for Fourth Amendment purposes that there is no reasonable expectation of privacy in trash one leaves outside a house (and thus that inspection of such trash is not a search for which a warrant is required). But that was in a residential setting where the trash was left in bags out on the curb. In a hospital case like *Froelich* the plaintiff would seem to have little control over his trash, and it's hard to imagine that there would be no liability if the defendant retrieved private and invasive hospital records from a trash barrel into which the plaintiff's small garbage can had been emptied. Maybe the court was swayed not only by the fact that the theft occurred outside Froelich's room but also by the fact that the hair the defendant obtained might not be considered embarrassing or private in itself.

On the second point—the fact that Froelich's piece of mind wasn't disturbed at the time the alleged invasion took place—it's hard to imagine too much turning on this;—hard to imagine, for example, that the result on facts like Berthiaume's would be much different if he had been unaware of the photography at the time but became aware of it later. Still, perhaps the harassing nature of the photography as it occurred in Berthiaume's case adds some oomph to his claim beyond what would have existed otherwise. It goes to whether a reasonable person would have found the intrusion offensive, which is the Restatement standard.

Q. What is the superficial similarity between *Froelich* and *Johnson v. K-Mart Corp.*? What is the distinction between them?
A. In both cases the plaintiffs' privacy was invaded by spies acting in the guise of employees; in both cases the defendant obtained information about the plaintiffs without their consent; and in neither case did the plaintiffs realize this when it was occurring. *Froelich* might seem the worse case because it occurred in a hospital and without any consent, fraudulently induced or otherwise, on the part of the plaintiff. Yet there was liability only in *Johnson*. Why?

Maybe the distinction involves what it was the defendant obtained through these invasive means: damaging private information in *Johnson*, and pieces of hair in *Froelich*. Hair may have turn out to have embarrassing implications, as perhaps it did in *Froelich*, but by itself it doesn't reveal much; an ordinary person wouldn't be as upset about having some of his hair stolen (say, from a barber shop floor) as he would be about having a confession of alcoholism relayed to his boss. Then again, a reasonable person might be highly offended by an attempt to steal some of his hair for the purpose of proving he had a sexual relationship with someone else. (Should the reasonable person standard be applied in this sort of context-specific way?) Conceivably it also is relevant that the defendant in *Froelich* had an arguably legitimate use for the hair, whereas in *Johnson* the defendant admittedly had no legitimate use for much of the information obtained by its spies.

Q. What is the distinction between *Harkey v. Abate* and *Figured v. Paralegal Technical Services*?
A. That's easy: in *Figured* the plaintiff was observed only in public; in *Harkey* the plaintiffs were observed—or at least made vulnerable to observation—in private. The only tricky part of *Harkey* is the court's holding that whether there was *actual* observation of the plaintiffs was relevant only to damages, not to liability. It seems a little strange as a conceptual matter. If a phone call is recorded but the recording is never heard by anyone (the tape is ruined), is the caller's privacy invaded? But maybe this part of the holding should be understood as a practical rule of evidence—in other words, as a way to relieve the plaintiffs of the difficult burden of proving that they actually were watched. Any plaintiff will have trouble proving this, with the result (if such proof must be shown) that the defendant will rarely be held liable. The court's rule overcomes that problem—or does it? What are the plaintiffs' damages if they can't prove that the defendant actually watched them? There is an analogy to the lost-chance cases in the cause in fact chapter: perhaps the injury can be described as the plaintiffs' felt sense of risk that they *might* have been seen and never will know for sure.

Q. Can *Elmore v. Atlantic Zayre* be reconciled with *Froelich v. Werbin*? With *Johnson v. K-Mart Corp.*?
A. Many students find the result in the *Elmore* case repulsive, but that may be because they find prosecutions for sodomy repulsive. You can test this by trying a hypothetical variation on *Elmore* in which the plaintiff is similarly observed in a bathroom stall molesting a child or committing a robbery against someone he encountered in the restroom and forced into one of the stalls. He is arrested—and then sues Zayre for invading his privacy. If the privacy claim seems like a loser on those facts, then perhaps that shows that the court in *Elmore* got the principle right, and that the problem is that Georgia had underlying criminal prohibitions that some find objectionable. But perhaps some would still try to tie

the privacy point to the criminal law point by saying the hypotheticals just offered are different from *Elmore* because the intrusion was necessary to protect a third party, whereas consensual sex and drug use are victimless crimes that don't justify spying.

A difficulty with all this is that one doesn't know whether the spying was justified until after it has occurred: it's not an invasion of privacy if you peek and catch someone in the act of doing something they shouldn't be; but if they're behaving themselves, it's an invasion after all. Or so it seems. Maybe it was important in *Elmore* that the defendants had indications of homosexual acts occurring in the restroom before they peeked. You can test this by combining our earlier case with the hypothetical offered a moment ago: the voyeuristic defendant in *Harkey* looks through a false mirror into a restroom stall, hoping for titillation; he quite unexpectedly observes a murder occurring, which he promptly reports. Has he committed an invasion of privacy?

Q. What result in *Shulman v. Group W Productions*?
A. The case proceeded on multiple theories. First, the court found no liability for publication of embarrassing private facts because it found that the broadcast was of public interest, citing *Cox Broadcasting*, *Florida Star*, and *Haynes*:

> The more difficult question is whether Ruth's appearance and words as she was extricated from the overturned car, placed in the helicopter and transported to the hospital were of legitimate public concern. Pursuant to the analysis outlined earlier, we conclude the disputed material was newsworthy as a matter of law. One of the dramatic and interesting aspects of the story as a whole is its focus on flight nurse Carnahan, who appears to be in charge of communications with other emergency workers, the hospital base and Ruth, and who leads the medical assistance to Ruth at the scene. Her work is portrayed as demanding and important and as involving a measure of personal risk (e.g., in crawling under the car to aid Ruth despite warnings that gasoline may be dripping from the car). The broadcast segment makes apparent that this type of emergency care requires not only medical knowledge, concentration and courage, but an ability to talk and listen to severely traumatized patients. One of the challenges Carnahan faces in assisting Ruth is the confusion, pain and fear that Ruth understandably feels in the aftermath of the accident. For that reason the broadcast video depicting Ruth's injured physical state (which was not luridly shown) and audio showing her disorientation and despair were substantially relevant to the segment's newsworthy subject matter. [...]
>
> One might argue that, while the contents of the broadcast were of legitimate interest in that they reflected on the nature and quality of emergency rescue services, the images and sounds that potentially allowed identification of Ruth as the accident victim were irrelevant and of no legitimate public interest in a broadcast that aired some months after the accident and had little or no value as "hot" news. (See *Briscoe*, 483 P.2d 34 [while reports of the facts of "long past" crimes are newsworthy, identification of the actor in such crimes "usually serves little independent public purpose"].) We do not take that view. It is difficult to see how the subject broadcast could have been edited to avoid completely any possible identification without severely undercutting its legitimate descriptive and narrative impact. As broadcast, the segment included neither Ruth's full name nor direct display of her face. She was nonetheless arguably identifiable by her first name (used in recorded dialogue), her voice, her general appearance and the recounted circumstances of the accident (which, as noted, had previously been published, with Ruth's full name and city of residence, in a newspaper). In a video documentary of this type, however, the use of that degree of truthful detail would seem not only relevant, but essential to the narrative.

As for intrusion upon seclusion, the court held that the plaintiff had a good claim for the recording made of the time she spent on the helicopter to the hospital, and possibly for some of the footage taken at the accident scene. From the court's opinion:

> Cameraman Cooke's mere presence at the accident scene and filming of the events occurring there cannot be deemed either a physical or sensory intrusion on plaintiffs' seclusion. Plaintiffs had no right of ownership or possession of the property where the rescue took place, nor any actual control of the premises. Nor could they have had a reasonable expectation that members of the media would be excluded or prevented from photographing the scene; for journalists to attend and record the scenes of accidents and rescues is in no way unusual or unexpected.

> Two aspects of defendants' conduct, however, raise triable issues of intrusion on seclusion. First, a triable issue exists as to whether both plaintiffs had an objectively reasonable expectation of privacy in the interior of the rescue helicopter, which served as an ambulance. Although the attendance of reporters and photographers at the scene of an accident is to be expected, we are aware of no law or custom permitting the press to ride in ambulances or enter hospital rooms during treatment without the patient's consent. Other than the two patients and Cooke, only three people were present in the helicopter, all Mercy Air staff. As the Court of Appeal observed, "[i]t is neither the custom nor the habit of our society that any member of the public at large or its media representatives may hitch a ride in an ambulance and ogle as paramedics care for an injured stranger."

> Second, Ruth was entitled to a degree of privacy in her conversations with Carnahan and other medical rescuers at the accident scene, and in Carnahan's conversations conveying medical information regarding Ruth to the hospital base. Cooke, perhaps, did not intrude into that zone of privacy merely by being present at a place where he could hear such conversations with unaided ears. But by placing a microphone on Carnahan's person, amplifying and recording what she said and heard, defendants may have listened in on conversations the parties could reasonably have expected to be private.

> The Court of Appeal held plaintiffs had no reasonable expectation of privacy at the accident scene itself because the scene was within the sight and hearing of members of the public. The summary judgment record, however, does not support the Court of Appeal's conclusion; instead, it reflects, at the least, the existence of triable issues as to the privacy of certain conversations at the accident scene, as in the helicopter. The videotapes (broadcast and raw footage) show the rescue did not take place "on a heavily traveled highway," as the Court of Appeal stated, but in a ditch many yards from and below the rural superhighway, which is raised somewhat at that point to bridge a nearby crossroad. From the tapes it appears unlikely the plaintiffs' extrication from their car and medical treatment at the scene could have been observed by any persons who, in the lower court's words, "passed by" on the roadway. Even more unlikely is that any passersby on the road could have heard Ruth's conversation with Nurse Carnahan or the other rescuers. [...]

> Whether Ruth expected her conversations with Nurse Carnahan or the other rescuers to remain private and whether any such expectation was reasonable are, on the state of the record before us, questions for the jury. We note, however, that several existing legal protections for communications could support the conclusion that Ruth possessed a reasonable expectation of privacy in her conversations with Nurse Carnahan and the other rescuers. A patient's conversation with a provider of medical care in the course of treatment including emergency treatment, carries a traditional and legally well-established expectation of privacy. [...]

We turn to the second element of the intrusion tort[:] [the] offensiveness of [the] intrusion, including its degree and setting and the intruder's "motives and objectives." [...]

On this summary judgment record, we believe a jury could find defendants' recording of Ruth's communications to Carnahan and other rescuers, and filming in the air ambulance, to be "'highly offensive to a reasonable person.'" With regard to the depth of the intrusion, a reasonable jury could find highly offensive the placement of a microphone on a medical rescuer in order to intercept what would otherwise be private conversations with an injured patient. In that setting, as defendants could and should have foreseen, the patient would not know her words were being recorded and would not have occasion to ask about, and object or consent to, recording. Defendants, it could reasonably be said, took calculated advantage of the patient's "vulnerability and confusion." Arguably, the last thing an injured accident victim should have to worry about while being pried from her wrecked car is that a television producer may be recording everything she says to medical personnel for the possible edification and entertainment of casual television viewers.

For much the same reason, a jury could reasonably regard entering and riding in an ambulance—whether on the ground or in the air—with two seriously injured patients to be an egregious intrusion on a place of expected seclusion. Again, the patients, at least in this case, were hardly in a position to keep careful watch on who was riding with them, or to inquire as to everyone's business and consent or object to their presence. A jury could reasonably believe that fundamental respect for human dignity requires the patients' anxious journey be taken only with those whose care is solely for them and out of sight of the prying eyes (or cameras) of others.

Nor can we say as a matter of law that defendants' motive—to gather usable material for a potentially newsworthy story—necessarily privileged their intrusive conduct as a matter of common law tort liability. A reasonable jury could conclude the producers' desire to get footage that would convey the "feel" of the event—the real sights and sounds of a difficult rescue—did not justify either placing a microphone on Nurse Carnahan or filming inside the rescue helicopter. Although defendants' purposes could scarcely be regarded as evil or malicious (in the colloquial sense), their behavior could, even in light of their motives, be thought to show a highly offensive lack of sensitivity and respect for plaintiffs' privacy. A reasonable jury could find that defendants, in placing a microphone on an emergency treatment nurse and recording her conversation with a distressed, disoriented and severely injured patient, without the patient's knowledge or consent, acted with highly offensive disrespect for the patient's personal privacy[.]

SECTION D. APPROPRIATION OF NAME OR LIKENESS

Relatively expendable cases: *Cardtoons, L.C. v. MLBPA* and *Carson v. Here's Johnny Portable Toilets.*

White v. Samsung Electronics, Inc. (D displays robot dressed to look like Vanna White in advertisements; L)
Anderson v. Fisher Broadcasting Co. (P's likeness used in advertisement for news show; NL)
Zacchini vs. Scripps-Howard Broadcasting Co. (D broadcasts film of P's human cannonball act; L)
Eastwood v. National Enquirer (D knowingly publishes false cover story about Clint Eastwood; L)

This is a lively and difficult branch of privacy law. You can organize it around a general discussion of whether and why there ought to be a right of publicity at all. Anyone can appreciate the trademark-type point that in an age of mass advertising, a person should not have to tolerate the publication of his picture in close association with a product he does not endorse. In addition to the risks of confusion and dilution this creates, it may in some cases reduce incentives to create strong reputations and personae in the first place (how realistic is this concern?). At the same time, though, there are benefits to having a rich public domain in which artists, critics, and others can parody and otherwise present someone's likeness without their consent. The cases try to draw lines that recognize both interests, perhaps with mixed success from the standpoint of clarity and coherence.

Q. What is the distinction between *Anderson v. Fisher Broadcasting Co.* and *White v. Samsung Electronics*?
A. The superficial similarity is that in both cases the defendant ran television commercials featuring the defendant's likeness; indeed, in *Anderson* it was actual film of the plaintiff, whereas in *White* it was merely a robot that nobody could have mistaken for the plaintiff. Yet *White* was the case of liability. Why?

The clearest line the court *Anderson* draws is between plaintiffs whose likenesses are used to suggest that they endorse the defendant's products and plaintiffs whose likenesses are used in other ways. This idea makes a certain amount of sense; as noted above, the most appealing cases for invasion of privacy claims of this sort are the ones where the consumer might be confused into thinking that the plaintiff chose to endorse the product, or where the plaintiff's ability to market his likeness is diluted because it has been overused by others without compensation.

Those clearly aren't issues in *Anderson*; that is the court's point in saying that the defendant deprived Anderson of no economic value. But are they issues in *White*, either? It seems unlikely that anyone would have inferred from the robot in the Samsung ad that White had agreed to endorse their products. It also seems unlikely that the ad would have reduced White's ability to market her likeness for real endorsements. Perhaps the court thought it best to have a reasonably clear rule against any sort of appropriation of Samsung's sort; even if the rule didn't serve its purposes in any clear way in White's case, it might serve them in the general run of cases—and separating the cases where there is a real threat of dilution from those where there isn't might just be too much trouble. But is that true? Think of the case where an advertiser uses a Bette Midler sound-alike in an ad. That case might implicate the purposes behind the rule; and would distinguishing Midler's situation from White's be a sticky problem in practice? An analysis of the likelihood of confusion in each case would seem to take care of it.

The other distinction that *Anderson* draws involves not the plaintiff's interest but the nature of the defendant's use of his likeness. There are commercial and noncommercial uses. A commercial use involves an attempt to get people to buy things because they see them associated with the plaintiff's likeness. A classic noncommercial use would be a newspaper story of general interest about a real person. The latter can't become a "misappropriation" claim without seriously impairing the production of media products and the information they supply to the public (we're setting aside for now claims based on the public disclosure of embarrassing private facts). And this isn't changed by the fact that the media outlets in question are operated for profit; for we currently depend heavily on for-profit enterprises to produce information.

What makes the *Anderson* facts a little tricky is that the plaintiff's face wasn't just used on a newscast; it was used on an *advertisement* for a newscast, making the case an intermediate one between the pure news story and the pure commercial. But if the television station can broadcast the plaintiff's image as part of a segment on its newscast, then why can't it also offer a clip of the segment at some other hour to inform viewers that an interesting newscast will be shown later at night? This use of the plaintiff's likeness is awkward because it highlights more dramatically the fact that even in its news-broadcasting capacity a television station is a business trying to get high ratings so it can sell advertisements. But it still would seem hard to find a good way to cleanly separate a case like Anderson's from a case where a person sues because his face figured in a televised news story where he wished it hadn't appeared because he's an introvert.

From the *Fisher* opinion:

Sensitivity about reproduction of one's likeness is not a 19th century refinement of western civilization, as is sometimes supposed; many cultures have feared the magical power conferred by possession of a person's image. The settlers who brought the common law to the Oregon Territory could find that this sensitivity preceded their arrival. Northwest native people such as the Chinook, according to Herbert Spencer, "if photographed, 'fancied that their spirit thus passed into the keeping of others, who could torment it at pleasure,'" an apprehension that plaintiff, at least, would not consider unrealistic today. Civil law systems derive limits on the unconsented publication of photographs by subsuming a right to one's own likeness under a "right of personality." [...]

Q. What is the distinction between *Zacchini vs. Scripps-Howard Broadcasting Co.* and *Anderson v. Fisher Broadcasting Co.*?

A. In both cases film of the plaintiff was shown by a television station on its newscast, and in both cases the footage was likely of interest to viewers. The difference lies not in what the defendant did with the footage but on the plaintiff's side of the equation. In *Zacchini* the broadcast of the footage threatened to deprive the plaintiff of the economic value of his performance, since people might watch the film as a substitute for paying to see Zacchini at the fair. This in turn might reduce Zacchini's incentive to perform at all. There is no comparable concern in the *Anderson* case; the plaintiff had been in an accident and was in no position to derive any economic benefit from it, so there is no need to worry that showing film of him would create any bad incentives.

Another way to look at the cases is to say that in *Zacchini* the defendant was doing an end-run around a transaction that was waiting to happen: a deal in which the television station paid Zacchini for the right to broadcast his performance for the entertainment of its views. But wasn't a similar deal possible in *Anderson*? The station could have negotiated with the plaintiff for the right to show footage of him, too—and maybe he would have charged more than Zacchini if he really didn't want his face on television. But even if transaction costs were similar in these two particular cases, they probably will tend to be higher in cases like *Anderson* where the subject of the footage is a random participant in a news event whose name may not even be known to the network.

Q. What is the distinction between *Eastwood v. National Enquirer* and *Anderson v. Fisher Broadcasting Co.*?

A. In both cases film of the plaintiff was used by a news outlet to illustrate a story that might be of interest to a news outlet. And *Eastwood* wasn't a case like *Zacchini* where the defendant's acts might have taken away Eastwood's incentive to build his persona as an entertainer; nor was there any implied endorsement of the defendant's publication. The distinction this time is that the story about Eastwood was (allegedly) false—and knowingly so. The court's theory is that the *Enquirer* gained a commercial advantage by putting Eastwood's face on its cover. This isn't actionable if the *Enquirer* does it in the course of newsgathering and reporting; news accounts are exempt from liability. But if the story is a "calculated falsehood," then in effect the *Enquirer* is selling fiction about Eastwood and using his picture to sell it. Though Eastwood is unlikely to want to market fiction of a similar type, he does market fiction of other kinds—movies—and his likeness makes them more appealing to some consumers. Still, the issue can't quite be that the story was fiction, because fiction gets more protection than this case suggests (see below). The point must instead be that the plaintiff was passing off the story as real but that it actually was fiction; this meant that the only available exemption was the doctrine that protects news coverage, which turns out not to be available because it doesn't extend to deliberate falsehoods. Lies have less social value than fiction.

Q. What if the defendant television station in *Anderson* had been wrong to portray the plaintiff as the victim of an accident? Suppose that he actually was in great pain because he just slipped and fell on some ice; the station got the footage mixed up. Different result under *Eastwood*?

A.   No. First, it was important in Eastwood's case that the falsehood was deliberate; media outlets don't commit actionable invasions of privacy every time they turn out to be wrong in what they say about someone they portray. Second, it seemed important to the court in *Eastwood* that the defendant's use of his picture supplied it with a commercial advantage. That probably wasn't true in *Anderson*, where the audience was unlikely to care whether the story was about the plaintiff in particular or about somebody else. A "false light" claim could be a possibility on these facts (see the next section of the chapter), but it seems doubtful.

Rogers v. Grimaldi (D produces movie called "Ginger and Fred" that isn't really about Ginger and Fred; NL)
Estate of Presley v. Russen (L for Elvis impersonator)
Cardtoons, L.C. v. Major League Baseball Players Association (NL for creators of cards parodying baseball players)
Carson v. Here's Johnny Portable Toilets, Inc. (title is self explanatory; L)
Montana v. San Jose Mercury News (D newspaper sells posters featuring picture of Joe Montana, who sues; NL)

Q.   What is the distinction between *Rogers v. Grimaldi* and *White v. Samsung Electronics*?
A.   In both cases the defendant did not portray the plaintiff directly but used symbols, visual or linguistic, to get some mileage out of the audience's familiarity with the plaintiff. The distinction is that in *Rogers* the usage was part of the defendant's "artistic expression," whereas in *White* the usage was part of an attempt to sell TV sets. But what is the difference between works of art and commercials? Many artists, certainly including many filmmakers, create their works because they hope to make a lot of money from them. And many commercials represent large investments of creative energy; there have been movies made that collect great commercials, and the best commercials are more ingenious than the worst movies.

Perhaps the point of the difference involves the markets involved. Celebrities have endorsement options—various ways they can sell the right to associate their likenesses with a product in commercials like Samsung's. Courts worry that if a likeness can be appropriated without compensation, this will reduce the incentive to invest in the creation of a marketable reputation in the first place and perhaps mislead the public. But these risks seem lower if the defendant merely has the right to talk about the plaintiff and refer to her, even in the title of the movie; and the costs of liability here would be greater, because creators of fiction would have to steer clear of many references to modern culture unless they wanted to negotiate with the people who are the subjects of their references.

Still, it's easy to appreciate Rogers's position. She probably thought that some people were going to the movie because of their fond associations with the original Ginger and Fred, whether or not they expected Ginger and Fred to be in the movie—as probably a few of them did. From the opinion:

> Rogers has submitted a market research survey dated July 1986 which reports that based on approximately 200 interviews in Boston and New York (Staten Island) 43% of those exposed to the Film's title only connected the Film with Rogers and that 27% of those exposed to the Film's advertisement connected the Film with Rogers. Rogers also learned during discovery that MGM had devised several promotional ideas for marketing the Film on the strength of the public's familiarity with Ginger Rogers and Fred Astaire. These ideas included using still photographs of Ginger Rogers and Fred Astaire, requesting that guests invited to the New York premiere of the Film "Dress: Ginger or Fred," and using a "Ginger and Fred" dance cane, an item associated with Fred Astaire, despite the fact that the male lead in the Film does not use a cane during dance routines. Only the latter suggestion was ultimately implemented.

Q.   What is the distinction between *Rogers v. Grimaldi* and *Eastwood v. National Enquirer*?

A. In both cases the defendant in effect published fiction that was made more attractive by the defendant's prominent use of the plaintiff's name or likeness to promote it—on the cover (*Eastwood*) or in the title (*Rogers*). The difference seems to involve the court's special distaste for attempts to pass off fiction as news, as discussed a moment ago, though one can ask whether the readers of the *Enquirer* really think they are getting anything other than fiction much of the time anyway.

Q. Hypothetical: in *Guglielmi v. Spelling-Goldberg Productions*, 603 P.2d 454 (Cal. 1979), the defendant published a "fictionalized" television movie about the life of the early Hollywood film star Rudolph Valentino, who had died more than fifty years earlier (in 1926). The defendant didn't get the consent of Valentino or his heirs, who therefore sued for damages. What result?

A. No liability, for the immediate reason that the right of publicity dies with its holder—in the view of this court (others disagree). Several of the Justices also thought, however, that the claim failed on First Amendment grounds:

> [A]ppellant claims that the film is not entitled to constitutional protection because respondents acted with "knowledge or reckless disregard of the falsity" of their broadcast concerning Valentino. However, appellant's effort to import the "actual malice" standard of liability in defamation actions of *New York Times Co. v. Sullivan*, 376 U.S. 254 (1964), is misguided. That standard reflects the Supreme Court's recognition that while defamatory false statements of fact have no constitutional value, such statements are inevitable in the continuing debate on public issues. Accordingly, to provide adequate protection to "speech that matters," the court held that even false statements of fact concerning public figures and officials are not actionable unless they are published with knowledge of their falsity or reckless disregard for the truth.
>
> No such constitutional dichotomy exists in this area between truthful and fictional accounts. They have equal constitutional stature and each is as likely to fulfill the objectives underlying the constitutional guarantees of free expression. Moreover, in defamation cases, the concern is with defamatory lies masquerading as truth. In contrast, the author who denotes his work as fiction proclaims his literary license and indifference to "the facts." There is no pretense. All fiction, by definition, eschews an obligation to be faithful to historical truth. Every fiction writer knows his creation is in some sense "false." That is the nature of the art. Therefore, where fiction is the medium as alleged by appellant in this case and as evident in the film's title, *A Romantic Fiction*, it is meaningless to charge that the author "knew" his work was false. [...]
>
> While few courts have addressed the question of the parameters of the right of publicity in the context of expressive activities, their response has been consistent. Whether the publication involved was factual and biographical or fictional, the right of publicity has not been held to outweigh the value of free expression. Any other conclusion would allow reports and commentaries on the thoughts and conduct of public and prominent persons to be subject to censorship under the guise of preventing the dissipation of the publicity value of a person's identity. Moreover, the creation of historical novels and other works inspired by actual events and people would be off limits to the fictional author. An important avenue of self-expression would be blocked and the marketplace of ideas would be diminished. As one commentator recently observed, "it is difficult to imagine anything more unsuitable, or more vulnerable under the First Amendment, than compulsory payment, under a theory of appropriation, for the use made of (an individual's identity in a work of fiction)." Hill, *Defamation and Privacy Under the First Amendment*, 76 Colum.L.Rev. 1205 (1976). [...]
>
> In contrast, the facts underlying *Lugosi v. Universal Pictures*, 603 P.2d 425 (1979), are substantially different than those in the present case. *Lugosi* involved the use of Bela Lugosi's likeness in connection with the sale of such commercial products "as plastic toy pencil

sharpeners, soap products, target games, candy dispensers and beverage stirring rods." These objects, unlike motion pictures, are not vehicles through which ideas and opinions are regularly disseminated. This case involves the use of a celebrity's identity in a constitutionally protected medium of expression, a work of fiction on film. *Lugosi* simply did not address the viability of a cause of action for appropriation of the right of publicity under these circumstances.

Q. What is the distinction between *Estate of Presley v. Russen* and *Rogers v. Grimaldi*?

A. In *Estate of Presley* the defendant's show presented an imitation of Presley, whereas in *Rogers* the defendant's movie used the plaintiff's name as a basis for commentary and expression of something other than the plaintiff's own creativity. So there would be liability for a movie called *Ginger and Fred* that presented people who look like Ginger and Fred imitating their dances. Unfortunately this puts the court in *Estate of Presley* into the unhappy position of needing to announce that the defendant's show there "serves primarily to commercially exploit the likeness of Elvis Presley without contributing anything of substantial value to society." This seems a hard claim to back up from the standpoint of an Elvis fan. Maybe it would be stronger if Elvis still were alive and losing money to impersonators who were thinner than he was and who could sing his songs better than he could. Given that he's dead, he isn't losing anything to the impersonator. But maybe the issue then becomes just whether these claims survive death. We've seen that some courts say they don't. The position that they do survive might be based on the thought that people will work harder to build reputations and personae if they know their descendents will be the exclusive beneficiaries of them.

Q. What is the distinction between *Cardtoons, L.C. v. Major League Baseball Players Association* and *White v. Samsung Electronics*?

A. First the similarities: in *Cardtoons*, as in *White*, the defendant published images that were similar to the plaintiff's likeness, though nobody would think they were one and the same; and in neither case would anybody be likely to infer that the plaintiff endorsed the defendant's products. Possible distinctions are, first, that *White* involved an advertisement, whereas the likenesses used in *Cardtoons* were embedded in the defendant's expression. Naturally this raises the usual problems of separating art from pure commercial usage. Second, the cards in *Cardtoons* more plainly were parodies offering criticism of public figures. The cost of forbidding them, or of forcing their makers to pay the ballplayers who were being criticized, would be high; we would lose potentially valuable criticism and commentary. The court in *Cardtoons* also thought that the defendant's cards would neither steal a noticeable amount of business away from the ballplayers nor decrease any incentive of theirs worth worrying about (though it might reduce their incentive to engage in behavior that invites parody, since they can be parodied for free). Some of these objections would have been strong in *White* as well. They point up the conjectural nature of the analysis that often supports arguments in this area: seat of the pants claims about how incentives will be affected and what opportunities will be lost if the defendant is allowed to persist.

Q. What is the distinction between the *Cardtoons* case and *Estate of Presley v. Russen*?

A. Both involved using near-likenesses of the plaintiffs for their entertainment value. *Cardtoons* might seem like the better case for liability because the ballplayers there were alive and had their own cards to sell. But *Estate of Presley* is the liability case because the court there didn't think the defendant's performances had any critical content or social value the way that the cards in *Cardtoons* did. Maybe *Estate of Presley* would have come out differently if the Elvis impersonator took the time to throw in some biting ridicule of Elvis's personal life or the costs of celebrity generally.

Q. What is the distinction between *Carson v. Here's Johnny Portable Toilets, Inc.* and *Rogers v. Grimaldi*?

A. In both cases the plaintiffs' names were used to refer to something other than themselves. In either case it was possible for consumers to be misled, at least momentarily, about the connection between the plaintiffs and the products with which their names were being associated. But in *Rogers* the usage was in the service of an artwork, whereas in *Carson* it was in the service of selling toilets. And in *Carson* it might seem more plausible that a consumer would think that Carson had endorsed the defendant's product (Carson did have a line of suits he endorsed that were advertised using his picture and the words "Here's Johnny" overhead).

Q. Hypothetical: in *Hirsch v. S.C. Johnson & Son, Inc.*, 280 N.W.2d 129 (Wis. 1979), the plaintiff was Elroy Hirsch, a famous football player from the mid-20th century. He was associated most famously with the Los Angeles Rams, for whom he was a running back from 1949 until 1957. While playing football at the University of Wisconsin, he was given the nickname "Crazy Legs" Hirsch because of his distinctive running style. In the 1950s there was a movie made of his life called "Crazylegs All American." He lent his name to various products for endorsement purposes. The defendants produced a shaving gel for women called "Crazylegs." Hirsch sued for unauthorized use of his nickname. What result?
A. The trial court dismissed the claim; the Wisconsin Supreme Court reversed:

> The fact that the name, "Crazylegs," used by Johnson, was a nickname rather than Hirsch's actual name does not preclude a cause of action. All that is required is that the name clearly identify the wronged person. In the instant case, it is not disputed at this juncture of the case that the nickname identified the plaintiff Hirsch. It is argued that there were others who were known by the same name. This, however, does not vitiate the existence of a cause of action. It may, however, if sufficient proof were adduced, affect the quantum of damages should the jury impose liability or it might preclude liability altogether. Prosser points out "that a stage or other fictitious name can be so identified with the plaintiff that he is entitled to protection against its use." 49 Cal.L.Rev. at 404. He writes that it would be absurd to say that Samuel L. Clemens would have a cause of action if that name had been used in advertising, but he would not have one for the use of "Mark Twain." If a fictitious name is used in a context which tends to indicate that the name is that of the plaintiff, the factual case for identity is strengthened. Prosser at 403.

> The record shows that Johnson's first promotion of the product, "Crazylegs," was the sponsoring of a running event for women and the use of a television commercial similar to the "Crazylegs" cheer initiated at University of Wisconsin football games when Elroy Hirsch became athletic director. These facts may augment and further identify the sports context in which the name, "Crazylegs," has been particularly prominent. The question whether "Crazylegs" identifies Elroy Hirsch, however, is one of fact to be determined by the jury on remand, and full inquiry into that fact is not foreclosed by the defendants' concessions in the present procedural posture of the case.

Q. What is the distinction between *Carson v. Here's Johnny Portable Toilets* and *Cardtoons, L.C. v. Major League Baseball Players Association*?
A. The usual: in *Cardtoons* there was an attempt at social commentary; in *Carson* there was merely an attempt at promotion.

Q. What result in *Montana v. San Jose Mercury News*?
A. No liability; the court thought the First Amendment protected the defendant's sales. The short version: "In summary, the First Amendment protects the posters complained about here for two distinct reasons: first, because the posters themselves report newsworthy items of public interest, and second, because a newspaper has a constitutional right to promote itself by reproducing its originally protected articles or photographs." The long version:

> In the instant case, there can be no question that the full page newspaper accounts of Super Bowls XXIII and XXIV, and of the 49'ers' four championships in a single decade, constituted publication of matters in the public interest entitled to First Amendment protection. Montana, indeed, concedes as much. The question he raises in this appeal is whether the relatively

contemporaneous reproduction of these pages, in poster form, for resale, is similarly entitled to First Amendment protection. We conclude that it is. This is because Montana's name and likeness appeared in the posters for precisely the same reason they appeared on the original newspaper front pages: because Montana was a major player in contemporaneous newsworthy sports events. Under these circumstances, Montana's claim that SJMN used his face and name solely to extract the commercial value from them fails. [...]

Additionally, SJMN had a right to republish its front page sports stories to show the quality of its work product. It is well established that "a person's photograph originally published in one issue of a periodical as a newsworthy subject (and therefore concededly exempt from the statutory prohibitions) may be republished subsequently in another medium as an advertisement for the periodical itself, illustrating the quality and content of the periodical, without the person's written consent." (*Booth v. Curtis Publishing Company*, 223 N.Y.S.2d 737 (1962). [...]

This same rule was applied in *Cher v. Forum Intern., Ltd.* 692 F.2d 634 (9th Cir.1982). In that case, actress/singer Cher had been interviewed by a talk show host in connection with a planned cover story on her in Us magazine. However, Cher and the magazine had a falling out, and plans for the story were dropped. The interviewer then sold the Cher interview to the publishers of Star, a tabloid, and Forum, a magazine. Cher sued, saying that her reputation was "degraded by the suggestion that she would give an exclusive interview to [those] publication[s]." Advertisements about Cher's interview in Forum appeared in Star, Penthouse, Forum, and the New York Daily News, falsely stating that Cher would divulge secrets to Forum that she " 'won't tell People and would never tell Us.' "

Applying California law, the court held that the publication of the interview in Forum was protected by the First Amendment. The Ninth Circuit court pointed out that the California Supreme "Court has acknowledged that 'the right of publicity has not been held to outweigh the value of free expression. Any other conclusion would allow reports and commentaries on the thoughts and conduct of public and prominent persons to be subject to censorship under the guise of preventing the dissipation of the publicity value of a person's identity.'" (citing *Guglielmi v. Spelling-Goldberg Productions* (concurring op.).

The court noted that although "California law permits recovery for the unauthorized use of one's likeness or name for commercial purposes [citations] [,] [n]o action under this theory will lie ... solely for publication which is protected by the First Amendment. Constitutional protection extends to the truthful use of a public figure's name and likeness in advertising which is merely an adjunct of the protected publication and promotes only the protected publication. Advertising to promote a news medium, accordingly, is not actionable under an appropriation of publicity theory so long as the advertising does not falsely claim that the public figure endorses that news medium." See also *Namath v. Sports Illustrated*, 371 N.Y.S.2d 10 (N.Y. App. 1975) (no violation of right of privacy where photo of Namath from 1969 Super Bowl game, which had originally appeared in Sports Illustrated, was used in advertisements for Sports Illustrated in *Cosmopolitan* (with the heading, "The Man You Love Loves Joe Namath") and in *Life* (with the heading, "How to get Close to Joe Namath")).

At the hearing on the summary judgment motion in this case, SJMN submitted undisputed evidence that it sold the posters to advertise the quality and content of its newspaper. The posters were effective in this regard: they were exact reproductions of pages from the paper. They contained no additional information not included on the newspaper pages themselves, and they did not state or imply that Montana endorsed the newspaper. SJMN also submitted evidence showing it set the price of the posters with the intent simply to recover its costs. Where, as here, a newspaper page covering newsworthy events is reproduced for the purpose of showing the quality and content of the newspaper, the subsequent reproduction is exempt from the statutory and common law prohibitions.

SECTION E. FALSE LIGHT

Time, Inc., v. Hill (D published story suggesting that P was abused by convicts during kidnapping; L if D acted with actual malice in *New York Times v. Sullivan* sense)
Zeran v. Diamond Broadcasting, Inc. (D's radio hosts negligently read P's first name and phone number on the air, associating it with tasteless t-shirt sales unconnected with P; NL because there was no action malice)
Douglass v. Hustler Magazine (P agrees to appear in *Playboy* but her pictures end up in *Hustler*; L)
Cox v. Hatch (Ps appear in photographs next to Orrin Hatch; NL)
Peoples Bank & Trust Co. v. Globe International Publishing, Inc. (P's picture used to illustrate scandalous tabloid story about someone else; L)
Mineer v. Williams (P's decedent maligned on talk show; NL because decedent's rights died with him)

False light is the most suspect of the four privacy torts. It's not clear if it really covers much ground that isn't covered as well—or better—by defamation law or other tort doctrines; and any additional coverage it does add may be considered constitutionally suspect. But false light may have some small office to fill in situations where the defendant does not publish false facts about the plaintiff that rise to the level of defamation but does publicize the plaintiff's likeness in an objectionable context. This unit typically will not quite consume a whole class session.

Q. What is the superficial similarity between *Douglass v. Hustler Magazine* and *Zeran v. Diamond Broadcasting, Inc.*? What is the distinction between them?
A. In both cases the defendant implied that the plaintiff made decisions that showed terrible taste. The falsity of the "light" was a closer question in *Douglass* than in *Zeran* because in *Douglass* the plaintiff did at least consent to appear nude in *Playboy*. The question was whether her apparently voluntary (but in fact involuntary) appearance in *Hustler* made a statement that put her in a light different enough from the truth to be actionable. In *Zeran* the plaintiff had nothing to do with the claims about him made on the radio (though he wasn't identified by his full name, much less photographed, by the defendant). So why is *Douglass* the case of liability? Because having just barely cleared the "false light" hurdle (element "a" of the Restatement test), Douglass clears the second hurdle—actual malice—while Zeran did not (Oklahoma law required him to make such a showing despite being a private figure; other jurisdictions would not have imposed such a requirement). Said the court in *Douglass*:

> With regard to "actual malice" in representing her as voluntarily associating with the magazine, the only question is whether Hustler knew that it was acting without authorization—knew, in other words, that Douglass was not voluntarily associating herself with the magazine—or didn't care. Hustler argues that it relied on Gregory to supply authentic releases and cannot be found to have acted with actual malice if he submitted forged ones. The absence of any release from the other woman in the "Ripped-Off" pictorial undermines this claim; but a more important point is that Gregory was Hustler's photography editor, acting within the scope of his employment, so that his knowledge of the falsity of the releases was the corporation's knowledge. It makes no difference whether in submitting the photographs he was acting as an independent contractor, as Hustler argues, or as an employee. As photography editor, which is to say in his capacity as an employee, he had some—it does not matter precisely how much—responsibility for the provenance of the photographs that were published. If someone had submitted nude photographs of Robyn Douglass to him without a release and he had told his superiors there was a release, he

would have been acting within the scope of his employment. It makes no difference that in fact he was the seller as well as the buying agent. The doctrine of respondeat superior is fully applicable to suits for defamation and invasion of privacy, notwithstanding the limitations that the First Amendment has been held to place on these torts.

Q. Can the Restatement illustration in the casebook text be squared with *Cox v. Hatch*?
A. Probably not. Remember that *Cox* said "at most, the photograph can be construed to imply that the plaintiffs are members of the Republican Party or that they supported Hatch's reelection. However, attribution of membership in a political party in the United States that is a mainstream party and not at odds with the fundamental social order is not defamatory, nor is attribution of support for a candidate from one of those parties." Yet that's about what happens in the Restatement illustration. One possible distinction on the facts (setting aside the court's language in *Cox*) is that *Cox* involved a photograph rather than a signature on a petition; the latter is a far clearer signal of support than allowing oneself to be photographed next to a political figure. As a matter of policy it might be pretty onerous to ask political candidates to get consent from everyone with whom they appear on pictures published by their campaigns. This could be a costly process (privately for the candidate but also for the public if they get to see less of the candidate) and with pretty slender apparent gains to justify it. It would not be comparably onerous to ask the circulator of a petition to remove the names of people who discovered that they signed mistakenly.

Q. What is the distinction between *Peoples Bank & Trust Co. v. Globe International Publishing* and *Cox v. Hatch*?
A. The plaintiff's photograph in the *Peoples Bank* case was associated with a claim that she conducted an extramarital affair (it's not clear whether the story suggested that she was married, that he was married, or that both were married). This is considered offensive to a reasonable person in a way that membership in the Republican party is not, even though some people might object more to the latter claim that to the former. Query whether the plaintiff in *Peoples Bank* might also have had a good claim based on the *Eastwood* case in the prior section of the chapter.

CHAPTER 13

NUISANCE

SECTION A. DEFINITIONS AND STANDARDS

Candidates for cases to cut: *Rockenbach* and *Adkins*.

Bamford v. Turnley (D sued by neighbor for creating nuisance with his brickmaking operation; L)
Jost v. Dairyland Power Cooperative (L for nuisance; evidence of the utility of D's conduct properly omitted)
Carpenter v. Double R Cattle Company (NL for nuisance because of the utility of the defendant's conduct)
Theoretical materials

Q. Baron Bramwell takes the position in *Bamford v. Turnley* that compensation should be paid to a plaintiff damaged by a nuisance even if the gains from the defendant's activities outweigh the costs. Why? And is the idea that the plaintiff should receive damages or an injunction?

A. Bramwell was imagining an injunction—but one which of course could be dissolved on an appropriate payment from the defendant to the plaintiff, thus providing the plaintiff with the compensation Bramwell describes. (See next question.) Economists view the requirement that the plaintiff be compensated in a case like this as merely having evidentiary value: only if the defendant compensates the plaintiffs will we really know whether the defendant's activities create more benefits for him than costs to them. If the evidentiary uncertainties are set to one side, then the orthodox economic view is that no compensation should be paid if the activity's cost-benefit ratio is favorable—for then the defendant has done nothing wrong. It's just a case of conflicting property uses that is most cheaply resolved by requiring the plaintiff to endure the discomfort or move.

The materials on nuisance are interesting to teach in part because they allow these economic ideas, familiar from negligence law, to be examined in a setting where their implications are stark: if the Hand formula approach is taken, the "P" in these cases often will be 1; so the defendant may be able to inflict certain and substantial ongoing costs on the plaintiff without paying for them. The objection to this view can come on distributive or fairness grounds, or on a ground that commits to a strong and particular view of property rights. But this last position has to be examined carefully. If one says that there should be liability because the plaintiff's property rights are being invaded, a circularity appears: what *are* the plaintiff's property rights? It's pretty clearly not the right to exclude small amounts of noise or light from passing over the plaintiff's property; so how do we define what rights come with ownership? Cost-benefit analysis provides one answer; Epstein's proposal, shown in this section, offers an alternative. The *Jost* and *Carpenter* cases are meant to show how two versions of these approaches can sound in practice and so provide grist for discussion along these same lines.

Q. Bramwell offers this possible reservation about the position he takes: "by injunction or by abatement of the nuisance a man who would not accept a pecuniary compensation might put a stop to works of great value, and much more than enough to compensate him." How serious a concern should this be?

A. This question presents a chance to discuss the Coase theorem and Calabresi and Melamed's famous article. If transaction costs are low, Bramwell's concern might seem to be a non-issue from an economic standpoint; if the plaintiff won't accept whatever large amount the defendant has offered to dissolve the injunction, then evidently the rights at stake are worth more to the plaintiff than they are to the defendant—so from the standpoint of efficiency there is no reason the rights *should* change hands. (The plaintiff's high valuation of his rights may seem idiosyncratic, but so what?) But if transaction costs are high there is an economic argument for awarding damages, for they can be viewed as approximating the transaction the parties would make for themselves if they could. The hard part then becomes determining when transaction costs are high. If there are lots of parties, there are dangers of strategic behavior by some of them (holdouts and free riders); if there are only two parties, there are dangers of other types of strategic behavior that arise from bilateral monopolies—bluff and bluster that can draw out or torpedo negotiations. And then what if it turns out that the reason the parties can't reach an agreement is that they have come to loathe each other or aren't comfortable exchanging cash because of norms against it that are in the picture? Should those be labeled "transaction costs"?

These general ideas no doubt are familiar to most torts teachers; they can be explored in any number of familiar places in the literature. Some excerpts from that literature are given below to accompany the part of the chapter on remedies in nuisance cases; some of the issues flagged here can be postponed until (or revisited during) that section of the chapter. The particular issues that arise from enmity between the parties are treated in some detail in Farnsworth, *The Economics of Enmity*, 69 U.Chi.L.Rev. 211 (2002).

Rockenbach v. Apostle (L for opening funeral home in residential neighborhood)
Adkins v. Thomas Solvent Co. (NL for D whose contamination of groundwater didn't reach the plaintiffs' properties, even though the plaintiffs' property values were driven down by the fear of contamination)

Q. What is the distinction between *Rockenbach v. Apostle* and *Adkins v. Thomas Solvent Co.*?
A. First the superficial similarity: both cases involve nuisance claims based on mental impressions, including in both cases some impressions that are unfounded (the court in *Rockenbach* approves the idea that a "dread of communicable diseases, not well founded, but nevertheless present in the mind of the normal layman" is entitled to some weight, as it may contribute to "depression"). One distinction, which the majority in *Adkins* thought important, was that the plaintiffs in *Adkins* were not alleging that they themselves were suffering at all; *they* understood that they were in no danger. Their only harm was in the reduction of their property values. In *Rockenbach* the plaintiffs themselves were in danger of being depressed by the funeral home and presumably could have recovered some damages for this even if the market value of their homes had not been affected—though notice the possible oddity of preferring the claims of plaintiffs who suffer only intangible harms (distress) to those who suffer no distress but real economic damage. (Of course for purposes of discussion one must assume the plaintiffs in *Adkins* would be able to show that their property values in fact went down.)

A distinction cutting the other way in *Adkins*, and perhaps suggesting that both cases were wrongly decided, is that in *Adkins* the plaintiffs at least were able to allege some independently tortious conduct by the defendants: maybe they had in fact contaminated the nearby groundwater, and maybe this act caused damage to property values beyond the point where the experts believed the contamination had stopped.

The cases also create openings for other points about policy. If liability is found in *Rockenbach*, the funeral home can simply be moved to a more commercial area of town. If there is liability in *Adkins*, however, the consequences are less clear and more worrisome. The defendant may have little control over the bad publicity it receives, so to tie its liability to public opinion of the dangers it has caused, as it affects market values in the area, threatens to create not only cascading liability but also opportunities for mischief: the worse the public's impression of the defendant's conduct, the more they owe, so that anyone who engages in public hand-wringing about the contamination will indirectly increase the defendant's liability even if the defendant in fact hasn't caused any real harm to anyone.

Q. Is there any way the dissenter in *Adkins* might have distinguished that case from the hypothetical the majority offers about people with AIDS being considered a nuisance?
A. What the dissenter did say was this:

The "conditions" on adjoining property enumerated by the majority [in the hypotheticals] are not only "lawful," but may be accorded special legal protection on constitutional or statutory grounds. No constitutional or statutory protection attaches to the condition the instant defendants are alleged to have created or maintained on their property.

Apart from this appeal to statutory and constitutional protections, there seems to be no escape from judicial judgments about the normative status of the private preferences that the alleged nuisance offends. Questions of right to one side, perhaps a more basic policy impulse lies behind the dissent's reaction: holding diseased human beings to be a nuisance would be more troubling than finding liability when the defendant is a manufacturing plant, even when both cases involve pandering to irrational beliefs. A manufacturing plant can be removed farther away from residential areas with no great difficulty. Telling a class of people that they have to locate themselves far from residential areas is more troubling, because the cost this imposes on them is much greater. It doesn't just include the cost of relocating and driving back and forth to their distant homes (which are costs the manufacturing plant also would incur, more or less). It also includes the costs of being isolated from the community at large in which most people live—a kind of ostracism.

By the way, for a case rejecting the notion that a funeral home is a nuisance, see *Pearson & Son v. Bonnie*, 272 S.W. 375 (Ky. App. 1925). The plaintiffs sued to prevent the defendant from operating a funeral home in their residential neighborhood. The trial court found that the defendant's business would constitute a nuisance:

> That the presence of [the funeral home] would depress the value of neighboring property admits of no doubt at all. Even defendants' witnesses (or some of them) admit their strong disinclination to live next or near to such an establishment. It is true that the members of the families of undertakers seem not to share this feeling. It is their custom, apparently, to dwell in the upper stories of buildings devoted to the family business. And defendants have introduced several other witnesses, and among them several women, who dwell near the present establishment of defendants, at Third and Chestnut streets, and who find no inconvenience, whether of body or of mind, from the association. Indeed, one of them expressed a strong partiality for such a neighbor, and had even requested that some of the windows be left open in order that she might the better hear the singing of funeral hymns. But this is a stoic or philosophic mood not genial to the average person, and I think there is no manner of doubt that the sale and rental of property in this neighborhood will be materially diminished, if this business is conducted as proposed.

The court of appeals reversed:

> [T]he location of a lawful business is not rendered inappropriate simply because the value of adjacent property is thereby depreciated and the sentiments and feelings of the owners are touched. One living in a city must necessarily submit to the annoyances which are incidental to city life and to risk the march of trade and business progress. Without trade, the largest city would soon languish and become a mere shell. Without residents, it would be like the snow on the bosom of the desert. It is a difficult matter at all times to strike the true medium between the conflicting interests and tastes of people in a densely populated municipality. But at least until the state steps in and, acting for its people as a whole, undertakes under its police power to zone a city, the inhabitants thereof must risk the rise and fall in value of their property occasioned, not by a material invasion of its physical enjoyment, but only by the establishment of a business or building though accompanied by a sentimental repugnance to the same. [...]

SECTION B. COMING TO THE NUISANCE

If you want the shortened version, cut *St. Helen's Smelting Co. v. Tipping* and the note after it. Think twice, though; it's an interesting case.

Oehler v. Levy (L for defendant despite fact that plaintiff came to the nuisance)
Powell v. Superior Portland Cement, Inc. (NL for nuisance because plaintiff came to it, moving in near the defendant's factory in a "company town")
St. Helen's Smelting Co. v. Tipping (L for industrial nuisance with various qualifications)

Q. Why isn't coming to the "coming to the nuisance" every bit as solid a defense as assumption of risk, which it closely resembles?
A. Apart from the arguments sketched in the text, there is the danger that such a doctrine would give landowners an incentive to bring suits prematurely to complain about possible nuisances that don't really trouble them. They might worry that if they don't bring such early suits, they will be estopped from complaining later if they decide they want to use their land for residential purposes. Disallowing a "coming to the nuisance" defense allows the neighbors to wait and sue only if and when the conflict becomes serious as a practical matter, perhaps allowing the other suits that would have been brought early to dry up and blow away on their own (as the defendant moves away for other reasons, etc.).

Q. What is the distinction between *Powell v. Superior Portland Cement* and *Oehler v. Levy*?
A. For one thing, the court in *Oehler* indicated that its result might depend on the notion that the value of residential living in the contested area was greater than the value of permitting the defendant's stables to remain there. That might not have been true in *Powell*, though, where the facts suggested that much of the value of the plaintiff's property depended on the existence of the factory nearby. Also (and relatedly), in *Oehler* the character of the neighborhood was changing, and there apparently was no reason to think the defendant couldn't effectively move its operations elsewhere. In *Powell* there appears to have been no such evolution occurring, and there was reason to doubt that the defendant's factory, which depended on the nearby limestone deposits, effectively could be moved someplace where it wouldn't cause such problems.

Q. The *Tipping* case distinguishes between physical damage and personal discomfort caused by alleged nuisances. The opinion of the Lord Chancellor (Westbury) suggests that liability for property damage is stricter than liability for personal discomfort; cases of the latter sort may be defeated by showing that the plaintiff's discomfort was caused by important commercial activities. Why this distinction?
A. Some students may be surprised by this idea in *Tipping*, since they might regard personal discomfort as more important than property damage. The distinction presumably is meant to capture certain practical features of these situations. Many industrial activities produce odors that are unpleasant to those living nearby but that don't do any harm to the property. Courts might have reservations about these claims on several grounds: it's easier for fumes to irritate the senses of a human being than to damage his property, and correspondingly harder to avoid the former injuries without seriously impeding industrial development; personal discomfort often will be distributed fairly evenly among the nearby population; and proving the seriousness of the plaintiff's discomfort and quantifying it are likely to be formidable problems. In cases involving physical damage the proof of harm and the process of measuring it are likely to be more easily overcome, and some people in the area may be much more affected than others.

The significance of the *Tipping* case is not entirely apparent on its face. The court upholds liability for the defendant, but qualifies it in somewhat vague ways such as the distinction just discussed. Over the long run the *Tipping* case came to be commonly regarded as introducing the idea of balancing the utility of the defendant's conduct against the plaintiff's interests. The case is not itself an important authority in American courts, but of course this part of the theory with which it is identified has adherents, as we saw at the start of the chapter.

Q. Given the ghastly conditions that Brenner describes (in his discussion of the *Tipping* case), why do you suppose the case reports from the 19th century are not full of reports of nuisance cases being brought to complain about them?

A. Brenner suggests these reasons:

> 1. The ruling in the *St. Helen's* case that nearly all injuries were excluded as "trifling inconveniences" unless they involved physical damage to property.

> 2. The ruling in *St. Helen's* that damages could only be recovered for visible injuries accompanied by a fall in the property's value. Property values often rose rather than fell in contaminated areas. It sometimes was said at the time that these increases in property values compensated neighbors for the harm to them, but as Brenner points out, tenants who did not own their property did not so benefit—yet nuisance law was in part meant for their benefit.

> 3. The legal requirement that the state of the neighborhood be taken into account in assessing liability. Many towns were in such bad shape that this amounted to no possible liability as a practical matter.

> 4. The cost of going to court was too much for most laborers working in such towns. Notice that the plaintiff in the *St. Helen's* case was the wealthy owner of a large estate.

> Richard Posner adds the suggestion that in some cases if a plaintiff were successful it might either cause the plant to move or increase its costs, resulting either way in the plaintiff being out of a job, getting a lower wage, or suffering collateral consequences if he made his livelihood in the community and was dependent on its economic health.

Section C. Sensitivity and Spite

An abbreviated version of this section would just assign *Rogers v. Elliott*, *Christie v. Davey* (or *Barger v. Barringer*, a traditional spite fence case; *Christie* is more fun, *Barger* more practical), and the *Fontainebleau Hotel* decision.

Rogers v. Elliott (NL for convulsions caused by ringing church bell because P was extrasensitive)
Amphitheaters, Inc. v. Portland Meadows (NL for lights at racetrack that interfere with drive-in movie theater next door; the latter was an extrasensitive use of the property)
Page County Appliance Center v. Honeywell, Inc. (problem: D's computers ruin television reception at P's store; L, since latter was not an extrasensitive use)
Poole v. Lowell Dunn Co. (L; court rejects hypersensitivity doctrine)

Q. Why does it matter if a plaintiff is "extrasensitive"? If the defendant's activities are, in fact, causing great costs to the plaintiff (costs which, let us imagine, may exceed the benefits of the activity for the defendant), why should the plaintiff's special vulnerability make his claim any weaker?

A. Maybe the idea is that planning decisions about land use, and the investments that ride on them, often have to be made before a potential defendant has knowledge of the idiosyncrasies of nearby neighbors. In making those decisions the planner ought to be able to assume that those nearby will be "reasonable" people—i.e., ordinary. Another possibility is that the extrasensitivity doctrine can be understood as a kind of argument about activity levels: it suggests that the cost to the plaintiff of relocating to someplace where his sensitivities aren't offended may be cheaper than asking the defendant to move. Yet another possibility is that in a case like *Rogers*, the plaintiff's extransensitive reaction may be offset by pleasure taken by others (those who enjoy the bells)—but the others have no feasible way to organize and give effect to their preferences.

Q. What was the relevance of the defendant's motive in *Rogers v. Elliott*?
A. None, because the motive wasn't proven to the court's satisfaction. The parties had had their differences in the past, and it's hard to resist the implication that the defendant was gratifying his dislike of the plaintiff by ringing the bell. On the other hand he *normally* rang the bell, so the claim regarding malice has to be that the defendant would have desisted for anyone else against whom he had no grudge, and this is hard to prove (the defendant denied it). Causation in this sense evidently must be shown; the fact that the defendant took malicious glee in carrying out his regular and lawful actions cannot turn them into a source of liability. And the court says that the evidence must be something more than mere implications of malice from the defendant's acts. This obviously is going to make it hard for the plaintiff to put together a successful claim, which is the way the court wants it: "implications" of malice can be generated all too easily, so if anything in law is going to depend on malice, it had better come with a stiff proof requirement.

Q. Most jurisdictions agree that a tortfeasor takes his victim as he finds him—the "eggshell skull rule." Yet most of them consider it a good defense to a nuisance claim that the plaintiff is extrasensitive. Can these two positions be reconciled?
A. They probably can be reconciled. One must distinguish between liability and damages. In an eggshell-skull case involving an alleged battery or negligent act by the defendant, the defendant's liability still must be shown by reference to a reasonable person standard: the defendant's touching of the plaintiff will not be a battery if he reasonably expected that a reasonable person would have licensed it; and the defendant's act will not be held negligent, either, if his conduct was reasonable—and in judging this we entitle him to assume that other people will be reasonable, not idiosyncratic. To make this more concrete, the point is that jostling someone on a subway does not become a battery (or a negligent act) just because the victim turns out to have a dread of being touched, weak shoulder that collapses as a result, or some other form of extrasensitivity. In this sense the extrasensitivity point does carry over to other areas of tort law.

The eggshell skull principle takes its bite at the damages phase. The point can be brought out in the nuisance setting with a different question. Suppose that the defendant's lights in the *Amphitheaters* case were conceded to have been a nuisance to normal neighbors of the defendant as well as to the movie theater. What damages would the theater be allowed to collect? Would the plaintiff movie theater be limited to collecting the damages that a normal, non-extrasensitive user would collect? The answer should be no, at least according to the eggshell skull principle: *once liability is established*, the defendant is on the hook for all of the plaintiff's damages even if they are unexpectedly large. Nothing in *Rogers* or the *Amphitheaters* case is to the contrary.

Q. What result in *Page County Appliance Center v. Honeywell, Inc.*?
A. Liability. From the court's opinion:

> In the case before us, ITT asserts the Appliance Center's display televisions constituted a hypersensitive use of its premises as a matter of law, and equates this situation to cases involving light thrown on outdoor theater screens in which light-throwing defendants have carried the day. Several of those cases are distinguishable both on facts and by the way the issue was raised.
>
> We cannot equate the rare outdoor theater screen with the ubiquitous television that exists, in various numbers, in almost every home. Clearly, the presence of televisions on any premises is not such an abnormal condition that we can say, as a matter of law, that the owner has engaged in a peculiarly sensitive use of the property. This consideration, as well as related considerations of

unreasonableness, gravity of harm, utility of conduct, and priority of occupation, are factual determinations that should have been submitted to the jury in this case. We find no trial court error in refusing to direct a verdict on this ground.

Christie v. Davey (L for malicious creation of noise to spite neighbor who gives music lessons; wonderful facts)
Mayor of Bradford v. Pickles (NL for maliciously interrupting flow of water to P's property)
Barger v. Barringer (L for building spite fence)
Fontainebleau Hotel Corp. v. Forty-Five Twenty-Five, Inc. (NL for building that throws neighboring beachfront hotel into shadow)
Hollywood Silver Fox Farm, Ltd. v. Emmett (problem: D fires guns to frighten P's vixens, hoping to induce P to remove sign advertising his fox farm; L)

Q. What is the distinction between *Christie v. Davey* and *Mayor of Bradford v. Pickles*?
A. In both cases the defendants maliciously (we can assume, given the courts' discussions) took actions that made the plaintiffs unhappy, probably in hopes of forcing the plaintiffs to make concessions to them; but there was liability only when the result was noise, not when it was the interruption of the flow of water to the plaintiff's property. The rationale probably has something to do with how the plaintiff's rights are defined. The plaintiff has a right not to be subjected to loud noise just for the purpose of making him miserable; in other words, he has a right to quiet unless there is a good (i.e., productive, non-malicious) reason to destroy it. He has no comparable right to receive a flow of water from his neighbor's property—not even a default right that gives way for good reason. Maybe the reason is that good motives and bad are harder to separate when we are concerned with the flow of water. A defendant may have all sorts of reasons for interfering with it, including the wish to make some money. Is this a bad reason? How do we figure out when malice becomes a sufficiently large share of the defendant's motive to justify liability? These could be problems in the noise case as well, but on the facts of *Christie* it was entirely clear that the defendant had no reason to make his music other than to annoy the plaintiff. On the other hand, the true goal of the defendant in *Christie* wasn't to annoy the plaintiff; it was to get the *plaintiff* to stop making noise. But it was found that the plaintiff had a right to make his noises, since they were innocent, so the defendant had no right to use annoyance as a weapon to get the plaintiff to stop.

Q. In *Rogers v. Elliott*, earlier in the section, we settled that if ringing the bell is not a nuisance, it doesn't turn into one just because the defendant feels a sense of malicious glee as he pulls the rope. How can this be squared with liability for spite fences?
A. The point in a spite fence case is that but for the spite, the fence would not have been built. The point in *Rogers* is that the bell would have been rung with or without the spite; and in that circumstance the addition of the spite does no causal work, so there can be no liability for it. But this may be too quick a resolution of the problem. Setting causation to one side, there generally is no liability for actions within the plaintiff's rights if they are taken for unkind reasons—though the "prima facie tort" doctrine, recognized in some jurisdictions, does permit liability in precisely that situation. The policy problem is that people do all sorts of things for all sorts of reasons that are hard to prove, and it's going to get messy if courts are called upon to identify and condemn those lawful acts done partly or wholly to annoy someone else. Many courts make exceptions to this principle for spite fences, though, perhaps because building a fence is a clearly defined act that often has pretty clear consequences for the defendant's neighbors; a relatively small expenditure by the defendant (you just pay for the fence once; no ongoing efforts are required) may be usable to create ongoing frustration for the plaintiff. It's a little easier to fathom what's going on between the parties in such a case than in a situation where, say, the defendant erects a large building rather than a small fence (see *Fontainbleau* below) or where the defendant lets his barking dogs into the back yard at annoying hours. Maybe these latter cases should be considered nuisances or maybe not, but making them depend on the defendant's motives will create hard problems of

proof. (The defendant in *Christie v. Davey* went the extra mile to cure the plaintiff's evidentiary difficulties on this score.)

For another interesting spite fence opinion (and a further source of ideas to offer in class), see *Burke v. Smith*, 37. N.W. 838 (Mich. 1888). The parties were neighbors in Kalamazoo. Between their properties Smith built a fence eleven feet high that blocked light from reaching Burke's windows. Burke sued in chancery court, where the fence was held to be a nuisance; the Michigan Supreme Court affirmed:

> The moral law imposes upon every man the duty of doing unto others as he would that they should do unto him; and the common law ought to, and in my opinion does, require him to so use his own privileges and property as not to injure the rights of others maliciously, and without necessity. It is true that he can use his own property, if for his own benefit or advantage, in many cases to the injury of his neighbor; and such neighbor has no redress, because the owner of the property is exercising a legal right which infringes on no legal right of the order. Therefore, and under this principle, the defendant might have erected a building for useful or ornamental purposes, and shut out the light and air from complainant's windows; but when he erected these "screens" or "obscurers" for no useful or ornamental purpose, but out of pure malice against his neighbor, it seems to me a different principle must prevail. I do not think the common law permits a man to be deprived of water, air, or light for the mere gratification of malice. No one has an exclusive property in any of these elements except as the same may exist or be confined entirely on his own premises. If a pond of water lies entirely within his lands, without inlet and outlet, he may do with it as he pleases while he keeps it upon his own premises. He may also use as he pleases what air or light he can keep and hold within his dominion upon his own lands. But to the air and light between the earth and the heavens the right of each man is more or less dependent upon that of his neighbor. His neighbor must bear the inconvenience and annoyance that the legal and beneficial use of his premises engenders in this respect, if such use falls short of what the law treats as a nuisance; but the right to use one's premises to shut out or curtail the use of either of these elements by his neighbor, out of mere malice and wickedness, when such use is not beneficial to him in any sense, does not exist in law or equity.

> It is said that the adoption of statutes in several of the states making this kind of injury actionable shows that the courts have no right to furnish the redress without statutory authority. It has always been the pride of the common law that it permitted no wrong with damage, without a remedy. In all the cases where this class of injuries have occurred, proceeding alone from the malice of the defendant, it is held to be a wrong accompanied by damage. That courts have failed to apply the remedy has ever been felt a reproach to the administration of the law; and the fact that the people have regarded this neglect of duty on the part of the courts so gross as to make that duty imperative by statutory law furnishes no evidence of the creation of a new right or the giving of a new remedy, but is a severe criticism upon the courts for an omission of duty already existing, and now imposed by statute upon them, which is only confirmatory of the common law.

Q. Is there a satisfactory distinction between *Barger v. Barringer* and *Mayor of Bradford v. Pickles*?

A. In the one case (*Pickles*) the defendant maliciously blocks the flow of water to the plaintiff's property—or again we can *assume* it was malicious because the court says it makes no difference); in the other case (*Barger*) the defendant maliciously blocks the flow of light to the plaintiff's property. It could be that we should distinguish between the flow of light, which everyone needs (especially in an age where artificial light was harder to come by), and the flow of water in a case like *Pickles*, which was valued for its commercial potential. On this view you have to play down the *Barringer* court's lumping of light with water as among life's essentials; there are different uses of water that may have different implications for its blockage by a neighbor.

But the cases finding liability for spite fences can also be viewed just as departures from the *Pickles* approach, so that the interesting question is just which approach seems preferable. You can look at the issue from an administrative standpoint and compare the costs of the various types of false positives and false negatives that the two rules can produce (malice matters or it doesn't). You can consider whether allowing spite fences creates the potential for escalating feuds. You can consider whether moral considerations have a place in legal judgments about how people exercise their rights.

Q. What is the distinction between *Barger v. Barringer* and *Fontainebleau Hotel Corp. v. Forty-Five Twenty-Five, Inc.?*

A. *Barger* condemns fences built "solely to inflict upon [the plaintiff] humiliation," etc.; *Fontainebleau* says there is no liability for a structure that blocks light that "may have been erected partly for spite." So they aren't quite inconsistent. They agree (and other cases say as well) that liability for a spite fence is defeated if the fence serves a genuinely useful purpose; for liability to attach, spite needs to be the only motive for the structure. The reason for this strong requirement probably is that the courts don't want to get into the business of stopping people from building useful structures on their property just because the construction also satisfies bad motives. Lots of things may fit that description. The point about a fence built solely for spite is not just that the owner is acting badly; it's that we also know (by hypothesis) that the fence is serving no *good* purpose that will be frustrated by a finding of liability. If a structure is much larger than a fence (like a hotel), it also may seem inherently less plausible that it was driven by spite; it would be a rare fit of spite that would drive a defendant to spend millions of dollars for no other reason than to erect a building as a monument to it.

When he wrote his own casebook back in the early 1980s, Posner suggested that *Fontainebleau* and the spite fence cases both should be actionable "without regard to nuisance theory, on the ground that they involve simply socially nonproductive, socially barren, efforts to increase the defendant's utility at the expense of the plaintiff's. The resources used in these efforts are wasted in terms of raising total social utility."

Q. What result in *Hollywood Silver Fox Farm, Ltd. v. Emmett?*

A. Liability. Said the trial court:

> Mr. Roche, who put the case for the defendant extremely well, submitted that the defendant was entitled to shoot on his own land, and that even if his conduct was malicious he had not committed any actionable wrong. In support of his argument, Mr. Roche relied mainly on the decision of the House of Lords in the case of *Bradford Corporation v. Pickles*. In that case the Corporation of Bradford sought to restrain Mr. Pickles from sinking a shaft on land which belonged to him because, according to their view, his object in sinking the shaft was to draw away from their land water which would otherwise come into their reservoirs. Mr. Pickles, they said, was acting maliciously, his sole object being to do harm to the Corporation. The House of Lords decided once and for all that in such a case the motive of the defendant is immaterial. [...]
>
> In the case of *Ibbotson v Peat*, [3 H. & C. 644 (1865)] a precedent for the statement of claim in this action is to be found. Mr Ibbotson was a land-owner at Brampton in the county of Derby and his land adjoined a grouse moor belonging to the Duke of Rutland. Mr Ibbotson, for the purpose of inducing the grouse on the Duke of Rutland's land to come on to his own, put on his own land quantities of corn on which grouse feed and thereby lured and enticed the grouse to come away from the Duke's land. The defendant Peat was in the employ of the Duke of Rutland and, minded to prevent Mr Ibbotson, the plaintiff, from getting advantage from such ungentlemanly conduct, let off fireworks, rockets and bombs, as near as he could get to Mr Ibbotson's land, for the purpose of frightening the grouse attracted by the corn away back to the Duke's land. In answer to the claim in that case, the defendant said, by a plea, that he was justified in letting off the rockets and bombs, because of the improper conduct of the defendant in luring away the grouse. The question was whether that was a good plea. It was decided that it was not a good plea. But, at the same time, the court expressed the opinion that the declaration alleging nuisance by noise

intentionally made for the purpose of injuring the plaintiff was a good cause of action and if no plea were filed judgment would necessarily be entered for the plaintiff. [...]

In my opinion the decision of the House of Lords in *Bradford Corporation v. Pickles* has no bearing on such cases as this. I therefore think that the plaintiff is entitled to maintain this action. I think also that in the circumstances an injunction should be granted restraining the defendant from committing a nuisance by the discharge of firearms or the making of other loud noises in the vicinity of the Hollywood Silver Fox Farm during the breeding season—namely, between January 1 and June 15—so as to alarm or disturb the foxes kept by the plaintiffs at the said farm, or otherwise to injure the plaintiff company.

SECTION D. REMEDIES

The key issues here can all be taught from *Boomer v. Atlantic Cement* if you don't want to assign the rest.

Madison v. Ducktown Sulphur, Copper & Iron Co. (court declines to enjoin D's nuisance because its value greatly exceeds the value of P's property; damages awarded instead)
Whalen v. Union Bag & Paper Co. (court enjoins D's nuisance despite fact that its value greatly exceeds the value of P's property)
Boomer v. Atlantic Cement Co. (court declines to enjoin D's nuisance because its value greatly exceeds the value of P's property; awards permanent damages)
Spur Industries v. Del E. Webb Development Co. ("rule 4" case in which court orders D to move its feedlot, but requires P to pay D's expenses)
Theoretical materials

These materials recapitulate the questions about the Coase theorem raised at the start of the chapter: if the court had entered an injunction in the *Madison* case, would there have been bargaining between the parties afterwards? What would it have looked like? Why shouldn't it have been allowed to occur? Do cases denying injunctions amount to instances of private eminent domain?

Since nuisance remedies are most interesting for the theoretical issues they raise, we think it will be most helpful here to offer excerpts from some of the secondary literature discussing them.

a. First is the canonical discussion in Calabresi and Melamed, *Property Rules, Liability Rules, and Alienability: One View of the Cathedral*, 85 Harv. L. Rev. 1089 (1972). Any reader of this manual probably is familiar with that article, but for the sake of convenience and refreshment here is its famous discussion of the issue at hand:

Traditionally [...] the nuisance-pollution problem is viewed in terms of three rules. First, Taney may not pollute unless his neighbor (his only neighbor let us assume), Marshall, allows it (Marshall may enjoin Taney's nuisance). Second, Taney may pollute but must compensate Marshall for damages caused (nuisance is found but the remedy is limited to damages). Third, Taney may pollute at will and can only be stopped by Marshall if Marshall pays him off (Taney's pollution is not held to be a nuisance to Marshall). In our terminology rules one and two (nuisance with injunction, and with damages only) are entitlements to Marshall. The first is an entitlement to be free from pollution and is protected by a property rule; the second is also an entitlement to be free from pollution but is protected only by a liability rule. Rule three (no nuisance) is instead an entitlement to Taney protected by a property rule, for only by buying Taney out at Taney's price can Marshall end the pollution.

The very statement of these rules in the context of our framework suggests that something is missing. Missing is a fourth rule representing an entitlement in Taney to pollute, but an entitlement which is protected only by a liability rule. The fourth rule, really a kind of partial eminent domain coupled with a benefits tax, can be stated as follows: Marshall may stop Taney from polluting, but if he does he must compensate Taney.

As a practical matter it will be easy to see why [legal writers] have ignored this rule. Unlike the first three it does not often lend itself to judicial imposition for a number of good legal process reasons. For example, even if Taney's injuries could practicably be measured, apportionment of the duty of compensation among many Marshalls would present problems for which courts are not well suited. If only those Marshalls who voluntarily asserted the right to enjoin Taney's pollution were required to pay the compensation, there would be insuperable freeloader problems. If, on the other hand, the liability rule entitled one of the Marshalls alone to enjoin the pollution and required all the benefited Marshalls to pay their share of the compensation, the courts would be faced with the immensely difficult task of determining who was benefited how much and imposing a benefits tax accordingly, all the while observing procedural limits within which courts are expected to function.

The fourth rule is thus not part of the cases legal scholars read when they study nuisance law, and is therefore easily ignored by them. But it is available, and may sometimes make more sense than any of the three competing approaches. Indeed, in one form or another, it may well be the most frequent device employed. To appreciate the utility of the fourth rule and to compare it with the other three rules, we will examine why we might choose any of the given rules.

We would employ rule one (entitlement to be free from pollution protected by a property rule) from an economic efficiency point of view if we believed that the polluter, Taney, could avoid or reduce the costs of pollution more cheaply than the pollutee, Marshall. Or to put it another way, Taney would be enjoinable if he were in a better position to balance the costs of polluting against the costs of not polluting. We would employ rule three (entitlement to pollute protected by a property rule) again solely from an economic efficiency standpoint, if we made the converse judgment on who could best balance the harm of pollution against its avoidance costs. If we were wrong in our judgments and if transactions between Marshall and Taney were costless or even very cheap, the entitlement under rules one or three would be traded and an economically efficient result would occur in either case. [...] Wherever transactions between Taney and Marshall are easy, and wherever economic efficiency is our goal, we could employ entitlements protected by property rules even though we would not be sure that the entitlement chosen was the right one. Transactions as described above would cure the error. While the entitlement might have important distributional effects, it would not substantially undercut economic efficiency.

The moment we assume, however, that transactions are not cheap, the situation changes dramatically. Assume we enjoin Taney and there are 10,000 injured Marshalls. Now even if the right to pollute is worth more to Taney than the right to be free from pollution is to the sum of the Marshalls, the injunction will probably stand. The cost of buying out all the Marshalls, given holdout problems, is likely to be too great, and an equivalent of eminent domain in Taney would be needed to alter the initial injunction. Conversely, if we denied a nuisance remedy, the 10,000 Marshalls could only with enormous difficulty, given freeloader problems, get together to buy out even one Taney and prevent the pollution. This would be so even if the pollution harm was greater than the value to Taney of the right to pollute.

If, however, transaction costs are not symmetrical, we may still be able to use the property rule. Assume that Taney can buy the Marshalls' entitlements easily because holdouts are for some reason absent, but that the Marshalls have great freeloader problems in buying out Taney. In this situation the entitlement should be granted to the Marshalls unless we are sure the Marshalls are the cheapest avoiders of pollution costs. Where we do not know the identity of the cheapest cost avoider it is better to entitle the Marshalls to be free of pollution because, even if we are wrong in our initial placement of the entitlement, that is, even if the Marshalls are the cheapest cost avoiders, Taney will buy out the Marshalls and economic efficiency will be achieved. Had we chosen the converse entitlement and been wrong, the Marshalls could not have bought out Taney. Unfortunately, transaction costs are often high on both sides and an initial entitlement, though incorrect in terms of economic efficiency, will not be altered in the market place.

Under these circumstances—and they are normal ones in the pollution area—we are likely to turn to liability rules whenever we are uncertain whether the polluter or the pollutees can most cheaply avoid the cost of pollution. We are only likely to use liability rules where we are uncertain because, if we are certain, the costs of liability rules—essentially the costs of collectively valuing the damages to all concerned plus the cost in coercion to those who would not sell at the collectively determined figure—are unnecessary. They are unnecessary because transaction costs and bargaining barriers become irrelevant when we are certain who is the cheapest cost avoider; economic efficiency will be attained without transactions by making the correct initial entitlement.

As a practical matter we often are uncertain who the cheapest cost avoider is. In such cases, traditional legal doctrine tends to find a nuisance but imposes only damages on Taney payable to the Marshalls. This way, if the amount of damages Taney is made to pay is close to the injury caused, economic efficiency will have had its due; if he cannot make a go of it, the nuisance was not worth its costs. The entitlement to the Marshalls to be free from pollution unless compensated, however, will have been given not because it was thought that polluting was probably worth less to Taney than freedom from pollution was worth to the Marshalls, nor even because on some distributional basis we preferred to charge the cost to Taney rather than to the Marshalls. It was so placed simply because we did not know whether Taney desired to pollute more than the Marshalls desired to be free from pollution, and the only way we thought we could test out the value of the pollution was by the only liability rule we thought we had. […]

Rule four gives at least the possibility that the opposite entitlement may also lead to economic efficiency in a situation of uncertainty. Suppose for the moment that a mechanism exists for collectively assessing the damage resulting to Taney from being stopped from polluting by the Marshalls, and a mechanism also exists for collectively assessing the benefit to each of the Marshalls from such cessation. Then—assuming the same degree of accuracy in collective valuation as exists in rule two (the nuisance damage rule)—the Marshalls would stop the pollution if it harmed them more than it benefited Taney. If this is possible, then even if we thought it necessary to use a liability rule, we would still be free to give the entitlement to Taney or Marshall for whatever reasons, efficiency or distributional, we desired. […]

The introduction of distributional considerations makes the existence of the fourth possibility even more significant. […] Assume a factory which, by using cheap coal, pollutes a very wealthy section of town and employs many low income workers to produce a product purchased primarily by the poor; assume also a distributional goal that favors equality of wealth. Rule one—enjoin the nuisance—would possibly have desirable economic efficiency results (if the pollution hurt the homeowners more than it saved the factory in coal costs), but it would have disastrous distribution effects. It would also have undesirable efficiency effects if the initial judgment on costs of avoidance had been wrong and transaction costs were high. Rule two—nuisance damages—would allow a testing of the economic efficiency of eliminating the pollution, even in the presence of high transaction costs, but would quite possibly put the factory out of business or diminish output and thus have the same income distribution effects as rule one. Rule three—no nuisance—would have favorable distributional effects since it might protect the income of the workers. But if the pollution harm was greater to the homeowners than the cost of avoiding it by using a better coal, and if transaction costs—holdout problems—were such that homeowners could not unite to pay the factory to use better coal, rule three would have unsatisfactory efficiency effects. Rule four—payment of damages to the factory after allowing the homeowners to compel it to use better coal, and assessment of the cost of these damages to the homeowners—would be the only one which would accomplish both the distributional and efficiency goals.

An equally good hypothetical for any of the rules can be constructed. Moreover, the problems of coercion may as a practical matter be extremely severe under rule four. How do the homeowners decide to stop the factory's use of low grade coal? How do we assess the damages and their proportional allocation in terms of benefits to the homeowners? But equivalent problems may often be as great for rule two. How do we value the damages to each of the many homeowners? How do we inform the homeowners of their rights to damages? How do we evaluate and limit the administrative expenses of the court actions this solution implies?

The seriousness of the problem depends under each of the liability rules on the number of people whose "benefits" or "damages" one is assessing and the expense and likelihood of error in such assessment. [...] The relative ease of making such assessments through different institutions may explain why we often employ the courts for rule two and get to rule four—when we do get there—only through political bodies which may, for example, prohibit pollution, or "take" the entitlement to build a supersonic plane by a kind of eminent domain, paying compensation to those injured by these decisions.

b. From A. Douglas Melamed, *Remarks: A Public Law Perspective*, 106 Yale L.J. 2209 (1997):

Rule 4 is alive and well—at least in Washington. As everyone knows, the traditional private law litigation process does not readily lend itself to Rule 4, particularly where there are large numbers on the plaintiff/victim/payor side, and Rule 4 is thus not common in the private litigation context. The notorious exception, the *Spur Industries* case, did not have a large number problem; maybe that is why it was able to find a use for Rule 4.

The government can overcome the large number problem, as it does in the paradigmatic eminent domain case. That much is obvious. What is perhaps less obvious is that, in the public law domain, the government uses Rule 4 all the time. For example, television broadcasters are in effect required to give up what many had thought to be their preexisting entitlement to broadcast violent programming if their viewers want to see it and their advertisers are willing to sponsor it; as compensation, the broadcasters are given free use of additional spectrum to accommodate the transition to the digital age. In a similar vein, the 1996 Telecommunications Act requires local telephone companies to make their facilities available to their would-be rivals in local telephony and compensates the phone companies by permitting them to enter into the long distance business that had previously been foreclosed to them. And, in at least two recent instances, the Federal Trade Commission has compromised the right of private entities to carry on their businesses by assuming oversight authority over them—in one case, a blank check to impose divestiture or other injunctive remedies as the Commission sees fit—and compensated the parties by permitting them to consummate an otherwise problematic merger. There are countless examples like this in the public sector. While they often have some of the trappings of a bargain, they ultimately can be called Rule 4-type remedies—or, in the case of the telephone companies and the long distance carriers whose own market positions are threatened, combinations of Rule 4 and Rule 2—because the consent of the private parties is not required.

c.   Another wrinkle was added in Krier and Schwab, *Property Rules and Liability Rules: The Cathedral in Another Light*, 70 N.Y.U. L. Rev. 440 (1995); in their scheme "P" refers to "polluter" and "R" to "resident":

> The point of liability rules—at least one of their central purposes—is to serve as a substitute for bargaining when transaction costs are high.   Rule two plays this role when asymmetric information costs or justice preferences (or both) point in the direction of an entitlement in R, protected only by a damages remedy.   P can force a sale, but the idea is that a reasonably accurate estimate of R's damages will lead P to compare its avoidance cost to R's damages and choose the cheaper, which might be to pollute and pay, or might be to abate.   Ordinary bilateral bargaining, thought to be too bogged down by transaction costs, is converted into unilateral bargaining, with P acting on its own account but with the judge acting on R's account, as a sort of proxy.   We get at least the illusion of a market test—an important objective of the whole business—that will accord more or less with reality depending upon the accuracy of the (objective) damages, the presence or absence of difficult tradeoffs when all the relevant considerations (information, justice, etc.) don't cut the same way, and so on.
>
> Rule four, an entitlement in P protected by damages, seems to open up vast new frontiers for liability rules.   It lets us once again accommodate high-transaction-cost cases (or so we like to imagine) but at the same time it allows us to act on a justice preference for P, or take advantage of asymmetric information.   Suppose, for example, that the judge is either indifferent on the question of justice or has a preference for P, and suppose also that the judge has a good notion of P's avoidance cost but not of R's damages.   Rule four handles the case.   Award the entitlement to P, determine P's damages (avoidance cost), and tell R to pay up or shut up.   If R's damages exceed P's avoidance cost, R will pay up (the efficient result); otherwise R will shut up (efficient again).   Under rule four, the judge acts as a proxy for P rather than R, and R decides whether to accept the judge's offer on behalf of P.   Rule four can, in principle, promote just and efficient results in exactly the fashion of rule two, but at the same time it can accommodate instances that rule two cannot (and vice versa).   Rule four can also, like rule two, create the illusion of a market test, and for the same reasons.   The two rules look to be mirror images of each other.
>
> But they are not.   At least with respect to the typical R v. P case, rule four is paradoxical in that it reintroduces the very problem it is meant to solve.   Litigation arising from environmental pollution and like problems (our stock example) generally involves not a single P and a single R, but rather a single P and multiple Rs.   Rule four asks those multiple Rs to agree on a choice—either to pay P's damages (avoidance cost) as set by the court, or to be quiet and go away.   But in posing such a choice to a group of choosers, rule four gives rise, necessarily, to the same problems of free riding and strategic bargaining, the same transaction costs, that were the reason for opting for a liability rule in the first place! [...]
>
> Let us quickly make the same point another way, and then use that way to indicate a path out of the paradox.   Above we referred to *Spur Industries* as a multiple-party case, when nominally at least it appears to have been otherwise, a simple contest between an innocent P (Spur Industries) and a guilty R (Del Webb).   Suppose for a moment that these two parties would bargain cooperatively rather than strategically, for which reason the court is inclined to use property rule three, with Spur Industries entitled to continue its operations unless Del Webb could induce it to do otherwise through bilateral negotiations.   This would be a bad approach for the court to take,

even on the assumption of cooperative bargaining, because Del Webb would likely offer too little to Spur Industries, relative to the social costs involved. Del Webb would be interested primarily in the marginal units it had been unable to sell in consequence of the pollution; it would be less concerned, if concerned at all, about the retirees who had already bought into the development. Its smaller stake made it a bad proxy for the residents of Sun City, yet those were the people whom the court regarded as the real parties in interest.

In any event, in the actual case, the court decided to use a liability rule. It could not use liability rule two because justice demanded that the entitlement be in Spur Industries. So it invented liability rule four, but in a way that seemed to foreclose any market test: Spur Industries, it said, had to go, and Del Webb, it said, had to pay. Despite such an ultimatum, however, Spur Industries and Del Webb would presumably remain free to bargain after the liability-rule judgment was entered, just as they would have been free to do so after a property-rule judgment. But Del Webb would again be a bad proxy, for the reasons discussed above. The residents would be in no position to bargain with Spur Industries, either. Collective action problems, not to mention justice considerations, foreclosed a judgment that Spur Industries could remain unless the residents paid its removal costs, and common sense foreclosed a judgment that Spur Industries could remain unless the residents voted to have Del Webb pay those costs (the outcome would be preordained). And rule two, as we said, was of no avail: Spur Industries, as an innocent party, could not justly be held liable in damages.

So what can be done? Consider the following:

Rule four entails what aptly can be called reverse damages, since in such cases nominal plaintiffs end up liable to nominal defendants. Yet while reverse damages can work wonders in some cases, they cannot work them in all. In particular, they are paradoxically impotent in the typical case of multiple Rs—a case like *Spur Industries*—simply because multiple parties are bad choosers. This implies a principle, a best-chooser axiom:

All other things being equal, when liability rules are used the party who is the best chooser should be confronted with the decision whether or not to force a sale upon the other party.

In most instances, the best chooser will be the smallest-number party—the feedlot operator in *Spur Industries*. But, for justice reasons already discussed, we cannot take the conventional path of rule two, which would make Spur Industries choose between paying damages to the citizens of Sun City or closing down. Similarly, for justice reasons and collective action reasons already discussed, we cannot use conventional rule four, which would have the citizens choose between compensating Spur Industries for closing or putting up with the stench.

There is another alternative. Bear in mind that the market-test principle underlying liability rules requires that some party—now seen as the best chooser—compare its own opportunity cost to the opportunity cost (figured by the judge) of the other party or parties. Usually the best chooser will be a single entity. Hence, in a case like *Spur Industries*, where Spur Industries (the feedlot owner) is the best chooser, we need (1) a way to confront Spur Industries with the social costs (the damages to the residents) that it would impose if the nuisance were to stay in place, such that Spur Industries would then compare those damage costs to its avoidance costs. But, for justice reasons, we also need (2) a way that doesn't make Spur Industries pay.

The solution? Simply reverse the reverse damages; do the double reverse twist. First, have the judge estimate as damages the residents' social costs mentioned in (1). The damages are objectively measured, of course; indeed, they are exactly the damages the judge would calculate in a conventional rule two case like *Boomer*. Next, have the judge enter the following peculiar order: If Spur Industries moves, the residents must pay Spur Industries the residents' damages set by the judge; if Spur Industries stays, it will get nothing. Peculiar, but it works. The judgment is just (in the terms in which we are thinking about that norm here), and it promotes the efficient result.

d. From Saul Levmore, *Unifying Remedies: Property Rules, Liability Rules, and Startling Rules*, 106 Yale L.J. 2149 (1997), which treats the Krier-Schwab suggestion as "Rule 5":

If a judge follows Krier-Schwab and allows the defendant, A, to continue on as before or instead choose to stop but then collect B's (projected but not yet suffered) damages, B may well be sorry that she brought her complaint. It is not just that legal fees will have been wasted either when B loses, in the manner of Rule 3, and the injunction against A is denied, or when A opts for Rule 5 (A stops and collects B's gain from this cessation) so that B gets what she asked for in harm-preventing terms, but only by paying her full reservation price. The problem from B's perspective is that B might not have been willing to pay this amount in order to stop A. Armed with the legal right to be free of pollution, B might have demanded $100,000, for example, before allowing A to send effluents her way, so that B's damages from A's operation can fairly be said to amount to $100,000; but this does not mean that B could or would pay this amount to stop A, if the law requires B to pay in order to change the status quo of A's operation. The wealth effect of the property right might itself cause B to spend something less than $100,000 on clean air. This well-known offer-asking differential, or endowment effect, may often be small enough to ignore, but inasmuch as every penny of B's potential gain from A's cessation is here sought, the problem is likely to be present and significant in most instances. There is something of an analogy here to the annoying insistence of a teacher that a student's request for the regrading of an exam will be entertained only on the condition that the student bear the risk that, when the exam is reviewed, it may be determined that the grade should be decreased rather than increased.

A subtle (or even subconscious) comprehension of this problem may well be at the heart of what is startling about the Krier-Schwab innovation. B complains that A's smokestack configuration causes B $100,000 in harm, and the shocking suggestion is that A can go on as before or choose to shut down (or alter the smokestack) and collect $100,000 from B. Even readers who are unfamiliar with the offer-asking literature may intuit that B is not indifferent, but is now worse off than before. None of the other rules threatens B in this manner. Indeed, the companion rule, 5CE, introduced by Krier-Schwab as theoretically isomorphic to Rule 5, does not seem at all startling. It will be recalled that this companion rule also draws on the restitution idea as it offers A the choice between stopping (Rule 1) and continuing at the cost of paying (to B) A's own gains from continuing rather than stopping (Rule 5CE). The fact that this proposal does not seem nearly as interesting as its partner, Rule 5 (A stops and collects B's gain from cessation), suggests again that it is neither the choosing function nor the restitutionary quality that generates surprise, but rather the fact that only in Rule 5 is it the case that B can emerge worse off than before.

It goes almost without saying that Rule 5 (A stops itself and collects B's gain from this cessation) must be deployed cautiously. As noted earlier, there is the moral hazard that A will engage in an activity in order to induce a complaint and then profit from stopping and collecting. The possibility that a judge will use Rule 3 (A may continue as before) presents much less of an encouragement for A's strategic, inefficient location; not only is the potential payment from B greater in Rule 5, but also with Rule 3, B can simply decline to offer to pay A, so that A will lose out if it has located simply to extract payment from B. In contrast, Rule 5 forces B to pay at A's insistence and, therefore, poses more of a moral hazard problem. Put differently, if Rule 5 is in each judge's portfolio, then there is the risk that B will be truly harmed by an antisocial, inefficient A, but will nevertheless decline to object for fear that she will trigger a Rule 5 decision and be yet worse off. B must think that there is a substantial chance of victory in the form of the judicial imposition of Rule 1 (A is stopped), Rule 2 (A pays B), or any of a number of other rules in order to complain about A's wrong.

e. From Dobris, *Boomer Twenty Years Later: An Introduction, with Some Footnotes About "Theory"*, 54 Alb. L. Rev. 171 (1990):

> The property scholars' love affair with the notion that damages are superior to the permanent injunction as a remedy for nuisance has its direct origins in the *Boomer* decision. Such a result is not difficult to understand, because *Boomer* went so much further than the typical case in vindicating hard-to-monetize damages for the plaintiff. On remand, the plaintiffs received much more than the difference between the market value of the property without the servitude and with the servitude, which had heretofore been the standard measure of damages. Thus, the usual complaint that damage awards insufficiently compensate losses that are hard-to-monetize (for example, subjective losses), did not seem as compelling after *Boomer*. The *Boomer* plaintiffs won a square deal in dollar terms.

> Why are damages the darling of the property scholars? [...] I think one reason is that justice seems to require compensating people for harms actually endured. Treating the injunction as the primary nuisance remedy sometimes has kept that from happening. Doctrines that fail to compensate plaintiffs who have been harmed leave us a little cold in the last decade of the twentieth century. Providing a damage remedy forces the polluter to consider the damage done to the plaintiff by operating the plant, without compelling the defendant to disgorge an inordinate share of profits. Damages allow the court to avoid the "balance of the equities" test at the level of "was there a nuisance?" This method allows the court to provide relief to the plaintiff without having to shut down an industry with great utility, such as the Atlantic cement plant.

f. From Richard Epstein, *Too Pragmatic by Half* (review of Farber, *Eco-Pragmatism: Making Sensible Environmental Decisions in an Uncertain World*), 109 Yale L.J. 1639 (2000):

> [The court in *Boomer* should have stuck] to its traditional rule and issue[d] an injunction against the cement factory instead of allowing it to escape with the payment of permanent damages. To be sure, that rule could cause dislocation to the local communities whose plants are closed down. But it is most unwise to evaluate the soundness of automatic injunctive relief simply by looking at its consequences for community life only after the construction of the cement plant. If the common-law rule were clearly established before plant construction, Atlantic Cement would pursue an appropriate development course. No longer would it simply construct expensive facilities in the hope that it would be able to tough out the legal challenges down the road. Now it would seek to resolve the conflicts with neighbors before a sorry impasse of the sort found in *Boomer* arose. The Atlantic Cement Company could have constructed its plant in a more remote location so as to avoid the conflicts; it could have purchased the nearby lands or servitudes over them, so as to internalize the losses before the plant went into operation; or it could have had the state condemn the nearby lands to make way for plant construction—at least if that initiative could pass muster under the "public use" limitation of the Takings Clause. To this last tactic, one might protest that the construction of a private cement plant (as opposed to a grist mill obliged to take all customers) does not pass the public-use test. But if this objection to legislative condemnation is valid, then it cannot be skirted by allowing judicial action to step in where legislative action would be unconstitutional.